SAUNDERS BOOKS IN PSYCHOLOGY

Robert D. Singer, *Consulting Editor*

Gorsuch, *Factor Analysis*

Hardych and Petrinovich, *Introduction to Statistics for the Behavioral Sciences*

Johnson, *Aggression in Man and Animals*

Kaufmann, *Introduction to the Study of Human Behavior*

L'Abate and Curtis, *Teaching the Exceptional Child*

Sattler, *Assessment of Children's Intelligence*

Singer and Singer, *Psychological Development in Children*

Skinner, *Neuroscience: A Laboratory Manual*

Stotland and Canon, *Social Psychology: A Cognitive Approach*

Wallace, *Psychology: A Social Science*

Assessment of Children's Intelligence

Jerome M. Sattler

Professor of Psychology
San Diego State University
San Diego, California

W. B. SAUNDERS COMPANY
PHILADELPHIA • LONDON • TORONTO • 1974

W. B. Saunders Company: West Washington Square
                           Philadelphia, Pa.   19105

                           12 Dyott Street
                           London, WC1A   1DB

                           833 Oxford Street
                           Toronto, Ontario M8Z   5T9, Canada

Assessment of Children's Intelligence

ISBN 0-7216-7943-9

Last digit is the print number: 9   8   7   6   5   4   3   2   1

To

VIRGINIA, HEIDI, and DAVID

and to my parents,

NATHAN and PEARL

PREFACE

A course in individual intelligence testing often represents the culmination of the student's undergraduate career in psychology and entry into graduate education, especially for those beginning a program of study in clinical or school psychology. The course is a synthesis of personality theory, developmental psychology, test theory, experimental psychology, and even English composition. The student arrives at the doorstep with anticipation and excitement. What he is now going to encounter is no more mere "book learning," but a live examinee who is going to be "examined." The tests he will probably learn to administer include the Stanford-Binet, the Wechsler Intelligence Scale for Children, and the Wechsler Preschool and Primary Scale of Intelligence. These tests are considered the most reliable and valid instruments for the assessment of children's intelligence. They are international in reputation, with the Stanford-Binet having gone through three American revisions. What an experience to anticipate!

The student soon finds that administration of the scales is but a minor factor, and that observations, organization, recommendations, and other aspects of report writing and communication must be struggled with step by step, word by word, and, at times, comma by comma. He is not sure what to say, how to say it, or what meaning and implications the results may have, either for the examinee or for the reader. This text has three main goals. The first is to assist the student with the process of psychological evaluation. In this respect, it is not intended as the final answer, but rather as a guide which contains information related to (a) theories and issues concerned with intelligence and intelligence testing, (b) the use of tests with minority group children, (c) problems encountered in test administration, (d) the use of quantitative and qualitative devices to assist in test interpretation, (e) the diagnostic process and the evaluation of children with a variety of psychopathologic conditions, (f) report writing, and (g) the consultation process. Thus, this text is designed to aid the student's education in the wide range of challenges which are involved in psychological evaluations.

The second goal has also guided selection of material. The pioneer clinicians were extremely knowledgeable, and to show the depth of their skills, their thoughts and work are noted whenever appropriate. This focus was selected because the rich and extensive literature on intelligence testing of children remains buried in the dusty recesses of numerous books, monographs, and journals. The findings and insights of many of our pioneer clinicians, educators, and investigators have been filtered through the years so that now their contributions cannot be easily recognized. This book clearly brings out their contributions.

A third purpose of the text is to summarize and integrate the findings of many studies that have been concerned with individual intelligence tests and with variables in the testing situation. Some of this material is of minor importance in the assessment process, but it is included to enable the interested reader to evaluate the attempts that have been made to use tests as research and clinical instruments and to provide a readily available source for those interested in the history of selected research on intelligence testing.

One chapter in the text discusses the Peabody Picture Vocabulary Test, a popular nonverbal test of intelligence, and a variety of other nonverbal, individually administered intelligence tests including the Quick Test, Pictorial Test of Intelligence, Columbia Mental Maturity Scale, and Leiter International Performance Scale. The Slosson Intelligence Test, a verbal intelligence test, also is discussed. There are many other important and useful individually administered intelligence and ability tests (e.g., Draw-a-Man, Porteus Mazes, and Illinois Test of Psycholinguistic Abilities) that are not covered in the text. Their omission is simply a result of limitations of space and time and is not in any way a reflection on their merits.

The text is limited in a number of ways. It does not present a thorough discussion of the nature of intelligence. Rather, it offers some important thoughts selected to provide a foundation for understanding intelligence theory in relation to individual intelligence tests. The text describes the major problems found in report writing, but does not offer an extensive discussion of grammar, style, and organization. Finally, it merely skims the surface of psychopathology, touching on major symptoms and patterns found in the predominant forms of childhood disturbance and emphasizing the role that intelligence plays in child psychopathology.

The text is designed for students in psychology and education. It is highly recommended that the student have had courses in tests and measurement, developmental psychology, and abnormal psychology (including abnormal child psychology) before he begins his study of individual intelligence tests as assessment tools. Some parts of the text, especially those concerned with research studies, diagnostic applications, and consultation, should be of benefit to clinical child psychologists, school psychologists, and psychometrists.

The underlying assumption of the text is that individually administered intelligence tests, such as the Stanford-Binet, the WISC, and the WPPSI, have much more to offer than just an "IQ." It would be a waste of valuable time if the psychologist's only goal were to produce an IQ. There are many well standardized instruments in the field of psychology and education that, under appropriate conditions, provide valid measures of intelligence. However, a thorough analysis of a child's performance on the Stanford-Binet, the WISC, or the WPPSI permits the examiner to gain an understanding of certain cognitive and conative features that no paper-and-pencil, group-administered test can provide. The text, it is hoped, will enable the examiner to use the Stanford-Binet, the WISC, and the WPPSI, which are delicate yet sturdy instruments, to provide each examinee the opportunities—educational, social, and emotional—with which to develop his maximum potentials.

There are a number of people I wish to acknowledge who were instrumental in my education and who contributed to the development of the book. I owe a great debt to two fine teachers, John W. Chotlos and Fritz Heider, who guided me as a student at the University of Kansas toward an outlook in psychology that emphasized the human concern and the necessity of a careful, descriptive approach to human problems. They have been a constant source of inspiration. I am grateful to the clinical psychology program at the University of Kansas, headed by M. Eric Wright, for providing me with the education needed to complete my studies in psychology.

My colleague, William A. Hillix, read every chapter and generously gave of his time to discuss with me various aspects of the text. He helped in innumerable ways to make the text more cogent and useful. Ralph Mason Dreger also read the entire manuscript and was an invaluable guide to organization, in addition to providing guidance on many other points. The wisdom and insight of Drs. Hillix and Dreger have made the book more knowledgeable and readable. I also have benefited from the careful comments on the entire manuscript made by Fredrick B. Davis, who was especially helpful in providing valuable suggestions about the statistical aspects of tests. Alan O. Ross and my colleague, Edward A. Jacobson, also read the entire manuscript and provided helpful suggestions. George C. Gross made many valuable comments on the first 10 chapters. Nancy E. Anderson provided many of the references that were used in evaluating the Peabody Picture Vocabulary Test. Her contribution makes her a co-author of the section on this test. Catherine Campisi also was helpful in providing comments on various chapters. The author, who usually but not always followed the advice of his readers, accepts final responsibility for the material contained in the text.

I also wish to thank Robert D. Singer, consulting editor of the Saunders psychology series, and Baxter Venable, the psychology and education editor at Saunders, for their support, encouragement, and sustained interest in the project. The advice of Baxter Venable was especially helpful in developing the content of some chapters. I am grateful to my able secretary, Diane Dietz, who typed the numerous drafts of each chapter, and to the secretaries at the Word Processing Center at San Diego State University, who typed various chapters of the book. The interlibrary loan service at San Diego State University, headed by Ann Wright and formerly by Mildred LeCompte, was helpful in enabling me to obtain many references. Part of the research cited in the book was performed under grants from the U.S. Department of Health, Education, and Welfare, Office of Education (OEG-4-7-078-057) and Social and Rehabilitation Service (15-P-55277/9-02). Their support has been appreciated. I wish to thank the Universiti Kebangsaan, Malaysia, where I was a Fullbright Lecturer, for providing me with the support needed to complete the last phases of the book.

I am also grateful to my students who have patiently and, at times, not so patiently struggled with me in becoming masters of psychological testing. During the many years in which this book was being written, my wife, Virginia R. Sattler, has been a constant source of encouragement. She has assisted me in numerous ways, such as by listening to many of my ideas about the development of the text, by reading and proofreading portions of chapters, and by typing some sections. She and my two children, Heidi and David, were understanding of those lost days at the pool or beach when I was too busy writing this book.

I am grateful to the authors and publishers who kindly permitted the use of tables, figures, and written materials. In addition to the acknowledgements that are shown in each table and figure, acknowledgement is made to the following sources to quote and reproduce materials:

Harvard University Press — pages 308–310 and 485 from E. M. Taylor, *Psychological Appraisal of Children with Cerebral Defects,* copyright 1959 by the Commonwealth Fund.

Society for Projective Techniques & Personality Assessment and R. J. Craig — for reprinting, with some changes, the case illustration from R. J. Craig, "An Illustration of the Wechsler Picture Arrangement Subtest as a Thematic

Technique," *Journal of Projective Techniques and Personality Assessment,* **33,** pp. 286–289. Copyright 1969, Society for Projective Techniques & Personality Assessment, reprinted by permission.

Rosa A. Hagin—for reprinting, with some changes, the case illustrations for the WPPSI from R. A. Hagin, A. A. Silver, and C. J. Corwin, "Clinical Diagnostic Use of the WPPSI in Predicting Learning Disabilities in Grade One," in R. S. Morrow (Chm.), Diagnostic and Educational Application of the Wechsler Preschool and Primary Scale of Intelligence (WPPSI). Symposium presented at the American Psychological Association, Miami, September 1970.

American Psychological Association and E. K. Sarason—for reprinting, with some changes, the case illustration from E. K. Sarason and S. B. Sarason, "A Problem in Diagnosing Feeblemindedness," *Journal of Abnormal and Social Psychology,* **40,** pp. 326–329. Copyright 1945, American Psychological Association, reprinted by permission.

JEROME M. SATTLER

CONTENTS

Section 3.

STANFORD-BINET INTELLIGENCE SCALE 85

Chapter 8

THE DEVELOPMENT OF THE STANFORD-BINET 87

Chapter 9

ADMINISTERING THE STANFORD-BINET 107

Chapter 10

INTERPRETING THE STANFORD-BINET 127

LIST OF TABLES

SECTION 1

INTRODUCTION AND GENERAL CONSIDERATIONS

An understanding of intelligence testing can be facilitated by a knowledge of the historical as well as contemporary forces and issues that have played and are playing a role in shaping the development and use of tests. Section 1 covers a broad spectrum of issues, touching lightly on the surface, but in the process an orientation is provided that should serve as a ground for understanding and evaluating much of the material which follows in other parts of the text.

Chapter 1 details the steps that are faced by the examiner in performing a psychological evaluation. Chapter 2 serves as an introduction to the work of some of the leading men in the history of intelligence testing and considers issues related to definitions and conceptions of intelligence. Some attempt is made to integrate current conceptions of intelligence. Chapter 3 deals with some of the factors that affect the development of intelligence and that should be considered in evaluating the merits of intelligence tests. Chapter 4 is devoted to a systematic review of issues involved in testing minority group children. The future of intelligence testing in schools may rest in large part on the manner in which the issues discussed in Chapter 4 are resolved.

CHAPTER 1

INTRODUCTION

The assessment of intelligence, the major focus of this book, is a complex activity. It calls for many skills on the part of the examiner, ranging from the ability to work with children (and adults) to a knowledge of statistics and test construction. But these abilities are only a beginning. The assessment of intelligence does not end with giving a test, recording and scoring responses, and arriving at a test score. It involves communicating the findings to interested parties, interpreting the results to parents and examinees on occasion, and participating in decision-making activities. One last point deserves consideration. Progress in assessment cannot occur without research. Many factors bear investigation. It is important that test reliabilities and validities be established with various populations, that hypotheses concerning test functions be validated, and that procedural changes be investigated. In addition, familiarity with previous research and the problems involved with such research will provide the examiner with a base from which he can evaluate his own testing techniques.

The material contained in this book is aimed at providing the examiner with the knowledge that he will need to evaluate and to use a variety of individual intelligence tests and to carry out the assessment task. It is understood that the examiner will have a background in statistics, in tests and measurement, and in child development. Those individuals working with emotionally disturbed children should have a thorough background in child psychopathology. The book is not meant to be a substitute for test manuals or for texts in child psychopathology. It supplements some of the material contained in test manuals, but goes further by considering many additional facets of tests and of the assessment process.

Mastery of the assessment process requires supervised experience. Supervision is especially needed in the beginning phase of the student's career. Supervision should cover all phases of the assessment process, including test administration, scoring, report writing, and consultation. If possible, many different types of children should be examined—normal and emotionally disturbed, retarded and gifted, and physically handicapped children as well—in a variety of settings.

OUTLINE OF THE ASSESSMENT PROCESS

Let us consider some of the tasks that are required in the assessment process and the ways this book will aid the examiner.

Selecting a Test

One of the first tasks which the examiner has is to select a test which will answer the questions posed by the referring agency or individual. In order to do this well, the examiner will have to know the characteristics of many of the available individual intelligence tests. The examiner will find in this book information and evaluative comments about a variety of individual intelligence tests. Those interested in reading about a particular test can turn directly to the specific chapter or chapters.

Administering the Test

The next task the examiner faces is administering the test. He will have to learn how to use the manual for the appropriate test. Knowing what is in the manual and in the present book will aid the examiner in learning how to administer the test properly. The book contains information on the completion of record booklets, general administrative procedures, considerations on violating standard procedures, testing-of-limit procedures, the physical abilities required for taking tests, ethnic minority group testing, and examiner-examinee variables. The examiner will be provided with practical suggestions, research findings, and the observations and insights of many psychologists and educators who have had considerable experience with intelligence tests.

Scoring the Test

Concurrently with administering the test, the examiner is required to score the child's responses. If he is going to score the test accurately, he should be familiar with research findings concerning scoring bias, halo effects, errors in test scoring, and difficulty in using scoring criteria. There will be special problems with tests having insufficient scoring examples. In connection with scoring, there also will be problems with tests that do not have adequate IQ ranges so that extrapolated IQ's may be used on some occasions. Special problems also are encountered in evaluating the responses of the sensory or motor disabled and with autistic and schizophrenic children. This book devotes special attention to scoring problems.

Observing Behavior

Another activity which takes place concurrently with administering the test is the observation of the child's general behavior and of behavior associated with test items. The observation of behavior constitutes an important part of the assessment process. An evaluation of the child's attitudes, language, and visual-motor abilities, for example, can aid the examiner in interpreting the child's performance and in making recommendations. Specific suggestions are made in this book for observing and evaluating general behavior and specific behavior connected with various test items.

Writing the Report

After the test is scored, the examiner will have to write reports. Reports necessitate interpreting results and making recommendations, in addition to reporting test results. Specific suggestions for interpreting test results are contained throughout the book. Tables have been constructed to aid the examiner in quickly finding minimum differences between subtest scaled scores on the Wechsler Intelligence Scale for Children (WISC) and Wechsler Preschool and Primary Scale of Intelligence (WPPSI) that are statistically significant. The interpretative rationales for many of the tests and subtests are described to assist in evaluating the child's performance. Extensive diagnostic examples also are available in the book to aid the examiner in formulating hypotheses about the child. Readers particularly interested in diagnostic considerations can turn directly to Chapter 19 to see how intelligence tests and, in particular, the Stanford-Binet and WISC provide useful information to assist in the diagnostic process.

Many additional aids to report writing are contained in the book. Sample reports cover normal as well as emotionally disturbed children. These reports are illustrative and are meant only as general guides. Many examples of communication problems are illustrated. Research findings concerned with report writing can be useful in aiding the examiner to evaluate his own reports, and such findings are surveyed systematically.

Consulting Activities

After the report is written, the examiner may desire to meet with the child to discuss the results or may need to discuss the results with the child's parents or with the referral source. In addition, the examiner may be called upon to present his results at a staff conference. In some cases, clients or parents may be defensive. In hospitals, special problems may arise in working with other professionals. The examiner, if he knows his subject matter extremely well, will be in a firm position to present and defend his findings clearly and systematically. A knowledge of the history of intelligence testing, for example, will help him to defend his statements by citing relevant findings and theories when necessary. Using intelligence tests with ethnic minority group children will require considerable skill and judgment. The examiner, too, should be cognizant of the problems involved with confidentiality and record keeping. These and other topics are discussed in the book in order to aid the examiner in his work in a variety of settings.

Conducting Research

Finally, the examiner may find himself doing research on intelligence testing. Much of the material in the book is relevant for that task. A knowledge of research and research problems may stimulate the examiner to design and conduct his own investigations.

The above steps are not necessarily in chronological sequence. While they depict the usual sequence that many students will meet, some students may find themselves engaged in research investigations before they learn to administer tests or concurrently with their study of tests. Other students, too, may be using psychological reports in their professional work long before they actually administer tests. Thus, the particular sequence of activities which brings the student into contact with intelligence tests may vary, but proper and knowledgeable use of test results is always the aim.

SUMMARY

Chapter 1 provides an overview of the tasks faced by the examiner in conducting a psychological evaluation. The assessment process consists of selecting, administering, and scoring a test, observing behavior, report writing, and, on some occasions, consultation through conferences. The assessment process also may generate research activities. The text provides information about each step in the assessment process.

CHAPTER 2

HISTORICAL SURVEY AND THEORIES OF INTELLIGENCE

INTRODUCTION

Before examining the history of intelligence testing and the various definitions of intelligence that have been proposed, we should examine various approaches to the concept of intelligence. Themes in the history of intelligence reveal that there has been a general progression from a stage in which there was no accepted definition of intelligence or method of testing intelligence to gradually developing a conception of intelligence based in part on logical and empirical approaches. It is often stated that there is no such thing as intelligence; however, we have gradually constructed the notion of intelligence through our very attempts to study intelligence.

We will see that, historically, somewhat intuitional and trial-and-error approaches were first offered, and then superseded by more systematic, logical, and empirical approaches. One of the things that define intelligence is its correlations with some kinds of criteria. When items failed to correlate with various criteria, they were discarded and replaced with other items. Another thing that occurs in the development of intelligence tests is that test constructors look at a task, a prototypical activity, and analyze the activities that are required for its proper execution. This analysis then leads to the development of specific kinds of items that are brought together to form a test.

As a result of empirical and theoretical work, factor analytic approaches evolved. Factor analysis is a statistical way of sorting out components which are related to overall task performance. Factor analytic approaches also went through trial-and-error phases. Now we have logical and statistical models of intelligence, and these too are going through trial-and-error phases. Factor analytic approaches have evolved from an analysis of "randomly" selected items to a situation in which logical analysis guides the selection of items and factor analytic techniques then test the logical analysis. Thus, at present, there tends to be a wedding of logical and statistical approaches.

Definitions of intelligence tend to follow from different theoretical views of intelligence. Some definitions emphasize correlations and some emphasize the functions which appear to be logically related to intelligence. Another approach is highly operational; it tells us that intelligence is what intelligence tests measure. This latter approach provides little in the way of a substantive contribution to our understanding of intelligence. The condensed history which follows shows us some of the men responsible for the trends that have taken place in the field of intelligence and summarizes some of the definitions of intelligence.

We will see that theories of intelligence are beginning to show a coalescing of views. Whatever position the student adopts toward definitions of intelligence, it is still important to recognize that the unique learning history of the individual determines the ways in which he uses his intelligence.

BRIEF HISTORICAL SURVEY

Interest in intelligence and in intelligence testing was an inherent part of the movement, beginning in the latter part of the nineteenth century, which brought psychology into being as a separate discipline. Intelligence testing had its roots in the fields of general psychology and measurement. The psychophysical methods developed by E. H. Weber (1795–1878) and G. T. Fechner (1801–1887), the study of difference limens by G. E. Müller (1850–1934) and F. M. Urban, and the statistical studies of higher mental processes initiated by Sir Francis Galton (1822–1911) formed the background for much of the work that would take place in the twentieth century.

Galton was very active in the field of mental measurement and, in particular, in the study of the inheritance of intellectual ability, mental imagery, and the development of statistical methods. His concern with individual differences led him to set up a psychometric laboratory at the International Health Exhibition in 1884, which later was re-established at University College, London. The laboratory was open to the public, and for a small fee provided measures of physical and mental capacities. Galton assumed that the ability to make fine sensory discriminations was correlated with intelligence, and this assumption, which generally proved to be invalid, may have been instrumental in limiting the progress of his work (Akhurst, 1970). K. Pearson, who contributed to the study of eugenics, anthropology, and psychology and who developed the correlation coefficient, was also active in England.

In America the mental testing movement grew out of the study of individual differences. James McKeen Cattell (1860–1944), who studied with Wundt in Germany and who visited Galton in England, published work in the area of individual differences. Working at the University of Pennsylvania, Cattell contributed to the development of statistical procedures that were necessary for the evaluation and application of tests. He used the term "mental test" in an article published in 1890.

Other individuals in the United States were also active at the turn of the century. J. Jastrow at the University of Wisconsin demonstrated in 1893 at the Columbian Exposition in Chicago a series of tests that were similar to those developed by Cattell. In the early 1890's F. Boas at Clark University and J. Gilbert in New Haven were also studying how children responded to various types of tests.

C. Wissler (1901) was one of the first investigators who sought to determine the validity of some of the tests that were thought to be related to cognitive processes. Most of the tests that he used were measures of simple sensory functions. Using the correlational methods of Galton and Pearson, he found that the relationships among the test scores and between the test scores and school grades were very low. S. E. Sharp (1898) reported in another study that tests similar to those used by Binet and Henri were measuring many different functions—a result which was contrary to the claim that was being made for them—and were giving unreliable results. These two studies, in spite of their methodological shortcomings, dealt early blows to the mental testing movement.

In Germany in 1889 E. Kraepelin, working in the field of psychopathology, was introducing more complex tests—such as tests of perception, memory, motor functions, and attention—for measuring mental functions. H. Münsterberg (1891) was also studying various types of perceptual, memory, reading, and information tests with children. The work of H. Ebbinghaus (1897), which dealt with tests of memory, computation, and sentence completion, was also related to the early development of tests.

At about the same time in France, A. Binet, V. Henri, and T. Simon were developing methods for the study of a variety of mental functions. Binet found the key to the measurement of intelligence by focusing on higher mental processes instead of on simple sensory functions. Developments in the field of intelligence testing proceeded in somewhat different fashions in England, America, Germany, and France. English workers were concerned with statistical analyses; the Americans focused upon implementation of the Binet ideas of a scale together with statistical methods of treating test data; the Germans emphasized the study of psychopathology and more complex mental functions; and the French focused on clinical experimentation (cf. McConnell, 1930). Further details concerning the intelligence testing movement may be found in Boring (1950), Peterson (1925), and Tuddenham (1962).

MEANINGS ASSOCIATED WITH AND DEFINITIONS OF INTELLIGENCE

Three Meanings Associated with Intelligence

Vernon (1969) described three different meanings associated with the term "intelligence"; the first two were initially formulated by Hebb (1966), while the third was developed by Vernon. First, "intelligence" is used to mean the innate capacity of the individual, his genetic equipment. This form of intelligence can never be measured directly. It has been termed *intelligence A,* the genotypic form, and is lowered by deficiencies in general plasticity and in genes relevant to special aptitudes and abilities. Cattell's (1963) concept of fluid intelligence is similar to intelligence A.

A second meaning of "intelligence" refers to what the individual does, or to his observed behavior. It results from an interaction of genes with the prenatal and postnatal environment. It is termed *intelligence B,* the phenotypic form. "Psychologically, Intelligence B is the cumulative total of the schemata or mental plans built up through the individual's interaction with his environment, insofar as his constitutional equipment allows [Vernon, 1969, p. 23]." Intelligence B can be lowered by constitutional handicaps, such as brain damage, and by environmental factors, such as limited satisfaction of biological and social needs, limited perceptual and kinesthetic experience, inadequate linguistic and conceptual stimulation, a nondemanding and undemocratic family climate, and inadequacies in schooling, language fluency, self-concept, and interests. Hebb (1966) pointed out that intelligence A and intelligence B are not wholly separate or independent of each other. Intelligence A, of course, enters into and is a necessary component of intelligence B. Cattell's (1963) concept of crystallized intelligence is similar to intelligence B.

A third meaning of "intelligence," *intelligence C,* refers to the results obtained on an intelligence test (with the exception of the Stanford-Binet and its derivatives). This meaning of "intelligence" may differ from what most people regard as intelligent behavior. A number of extrinsic handicaps, especially found among disadvantaged children and among those from underdeveloped nations, can serve to lower test performance, including (*a*) the examinee's unfamiliarity with the test situation and his lack of motivation; (*b*) difficulties associated with the item format and testing conditions; (*c*) mistrust of the examiner, and anxiety and excitement; and (*d*) difficulties in understanding the instructions or in communicating the responses. These extrinsic handicaps, of course, also affect Stanford-Binet scores.

Vernon believed that the Stanford-Binet, or the Verbal Scale of the WISC, thoroughly samples intelligence B of Western children. In contrast, specialized tests, such as verbal, mechanical, or nonverbal ones, sample many different types of abilities, and therefore come under intelligence C. The Stanford-Binet is particularly valuable in measuring intelligence B, which in Western civilization primarily refers to the grasping of relations and to symbolic thinking, because it contains material which reflects children's thinking.

Definitions of Intelligence

Defining intelligence is not an easy matter. In a famous symposium conducted in 1921 (*Journal of Educational Psychology*), 13 psychologists gave 13 different views about the nature of intelligence, although there was much in common in their definitions. Terman (1921), one of the participating psychologists, defined intelligence as the ability to carry on "abstract thinking." He was well aware of the danger of placing too much emphasis on the results of one particular test: "We must guard against defining intelligence solely in terms of ability to pass the tests of a given intelligence scale. It should go without saying that no existing scale is capable of adequately measuring the ability to deal with all possible kinds of material on all intelligence levels [p. 131]." His comments are still very appropriate today.

Binet (Binet & Simon, 1905) regarded intelligence (as Chapter 8 describes in detail) as a collection of faculties: judgment, practical sense, initiative, and the ability to adapt oneself to circumstances. However, his selection of tests was based on an empirical criterion, namely, those tests which differentiated older from younger children. What he thought the tests were measuring was based only upon his opinion; the tests were not originally selected on the basis of factor analysis.

Wechsler (1958) defined intelligence as "the aggregate or global capacity of the individual to act purposefully, to think rationally and to deal effectively with his environment [p. 7]." This definition implies that intelligence is composed of qualitatively different elements or abilities. However, it is not the mere sum of abilities that defines intelligence, because intelligent behavior is also affected by the way in which the abilities are combined and by the individual's drive and incentive. Wechsler recognized that while it is possible to measure various aspects of intellectual ability, the obtained scores are not identical with what is meant by intelligence. Wechsler has taken a pragmatic view of intelligence, stating that intelligence is known by what it enables us to do. However, as Guilford (1967) noted, Wechsler failed to supply empirical referents for such terms as "aggregate," "global," "purposefully," and "rationally."

Intelligence, according to Piaget (Elkind, 1969), is an extension of biological adaptation, consisting of the processes of assimilation (processes responsive to inner promptings) and of accommodation (processes responsive to environmental intrusions). Assimilative processes permit intelligence to go beyond a passive coping with reality, while accommodative processes operate to prevent intelligence from constructing representations of reality which have no correspondence with the real world. Intelligence represents the rational processes, the processes which show the greatest independence of environmental and internal regulation.

FACTOR ANALYTIC THEORIES OF INTELLIGENCE

Spearman

C. E. Spearman (1927) was one of the early proponents of a factor analytic approach to intelligence. Spearman proposed a two-factor theory of intelligence to account for the patterns of correlations which he observed among group tests of intelligence. The theory stated that a general factor (g) plus one specific factor per test can account for performance on intelligence tests. Any intellectual activity involves both a general factor, which it shares with all other intellectual activities, and a specific factor which it shares with none.

Thorndike

E. L. Thorndike's (1927) approach to intelligence was based on the premise that intelligence is comprised of a multitude of separate elements, each representing a distinct ability. He believed that certain mental activities have elements in common and combine to form clusters. Three such clusters were identified, namely, social intelligence (or dealing with people), concrete intelligence (or dealing with things), and abstract intelligence (or dealing with verbal and mathematical symbols). However, factor analytic methods were not used to obtain these clusters.

Thurstone

The factor analytic theorist who was most divergent from Spearman was L. L. Thurstone (1938), who used the centroid method of factor analysis. In the centroid method, factors are extracted from a correlation matrix in which the first axis passes through the center of gravity of the system. Thurstone extracted the following seven important group factors or, as he labelled them, "primary mental abilities": verbal meaning, number facility, inductive reasoning, perceptual speed, spatial relations, memory, and verbal fluency. Tests were developed to measure these factors (Primary Mental Abilities Tests). While Thurstone's multidimensional theory at first eliminated g as a significant component of mental functioning, the primary factors were found to correlate moderately among themselves, leading Thurstone to postulate the existence of a second-order factor which may be related to g.

Guilford

The most prominent multifactor theorist in the United States is J. P. Guilford (1967). He developed the Structure of Intellect model as a way of organizing intellectual factors into a system. The model is three dimensional, with one dimension representing operation categories, a second dimension representing content categories, and a third dimension representing product categories. Thus, intellective tasks can be understood by the kind of *mental operation* performed, the type of *content* on which the mental operation is performed, and the resulting *product*. The model proposes five different kinds of operations (cognition, memory, divergent thinking, convergent thinking, and evaluation), four types of content (figural, symbolic, semantic, and behavioral), and six products (units, classes, relations, systems, transformations, and implications). Thus, 120 possible factors ($5 \times 4 \times 6$) are postulated in accordance with the model. The Structure of Intellect model also is described in Chapters 10, 13, and 16 for the Stanford-Binet, WISC, and WPPSI, respectively.

Guilford's model has been criticized by Eysenck (1967) for failing to reproduce the essentially hierarchical nature of intelligence test data. Eysenck, following McNemar (1964), noted that the one outstanding fact which recurs in most studies of intelligence tests is the universality of positive correlations among all relevant tests, and the positive correlations between different factors. The failure to mention any central feature in the model thus reduces its value.

Vernon (1961) also had reservations about Guilford's model. He noted that proof is lacking for the existence of the large number of factors in the model. The model, too, has not been frequently used in other laboratories. Finally, validity evidence is lacking to demonstrate that the new factors give additional information about thinking in everyday life.

Vernon

A hierarchical theory of intelligence has been developed by P. E. Vernon (1950). The highest level is a general intellective factor (g), followed by two major group factors—Verbal-Educational (V:ED) and Practical-Mechanical-Spatial (K:M). Each of these group factors is further broken down into minor group factors. Specific factors, peculiar to certain tests, form the last level. The theory synthesizes the work of Spearman and Thurstone, but gives central importance to g.

Cattell

R. B. Cattell (1963) proposed that general intelligence is composed of two factors—fluid intelligence and crystallized intelligence. These factors are viewed as distinct but correlated. Fluid intelligence is a basic capacity for learning and problem solving, independent of education and experience. Fluid intelligence is general to many different fields, and is used in tasks requiring adaptation to new situations. Crystallized intelligence is the result of the interaction of the individual's fluid intelligence and his culture; it consists of learned knowledge and skills.

OTHER APPROACHES TO INTELLIGENCE

Jensen

A. R. Jensen (1970a, 1970b, 1970c) from his experimental work on memory and intelligence and from his survey of intelligence test literature has synthesized many important issues related to intelligence testing. We review first his general conception of intelligence and then his theory of intelligence.

Jensen's Approach to Intelligence and Intelligence Testing. Jensen (1970c) sees intelligence as an attribute of persons. Intelligence is in the same domain as temperature. The thermometer allows for the objective measurement of temperature; the intelligence test allows for the objective measurement of intelligence. Intelligence, unlike temperature, is multidimensional, so that persons have different ranks on different kinds of intelligence tests.

The primary abilities included in the concept of intelligence, from a psychological viewpoint, are conceptual learning ability, abstract or symbolic reasoning ability, and abstract or verbal problem-solving ability. These abilities represent only a segment of the spectrum of intellectual abilities. They are emphasized on most standard intelligence tests because they are abilities that are needed for school work and for many occupations. The similarity in the composition of different tests, observed through high intercorrelations among tests, indicates that there is a large general factor (g) which tests share in common.

The IQ is related to socially valued criteria. The prestige value of occupations, upward social mobility, and scholastic success, for example, are substantially related to measured intelligence. Jensen recognized that the predictive validity of the IQ is much less accurate for individuals than for groups. Unassessed traits or unpredictable unusual future circumstances may radically alter the course of an individual's intellectual development. Consequently, caution must be used in the assessment of individuals, especially in predicting future intelligence.

Jensen (1970b) suggested that the concepts of intellectual breadth and altitude are useful in understanding the composition of intelligence tests. General information and vocabulary tests measure intellectual breadth, while tests involving problem solving measure altitude. The breadth factor depends on amount and range of exposure as well as on the individual's interests and values. Breadth and altitude measures are highly correlated with g, but test content reflecting breadth, such as is found on the Peabody Picture Vocabulary Test, is extensively influenced by environment and training. The altitude factor seems to be more dependent on innate endowment than the breadth factor. Cattell's (1963) fluid intelligence is similar to the altitude component, while crystallized intelligence is similar to the breadth component.

Jensen's Associative-Ability and Cognitive-Ability Theory. Jensen's (1970a) theory of mental functioning seems to explain the results of numerous investigations which have studied cognitive processes of minority group children. He postulated the existence of two types of abilities, "associative ability" and "cognitive ability." The two types of abilities are viewed as having underlying genetic processes that are essentially different. While the abilities may be correlated, they also may have different developmental rates. Cognitive functions are partly dependent on associative functions, but the reverse does not hold. Current behavioral tests are likely to measure both levels, but different tests measure the abilities to different degrees. Examples of tasks measuring associative abilities are digit-span memory, free recall, serial learning, and paired-associate learning. Cognitive abilities are in part measured by conceptual- and abstract-reasoning tasks.

Standard intelligence tests are usually a mixture of associative and cognitive functions, but most measure cognitive ability. Spearman's g factor is a major factor in most intelligence tests. In the WISC, Digit Span forward and Digit Symbol subtests are relatively pure measures of associative abilities. The Vocabulary subtest and Information subtest contain items which depend upon previous learning. Associative abilities are involved in these two subtests (and others), especially for the easier, more concrete words and simple factual-content questions. The Arithmetic reasoning problems, especially the more difficult ones, the Similarities items, and the Block Design items likely reflect cognitive abilities. Jensen classified the Porteus Maze Test as being more a measure of associative than of cognitive processes. Tests of immediate memory span are good measures of associative processes.

Associative and cognitive abilities are essentially orthogonal to (uncorrelated with) Cattell's (1963) fluid and crystallized general intelligence. Digit Span tests measure fluid intelligence *and* associative abilities, while the Progressive Matrices test and Cattell's Culture Fair Intelligence Test measure fluid intelligence *and* cognitive abilities.

Socioeconomic status is postulated to be largely independent of associative abilities, but correlated with cognitive abilities. The hypothetical growth curves that are shown in Figure 2–1 for associative and cognitive abilities in middle and low socioeconomic classes suggest that in both classes, associative abilities are nearly equal throughout the developmental period, while cognitive abilities are not. Cognitive abilities show a progressively widening cleavage in development, in favor of the middle and upper socioeconomic classes.

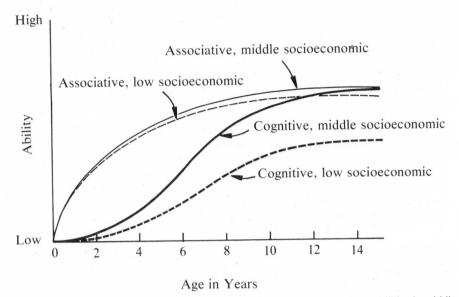

Age in Years

Figure 2–1. Hypothetical growth curves for associative and cognitive abilities in middle socioeconomic and low socioeconomic classes. (Reprinted, with a change in notation, by permission of the publisher and author from A. R. Jensen, "A Theory of Primary and Secondary Familial Mental Retardation," in N. R. Ellis (Ed.), *International Review of Research in Mental Retardation,* Vol. 4, p. 63. Copyright 1970, Academic Press.)

The hypothetical growth curves can help to explain the finding that low socioeconomic children do progressively poorer in school ("cumulative deficit" theory). The school's curriculum becomes increasingly abstract and conceptual (involving cognitive abilities) with advancing grades, and children with below-average cognitive ability, regardless of their associative ability standing, will therefore be at an increasing disadvantage. Jensen proposed that the educational process for low socioeconomic children with below-average cognitive ability be revitalized, by having instruction in the basic school subjects more in accord with associative processes than with the cognitive processes currently employed.

Jensen suggested that memory span is a more adequate measure of general intelligence than is generally believed. However, memory span is not a unitary ability. Digit Span forward appears to be an almost pure measure of associative abilities, while Digit Span reversed, a task calling for a transformation of input, involves some cognitive ability. Digit Span has a substantial correlation with IQ in the normative population of the Wechsler and Stanford-Binet tests, but in the low socioeconomic classes the correlation is negligible. Jensen attributed this finding to a deficiency in cognitive mechanisms in the low socioeconomic classes. Digit Span tests and general IQ tests, therefore, appear to measure different mental abilities.

In severe grades of mental retardation, associative and cognitive abilities are both markedly deficient. It is in the area of the milder forms of mental retardation, especially those termed "familial," where Jensen's theory takes on importance. He proposed that *primary retardation* be the term used to refer to deficiency in associative abilities, and *secondary retardation,* the term for deficiency in cognitive abilities. Individuals who achieve IQ's on conventional tests in the range between -1 and -2 standard deviations below the mean (e.g., IQ's of 70 to 85) are largely from groups called "culturally disadvantaged." It is unfortunate that these individuals are labeled "retarded," because many of them are average in associative abilities. Further, once they leave school, they are not perceived as being retarded. Jensen maintained that these children are, in actuality, neither "slow learners" nor possessors of a pattern of abilities that is the result of cultural deprivation. Jensen marshaled an impressive array of evidence to support his theory. While his theory is not without criticism (e.g., Humphreys & Dachler, 1969; Voyat, 1970), he has given the fields of psychology and education a stimulus for action and has shown how intelligence tests can aid not only in the understanding of mental ability, but also in the application of teaching methods.

Burt

Burt (1955) observed that evidence from different branches of psychology leads to the notion that mental capacity is cognitive, general, and innate. Differences in intelligence seem to depend on the combined action of numerous genes whose influence is similar, small, and cumulative. It is important to distinguish between intelligence as an abstract component of the individual's genetic constitution and intelligence as an observable and empirically measurable trait. Evidence suggests that at least 75% of the measured variance in IQ is attributable to genetic factors, and less than 25% to environmental conditions. (For further information about the issue of genetic factors and intelligence see, for example, Bloom, 1964; Burt, 1958; Butcher, 1968; Hunt, 1961; Jensen, 1969; Vernon, 1969.)

Wesman

Part of the confusion concerning definitions and ways of measuring intelligence, according to Wesman (1968), is a result of the failure to understand that (a) intelligence is an attribute, not an entity; and (b) intelligence is the summation of the learning experiences of the individual. Tests with different names (e.g., intelligence, achievement, or aptitude) are for the most part measuring similar abilities; the name merely reflects different criteria that have been selected for investigation. All ability tests measure what the examinee has learned. Wesman also pointed out that factors obtained from factor analytic studies should be considered descriptive categories and not a reflection of underlying entities.

SUMMARY

The field of intelligence testing grew from the soil nourished by the early experimental psychologists who were developing psychophysical methods (e.g., Weber, Fechner, Müller, and Urban), and by the pioneering efforts of Galton in England, Cattell in America, Kraepelin in Germany, and Binet and Simon in France. The focus on higher mental processes enabled Binet to develop a useful test of intelligence.

Vernon described three different meanings associated with the term "intelligence." Intelligence A refers to the genotypic form (genetic level); it can never be measured directly. Intelligence B refers to the phenotypic form (observed behavior); it represents the mental processes that develop as a result of genetic factors in interaction with the environment. Intelligence C refers to the results that are obtained by an individual on an intelligence test.

The definition of intelligence continues to be a problem. Terman focused on abstract thinking as the essential part of intelligence; Binet focused on a varied set of qualities including judgment, common sense, initiative, and adaptation; Wechsler stressed the qualities of purposefulness, rationality, and ability to deal effectively with the environment; and Piaget emphasized the biological adaptive processes of assimilation and accommodation.

Concurrently with the development of statistical methods for the evaluation of large amounts of data, factor analytic theories of intelligence arrived on the scene. Spearman proposed a two-factor theory, emphasizing a general factor (g) and one or more specific factors (s). Thorndike described three kinds of intelligence—social, concrete, and abstract. Thurstone found at least seven group factors, and in his later work postulated a second-order factor which may be similar to g. Guilford's three-dimensional Structure of Intellect model (operations, contents, and products) results in 120 possible factors. Vernon's hierarchical approach to intelligence emphasizes the g factor, followed by Verbal-Educational and Practical-Mechanical-Spatial group factors, which are in turn further broken down into minor group factors. Cattell postulated that there are two kinds of factors in general intelligence: fluid intelligence (capacity independent of experience) and crystallized intelligence (learned knowledge).

Jensen impressively argued that intelligence tests are valuable tools which provide reliable and valid measures of abilities that are needed in our society. However, he also pointed out that the predictive validity of the IQ is less certain for an individual than for groups. His associative-ability and cognitive-ability theory is an attempt to demarcate two separate but partially dependent mental functions. Associative ability is represented by memory and serial learning tasks, and cognitive ability is represented by abstract reasoning tasks. Jensen, in maintaining that socioeconomic status is largely independent of associative abilities, but not of cognitive abilities, has attempted to account for the progressive difficulty children from low socioeconomic classes have in school.

Theories of intelligence are beginning to show a coalescing of views, stressing the importance of both innate and developmental influences. Intelligence is viewed as being a central, "fluid" kind of genetically determined basic ability which is modified by experience. However, the ways in which people use their intelligence are determined by the unique learning history of the individual.

CHAPTER 3

ISSUES RELATED TO THE MEASUREMENT OF INTELLIGENCE

Psychologists have searched for variables which may affect, and are related to, the measurement of intelligence. They have examined such areas as the stability of intelligence, factors affecting mental growth, infant tests, the concept of mental age, and cultural factors as they are related to intelligence. These areas, especially as they relate to an evaluation of the assets and limitations of intelligence testing, are discussed in the present chapter. The issues considered in the chapter should guide the examiner in evaluating the results of examinations, especially when making recommendations.

STABILITY AND CHANGE OF INTELLIGENCE

In attempting to determine the constancy of the IQ, that is, the extent to which a child's IQ remains the same from one test session to another, two separate issues should be considered (Anastasi, 1958). One issue involves the prediction of the IQ at a later date, while the other issue concerns the extent to which the IQ provides an index of the regularity of intellectual development. The latter issue refers to how stable an individual's IQ is over a period of time. The prediction of IQ at a later date from an IQ score depends on such factors as (a) reliability of measures; (b) extent to which items attempted measure the same functions at each level; (c) differential learnings between testings; (d) time interval between tests; (e) age at which the initial test is administered; and (f) shapes of distributions of scores at each testing. With respect to (d) and (e), research has shown that the shorter the test-retest interval, the higher the correlation; and the older the examinee, the greater the constancy of the IQ. Generally, the predictive value of the IQ, Anastasi concluded, is fairly high. However, as an index of the regularity of intellectual development, the IQ fails. Over an interval of time, any one individual may show large shifts in the scores he obtains. Changes as great as 50 points have been reported (Honzik, Macfarlane, & Allen, 1948). IQ's obtained prior to age six must be interpreted with discretion (Bradway, 1944, 1945a).

Bloom (1964) reviewed longitudinal studies of intelligence which used the Stanford-Binet and other intelligence tests. He concluded that the variation in intelligence at age 17 can be accounted for by the following developmental pattern: 20% is developed by age 1, 50% by age 4, 80% by age 8, and 92% by age 13. This pattern shows differentially accelerated growth, with very rapid growth of intelligence in the early years. As much development takes place during the first four years of life as in the next 13 years.

Bloom also pointed out that the stability of intelligence is greater for shorter time periods than for longer time periods. The stability of measured intelligence increases with age. The effects of extreme environments may change IQ by about 20 points. The evidence on stability of the IQ, it is well to remember, is based upon measured intelligence and not on intelligence as it may be revealed in natural conditions or on tests which may be developed in the future. "Intelligence is a developmental concept, just as is height, weight, or strength [p. 68]." Bloom cautioned that no decisions of any significance should be made about a child on the basis of a single test administration during the first few years of life. Further, "a single early measure of general intelligence cannot be the basis for a long-term decision about an individual [p. 88]." Error variation is reduced when the results of several test administrations are combined, but the notion of an absolutely constant IQ must be questioned. Bloom concluded that major changes in a characteristic are very difficult to produce after it has reached a high level of stability. However, at any time it is likely that individuals can be helped to learn better ways of using their abilities.

Wallin's (1940) observations concerning fluctuations in individual intelligence test performance are also instructive. Fluctuations may be a result of "resistances, emotional upsets, distraction, fear of the examiner, dislike for the tests, lack of intellectual stimulation in the subject's ordinary social and intellectual environment, illnesses, and injuries [p. 216]." In addition, defects in test construction, scoring and administration problems, and hereditary or constitutional factors may contribute to changes in test scores. Accelerations in intellectual growth may be associated with "improved physical health, a stimulating social and educational environment, or freedom from hampering conflicts, fears, and anxieties [p. 216]." He concluded:

It is indisputable that fluctuations do occur whether the children are normal or abnormal, whether the retests are given by the same or different examiners, or whether the retests are given infrequently or in a long series of retests at six months' intervals. These fluctuations may be genuine or illusory. They may be partly correct and partly misleading. They may be exaggerated or minimized by the testing or scoring techniques. They may be caused by endogenous or exogenous factors. They may represent the effects of practice or of emotion inhibitions. They may be permanent or temporary. They may be subject to remediation or they may prove to be highly resistant to modification [p. 220].

Wallin recommended that classifications and assignments be made tentatively, subject to revision in the light of fuller knowledge.

FACTORS AFFECTING MENTAL GROWTH AND IQ CHANGES

Studies which have investigated familial and personality factors, and to some extent biological factors, have identified various factors associated with the rate of mental growth and with changes in the level of intellectual development. Some of these studies are reviewed in this part of the chapter.

Familial Conditions

Variables in the familial environment that may be related to the mental growth of children were studied in a sample of children who were followed from 21 months of age to 30 years of age (Honzik, 1967). Children were found to obtain high IQ's when there was evidence of parental ability; maternal concern, energy, and worrisomeness; and concern by both parents about their children's achievement. The relevant affectional milieu which affected the rate of mental growth was found to be different for males and females. Sons obtained high IQ's with a close mother-son relationship and when father had occupational success and satisfaction, whereas daughters obtained high IQ's with a friendly father and with compatible parents. At the age of 8 years, children obtained higher IQ's when their parents were demanding (e.g., ambitious for their children) than when they were neutral, whereas lower IQ's were obtained when parents were unconcerned about their children (i.e., few ambitions for their children or indifferent to success or failure). Honzik's results suggested that both biological factors and patterns of interaction within the family affect rate of mental growth. These results generally confirmed those of an earlier investigation by Honzik and her co-workers (Honzik et al., 1948). Bradway and Robinson (1961) supported the contention that biological factors affect IQ change. They found that significant position changes in the distribution of IQ's from preschool to adolescent years were related to ancestral intelligence. Changes between adolescence and adulthood showed no such relationship.

Other studies have also reported that changes in IQ level were related to familial environmental variables. In one study which covered a three-year period, children reared in warm, democratic homes gained in IQ points, whereas those reared in less emotionally gratifying homes either did not gain or obtained lower IQ's (Baldwin, Kalhorn, & Breese, 1945). Similarly, in another investigation, parents who used democratic principles, such as justification of policy and readiness of explanation, tended to have children who increased their IQ's on successive tests (Sontag, Baker, & Nelson, 1958).

The relationship between disciplinary atmosphere in the home and intellectual development has also been studied (Kent & Davis, 1957). Higher Stanford-Binet (Form M) IQ's were obtained by children coming from demanding homes (M IQ = 124) than by children coming from normal homes (M IQ = 110), overanxious homes (M IQ = 107), or unconcerned homes (M IQ = 97). On the four WISC Performance Scale subtests that were administered, the only significant finding was that the children coming from normal homes obtained significantly higher IQ's (M IQ = 110) than those coming from overanxious homes (M IQ = 101). While children coming from demanding homes obtained the highest Stanford-Binet IQ's, they were also judged to be more restless, tense, ill-at-ease, and overanxious to succeed than children coming from normal homes. Most children coming from unconcerned homes (8 out of 9) showed signs of emotional disturbance, such as apathy and lack of spontaneity. The less efficient WISC performance of the children from overanxious homes was attributed to their deficiency in practical abilities; explanations based on situational factors which may have interfered with test performance were ruled out by the investigators. Overall, the results indicated that discipline in the home significantly affected intellectual development.

Personality and General Correlates

Children during the period between 3 and 12 years of age who showed gains in Stanford-Binet IQ have been found to have an aggressive, self-assured mastery of tasks and a competitive independent pattern, while those who showed losses in IQ have been found to have a passive, infantile dependency pattern (Sontag, Baker, & Nelson, 1955). These findings were essentially supported in other investigations which have reported that, during the developmental period from 6 to 10 years of age, aggressiveness, self-initiation, high need-achievement, competitive striving, and curiosity about nature were correlated with gains in IQ's (Kagan, Sontag, Baker, & Nelson, 1958; Sontag et al., 1958). Acceleration or deceleration of intellectual level during the period between 4 and 6 years of age appears to be associated with such factors as maturational or physiological changes and the emotional relationship between child and parents (Sontag et al., 1958).

In an investigation of some correlates associated with IQ change, a group of children were selected who showed changes in their Stanford-Binet (Form L) IQ's when first tested at 3 to 5 years of age and then retested at 6 to 7 years of age. Children who increased their IQ's, in comparison with those who decreased their IQ's, were more often (a) born prematurely, (b) of high socioeconomic status, (c) constant in their emotional adjustment, and (d) unimpaired on other measures of psychological functioning (Wiener, Rider, & Oppel, 1963).

Personality variables obtained from the Children's Personality Questionnaire have been found to be related to intellectual level in a sample of children between the ages of 10 and 13 (Kirkendall & Ismail, 1970). Children in the superior intelligence group were rated as being more outgoing, warmhearted, emotionally stable, calm, gay, enthusiastic, forthright, and natural than children in either the normal or low intelligence groups. Overall, children with superior intellectual ability tended to be better adjusted emotionally than those of normal or low intellectual ability. Another study indicated that boys who were socially dependent at age 2 tended as 6-year-olds to have a less abstract cognitive style and lower WISC Performance Scale IQ's, but not lower Verbal Scale IQ's, than boys who were less dependent (Wender, Pedersen, & Waldrop, 1967).

INFANT TESTS

While measures of sensorimotor adaptation in infancy have not been found to be *highly* predictive of later intelligent behavior (cf. Thomas, 1970), recent research indicates that infant mental development is related to later intelligence (Ireton, Thwing, & Gravem, 1970; Werner, Honzik, & Smith, 1968; Willerman, Broman, & Fiedler, 1970). These studies provide some support for Piaget's (Flavell, 1963) and Bruner's (1966) claim that certain behavioral phenomena of infancy are manifestations of intelligent behavior in that they represent the child's attempts to operate on his environment, and that such operations provide analogues to later intelligent behavior (Ireton et al., 1970).

MENTAL AGE

Mental age (MA) divided by chronological age (CA) and multiplied by 100 produces the ratio IQ. The MA provides an age-equivalent for the examinee's raw score, whereas the IQ indicates an examinee's performance relative to that of examinees who are at his own chronological age. Mental age can be defined as the degree of general mental ability possessed by the average child of a chronological age corresponding to that of the examinee. This definition does not allow, in practice, for the existence of "natural" mental-age units beyond that of the highest level reached by the average person (at about age 15 to 20). Thus, the concept of IQ (a ratio to show "brightness") cannot be properly derived for superior children or for any adult by means of the conventional ratio IQ. Such serious limitations suggest that a "brightness coefficient" — an IQ — should never have been derived by the ratio method. Binet never used the IQ measure for his scale.

The concept of mental age may be interpreted grossly as cognitive level or vice versa (Kohlberg & Zigler, 1967). Mental age, as a unit of measurement, also possesses a high degree of generality (Stroud, 1957). However, mental age scores, while easily calculated and easily understood, have limitations that are often overlooked (British Psychological Society, 1958; Greene, 1941). First, mental growth shows a decrement from year to year so that the difference between mental ages of two and three is much greater than the difference between mental ages 10 and 11. Second, after the age of 13, the concept of mental age changes. The mean mental age does not increase as rapidly as chronological age. The highest mental age possible on the Stanford-Binet is 22–10, but this figure does not represent the achievement of an average American at an age of 22 years and 10 months; it is the mental age of a superior person. An average adult only achieves a mental age of 15–9. Thus, the original meaning of mental age, as representing the average of a particular age group, is lost for adults.

Third, the abilities measured at different mental ages may not be the same. Fourth, the same mental ages at different chronological ages may have different meanings. For example,

A ten-year-old with a mental age of six will differ from a normal six-year-old in physical development and skills; his interests and experience may be more like those of his age group although their range and his understanding of them will be poorer. He will perhaps be less curious, spontaneous and active; the quality of his learning and remembering will be poorer [Tansley & Gulliford, 1960, p. 43].

Fifth, even the same mental age at the same chronological age may have different meanings. Thus, children with the same mental age may not be able to do the same grade of work or make the same rate of progress in school (Murdoch, 1918).

SOCIOECONOMIC FACTORS AND INTELLIGENCE

In this part of Chapter 3 we review briefly some general findings that are related to socioeconomic level, urban-rural status, and intelligence. The next chapter (Chapter 4) considers in depth the factors that are involved in the intelligence testing of ethnic minority group children, and socioeconomic status is one such factor.

High socioeconomic groups obtain, on the average, higher IQ's than low socioeconomic groups (Havighurst & Janke, 1944; Janke & Havighurst, 1945). "The relationship of measured intelligence to socio-economic level is," according to Tyler (1965), "one of the best documented findings in mental-test history [p. 336]." The studies by Werner et al. (1968) and by Willerman et al. (1970) that were cited in the previous part of the chapter concerning infant tests also indicated that infant developmental status interacts with socioeconomic status. Low scores on infant developmental scales are more likely to result in poorer intellectual performance at later ages (4 and 10 years) in the context of low socioeconomic status than in the context of high socioeconomic status. Urban children usually perform at a higher level than rural children (Jones, Conrad, & Blanchard, 1932; Lehmann, 1959, McNemar, 1942).

THE TESTING OF INTELLIGENCE: PRO AND CON

Theories of intelligence, as we have seen in Chapter 2, have begun to show some type of consolidation. A view is emerging which emphasizes the interplay of biological and environmental factors in the development of cognitive ability. However, there still remains a gap between theories of intelligence and the ways in which intelligence is measured. In this section, we cover some of the limitations as well as the assets of intelligence testing. In a way, the entire text can be seen as providing material which shows the values and limitations of intelligence testing. We first consider some of the difficulties with the testing of intelligence, and then discuss some of the values of testing. The limitations and assets are here considered primarily in terms of a single test score derived from tests.

Limitations of Intelligence Testing and Intelligence Tests

IQ Limited in Predicting Occupational Success. Perhaps one of the most serious limitations of intelligence testing is that the score obtained from the test, the IQ, has a limited relationship to the individual's true occupational potentials (Hudson, 1971). Having a high IQ, for example, is no guarantee of success as a doctor, lawyer, or teacher. A similar thesis is offered by Kagan (1971), who pointed out that the use of power for benevolent or malevolent ends has usually been independent of level of intelligence. For many occupations, Kagan stated, the IQ should not be the primary characteristic for which an individual is screened. Tests should not be used to sort children into stereotyped categories that interfere with their ability to enter professional occupations.

Hudson extended his argument about the limited predictive utility of the IQ by pointing out the biases inherent in intelligence tests. Intelligence tests

favour those with a taste for convergent, analytic, scientific modes of thought; leaving the more divergent, more imaginative, and more artistic at a disadvantage. And it is a sobering reflection, in this context, that whilst conventional I.Q. tests favour scientists against arts specialists, they do not correlate with any known index of adult scientific skill. Gifted scientists are no more likely to have high I.Q.'s than their less gifted colleagues [p. 285].

Hudson recognized that while intelligence tests measure ability, they also can be said to be social mechanisms which are used by people with similar values to pass on educational advantages to children who resemble themselves (cf. Kagan, 1971). Both of these points, Hudson believed, are oversimplifications; only future research will extend our knowledge of the complexities involved in intelligence testing.

IQ Limited in Predicting Nonacademic Skills. The IQ is not only limited in predicting success, but it is also limited in predicting nontest or nonacademic intellectual activity (Masland, Sarason, & Gladwin, 1958). Littell (1960) observed: "... the nature of the test situation rules out problem solving which takes place outside of a one-to-one relationship with another person or which involves any but very short periods of time [p. 135]."

Thorndike (1921), in assessing the 1916 Stanford-Binet, recognized that for a child who has normal educational opportunities, the Stanford-Binet will predict accurately how he will respond to academic material. However, the test results will be less helpful in determining

how well he will respond to thinking about a machine that he tends, crops that he grows, merchandise that he buys and sells and other concrete realities that he encounters in the laboratory, field, shop and office. It may prophesy still less accurately how well he will succeed in thinking about people and their passions and in responding to these [p. 126].

Misuse of Intelligence Tests as Measures of Innate Capacity. It is important to recognize, according to Masland, Sarason, and Gladwin (1958) and to Sarason and Doris (1969), that intelligence is not a thing, that the testing situation is not representative of all problem solving situations, and that it is difficult to arrive at conclusions about capacity from test results. Similarly, Stodolsky and Lesser (1967) suggested that intelligence tests do not measure something innate, fixed, and pre-determined. Rather, intelligence tests can be thought of as samples of learning based on general experiences. The score reflects the richness of the milieu in which the child functions and the extent to which he has been able to profit from his milieu.

Earl (1961) noted that the Binet and Simon scale was intended to test common sense. "Its subsequent misuse, as a test of innate general intelligence in child or adult, educated or illiterate, would have shocked its great author [pp. 9–10]." Earl believed that "the IQ is perhaps the supreme example of the vicious practice of sacrificing psychological thinking to statistical convenience [p. 11]."

Gallagher and Moss (1963) suggested that intelligence tests should be considered as "school aptitude tests" or "diagnostic tests," but not as tests that provide a genetic patterning of the child. When exceptional children are tested in a school setting, the examiner's "major concern is with the abilities shown by this youngster at this time and what he can be expected to do in the school setting [p. 4]."

Intelligence Tests Provide Limited Information.   The intelligence test is multidimensional, yet it provides only a single IQ score (Guilford, 1956; McFie, 1961; Sarason & Doris, 1969; Sigel, 1963). General intelligence scales cannot provide an exhaustive foundation for the study of abilities, because children are capable of many more functions than are represented in general intelligence scales (Dingman & Meyers, 1966).

Processes Underlying Response Are Not Measured.   The test response indicates "what" the examinee can do; it does not indicate the processes underlying the responses (Haeussermann, 1958; Sigel, 1963). The test provides limited information about how the solution was arrived at, whether impaired areas of functioning were detoured in responding to the task, or what were the reasons for failure. Sigel noted that "a correct answer to an analogies item, for example, may be a function of particular learning, perceptual discrimination, syllogistic reasoning, or any combination of these [p. 40]."

Penalizing Nonconventional Responses.   Test manuals fail to consider as being correct responses which deviate from those prescribed. Therefore, nonconventional, original, or novel responses are penalized (Sigel, 1963). Minority group children may be also penalized for giving responses which are appropriate for their milieu (see Chapter 4).

Confusion of Functions of Testing.   Three major functions of intelligence testing are often confused with each other: namely, to predict school performance, to determine patterning of abilities, and to clarify the child's problems (Gallagher & Moss, 1963). Intelligence test scores provide useful information about how the examinee is functioning at the time of testing; prediction of later performance is much less valid. It is especially important that educational decisions not be made on the basis of an IQ obtained in the distant past, because IQ's, as we have seen, fluctuate, and because even the same intelligence test may measure different abilities at different age levels.

Intelligence Tests Restrict Understanding of Mental Abilities.   Dingman and Meyers (1966) believed that the use of the WISC and Stanford-Binet in factor analytic studies has beclouded the issues regarding mental abilities and has slowed the search for wider spectra of human abilities in childhood. A similar criticism has been made by Nunnally (1967), who pointed out that since Binet and Simon designed their tests from the global end products of intellectual functioning, their work may have been harmful, in the sense that subsequent studies of human abilities have failed to teach us much about the nature of human intellect.

Assets of Individual Intelligence Tests

The shortcomings of individual intelligence tests and intelligence testing, which have been discussed in the previous section and which are discussed in other chapters of the text, must be recognized and incorporated into the assessment process. Some of the shortcomings have even been said to mean that intelligence tests *limit* our understanding of intelligence (cf. Sigel, 1963). Even the most fervent proponents of intelligence testing recognize the many limitations that exist with current tests and procedures. However, tests also are valuable and contribute in many ways to decision-making processes in schools and clinics, and these contributions, too, should be recognized. Throughout the text, as well as in this chapter, the assets and limitations of intelligence tests will become apparent. In addition to the IQ, other kinds of information, as the remainder of the text shows, are inferred from the results of intelligence testing. Consequently, many of the objections raised to intelligence testing are obviated by a more differentiated type of analysis of the intelligence test. Some of the assets of intelligence tests may be summarized as follows.

Despite the frequent criticisms leveled against the IQ, a child's IQ, obtained in a standard situation, has more demonstrated behavioral correlates than any other psychological measure (Kohlberg & Zigler, 1967). Individual intelligence tests adequately predict scholastic achievement, yield a more useful picture of cognitive development than group tests, and aid in clinical situations (Butcher, 1968). Vernon (1969) recognized that while the intelligence test gives a better estimate of potentiality than other measures of achievement, its main usefulness lies in its ability to predict "educability or trainability because of its greater generality, and because it samples the reasoning capacities developed outside school which the child should be able to apply in school, e.g., to new subjects [p. 27]."

Tests permit the measurement of change, provide information about the individual's initial status, and help in understanding the nature of intelligence and the effects of environmental variables (Anastasi, 1967). While none of the current standardized intelligence tests provide for a thorough and detailed assessment of the individual's cognitive make-up, they do make their contribution to the assessment process.

SUMMARY

General issues concerning the measurement of intelligence have been discussed in Chapter 3. In evaluating the constancy of the IQ, one must consider the issues of prediction and regularity of intellectual development. Prediction is good for short periods of time and for older children. However, the IQ fails in providing a stable index of development, because large shifts can occur over an extended time interval. Intelligence is a developmental concept. During the first four years of life, as much development takes place as in the next 13 years.

The family environment can affect rate of mental growth. High IQ's have been found to be associated with such factors as parental ability; maternal concern, energy, and worrisomeness; and parental concern about achievement. The affectional milieu which is related to rate of mental growth may be different for males and females. A democratic home environment appears to facilitate intellectual development. Children from demanding home environments have high IQ's, but they also are more anxious than children from normal home environments.

Gains and losses in IQ have also been associated with different types of personality patterns in children. Children who gain in IQ have been found to be self-assured and competitive, while children who show losses in IQ are more likely to be passive and dependent. Prematurity, high socioeconomic status, and constancy of emotional adjustment also are related to increases in IQ from preschool to school ages. Well-adjusted adolescents have been found more frequently in bright than in normal and low ability groups.

Limitations are associated with use of the mental-age concept on the Stanford-Binet. (*a*) The concept of mental age for test purposes, defined as the degree of general mental ability possessed by the average child of a chronological age corresponding to that of the examinee, breaks down for superior children or for adults when it is used in the ratio IQ. (*b*) Different abilities may be measured at different mental ages. (*c*) The same mental age at different chronological ages may indicate different things. (*d*) Children with the same mental age at the same chronological age may have different abilities. However, in spite of these difficulties, mental age provides an index of the child's cognitive level and possesses a high degree of generality.

The following are some relationships between cultural factors and intelligence: Intelligence level is positively associated with socioeconomic status. Urban children usually obtain higher IQ's than rural children.

The limitations of intelligence testing are as follows:
1. The IQ is limited in predicting occupational success.
2. The IQ is limited in predicting nonacademic skills.
3. Intelligence tests do not provide measures of innate capacity.
4. Intelligence tests provide limited information about the domain of cognitive functions.
5. Intelligence tests do not measure the processes underlying the test responses.
6. Intelligence tests penalize nonconventional responses.
7. Intelligence tests may be unreliable for long range predictions.

The IQ obtained on a standard intelligence test has more demonstrated behavioral correlates than any other psychological measure. Intelligence tests provide some information about cognitive development, useful information about the child's ability to profit from school, and guideposts for measuring change and for evaluating the effects of environmental variables. The assets of intelligence tests are mentioned only briefly in Chapter 3 because material is included throughout the text to illustrate how individual intelligence tests are useful in school and clinical situations.

CHAPTER 4

TESTING MINORITY GROUP CHILDREN[1]

In keeping with the main theme of the present text, to elucidate the issues and problems concerned with the use of individual intelligence tests, the present chapter considers the factors involved in administering intelligence tests to children of minority groups. Sociocultural factors are also examined, especially as they relate to attitudes and perceptions toward tests and the testing situation. Material related to racial and ethnic group differences in intelligence is outside of the scope of the text. However, those interested in pursuing this topic can consult relevant sources (e.g., Bereiter, 1969; Cronbach, 1969; Crow, 1969; Dreger & Miller, 1968; Elkind, 1969; Eysenck, 1971; Hirsch, 1970; Hudson, 1971; Hunt, 1969; Jensen, 1969; Kagan, 1969; Shuey, 1966).

Minority group children represent heterogeneous groups of children, so that it becomes difficult to know what group or groups of children should be so classified. Valentine (1971), for example, found in one single urban community 14 different Afro-American subgroups, each with more or less distinct cultures. The label "minority group children" is used to designate individuals whose values, customs, patterns of thought, language, or even interests are significantly different from the prevailing pattern of the society in which they live (Liddle, 1967). The groups from which minority group children come include Negroes; Mexicans; Indians; Appalachian whites; Puerto Ricans; and children of foreign-born, migrant farm workers, and unskilled laborers.

The use of such labels as "culturally handicapped," "culturally disadvantaged," or "culturally deprived" to designate minority group children has been unfortunate, because these terms have value implications. No one has the right to degrade a subculture that does not conform to the patterns of the majority group. Certain behaviors in lower-status groups may be both healthy and justified, because life conditions differ markedly from those of the dominant culture (Barnes, 1971). The extent to which a group is handicapped may lie only in the eyes of the beholder. This chapter therefore uses the term "minority group" instead of alternatives which may have pejorative connotations.

Although intelligence testing still constitutes one of the important links in the educational chain, some believe it must be discarded because it allegedly has become a tool of the white majority — a tool that is being used to suppress the rights of ethnic minority children and, in particular, of Negro children

---

[1]A version of Chapter 4 appeared in *The First Review of Special Education* (Sattler, 1973a).

(Davis, 1971; Williams, 1970a). The issues concerning intelligence testing of minority group children are complex, for they are woven into the very fabric of society. Test results have an impact on the individual's self-esteem, influence his life chances, and engage his deepest political and social attitudes (Brim, 1965).

BIAS OF INTELLIGENCE TESTS AND TESTING

Arguments Against Use of Intelligence Tests

Numerous arguments against the use of standard intelligence tests with minority group children have appeared (Anastasi, 1967; Berdie, 1965; Clark, 1967; Eells, Davis, Havighurst, Herrick, & Tyler, 1951; Halpern, 1971; Johnson & Medinnus, 1965; Kagan, 1968, 1971; Leland, 1971; Levine, 1966; Masland, Sarason, & Gladwin, 1958; Mundy & Maxwell, 1958; Palmer, 1970; Riessman, 1962; Sarason & Doris, 1969; Schmideberg, 1970; Schubert, 1967; Williams, 1970a, 1970b, 1970c, 1971; Zigler & Butterfield, 1968). Standard intelligence tests are said to have a strong white, Anglo-Saxon, middle class bias, and that minority group children are handicapped in taking tests because of deficiencies in motivation, test practice, and reading. In addition, rapport problems are postulated, especially when the examinee is black and the examiner is white (see pages 31 and 32 for further discussion concerning the examiner's race). Intelligence tests, too, are said to be more related to nonschool problem-solving experiences of middle class children than to those of lower class children (Masland et al., 1958; Sarason & Doris, 1969).

Western culture emphasizes achievement and problem solving, and in this culture it is necessary for a child to recognize and to accept intellectual challenge by the time he begins school. However, minority group children may fail to comprehend and to accept the achievement aspects of the test situation (Palmer, 1970). They may view it as an enjoyable child-adult encounter, rather than as a time to achieve; or, if the problem-solving aspects of the situation are recognized, they may be ignored or be responded to on an associative level.

Arguments Offered by the Association of Black Psychologists

The Association of Black Psychologists also maintained that current standardized tests should not be used to test black children (Williams, 1970a):

The Association of Black Psychologists fully supports those parents who have chosen to defend their rights by refusing to allow their children and themselves to be subjected to achievement, intelligence, aptitude and performance tests which have been and are being used to—A. Label Black people as uneducable. B. Place Black children in 'special' classes and schools. C. Perpetuate inferior education in Blacks. D. Assign Black children to educational tracts [sic]. E. Deny Black students higher educational opportunities. F. Destroy positive growth and development of Black people [p. 5].

Conventional intelligence and ability tests are said to be unfair to black children, endangering their future in many ways, one of which is to place them in slow tracks in school (Williams, 1970a). A teacher, led to believe that the low test scores of black children mean that they are slow, treats them with an expectancy of "slow performance," thereby producing a self-fulfilling prophecy. The evidence to support the teacher expectancy and self-fulfilling prophecy phenomena, however, is by no means conclusive. The pitfalls of Rosenthal and Jacobson's (1968) study have been pointed out by Snow (1969) and Thorndike (1968), and other studies have failed to document the expectancy effect

(Claiborn, 1969; Fleming & Anttonen, 1971; Ginsburg, 1970; Gozali & Meyen, 1970).

Black children have also been said to develop unique verbal skills that are neither measured by conventional tests nor accepted in the middle class-oriented classroom (Williams, 1970b). Traditional ability tests may also violate the ethnic minority child's civil and constitutional rights under the provisions of the Fourteenth Amendment for equal protection under the law (Williams, 1971). Court cases, cited by Williams, involve issues related to the use of psychological tests in testing minority groups in the schools, placement of minority group children in special classes, and selection of children for the track system.

Illustrations of Bias of Intelligence Tests

The cultural bias of intelligence tests can be seen in the following illustrations (Williams, 1970c). According to Williams, responses to the Stanford-Binet question, "What's the thing for you to do if another boy hits you without meaning to do it?," are dependent on the child's type of neighborhood. In many black communities, the response "Walk away" would mean suicide. Children in black communities are taught to hit back as a means of survival. However, "Hit him back" receives zero credit on the Stanford-Binet. This and other examples are used to support the contention that neither test items nor much of the school's curriculum is relevant to the black experience. The poor performance of Negro children on conventional intelligence tests is attributed to the biased content of the tests; i.e., the test material is drawn from outside the black culture.

The bias of psychometric tests is especially evident when questionable responses are given a score of zero (Hewitt & Massey, 1969). During a test, the examiner-examinee relationship is fraught with communication problems. When a middle class white examiner tests a black ghetto child, the examiner's enunciation of words may not be clear to the examinee; the examinee, in turn, may use words that cannot be understood by the examiner. Phrases used by black ghetto children may have special meaning, although superficially the phrases are awkward, incorrect, or appear to be invented. The test stimuli, too, are vulnerable to cultural bias. Test stimuli that may appear to be *incomplete* to the child who is *not* from an impoverished environment (e.g., items on the Mutilated Pictures test at year-level VI of the Stanford-Binet or items on the WISC Picture Completion subtest) may appear to be *complete* to the ghetto child.

To illustrate the bias of test stimuli, Hewitt and Massey gave an example of a WISC Picture Completion item which requires the identification of a tooth missing from a comb. The ghetto child seldom sees a complete comb. To him, a comb is useful even when teeth are missing, to be replaced when it is no longer of any use; i.e., a toothless comb is a commonplace item, not a rarity. The ghetto child may respond by saying "hair" or "brush" or "hand." "Additionally, the physical aspects of Negro hair make it difficult to comb and the kinkiness often breaks off teeth more readily than does straight hair. Both economics and physiology influence this question [p. 36]."

Hewitt and Massey believed that standard IQ tests are based, in large part, on skills and information acquired in the school. Such tests, therefore, unfairly assess the intellectual skills of the ghetto child who views the school negatively. They concluded that standard intelligence tests will become diagnostic of mental ability only when the educational process is made applicable to the Negro student's life and learning style.

Hewitt and Massey's presentation lacked adequate item-analysis data; until more data are obtained, their illustrations stand as interesting speculations, rather than as a demonstration of the cultural bias of the WISC. Their statement concerning the relationship between IQ tests and information acquired in the schools is not supported by data, nor do they provide data concerning: (a) whether negative attitudes toward school affect learning, (b) whether poor learning promotes negative attitudes toward school, or (c) whether poor learning is some combination of (a) and (b). While phonetic variation studies have shown that middle class white speakers were able to communicate effectively with Negro children (Crown, 1970; Eisenberg, Berlin, Dill, & Frank, 1968; Peisach, 1965; Quay, 1971; Weener, 1969), less is known about the extent to which white examiners or middle class black examiners are able to understand the communications of poor black children. A common complaint in desegregated schools now is "I just can't understand them [poor black children]." Yet these same children communicate exceedingly well with their own peers. The black in the south, and to a lesser degree in the north, has spent 350 years perfecting a communication system that will exclude whites and, incidentally, white-oriented blacks. It is no wonder "I can't understand them" (R. M. Dreger, March 1972, personal communication).

Reasons for Poor Performance

A variety of reasons might account for the poor performance of minority group children on standardized intelligence tests (Zigler & Butterfield, 1968). While the children may have an adequate storage and retrieval system to answer questions correctly, they may fail in practice, because they have not been exposed to the material. For example, to the question, "What is a gown?" which appears on the Stanford-Binet, they may respond incorrectly because they have never heard the word "gown." Motivational factors may affect the performance of some minority group children; they know what a gown is, but respond with "I don't know" in order to terminate as quickly as possible the unpleasantness of interacting with a strange and demanding adult. Thus, when low IQ scores or changes in IQ test performances occur, they may be due to modifications in test content or in motivational factors, neither of which has much to do with the children's thinking abilities.

Studies have suggested that minority group children, in comparison with middle class children, are more wary of adults, more motivated toward securing adults' attention and praise, less motivated to be correct for the sake of correctness alone, and willing to settle for lower levels of achievement success (cf. Zigler & Butterfield, 1968). The results of Zigler and Butterfield's own investigation suggested that minority group children (Negro and white) suffer from emotional and motivational deficits which decrease their usual intellectual performance.

Poverty: the Main Characteristic of Minority Groups

Formal testing procedures appear to identify those individuals who cannot compete in our technologically-oriented culture (Leland, 1971). Tests therefore become major instruments for casting out the physically sick, the uneducated, and those with special personal problems. The poor, as a group, are the most vulnerable, and it is *poverty* that is the main characteristic of minority groups. The adaptive strategies of the poor are not always conducive to good test performance. They may cope poorly with external pressures and experience failure—even in areas where they have some cognitive strengths—because they feel that things often happen to them in spite of themselves and without their participation. Testing situations may arouse tension and feelings of suspicion in the poor child. He may react with aggression or with nonparticipating resistance, but simultaneously feel that it is important to establish a friendly relationship with the examiner. A heightened preoccupation with his relationship with the examiner may, in turn, reduce the saliency of the test questions. Such strategies leave the poor child ill-equipped to cope with tests. Leland made the telling observation that when a child who performs adequately in his own environment is given a label as a result of testing, the label makes him visible to others. Testing for special reasons (by referral) thereby makes an otherwise unlabeled person visible and begins to create social problems where previously none had existed.

Position of the Society for the Psychological Study of Social Issues

A work group of the Society for the Psychological Study of Social Issues (Division 9 of the American Psychological Association) presented a sound discussion of some of the issues involved in the use of current standardized tests with minority groups (Deutsch, Fishman, Kogan, North, & Whiteman, 1964). The following material is a condensation of their presentation. The three critical issues in testing minority group children involve whether tests (a) reliably differentiate among members of minority groups, (b) have predictive validity, and (c) are interpreted adequately.

Reliability data for specific minority groups are not presented in test manuals, including the manuals for the Stanford-Binet, WISC, and WPPSI. Such data are badly needed, especially by institutions that test minority groups. The following trends emerge from studies investigating the characteristics of minority group children that affect their test performance and test results:

. . . it may be hypothesized that in contrast to the middle-class child the lower-class child will tend to be less verbal, more fearful of strangers, less self-confident, less motivated toward scholastic and academic achievement, less competitive in the intellectual realm, more "irritable," less conforming to middle-class norms of behavior and conduct, more apt to be bilingual, less exposed to intellectually stimulating materials in the home, less varied in recreational outlets, less knowledgeable about the world outside his immediate neighborhood, and more likely to attend inferior schools [Deutsch et al., 1964, p. 132].

The examiner has the responsibility, whenever there is a doubt about test reliability for the sample of children that he is testing, for presenting the results in a cautious manner. Critical decisions should not be made on the basis of the "face value" results. Careful study of individual responses will help in determining the extent to which the overall performance is representative of the child's ability.

The work group pointed out that minority group status is not a crucial consideration when an examinee is being compared to a specific norm group. However, the examinee's minority group status *is* important when his scores are explained, or when they are used to make long-range predictions.

For example, no inequity is necessarily involved if a culturally disadvantaged child is simply reported to have an IQ of 84 and a percentile rank of 16 on the national norms for a certain intelligence test. However, if this is interpreted as meaning that the child ranks or will rank no higher in learning ability than does a middle-class, native born American child of the same IQ, the interpretation might well be erroneous [Deutsch et al., 1964, p. 134].

The final issue discussed by the work group concerned the interpretation of test results. Errors in test interpretation stem from several sources. For example, responses deviating from the norm of the majority culture may be typical of a minority group and hence not deviant at all (cf. Ellenberger, 1960). Test performance should always be interpreted in light of the child's life experiences. Another source of error relates to construct and content validity. The content of a test may, for some groups, tap motivation as well as the trait purportedly being measured. In addition, the test procedures, which include ways in which questions are asked and responses given, may affect the child's performance. By becoming familiar with the cultural and social background of minority group children, the examiner may avoid misevaluating test performance.

Tests and Discriminatory Practices in School

Mercer (1971) reported data which seemed to support Berdie's (1965) observation that tests may actually lead to and encourage discriminatory practices. Mercer studied the relationship between membership in ethnic minority groups and placement in classes for the mentally retarded in public schools in Riverside, California. While the percentage of children in ethnic groups tested by psychologists closely approximated the ethnic distribution of the entire school population, there was a disproportionate number of Mexican American and Negro children obtaining IQ's below 80. In addition, there were disproportionately more Mexican American children, but not Negro children, than Anglo-Americans recommended for placement and finally placed in classes for the mentally retarded. Mercer believed that a "defect hypothesis" (i.e., that mental retardates suffer from specific physiological and cognitive defects over and above their slower rate of development) or a genetic hypothesis could not account for her findings. Instead, she proposed an alternate hypothesis: children from low socioeconomic groups or from ethnic minority groups are more vulnerable to being labeled mentally retarded, because clinical measures (primarily, intelligence tests) are interpreted from a culture-bound perspective.

Challenge to Cognitive Deficit Theory

An important article by Cole and Bruner (1971) challenged many prevalent views concerning the psychological processes operating in individuals designated as "culturally deprived." Using material from such diverse fields as anthropology, sociology, linguistics, and psychology, Cole and Bruner marshaled an impressive set of arguments to refute the notion that individuals from certain subcultural groups have cognitive deficits. Labov's (1970) work, in particular, played a crucial role in their analysis. Labov pointed out that in an assessment situation, the only thing controlled is the superficial form of the stimulus—the test question. The examinee's interpretation of the stimulus and the response he believes is appropriate are completely uncontrolled. Therefore, studies on the verbal capacities of children, which often are included in investigations of subcultural differences in cognitive capacity, cannot be valid if the crucial intervening variables of *interpretation* and *motivation* are uncontrolled. Labov also noted that the traditional assessment situation elicits deliberately defensive behavior from Negro examinees. Because the Negro child expects that talking openly will expose him to insult and harm, he may not try to answer the questions. The linguistically deficient child in the assessment situation may demonstrate powerful reasoning and debating skills in his own environment.

Cole and Bruner argued:

Those groups ordinarily diagnosed as culturally deprived have the same underlying competence as those in the mainstream of the dominant culture, *the differences in performance being accounted for by the situations and contexts in which the competence is expressed* [p. 870].

However, they also recognized that a ghetto inhabitant's language training may make him unfit for jobs in the middle class culture. The assumptions that situational factors are often important determinants of psychological performance and that different cultural groups are likely to respond differently to any given situation led Cole and Bruner to propose a change in traditional ways of psychological experimentation by incorporating "representative design" (Bruns-wik, 1956) and an analysis of the "ecological significance" of stimulation.

Cole and Bruner indicated that the assessment of competence requires a determination of "first, whether a competence is expressed in a particular situation and, second, what the significance of that situation is for the person's ability to cope with life in his own milieu [p. 874]." The label "cultural *deprivation*," Cole and Bruner maintained, "represents a special case of cultural *difference* that arises when an individual is faced with demands to perform in a manner inconsistent with his past (cultural) experience [p. 874]."

Valentine (1971) suggested that neither the deficit model (cf. Zigler & Butterfield, 1968) nor the difference formulation (cf. Baratz & Baratz, 1970) is adequate in accounting for Afro-American behavior. Instead, he argued for a biculturation model. According to Valentine, biculturation is the

key concept for making sense out of ethnicity and related matters: the collective behavior and social life of the Black community is bicultural in the sense that each Afro-American ethnic segment draws upon both a distinctive repertoire of standardized Afro-American group behavior and, simultaneously, patterns derived from the mainstream cultural system of Euro-American derivation [p. 143].

Afro-Americans are bicultural and bidialectical, and, far from being either deficient or merely different in culture, often have a richer repertoire of life styles than middle class whites. The thread linking the authors in this section is that the behavior of cultural minorities is seen as valid in its own right and not inferior or deprived.

NEGRO EXAMINEES AND EXAMINERS' RACE

The examiner's race as a variable which may affect Negro examinees' performance has been considered an important variable in the field of intelligence testing, almost from the beginning of the testing movement. Many writers maintained that differences in racial membership affect the examiner-examinee relationship (Anastasi, 1958; Anastasi & Foley, 1949; Barnes, 1969; Blackwood, 1927; Brown, 1944; Deutsch et al., 1964; Garth, 1922; Hilgard, 1957; Klineberg, 1935, 1944; Pettigrew, 1964; Pressey & Teter, 1919; Riessman, 1962; Strong, 1913). Testing Negro children in the south may present a special problem for the white examiner because the children may have an attitude of fear and suspicion that can interfere with their performance (Klineberg, 1935). According to the above writers, Negro examinees, when tested by white examiners, may display behaviors that reflect their discomfort in the test situation. They may show fear and suspicion, verbal constriction, strained and unnatural reactions, and a facade of stupidity to avoid appearing "uppity." They may also score low to avoid personal threat. The test situation, too, may be viewed by Negroes as a means for white persons, not blacks, to get ahead in society (Pettigrew, 1964). While many of these behaviors, patterns, and perceptions are likely to exist and are important phenomena in their own right, there is no way of knowing to what extent they affect the examinee's scores (Sattler, 1970).

The examiner, too, must be cognizant of the possibility that his views of the Negro may affect his ability to establish rapport. Recent research indicates "that although the United States white's view of Negroes may be becoming somewhat less negative, it is still radically different from his view of white Americans [Brigham, 1971, p. 20]." The examiner must guard against permitting stereotypes of the Negro (e.g., superstitious, lazy, happy-go-lucky, and musical—Hartsough & Fontana, 1970) to affect his work.

When research studies are reviewed, the results suggest that the examiner's race does not usually affect the performance of Negro or white subjects on individual or group-administered intelligence tests. Thus, studies using standard intelligence tests have usually reported that the examiner-race variable was not significant (Caldwell & Knight, 1970; Costello, 1970; Crown, 1970; Lipsitz, 1969; Miller & Phillips, 1966; Pelosi, 1968), although one study reported a significant examiner-race variable (Forrester & Klaus, 1964) and two studies found that the examiner's race played a significant role with some groups but not with others (Abramson, 1969; Canady, 1936, as analyzed by Sattler, 1966a). Shuey (1966), from her review of literature, concluded that white examiners do not adversely affect the IQ's of Negro examinees. It is crucial to note that such studies are still too few in number, and often too faulty in design, to permit firm generalizations concerning the effect of the examiner's race on children's performance on intelligence tests. For example, the small number of examiners used in many studies confounds individual differences and race differences among examiners. Until very recently, cross-examiner studies have been virtually nil (cf. Sattler, 1973c).

CULTURE-FAIR TESTS

Attempts to develop culture-free and culture-fair tests have not been successful, because of the failure to recognize that intelligence, in part, is the summation of the learning experiences of an individual (Wesman, 1968). Therefore, intelligence tests cannot be created so that differential exposure to learning has no influence on scores. If the intent is to predict the individual's ability to learn the content of the more general culture, tests designed for the subculture will be less relevant than those which sample from the general culture. The acquisition of conventional verbal abilities will be needed if an individual is to progress in the general educational system and in the general culture. No test can be regarded as culture-fair (Anastasi, 1961; Vernon, 1965). Developing new types of tests which will both predict socially useful criteria and not be influenced by skills valued in the dominant culture will be extremely difficult (Bennett, 1970).

Nonverbal tests are also not culture-free, because they depend upon the ability to reason logically — an ability which is bound to middle class ways of thinking, i.e., to analytic ways of thinking (Cohen, 1969). The analytic way of thinking and the relational way of thinking are two of the basic cognitive styles. Cognitive styles are methods by which individuals select and process information. They are independent of native ability and definable without reference to specific substantive content. The analytic cognitive style consists of (a) abstracting salient information from a stimulus or a situation, (b) a stimulus-centered orientation to reality, and (c) a focusing on specific parts. The relational cognitive style consists of (a) a descriptive mode of abstraction, (b) a self-centered orientation to reality, and (c) a focusing on the global characteristics of a stimulus.

For Negro children, nonverbal tests (or sections of tests) have been found to be as difficult as or more difficult than verbal tests. These data do not permit one to determine the extent to which nonverbal tests are culture-bound; they simply indicate that Negro children obtain different scores on verbal and nonverbal tests. For example, on the WISC, the Performance Scale has been found to be as difficult as or more difficult than the Verbal Scale for Negro children (Atchison, 1955; Caldwell & Smith, 1968; Cole & Hunter, 1971; Goffeney, Henderson, & Butler, 1971; Hughes & Lessler, 1965; Teahan & Drews, 1962). Cattell's Culture Fair Intelligence Test has not been found to have any advantage over the Stanford-Binet in testing Negro disadvantaged children (Willard,

1968). When Form L of the Stanford-Binet (primarily verbal) has been compared with the Raven's Progressive Matrices (nonverbal) in a sample of 7- to 9-year-old low socioeconomic status Negro and white children, the results showed that Stanford-Binet scores were similar for the two ethnic groups, while Progressive Matrices scores were significantly lower for the Negro than for the white children (Higgins & Sivers, 1958). Thus, the Stanford-Binet was said to have less ethnic bias than the Progressive Matrices. However, what is most important is which test is more valid for the purposes for which it is being used.

Other studies have reported similar trends. Negro preschoolers have been found to obtain higher Stanford-Binet IQ's than Leiter IQ's (Costello & Dickie, 1970). The highly verbal administration of the Stanford-Binet was found to be somewhat more reassuring to the lower class children and to young children than the procedures used with the Leiter. The Davis-Eells Test of General Intelligence on Problem-Solving Ability has been found to be as influenced by cultural factors as other measures of intelligence and achievement in a sample of Anglo-American and Mexican American children in grades 2 through 5 (Stablein, Willey, & Thomson, 1961).

Tests on the Stanford-Binet and Wechsler scales which apparently have little socioeconomic status bias include Digit Span, Block Design, and Mazes (Jensen, 1970b). The Stanford-Binet may be less status-fair than the Wechsler scales because tests of the same content (e.g., Vocabulary and Digit Span) do not appear at every year level of the former. Therefore, year levels may differ in their status-fair properties. It is theoretically possible that the discontinuance procedures might prevent some children from taking tests that are potentially less status biased at a higher year level. This assumes that the higher year level is less biased than the lower year level. The point-scale format of the Wechsler scales does not have such problems. It is not known to what extent the year-level format of the Stanford-Binet produces status bias; this is a question for further investigation.

Jensen listed three ways to judge the status fairness of a test. First, the predictive validity of a test can be studied for different groups in the population. If different predictive validities are found, and if the differences cannot be attributed to differences in variance in the test scores or in the criterion scores, the test is probably biased in favor of some groups. Second, tests having many culturally loaded items are less likely to be status fair than tests with few culturally loaded items. Third, tests that are highly resistant to practice gains may be more a measure of internally regulated developmental processes than of environmental influences.

Jensen (1970b) proposed that "a test is status fair to the degree that its correlation with 'Intelligence A' [genotypic form, related to the innate capacity of the individual; see Chapter 2] in the population in which the test is used approaches unity [p. 80]." This means that the higher the correlation between phenotype (test) and genotype (intelligence A), the higher the fairness of the test. The Stanford-Binet, Jensen stated, has a phenotype-genotype correlation of approximately .90 in the normative Caucasian population, a figure which is the square root of the heritability of intelligence test scores. The average value of estimates of heritability is about .80, "which means that about 80 per cent of the true-score variance on intelligence tests is attributable to genetic factors and about 20 per cent is attributable to nongenetic factors [p. 80]." However, Jensen also indicated that, at present, there are not adequate data to estimate the heritability of intelligence test scores in the American Negro population.

Jensen (February 1972, personal communication) also stated that it is important to recognize that such statements as "no test can be regarded as culture-fair" or "culture-fair tests are not free of all cultural influences" *and* "there is no line which is perfectly straight" are comparable. Culture-fairness is not either-or, but a dimension (or a number of dimensions) along which various tests can range. The fact that no test lies at either of the end points of this continuum does not invalidate the continuum or the differences in culture loading between tests lying at various points along the continuum.

The analogy between tests of culture-fairness and straight lines provided by Jensen must be viewed with caution, as should be the implication that culture-fairness is a simple determinate dimension along which tests clearly lie. It may be important that the statement "there is no test that is culture-fair" is true in a somewhat *different* sense from "there is no line which is perfectly straight." Lines can, *in principle,* approach perfect straightness, and we know pretty precisely what is meant by that. Perhaps tests *cannot,* in principle, approach culture fairness. This may well be the case because "culture fairness" is not a well defined term, as "straight line" is, and in fact the definitions accepted by Negro and white subgroups differ. For example, it can be argued that if the predictability in the minority group is as good as in the majority group, the test is possibly fair. The minority group might well argue that the very *use* of the test is unfair because its predictive abilities can be used to deprive people of their place in society. In a sense, *no test can be culture-fair if the culture is not fair.*

The reason (or one reason) for this is that the *criterial* behaviors must be culture dependent. Why predict academic performance? Why choose certain symbol-manipulative abilities as intelligent behaviors? These behaviors are selected because the dominant culture values them.

What is the dimension along which tests vary when they vary in culture fairness? If members of different cultures vary, it may be that the variation is genetically rather than culturally produced. Or it may be that the test isn't culturally fair. How to find out which? This can be accomplished only by distributing members of the cultures in question into each other's culture so that culture can be held constant in some comparisons and genetics in others. If the subculture is shown to make no difference in responses to certain items, then we might say that those items were culturally fair. But why should those items in particular constitute a test of anything in particular, say intelligence? The above discussion points out some of the difficulties in defining and determining culture-fairness.

TEST PROCEDURES

Group vs. Individual Tests

The difference between scores obtained on individually administered tests and group-administered tests is of interest. Low socioeconomic status children may be more distracted in a classroom testing situation than when they are tested individually. Jensen (1970a) suggested that results of studies which have indicated that there is a greater discrepancy between group and individual test scores for low socioeconomic status children than for middle class children might have been due to the extrinsic factors in the group-testing situation (e.g., test procedures, instructions, and forms) which might have interfered with the children's performance.

Modifications in Test Procedures

Minority group preschool children (Negro and white) have been found to obtain higher scores on the Stanford-Binet (Form L-M) when a test administration procedure allowed them to obtain a maximum number of successes early in the testing experience than when the standard procedure was used (Zigler & Butterfield, 1968). On the Peabody Picture Vocabulary Test, randomizing the difficulty level of the items (along with other procedural changes) led to higher scores than did the standard procedure in a group of Negro preschool children (Ali & Costello, 1971). The dialect (standard English or Negro dialect) in which the Stanford-Binet (Form L-M) (Quay, 1971) or the Wechsler Preschool and Primary Scale of Intelligence (Crown, 1970) was administered failed to affect significantly the IQ's obtained by Negro children. Interestingly, in Quay's study, the actual speech of the children was predominantly in dialect in both language conditions of test administration, while comprehension of standard English and dialect was equal. Other studies or findings have shown that reinforcement conditions (e.g., praise or candy) have not significantly affected Negro children's Stanford-Binet scores (Tiber & Kennedy, 1964; Quay, 1971), and that feedback and reward led to significantly higher WISC Verbal Scale scores of lower class white children but not of lower class Negro or middle class white children (Sweet, 1969).

MEXICAN AMERICANS

Five million Mexican Americans are concentrated in five states—California, Texas, Arizona, Colorado and New Mexico. The use of Spanish is declining among native-born Mexican Americans, being used less frequently in large cities in California than in small cities in Texas. The decline in use is most prominent among middle class Mexican Americans (Moore, 1970).

Bilingualism

Mexican American children usually have to learn English as a second language and then are required to use this second language in their school work (Manuel, 1965). Spanish, however, is the language they use outside of school. It is spoken at home and in the community, but is seldom used in reading. Because of this form of bilingualism, many children fail to develop a sufficient mastery of either language, and learning is more difficult under such conditions.

Whether or not bilingualism constitutes a handicap depends upon the way in which the two languages have been learned (Anastasi & Cordova, 1953). The child who learns one language at home and another at school may be limited in his mastery of both languages, whereas the child who learns to express himself in at least one language in all types of situations will have minimal handicaps, if any. In a recent review of bilingualism and intelligence, Darcy (1963) concluded:

While the bulk of evidence indicates that bilingual children receive significantly lower scores on verbal intelligence tests than comparable monoglots, this inferiority does not hold if the tests are of a non-verbal type, particularly if the monolingual and the bilingual subjects are of the same socioeconomic class [p. 280].

Speech Difficulties

Because Mexican American children often speak Spanish as their primary language, the Anglo-American examiner may have difficulty communicating with the Mexican American examinee. The patterns of speech inculcated by use of the primary language, Spanish, can interfere with the correct speaking of English (Beberfall, 1958; Chavez, 1956; Perales, 1965). Speech patterns of bilingual Mexican American children often are a complex mixture of both English and Spanish, and the children may never become proficient in speaking either language (Holland, 1960). Language barriers arise from (*a*) the different sound that the same letters have in Spanish and English (e.g., *i* in "hit" or "miss" may be pronounced as *ee* as in "meet"), and *(b)* the variations in concepts that exist between the two cultures (e.g., "nose" in some Spanish localities is plural, so that a child may say "I hit *them* against the door") (Chavez, 1956).

Spanish-speaking children can encounter three types of difficulties when they speak their own language (Perales, 1965). First, because their Spanish vocabulary is limited, they may borrow from a limited English vocabulary to complete expressions begun in Spanish. Students may use such expressions as "*yo le dije que* I wouldn't do it" (I said to him that I wouldn't do it) and "*El fue,* but I stayed in *la casa*" (He went, but I stayed in the house). Second, they may give English words Spanish pronunciations and meanings (called *pochismos*). For example, a Spanish speaker may use the word *huachar* (from the English verb "to watch") instead of the correct Spanish verb *mirar,* or the word *chuzar* (from the English verb "to choose") instead of the correct Spanish word *escoger.* Third, they may have difficulties in pronunciation and enunciation. They may say, for example, "*Nos juimos con eos*" for "*Nos fuimos con ellos*" (We went with them).

Rapport

Stereotypes held by either the Anglo examiner toward the Mexican American examinee, or by the Mexican American examinee toward the Anglo examiner, may interfere with rapport. The two ethnic groups are keenly aware of the differences that divide them, and feelings of resentment — stemming from a mutual lack of understanding — are prominent (Madsen, 1964). Anglos generally know little about Mexican American customs and values (Clark, 1959), nor are they knowledgeable about the conditions that exist in the *barrio* (section of a town in which Mexican Americans live) (Burma, 1954). The examinee's language may serve as a reduced cue for group identification and, like skin color, it may influence the examiner-examinee relationship (Anastasi & Cordova, 1953).

Anglo-Americans are said to hold distorted images about Mexican Americans. Mexican Americans are characterized as being unclean, prone to drunkenness, criminal, deceitful, and of low morality (Simmons, 1961). More favorably, they are stereotyped as being musical and romantic, and having a love of flowers. Most of the Mexican Americans' images of the Anglo are formed on the basis of the Anglos' attitude toward them. Anglos are viewed as stolid, phlegmatic, cold-hearted, and distant, and are said to be braggarts, conceited, inconstant, and insincere. The favorable views are that Anglos have initiative, ambition, and industriousness.

Some of the stereotypes have no discernible basis in fact, while others may have at least a kernel of truth. Few if any of the stereotypes are valid and none is demonstrably true of all individuals. The negative images on the part of the Mexican American about Anglo-Americans are primarily defensive rather than justificatory. The Anglo-American stereotypes of the Mexican American as being child-like and irresponsible support the prejudiced notion that Mexican Americans are capable only of subordinate status. Anglo stereotypes provide an easy rationalization for maintaining the status quo, thus making unnecessary any attempts to improve conditions for Mexican Americans (Saunders, 1954).

Inappropriateness of Intelligence Tests

Arguments against the validity of standardized intelligence tests in the assessment of Mexican American children center around the personal, social, and cultural differences between Mexican American children and the normative groups. Intelligence tests fail to measure adequately the intelligence of Mexican American children because the language and content of the tests are inappropriate, the group is not represented in the norms, and the testing situation is atypical (Ramirez & Gonzalez, 1971). An additional criticism, which may stimulate the development of new tests, is that standard tests are not suitable for Mexican American children, because their cognitive style may be primarily relational while the tests require an analytic mode. However, more information is needed about the relationship between cognitive styles and ethnic group membership. (Cognitive styles are also discussed under "Culture-fair Tests" in this chapter.)

Over 35 years ago the necessity to consider the characteristics of the normative group and the examinee population was recognized: "A test is valid only to the extent that the items of the test are as common to each child tested as they were to the children upon whom the norms were based [Sanchez, 1934, p. 766]." Sanchez found that the 1916 Stanford-Binet presents vocabulary difficulties for Spanish-speaking children. Many words were used in the 1916 Stanford-Binet, either in the specific directions or in specific responses required by the tests, that are not in the standard vocabulary of Spanish-speaking children. Because mentally retarded Mexican American children have been found to perform better on the Arthur Performance Scale than Anglos of comparable age and intelligence, Shotwell (1945) concluded that standard intelligence tests are not valid for the assessment of Mexican Americans and other racial groups. However, this conclusion is questionable, because the sample was from a limited segment of the IQ distribution and no other ethnic groups were studied.

In another investigation, Mexican American children between the ages of 6 and 16 also were found to obtain significantly lower scores on the Stanford-Binet (form not indicated) than on the Arthur Performance Scale (Cook & Arthur, 1951). The results were attributed to limited language facility and to cultural differences between the Mexican American children and the normative group. A study of the Stanford-Binet (Form L) performance of Mexican American children from both the upper and lower socioeconomic classes indicated that the Stanford-Binet provides a valid measure of the intellectual level of upper class, but not of lower class, Mexican American children (Kidd, 1962). Only three tests in the scale were found to yield the same scores, on the average, for children from the two cultures: Paper Cutting at year-levels IX and XI and Memory for Designs at year-level IX.

Translating a Test or Test Directions

Spanish has been used, either in the test directions only or in the complete test, to administer standardized intelligence tests to Spanish-speaking children. In one study, Form M of the Stanford-Binet was first administered in English to Mexican American bilingual fourth-grade pupils (Keston & Jimenez, 1954). Four weeks later, Form L of the Stanford-Binet was administered in Spanish. On Form M, the mean IQ was 86; on Form L the mean IQ was 72. Scores on the English version were thus significantly higher than scores on the Spanish version. Students who performed better on the Spanish version than on the English version were usually low-ability students. The investigators theorized that the sample had a higher level of development in the English language than in the Spanish language. The Spanish translation is not suited to bilingual Mexican American children, because the Spanish spoken by the children contains archaisms, contaminations, and Anglicisms. The development of proficiency in the Spanish language may cease when Mexican American children enter grade school and begin their formal education in the English language. The investigators concluded that while the English version of the Stanford-Binet does not give an accurate measure of the intelligence of bilingual Mexican American children, it gives a fairer and more accurate result than the Spanish version.

Chandler and Plakos (1969) set out to evaluate whether Mexican American children in classes for the educable mentally retarded might have been placed incorrectly, on the basis of scores obtained on the English version of the WISC. They used the Spanish version of the WISC, *Escala de Inteligencia Wechsler para Niños,* which was standardized in Puerto Rico and published by The Psychological Corporation. However, the investigators modified the Spanish version of the WISC, because some of the items are apparently not applicable for Mexican American children. The Puerto Rican norms, however, were still used. In order to make the test applicable to Mexican Americans, whose native tongue is a Spanish idiomatic to various regions in Mexico, some words were changed, such as *bola* to *pelota* and *concreto* to *cemento;* acceptable answers were expanded, so that to the question "Where is Chile?" credit was given to "in a can" or "in a field" or "in a store." Using the modified Spanish version of the WISC, the children obtained an increase of 12.45 points over their scores on the English version of the WISC. The investigators concluded that many Mexican American children may have been placed in educable mentally retarded classes solely on the basis of performance on an invalid test (i.e., the English version of the WISC). Their procedure, however, warranted no such conclusion. Not only were standard procedures violated in administering the Spanish version of the WISC, thereby making use of the Puerto Rican norms inappropriate, but, in addition, validity data for the scores obtained on the Spanish version of the WISC by the Mexican American children were not presented.

The Sweetwater Union High School District of Southern California agrees with Chandler and Plakos in stating that the Puerto Rican version of the WISC presents problems for use with Mexican American children (M. Grossman & H. Teller, July 1971, personal communication). A number of examples point out needed modifications. On the Information subtest, the question concerning the distance between New York and Puerto Rico is inappropriate for Mexican American children. A suggested substitution is the distance between Mexico D. F. and Monterey for children educated in Mexico, or the distance between New York and Chicago for those educated in the United States. A substitute for the number of pounds in a ton might be the number of meters in a kilometer. On the Arithmetic subtest, *bolitas de vidrio* could be replaced with *canicas* for the word "marbles." These and other examples indicate that the Puerto Rican version of the WISC should not be used without modification in the testing of Mexican American children. Modifications, however, are not the final answer until questions of reliability and validity are answered.

Galvan (1967) administered the WISC in English and in Spanish to bilingual and culturally deprived Mexican American children who were in grades 3, 4, and 5. Giving the WISC in Spanish was found to facilitate performance, primarily on the Verbal Scale. However, the validity of the two language versions was equal, as noted by the .46 correlation between the California Achievement Test and the WISC given in Spanish, and the .52 correlation between the California Achievement Test and the WISC given in English. The correlation between the two Verbal Scales was .53, while the correlation between the two Performance Scales was .97. Palmer and Gaffney (1972), however, reported that translating the WISC into Spanish did not alter significantly the scores of fifth grade Mexican American children.

Holland (1960) sought to determine the effects of bilingual administration of the WISC Verbal Scale in a sample of Mexican American children in grades 1 through 5 who had been recommended for testing because of academic or emotional problems. The bilingual administration consisted of (*a*) giving the subtest instructions in English first, followed by repeating the instructions in

Spanish if the instructions were not understood or if only partially understood, and (*b*) giving credit to a correct answer given in either language. The test questions, however, were presented in English. The children obtained a mean bilingual Verbal Scale IQ of 85, a mean English Verbal Scale IQ of 81, and a mean Performance Scale IQ of 91. Differences between the two Verbal Scale IQ's decreased from the first grade to the fifth grade. Holland suggested that the English Verbal Scale IQ can be considered to represent the present level of functioning in English language skills. The bilingual Verbal Scale IQ may represent the future potential for verbal skills, when the examinee's knowledge of English is approximately equal to that of Spanish. Again, this conclusion is particularly questionable in view of the fact that *neither* language is adequate, and it is very doubtful whether "future potential" is adequately assessed by even the bilingual administration.

The studies which investigated the effects of translating test content or test instructions from English into Spanish thus have indicated that such procedures are fraught with hazards. Translation of a test makes it a hybrid belonging to neither culture. As Sanchez (1934) noted, translating a test may be of no value, if the items have not been experienced by the child. The need is for construction of tests in the native language, with native cultural norms, administered by native psychologists.

Performance on the WISC

The WISC, according to Hewitt and Massey (1969), may not be a suitable test for evaluating the intelligence of Mexican American children. Their passivity, or unwillingness to engage in competition, may cause them to do poorly on the timed subtests, especially on Block Design. The Coding subtest, however, may be the least culturally biased, in spite of its being a timed subtest; the Information and Comprehension subtests may be the most culturally biased. Mexican American children, too, are said to have difficulty with abstractions, in seeing alternatives, and in changing their problem-solving techniques. The above observations will remain as plausible but unconfirmed speculations until empirical support is presented.

The available research findings suggest that Mexican American children, especially those who are bilingual, obtain higher scores on the Performance Scale than on the Verbal Scale. For example, Altus (1953) compared the WISC scores of bilingual Mexican American children with those of monolingual Anglo-American children. The sample consisted of 11-year-old children who had been referred for screening for special classes for the mentally retarded. The Anglo children obtained significantly higher scores than the Mexican American children on the Full Scale and on the Verbal Scale, and on the Information, Comprehension, Similarities, Vocabulary, and Picture Completion subtests. However, the two groups did not obtain significantly different scores on the Performance Scale. Altus concluded that the retardation of bilingual Mexican American children appears to be a linguistic one. Bransford (1966) also reported that bilingual Mexican American children in special classes for the mentally retarded obtained higher Performance Scale IQ's than Verbal Scale IQ's, and that the disparity between the two IQ's continued with increasing age.

A somewhat different conclusion concerning the disparity between Verbal and Performance IQ's, as a function of increasing age, results from Fitch's (1966) investigation. In this study, a group of first- and second-grade bilingual Mexican American children was matched with fifth- and sixth-grade bilingual Mexican American children. The two groups therefore differed by five years in exposure to English. While the only significant difference between the two groups was on the Vocabulary subtest, in favor of the fifth-sixth graders, the disparity between the Verbal and Performance Scale IQ's was less for the older group than for the younger group (84 vs. 92 and 78 vs. 98, respectively).

The effects of both social class and ethnic origin, as variables related to the WISC scores of adolescent male and female Anglo-Americans and Mexican Americans from the middle and lower socioeconomic classes, were studied by Christiansen and Livermore (1970). The results indicated that social class was a more important factor than ethnic origin in differentiating among children. On all the WISC measures studied, lower class children obtained significantly lower scores than middle class children. However, Mexican American children also obtained significantly lower scores than Anglo-American children on combinations of WISC subtests measuring general intelligence, retention of verbal knowledge, and ability to use verbal skills in new situations. The investigators suggested that the bilingual nature of the Mexican American home makes it difficult for the children to acquire verbal skills needed in an Anglo culture.

Killian (1971) studied the WISC performance (together with performance on the Illinois Test of Psycholinguistic Abilities and Bender-Gestalt) of male and female Anglo-American, Mexican American monolingual, and Mexican American bilingual children, who were matched on school achievement and were attending kindergarten or first grade. The school achievement scores were slightly above average. The Full Scale and Performance Scale IQ's of the Anglo-American children (M IQ's = 98 and 97) were significantly higher than those of the Mexican American bilingual children (M IQ's = 88 and 90), but not significantly higher than those of the Mexican American monolingual children (M IQ's = 92 and 93). The Anglo-American children also obtained a significantly higher Verbal Scale IQ (M = 100) than both Mexican American groups (monolingual M IQ = 92, bilingual M IQ = 88).

Anglo-American children were significantly higher on the Comprehension and Picture Arrangement subtests than were the two Mexican American groups. In addition, at the kindergarten level, but not at the first grade level, Anglo-American children were significantly higher on the Information subtest than the Mexican American children. Scores on the Arithmetic, Vocabulary, Block Design, Object Assembly, and Coding subtests were not significantly different among the groups. Bilingualism did not generally play a significant role in distinguishing the performance of the two Mexican American groups.

The WISC results, together with findings on the other two tests, suggested to Killian that the Mexican American children did not have a profile indicating severe and early restriction of experience at home. Rather, their major difficulty seemed to be in the area of input, namely, problems with interpreting meaningful words and pictures that were presented in sequence. The results concerning the differential performance of the Anglo-American and Mexican American groups on the Information and Comprehension subtests were interpreted to mean that during the first grade the school is able, apparently, to increase the Mexican American child's general information knowledge, but is not as successful in enhancing his understanding of social skills and values.

In Killian's study there would be little reason to expect that the Mexican American children would have restricted experiences at home, because they were matched with Anglo-American children on achievement scores that were above average. An interesting way to interpret the results is to say that Mexican American children obtained a mean achievement test score equal to that obtained by Anglo-American children with a higher average IQ.

PUERTO RICAN CHILDREN

The problems involved in testing Puerto Rican children are likely to be similar to those involved in testing Mexican American children. For example, working in Puerto Rico, Roca (1955) translated and adapted the WISC and Stanford-Binet (Form L). Some items were found to be too difficult, while others were too easy. On the WISC Vocabulary subtest, for example, either words such as "spade," "mantis," "spangle," and "belfry" were too easy when translated into Spanish, or else they had different meanings. Items within subtests were also found to be of a different level of difficulty from the standard version. Thus, even after translation, a test may not be valid for Spanish-speaking children.

Talerico and Brown (1963) evaluated the WISC scores obtained by Puerto Rican children divided into three age groups (6–8, 9–11, 12–15); they had been attending a psychiatric clinic for children. In all three groups the Performance Scale IQ was higher than the Verbal Scale IQ by about 6 to 12 points. The largest differences between the IQ's on the two scales were in the two youngest age groups. In the total group, the three easiest subtests were Picture Completion, Block Design, and Object Assembly, while the three hardest subtests were Arithmetic, Information, and Vocabulary.

Degree of cooperation on the Stanford-Binet at the age of 3 years was found to have prognostic significance for Puerto Rican working class children but not for middle class white children (Hertzig & Birch, 1971). On retesting at the age of 6, the white children who were uncooperative at the age of 3 obtained scores which were similar to those obtained by the cooperative white children. However, the Puerto Rican children who were uncooperative at the age of 3 obtained scores on retest that were significantly lower than those obtained by the initially cooperative Puerto Rican children. The investigators suggested that the uncooperative Puerto Rican 3-year-old might have been displaying a pattern of functioning that is antithetical to the subsequent development of effective problem-solving skills. This conclusion may be justified, but another is possible: cooperative Puerto Rican children may be more advanced cognitively and thus more cooperative. Finally, it was suggested that intervention programs may be particularly suitable in modifying behavior style for the uncooperative children.

NORTH AMERICAN INDIAN CHILDREN

The appropriateness of using tests, standardized on white children, with North American Indian children has also been questioned. Turner and Penfold (1952) described some of the handicaps of North American Indian children that interfere with their educational morale and which are likely to affect their test performance. The children are said to lack confidence because of a long history of social failure, the absence of distinguished members, discrimination by whites, and failure of some members who have left the reservation. Additional handicaps include a lack of tradition of education, low socioeconomic level, low attendance in school, language deficiencies in the home, an inadequate school system, and low test motivation.

The traditional values of the Pueblo Indians, and to a lesser extent of the Navajo, contrast with those of the Anglo culture, and have been known to cause problems in the adjustment of Indian children to public schools (Zintz, 1962). The values of the Indian child include (a) a desire for harmony with nature instead of a mastery over nature; (b) a present time orientation rather than a future time orientation; (c) an explanation of natural phenomena by mythology and sorcery rather than by science, together with fear of the supernatural; (d) an aspiration to follow in the ways of old people, and to cooperate and maintain the status quo rather than to compete and climb the ladder of success; (e) a choice of anonymity and submissiveness over individuality and aggression; and (*f*) a desire to satisfy present needs and to share, in place of working to "get ahead" and saving for the future.

Other difficulties, some of which overlap with those mentioned in the previous paragraph, were described by McDiarmid (1971). Communication is difficult because of the many different dialects that are found among North American Indian tribes. Motivational problems arise because of differences between middle class white children and Indian children. Middle class white children, it is assumed, are test-wise and have culturally conditioned achievement motivation. These assumptions mean that they desire to do well, are able to attend carefully to directions, and have a sense of time and competition. Indian children, in contrast, are handicapped in these areas. Slowly changing seasons may be as important to them as clock time, and competitive individualism is punished. The examiner, too, may encounter difficulty in administering the test and in interpreting test results when he meets such behaviors as infrequent speech, limited responses to test questions, and speaking softly. In the comparative study of ethnic groups, McDiarmid favors the approach of Lesser, Fifer, and Clark (1965), which focuses on patterns of differences among ethnic groups rather than on the absolute amounts of differences.

There is some evidence that indicates that Indian children are more successful on the WISC Performance Scale than on the WISC Verbal Scale. Turner and Penfold (1952) reported that a sample of Indian children between 7 and 14 years obtained a Performance Scale IQ that was 11 points higher than their Verbal Scale IQ. Observations of test behavior indicated that there were few errors made on the Coding subtest, while much time was taken to answer the Verbal Scale items. Generally, the Indian children appeared to be in greater fear of making a mistake than has been observed in white children.

Cundick (1970) studied the performance of southwestern American Indian children in prekindergarten through sixth grade on four intelligence tests. On the WPPSI and WISC, available from prekindergarten through third grade, Verbal Scale IQ's were significantly lower than those for the normative groups (obtained from the test manuals) in all of the grades tested. Performance Scale IQ's, on the other hand, were significantly lower than the normative groups only at the prekindergarten level. Schooling thus did not seem to raise Verbal Scale IQ's for these children during their first four years of education. The mean Draw-a-Man IQ's, available for all of the grades studied, were very close to the expected mean IQ of 100 after the second grade. The Peabody Picture Vocabulary Test, also available for all grades studied, showed, in sharp contrast, a narrow range of mean IQ's (53 to 69), with IQ's dropping lower after the third grade. Cundick's study shows that American Indian children differ from test standardization groups differentially according to the functions measured. An implication of this study is that it is important to determine for each specific minority group the degree to which different tests are comparable.

VALUE AND VALIDITY OF INTELLIGENCE TESTS

Value

In Chapter 3, the assets as well as the limitations of intelligence tests were discussed. These considerations are, of course, pertinent to the evaluation of minority children as well. In the early part of Chapter 4, other kinds of arguments against the use of intelligence tests for evaluating ethnic minority children have been presented. One of the major arguments is that tests are used to justify discrimination. We now consider other factors that pertain to the usefulness of intelligence tests for minority group children.

Test scores of underprivileged minority children are useful indices of immediate or present functioning (McNemar, 1964). Tests point out differences among groups (Lorge, 1966). Because tests may reveal the inequalities of opportunity available to various groups, they may also provide the stimulus for social inventions to facilitate the maximum development of each individual's potentialities. Thus, knowing that differences exist may lead to the gradual disappearance of some kinds of bias. Minority groups should be favorably inclined toward use of ability tests, because tests constitute a universal, objective rather than prejudicial, standard of competence and potential (Brim, 1965). Other selection methods may decrease the opportunities of minority group children.

Concern about the social consequences of not using educational tests has been expressed (Ebel, 1964; Messick & Anderson, 1970). If educational tests are abandoned, it will become more difficult to encourage and reward individual efforts to learn. Programs will be difficult to evaluate, and educational opportunities might be based more on ancestry and influence, and less on aptitude and merit. Decisions on curriculum would be based less on evidence, and more on prejudice and caprice. Thus, the consequences of not testing might be to increase bias and discrimination.

Validity

Studies investigating the validity of standardized intelligence tests with populations of ethnic minority groups usually report validity coefficients which are similar to those obtained with white populations. An extensive investigation of the Stanford-Binet (Form L-M) with a sample of 1800 Negro elementary school children between the ages of 5 and 16 years who were living in the southeastern United States indicated that there was a .69 correlation between the Stanford-Binet MA and California Achievement Test scores; the Binet also correlated significantly with teachers' ratings ($r = .32$) and with grades in academic areas (r's $= .64$ to .70; Kennedy, Van de Riet, & White, 1963).

In other studies, the Stanford-Binet (Form L-M) was found to correlate significantly ($r = .67$) with the Metropolitan Achievement Test in a sample of disadvantaged children, 80% of whom were Negro, between the ages of 9 and 11 years (Bruininks & Feldman, 1970), and with reading achievement ($r = .57$) in a sample of second and third grade Negro boys (Bruininks, 1969). Individual tests in the Stanford-Binet were found to have generally the same level of difficulty in a sample of Negro and white children between the ages of 4 and 6 years enrolled in a Head Start program that they have in the normative population (Olivier & Barclay, 1967). Peabody Picture Vocabulary Test scores have been found to be related significantly to reading achievement scores in a sample of Negro first graders (Hall, 1969). Group tests of achievement and ability have also been found to correlate significantly with grade point average for twelfth grade Negro students (Boney, 1966), and to be valid predictors for first grade Negro children (Mitchell, 1962).

There have been at least two reports indicating that the WISC, as well as other intelligence tests, may not be appropriate for Negro children. In one study, southern Negro children between the ages of 10 and 13 years obtained low scores on the WISC; however, they seemed to be functioning effectively in their own environment (Young & Bright, 1954). The authors concluded that the WISC may not be valid for Negro children. In another study, of the four tests used (WISC, Revised Beta Examination, Ammons Full-Range Picture Vocabulary Test, and Porteus Maze Test), the Porteus Maze Test was the only one capable of differentiating southern Negro adolescents who were behaviorally retarded from those who were not behaviorally retarded (Cooper, York,

Daston, & Adams, 1967). However, significant correlations (r's = .38 to .61) have been found between the WISC and Wide Range Achievement Test in samples of 7-year-old white as well as Negro children (Henderson, Butler, & Goffeney, 1969).

The position taken by some writers—that IQ's are not valid for some persons because they are functioning effectively in their own environment—may not do justice to the concept of the validity of intelligence tests. "Effective functioning" in one's own environment is not the criterion by which the validity of the IQ is determined. The effectiveness of a person's functioning is in large part dependent upon his particular milieu. What is effective in one setting may be ineffective in another. Intelligence tests are intended to measure factors that pertain to the culture as a whole; therefore, their validity rests on criteria derived from the general culture and not from any specific subcultural group. Yet (as we have seen in the previous section of this chapter on culture-fair tests) this is precisely why minorities may legitimately object to perfectly "valid" intelligence tests. Why, philosophically, shouldn't the subgroup provide the criterial performances to be predicted?

RECOMMENDATIONS FOR ASSESSING MINORITY GROUP CHILDREN

Many different kinds of recommendations have appeared concerning the assessment of minority group children. Some have favored a moratorium on testing (Davis, 1971; Williams, 1970a), while others advocated ways in which testing can become a more useful tool in the educational process. One recommendation is for administering a wide range of mental tasks when testing minority children (Anastasi, 1961; Davis, 1971; Jensen, 1970a). Neither a single test score nor any small number of scores can provide an adequate picture of the intellectual abilities of a group (Anastasi). The sampling of cognitive abilities is especially important in order to discover the strengths and weaknesses of children from educationally disadvantaged backgrounds, since there may be more variability in their pattern of abilities than in the pattern of children who are not disadvantaged (Jensen). Jensen also advocated the use of tests of g that are free from obvious cultural content for the assessment of educationally disadvantaged children, in order to select children with potentially strong academic aptitude. Examples of such tests are the Progressive Matrices (Raven, 1960), Culture Fair Intelligence Test (Cattell, 1959), and Domino Test (Gough & Domino, 1963).

Correcting the culture-bound perspective of current intelligence tests would require the establishment of separate norms for various sociocultural groups (Mercer, 1971). A person's score on an intelligence test would then be interpreted with reference both to standard norms and to his own sociocultural group norms. The former comparison would reflect how the person stands in relationship to the general population of the United States, while the latter comparison would reflect the amount of knowledge the person has acquired about the culture of the dominant society as compared to others who have had comparable opportunities to learn. A score interpreted with reference to the standard norms might indicate how well the person might currently be able to participate in the dominant culture, while a score interpreted with reference to the sociocultural norms might indicate the probability that the person might reach a particular level in the dominant culture, if given adequate educational experiences. However, interpreting this score in this way would be guesswork until it was demonstrated that educational experiences could indeed make the person capable of reaching the "expected" level in the dominant culture.

There is a need for the development of tests that will better reflect the potential intelligence of children from minority groups and a need to make intelligent and accurate interpretations of results, particularly when the results are used as a basis for making school judgments and class assignments of children that will affect their future lives (Clark, 1960). Present and future tests are needed to evaluate the psychological processes by which children learn; tests should not be used solely to sample what has been learned and to infer the capacity to learn from their scores (Newland, 1970). Changing the curriculum and teaching approaches for black children, rather than devising new tests, is another suggested approach, because abolishing tests will not remove the adverse conditions that black children find in the community and in the schools (Milgram, 1970).

The assessment of Mexican American children may improve when changes are made both in the educational system and in some of the children's attitudes, perceptions, and behaviors (Ramirez, Taylor, & Petersen, 1971). Two approaches that may prove valuable are bilingual education, since it may lead to greater facility in both English and Spanish, and involving the parents in the educational process by helping them learn ways of reinforcing their child's achievements. In working with Mexican American children (as well as with children from other groups), it is important to understand the examinee's culture and community. The examiner who is able to help Mexican American children feel pride in their native language and culture and to learn Spanish himself, will be making important strides in facilitating the educational process (Nava, 1970).

Alternatives to the standard goals of classification in the assessment process are being offered. The proper task of testing is to discover ways to help the individual; it should not be to exclude individuals from entering courses of study or occupations (E. B. Williams, 1971). Education should change from focusing on the selection of individuals, to gaining more knowledge about individuals and ways in which they can be served. Who is to determine the standard and for whose benefit has the standard been defined? asked Williams. The need for educational reform has also led to the development, in many fields of learning, of individualized instruction involving self-paced learning (Holtzman, 1971). The curriculum consists of units of instruction or modules which are linked together. Testing consists of evaluating the extent to which the individual has met the training objectives (e.g., the learning of modules), rather than normative testing for measuring individual differences.

Members of minority groups who have encountered prejudice and exclusion tend to respond to intelligence testing as simply another means to implement prejudice, however unjustifiable that response may be. But the views of E. B. Williams and Holtzman seem to be ones that everyone could agree to. Their aims are not to exclude anyone from any program; they aim simply to help the individual.

The classroom teacher involved with educating children from "disadvantaged" cultural groups (a) should recognize that educational difficulties displayed by the children represent a difference, rather than a special kind of intellectual difficulty, and (b) should concentrate on how to get the child to transfer skills he already possesses to the tasks at hand, rather than attempt to create new intellectual structures (Cole & Bruner, 1971). A social-systems approach in place of the modal approach to the study of lower-status children (and, in particular, black children) might prove to be valuable (Barnes, 1971). The modal approach focuses on the individual or his family, and emphasizes mental health, treatment, and pathology. The social-systems approach emphasizes the interdependence of child and family with other levels of society, the heterogeneity of blacks (and other oppressed groups), the recognition of the black community as a complex social system, and the shift of focus from behaviors of individuals to recurrent interchanges between people. It will be necessary to recognize explicitly the minority child's community, group, and culture in order to break his familiar cycle of educational failure.

The handicaps of minority group children are often so great that their test scores may have meanings different from those of nonminority group children, even when the scores are numerically the same (Deutsch et al., 1964). Test scores should not be accepted as fixed levels of either performance or potential; instead, they may be used to determine the magnitude of the deprivation that is to be overcome by a planned program of remedial activities. Scores can also be used to compare disadvantaged children with one another. Still another way in which scores can be useful is to compare the child's current test performance with his previous test performance. In the last analysis, the examiner and other test users must accept the responsibilities involved in interpreting and in using educational and psychological tests.

Many comparisons depend upon tests, but they also depend upon *our* intelligence, our good will, and our sense of responsibility to make the proper comparison at the proper time and to undertake proper remedial and compensatory action as a result. The misuse of tests with minority group children, or in any situation, is a serious breach of professional ethics. Their proper use is a sign of professional and personal maturity [Deutsch et al., 1964, p. 144].

CONCLUDING REMARKS

There may be no answer to the question of whether or not current standardized intelligence tests should be used in the assessment of minority group children, because the question is not properly phrased. The better question is, "When and how should they be used?" Another question: "How can assessment be improved?" Obviously, when the social and cultural backgrounds of children differ markedly from those of the normative group, standard tests should not be used in decision-making situations. While there is evidence that indicates that intelligence tests have acceptable levels of concurrent validity for some minority groups, for other groups validity data are sparse. What especially is important to consider is the type of validity in question. For example, little is known about the long-range predictive validity of intelligence tests for minority group children. Additional research is sorely needed. Objections to intelligence tests may be overcome if tests are used as measures of outcomes of education and not as screening devices (Thorndike, 1971).

The lack of supporting data for the statements of many writers concerning the effects of the examiner's race on the examinee's performance does not mean that the examiner can be indifferent to the examinee's race. He must be extremely careful when testing examinees of races or cultures other than his own. He should be alert to any nuances in his or the examinee's performance that suggest that an invalid performance is in the making. Every attempt must be made to elicit the examinee's best performance, without, in the process, modifying standard procedures. A competent examiner should have the resources to *administer* an individual test of intelligence to examinees of different races and cultures. However, the problems of test standardization, cultural deprivation, and cultural milieu all transcend the examiner-examinee relationship in affecting the examinee's performance. Cultural gaps between the examiner and examinee can create communication problems that affect not only rapport but also the examinee's ability to understand and to respond to the test questions according to the intent of the test constructors. Testing examinees from cultures different from that of the examiner is a demanding task; there are no simple solutions. The problem, of course, is exaggerated when the examinee belongs to a culture different from that of the standardization group.

If there is a need to evaluate minority group children, which test or tests can be used? Minority groups do not appear to accept any of the available standard intelligence tests. Although educators and psychologists must be responsive to the needs of minority group children and acknowledge the pleas of individuals like R. L. Williams, they will likely need to use tests in their educational programs. The shortcomings and hazards of using standardized intelligence tests with minority group children have been documented in this chapter. In addition, excellent recommendations have appeared that may pave the way for more appropriate uses of tests. I support the position presented by the work group of the Society for the Psychological Study of Social Issues (Deutsch et al., 1964). Standardized intelligence tests may be used, but only if their shortcomings and difficulties are recognized when applied to the evaluation of children coming from minority groups. Tests should never be used if they do not contribute to the development of the child or to the body of knowledge of a field of study. Obviously, no tests should be used in ways or under conditions that would physically or emotionally harm any child. However, it is difficult to spell out convincingly how tests *do* contribute, especially if the audience represents ethnic minority group members. Tests are needed that can evaluate the thought processes, modes of perceiving, and modes of expression for different cultures, and that also accord some recognition to the differing contents in different cultures. Finally, subgroups in the culture may wish to construct their own specific tests to predict what they want predicted, if it differs from what the dominant culture wants predicted.

SUMMARY

"Minority group children" has been selected as the term to designate children who come from groups whose sociocultural patterns differ from those of the society in which they live. Poverty appears to be the main characteristic of the minority groups that are the focus of this chapter. Intelligence testing of minority group children involves complex issues, which reflect many facets of our society. Tests, it has been said, provide one of the means that society uses to prevent individuals from achieving valued positions in the society.

The following are the principal arguments against intelligence testing of minority group children:

1. Tests have a white, Anglo-Saxon, middle class bias.
2. Minority group children are deficient in motivation, test practice, and reading skills, and therefore are handicapped in taking tests.
3. Examiner-examinee rapport problems are present.
4. Tests do not reflect the problem-solving experiences of lower class children.
5. Minority group children fail to comprehend fully the achievement aspects of the test situation.

The reasons why minority group children are poor achievers on tests include the following:

1. They have had limited exposure to the test materials.
2. Their choice of adaptive strategies in the test situation may be inadequate (e.g., desiring to terminate the testing session as soon as possible or focusing on the examiner instead of on the test questions).
3. Emotional conflicts are aroused in the test situation (e.g., suspicion, aggression, or resistance).

The Association of Black Psychologists has branded tests as being instruments which are antithetical to the rights of black children. R. L. Williams, one of the leading spokesmen for the group, has argued that tests have contributed to the self-fulfilling prophecy: The low test scores of black children have led teachers to treat black children in ways that will conform to their expectations. However, there is little evidence to support the self-fulfilling prophecy phenomenon in the classroom. Williams, along with Hewitt and Massey, provided, without research data, graphic illustrations of the possible cultural bias of some Stanford-Binet and WISC questions.

A knowledgeable use of tests is based on (a) reliability data for the respective minority groups, and such data are often not available; (b) a recognition of the difficulty in making long range predictions; and (c) a thorough understanding of the examinee's cultural background. Tests cannot adequately assess the verbal capacities of black children, according to Labov, because the situation in which the tests are administered does not take into account either the child's interpretation of the situation or his motivations. Thus, the linguistically *deficient* child in the assessment situation may be linguistically *sufficient* in his own environment.

Although the examiner's race has been postulated to play a role in the testing situation, the available limited research studies have failed to provide systematic support for this assumption. So-called "culture-fair tests" do not provide more valid measures of the abilities of minority group children than standard tests, because culture-fair tests also require analytical ways of thinking. Some modifications in test procedures have been found to facilitate the performance of Negro children; others do not.

The following are some difficulties in assessing Mexican American children:

1. Their cultural values may be different from those of the standardization group.

2. They may be inadequate in their comprehension of English.

3. The examiner's stereotypes of the child and the child's stereotypes of the examiner may interfere with rapport.

4. Tests may not be valid because (a) they contain inappropriate language and content; (b) they do not include the group in the norms; (c) the testing situation is atypical; and (d) they do not measure relational ways of thinking.

Translating a test or test directions has not proven to be a viable procedure in testing Mexican American and Puerto Rican children. For example, translating a test is of no value if the child has not been exposed to materials which are similar to those contained on the test. Further, many Mexican American children may be deficient in both English and Spanish. What is needed are tests that are constructed in the native language, with native cultural norms, administered by native psychologists.

On the WISC, Mexican American children are likely to obtain higher Performance Scale IQ's than Verbal Scale IQ's, a result which, in part, may be related to their limited proficiency in English.

The sociocultural values of North American Indian children — such as a de-emphasis on competitive individualism and achievement motivation and an emphasis on harmony with nature and the present time — are likely to interfere with their performance on many standardized intelligence tests.

Tests are valuable for minority group children in providing (a) useful indices of present functioning, (b) a universal standard of competence and potential, and (c) a stimulus for change. Acceptable validity coefficients have been reported for different kinds of individual intelligence tests for Negro children using grades and achievement test scores as the criteria.

The following kinds of recommendations have been made for the use of tests:

1. An immediate moratorium on all testing.

2. Administering a wide range of tests, especially those which measure g.

3. Establishing separate norms for various sociocultural groups.

4. Devising tests that will better measure intellectual potential and the processes by which children learn.

5. Changing the teaching curriculum and developing new teaching approaches instead of devising new tests.

6. Using tests to find ways of helping the individual (e.g., focusing on training objectives instead of normative testing).

7. Emphasizing tests as measures of outcomes of education and not as screening devices.

A responsible use of tests stresses the recognition of their shortcomings and limitations. In using tests to evaluate minority group children, special efforts must be made to study and learn about the cultural patterns of these children.

SECTION 2

ADMINISTERING INDIVIDUAL INTELLIGENCE TESTS

The three chapters in Section 2 form a cluster concerned with general issues involved in administering individual intelligence tests. The material in this section should be of value in most assessment situations in which individual intelligence tests are used. Chapter 5 considers the role of the examiner in the intelligence testing situation. It makes suggestions for test administration and reviews research studies involving examiner variables. Chapter 6 examines the examiner-examinee relationship, citing both descriptive material and research studies involving rapport, incentives, and pretest variables. Chapter 7 is primarily a "how to do it" chapter, which emphasizes techniques for working with various types of children, including emotionally disturbed, brain-injured, and physically handicapped children.

CHAPTER 5

THE ROLE OF THE EXAMINER IN ADMINISTERING INDIVIDUAL INTELLIGENCE TESTS

The problems involved in the administration of an individual intelligence test encompass numerous areas in addition to the mastery of the standard test procedures. Some of the additional factors that may affect the child's performance are the conditions under which the test is administered; the examiner's style, personality, and sex; and the procedures used to administer the various scales or tests. The present chapter considers these and related areas, and reviews the relevant research literature. In Chapter 6, an additional important area of consideration—the interpersonal relationship between the examiner and examinee—is discussed.

WHEN TO ADMINISTER AN INDIVIDUAL INTELLIGENCE TEST

Time is a precious commodity. Examiners, be they psychologists, counselors, or educators, find numerous demands on their time; they realize that time must be preserved carefully, especially for those activities deemed productive. Consider the reasons for administering an individual intelligence test. How important is it for the test to be administered? Will a group test be as effective as an individual test in answering the referral question? Are there any motivational, personality, linguistic, or physically disabling factors that may impair the examinee's performance on a group intelligence test? An individual test should be administered primarily when there is reason to question the validity of the results of a group test or when careful evaluation of the examinee's performance is desired. The examiner should also discuss the reasons for individual assessment with referral sources in order to familiarize them with the values and limitations of individual testing. Such discussion may lead to reducing the number of children referred for individual testing. In turn, children most in need of individual testing will be provided with prompt and intensive services.

TEST CONDITIONS

Ideally, the examination room should be one which minimizes external sources of distraction and maximizes the examinee's motivation. The varied conditions which the examiner will meet on the job will invariably fall short of the ideal. He therefore must try to secure those conditions which approximate the ideal, yet must never test when the conditions would adversely affect the child's performance. We can be somewhat heartened by Bateman's (1968) findings which showed that non-optimum testing conditions may yield valid IQ's when mentally retarded children are tested. Bateman had mentally retarded children attending a summer day camp take the Stanford-Binet (Form L-M) under adverse conditions. Thirty-five minutes were allotted for the administration of the test, the noise level was high, the heat was extreme, the lighting was poor, and the table and chair sizes were improper. Yet in spite of these conditions, the IQ's obtained by the children were only .39 points lower than those they had obtained on previous tests. Bateman concluded that, even when it is necessary to examine children under testing conditions similar to those used in her study, the validity of the obtained IQ's should not be affected substantially.

THE EXAMINER

The administration of a standard psychological test has been viewed, almost from the inception of the field of individual testing, as a procedure that requires skill and training. Whipple (1912) noted that it is difficult for novice examiners to administer the Binet-Simon tests: "No one who has drilled students in the laboratory has failed to be struck with the impossibility of laying down fool-proof directions for the conduct by an amateur of a psychological test [p. 119]." Moreover, examiners need "special drill in the handling of what is really an exceedingly delicate psychological instrument [p. 119]." Kuhlmann (1914) made parallel observations, noting that examiners may not be familiar with the test directions and with scoring rules. They may have difficulty in adapting test procedures and in interpreting responses on those occasions that are not covered by the test directions. They may not be able to adapt themselves to the child's level; consequently, they cannot elicit the child's best efforts. Finally, Kuhlmann pointed out that some examiners do not appreciate the absolute necessity of adhering strictly to all rules of testing and the need for careful, painstaking work.

Stern (1914) also foresaw well the requirements for the development of testing skills:

It must be understood that tests of intelligence are not easy to conduct. Their administration demands extended practice, psychological training, and a critical mind. Thus, for instance, the average teacher, whose work has been with the wholly different methods of pedagogical questioning and examining, is very apt to apply psychological tests in those forms in which their value would be positively illusory. If, accordingly, the use of tests for practical purposes shall attain any very large currency, the training of a specially psychologically drilled personnel will become a necessity. School psychologists would then take their place side by side with the school physicians [pp. 11–12].

One of the earliest descriptions of the examiner's role was given by Mateer (1924), who ably summarized the kinds of requirements necessary for the work of the psychological examiner.

The clinical psychologist makes the personality of the laboratory in which he works. It is dependent upon him for its formulation of the ideals which shall control its advance lines of work. He must, to further his own work, be broad-minded and as broadly educated as possible. His specialized training should include more than the modes and methods of his special work. He must be intelligently ignorant, sympathetic but impersonal, not overemotional nor yet unemotional, capable of holding a critical perspective. He must be tactful and in sympathy with his patients. His relation to them should be one of evoking confidence. He must be widely enough trained to be automatically cognizant of and plan for all sorts of chance clinic problems, such as fatigue, hunger, antagonism, shyness, illness, and difficult parents. He must naturally combine the handling of the patient with the education of those responsible for him. He must always be fair, just, patient, repaid for all effort made by his interest in the individual handled. Perfunctoriness is the final test of clinical unfitness [p. 438].

The examiner's personality and manner play an important role in the test situation. He is more than a mere recorder "of processes and images such as the pure experimentalist records [Mateer, 1924, p. 68]." He must consider the examinee's motivation, social group, and family, and in order to be successful, should have tact, the ability to explore the examinee's limits, and a liking for children. Flexibility is required; the procedures set for one child may not work with another child. Undesirable types of examiners described by Mateer are first, those who are excitable, over-emotional, and verbalistic, and who tend to exaggerate the examinee's symptoms. Second, there are antagonistic but usually phlegmatic examiners who refuse to believe any of the symptoms they find during the examination. Children tested by such examiners may receive higher mental ages than justified, because they are given the benefit of the doubt. Third, there are examiners who are too restrained, unemotional, and indifferent, and who tend to see the case as being only part of their day's work.

Mateer anticipated the work of Schafer (1954), who described how various examiner roles and personality styles enter into the interpersonal dynamics of the test situation. There are four aspects of examiner roles, according to Schafer, which are constants in the testing situation, regardless of specific examiner characteristics. First, there is the voyeuristic aspect of the examiner's role. The examiner looks at the examinee and uncovers material, but does not commit himself to the relationship. Second, the examiner is in an autocratic position. He dominates the relationship and shares little. Third, there are the oracular aspects of the role. Inferences are made from signs, predictions are made, and advice is given, either implicitly or explicitly. Fourth, there is the saintly aspect of the role. The examiner is in a position to help the examinee. Examiners develop means by which to cope with each of these aspects. However, the process-oriented relationship, which is described in Chapter 6, and some recent proposals for the examiner-examinee relationship, which are described in Chapter 26, can be effective means for modifying some of the above roles.

Schafer described eight types of examiner personality styles. Each style may be present in each examiner, with one or more of the styles being dominant on a particular occasion. The styles are as follows: (a) the examiner with an uncertain sense of personal identity; (b) the socially inhibited or withdrawn examiner; (c) the dependent examiner; (d) the examiner with rigid defenses against dependent needs; (e) the rigidly intellectualistic examiner; (f) the sadistic examiner; (g) the examiner with rigid defenses against hostility; and (h) the masochistic examiner. On many occasions none of these orientations will disrupt the examination. However, they have been described by Schafer in order to alert the examiner to the potential disruptive nature of these roles in the testing situation. The examiner would do well to monitor his own behavior in order to note instances of these personality styles when he is administering tests.

Examiner Halo Effects

The examiner must try to prevent his test administration from being influenced by his impression of the examinee—the "halo" effect. For example, examiners may overrate the responses of a child whom they perceive as "bright" and underrate the responses of a child who appears "dull." In the testing of handicapped children, the halo effect may occur in the following way:

Motivated by a feeling of sympathy often reinforced by seeing the physical energy expended by so many palsied children in following instructions, the examiner easily believes his hope, i.e., that the child knows more than he can express, and hence overestimates the child's ability [Burgemeister, 1962, p. 117].

Binet and Wechsler carefully sought to diminish halo effects by their standardization procedures. Yet Goodenough (1949) pointed out that most of us too rarely take precautions to avoid it.

There is some evidence from social-psychological literature that an experimenter's hypotheses (or expectancies) may exert some subtle influence over a subject's performance. An experimenter's hypothesis may affect how he behaves with a subject, and early data returns in an experiment may lead to the development of experimenter expectancies that can subtly affect the experimenter's behavior in later interactions with the subject (Rosenthal, 1966). Administering an individual intelligence test is somewhat analogous to conducting an experiment. Prior information about the examinee's ability level and classroom performance, and impressions resulting from the information obtained from the responses to early test questions, may lead the examiner to formulate a hypothesis, albeit vague, regarding the examinee's level of intelligence. Studies that have investigated the effects of expectancy on the examiner's behavior or on the results he obtains from examinees are reviewed in the latter part of this chapter.

SUGGESTIONS FOR ADMINISTERING INDIVIDUAL INTELLIGENCE TESTS

When the examiner encounters an examinee for the first time, anxiety is likely to be the examiner's companion. He has all at once become a juggler, having to do such things as keep the materials ready, be friendly with the examinee, present the instructions verbatim, respond appropriately to the examinee, record as precisely as possible the examinee's responses, observe the examinee's behavior and, finally, score the responses. In time, many of these procedures become routine, but even the most experienced examiner will need to review his test procedures periodically. The test manuals usually present many useful and important suggestions for administering the various tests; in each case they should be studied carefully. The following suggestions serve to supplement or to re-emphasize a number of selected points that are often presented in test manuals.

General Suggestions

We begin with some general suggestions by citing Goddard's (1911) advice for administering the Binet-Simon scale; this advice is remarkably pertinent for the administration of all individually administered intelligence tests. The child should not be given too much help or discouraged. The examiner should not begin with any preconceived notions about how the child will perform or about how much he knows. He should not give credit to a child merely because he feels certain that the child could do the problem under other conditions. Finally, the examiner should follow the manual carefully.

The instructions for the various tests should be read verbatim, in an even and relaxed manner, avoiding a wooden or machine-like approach. Digits should be read at the rate of one per second. Memory items should not be repeated. The instructions used for the first trial of a test or subtest can be repeated on succeeding trials or items. The directions should be learned well; ideally, they should be memorized.

The examiner should maintain control of the situation. He should not allow the child to turn pages in the manual, to play with the test materials, or to have pencils, pens, or toys in his hands, except when they are needed for a test. If the examiner is uncertain about what the child said, he should ask the child to repeat his response. To minimize the number of these situations, the examiner must pay close attention to the child's responses. On tests that have time limits, unless the manual says otherwise, the child should not be told how much time is allotted to the task. If the child asks, he should be told to give his answer as soon as he knows it, or something similar. The examiner should seldom accept the first "I don't know" response given by the child but should ask him to try again, unless the question appears to be too difficult for him. The child should be asked to explain his answer further when the response is incomplete or when it borders on a correct response but is not correct as it stands. However, obviously incorrect responses should not be probed. If the child asks to have part of a question repeated, it is preferable to repeat the entire question. The child should not be told whether his responses are correct. If asked, the examiner can say that it is against the rules to tell the answers, or that he can ask about one or two of his answers at the end of the examination, if he is still interested in discussing them at that time.

The examiner should immediately record the child's answer in the appropriate space provided on the record booklet. The response should be recorded as accurately as possible. Judgment will have to be exercised in recording (or in not recording) parts of the child's response that have limited relevance to the test question.

The child's responses should be scored as soon as they are given. On the Stanford-Binet, tests that may fall at the basal and ceiling levels *must* be scored during the examination proper. Failure to follow this procedure may result in an invalid test administration, because a basal level and a ceiling level should be established if standard procedures are to be followed. Similarly, on the WISC and WPPSI, discontinuance procedures cannot be followed unless responses are immediately scored. However, on the Stanford-Binet, when responses that are difficult to score occur on tests falling between the basal and ceiling year levels, the examiner may score or re-score them carefully after the examination is completed. A question mark can be placed to the left of such responses in order to identify them easily when they are checked. A similar procedure can be followed for the WISC and WPPSI. However, the examiner should try to score as many responses as possible during the examination.

The examples shown in the various test manuals for scoring the responses are guides. They are *not* meant to be the *only correct* answers, with the exception of those problems that have only one correct answer or for which the manual lists the only acceptable responses. The examiner should study the scoring criteria for each test or subtest. In arriving at a score, he should follow the intent of the item, that is, the philosophy of the scoring guide. He must shield from the child, as unobtrusively as possible, the scores that are recorded in the record booklet. At the conclusion of the examination, he may give the child a small gift. A piece of blank paper or candy is acceptable. The paper cuttings from the Stanford-Binet should not be given as gifts, because they may provide cues to other children.

Departures from Standard Procedures

There are major problems involved with departing from standard procedures during the actual test administration. The importance of following standard procedures was stressed by Terman and Merrill (1960): "The discipline of the laboratory has furnished the training ground for instilling respect for standard procedures [p. 47]." However, in requiring standard test procedures, test authors do not take into account variability among examinees or the possibility that a more accurate estimate of intellectual ability can be obtained, on some occasions, by "violation" of standard procedures. The examiner who deems it desirable to go beyond the standard test instructions in order to assess present or potential intellectual ability usually has read that such procedures may interfere with or affect the final test results. For example, Cronbach (1960) pointed out that "any departure from standard administrative practice changes the meaning of scores [p. 185]." Other writers, too, have stated that test norms cannot be used when standardized tests have been altered (e.g., Braen & Masling, 1959; Strother, 1945).

Eisenson (1954) noted that there may be occasions when standard administrative procedures should not be followed. For example, tests administered to aphasic patients

should be used to aid in formulating clinical judgments rather than as a means of trying to get a quantitative index. . . . Modifications in administering the tests and of evaluating the responses are usually necessary, or at least desirable, in order to elicit the clearest picture of the patient's intellectual functioning. Time limits may be ignored and roundabout definitions accepted [p. 4].

He recognized that such modifications preclude the use of test norms.

Newland (1963) illustrated well other alternatives available to the examiner in making test adaptations:

. . . the examiner may read the standardized test items to blind subjects, may allow a child to use a typewriter in giving his responses if he has a major speech or handwriting problem, may observe the eye movements of the subject as he identifies parts of a test item (where other children might write or point with their fingers in responding), might start with motor items rather than with verbal items in the case of a child whose problem involves the communication area, or might even rearrange some Binet items into WISC form if research warranted taking such liberties with the material [p. 69].

Contingency Reinforcement Procedures. The following case demonstrates how contingency reinforcement procedures can be effective in enhancing a child's performance in the testing situation. An 11-year-old girl achieved an IQ in the normal range (IQ = 101) when first tested with the WISC, and IQ's in the mentally retarded range (IQ's = 62, 51 and 65) when tested over a two-year period of time on three other occasions (Miller, 1969). However, outside of the testing situation, she seemed to function in the normal range. On the Verbal Scale subtests she failed many items by saying that she did not know the answer or by making inaccurate replies. On the Performance Scale subtests, she haphazardly manipulated many of the materials and generally made little effort to complete the items. Neurological evidence was negative. When she was tested for a fifth time, a monetary reward incentive procedure was used. Chips, which were to be exchanged for money, were given for correct responses and for bonus credits. This procedure resulted in the child's achieving an IQ of 106. Interestingly, performance on the Digit Span subtest at first did not improve. However, she performed at a normal level when the contingency was changed from one chip per correct series to one chip for each digit in the series when the entire series was repeated without error. This case illustrates the importance of flexible administrative procedures that are designed to encourage children to participate in the testing situation, and of the importance of comparing the test results with the child's behavior outside of the testing situation.

Use of Norms When Departures from Standard Procedures Occur.
In order to be able to use the test norms with confidence, the test items must be administered according to standard procedures. This means, for example, that the examiner must use the exact words of the questions, the specific test materials, and the specified time limits. However, while test content and test materials are standardized, one doesn't really know about the effects of small deviations in test procedures. Each test has a standard error and this reflects the nuances in the examiner-examinee relationship, the conditions of the examination, the time of day, and other similar factors. When a small change occurs in rapport or in other aspects of the test situation, it is hoped that these changes will keep the resulting score within the range of the standard error, but this will never be precisely known.

The examiner should consider when standard norms can be used and when they cannot be used. What does it mean to use them and be wrong? Can intuitive or conventional wisdom serve the examiner as a partial guide in the absence of formal standardization procedures? The answer to the latter question is a qualified "yes," depending on the extent to which modifications or violations have occurred. We have seen that one cannot standardize every little adaptation or test administration procedure. What is most crucial, however, is that standard procedures be followed in test administration and in test scoring. The use of a multiple-choice procedure for administering a test that calls for the child to provide a definition appears to be a major departure from standard procedures. In such a case, the use of test norms is highly questionable.

Comment on Departures from Standard Procedures. The above material suggests that while standard administrative procedures are the rule, exceptions may occasionally be made in order to obtain some estimate of the child's ability without regard for norms. However, wherever possible, standard procedures should be followed. On those occasions when modifications must be used, such information should be clearly conveyed in the report and the resulting scores interpreted in light of the modifications. The scores may be less precise, and predictions about future levels of functioning are likely to be more gross than would otherwise be the case. Suggestions for modifying the Stanford-Binet and WISC appear in Chapters 9 and 12.

Testing of Limits

The standard administrative procedures should be followed, if possible, in all cases. The only exceptions are those discussed in the test manuals (e.g., changing order of tests if necessary, eliminating spoiled tests, etc.) or when testing handicapped children. However, there are times at which the examiner desires to go beyond the standard test procedures (testing of limits) in order to gain additional information about the child's abilities. These occasions may be infrequent, but when they occur, the information gained from testing-of-limits procedures can be helpful, especially in clinical settings. Any successes obtained during testing of limits, of course, cannot be credited to the child's scores. *All testing-of-limits techniques should be used only after the scale has been administered using standard procedures.* The reason why this principle should be followed is that the additional cues on one item may facilitate the child's performance on the remaining items of a test or subtest. Such findings were recently reported for the Block Design and Picture Arrangement subtests of the WISC and Wechsler-Bellevue (Sattler, 1969). Many different testing-of-limits procedures may be used, some of which are described below.

1. Additional Cues. How much help is necessary for the child to answer a question correctly? To answer this question, the examiner may provide a series of cues to the child. He can show him the first step in solving the problem, after which he can provide a series of additional steps if needed. Or the examiner might begin by asking the child how he went about trying to solve the problem. This question can be followed by asking the child to try to answer the problem again, or by providing the first step in reaching the correct solution, or by informing him where his method was wrong and then asking him to try again. The more cues that are needed before success is achieved, the greater the degree of possible learning disability or cognitive deficit.

2. Establishing Methods Used by the Examinee.   There are many different ways of solving the test questions. To learn how the child went about solving the problem, the examiner may simply ask him what method he used. Some children will be able to verbalize their method, while others will not, even though they have answered correctly. In asking about the method of problem-solving, the examiner may also learn how well the child understood the task. To take one example, the digit tests can be solved by grouping the digits in pairs of two, three, or more digit sequences, by recalling them as a number (4–1–3 as four hundred and thirteen), or by recalling them as distinct digits in sequence. The method used may be related to learning efficiency or to personality features, or it may have no particular import.

3. Additional Time Limits.   When the child fails a test because of time limits, the examiner can re-administer the test without time limits (after the examination has been completed), in order to determine whether the child can solve the problem.

4. Alternate Scoring.   As a result of the help provided during the testing-of-limits phase, the child may pass tests. During the test proper, too, the child may solve a problem after the time limit has been reached. In such cases, an alternate IQ can be calculated, and both the standard and alternate scores reported. However, the alternate IQ must be interpreted cautiously because it has no normative basis. Little is known about the meaning of alternate scores, but it is possible that they are related to learning potential.

RESEARCH STUDIES ON EXAMINER EFFECTS

We now turn to research studies that have focused on various examiner variables. The topics covered include expectancy-effect studies, general examiner studies, and studies of the examiner's experience, sex, and other specific characteristics. The examiner race variable has been considered previously in Chapter 4. Problems associated with the examiner's scoring of test responses also are considered in Chapters 9, 13, and 16, which discuss the Stanford-Binet, WISC, and WPPSI, respectively.

Expectancy Effects

In the studies that have investigated expectancy effects, prior information about the examinees was furnished to the examiner. The investigations followed one of two approaches. In one approach, the examiners scored responses that had been preselected by the investigators, while in the other, examiners administered tests to subjects who were "naive" with respect to the purposes of the experiment. In the five studies reviewed that used preselected responses, significant expectancy effects were found in each case, although the effects were not uniform across all subtests.

One series of studies used a paradigm that consisted of presenting ambiguous responses for WISC and WAIS subtests to graduate student examiners under different guises. When supposedly given by bright examinees, the ambiguous responses received more credit than the same responses when supposedly given by dull examinees. This relationship occurred in a variety of situations, including presenting written responses on a sheet, tape-recorded responses, and responses given by examinee-accomplices (Sattler, Hillix, & Neher, 1970; Sattler & Winget, 1970). When both ambiguous and nonambiguous responses have been used, the expectancy effect also has been found to affect scores significantly in the predicted direction whether the ratings were by graduate or by undergraduate students (Egeland, 1969; Simon, 1969). In another study, the degree to which the examiners (undergraduates) liked the examinee and found him to be warm was related significantly to their scoring of preselected WAIS responses (Donahue & Sattler, 1971).

In seven studies in which examiners tested subjects, three have reported significant expectancy effects (Hersh, 1971; Larrabee & Kleinsasser, 1967; Schroeder & Kleinsasser, 1972) and four have not (Dangel, 1970; Ekren, 1962; Gillingham, 1970; Saunders & Vitro, 1971). The primary difference among studies with these two outcomes is that in two of the three studies with significant expectancy effects, each examiner tested only two children, one under a positive expectancy and the other under a negative expectancy. In the studies reporting nonsignificant effects, the examiners tested four, five, six, or eight subjects. Perhaps expectancy effects are less powerful in situations in which the examiner tests a number of examinees.

The expectancy effect is relevant not only to scoring but also to other decisions made by examiners. For example, Hersh reported that under positive expectancies, examiners began the Stanford-Binet at a year level that was higher than the year level selected under negative expectancies. Like Hersh, Sattler and Winget found that under positive expectancies examiners rated examinees in a more favorable light and made more favorable recommendations than they did for examinees who were tested under negative expectancies. Although Dangel did not find that the expectancy effect influenced the examiners' scoring, expectancies did play a role in affecting the examiners' predictions about the child's future behavior.

The studies reviewed indicate that pretest information plays a role in the overall evaluation of the examinee and, on occasion, in scoring responses and in administering the test. The existence of expectancies regarding an examinee's probable level of performance does not mean that scoring bias will necessarily occur (cf. Simon, 1969). Rather, the research studies point out that examiners must guard against the occurrence of halo effects when administering intelligence tests. The processes by which pretest information affects the examiner's performance are still unclear. We do know, however, that when expectancies are disconfirmed, examiners may avoid eye contact with the examinee (Johnson, 1970). Further studies will be helpful in uncovering the ways in which expectancies become translated into overt and covert behavior.

Information about how expectancies may play a role in the testing situation also is available from studies that have examined the behaviors and judgments made by student teachers. For example, in one study, student teachers who received favorable expectancies were more effective in teaching children words during a 10-minute interaction than those receiving unfavorable expectancies (Beez, 1968). In another study in which intelligence level and achievement level were held constant, socioeconomic class was found to play a significant role in the predictions made by student teachers (Miller, McLaughlin, Haddon, & Chansky, 1968). Lower estimates of academic achievement, classroom citizenship, and life attainments were given to pupils coming from lower class backgrounds than to pupils coming from middle class backgrounds. Thus, socioeconomic class was shown to be a powerful influence in affecting the judgments of student raters.

Eliminating halo effects in scoring, administering, and evaluating intelligence tests is a difficult goal. One possible approach is to have examiners administer tests without prior knowledge of the examinee's abilities (cf. Schroeder & Kleinsasser, 1972). However, even if this procedure were followed, the examiner, after administering the initial subtest on the WISC or after the first few tests on the Stanford-Binet, would probably begin to develop expectancies. Further, testing without prior knowledge would prevent the examiner from being in a position to determine the appropriateness of the request for testing and to explore strategies with the referral source (cf. Hersh, 1971). It probably is impossible to eliminate the examiner's positive or negative evaluations of the child; however, it should be possible to minimize the influence of these reactions upon the examiner's rating of the child's test responses. The examiner must become aware of his reactions to the child, and be especially alert to possible halo effects in his scoring of the child's ambiguous responses.

General Examiner Studies

There are two main formats that have been used by investigators to study examiner differences. The formats parallel those encountered in research studies on the halo effect. One format involves determining the extent to which examiners who are faced with the same set of responses differ in their scoring of responses. The second concerns the evaluation of scores obtained by examiners. Involved in this second area are issues dealing with the examiner's effect on the examinee and the examiner's judgment of the examinee's performance. The last issue is also associated with halo effects.

The research literature conclusively demonstrates that examiners differ in the scores they give to ambiguous responses; however, studies concerned with overall scores (IQ's) or with nonambiguous responses are less clear-cut. Using ambiguous responses, examiner differences have been found for Stanford-Binet responses (Sattler & Ryan, 1973a; Wrightstone, 1941) and for responses to tests in the Wechsler series (Mahan, 1963; Massey, 1964; Miller & Chansky, 1972; Miller, Chansky, & Gredler, 1970; Plumb & Charles, 1955; Sattler, Winget, & Roth, 1969; Schwartz, 1966; Scottish Council for Research in Education, 1967; Walker, Hunt, & Schwartz, 1965). While it is difficult to determine the frequency with which ambiguous responses occur on tests, the fact that considerable variability exists in the scores examiners give to ambiguous responses indicates that examinees' IQ's may be dependent, in part, on the particular examiner performing the evaluation. Improved scoring manuals may help to reduce this source of examiner variability.

In attempting to determine whether examiners differ in the IQ's or subtest scores they assign, many investigators selected data from field settings; that is, from protocols taken from clinic files or from research investigations. Therefore, most studies did not experimentally manipulate the examiner variable—random selection of examiners or random assignment of examinees to examiners was not employed. The experimental design limitations make caution necessary in interpreting some of the studies related to examiner differences. In addition, some studies (e.g., Cattell, 1937; Cieutat, 1965) failed to report or to employ appropriate statistical procedures (Sattler, 1966b; Sattler & Theye, 1967).

Reports in which the Stanford-Binet and Wechsler tests were used indicate that both significant differences (Bennett, 1970; Cattell, 1937; Cieutat, 1965; Cieutat & Flick, 1967; Cohen, 1950, 1965; Curr & Gourlay, 1956; Davis, Peacock, Fitzpatrick, & Mulhern, 1969; Di Lorenzo & Nagler, 1968; Green, 1960–62; Kaspar, Throne, & Schulman, 1968; Schwartz & Flanigan, 1971; Smith & May, 1967; Thomas, Hertzig, Dryman & Fernandez, 1971) and nonsignificant differences (Green, 1960–62; Krebs, 1969; Nichols, 1959; Sattler, 1969; Schachter & Apgar, 1958) exist among examiners in the scores they obtain. In spite of the methodological problems encountered in studies evaluating examiner effects, there is some evidence to suggest that examiners occasionally differ among themselves in the scores they obtain, although differences among examiners in the scores they obtain is by no means pervasive. The specific reasons for such differences are not usually known. However, in one study (Thomas et al., 1971) an analysis of the psychological reports and interviews with the two examiners indicated that the one examiner who obtained higher IQ's than the other examiner (*a*) used more positive terms in her reports to describe the examiner-child interaction and the child's approach to the test demands, (*b*) spent more time in establishing rapport, and (*c*) always encouraged the child to try to answer the test questions. The research reports provide no justification for assuming that significant differences will be found among any given group of examiners. The examiner's goal is to strive for the highest level of competence and skill. In reaching for this goal, he is attempting to reduce to a minimum and, ideally, to eliminate completely any examiner sources that contribute to test invalidity or unreliability. "Extraneous" sources that contribute to examinee variability cannot be controlled, but there is no reason to accept extraneous sources that contribute to the examiner's variability.

Examiner's Experience

Studies that have evaluated the examiner's experience as a variable that may affect scores on the Stanford-Binet and Wechsler tests report nonsignificant findings (Curr & Gourlay, 1956; Davis et al., 1969; Jordan, 1932; Kaspar et al., 1968; Masling, 1959; Plumb & Charles, 1955; Sattler & Ryan, 1973a; Schwartz, 1966) as well as significant findings (LaCrosse, 1964; Smith, May, & Lebovitz, 1966). In the latter two studies, the examinees were Negro children while the examiners were of either the Negro or the white race. Consequently, the difference in the racial memberships of the examinees and examiners complicated the generality of the findings. Kaspar et al. (1968b) proposed that experienced examiners may develop personal standards for scoring that are not shared with other experienced examiners. Overall, the studies indicate that the examiner's experience is not of critical importance in affecting test scores. It is probable that, once a certain level of proficiency is reached, the variable of experience as a factor that affects test procedures or the examinee's performance is no longer important. Some examiners with minimal experience may be better in establishing rapport and in obtaining valid test scores than those with extensive experience.

Examiner's Sex

Studies of examiner effects have employed both male and female examiners, but few have systematically evaluated the role of the examiner's sex. Those that have done so indicate that, while the examiner's sex may interact with the examinee's sex in affecting performance on selected tests or subtests, no systematic trends have emerged. Pedersen, Shinedling, and Johnson (1968), for example, reported that on the WISC Arithmetic subtest female examiners obtained higher scores from female examinees than from male examinees, whereas male examiners tended to obtain higher scores from male examinees than from female examinees. However, Quereshi (1968) failed to find significant examiner sex effects for the same WISC subtest, while finding that the examiner's sex was a significant main effect as well as an interactant for other subtests and scales. The direction of differences for male and female examiners was, in part, a function of the particular subtest, the examinee's sex, and the examinee's age. In two studies using the Stanford-Binet, Cieutat and Flick (1967) failed to find significant examiner sex effects and, while the examiner's sex was a significant variable in the Smith et al. (1966) study, the results were difficult to interpret because consistent trends were not evident.

Specific Examiner Characteristics

Egeland (1967) studied the interaction between the anxiety level of the examiner and the anxiety level of the examinee. One high-anxious examiner and one low-anxious examiner administered the WISC to high- and low-anxious fifth graders. The anxiety level of the examiner was measured by the Manifest Anxiety Scale, whereas the anxiety level of the examinee was measured by the Childrens' Manifest Anxiety Scale. The examiners' anxiety level was not found to affect significantly IQ's on the Full Scale or on the Performance Scale. However, on the Verbal Scale the high-anxious examiner obtained significantly higher IQ's than the low-anxious examiner (114 vs. 108), a result of the fact that the low-anxious examinees obtained higher scores under the high-anxious examiner than under the low-anxious examiner (122 vs. 110). The generality of these findings may be limited, since only two examiners were studied.

Instead of studying a personality variable, Sattler and Martin (1971) set out to determine the effects of anxious and nonanxious examiner roles on WISC Information and Coding subtest scores. The examiners were eight female Canadian undergraduates who were trained to administer the two subtests, while the examinees were sixth-grade Canadian males. In the anxious role, the examiner moved around in her chair, played with her pencil, spoke in a low tone of voice, and stuttered occasionally. In the nonanxious role, standard test conditions were maintained. The results showed that the role effect was not significant. While the findings are limited to the two subtests and to the specific procedures employed in the study, they do indicate that certain examiner behaviors may not significantly affect the performance of children.

Sattler (1973b) intercorrelated 24 examiner variables obtained from a sample of graduate student examiners who had scored Stanford-Binet responses. The variables included scoring style (number of plus responses), scoring accuracy, personality scores (Personality Research Form), ability level (Graduate Record Examination), F Scale, age, and major. The results indicated that neither scoring style nor scoring accuracy correlated significantly with any of the variables. The findings of this study, however, are not generalizable to actual test situations.

SUMMARY

The examiner's role begins as soon as he becomes a member of the professional community. It is his responsibility to work with the referral sources in helping them to understand the assets and limitations of individual intelligence tests. Once a decision to evaluate a child has been made, the examiner should try to insure that optimum testing conditions are provided. While it goes without saying that the examiner must learn his instruments well, he also must be aware of his own personality and strive to overcome problem areas that may impede his work with children.

There are no set rules for working with children. A flexible approach is needed within the context of following the standard procedures described in test manuals. Generally, responses should be scored immediately after they are given by the child. The scoring samples in test manuals are guides; in most cases, they are not meant to be the only correct responses. Departures from standard procedures may be needed when testing handicapped children. However, the resulting scores must then be considered as being less precise estimates of intelligence. On some occasions it is useful to test limits in order to determine how much help the child needs before solving a problem. Such procedures should be attempted after the standard test has been completed.

Halo effects are universal problems that arise in the course of conducting an examination. There is substantial evidence that halo effects at times operate in the scoring of test reponses, with bright examinees receiving more credit than dull examinees for the same responses. When examiners are provided with information about the examinee's probable level of performance, they are on some occasions likely to obtain better scores from examinees purported to be bright than from examinees purported to be dull. One of the steps that may be necessary in reducing halo effects is the recognition of their occurrence.

Examiners have been found to differ among themselves in their scoring of test responses and in the scores that they obtain from examinees. However, the sources for these differences have not been established. The examiner's experience does not appear to play a crucial role in the scores given to test responses. The examiner's sex is usually not a critical factor in affecting the child's performance. Children do not usually appear to be affected significantly by either the examiner's anxiety level or by examiner behaviors indicative of anxiety. Examiners' personality variables have not been shown to be associated significantly with scoring style and scoring accuracy.

CHAPTER 6

THE EXAMINER-EXAMINEE RELATIONSHIP

It is obvious that valid test results depend on the child's cooperation (cf. Bronner, Healy, Lowe, & Shimberg, 1927; Goodenough, 1949; Gunzburg, 1961). Consequently, the establishment of a harmonious relationship is an important goal. The examiner should aim to have the child perform at his optimum level of efficiency. With young children, the test may be referred to as a game, and the examination carried out in a game-like spirit. Goddard's (1910) suggestions, which were made over 60 years ago, still stand as a guide for good testing procedures: "*At all events get down to the level of the child.* Never tell a child his answer is wrong. Always encourage [p. 146]." When a child fails, try to understand why.

INTRODUCING THE EXAMINATION AND ESTABLISHING RAPPORT

Bingham (1937) offered a number of valuable suggestions applicable to the testing situation. The examiner should use the child's first name when he meets him and also should give his name to the child. He should give the child a frank and brief account of the purpose of the examination. However, the opening statement need not be standardized. It should be flexible and adaptable to the child's attitude. The introductory talk should be kept to a minimum. The examiner's manner should be one of confidence and encouragement, making it clear that he wants the child to make the best possible score. He should convey to the child that he is sincerely interested in seeing him succeed, not in showing him up or in catching him in error. While the child is working, he should be observed inconspicuously. He should not be stared at, confronted with a stopwatch, or have anything done in his presence that might distract, embarrass, or irritate him. The examiner should try to be inconspicuous when recording observations and scoring responses.

The child should be helped to feel at ease. He should be encouraged to give a response to each question. His interest level should be maintained. Fatigue is an indication that testing should be discontinued. Because directions for every situation that may arise cannot be given, the examiner must be prepared to use tact and common sense in meeting difficulties. He should avoid stereotyped and routine manners of interacting with the child.

Rapport can be facilitated by starting immediately with the test material, giving brief, natural, and casual praise for success (Martin, 1941). In administering the Stanford-Binet, the examiner may help anxious examinees by beginning the examination with one or two tests below their probable basal level. (A similar procedure can be used with the WISC and WPPSI on those subtests that have easier items that are not routinely administered.) The impersonality of the intelligence tests' questions, coupled with the experience of success in answering questions, should help the child to relax more quickly than almost any other procedure.

NEGATIVISM AND BLOCKING

Carter and Bowles (1948) indicated that individual intelligence tests are "heavily weighted with tasks in which the examiner plays a prominent role, and since such tasks are found to stimulate negativistic behavior frequently, test scores sometimes reflect negativism as much as or more than the behavior equipment the tasks supposedly sample [pp. 128–129]." Carter and Bowles's observations do not, of course, characterize the behavior of all children. On most occasions, few children will react in a negativistic way or outrightly refuse to respond to the test questions. A short interchange between examiner and child is frequently all that is needed to establish rapport. Gunzburg (1961) suggested that when children are only superficially cooperative, "The modulations of the examiner's voice and his facial expression will have to play a great part in overcoming the lack of real interest and motivation, the anxiety and resentment, the shyness and the tendency of giving in too soon, which may be hidden very successfully behind a semblance of co-operation [pp. 250–251]."

Some techniques are not effective in establishing rapport and in motivating the child. For example, statements made by the examiner that are in conflict with the quality of the response may increase the incidence of blocking and refusal to respond (Cole, 1953). The examiner who has been using praise excessively will find difficulties in continuing to use it when the test questions become more difficult. The examiner then becomes "confronted with the alternatives of either abandoning his previous approach, with the obvious implication that praise is no longer deserved, or continuing to praise in situations where the subject himself is aware that performance is inadequate [Cole, 1953, pp. 133–134]." Praising the child *for his effort* rather than for the results of his effort, a subtle but important distinction, may help to reduce some of the problems associated with the use of praise.

Cole suggested that blocking can be reduced by capturing the child's frame of reference. The child should be shown that his situation is understood. This can be accomplished by showing acceptance of his attitudes toward the examination and recognition that the questions are getting harder, and by verbally acknowledging his reactions. In general, rapport can be facilitated by showing the child respect.

TESTING PRESCHOOL CHILDREN

Preschool children are likely to be challenging to test. They have little interest in their performance, their social behavior is not advanced, they follow their own impulses, they are difficult to coerce, and they express their feelings easily. A useful framework for testing and working with preschool children has been provided by Goodenough (1949) and by Read (1960). Their major points are presented below. The reader is encouraged to consult both sources for detailed comments concerning work with preschool children.

Goodenough's (1949) major points are as follows:

1. The testing room should be attractive to the child.

2. The testing materials should be arranged systematically.

3. The testing materials, toys, and other necessary equipment should be kept at hand but out of sight.

4. The child should not be urged to respond before he is ready.

5. The child should be physically comfortable before beginning the examination.

6. Instructions for test administration should be followed exactly.

7. The speed of administering the tests should be adjusted to the personality of the child.

8. The examiner's voice should be kept low in pitch.

9. The child should be prepared for each kind of test.

10. Remarks made by the child should not be ignored.

11. Adequate praise should be given.

12. The examiner should watch for early signs of boredom, fatigue, physical discomfort, or emotional distress, and take appropriate action before such conditions become acute.

13. The examiner should be playful and friendly, but always maintaining control of the situation.

14. The examiner should try to have the child cooperate actively at all times.

Read's (1960) major points augment those of Goodenough:

1. Give the child a choice only when you intend to leave the situation up to him.

2. Use words and tone of voice that will help the child feel confident and reassured.

3. Never attempt to change behavior by acts that may make the child feel less respect for himself.

4. Avoid motivating the child by making comparisons between him and another child or by encouraging competition.

5. Redirection is most effective when it is consistent with the child's motives or interests.

6. The most effective way of handling problems is to foresee or to forestall them.

7. Limits on the child's allowable behavior, when necessary, should be clearly defined and consistently maintained.

To augment point 7, the examiner should be sure that the child clearly understands the limits that are set. While consistency is necessary, the examiner should not be inflexible or afraid. He should accept the child's need to "test out" the limits. He should adapt limits to the child's needs, giving him time to accept them while at the same time respecting his feelings.

The examiner must try to accept the child as he is, with his feelings and behavior, knowing that there are reasons for the way he feels and acts. He must help the child to find acceptable outlets for his feelings. He must try to meet the child's needs. Skills acquired in handling young children can aid in helping them gain confidence in their abilities. Increased confidence may enhance the child's cooperativeness and willingness to respond to the tests.

Finally, the examiner needs to be aware of the feelings of the parents. Parents have limited experience with testing; they may lack knowledge about the meaning of test results. They may be anxious about their child's behavior and defensive about their child's needing testing. Giving realistic reassurance whenever possible can help to alleviate some of their anxieties.

GENERAL COMMENT CONCERNING TESTING SKILLS

The examiner's competence is judged not only by his ability to establish rapport with the child and to administer tests in a standardized manner, but also by his ability to observe and to record the child's behavior. The psychologist's skill lies in his ability to obtain cooperation from the most intractable child under conditions that depart as little as possible from standardized procedures (Shapiro, 1951). However, subjective factors — such as examiner's style, child's physical and mental condition, physical environment, interruptions during testing, examiner's preparation, and language difficulties of the child — invariably will enter into the testing situation to reduce its objectivity (Louttit, 1957). It is also important to note that not all examiners will be (or should be expected to be) equally effective in working with preschool children or with handicapped children.

EXAMINEE'S ATTITUDES AND EXPECTATIONS

Fiske's (1967) study of adults' reactions to a variety of tests — including intelligence, interest, and projective tests — can be helpful in understanding how children, too, may react to tests. Fiske pointed out that examinees are likely to have some idea about the purposes of tests and do react to being tested. Standardizing test procedures does not insure objectivity, because children will react in different ways. The examinee in the test situation usually recognizes that he is being judged, and that the test holds the possibility that he may be found wanting. Tests of ability, which present clearly defined tasks, tend to minimize the potential intrusion during the testing session of many diverse examinee evaluations and feelings. Personality tests, on the other hand, are inadequate in controlling such sources of variance. Fiske concluded that the examiner should learn from the examinee what he thinks about the purposes of being tested, how he evaluated the test, and what his feelings were about the test.

The examiner in the testing situation is actively trying to accomplish his clinical aims; conversely, the child who is relatively unprotected by age, experience, skill, and insight is reactively attempting to control the situation (Engel, 1960). The youngster is seldom aware of his explicit role in the diagnostic process. Some children may try to control the situation by requesting water frequently or by being silently negativistic, whereas some examiners may control the situation by never varying from the test procedures. Engel wisely advised that the examiner should be alert to nonverbal forms of communication and to time and space considerations, and should observe any regressive behaviors that might occur during the examination.

PROCESS-ORIENTED RELATIONSHIP

We have seen that testing is much more than a routine automatic procedure. The examiner must be vigilant, making certain that the examinee has the necessary physical abilities to proceed with the test, observing when the examinee is or is not making his best effort, and deciding when to offer encouragement and praise. Timing is a key to successful testing.

In Chapter 26, which deals with the consultation process, issues are discussed that also pertain to test administration. As a forerunner to Chapter 26, and as a way of codifying some of the issues discussed in the present chapter, we now consider how a process-oriented relationship can enhance the psychological evaluation. The major characteristics of the process-oriented relationship have been described by Leventhal, Slepian, Gluck, and Rosenblatt (1962). In the process-oriented relationship, the child is encouraged to participate actively in the testing process. The examiner's role becomes one of being a helper and not just an observer. In establishing rapport, the child's feelings, including misconceptions and resistances, are accepted and dealt with. In the process-oriented diagnostic workup, factual information is sought, but allowed to emerge in the context of the examiner-child relationship. The process-oriented relationship considers six essential areas.

1. What is the problem as the child sees it?
2. What does the child see as the basis for the problem?
3. What are the child's feelings about the problem? For example, how concerned is he?
4. What can and should be done about the problem? What alternatives exist as possible approaches to solutions?
5. How can testing play a role as a helping process, or as part of one?
6. How can the test findings be interpreted to the child in a way that will be beneficial to him?

Areas 1 through 5 are considered with the child, usually before formal testing has begun. The process-oriented procedure offers a number of advantages. The examiner, before he begins testing, may have a better idea of the child's set, orientation, and preconceptions. Second, more meaningful material may be elicited. Third, the testing experience helps to introduce the child to clinical help. The process-oriented procedure can potentially provide a more meaningful testing relationship for both the child and the examiner.

Keeping with the process-oriented procedure, Shore (1962) suggested that the examiner should try to determine how the child perceives the testing situation during the pretest phase and then make active efforts to clarify and correct any unusual views that the child may have toward testing. The child should be informed what is to be done with the tests after they have been completed, and how he may find out about the results. During the examination proper, the child may engage in some behaviors that will perplex the examiner. On these occasions, the examiner must decide, for example, whether a particular behavior reflects true helplessness or whether it is manipulative. The examiner then must take appropriate action. Help in the form of support and encouragement should be given whenever it is necessary to keep the child interested in the tasks.

CHECKLIST FOR EVALUATING THE EXAMINER-EXAMINEE RELATIONSHIP

The following list of questions is intended as a guide for the examiner. The list can also be used as a checklist by an observer. The novice examiner, especially, is encouraged to answer each question carefully after an examination has been completed.

Examiner-Examinee Relationship

1. Did the examiner prepare the examinee for the examination?
2. Was the examiner friendly?

3. Was the examiner free from distracting mannerisms?
4. Was the examiner sympathetic and interested?
5. Was the examiner's appearance appropriate?
6. Was the examiner's voice audible and pleasant?
7. Did the examiner accept the examinee's attitudes?
8. Was the examiner biased? If so, in what ways?
9. Did the examiner seem at ease?
10. Did the examinee seem at ease?[1]

The Examination

1. Was the atmosphere permissive?
2. Was the pace of the examination appropriate to the examinee's abilities?
3. Were the examiner's vocabulary and concepts suited to the examinee?
4. Were test procedures adequately explained to the examinee?
5. Was the examiner aware of signs of fatigue?
6. Was fatigue handled adequately?
7. Was the examiner aware of emotional upsets?
8. Was emotionality handled adequately?
9. Did the examiner include critical material (material containing the solution) in his explanations?
10. Did the examiner strive to have the examinee clarify vague responses through additional questioning?
11. Were inquiries made in a nonthreatening manner?
12. Was the examinee praised appropriately?
13. Did disruptions in testing arise? If so, how did the examiner handle them?
14. Were tests given hurriedly?
15. Did the examiner manipulate materials with ease and confidence?
16. Did the examiner follow the standardized procedures carefully?
17. Were responses recorded in the record booklet and scored?
18. How was the examination terminated?

EXAMINER-EXAMINEE RESEARCH STUDIES

Several attempts have been made to study how the examiner-examinee relationship might affect the examinee's performance on intelligence tests. Studies in this area may be classified into one of two general groups. In one, the examiner-examinee relationship was varied throughout the entire administration of the test. In the other, only pretest conditions were manipulated, while standard rapport conditions were maintained during the test proper. We now turn to the research studies.

Variables Affecting Examiner-Examinee Relationship During Testing

Rapport. A series of studies has appeared which can be viewed as evaluating how rapport, which is systematically varied during the test administration, affects the child's performance. A recent study used two rapport condi-

---

[1]Chapter 25 presents a detailed list of questions that focus on the examinee's test behavior and attitudes.

tions—enhanced rapport and neutral rapport—in evaluating their effects on the WISC scores of bright children in the first through seventh grades (Feldman & Sullivan, 1971). In the enhanced-rapport condition, the examiner initiated and sustained friendly conversation and used positive verbal reinforcement during the examination. In the neutral-rapport condition, the examiner responded to the examinee, but he neither initiated conversation nor gave reinforcements for correct answers. In grades 5 to 7, the mean IQ in the enhanced-rapport condition was considerably higher than the mean IQ in the neutral-rapport condition (122 vs. 109), whereas in grades 1 to 3, the mean IQ's were much closer together (119 vs. 116). More spontaneous responses, more multiple responses, and fewer "I don't know" responses also occurred in the enhanced-rapport condition than in the neutral-rapport condition, although these effects were more likely to occur in the older than in the younger group. The investigators concluded that older children (in comparison to younger children) may be more prone to take notice of and respond to the sociability of the examiner, and that enhanced rapport encourages a child to increase his level of verbal expressiveness.

In a similar study, however, a "tough" examiner role (no effort made to establish rapport prior to testing, cold and aloof atmosphere during testing, and no praise or encouragement) and a "tender" examiner role (a warm and friendly atmosphere, with praise and encouragement during examination) failed to establish significant examiner-role effects on the Stanford-Binet and WISC scores obtained by 13-year-old institutionalized mentally retarded children (Silverstein, Mohan, Franken, & Rhone, 1964). Another study reported that Negro preschool children attending a Head Start program obtained higher Peabody Picture Vocabulary Test scores when the difficulty level of the items was randomized and when detailed instructions and verbal reinforcements were used than when standard procedures were used (Ali & Costello, 1971).

Studies also have investigated the effect of discouraging the examinee during his performance. One study examined the effects of verbal approval and disapproval upon scores obtained on four WISC subtests (Arithmetic, Digit Span, Picture Arrangement, and Block Design) by third and fourth grade children (Witmer, Bornstein, & Dunham, 1971). The sample was from the upper middle class and had obtained a mean IQ of 112 on the Primary Mental Abilities Test. Two examiners served in the study. In the verbal-approval condition, such statements as "Good," "Fine," and "That was good" were given after the first response in each subtest and between subtests. In the verbal-disapproval condition, the examiner said "I thought you could do better than that" after the first response, and "That wasn't so good" between subtests. A neutral condition also was used. The children obtained significantly higher scores in the approval condition (standard score = 48) than in the disapproval condition (standard score = 42). However, the approval condition did not yield scores that were significantly higher than those obtained in the neutral condition (standard score = 44).

Other studies also have shown, for the most part, that discouragement during the examination lowers the scores obtained by children. Discouragement significantly lowered Stanford-Binet (Forms L and M) scores of eighth-grade children (Gordon & Durea, 1948) and Form L scores of above-average fifth- and sixth-grade children (Pierstorff, 1951). However, three different incentive conditions—verbal praise, verbal reproof, and awards of candy—had no significant effect on the Stanford-Binet (Form L-M) scores obtained by second- and third-grade white and Negro children (Tiber & Kennedy, 1964). (The latter study also is an incentive study.)

Incentives.   We now turn to a group of studies that directly examined the effects of various kinds of verbal and material incentives on the scores obtained by children. One of the earliest studies in this area investigated the effects of money and praise incentives on the Stanford-Binet (Forms L and M) scores of white and Negro children in the age range of 7 to 14 years (Klugman, 1944). The scores of Negro children but not of white children were found to be significantly affected by the incentives (higher scores with money than with praise: M IQ = 100 vs. M IQ = 96). In another study, feedback (telling child when his response was correct) and reward (giving child chips — to be exchanged for money — when his response was correct), given by four white female examiners, were studied as variables that might affect the WISC Verbal Scale scores of middle class white, lower class white, and lower class Negro children between the ages of 6 and 13 years (Sweet, 1969). Neither of the treatment conditions significantly affected the scores of the middle class white and lower class Negro children. However, in the lower class white group, both treatment conditions resulted in significantly higher scores than those obtained in the control group.

The effects of social and token reinforcement on the WISC Block Design performance of fourth graders, who had achieved IQ's between 80 and 120 on the Lorge-Thorndike Intelligence Test, were the focus of another investigation (Bergan, McManis, & Melchert, 1971). A test-retest design was used, with a three-week interval between tests. In the social reinforcement condition, a positive verbal statement was made by the examiner ("Good," "Fine," "Right," etc.) immediately after the child made a correct block placement. In the token reinforcement condition, the child was given a white chip every time he put a block in the right place and a red chip when he finished a design correctly; at the end of the subtest, the chips were exchanged for money. The results were complicated, because reinforcement effects were dependent partly on the sex of the child. Boys showed significant gains in accuracy only under token reinforcement and significant speed gains only under social reinforcement, while girls showed significant gains in accuracy but losses in speed in all three conditions.

Candy as a reinforcer usually has not been found to be different from verbal reinforcers in affecting children's performance, as the studies below indicate. However, the effectiveness of the reinforcers in these studies is difficult to evaluate, because a neutral (control) condition was not employed. Verbal approval ("Very, very good") and material reinforcement (a piece of candy) were not found to differ significantly in affecting the WISC Block Design scores of Negro and white second and fifth graders (Cohen, 1970). Similarly, 4-year-old Negro children given praise did not differ in their Stanford-Binet (Form L-M) scores from children given candy (Quay, 1971). Finally, the study by Tiber and Kennedy (1964) cited above also failed to find that candy differed significantly from other reinforcers.

Comment on Examiner-Examinee Research Studies

While the results of Feldman and Sullivan's (1971) study are important, a number of problems exist in the design of the experiment. The "enhanced rapport" condition appears to be a misnomer, because its description is similar to what is used (or at least advocated by most test manuals) in standard testing situations. The neutral condition, rather than being "neutral," appears to have been one that may have been aversive to the children. Further, there does not appear to have been any control for the sex of the examiner or for the effects of the examiner's expectations on the examinee's performance. Thus, the results seem to reflect how a standard testing condition compares with a potentially aversive testing condition.

The difficulty with studies of the type conducted by Witmer, Bornstein, and Dunham (1971) is that examiner bias was not controlled. Consequently, the examiners may have subtly altered their administrative procedures to conform to the respective conditions. For example, in the approval condition, they may have been more friendly, more precise in their communications, and more lenient in their administration than they were in the disapproval condition. Second, when verbal disapproval was given after the first item of each subtest, it was not based on any meaningful behavior of the child. For example, when the child was told that he could do better after responding correctly to the first Arithmetic problem, he may have become perplexed, perhaps about himself as well as about the examiner. The communication was disjointed with the child's actual behavior and with the test situation. It is remarkable that the children still performed under such conditions. If investigators are interested in studying the effects of disapproval and approval, they should attempt to make reinforcing statements that either are somewhat congruent with the child's behavior or are not flagrantly in conflict with the child's behavior. In the present experiment, the remarks that were made between the subtests appear to be less incongruent than those made after each response.

Bergan, McManis, and Melchert (1971) concluded that the use of extrinsic reinforcement during the administration of the WISC Block Design subtest may seriously bias the child's performance. However, the conclusion seems to be somewhat premature. Girls, for example, obtained significantly higher scores in the control condition as well as in the reinforcement conditions; practice may account for these results. Boys in the control condition gained 10 points; in the social-reinforcement condition, 12 points; and in the token-reinforcement condition, 16 points. While only the results for the token-reinforcement condition were significant, gains did occur in the other two conditions. Further, it is important to know the significance of the differential gain between the control and token-reinforcement conditions, but this comparison was not made. At any rate, the major problem with the research design, with respect to standard testing procedures, is that the reinforcements were given after each block placement, a procedure which should not be used normally in administering the Block Design subtest or, for that matter, in administering any subtest or test. The child should be permitted to work without any feedback once he has started the task. In standard testing conditions, the praise or reinforcement should come between tasks, and then only when necessary. Finally, the reinforcements were administered on the retest and not on the test proper. Any conclusions would therefore be limited to the retest phase only. Consequently, further experimentation would be helpful in evaluating the effects of social and token reinforcement on intelligence test performance.

Pretest Variables Affecting the Examiner-Examinee Relationship

Attempts have been made to evaluate the effects of the examiner-examinee relationship, prior to the actual administration of the test, upon the examinee's performance. One of the early studies in this area concerned the effects of three different types of social relationships on the scores obtained by 3-year-old children on the Stanford-Binet (Sacks, 1952). First, Form L was administered under standard conditions. Then, for a 10-day period before Form M was administered, the examiner established three different types of relationships with the children. In the "good" relationship group, she showed interest in the children, talked with them, and played games with them. In the "poor" relationship group, she sat off to one side of the room, did not honor their requests for help, wore a dull facial expression, and tried to get the children to dislike her without distrusting her. A third group served as the control. On the retest, which was administered under standard conditions, the good relationship group gained 14 IQ points; the poor relationship group, 5 IQ points; and the control group, 2 IQ points. These results indicated that the children in the good relationship group obtained significantly higher scores than those in the other two groups.

The effects of prior contact with the examiner on the WISC Full Scale IQ's obtained by third-grade children have been investigated recently (Tyson, 1968). Three conditions were established, similar to those used by Sacks (1952). In the "warm" pretest contact condition, the examiner wore a bright dress, asked the child about his pets, friends, and favorite games, paid attention to what he said, praised him, and offered him cookies. In the "cold" pretest contact condition, the examiner wore a drab dress, did not look at the child, did not allow him enough time to answer questions, frowned from time to time, and engaged in other assorted behaviors. In the third condition, there was no contact prior to testing. The pretest contact occurred several days before the actual testing took place. During the actual testing, the examiners (five females) maintained their usual testing rapport. The results showed that IQ's did not differ significantly among the groups. Variations in the warmth and coldness of pretest contact, therefore, had no effect on the IQ's obtained by the children. However, another study reported that in a sample of children between 7 and 14 years of age a "rigid" examiner role prior to testing led to lower WISC subtest scores than a "rapport" examiner role, primarily on those subtests administered early in the series (Exner, 1966).

Pretest procedures were the focus of another study, which examined the WPPSI scores of 4- and 5-year-old middle class white, lower class white, and lower class Negro children (Kinnie, 1970). All children were first administered the WPPSI under standard procedures. Then three experimental groups and a control group were formed. In the familiarizing group, middle class white adults, similar to those who would be administering the retest, spent some time with the children. In the language-and-materials group, the children were exposed to the type of language and materials that are used in the WPPSI. In the test-like group, the children were given practice in taking tests. After an average lapse of nine weeks, the WPPSI was readministered by 10 female, white, middle class volunteers. Greater gains in WPPSI IQ's were obtained by children in the familiarizing and language-and-materials groups than in the test-like and control groups. Increases in the WPPSI IQ's were almost entirely on the Performance Scale subtests. In the experimental groups, changes ranged from -1 to 6 IQ points for the Full Scale, from -4 to 5 IQ points for the Verbal Scale, and from 2 to 11 IQ points for the Performance Scale. The Full Scale mean change in the control group was 1 IQ point. Treatment effects also were similar in the two socioeconomic classes and in the two ethnic groups. The extent to which similar findings would appear when Negro children are exposed to Negro adults and then are tested by Negro examiners is not known.

Other studies have also found that the examiner-examinee relationship may occasionally play a role in affecting test scores. Normal children administered an individual intelligence test by examiners they preferred were found to obtain higher scores than children tested by nonpreferred examiners (Hata, Tsudzuki, Kuze, & Emi, 1958). Mentally retarded children, too, obtained higher scores on an individual intelligence test when tested by a familiar examiner than when tested by an unfamiliar examiner (Tsudzuki, Hata, & Kuze, 1956). However, familiarity with the examiner did not affect the 1916 Stanford-Binet scores obtained by normal children between 3 and 8 years of age (Marine, 1929).

The effects of aversive experiences immediately prior to being administered intelligence tests also have been studied. The Stanford-Binet (Forms L and M) IQ's of 9-year-old boys were lower after a failure experience, while a success experience did not significantly affect their IQ's (Lantz, 1945). A frustration experience (e.g., interruption of a marble game task and withholding of a promised reward) prior to being administered the WISC Coding subtest led to significantly lower Coding scores in samples (*a*) of 8-year-old boys with a history of anti-social acts (Solkoff & Chrisien, 1963), (*b*) of 9-year-old brain-injured boys (Solkoff, 1964), and (*c*) of normal 5- to 9-year-old boys, but not of girls (Solkoff, Todd, & Screven, 1964). We do not know, however, about how frustration affects performance on other WISC subtests. Pretest instructions designed to induce test anxiety (i.e., that the test was very important and that the results would be placed in the records) and motivation during the test proper (i.e., use of money as an incentive) did not produce significant differences in Digit Span performance of 14-year-old mentally retarded children (Keller, 1957).

SUMMARY

The psychological examination aims to elicit the child's best effort and, in order to do so, rapport should be established early in the test session. Sources of difficulty that may interfere with the child's performance should be dealt with as early as possible during the examination. However, standard test procedures should not be violated in the process without excellent reasons.

The administration of a psychological test cannot be thought of simply as a process of following objective standardized procedures. The testing situation represents the interplay of examiner, examinee, and situational factors, in addition to test content and test procedures. The child's perceptions and attitudes, in particular, must be considered as an inherent part of the evaluation. The process-oriented relationship stresses the active participation of the child in the testing process. The examiner becomes an active participant in the relationship, and foregoes his former role of merely being a test observer and recorder.

Research studies that have focused on the examiner-examinee relationship have reported that when the examiner gives praise, or engages in other rapport-inducing behaviors, some groups of children are likely to obtain higher scores than under neutral or aversive conditions. Discouragement usually reduces the scores obtained by children. Incentives, in the form of money or chips, at times significantly affect performance, whereas candy, as a reinforcer, does not appear to differ significantly from verbal approval. Methodological difficulties, however, are evident in many studies that have investigated the effects of rapport and incentives on intelligence test performance.

The pretest examiner-examinee relationship has been found in many studies to affect children's performance. However, the procedures used, the groups studied, and the tests administered all appear to be important variables in determining whether pretest variables play a significant role. WPPSI Performance Scale scores may be more influenced by pretest conditions than WPPSI Verbal Scale scores. A frustration experience prior to being administered the WISC Coding subtest is likely to result in a decrement in performance, but little is known about the effects of frustration on other WISC subtest scores. Finally, when scores on the second administration of a test are affected by the intervening examiner-examinee relationship, the findings do not permit generalization to situations in which the test is administered for the first time.

CHAPTER 7

SUGGESTIONS FOR TESTING CHILDREN WITH SPECIAL PROBLEMS

In the previous two chapters we considered some general issues that were related to administering individual intelligence tests. In the present chapter, suggestions for administering tests to children with special problems are discussed. Physically handicapped children and, of course, emotionally disturbed or brain-injured children present particular problems; such children will test the resources of even the most competent and experienced examiner. A careful study of the material in this chapter will alert the examiner to some of the problems that he may encounter in the testing of children and will provide him with some suggestions to aid him in overcoming testing problems. The general principles and procedures of testing and test interpretation that are used for nonhandicapped children are also used for handicapped children (Goldman, 1961).

While every attempt should be made to administer a standardized test to handicapped children, there will be occasions when testing is not possible. Children who are actively psychotic, severely cerebral-palsied, or markedly deficient in attention and motivation, whether as a result of mental retardation or some other specific condition, may prove to be untestable (Goldman, 1961). In such cases, the examiner should report his observations of the child's behavior and try to reschedule testing at a later date.

THE CHILD WITH SPECIAL PROBLEMS

Underlying the various types of problems that children present are a number of commonalities. The child with a special problem is first a child, with all that means in terms of immaturities of various kinds. Secondly, something has interfered with his development, with what Virginia Axline calls the "spiral of growth." Third, whatever else he is doing, he is attempting to cope with the world, not only with his immature judgment and his incapacities but with a special handicap that either may prevent his adequate coping or, in some cases, may spur him to overcompensation. All of the different groups of children with special problems are engaging in behavior that may have adaptive significance. Fourth, failures in the coping process bring frustration, and frustration may generate excessive moving toward, moving against, or moving away from behaviors (Karen Horney). The result of frustration is probably best illustrated in the brain-injured child of normal or sometimes even superior intelligence, who knows what he wants to do and should be doing but is helpless in attempting to accomplish that which he strives to do.

TESTING PROBLEM CHILDREN

The role of the examiner is different from the role of a therapist or teacher, and difficulties may arise when techniques associated with these roles are applied in the examination setting. The object of the examination is to evaluate the child's performance and not to "work through" problems or to "teach" material (Kicklighter, 1966b). When children are difficult to test, the examiner should try to find a procedure that will help the child to be less resistant. Kicklighter suggested that if alternatives are presented to the *negative* child, the examiner should make certain that each alternative is acceptable. Thus, "Would you like to do this or that?" should be used rather than "Would you like to do this?" The examiner should involve the *frightened* child as early as possible in the testing situation, rather than spending time in explaining the testing procedures to him. For the *nonspeaking* child, it may be helpful to begin with performance-type material. Occasionally, communication may be facilitated by using a third source, such as a person, an object, or a doll to present the material. Whispering the questions may stimulate the nonspeaking child to whisper back his answers. For the *distractible-hyperactive* child, the examiner should try to give the tests as quickly as possible. Distractibility can be reduced also by gently holding the child's hands or arms or head.

Shapiro (1951) describes an incident which reveals the success of a flexible administrative approach:

The psychologist had to give a Binet to a 4-year[-old] girl whose main complaint was that she did not talk. He hit upon the expedient of placing the little girl on his knee and giving her a kiss for every item which she completed, regardless of whether it was right or wrong. Every item was presented and every response scored rigorously according to the instructions in the manual — with the one exception of the reward for responses. The patient completed enough of the test to show that mental defect was not to be considered in her case, and she walked out of the testing room talking to and kissing everybody that she met [p. 754].

TESTING PSYCHOPATHOLOGICAL GROUPS

Administering an intelligence test to children who are mentally ill requires constant intensive effort. While most emotionally disturbed children should not feel threatened by intelligence tests (Garner, 1966), the examiner must be patient because the work may be hard, annoying, wearing, and intense (Dearborn, 1926). It is important to try to relate to the child as a person (Towbin, 1964). Tact, diplomacy, patience, ingenuity, and understanding of emotional difficulties are essential, especially in testing schizophrenic children (cf. Wentworth, 1924). Questions should be read slowly and clearly. In some cases, two test sessions may be needed. Schizophrenic children may be difficult to test because they cannot concentrate well and because they may have preoccupations that impede their comprehension of the instructions (Hoskins & Jellinek, 1933). The child who is evasive will require still more care and still more time to administer the scale. *Common sense must be used at all times.* A child who is acutely disturbed should not be administered the scale; force should never be used (cf. Towbin, 1964). Several interviews may be necessary to coax the child characterized by infantilism out of his passivity, because he may have been deprived of any incentive to use and to develop his abilities; he may be totally unprepared to respond to the test situation (Haeussermann, 1958).

Children who are suspected of being schizophrenic are easier to test when they have average or above-average intelligence, when they can speak, and when they are cooperative; the assessment situation is more complicated when intelligence is low and when there is mutism (Mehr, 1952). For those who are mute, the Merrill-Palmer Scale may prove to be more useful than the Binet, WISC, or WPPSI (Rutter, 1966). Items from the Cattell Infant Intelligence Scale and from the Vineland Social Maturity Scale also can be used to assess general level of functioning of young schizophrenic children (Alpern, 1967). Schizophrenic children may differ from other cognitively handicapped children, primarily by virtue of having fewer motor disabilities.

TESTING BRAIN-INJURED CHILDREN

There are a number of procedures that can be used in handling problems that arise in the testing of brain-injured children (Berko, 1953; Mecham, Berko, & Berko, 1960; Mecham, Berko, Berko, & Palmer, 1966). Because the brain-injured child may be more fearful than other children, the child's parents or his teachers should inform him about the examination a day or two before it is scheduled. Similarly, the strangeness of the testing situation can be reduced by having the child visit the examining room shortly before the examination, meet the examiner, and handle the test materials. The test situation may pose a threat to the child's self-esteem, but the threat may be diminished by minimizing the "testing" features of the situation. The examiner can create a play atmosphere with younger children, while with fear-ridden children or with frustrated children the examiner might begin playing with test-like materials (e.g., form boards or puzzles).

Some brain-injured children who know an answer to a problem may require an inordinately long time to organize an appropriate response. They may sit quietly for a long time before responding, or they may make tentative, hesitant responses. On such occasions, the child should be permitted to proceed at his own pace, without being urged to respond. However, when the delay is excessive (e.g., over a minute), the problem should be repeated, because there exists the possibility that the child has forgotten the problem.

If *perseveration* occurs, the examiner should try to distract the child. One useful procedure is to interject a comment about the weather. This will give the child time to reorganize himself before returning to the task. Before beginning to test, the examiner must eliminate or minimize all potential sources of distraction in the testing room. The room should be quiet and objects and toys should be removed.

When the brain-injured child cannot cope with the test demands, he may become emotionally labile. An extreme form of emotional lability is termed "catastrophic reaction." Behaviors included in catastrophic reactions, besides extreme emotional lability, are sitting quietly and doing nothing, blanking out, or giving an apparently aberrant response as a way of leaving a difficult situation. Catastrophic reactions and lesser forms of emotional lability can be minimized by the following procedures: (*a*) introducing the testing procedures slowly and casually by permitting the child to play with the test materials; (*b*) avoiding any implications of failure in the child's performance; (*c*) avoiding sudden movements or noises; (*d*) introducing new materials gradually, reassuring the child that the new activities will be pleasant; (*e*) stopping testing, if the emotional lability becomes too severe, and then sitting quietly or going back to a test that the child has previously passed.

TESTING MENTALLY RETARDED CHILDREN

Mentally retarded children may behave during the examination (and on other occasions as well) in ways that are traditionally viewed as being negative.

Their behaviors are bothersome or frustrating to the examiner or to others. However, these same behaviors may have adaptive significance, by allowing the child to maintain self-esteem in the face of difficult intellectual or social demands (Hirsch, 1959). For example, aggressive, hyperactive behavior may represent an emergency reaction at finding oneself in a novel situation where the tasks are very difficult. Echolalia may serve as a way of establishing and maintaining a relationship. Persistent questioning may be an effort to ensure stability — a need to gain assurance that things will remain constant. Perseveration may be a means to enable the child to see him through the situation. Finally, denial may serve to cover the child's vulnerability.

Hirsch recommends a number of actions the examiner can take to cope with some of the behaviors shown by mentally retarded children. When the child tries to reverse roles with the examiner, the examiner should help him to become at ease and agree to alternate questions with him. By showing the child that he can be accepted without blame or ridicule, the examiner may diminish the child's need to keep control. Aggressive and hyperactive behavior may be reduced by beginning the examination with easy questions. Finally, to prevent the child from being constantly confronted with inadequacy, the examiner can alternate difficult tasks with easy ones. However, the potential problems involved in modifying test procedures must be recognized.

TESTING PHYSICALLY HANDICAPPED CHILDREN

The techniques used to test physically handicapped children encompass those used with normal children, but their application is more demanding. The normal child often needs little encouragement. He is accustomed to answering test questions and is likely to find the tasks challenging. The physically handicapped child, in contrast, may feel at a disadvantage in the test situation. His physical limitations may make him appear clumsy and awkward, with ensuing feelings of self-consciousness. However, his reactions to the test situation largely depend on how he perceives himself outside of the test situation.

Testing handicapped children poses the following kinds of problems (Russ & Soboloff, 1958): First, communication difficulties may exist. Speech and hearing deficiencies may produce false impressions about the child's intellectual ability. Second, the child may become fatigued easily, because he is unaccustomed to concentrated work for long periods of time. Third, if there are attention difficulties, they may be associated with physical deficiencies rather than with cognitive deficiencies. Fourth, rapport difficulties may occur with those children who have heightened dependency.

Prior to testing a physically handicapped child, it is important that the examiner determine the degree to which the child is physically able to respond to the tests (Allen, 1959; Sievers, 1950; Strother, 1945). The examiner should evaluate the child's (*a*) vision, hearing, speech, sitting balance, and arm-hand use; (*b*) reading and writing skills; and (*c*) ability to indicate "yes" or "no" by verbal or nonverbal means. The results of such an evaluation will aid in selecting and in administering the tests. Figure 7–1 shows a form developed by Katz (1954), which can be useful in recording the examiner's observations of the sensory and motor capacities of physically handicapped children. The physical abilities necessary for the Stanford-Binet are described in Chapter 9, while those for the WISC and WPPSI are presented in Chapter 12. Suggested modifications are also discussed in these chapters.

SURVEY OF DEGREE OF PHYSICAL HANDICAP

Name _____ Date _____

Date of birth _____ Diagnosis _____

Age _____ Sex _____ Rater's name _____

	NON-HANDICAPPING		HANDICAPPING		Comments
	Minimal	*Mild*	*Moderate*	*Severe*	
VISION	☐ No trouble with vision; no glasses needed	☐ Some correction needed; may wear glasses; not handicapped in seeing	☐ Quite handicapped in seeing; vision not correctible by glasses	☐ Almost blind Totally blind	Left eye Rt. eye
HEARING	☐ No trouble with hearing	☐ Some difficulty in hearing; may wear hearing aid satisfactorily	☐ Quite handi-capped in hearing; has difficulty when wearing hearing aid	☐ Almost deaf Totally deaf	Left ear Rt. ear
SPEECH (verbal)	☐ Speech can be under-stood with-out difficulty by a stranger	☐ Some difficulty in being under-stood by a stranger; able to get ideas across in speech	☐ Speech hard for a stranger or imme-diate family to understand; hard to get ideas across in speech	☐ Almost totally unable to commu-nicate by speech; totally without speech	
SITTING BALANCE	☐ No difficulty in sitting in a chair or at a table	☐ Some difficulty in sitting in a chair or at a table, but not handicapped in doing so	☐ Quite handicapped in sitting in a chair or at a table; needs a relaxation chair and tray	☐ Unable to main-tain sitting balance unless fully supported	
ARM-HAND USE	☐ No difficulty in using arms and hands for self-help activity	☐ Some difficulty in using arms and hands for self-help, but not handicapped in doing so	☐ Quite handicapped in using arms and hands for many self-help activi-ties	☐ Unable to use arms and hands for any self-help activity	Left arm Rt. arm
WALKING	☐ No difficulty in walking	☐ Braces needed; unsteady gait; but able to get around	☐ Quite handicapped in walking; cannot walk independently	☐ Unable to walk	Left leg Rt. leg

Figure 7–1. Survey of Degree of Physical Handicap. (Reprinted, with a change in nota-tion, by permission of the publisher and author from E. Katz, "A Survey of Degree of Physical Handicap," *Cerebral Palsy Review,* **15**(11), p. 10. Copyright 1954, Institute of Logopedics.)

Deaf Children

The testing of children with impaired hearing requires a high degree of skill and wide experience with deaf children (Reed, 1970). Because sight is the chief means by which deaf children receive stimuli, they are more likely to seek visual clues (e.g., facial expressions or movements of hands) to gain understanding about their performance (Murphy, 1957). The examiner must realize that even slight movements may furnish cues to the deaf child. Children with impaired hearing are extremely attentive to facial expressions for clues about their performance. Smiling, as though the child were being rewarded for a correct response, should be avoided when a wrong response has been given so that the child is not encouraged to continue to make similar responses.

For children who lip read, it is important that the lighting in the room and the child's position in relation to the examiner be appropriate. Examiners must be able to make the instructions understood without indicating the answer. Pantomime is not always successful in conveying to the examinee exactly what the examiner intends to communicate. While a simple demonstration will sometimes suffice, the demonstration itself may also indicate the answer. Responses that are given in pantomime by the examinee should be given credit only when there is no doubt about the accuracy of the answer (Bice & Cruickshank, 1966).

The necessity for considering whether a child may be deaf can be seen in the tragic case of a child who received an IQ of 29 on the Stanford-Binet, a score that led to her commitment to a hospital for the mentally retarded where she remained for five years (Vernon & Brown, 1964). She was re-evaluated with a performance test, and obtained an IQ of 113. Upon dismissal from the institution, she entered a school for the deaf and made good progress.

Hard-of-hearing children may give the impression of being able to understand directions and test questions, but on closer inspection their seeming comprehension may turn out to be an artifice. They may have learned how to play a role that allows them to avoid confronting a potentially embarrassing situation. In testing hard-of-hearing children, the examiner should begin with a performance measure and then, if it is indicated, give a verbal test. Representative performance tests include the WISC and WPPSI Performance Scales, Leiter International Performance Scale, Progressive Matrices, Ontario School Ability Examination, and Nebraska Test of Learning Aptitude.

Blind Children

The testing of blind children should pose few difficulties, although Pintner (1942) believed that partially-sighted children are probably handicapped in taking the usual standard intelligence tests. The verbal portions of standard intelligence tests provide the primary source of items. The Verbal Scale of the WISC and WPPSI and many of the Stanford-Binet tests can be administered to blind children. Performance items, as presently constituted in these three scales, do not readily adapt themselves for administration to blind children. The Hayes-Binet is often used in testing blind children. It is important that the partially-sighted child wear his glasses when he is tested and that the lighting conditions be adequate in the testing room (Margach & Kern, 1969).

Cerebral-Palsied Children

Cerebral-palsied children present particular difficulties when being tested. Their motor, speech, visual, and auditory difficulties may limit the applicability of standardized tests and make caution mandatory in interpreting test results (cf. Bice & Cruickshank, 1966; Garrett, 1952; Lord, 1937). Cerebral-palsied children frequently perform motor tasks in a slow and laborious manner and therefore are at a particular disadvantage when time limits are imposed. Interpreting their test failures is difficult, because the examiner is not always certain whether the failure is a result of the child's physical disability or of his limited mental ability (Garrett, 1952). Some writers are of the opinion that when standardized tests are given to severely handicapped cerebral-palsied children, the scores may tend to underestimate the children's ability in proportion to the severity of their handicaps (Katz, 1955; McIntire, 1938). However, in spite of the difficulties in using standard tests, it is still important to compare the cerebral-palsied child's performance with that of the normal child, because the latter sets the standards in the world at large (Allen, 1959; Maurer, 1940; Michal-Smith, 1955).

Because many cerebral-palsied children talk adequately and have at least one good hand, modifications in administering the tests may not be necessary. However, when serious physical limitations exist, modifications are needed. Bice and Cruickshank (1966) suggested that tests requiring the least modification be used:

If the subject has good hands and poor speech, performance tests are appropriate. If the opposite is true, verbal tests may have priority. In the majority of cases, the examiner will be able to give at least part of both these types of tests. At times it is necessary to omit tests. A child who can neither walk nor use a wheel chair cannot be asked to go to a chair to place a pencil, or go to a door and open it. Scores can be prorated as necessary [p. 103].

While some writers have questioned whether the initial IQ's obtained by cerebral-palsied children are reliable and valid (Mecham et al., 1960; Russ & Soboloff, 1958; Sievers, 1950), research studies and follow-up reports indicate that the initial test results have a satisfactory degree of reliability and validity (Crowell & Crowell, 1954; Klapper & Birch, 1966; Kogan, 1957; Portenier, 1942; Taylor, 1961). However, caution is still needed in using the first scores as the sole criterion in long-range planning, not only for cerebral-palsied children, but for all children examined by an intelligence test (cf. Mecham et al., 1960).

SUMMARY

Administering standardized intelligence tests to emotionally disturbed children, brain-injured children, mentally retarded children, and physically handicapped children requires patience, understanding, and flexibility. A careful study of the suggestions that have been made for each of these groups should prove to be valuable to examiners. We have seen that time limitations may not be appropriate for certain groups, that deaf children will not be able to respond to oral-verbal items while blind children will not be able to take performance tests, that the cerebral-palsied child will have difficulty on performance items, and that the examination may take days rather than hours to administer. Those examiners who master the necessary techniques for administering intelligence tests to handicapped children should find their work rewarding.

SECTION 3

STANFORD-BINET INTELLIGENCE SCALE

Section 3 is devoted to the Stanford-Binet Intelligence Scale. Chapter 8 presents a detailed history of Alfred Binet's work as it pertains to the development of the Binet-Simon scales. The modifications and revisions of the scales that took place in the United States are discussed in detail, with critical commentary accompanying the reviews for each revision. Chapter 9 considers factors involved in administering the Stanford-Binet; the chapter complements the Stanford-Binet manual. Part of Chapter 9 also describes the mechanics of completing the record booklet and should be of particular help to the beginning examiner. Chapter 10 describes the results of factor analytic investigations of the Stanford-Binet and discusses a number of current views for classifying Stanford-Binet tests. Chapter 10 also presents the standard deviation method for evaluating the child's performance on the Stanford-Binet and discusses scatter analysis. Applications of the Stanford-Binet to the field of psychopathology are presented in Section 5.

CHAPTER 8

THE DEVELOPMENT OF THE STANFORD-BINET

Our study of the Stanford-Binet Intelligence Scale begins by turning to the historical developments that shaped the scale. This chapter includes a discussion of Alfred Binet's personal biography and professional development, examines his collaboration with Henri and Simon in originating intellectual measurement, and discusses further developments (including many adaptations) of the Stanford-Binet scales in America, but with emphasis on the Stanford revisions.

Alfred Binet, the man primarily responsible for the construction of the scale, was born in Nice, France on July 8, 1857, to well educated parents: a physician father and an artist mother. He died on October 18, 1911. Throughout his career, Binet brought a varied set of skills and interests to the study of thinking and intelligence. Both science and art were open to him. He wrote in a lucid and entertaining style, was willing to inquire and question provocatively, and had a streak of both the journalist and the reformer (Reeves, 1965). Because of his many contributions to the field of intelligence, Binet has been referred to as the father of intelligence testing (Pintner, 1931).

Binet's interest lay first in law, later in biology, and finally in psychology. He was an indefatigable worker, publishing about 336 books and articles during his career; however, Ellenberger (1970) noted that Binet "unfortunately scattered his activities in many fields and never succeeded in creating the final work in which he would have concentrated the result of his life's work [p. 356]." Binet also met with failure in obtaining professorships, losing out to Pierre Janet at the College de France and to Georges Dumas at the Sorbonne.

Three phases in Binet's career in psychology can be distinguished (Varon, 1935). For the first part of his career (1880 to 1890), he adhered to associationistic psychology. He entered his second phase (1890 to 1895) with an interest in mental development and organization but without a theoretical focus. In the third phase of his career (1895 to 1911) he pursued a qualitative and quantitative study of individual differences.

FIRST PHASE

During the 1880's Binet published a number of articles on associationism, the first one at the age of 23. In this decade his work with Charcot and Féré at the Salpêtrière stimulated his interests in such areas as hallucinations and perception, hypnosis and suggestibility, abnormal psychology, and somnambulism. As we shall see, some of these areas of interest helped Binet in the development of the Binet-Simon scales. Binet found problems with the approach of associationism, which emphasized contiguity and resemblance in memory. Subsequently he discarded it, for he held that recall was directed mainly by attention and will. Then he entered the second period of his career. Wolf (1964) characterized the first part of Binet's career as a period of controversy and defeat.

SECOND PHASE

In 1892, Binet became adjunct director of the Laboratory of Physiological Psychology at the Sorbonne; three years later, he became director, a position that he held until his death at the age of 54. In 1895 he founded the journal *L'Année Psychologique,* which became the primary source for his future publications. About 1890, Binet (1890a) began to observe carefully the development of his two young daughters. Experiments with his children enabled him to gain information about mental organization, mental development, mental measurement, and other phenomena, including instinctive behavior, individual differences, and personality. His first definition of intelligence was linked to perception. "What is called intelligence in the narrow sense of the word consists of two principal things: first, perceiving the external world, and then taking up these perceptions again in the memorial state, handling them again, and meditating on them [Binet, 1890b, p. 582]." Binet emphasized that in the process of perception the whole is genetically prior to its parts. He discovered that the 4-year-old child defines words primarily in terms of use; for example, "A fork is for eating." Thus, the foundation for the Vocabulary test was laid (Binet, 1890b).

During the early 1890's Binet not only studied mental organization, but also investigated consciousness, perception, rotary movements in insects, individuals who possessed excellent powers of calculating, chess players, synesthesis, and speed in graphic movements. His work represented "a groping after a method of experimenting with normal subjects, and still more, a groping after the problems with which such experiments ought to deal [Varon, 1935, p. 31]." His work of this period culminated in the publication of *Introduction à la Psychologie Expérimentale* in 1894. Binet's approach to experimental psychology emphasized a study of complex functions, the use of reliable measures, observation, and comparative introspection.

THIRD PHASE

During the third phase of his career, which lasted from 1895 to 1911, Binet's primary interest was in the qualitative and quantitative study of individual differences. Psychology, for Binet, should be empirical and separated from metaphysics; it was to become a science of observation and experimentation. *L'Année Psychologique* served as the medium through which he was able to pursue his goal. Binet, in collaboration with Victor Henri (1872–1940), set out to apply the scientific method to the study of individual differences. They wanted to devise tests that not only would differentiate between two individuals but also would throw light on the particular make-up of the individual himself. They noted that previous work (see Chapter 2) had been ineffective in studying individual differences because it placed too exclusive an emphasis on sensory factors and focused on special, limited abilities of minor significance. Differences among individuals are most marked in the complex and higher mental processes; individuals differ least in elementary processes. They considered memory, reasoning, and judgment as best serving to differentiate individuals. Memory tests would provide information about general powers of acquisition, voluntary concentration of attention, tastes and tendencies, general mental disposition (reflected, for example, by errors or omissions), and power of comprehension (Binet & Henri, 1895c).

Binet and Henri went further than theorizing. They proposed a series of specific tests to study individual differences, though these tests were not in all cases original. Furthermore, Binet and Henri were good test constructors; they held that tests should (*a*) be simple, clear, short, and reliable, (*b*) be given within a 60- to 90-minute testing period, (*c*) have clear scoring principles that are independent of the examiner, and (*d*) require no complicated apparatus.

They were also concerned with questions of validity, because they were interested in determining how the abilities measured by the tests improved with age and with school attainment, and how the test scores were related to teachers' ratings. They recognized that the test questions must be appropriate to the child's milieu (Wolf, 1969a). The key to individual differences centered in the study of the following processes: "Memory, nature of mental images, imagination, attention, faculty of comprehension, suggestibility, esthetic appreciation, moral sentiments, muscular force and force of will, and ability and acuity of observation [Binet & Henri, 1895c, p. 434]." The following representative tests were offered as the means by which these 10 processes could be measured:

1. Memory:
   a. visual memory of a geometrical design
   b. memory of a sentence
   c. memory of musical notes
   d. memory of colors
   e. memory of digits
2. Images:
   a. reproduce from memory 12 randomly selected letters in three rows of four letters each
3. Imagination:
   a. ink-blot
   b. abstract words
   c. composition or completion of a picture
   d. construction of as many phrases as possible containing three specified nouns
   e. development of a theme
4. Attention:
   a. reproduction by memory of a line of given length in several successive trials
   b. speed and number of errors in crossing out the *a*'s on a printed page
   c. counting strokes of two metronomes going at slightly different speeds
   d. execution of several acts simultaneously
5. Comprehension:
   a. description of the movements made by a sewing machine or a crawling insect in a given period of time
   b. similarities and differences in synonyms
   c. criticisms of inexact or incorrect sentences
6. Suggestibility:
   a. showing lines of different length and detection of odors; in each case some manipulation made to study suggestibility

  b. imagination through anticipation
  c. emotional disposition (apprehension due to suggestion)
  d. involuntary movements
7. Esthetic appreciation:
  a. comparing preferences for colors with preferences of artists
  b. associations to colored squares
  c. understanding of musical phrases
8. Moral sentiments:
  a. observe reactions to pictures portraying various themes
9. Muscular force and force of will:
  a. lifting weights — dynamometer
10. Motor skill and visual judgment:
  a. putting a needle through a small hole
  b. tapping test
  c. estimation of how many times one line is contained in another longer line

Binet and Henri defined higher mental processes primarily in functional terms. They viewed memory as an intellectual process that was facilitated by understanding. Attention was seen as having the characteristics of a process; it included the measurement of duration and scope. Comprehension, considered to be a complex function, referred to common sense and judgment, and included the talent of observation and the spirit of ingenuity. Suggestibility pertained to the influence that one person exerts over another. These definitions, in spite of their seeming simplicity, have not changed considerably over the years.

Mental tests, Binet and Henri concluded, ought to be sufficiently varied to measure a large number of higher complex functions. They recognized that their series of tests was tentative and in need of revisions, which were to be determined by experimentation; initially, neither were results given nor suggestions made regarding standardization of the tests into a scale. Nevertheless, their work was a necessary beginning, and their series of tests established a basis for the development of the 1905 scale.

Binet and Henri gave continuous attention to the measurement of higher complex functions. The first extensive investigation of memory of words and of sentences appeared in two important papers published in 1895 by Binet and Henri (1895a, 1895b). Verbal memory received emphasis in their work, since it was seen as the chief foundation of school instruction and as a basic factor in all forms of language. However, later developments in the field of intelligence testing showed that their belief in the importance of memory tests as indicators of intelligence was somewhat misplaced.

In order to study tests of attention, Binet (1903) asked a school director and a class teacher to select children whom they considered to be intelligent ($N = 5$) or not intelligent ($N = 6$). Tests successful in differentiating the two groups included copying digits, tactile sensibility, and cancellation of letters from a printed page; other tests, such as choice reaction time, quick perception of words, and speed of work, were not successful. The intelligent children, in comparison with the less intelligent children, were quicker and more accurate in their solution of tasks. Binet defined attention, on the basis of these studies, as mental adaptation to a new situation. Speed of carrying out routine acts, he concluded, was not related to intelligence. Binet also sought to classify people into types (such as emotional, intellectual, and stable) through the study of such variables as memory, capillary circulation and pressure, suggestibility, graphology, and mental fatigue. Twenty tests measuring complex processes were described in his 1903 book on intelligence, *L'Etude Expérimentale de L'Intelligence*.

The impetus for the construction of the first scale came from the Minister of Public Instruction in Paris in 1904, when he appointed a committee to find a method that could separate the subnormal (mentally retarded) from the normal child in the schools. Binet, a member of the committee, began work on the problem by assuming that the difference between the two groups was one of intelligence. In collaboration with Theodore Simon (1873–1961), who was a physician (Wolf, 1961), 30 tests were devised that could be rated objectively and that could differentiate the mentally retarded from the normal (Binet & Simon, 1905). The tests represented an evolution of those studied by Binet, Henri, Simon, and others. They required execution of simple commands; coordination of movement of head and eye; prehension provoked by a tactile or visual stimulus; recognition of food; verbal knowledge of objects; ability to define words; knowledge of pictures; designation of objects; suggestibility; and completion of sentences. The tests, termed the 1905 scale, were given to subnormal children at the Salpêtrière and to subnormal and normal children in the primary schools of Paris.

The object of the 1905 scale was to devise a measure of the intellectual capacities of school children. It was not to be used in the treatment of the mentally retarded, nor was it to be applied to the study of organic brain damage. In fact, the study of mental disorganization was not even under consideration at this time. Binet and Simon aimed, at first, simply to determine the level of intelligence of school children.

The 1905 scale had many features that Binet and Simon believed to be important for an assessment of intelligence. The scale measured general mental development and judgment rather than an assortment of specific functions. Administration time was short, tests were arranged in order of difficulty rather than by type, and they were scored with whole, half, or no credit. The scale, unlike previous attempts to measure intelligence, sought to measure a wide variety of complex mental processes, rather than simple sensory-motor functions. In their 1905 article, "New Methods for the Diagnosis of the Intellectual Level of Abnormal Children," Binet and Simon presented their original scale, the idea of a graded series of tests, the concept of intelligence (see below), and some qualities associated with an intelligence test.

The so-called 1908 scale was described in their later article, "The Development of Intelligence in Children" (Binet & Simon, 1908). Tests were grouped according to age, and the concept of mental age was introduced. The beginning of test standardization can be seen in their approach to item placement: each item was placed at an age level where 60% to 90% of normal children passed it. In their last revision, the 1911 scale, further refinements were made, particularly in selecting tests that would differentiate intelligence from academic knowledge. The 1911 scale is described in Binet's (1911) article, "New Researches about the Measurement of Intellectual Level of School Children."

BINET'S AND SIMON'S APPROACH TO MENTAL AGE AND INTELLIGENCE

Binet can be credited with the popularization of the mental-age concept, although it did not originate with him (Peterson, 1925; Pintner, 1931; Woodrow, 1919). One of the earliest references to the mental-age concept was made by Esquirol (1838), who noted that an idiot was not capable of acquiring knowledge common to other persons of his own age. Duncan and Millard (1866), as well as Down (1887), suggested that a useful method for understanding mental retardation was to compare a mentally retarded child with younger children, although tests were not used for this purpose. Another reference to mental age appeared in a report by Hall (1848), in which he cited the testimony of a psychiatrist who had stated that the defendant in a murder trial, an adult, had knowledge equal to that of a 3-year-old child. It remained for Binet, however, to refine the concept of mental age and to make it definite and concrete.

Binet and Simon recognized that mental faculties, which they considered to be abilities, are independent and unequal within each subject. The tests in the 1905 scale were thought to measure various faculties. They considered intelligence to be a composite of such abilities as comprehension, invention, direction, and censorship. Nevertheless, as Kendig and Richmond (1940) noted, their scale yielded only one score measuring general level of intelligence. The 1905 scale, like all later ones, failed to provide scores for the mental processes measured by the separate tests. Only with the Vocabulary test was there an attempt to measure the same ability throughout the scale.

In developing their scale, Binet and Simon first approached the problem of defining intelligence by describing *judgment* (which included good sense, practical sense, initiative, and the ability to adapt oneself to events) as the *sine qua non* of normality or as the essential faculty of intelligence: "To judge well, to comprehend well, to reason well, these are the essential activites of intelligence [Binet & Simon, 1905, p. 192]." Intelligence was not considered to be the same as scholastic aptitude (Binet & Simon, 1908). Furthermore, they attempted to delineate two separate processes that they thought were involved in intelligence. One process, maturity, includes the development of judgment and comprehension and the ability to make further acquisitions. The other process, rectitude, refers to the correctness of intelligence, or the extent of foolishness associated with interpretations or judgments. However, such a distinction is somewhat artificial, and Binet and Simon also regarded it as tentative (Peterson, 1925).

Their study of the mentally retarded helped them to clarify further the concept of intelligence (Binet & Simon, 1909a). Normal intellectual functioning is distinguished from retarded intellectual functioning by three distinct elements that work together and form part of a single process: *direction of thought* (its complexity and persistence), *adaptation* (ability to differentiate), and *self-criticism*. These three elements may be paraphrased as follows: (*a*) the ability to take and maintain a given mental set; (*b*) the capacity to make adaptations for the purpose of attaining a desired end; and (*c*) the power of auto-criticism (Terman, 1916). These elements were also included in a functional definition of thought. Although Binet and Simon did not have a well-formulated definition of intelligence, no earlier definition was as concise in emphasizing the active and organized properties of intelligence.

CONCLUDING COMMENTS CONCERNING BINET AND SIMON

Before we turn to American revisions of the scale, other facets of the work of Binet and Simon should be considered briefly. Their work extended beyond intellectual measurement. Binet and Simon were interested in classifying individuals with reference to each other, not in measurement purely in the physical sense. Even when working on the 1908 and 1911 revisions, Binet maintained his interests in many areas that had engaged him in the course of his professional career. Research was conducted on teachers' preferences for academic subjects, language and thought, palmistry, mental deficiency, and insanity. Binet tried many methods (including head movements, aethesiometry, graphology, and palmistry) before arriving at his final scales.

Binet and Simon increasingly became concerned with intellectual functioning in mental illness. They learned that the general paretic had a *disturbance* in the functioning of intelligence, whereas the imbecile had an *arrest* in the development of intelligence; this is a distinction that is still very important. Binet and Simon suggested that the paretic's difficulties with memory, flow of words, arithmetic calculation, and perception represented a lack of evocation of ideas—a failure of an essential part of adaptation. Senility, in contrast, concerns the loss of memory and not functional inertia. Consequently, the senile person recognizes that he is losing his ability, whereas the paretic does not (Binet & Simon, 1909b). Murphy (1968) also recognized Binet's interest in the clinical application of the scales. He noted that:

Binet had been a tester of intellectual powers, and a sophisticated student of ego organization, long before he was charged by the French Minister of Public Instruction in 1904 to differentiate the clinical group of the mental defectives from those capable of doing the normal work of the schools. It was a clinical purpose that Binet's work served, and it was a methodological sophistication, with fifteen years of prior work with testing, that made possible the 1905 scale [p. 22].

The scales represent a gradual evolution. They were successful because they were simple and practical, the directions were definite and exact, the tasks were brief and varied, and the tests were placed at year levels (Mateer, 1924). Terman (1916) also recognized that the scales were successful because they used age standards or norms in the measurement of intelligence, they tested complex instead of simple and elementary processes, and they provided a general level of intelligence. It is ironic that while Binet was convinced that intelligence is embedded in the total personality, his tests have become instrumental in giving to the concept of "intelligence" a relatively independent existence (Wolf, 1969a).

The Binet-Simon scales, almost from their inception, were recognized as being extremely valuable for the diagnosis of mental retardation (Burt, 1914). The scales achieved great popularity in many countries, including France, Belgium, Switzerland, Italy, Russia, Sweden, England, and America. Butcher (1968) aptly summarized the work of Binet and Simon as follows:

Binet and Simon were concerned to sample broadly the intellectual performances of which typical children at particular ages would be capable, including as little as possible that was distinctively scholastic, but taking equal pains to retain a broad conception of intellectual progress and, above all, to tie down the items to what children actually were found able to perform as distinct from any purely theoretical ideas of what they ought to be able to [p. 220].

This section is concluded by citing Burt's (1914) tribute to the Binet-Simon scales, a tribute which contains a glimpse of the range of Binet's and Simon's contribution to the testing movement.

As a provisional but practicable plan for testing mental deficiency, as a rough but intelligible method of interpreting the results, as a pioneer investigation of the general course of mental development, as a demonstration of the richness of the higher, more complex, and more ordinary mental processes, as a protest against the mere examination of acuity of sensation, of speed of reaction, or of anatomical peculiarities, as a means of interesting the teacher, the doctor, and the social worker in the measurement of psychological capacities by psychological devices, as a prolific source of inspiration and suggestion, and, finally, as a stimulus to scientific discussion and enquiry, in these and many other ways the Binet scheme remains a marvel and a masterpiece [pp. 149–150].

THE BINET-SIMON SCALE IN AMERICA

The Binet-Simon scales were accepted readily by many investigators in the United States, but revisions were needed. (For information concerning the scale in other countries, consult Peterson, 1925.) Goddard, the director of the Psychological Laboratory at the Vineland Training School, introduced the 1905 scale to the United States in 1908 (Goddard, 1908), and, two years later, the 1908 scale (Goddard, 1910). Goddard adapted the 1908 scale with as few revisions as possible, and standardized it on 2000 American children. For many years this version was the one most commonly used. The early use of the scale was almost entirely restricted to the evaluation of the mentally retarded. Goddard, too, altered Binet's conception of intelligence by substituting for "Binet's *idea* of intelligence as a shifting complex of inter-related functions, the concept of a single, underlying function (faculty) of intelligence. Further, he believed that this unitary function was largely determined by heredity, a view much at variance with Binet's optimistic proposals for mental orthopedics [Tuddenham, 1962, p. 490]."

Other translations and references to the scales appeared about the same time. Whipple (1910) described the scales in *Manual of Mental and Physical Tests*. Huey (1910) published a translation of the 1908 scale, as did Wallin (1911) and Kuhlmann (1912). The National Education Association in 1909 cited the Goddard revision of the 1908 scale as a test that could be used with exceptional children and with mentally retarded children (Bruner, Barnes, & Dearborn, 1909). Kuhlmann (1922) also published a second version of the Binet-Simon scales. His first version had adhered closely to the original 1908 scale, but his second version introduced many new tests covering ages 6 months to 15 years. Kuhlmann's most original contribution was to standardize the scale for children below the age of 3 years. Yerkes, Bridges, and Hardwick (1915) also made use of the Binet-Simon tests, but arranged them in a point-scale format because they felt that such an arrangement would facilitate the measurement of mental ability. These authors objected to the grouping of tests into age levels in the Binet-Simon scales, and to the complex administrative procedures required of the examiner. They also objected to the basal age concept, for it easily could lead to an inappropriate inference about level of mental functioning.

Terman in 1911 commented that the 1908 scale had great practical and theoretical value, and suggested a number of additional tests, including interpretation of fables and the ball-and-field problem, that could be used to supplement the Binet-Simon scale (Terman, 1911). Terman also became interested in the intelligence testing of school children, and after studying Goddard's work, collaborated with Childs in publishing a tentative revision of the Binet-Simon scale in 1912 (Terman & Childs, 1912). This revision was modified, extended, and standardized during the next four years. The 1916 Stanford-Binet used the ideas of Binet and Simon, but Terman deserves credit for his thorough and accurate working out of the method suggested by Binet and his co-workers. A major contribution of the 1916 scale was its standardization.

Terman also adopted Stern's mental quotient concept, which is arrived at by dividing mental age by chronological age. Stern had originally introduced his idea in a paper delivered at the German Congress of Psychology in Berlin in April 1912 and described it in his book, *The Psychological Methods of Testing Intelligence* (Stern, 1914). Stern's rationale for the development of the mental quotient concept was, in part, as follows:

It is perfectly clear how valuable the measurement of mental retardation is, particularly in the investigation of abnormal children. It has, however, been shown recently that the simple computation of the absolute difference between the two ages is not entirely adequate for this purpose, because this difference does not mean the same thing at different ages. . . . Only when children of approximately equal age-levels are under investigation can this value suffice: for all other cases the introduction of the *mental quotient* will be recommended. . . . This value expresses not the difference, but the ratio of mental to chronological age and is thus partially independent of the absolute magnitude of chronological age. The formula is, then: mental quotient = mental age ÷ chronological age [pp. 41–42].

Terman and his associates renamed this ratio the intelligence quotient (IQ) when they produced the 1916 version of the Binet-Simon scale and called it the Stanford Revision and Extension of the Binet-Simon Intelligence Scale. Although the IQ has become an extremely useful means for classifying persons, Wolf (1969b) noted that it is questionable whether Binet "would have accepted even Terman's elaborate standardizations as a valid basis for calculating IQ's [p. 236]."

The Binet-Simon scale was also revised by Herring in 1922 (Herring, 1922). The Herring Revision, which contained 38 original tests arranged as a point scale and which provided a mental age and IQ, was available as an alternate form because of its high correlation ($r=.98$) with the 1916 Stanford-Binet. However, the Herring Revision had several faults, such as containing more tests that required reading than were found on the Stanford-Binet and producing IQ's at the superior levels that were not equivalent to those obtained on the Stanford-Binet (Carroll & Hollingworth, 1930).

The Binet-Simon scale helped to stimulate the development of clinical psychology in the United States and in other countries as well. Jenkins and Paterson (1961) have observed, "Probably no psychological innovation has had more impact on the societies of the Western world than the development of the Binet-Simon scales [p. 81]." Tuddenham (1962), too, expressed a similar belief:

The success of the Stanford-Binet was a triumph of pragmatism, but its importance must not be underestimated, for it demonstrated the feasibility of mental measurement and led to the development of other tests for many special purposes. Equally important, it led to a public acceptance of testing which had important consequences for education and industry, for the military, and for society generally [p. 494].

With the introduction of the scale, intelligence testing became a popular technique in many varied institutions throughout the country. The 1960 revision (Terman & Merrill, 1960) represents the latest and most modern development of Binet's original idea.

The intelligence testing movement developed without the backing of any particular school or system, and it grew because of practical demands (Heidbreder, 1933). The IQ concept also generated interest in the testing movement. Success came to Binet and Simon when they attempted to measure intelligence in general terms, abandoning the attempt to analyze intelligence into component parts. While there were many workers in the field of test construction during the Binet-Simon period (see Chapter 2), it was Binet's and Simon's work during the years from 1905 to 1911 that led to their scale receiving universal recognition as a practical means for the measurement of mental ability.

THE SCALES

As we have seen, Binet and Simon made two revisions of their 1905 scale, one in 1908 and one in 1911, and the popularity of the scales in the United States led to further revisions. This section of the chapter reviews only the scales as they were developed by Binet and Simon, by Terman, and by Terman and Merrill. Table 8–1 summarizes some of the major characteristics of the

Table 8-1. SOME CHARACTERISTICS OF THE BINET-SIMON AND STANFORD-BINET SCALES

SCALE YEAR	AUTHORS	NUMBER OF TESTS	YEAR LEVELS COVERED	MODIFICATIONS MADE IN REVISIONS	DIFFICULTIES
1905	Binet and Simon	30	Very low grade idiots to upper elementary grades		Poorly standardized ($N = 50$) Inadequate range Tests did not always discriminate No objective method for arriving at a total score
1908	Binet and Simon	59	III to XIII years of age	New tests added Some tests eliminated, especially those at the idiot level Tests grouped according to age commonly passed Mental age concept introduced	Inadequate standardization ($N = 203$) No credits given for fractions of a year Lower year level tests too easy, higher year level tests too difficult Scoring and administrative procedures inadequate Unequal number of tests at different year levels
1911	Binet and Simon	54	III years of age to Adult level	New tests added, some eliminated Credit given for fraction of a year Tests shifted More detailed scoring instructions Adult year level included	Almost same difficulties as those noted for 1908 scale; there were no fundamental changes
1916	Terman	90	III years of age to Superior-Adult-I level	New tests added Some tests revised Location changed for some tests Scoring and administrative procedures changed and better organized Introduced alternate tests Introduced IQ concept Representative sampling attempted	Poor standardization at extremes Only single form Inadequate standardization ($N = 1000$ native-born Californian children and 400 adults) Inadequate measure of adult mental capacity Too heavily weighted with verbal and abstract materials Inadequate scoring and administrative procedures at some points Some tests dated in the 1930's Some tests misplaced Too much credit for rote memory
1937	Terman and Merrill	129	II years of age to Superior-Adult-III level	Better standardization ($N = 3184$) Two forms (L and M) More performance tests at earlier year levels	Equal variability at all ages not present Sample somewhat higher in socioeconomic level than general population, and more urban than rural subjects included Some tests difficult to score Low ceiling with above average adolescents

Table 8-1. SOME CHARACTERISTICS OF THE BINET-SIMON AND STANFORD-BINET SCALES—CONTINUED

SCALE YEAR	AUTHORS	NUMBER OF TESTS	YEAR LEVELS COVERED	MODIFICATIONS MADE IN REVISIONS	DIFFICULTIES
1960	Terman and Merrill	142	II years of age to Superior-Adult-III level	One form (L-M), which incorporates best tests from Forms L and M New group of children used to check changes in test difficulty ($N=4498$) Some tests relocated, dropped, or rescored Substitution of deviation IQ for ratio IQ—standard score with $M=100$ and $SD=16$ Use of age 18 years as ceiling level rather than 16 years Clarification of scoring principles	Too heavily weighted with verbal materials Does not measure originality and creative abilities Inadequate for very superior students Abstract verbal tests appear at too low a level and rote memory tests appear at too high a level Restandardization procedures not appropriate

three Binet-Simon scales and of the three Terman and Terman-Merrill scales. The number of tests included in the Binet-Simon scales ranged from 30 to 59, while the number of tests in the three Terman and Terman-Merrill scales ranged from 90 to 142. Successive revisions were improvements on the former versions, although Berger (1970), as we will see in the discussion of the 1960 revision, had serious reservations about the construction of Form L-M. Tests were usually added, eliminated, and regrouped, and instructions were improved. The major difficulties with the Binet-Simon scales consisted of their inadequate standardization and their failure to provide partial year-level credits.

1905 Scale

The first published scale contained 30 tests, which were arranged in order of difficulty rather than by year levels. Some tentative standards were presented, which gave the number of tests that normal children would pass; also discussed were ranges of test successes and levels of mental retardation. Tests 1 through 9 were expected to be passed by 3-year-olds, and Tests 10, 11, 12, and 14 by 5-year-olds. On Test 13 younger children were found to be more suggestible than older ones. Test 16 was seen as being a good test to separate 7- from 5-year-olds. Differences between 7- and 9-year-olds and 9- and 11-year-olds were determined primarily by Tests 15 through 30, although specific criteria were not given that would enable the examiner to distinguish between 7- and 11-year-olds.

Binet and Simon found the scale useful for classifying mentally retarded persons, although the diagnostic criteria were somewhat crude. Idiots (adults) were not expected to go beyond Test 6, and imbeciles (adults) were not expected to pass beyond Test 15, but for morons no precise limit could be given. Language tests (particularly Test 27) appeared to be most effective in differentiating normals from morons, especially for morons who were between the chronological ages of 8 and 13 years. Binet and Simon recognized that the three divisions among the mentally retarded were not absolute, but they were selected so as to conform with medical usage current at that time. As Table 8–1 shows, many serious difficulties existed with the scale, including inadequate standardization and inadequate scoring criteria. The 1905 scale is presented below.

The 1905 Scale

1. Visual coordination. Noting the degree of coordination of movement of the head and eyes as a lighted match is passed slowly before the subject's eyes.

2. Prehension provoked tactually. A small wooden cube is to be placed in contact with the palm or back of the subject's hand. He must grasp it and carry it to his mouth, and his coordinated grasping and other movements are to be noted.

3. Prehension provoked visually. Same as 2, except that the object is placed within the subject's reach, but not in contact with him. The experimenter, to catch the child's attention, encourages him orally and with appropriate gestures to take the object.

4. Cognizance of food. A small bit of chocolate and a piece of wood of similar dimensions are successively shown the subject, and signs of his recognition of the food and attempts to take it are noted carefully.

5. Seeking food when a slight difficulty is interposed. A small piece of the chocolate, as used in the previous test, is wrapped in a piece of paper and given to the subject. Observations are made on his manner of getting the food and separating it from the paper.

6. The execution of simple orders and the imitation of gestures. The orders are mostly such as might be understood from the accompanying gestures alone.

(This is the limit for idiots as experimentally determined.)

7. Verbal knowledge of objects. The child is to touch his head, nose, ear, etc., and also to hand the experimenter on command a particular one of three well-known objects: cup, key, string.

8. Knowledge of objects in a picture as shown by finding them and pointing them out when they are called by name.

9. Naming objects designated in a picture.

(This is the upper limit of 3-year-old normal children. The three preceding tests are not in order of increasing difficulty, for whoever passes 7 usually passes 8 and 9 also.)

10. Immediate comparison of two lines for discrimination as to length.

11. Reproduction of series of three digits immediately after oral presentation.

12. Weight discrimination. Comparison of two weights—of 3 and 12 grams, of 6 and 15 grams, and of 3 and 15 grams.

13. Suggestibility. (*a*) Modification of 7: an object not among the three present is asked for. (*b*) Modification of 8: "Where [in the picture] is the *patapoum?* the *nitchevo?*" (These words have no meaning.) (*c*) Modification of 10: the two lines to be compared are of equal length.

(Test 13 is admitted to be a test not of intelligence but of "force of judgment" and "resistance of character.")

14. Definitions of familiar objects—*house, horse, fork, mamma.*

(This is the limit of 5-year-old normal children, except that they fail on Test 13.)

15. Repetition of sentences of 15 words each, immediately after hearing them spoken by the examiner.

(This is the limit of imbeciles.)

16. Giving differences between various pairs of familiar objects recalled in memory: (*a*) *paper* and *cardboard,* (*b*) *a fly* and *a butterfly,* and (*c*) *wood* and *glass.* (Test 16 alone effectively separated normal children of 5 and 7 years.)

17. Immediate memory of pictures of familiar objects. Thirteen pictures pasted on two pieces of cardboard are presented simultaneously. The subject looks at them for 30 seconds and then gives the names of those recalled.

18. Drawing from memory two different designs shown simultaneously for 10 seconds.

19. Repetition of series of digits after oral presentation. Three series of three digits each, three of four each, three of five, etc., are presented until not one of the three series in a group is repeated correctly. The number of digits in the highest series which the subject repeats is his score.

20. Giving from memory the resemblance among familiar objects: (*a*) *a wild poppy* (red) and *blood,* (*b*) *an ant, a fly, a butterfly,* and *a flea,* and (*c*) *a newspaper, a label,* and *a picture.*

21. Rapid discrimination of lines. A line of 30 cm. is compared successively with 15 lines varying from 35 down to 31 cm. A more difficult set of comparisons is then made of a line of 100 mm. with 12 lines varying from 103 to 101 mm.

22. Arranging in order five weights – 15, 12, 9, 6, and 3 grams – of equal size.

23. Identification of the missing weight from the series in Test 22 from which one is removed. The remaining weights are not in the right order. This test is given only when Test 22 is passed.

(This is given as the most probable limit of morons.)

24. Finding words to rhyme with a given word after the process has been illustrated.

25. Supplying missing words at the end of simple sentences, one for each sentence. This is the Ebbinghaus completion method simplified.

26. Construction of a sentence to embody three given words: *Paris, gutter, fortune.*

27. Making replies to 25 problem questions of graded difficulty; such as, "What is the thing to do when you are sleepy?" "Why is it better to continue with perseverance what one has started than to abandon it and start something else?"

(Test 27 alone reveals the moron.)

28. Giving the time that it would be if the large and the small hands of the clock were interchanged at four minutes to three and at 20 minutes after six. A much more difficult test is given those who succeed in the inversion; namely, to explain the impossibility of the precise transposition indicated.

29. Drawing what a quarto-folded paper with a piece cut out of the once-folded edge would look like if unfolded.

30. Giving distinctions between abstract terms; as between *liking* and *respecting* a person; between being *sad* and being *bored.*

1908 Scale

The 1908 scale was the first age scale. The tests were arranged into year levels by using an empirical procedure, that is, by actually determining what children could do. However, the sample size was limited, and the procedures for placing tests at specific year levels were not well developed. The first six tests of the 1905 scale were dropped because they were more suitable for infants than for 3-year-olds. Other tests, too, were eliminated and still others added. The 1908 scale was criticized for containing tests that were too dependent on school experiences. While they recognized this limitation, Binet and Simon were not yet ready to make significant changes in test content. (See Table 8–1 for other comments concerning the 1908 scale.)

With the introduction of the 1908 scale, Binet and Simon made more precise descriptions of the three divisions of mental retardation. Age levels 0–2 characterized idiots, 2–7 imbeciles, and 7 and above, morons. While these age levels were more formal than those proposed in the 1905 scale, Binet and Simon still failed to relate mental age to the degree of defectiveness in children. It remained for Stern in 1912 to deal successfully with this problem when he introduced the mental-quotient concept (Stern, 1914).

The 1908 scale constituted a significant advance over the 1905 scale, and it is considered an important milestone in the chronology of intelligence testing (Peterson, 1925). Placing the tests into age groups represents the most significant advance over the 1905 scale (Pintner, 1931). The 1908 scale's advantages over the 1905 scale also included the adoption of mental-age units that were easily understood, and the administration of several varied tests to each examinee.

Ayres (1911) evaluated the Binet-Simon scale shortly after it appeared in the United States. His perceptive analysis was to be echoed by many other writers in later years. Ayres believed that the tests predominantly reflected the child's ability to use words fluently, and only minimally his ability to act. Some tests depended on recent environmental experience, while others depended on the ability to read and write. Finally, he indicated that too great weight was given to tests requiring the ability to repeat words and numbers, to assemble puzzles, and to define abstract terms.

1911 Scale

In the 1911 scale, Binet and Simon changed the location of some tests. Four of the XI-year-level tests were raised to the XII-year level, and all of the XII-year-level tests to the XV-year level. The three XIII-year-level tests of the 1908 scale, with the addition of two new tests, became tests at the Adult-year level, which was a new year level. Tests too dependent on scholastic ability, such as reading and writing, and tests too dependent on knowledge that had been incidentally acquired, were eliminated. Other tests were shifted and new ones were introduced. Year-levels III, IV, and V were exactly the same as in the 1908 scale. At each year level there were five tests, except at year-level IV where only four tests appeared.

1916 Stanford-Binet Scale

A considerable amount of effort went into the 1916 revision (Terman, 1916). It represented the most thorough and extensive development of the Binet-Simon scales. Terman added some tests, revised others, changed locations, changed methods of scoring and administration, introduced alternative tests, and attempted representative sampling. The added tests, with alternatives, increased the number of tests from 54 to 90. Of the 36 new tests in the 1916 Stanford Revision, 27 were devised by Terman and his colleagues; two were borrowed from the Healy-Fernald series, one from Kuhlmann, and one from Bonser. The remaining five tests were modifications of earlier Binet tests (Terman, 1916). Six tests appeared in each year level so that a more convenient method of calculating mental age was available. Examinees older than 16 years of age were assigned the chronological age of 16, which was to be used in the calculation of the IQ. The scale ranged from year-level III to Superior-Adult-I level. Terman was also aware that on occasion a quick estimate of the child's intelligence was needed, and for such occasions he indicated four tests at each year level (with the exception of year-level XII, where six tests were designated) to be used as a short form of the scale.

In spite of the refinements, many difficulties remained. As can be seen in Table 8–1, standardization was still a problem. There was only one form, adult mental capacity was inadequately measured, verbal materials were too prominent, and scoring and administrative procedures were inadequate for some tests. Studies by Madden (1932), Stoke (1933), and Wallin (1929), for example, also showed that the tests at the VIII- and IX-year levels varied considerably in their level of difficulty. Porteus's (1922) criticisms of the tests in the scale (criticisms that have been applied also to successive revisions of the scale) were that the tests

favor the glib tongued, quick thinking child, the child who has had a good educational environment, the child who memorizes readily and to whom expression is easy, and who, therefore, shows good scholastic promise. On the other hand, they do not do justice to the child with capacity for achievement in manual and industrial pursuits, who is shy and unresponsive in oral tests, or who lacks facility in language expression, or whose mental operations are slow but sure, or who has been unfortunate in his educational background [p. 188].

Burt (1939) described the 1916 Stanford-Binet as forming "a convenient and practical method for quick clinical diagnosis rather than a reliable scientific instrument for statistical surveys [p. 256]."

1937 Revision

After a 21-year period, the 1916 scale was revised (Terman & Merrill, 1937). Flanagan (1938), while recognizing that some difficulties still existed with the scale, stated: "The publication of this book [*Measuring Intelligence*] is a milestone in the progress of the individual-testing of intelligence... [p. 133]." Additional items were introduced, the scale was better standardized, two forms were available, and there were more performance tests at the earlier year levels. New types of tests were more prevalent at the preschool and adult levels, and more use was made of differential scoring of the same test (Flanagan, 1938). In comparison with the 1916 revision, Table 8–2 shows that there was an increase in the nonverbal tests in year-levels II to V by 21 per cent in Form L and by only 3 per cent in Form M, while in year-levels XII through SA III the percentage of nonverbal tests was reduced in the two 1937 forms (Kennedy-Fraser, 1945). Improvement was made in memory tests (Kent, 1937), in the wording of questions, in year level assignments, and in the scoring of the Vocabulary test (Burt, 1939). The scale was extended downward to year-level II, with tests appearing at half-year levels between years II and V, and upward to the Superior-Adult-III level. Tests were also provided for year-levels XI and XIII.

In computing the IQ's of older examinees on the 1937 scales, the chronological age after 13 is computed by disregarding increasing fractions of successive chronological age increments. From 13 to 16, one out of every three additional months of chronological age is disregarded, and after 16 all of the chronological age is disregarded. Thus, for examinees 16 years of age or over, the chronological age divisor for computing the IQ is 15–0. The tables in the manual (Terman & Merrill, 1937) automatically take care of the reduced values for chronological ages after 13. The standard deviations in the 1937 forms ranged from 12.5 at year-level VI to 20.6 at year-level II-6. To adjust for this variability, Roberts and Mellone (1952) presented tables that made the IQ's comparable at different age levels. Tables of equivalent values for the 1916 and 1937 revisions were also published by Bernreuter and Carr (1938) and by Davis (1940).

The reliability coefficients for the scales range from .98 for subjects with IQ's below 70 to .90 for subjects with IQ's above 129. Corresponding standard errors of measurement range from 2.2 for subjects below 70 IQ to 5.2 for subjects above 129 IQ. The individual test correlations with the total score range

Table 8-2. PERCENTAGE OF NONVERBAL TESTS IN 1916 AND 1937 FORMS OF THE STANFORD-BINET

YEAR LEVELS	1916	1937 Form L	1937 Form M
II-V	38	59	41
VI-XII	19	19	12
XIII-SA III	38	26	21

(Reprinted by permission of the publisher from D. Kennedy-Fraser, *The Terman-Merrill Intelligence Scale in Scotland,* p. 30. Copyright © 1945, University of London Press.)

from .27 to .91; the median correlation is approximately .62. Validity coefficients indicate that the relationship between IQ and school success ranges from
.40 to .50 (Terman & Merrill, 1953).

Many other favorable comments were made about the 1937 scale in comparison with the 1916 revision. Krugman (1939) noted that the 1937 scale had
better statistical properties, standardization and validation, and directions.
Goodenough (1942) pointed out that it sampled abilities better and also
provided more stable IQ's over time. Burt (1939) commented that the scale
was more efficient for the diagnosis of mental retardation. He also believed that
there was some hope that the scale could "measure the child's general intelligence with a rough but reasonable degree of accuracy and at the same time
throw sidelights on the kind as well as on the nature and extent of the special
abilities or special defects that he displays [p. 260]." Vernon (1937) saw the
Stanford-Binet as partaking of both the clinical and the psychometric approaches: "It has the flexibility and the control of the subjective situation characteristic of the clinical interview, but at the same time sufficient objective control to yield a [reliable] measure of ability [p. 106]." McCandless (1953a)
noted that in the hands of a competent clinician the Stanford-Binet in conjunction with a performance test is remarkably informative.

Negative comments also took their place alongside the many favorable
ones. Weaknesses of the 1937 scale, in comparison to the 1916 scale, included
longer administration time, more scatter, and more variability of IQ scores
(Bernreuter & Carr, 1938; Goodenough, 1942; Krugman, 1939). The 1937
scale still placed too much emphasis on verbal material and on rote memory,
had confusing directions at times, and could not always be administered with a
single basal and final year (Krugman, 1939; McCandless, 1953a). Neither the
standard error of measurement of any particular IQ (Flanagan, 1938) nor the
standard error of the sample mean (Marks, 1947) could be determined by the
information contained in the manual or by the sampling procedures, respectively. McNemar (1942), however, later published standard errors of measurement, which are shown in Table C-4 in the Appendix.

Form M does not have a Vocabulary test, and therefore it is not possible to
obtain as much projective material from Form M as from Form L (McCandless, 1953a). Some felt that performance tests were inadequately represented
(Weider, Levi, & Risch, 1943), while others felt that there was an overweight-
ing with practical or manual tests (e.g., Burt, 1939). The scale was seen as being
unsuitable for use with adults (British Psychological Society, 1958; McCandless, 1953a), and as taking the setting of a school situation, thereby inhibiting
maximum efficiency in children, such as delinquents, who have adverse reactions to school (Weider et al., 1943). There was dissatisfaction with the ceiling
procedure, which leaves the examinee with a sense of failure, and with the
unpredictability of the time required to administer the test (McCandless,
1953a).

Irregularities in test placement were also found, but not always in the same
direction. Harriman (1939) reported that 200 fifth and sixth graders on Form L
had more success with tests at the XIII-year level (70% success) than with
tests at the XII-year level (63% success); other irregularities were also found in
per cent success. Mitchell (1941), in contrast, found that tests at year-level
XIII were more difficult than those at year-levels XII and XIV in a sample of
college freshman and senior medical students.

Cattell (1937), an advocate of the factor analytic approach to intelligence
testing, which partly emphasizes the use of special tests for the measurement of
abilities, found the Stanford-Binet wanting in several respects. He criticized the
scale for containing tests of scholastic attainment and life experience rather
than measuring g, for inadequate reliability and fine grading, for inadequacies at
higher mental ages, and for permitting special factors to play a large role in con-

tributing to the total score. He believed that the attachment of a single score to the measurement of a collection of abilities is meaningless; that the derived IQ does not mirror the true variability of intelligence; and that the personal relationship between the examiner and examinee may lead to unreliable test scores (see Chapter 6 for related material). Cattell in 1937 therefore concluded "that the Binet-Simon and its modifications constitute an obsolete instrument which ignores all that progress in the theory of mental testing which has been made in the last twenty years, and which should be replaced by more up-to-date measures of 'g' [p. 115]." Furthermore, the scale yields "a vague composite of ill-defined traits and abilities [p. 116]." While some of these criticisms are doubtlessly correct, Cattell's views are not completely justified. The 1937 Stanford-Binet has continued to yield acceptable validity coefficients (e.g., Watson, 1951) and has been subjected to factor analyses that have yielded a large first unrotated factor (see Chapter 10 for a summary of factor analytic studies). The scale's hardiness continues, in spite of its flaws, and, as we shall soon see, it has been further refined in the latest 1960 revision.

Critical comments concerning the applied and clinical use of the 1937 scale also appeared in a report by Krugman (1939), which was based on the responses he obtained to a questionnaire from 10 psychologists working at the New York City Bureau of Child Guidance. Krugman's summary well illustrates the views of many clinicians using the scale and probably reflects similar views currently existing toward the 1960 revision.

In general, then, these psychologists believe that there is something radically wrong with the content of the Revised Form L—that the verbal material is not fair to New York City children, that many tests are misplaced in the scale, that some material is not appropriate for clinic children, that instructions for administration are frequently inadequate, although, in the main, simpler than instructions for the old Stanford-Binet, and that criteria and scoring instructions are too often inadequate. Furthermore, although there is divided opinion on the matter of year-by-year testing, most of the psychologists agree that, in a clinic situation, more flexibility of administration is necessary [p. 597].

The use of individual testing procedures for the assessment of intelligence is not without its pitfalls. Kent (1937) pointed out that the age-grade method, used in the Stanford-Binet, is more cumbersome and uneconomical than a scoring system that evaluates responses by points because there are too many tests that add nothing to the scale's adequacy and because credit is not given for partial successes. (Yerkes et al. (1915) had similar objections; see page 94.) Kent also noted that oral tests present many difficulties for both examinees and examiners. First, "a test which calls for oral response discriminates very seriously against the child who by reason of speech defect or impediment is unable to make himself understood [p. 423]." Second, the procedures used on the Stanford-Binet are not sufficiently flexible for clinical subjects. Third, subjective examiner decisions are involved in the presentation of the vocabulary words and in the scoring of the vocabulary responses (see Chapter 5 for related material).

Kent's (1937) opinion of the Stanford-Binet (and of similar oral types of tests) was as follows:

It measures the subject's willingness to attempt a definition, not invariably his actual ability to offer an acceptable response. Subjects differ widely in respect to the standards of certainty which seem to them to justify a response. It is sometimes the highly intelligent person who is most reluctant to offer anything short of a definition worthy of the dictionary, and who will decline to answer at all rather than attempt a crude explanation which does not satisfy his own standard of definition [p. 425].

Kent also noted that the clinical subject may find the request to define words as unnatural and wholly remote from everyday experience. We use words at all times, but only rarely have occasion to define them. . . . A person unaccustomed to the use of the dictionary frequently feels bewildered when requested to define a word which has no familiar synonym. One who does not know how liberally the responses are scored may well feel trapped [pp. 425–426].

1960 Revision, Form L-M

The 1960 Form L-M revision (Terman & Merrill, 1960) was constructed by selecting from Form L and Form M those tests that showed an increase in the percentage passing the test with increase in age and those that correlated highly with the scale as a whole. The ratio of Form L to Form M tests in the new scale is about 9 to 7. Some tests were relocated, some eliminated, and some rescored. Instructions for test administration and scoring were improved, the formats for the test materials were redesigned to be more pleasing and more convenient (Neale, 1962), and the IQ tables were extended from age 16 to 18. The scale was not restandardized; instead a sample of 4,498 subjects who had taken the scale between 1950 and 1954 was used to check on changes in item difficulty. New material was not introduced, nor were the essential features of the scale changed. With the latest revision, only one form is available. Validity data were not presented with the revision; its validity rests on the fact that the same type of tests are used as in the 1937 scales (Balinsky, 1960).

One of the most important developments in Form L-M is the replacement of the 1937 scale's IQ tables, which represent the conventional ratio IQ, by tables devised by Pinneau, which present deviation IQ's for ages 2 through 18 years. The deviation IQ is basically a normalized standard score with a mean of 100 and a standard deviation of 16. It expresses the deviation of the ratio IQ from the mean ratio IQ at each age level. The deviation IQ controls for the variability in IQ distributions that was found to exist in various levels of the former revisions. A specific IQ at different ages in Form L-M indicates close to the same relative ability or standing regardless of the age of the examinee.

Berger (1970) was unhappy with the manner in which the deviation IQ's were constructed. He pointed out that deviation IQ's are different from deviation scores, which are linear transformations of raw score "distances" from the mean. Further, he noted that the deviation IQ tables in the Stanford-Binet manual should not be accepted as being valid until it has been demonstrated that, first, L-M ratio IQ's have the same distribution statistics as those observed on the 1937 scales and that, second, the 1960 revision employed representative samples. The revision procedures used with Form L-M prevented either of these conditions from being fulfilled. Consequently, Berger concluded that "there would appear to be no justification in interpreting L-M 'IQs' according to standard practice [p. 24]." Berger's analysis serves to remind us of the shortcomings of the deviation IQ as it is used on the Stanford-Binet (L-M), and of the necessity to employ careful standardization procedures in constructing new tests or in revising old ones.

Berger also found fault with the procedures that were used to substitute for restandardization. For example, he believed that item difficulty cannot be properly determined because an inappropriate mental age criterion was used to select the sample for revision. Second, the demographic characteristics of the sample were not sufficiently detailed so that the extent of bias in the sample can be determined. Fraser (1965), too, noted that changes in the composition of tests were made without restandardization. On the basis of these and other criticisms, Berger concluded that Form L-M provides MA's and IQ's that are of limited accuracy, a limitation that is in addition to those usually associated with intelligence test scores. Berger recommended that the 1937 forms continue to be used until the scale is restandardized.

The 1960 scale also has weaknesses common to all former revisions. It has been criticized for being too heavily weighted with verbal materials so that for some purposes it may not be useful. Like other tests of intelligence, it does not measure creative abilities. It is inadequate for superior students, although the latest revision is more effective than former ones for use with superior adolescents (Kennedy, Moon, Nelson, Lindner, & Turner, 1961). Also, it has abstract material at too low a level, and rote memory tests at too high a level (see Table 8-1). The 1960 revision, despite some of the difficulties associated with its standardization, still produces acceptable validity coefficients (cf. Himelstein, 1966) and remains as one of the standard instruments for the assessment of children's intelligence.

SUMMARY

Alfred Binet has been considered the father of intelligence testing because of his efforts in bringing forth a valuable tool for the assessment of intelligence. His interests were intertwined with the areas of developmental, clinical, and experimental psychology. His collaborators in the development of an intelligence scale included Victor Henri and Theodore Simon. These three men were good test constructors, being cognizant of both examinee and examiner factors that might affect the reliability and validity of test results. Their search for tests was guided by a concern for those that could shed light on higher mental processes. They were alert and flexible investigators, willing to discard tests that proved to be unreliable and willing to modify others when needed.

The first Binet-Simon scale—the so-called "1905 scale"—developed from a practical need of the public school system in Paris. The Minister of Public Instruction desired a means of separating mentally retarded from non-mentally retarded children, and it was to this problem that Binet and Simon addressed their work. The first scale represented the culmination of years of previous experimentation.

Binet and Simon considered judgment, comprehension, and reasoning as the essential parts of intelligence. The process of thinking was conceived of as having three interrelated parts: the ability to adopt and maintain a given set, the ability to make adaptations, and the ability to criticize oneself. While this conception of intelligence was not a precise one, it did emphasize the active and organized properties of intelligence. Through the use of the mental age concept, Binet and Simon found a means of ranking individuals.

The Binet-Simon scales were warmly received in many countries. Goddard, in the United States, was one of the leading proponents of the scales, and contributed by translating, adapting, and standardizing the scales. Huey, Wallin, and Kuhlmann were also engaged in translating and refining the scales during this same time period (approximately 1908 to 1912). A point-scale format of the scales was published by Yerkes, Bridges, and Hardwick in 1915.

Terman and Childs produced a revision of the Binet-Simon scale in 1912, and during the next four years completed a thorough standardization of the revised scale which, when published in 1916, was termed the "Stanford Revision and Extension of the Binet-Simon Intelligence Scale." With the 1916 scale, Terman introduced the IQ concept, a concept borrowed from Stern, who had referred to it as "mental quotient." Terman can be credited for his thorough and accurate working out of the procedures originally formulated by Binet and his co-workers.

The 1905 scale consisted of 30 tests arranged in order of difficulty. The year level format of tests was introduced in the 1908 scale, which contained 59 tests. The 1911 scale represented a further refinement of the scales and increased the range to include an adult year level while simultaneously decreasing the number of tests to 54. The first thoroughly American version of the scale, the 1916 Stanford-Binet, consisted of 90 tests, 36 of which were new. It ranged from year-level III to Superior Adult I. The 1937 Stanford-Binet appeared after a 21-year period. It extended the range from year-level II to Superior Adult III, increased the number of tests to 129, and had two forms, L and M. The 1960 Stanford-Binet (Form L-M) combined tests from the two 1937 forms, and in place of a restandardization, a sample of subjects who had previously taken the scale was used to evaluate difficulty levels of the tests. Form L-M replaced the ratio IQ with the deviation IQ.

The 1937 and 1960 forms of the Stanford-Binet have proved to be extremely reliable and valid instruments. However, the Stanford-Binet, like any measuring instrument, is far from perfect. The scales have been criticized for (a) placing too heavy emphasis on verbal and rote memory tests, (b) providing too few tests of g, (c) providing only one score (the IQ) to represent the complex nature of cognitive functions, (d) failing to measure creative abilities, and (e) being unsuitable for testing adults. Technical criticisms for all forms include the cumbersomeness of the age-scale format, scoring and administration difficulties, and low ceiling for gifted adolescents. A major problem of the 1937 forms was the unequal standard deviations at each year level. In the 1960 form, revision procedures were found to be inadequate, especially with respect to the construction of the deviation IQ's and the determination of difficulty levels for the tests.

The Binet-Simon scale was influential in stimulating the development of clinical psychology in the United States and in many other countries. The scales demonstrated that mental measurement was possible, and by so doing, led to the development of many other types of tests and to an acceptance by the public of testing. Consequently, the Binet-Simon scale has had an important impact on Western society, especially for education, industry, and the military.

CHAPTER 9

ADMINISTERING THE STANFORD-BINET

As seen in Chapters 5, 6, and 7, the administration of psychological tests is a demanding activity, yet it can be an extremely rewarding one. The standardized test procedures used in the Stanford-Binet, which have been carefully developed over the years, do not cover all contingencies. Some examinees will fail to obtain a basal or a ceiling level, while others have physcial handicaps that interfere with their performance on the scale. Psychologists, inquisitive about test procedures, have attempted to learn about such things as the effects of alterations in standardized procedures and the effects of obtaining more than one basal or ceiling level. This chapter focuses on test procedures in the administration of the Stanford-Binet. One section of the chapter describes the mechanics of completing the record booklet.

PHYSICAL ABILITIES NECESSARY FOR TAKING THE STANFORD-BINET

In order to respond to the Stanford-Binet tests, the examinee must possess specific physical abilities that entail both sensory and motor functions. Allen and Jefferson (1962), following the work of Katz (1956), presented an analysis of the physical abilities required for each Stanford-Binet test. Their analysis, shown in Table C-3 in the Appendix, is useful in enabling the examiner to determine (a) tests to which physically disabled examinees can respond, and (b) tests that can be modified for presentation. Their proposals for modifying some of the Stanford-Binet tests are discussed in a later part of this chapter (see pages 112–114).

Table C-3 shows that vision is necessary for most of the tests below year-level VIII. After year-level IX, tests usually require oral speech and reading comprehension, or oral speech and hearing ability. However, examinees who cannot speak should be encouraged to write their answers. If reading comprehension is present, hearing ability may be dispensed with as a necessary capacity for many tests after year-level VII.

WHERE TO BEGIN TESTING

It is important to start the examination at a year level that contains questions that are challenging to the examinee and yet have a high probability of being answered correctly. Starting with very easy tests may produce boredom and loss of interest, while starting with very difficult tests may produce anxiety and discouragement. Moreover, testing time can be reduced when a single basal level is found. The following points are important to consider in deciding where to begin the examination.

First, consider the examinee's chronological age. Most examinees with average intelligence usually will establish a basal level at a year level close to their chronological age. Testing may be begun at their chronological year level or one year level below their chronological age.

Second, the Vocabulary test can be administered first to examinees who are 6 years of age or older. This test provides a Vocabulary Age, which appears on the lower right-hand corner on the second from the last page of the record booklet. The examination can then be continued at the year level corresponding to the Vocabulary Age level. This year level will be at an even year level only from VI through XIV and then at every year level for the remainder of the scale. When examinees are younger than 6 years of age, the Vocabulary Age obtained from the Picture Vocabulary test is available when this test is administered first at year-level IV. Wells and Pedrini's (1967b) suggestion that the Picture Vocabulary test routinely be administered first to examinees younger than 6 years of age is not recommended, because the test would have to be administered out of sequence at year-levels II, II-6, and III. At these year levels the test is not the first one in the series of tests. Since it is not known to what extent changes in test order affect the examinee's performance, it is recommended that tests be administered in the order in which they are presented in the manual, so that difficulties associated with modifications in the standard procedures are avoided.

Third, background information may provide some guideposts. For example, if the examinee is being considered for an educable mentally retarded class, his mental age may be considerably below his chronological age. If placement in a gifted class is the purpose of the examination, the examinee's mental age may be considerably above his chronological age.

The above three points should be taken into account when determining entry into the scale. The examinee's chronological age, background information, and initial test performance will aid in selecting an appropriate year level. When one of the vocabulary tests is administered first, testing can be continued at the year level indicated by the Vocabulary Age, especially if this year level is close to the examinee's chronological age. For examinees whose Vocabulary Age is considerably above their chronological age, the examination can be begun at a year level midway between the Vocabulary Age year level and the chronological age year level. For example, suppose a 10-year-old examinee obtains a Vocabulary Age of 14. One possible entry point is at year-level XII, which is the level halfway between year-level X (representing the examinee's chronological age) and year-level XIV (representing the examinee's Vocabulary Age). If there is reason to believe that the examinee has superior intellectual ability (on the basis of background information or qualitative performance), testing could be continued at the Vocabulary Age year level, which, in the present example, is XIV. When examinees obtain a Vocabulary Age considerably below their chronological age, testing can be continued at a year level midway between the two ages. If testing has begun at a year level that is either too high or too low, the examiner can always change to another year level and continue testing at that level.

EFFECTS OF NOT HAVING A BASAL LEVEL OR A CEILING LEVEL

The Stanford-Binet requires that one basal level and one ceiling level be obtained in administering the scale. However, occasionally neither a basal level nor a ceiling level can be obtained. The former can occur in testing young mentally retarded children (and occasionally with young normal children as well), while the latter can occur in testing gifted adolescents. In such cases, the examiner has the choice of either disregarding the results and turning to another test that may be more valid, or of using the test results, recognizing that they may not be valid. While there is no definitive answer concerning the procedure to follow when a basal or ceiling level is not obtained, there are several guideposts and research data available.

If the examinee passes one test at year-level II, a basal age of 1–6 can be assumed and one month credit added for each test passed at year-level II (Sternlicht, 1965). This procedure resulted in a .90 correlation between the Kuhlmann Tests of Mental Development and the Stanford-Binet (Form L-M) in a group of mentally retarded children having mental ages between $1\frac{1}{2}$ and $2\frac{1}{2}$ years and chronological ages between 4 and 10 years. Thus, the suggested procedure appears to be warranted when a basal level cannot be established on the test.

The effects of not having a ceiling level on the Stanford-Binet (Form L-M) have also been investigated (Kennedy et al., 1961). The sample consisted of adolescents with superior intelligence, who were between the ages of 15 and 16 years, and who had passed some tests at the last level of the examination, Superior Adult III. The concurrent validity of the Stanford-Binet was studied by means of the Sequential Test of Educational Progress. The correlation between the Sequential Test and the Stanford-Binet was .50, and the correlation between the Sequential Test and the Wechsler Adult Intelligence Scale was .43. It was concluded that Form L-M of the Stanford-Binet is an effective though not ideal research instrument for the study of superior adolescents. It is likely that the larger the number of tests that are passed at the II-year-level, or failed at the Superior Adult III-year-level, the greater the probability is that the results are valid.

RANGE OF TESTING

The procedure of establishing one basal level and one ceiling level assumes that tests below the basal year level would have been passed had they been administered and that tests above the ceiling year level would have been failed had they been administered. However, these assumptions are not always valid, because children fail tests below their basal level and pass tests above their ceiling level (Bradway, 1943; Mitchell, 1941; Wile & Davis, 1941). Consequently, when, by design, the examination is administered by the establishment of more than one basal year level or more than one ceiling year level, the resulting IQ's can differ from those obtained by the standard method.

Investigators have been interested in determining the effects of establishing two successive ceiling year levels, while establishing the basal level in the usual manner. In one study, the Stanford-Binet (Form L) was administered to children (primarily mentally retarded) between the ages of 7 and 15 years (Berger & Speevack, 1940). A mean increase of 3.2 mental age months (range of two to 14 months) was obtained for 88 (42%) children in the sample when two ceiling levels were established. Tests passed after the first ceiling level by more than 10% of the 88 children included Picture Absurdities II (year-level X), Plan of Search (year-level XIII), Problems of Fact (year-level XIII), Response to Pictures (year-level XII), and Memory for Words (year-level XIII). In a second study (Berger & Speevack, 1942), the same procedure was used to administer Form M to children (primarily mentally retarded) who were in the same age range as those in the first study. A mean increase of 3.14 mental age months (range of two to 12 months) was found for 66 (32%) children. Tests passed after the first ceiling level by more than 10% of the 66 children included Repeating 4 Digits Reversed (year-level IX), Block Counting (year-level X), Word Naming: Animals (year-level X), Repeating 6 Digits (year-level X), Response to Pictures II: Messenger Boy (year-level XII), Repeating 5 Digits Reversed (year-level XII), and Problems of Fact (year-level XIII). While recognizing that prolonging the examination can increase fatigue and loss of rapport, Berger and Speevack still suggested that the examination be extended to the point at which two successive year levels of failure have been reached.

Another study also evaluated the effects of extending the ceiling year level on the IQ (Carlton, 1940). The Stanford-Binet (Form L) was administered to institutionalized mentally retarded adolescents. The children were tested until they failed all tests on three successive year levels. The results showed that after failing all tests at one level, 40 children (19%) still passed tests at levels above the first established ceiling level. The mean IQ gain was 1.88 points, with a range of 1 to 4 points. Carlton recommended that two successive year levels of failure be obtained when testing mentally retarded children at year levels from IX to XII.

The effects of wide-range testing, consisting of establishing two basal levels and two ceiling levels, have also been studied (Bradway, 1943). The Stanford-Binet (Form L) was administered to an unselected population of children between the ages of 11 and 15 years. One or more tests were failed below the first basal level by 57 (45%) children. Some children passed tests at the last level of the examination; therefore, a ceiling level could not be established. For those children having at least one ceiling level, 18 (28%) passed some tests above the first ceiling level. For the total group, the scores obtained under the two procedures did not significantly differ. IQ's obtained under the two procedures also correlated highly. Bradway concluded that the wide-range and standard procedures produce nearly identical results for a general population of 11- to 15-year-olds. Bradway noted that before a modification of standard procedures should be considered, the wide-range procedure in comparison to the standard procedure should yield more reliable and more valid results, or yield results that have greater prognostic value. There is little evidence to indicate that the wide-range procedure is more successful in any of these ways.

SUGGESTIONS FOR AND ISSUES INVOLVED IN ADMINISTERING THE STANFORD-BINET

General suggestions for administering individual intelligence tests have been discussed in Chapter 5. Specific suggestions for administering the Stanford-Binet are presented here. Test materials should be arranged from the examinee's left to his right, unless other instructions are given in the manual. On tests requiring the examinee to mark his response in the record booklet, expose the one page that is needed by folding the booklet at the centerfold. When a screen is needed, the white side of the cardboard doll may be used. All materials should be returned to the test kit immediately after they are used. While a stopwatch is not mandatory to administer the tests, it can be helpful. Of the 142 tests in the scale (including alternates), only 15 different tests are timed (see Table 9–1). There are no timed tests from year-level IV through year-level VIII. The instructions in the manual should be repeated on each new trial or part of a test.

An extremely detailed supplementary aid for administering the Stanford-Binet (Form L-M) has appeared recently (Pedrini & Pedrini, 1970). Detailed suggestions covering various phases of test administration—such as where to

Table 9-1. TIMED TESTS ON THE STANFORD-BINET (L-M)

YEAR LEVEL	TEST	TIME
II	Delayed Response	10 seconds
III	Stringing Beads	2 minutes
III-6	Sorting Buttons	2 minutes
IX, XI	Memory for Designs I	10 seconds
IX	Rhymes: Old Form	30 seconds
X	Word Meaning	1 minute
XII	Minkus Completion I	5 minutes
XIII	Dissected Sentences	1 minute
XIII	Copying a Bead Chain from Memory	2 minutes
XIV, AA, SA II	Ingenuity I	3 minutes
XIV	Ingenuity II	3 minutes
AA	Arithmetical Reasoning	1 minute
SA I	Minkus Completion II	5 minutes
SA II	Codes	3 minutes
SA III	Reasoning II	5 minutes

locate the test materials, rephrasing test questions, and procedures for handling the test materials—are presented. While beginning examiners may profit from reading the guide, its contents, in part, duplicate the material in the Stanford-Binet manual.

The problems associated with administering and scoring the scale and in completing the record booklet have been pointed out in a report by Pierce (1948). The following errors were observed in 88 Stanford-Binet (Forms L and M) protocols obtained from three examiners. Examiners must try to avoid these errors when they administer the Stanford-Binet.

1. Records were not readable. (Readable records are important because (a) they provide valuable data when future performance is compared with past performance; (b) errors in scoring and in calculations can be checked; and (c) clearly written responses and calculations are valuable for research purposes.)

2. Minus signs and plus signs were not filled in.

3. Some examiners credited a child who refused to respond if they felt that the child could adequately respond, while other examiners judged refusals as failures. (Refusals should not be counted.)

4. The halo effect was evident when examiners overestimated intelligence on tests that had inconclusive results.

5. Examiners undertested; they did not give the time and effort necessary to obtain maximum scores, especially when on retest the score was found to be equal to that of a previously obtained score.

6. Testing was stopped prematurely when the child had failed five of the six tests at a given year level.

7. Troublesome tests or time-consuming tests were omitted.

A study by Stott (1940) indicated that student-examiners' IQ's were related significantly ($r = .59$) to their ability to administer the Stanford-Binet, but not to their ability to interpret and to use the test results. IQ's were also found to be related significantly to testing efficiency ($C = .46$).

A recent report evaluated scoring patterns on the Stanford-Binet (Sattler & Ryan, 1973a). In one part of the study, the scores given by Terman and Merrill were compared with those given by 57 psychologists to 300 Stanford-Binet (Form L) responses that appeared in a supplementary scoring guide published by the New York City Board of Education (Wrightstone, 1941). The 300 responses were ones that could not be scored readily on the basis of the principles and examples given in the test manual. The results showed that a majority of the psychologists agreed with Terman and Merrill on 74% of the responses. Within the group of 57 psychologists, 90% or more agreement was found for only 9% of the 300 responses. A partial replication of the study was conducted by giving 65 of the 300 responses to clinical psychologists and graduate students. The results of this phase of the study were similar to those of the original one. The findings of both studies indicated that examiners differ in their scoring of Stanford-Binet responses. The supplementary scoring guides prepared by Pintner, Dragositz, and Kushner (1944) and by the New York City Board of Education (Wrightstone, 1941) are valuable sources to consult in scoring responses for Form L tests that appear on Form L-M.

Suggestions for Specific Tests

II, 2. Delayed Response. Use the three boxes that are closed on the top side and on four sides.

II, 3. Identifying Parts of the Body. Place the doll face up and flat on the surface of the table.

III-6, 1. Comparison of Balls. For each trial, alternate the horizontal position of the balls by using a 180 degree rotation.

III-6, 3. Discrimination of Animal Pictures. Do not touch the card after it is placed on the table. However, ask the examinee to point to the animal if his response is not clear.

VI, 6. Maze Tracing. In pointing to the sidewalk, the examiner can run the top of his pencil back and forth horizontally over a small area of the top of the maze, or he can run his pencil up and down vertically in approximately the same area (Pintner et al., 1944).

VIII, 2. Memory for Stories: The Wet Fall. Give the examinee a copy of the story *after* reading the instructions and the title of the story.

VIII, 4. Similarities and Differences. Do not probe on items *c* and *d*. If the examinee fails to give *both* a similarity and a difference for each item, he fails the item or items.

IX, 1. Paper Cutting. Remove scraps from the table after the test has been completed.

IX, 3; XI, 1. Memory for Designs I. Show the examinee the designs *after* reading the instructions. Give the examinee a blank portion of the record booklet for his drawings.

XIV, 2. Induction. Leave the cut sheets of paper unfolded, one on top of another. Do not ask for the rule unless the last response is correct.

Vocabulary. Older children may find it disconcerting to have the card pulled away from them after six consecutive failures. The child can be asked to look at the list to see if he knows any other words. Credit should be given for any successes (Pintner et al., 1944).

MODIFYING STANFORD-BINET TEST PROCEDURES

Many suggestions have been offered for modifying the administration of tests on the Stanford-Binet (see, for example, Allen & Jefferson, 1962; Sattler & Tozier, 1970; Taylor, 1961). Suggestions include presenting tests in a multiple-choice format, pantomiming responses, steadying the child's hand, enlarging objects, having the child point, and showing the child the test problems. Some modifications, such as a multiple-choice administration of the Picture Vocabulary test of the Stanford-Binet, may lead to an easier test by eliminating, in part, the recognition and recall elements required by the standard presentation (Burgemeister, 1962). IQ's obtained by using modified procedures, such as selecting only certain tests or changing methods of administering the tests, should be viewed cautiously (cf. Sattler & Tozier, 1970). The results obtained by use of modified procedures should be considered as a rough estimate of the child's level of intellectual functioning. (Chapters 4 and 5 also discuss modifications in test procedures.)

Alternating the order of administering difficult and easy tests on the Stanford-Binet (Form L) has been the focus of one study (Hutt, 1947). This alternation in administering the tests was termed the "adaptive method." The children, who were in kindergarten through ninth grade, were divided into a poorly-adjusted group and a well-adjusted group. The adaptive method of test administration resulted in significantly higher scores than the standard method of test administration for the poorly-adjusted group; however, the well-adjusted group obtained similar scores under both types of administration.

Another form of test administration has been termed "serial administration," that is, grouping tests of the same content together. When the Stanford-Binet (Forms L and M) was administered under conventional and serial orders to children who ranged in age from 5 to 18 years, the two orders of administration did not produce significantly different IQ's (Frandsen, McCullough, & Stone, 1950). In a nonexperimental study, two Stanford-Binet (Form L) IQ's were computed, one standard and one based upon tests that could be arranged serially (Spache, 1942). A group of gifted children between 2 and 9 years of age obtained similar IQ's with the two methods.

A pointing-scale method has been proposed for scoring the Stanford-Binet (Form L). It involves scoring only those tests that can be answered by pointing and then computing mental age by prorating (Katz, 1956). Cerebral-palsied preschool children were found to obtain equivalent IQ's under the standard and pointing-scale methods. However, normal children were not studied. Changing the size of the Stanford-Binet (Form L) test stimuli by enlarging the visual items was not found to affect significantly the scores obtained by partially-sighted children between the ages of 8 and 10 years (Livingston, 1957).

In Table C-3 of the Appendix, several tests are shown that are considered to be adaptable by Allen and Jefferson (1962). Most of these tests are at year-levels II through V. The adaptations consist of allowing the child to substitute pointing and other nonverbal response modalities for his limitations in arm-hand use and in speech. The following are examples of modifications proposed by Allen and Jefferson:

Three-Hole Form Board (year-level II, 1 and year-level II-6, Alternate)

Vision is necessary but the examiner may actually place the blocks in the form board recesses for the testee. The blocks are removed in the child's presence and each one is placed above its appropriate recess. By pantomime or orally the examiner indicates that each block is to be reinserted into its recess. Examiner points to the first block, the square, and then to the first recess, the square, and asks if it belongs there. Regardless of the "yes" or "no" signal, the tester goes on to the triangle and the circle recesses in turn inquiring if the square block belongs in either of these recesses. If the child selects the correct recess the block is appropriately placed. The same is done for the triangle and the circle blocks in that order [p. 43].

Identifying Objects by Use (year-level II-6, 1)

The instructions for the test are given: "Show me the one we drink out of."

Then pointing to the shoe he [the tester] asks, "Is it this one?" and waits for the prearranged response signal for "yes" or "no." Whether the choice is correct or not, the tester continues in a clockwise rotation stopping at the cup, penny, iron, knife, and the auto, inquiring, "Is it this one?" The same procedure is followed for each of the six objects on the card [p. 42].

Picture Memories (year-level III, 4)

After the instructions are given for Card (A),

The tester starts at the corner of the card and points to the dog, inquiring "Is it this one?" This is continued until the client has seen and responded to all the pictures in Card (A). The correctness of the choice is recorded. The same procedure is repeated with cards (b) and (B) until one correct answer is given [p. 42].

Comparison of Sticks (year-level III-6, Alternate)

The examiner arranges the two sticks in proper order and asks which of the two is longer. Pointing to the top one he says, "Is it this one?" After the visible response signal of "yes" or "no," the tester indicates the stick below it and repeats the question. The reply is noted and the entire procedure is continued until the criterion of three correct responses in three trials or five in six is met. In each instance the tester should point to the top and bottom sticks so as to avoid cueing the testee to the correct choice [p. 43].

Picture Identification (year-level IV, 4)

The pictures are placed before the testee. The tester states, "Show me the one that we cook on." Starting at the top, he points to each picture asking, "Is it this one?" and moves across the four rows pointing to each of the twelve pictures [p. 44].

The suggestions for modifying tests that have been offered by Allen and Jefferson are valuable because they provide an opportunity to evaluate a child who otherwise could not be administered the Stanford-Binet. However, until the effects of such modifications are studied, there is no way of determining to what extent the standard norms can be used.

Following the work of Katz (1956), an experimental modification of the Stanford-Binet (Form L-M) has appeared recently for tests located at year-levels II through V (Sattler & Anderson, 1973). The modifications consist of changing tests that require a verbal or motor response to a nonverbal pointing format or "yes-no" format. Most of the tests in the modified form are presented via pictures, and the child is asked to select the picture that best answers the question. In a group of normal preschool children, IQ's on the modified and standard forms were correlated significantly ($r = .91$), with means being less than two points apart (116.4 vs 115.2). The correlation between the modified form and the Peabody Picture Vocabulary Test was also significant ($r = .44$), although low. Similar findings were obtained with a group of cerebral-palsied preschool children.

When three different methods to compute Stanford-Binet (Form L) IQ's were used with cerebral-palsied children, 74% obtained identical IQ's with the different methods (Schonell, 1956). The first method was the standard method of computing the IQ (tested IQ); the second, a modified IQ, credited the child with passing tests that the examiner judged he would have passed if not for his disability; and the third, an estimated IQ, established an IQ based upon the examiner's estimate of the child's overall ability. Generally, the computational modifications provided similar test scores.

TESTING THE LIMITS ON THE STANFORD-BINET

We have seen in Chapter 5 that testing of limits is a procedure that sometimes may prove useful in obtaining additional qualitative information about the examinee. The most thorough and systematic procedures for testing the limits on the Stanford-Binet (and on other tests) have been presented by Taylor (1961). Her detailed suggestions for many of the Stanford-Binet tests are too numerous to summarize, but her suggestions for one test (Picture Vocabulary) are shown below. The reader is encouraged to study her work in full, and to consult her book whenever there is a need to test the limits.

Picture Vocabulary

... GESTURES. The same picture material may be used to study more specifically a child's ability to express himself without words. Show a knife (or airplane, ball, spoon) and ask, "Show me what it does" or "Show me what we do with it." For children who do not seem to understand language, show by a sample what is wanted of him.

Note: Does the child use varied appropriate gestures, or does he tend to use the same gestures with all pictures? Are his means of expression mostly manual, facial, or both? Is there any sign that he indicates objects of the same category in similar ways? Does he, for instance, describe animals by their sounds and movements, tools by their use? or does he point to a chair in the room to indicate a stool or chair? Observation of a child's use of gestures can be of considerable diagnostic significance with respect to development of communication.

... ALTERNATE NAMING. If the child has designated an object either in words or through gestures, E may ask, "What else could it be?" The child may or may not find a second response, produce a synonym, a better word, or a better gesture.

... POINTING. This picture material may also be used to investigate comprehension of language. Use all cards of a series at one time, or use them in groups of four to six. Present the material by asking, "Where is the spoon?" etc. . . . The child can indicate by pointing or nodding at the pictures, or in any other way he chooses. For a severely handicapped child who is unable to point accurately or to turn his head freely, the pictures may be spread far enough apart to avoid equivocal responses, yet near enough so that they all remain in the line of vision.

Note whether the child scans the field for the proper picture or responds haphazardly, pointing first to one, then to another. Does he point to the correct picture only? Does he know at least the general area in which it belongs? (Does he point to a fork when asked for a knife, for instance?) Does he seem to see all the pictures correctly, or does he make unexpected errors? Are they possibly due to sensory difficulties? Check whether a wrong picture is pointed to because of poor perception, eyesight, or hearing. Does he not *understand* or does he not *see* (or *hear*) the difference in the looks of a gun and knife, or the words house and horse?

... Experience shows that, in general, normal children are able to point out all pictures adequately before or at least at the same age they can find names for them. Often one may find children who can point correctly to something long before they are able to name it. It may often be important for the clinician to discover whether a child understands more language than he is able to express. The procedure is therefore of considerable value in all cases of speech retardation, as well as in those where sensory difficulties are suspected [pp. 309–310].

The above example illustrates that the child's performance can be meticulously examined by using a varied and flexible testing-of-limits procedure. Not only does Taylor provide specific questions, but she also presents helpful suggestions for analyzing the child's performance. While the Behavior and Attitude Checklist (see Chapter 25) provides information that should enable the examiner to evaluate general behavior and attitudes, Taylor focuses on specific features of the child's responses in relation to the testing-of-limits questions and in relation to the content and materials of specific tests.

SHORT FORMS OF THE STANFORD-BINET

Giving a short form of the Stanford-Binet can save considerable time and thereby make it possible to use the saved time to administer other tests or assessment devices. However, if the test questions themselves are seen as providing important stimuli that are useful for obtaining information about the examinee's cognitive make-up and personality, then shortening the examination will limit the amount of information available to the examiner. The reliability and validity of the short form, too, must be considered. While acceptable correlations between abbreviated scales and the full scale are usually reported, few investigators actually have given the short form. In most cases, the full scale was administered and the MA's and IQ's were obtained for the short form from the full scale. This procedure presents problems in interpreting the correlation coefficient because of overlapping tests in both forms. In addition, there is no way of assessing the effects of the altered order of test administration on the resulting score.

In studying abbreviated and full scales, it is important to distinguish between correlations obtained for a group, mean scores obtained on the scales, and differences in the IQ's obtained by any one individual examinee. A correlation coefficient of .99 between two scales still could result in a significant difference between the means obtained on the scales. Even when the correlation is high and mean difference between the two scales is small, one examinee may have large differences between the scores he obtains on the two scales.

Five types of short forms have been studied, namely, abbreviated tests (those so designated by Terman & Merrill (1937, 1960) and by Terman (1916)), modified abbreviated tests (Wright, 1942), tests arrived at by the limen method (Lorr & Meister, 1942), Vocabulary test alone, and a combination of tests from the Cattell Infant Intelligence Scale and the Stanford-Binet (Alpern & Kimberlin, 1970). These short forms, with relevant research concerning the short forms, are described in the following paragraphs.

Abbreviated Tests

The starred tests, four at each year level and half-year level, are used for the abbreviated scale. The resulting saving in time is approximately 33%. Early studies with the 1916 Stanford-Binet reported satisfactory correlations between the abbreviated and full scales (Brooks, 1929; Elwood, 1934). However, Elwood cautioned against the use of the abbreviated scale because differences between it and the full scale were as much as 17 months in MA in a mentally retarded sample and 14 months in MA in a normal sample.

Studies reporting on the efficacy of the abbreviated scale for the 1937 forms uniformly showed high correlations (.89 or higher) between the abbreviated and full scales (e.g., Birch, 1955; Brown, 1942; Kvaraceus, 1940; Shotwell & McCulloch, 1944; Spache, 1942; Spaulding, 1945; Wright, 1942). However, the range of difference in IQ points between the abbreviated and full scales was often considerable. For example, Wright reported a range of -17 to $+13$ points. Kvaraceus found two examinees with more than a 10-point difference, 25 examinees with a difference between 6 and 10 points, and 187 examinees with a difference between 0 and 5 points.

Studies using abbreviated tests for the 1960 form have involved mentally retarded children (Silverstein, 1963a, 1966; Silverstein & Fisher, 1961), Negro children (Kennedy et al., 1963), and children attending a child guidance clinic (Gayton, 1971). Correlations ranging from .92 to .99 between the abbreviated and full scales are reported in these studies.

Modified Abbreviated Tests

Wright (1942) proposed a method that consists of giving the four starred tests at each year level and six tests at the basal and ceiling year levels. This procedure results in a time saving of about 20%. A number of studies indicate that this procedure is somewhat more reliable than the Terman-Merrill abbreviated scale (e.g., Birch, 1955; Gayton, 1971; Silverstein, 1963a, 1966; Silverstein & Fisher, 1961; Wright, 1942).

Limen Method

The limen method, introduced by Lorr and Meister (1942), consists of finding the year level at which the examinee passes 50% of the tests. This year level then becomes the MA. When interpolation is necessary to arrive at the appropriate MA, tables are provided by the authors. The limen method uses about one-third of the tests and results in a time saving of about 66%. Lorr and Meister reported a .97 correlation between IQ's obtained by the limen and standard methods, and other studies have indicated that the limen method provides an adequate measure of intelligence (Birch, 1955; Meister & Kennedy, 1947; Meister & Kurko, 1951).

Vocabulary

Use of the Vocabulary score to obtain an MA, which then can be used to determine an IQ, is a much more precarious procedure than the procedures used with the abbreviated scales described above. Using MA's, correlations obtained between the Vocabulary test and full scale (e.g., .67 to .86 reported by Edwards (1963); .77 to .92 reported by Spache (1943)) are much lower than those reported for other abbreviated scales.

Cureton (1954) provided MA estimates based on the Vocabulary test raw scores of Form L. These MA estimates, shown in Table C-6 of the Appendix, range from ages 5–4 to 25–0. MA estimates are not provided for raw scores below 5. IQ's are computed from the MA's by dividing them by the CA up to age 13, and thereafter by the CA equivalents used with the 1937 Stanford-Binet. The IQ tables in the manual for the 1960 form can also be used to obtain the IQ. The standard error of measurement for the resulting IQ's is approximately 10 IQ points. Using Cureton's method, Benson (1963) correlated IQ's obtained on Form L-M with those obtained on the WAIS. The following coefficients were reported: .86 with the Full Scale, .89 with the Verbal Scale, and .60 with the Performance Scale. The standard error of measurement for the predicted WAIS Full Scale IQ was 6 points. Benson suggested that the Binet Vocabulary test provides a useful basis for estimating mental ability in the absence of pre-psychotic or organic factors. However, this short form may be applicable only to children whose general sociocultural background is similar to that of the Stanford-Binet standardization group.

Cattell-Binet Short Form

A short form of the Cattell Infant Intelligence Scale (Cattell, 1950) and Stanford-Binet (Form L-M) has been described, which may be useful for evaluating mentally retarded children (Alpern & Kimberlin, 1970). The form consists of two specific tests at each year level of the scales through year-level X. After year-level X, any two tests per year level may be used. The Cattell-Binet Short Form, which is shown in Table C-5 of the Appendix, is administered by obtaining a *triple* basal level and a *triple* ceiling level. The Revised IQ tables in the manual are used to obtain the IQ. For IQ's that are not found in the tables, the standard IQ formula ($IQ = MA/CA \times 100$) can be used. Satisfactory reliability (.97) and validity coefficients (.73 to .83) were obtained for the short form. The short form is efficient and economical, since it takes about 75% less time than the standard form and uses 37% of the tests of the full scales.

Comment on Short Forms of the Stanford-Binet

The abbreviated scales will usually provide a valid estimate of intelligence. The general trend that emerges from the studies is that the reliability of the abbreviated scale is increased as the number of tests used in the scale increases. Thus, the Wright method provides somewhat more reliable IQ's than the Terman-Merrill abbreviated scale method. The least reliable IQ's are given by use of the Vocabulary test alone. However, even the Vocabulary test provides a good approximation of mental age. As Silverstein (1966) observed, the abbreviated scale may justifiably be used when time is an important consideration.

It seems advisable, however, to administer the entire scale except when continuing the examination will cause a hardship to the examinee (cf. Spache, 1944). This recommendation applies particularly to those situations in which an IQ score will be used in conjunction with other material to make important decisions concerning the examinee, and when the scale is used as an assessment device to observe, record, and evaluate the child's ability. In screening situations, short forms appear to be acceptable as a means of arriving at an estimate of intelligence. However, it is important to recognize that while administration and scoring time is relatively short for the short form, the time involved in preparation, arranging for a meeting, and the like is similar for both long and short forms. The per cent time saving for short forms, therefore, is an overestimate when everything involved is considered.

THE RECORD BOOKLET

The proper completion of the record booklet helps in obtaining an accurate permanent test record, aids in the writing of the report (especially if the writing is delayed), and facilitates reviewing the scoring. Filling out the record booklet requires attending to many minor details; attending to them early in one's testing career will help to establish a worthwhile pattern to guide future test administrations. This part of the chapter discusses the proper completion of the record booklet, the notations in the record booklet, and some material related to test administration. The basic principles that apply to the Stanford-Binet are applicable to other tests. Accordingly, the material contained in this section on the record booklet of the Stanford-Binet is an example of the care that should be used in dealing with the record booklets of other tests.

Cover Page

On the cover page of the booklet all important identifying information must appear. The examinee's name, sex, address, date of test, birthdate, and age, and the examiner's name are usually necessary as a minimum. Below the identifying information part, there is a section labeled "Factors Affecting Test Performance." The completion of these ratings is optional because similar material should be discussed in the report, and because the record booklet is often not available to the reader of the report. However, the factors listed can provide useful guidelines for the examiner.

On the upper right-hand side of the cover page there is a small rectangle with the terms CA, MA, and IQ (see Figure 9–1). This section of the cover page is completed after administering the examination. For an examinee who is 4 years and 6 months of age and who has achieved a mental age of five years and two months, the CA and MA are expressed as follows: CA 4–6; MA 5–2. The first numeral indicates years; the second, months. It is not necessary to write "four years and six months" or some other expression, since it is assumed that those having access to the record booklet will understand the meaning of the two numerals. Figure 9–1, which is a reproduction of part of the right-hand side of the cover page, shows how the IQ is written.

The rectangle on the right-hand side of the cover page labeled "Test Summary" should also be completed after the test has been administered. Figure 9–1 illustrates, for an examinee of CA 4–6, the proper completion of this section of the booklet. The Arabic numerals in the "Yrs." column represent the basal age, which is the *lowest* level of the examination at which all tests were passed. No other numerals are written in the "Yrs." column. Since the basal age was at the IV-6-year level, the number 4 appears in the "Yrs." column and the number 6 in the "Mos." column. In the column labeled "Mos.," credit is allotted for those tests passed *above* the basal year level. As illustrated in Figure 9–1, four months' credit was given at year-level V because four tests were passed at this level; because each test passed receives *one* month's credit at year-level V, four months are credited. Opposite year-level VI, a 4 appears, which indicates that two tests were passed here—each test at this year level is allotted *two* months' credit. A zero (0) appears opposite year-level VII, indicating that all tests were failed here.

Opposite the term "Total," separate scores appear in the years-and-months columns. The 4 indicates the years' credit, and the 14 reflects the

CA	4–6
MA	5–2
IQ	115

Figure 9–1. Section of right-hand side of cover page of Stanford-Binet (L-M) Record Booklet. (Reprinted, with a change in notation, by permission of the publisher. Copyright 1960, Houghton Mifflin Company. All rights reserved.)

TEST SUMMARY	Yrs.	Mos.
IV-6	4	6
V		4
VI		4
VII		0
Total	4	14
MA Score	5–2	
Testing time	1 hr. & 30 min.	

months' credit. The MA then becomes the sum of these two credits, 5–2. The 5–2, indicating five years and two months, is obtained by adding the number of months' credit from the basal year to the number of months' credit obtained from the remaining year levels (6 + 8 = 14 months), and then adding this figure to the years' credit of the basal year (adding one year and two months to four years results in a total of five years and two months). Of course, there are other ways to compute the MA. For example, the basal credit is converted to months (in Figure 9–1, 4–6 is equal to 54 months); then the additional months earned (eight months) are added, giving the total months' credit (54 months + 8 months = 62 months). The total months' credit is then converted to years and months (62 months = five years and two months, 5–2). Recording the amount of time required for testing completes the "Test Summary" section.

Inside Booklet

Allotment of Credit.   On the first page and on all the remaining pages of the record booklet, space is provided for recording and scoring the examinee's responses. Table 9–2 shows the proper completion of year-level II of the booklet. The number of months' credit allotted for the passing of a test at year-level II is shown in the parentheses after "Year II." Similar information is provided at every year level. The differential credit within any year level is a function of the number of tests administered. Usually, either all tests are ad-

---

Table 9-2.   Year-Level II of Stanford-Binet (L-M) Record Booklet

Year II (6 tests, 1 month each; or 4 tests, 1½ months each)

[\ ]   1. *Three-Hole Form Board   (1+) [\ ]   a) ✓   b) ✓

[\ ]   2. Delayed Response   (2+) [3]   a) Middle ✓   b) Right ✓   c) Left ✓

[\ ]   3. *Identifying Parts of the Body (same as II-6, 2)   (4+) [5]

　　　　a) Hair ✓   b) Mouth ✓   c) Feet ✓   d) Ear ✓   e) Nose ✓

　　　　f) Hands ✓   g) Eyes ✓

[\ ]   4. Block Building: Tower   (±) [+]

[\ ]   5. *Picture Vocabulary (same as II-6, 4; III, 2; IV, 1)   (3+) [4]

1. airplane ✓	7. horse ✓	13. flag ✓
2. telephone ✓	8. knife ✓	14. cane ✓
3. hat ✓	9. coat ✓	15. arm ✓
4. ball ✓	10. ship ✓	16. pocket knife ✓
5. tree ✓	11. umbrella ✓	17. pitcher ✓
6. key ✓	12. foot ✓	18. leaf ✓

[\ ]   6. *Word Combinations   (±) [+]   Example___I go home.

____ Alternate. Identifying Objects by Name   (5+) [ ]

　　　　a) Dog_____   b) Ball_____   c) Engine_____   d) Bed_____

　　　　e) Doll_____   f) Scissors_____

6 Mos. credit at Year II

Table 9-3. CREDIT ALLOTTED FOR STANFORD-BINET (L-M) YEAR LEVELS

YEAR LEVELS	NUMBER OF TESTS	INDIVIDUAL TEST MONTHS' CREDIT	TOTAL MONTHS' CREDIT
II-V	6	1	6
VI-XIV	6	2	12
AA	8	2	16
SA I	6	4	24
SA II	6	5	30
SA III	6	6	36

ministered (omitting the alternates), or only those tests are administered that make up the short form. When all tests are administered, the first piece of information in the parentheses is applicable; when the short form of the examination is administered, the second piece of information applies. At year-level II, one month's credit is allotted for each test passed when six tests are administered; one and one-half months' credit is allotted when four tests are administered. Six months' credit is the maximum allotted for this year level. If, in exceptional cases, only three tests are administered, credit for each test is prorated (two months are credited for each test passed, in order to obtain the total of six months' credit).

The allotment of months' credit is partly a function of the specific year level of the examination. The over-all distribution of months' credit can be seen by studying Table 9–3, which presents the year levels, the allotted number of months' credit for each test, and the allotted total number of months' credit. The data of Table 9–3 are based upon the assumption that all tests at each year level of the examination (excluding alternates) are administered. As can be seen in Table 9–3, tests at the half-year levels (II through V) are each allotted one month's credit. The total number of months' credit allotted for any full year level from II through V is the same as the allotment for the next nine year levels (VI through XIV). Because year levels between II and V are divided into two parts (e.g., II and II-6), a total of 12 months can be earned in any one full year. After year-level XIV, the total months' credit allotted to each year level changes. Beginning with SA I, while the number of tests remains constant, more weight is given to each test. Thus, the allotment is 24 months' credit at SA I, 30 months at SA II, and 36 months at SA III. There are six tests at every half-year level and at every year level except at the AA year level, where eight tests are present.

Returning again to Table 9–2, notice that four of the six tests (Tests 1, 3, 5, and 6) have an asterisk preceding the name of the test. The asterisk denotes those tests administered in the short form. In the rectangle preceding the name of the first test, "Three-Hole Form Board," a 1 is written to indicate that the examinee received one month's credit for his performance on this test. The 1 appearing in all of the rectangles of year-level II means that the examinee was successful on all tests at this year level. After the name of the first test, "Three-Hole Form Board," a (1+) is printed, which indicates the minimum number of parts of the test that must be passed before credit is given. Thus, before credit is earned, one of the two parts of the first test must be passed; for the second test, "Delayed Response," two of the three parts must be successfully completed. Additional credit is not assigned when more parts of a test are passed than are required by the minimum number. For example, one month's credit is assigned for success either on both trials a and b of the "Three-Hole Form Board" or on one trial only. When all six tests are administered at year-levels II through V, no more than one month's credit can be assigned to a single test.

The number "1" is written in the bracket after the (1+) to indicate that performance was satisfactory on one of the two trials of the test. A "2" is written when both trials a and b are successfully completed. The examinee's success on trial a and failure on trial b are shown by a "correct mark" (√) on the line after the "a" and an "incorrect mark" (√̸) on the line after the "b."

The notations printed in the booklet for Test 2, "Delayed Response," are very similar to those appearing for Test 1. Note, however, that two of the three trials must be correct before credit is given. Note, also, that Test 2 is not administered in the short form, as shown by the absence of an asterisk before the name of the test.

Tests at More Than One Year Level.   Test 3, "Identifying Parts of the Body," contains a statement after the name of the test, which does not appear after the names of Test 1 and Test 2. The statement "same as II-6, 2" means that Test 3 is also administered as the second test (the 2 after the comma means second test) at year-level II-6. Similar information appears after the test names for all other tests occurring at more than one year level. When the same test appears at more than one year level, additional parts of the test must be correctly answered in order for the examinee to receive credit at the higher year level or levels. However, test content, administration, and scoring criteria do not change. The 4+ appearing after "same as II-6, 2" for Test 3 at year-level II indicates that four parts must be passed in order to give credit, whereas at year-level II-6, the 6+ in the parentheses after "same as II, 3" specifies that at least six parts must be passed to give credit. The number of parts needed for credit on each test is always indicated in the record booklet and in the test manual.

A useful procedure to follow when reaching a test that appears at more than one year level is to record the score at the level at which the test first appears and at each of the other year levels at which it also appears. Space for recording responses to a test appearing at more than one year level is always provided at the year level at which the test first appears. Thus, for example, if the examination is begun at year-level II-6, responses to the "Identifying-Parts-of-the-Body" test are recorded at year-level II, 3. However, no tests at year-level II are actually administered when the basal year level is established at year-level II-6. The space in the record booklet at year-level II is used to record the responses to the "Identifying-Parts-of-The-Body" test; the scoring criteria used to establish success or failure are, in this example, those indicated for year-level II-6. There are 11 tests (excluding alternates) appearing at more than one year level of the examination. The Vocabulary test occurs at all even-year levels from VI through XIV, and then at every year level from SA I to SA III.

Plus or Minus Scoring.   Test 4, "Block-Building: Tower," differs from the preceding three tests by not having trials or parts. This is indicated by the ± in the parentheses after the name of the test (see Table 9–2). The + recorded in the bracket after the (±) indicates that the examinee passed the test.

Tests at More Than One Year Level (Further Comments) and Establishing a Ceiling.   The year levels of the examination at which Test 5, "Picture Vocabulary," is administered are shown immediately after the name of the test. Similar information appears, as we have seen, after the "Identifying-Parts-of-the-Body" test. Test 5 occurs at four different year levels; namely II, II-6, III, and IV. The examiner must be alert to the fact that a score on the "Picture Vocabulary" test may indicate that credit for passing the test is assigned to *more than one year level*. As suggested earlier, it is important to note the score needed for credit at each of the other year levels at which the "Picture Vocabulary" test appears so that credit can be recorded and a valid test ceiling can be reached. For example, if 14 parts of the "Picture Vocabulary" test are passed, the examination usually should be continued to at least year-level IV-6 in order to establish a ceiling, even though all tests may have been failed at year-level III-6. The reason for continuing testing beyond the first year level at which all tests were failed is that, since a test at the IV-year level was passed (14 correct answers to the "Picture Vocabulary" test), the ceiling level should be established at a year level *above* IV. To recapitulate: continue testing in order to obtain a ceiling year level whenever a test is passed at a year level above the level at which all tests have been *first* failed.

Test 6 and Mos. Credit. Test 6, "Word Combinations," contains space for recording the specific word combination(s) produced by the examinee. In the example in Table 9–2, the alternate test "Identifying Objects By Name" was not administered and, thus, this part of the booklet remains incomplete. The 6 appearing opposite "Mos. credit at Year II" indicates the sum of months credited for the examinee's performance at year-level II.

Summary of Major Points and Other Useful Guides

As an overall guide to filling out the record booklet, the following points should be considered:

1. Record the examinee's responses to the test questions verbatim as soon as they are made. If additional paper is used, always indicate the test name or test number and year level at which the response occurred. Always use discretion in recording remarks that are not directly pertinent to the test questions. Such remarks may occasionally be noted if they provide useful information about the examinee's personality or test performance.

2. Indicate scores clearly by a check mark or a plus sign ($\vee$, +) or by a modified check mark or a minus sign ($\vee$, −) in the booklet.

3. Fill in the brackets with the appropriate number. This number depends on the number of *trials* or *parts* that have been successfully completed. It will vary from 0 to a maximum of 40, depending on the specific test administered.

4. In the rectangle preceding each test, write the number of months credited. This number ranges from 0 to 6, except when the short form is administered or when credit is prorated. Writing a number rather than a plus (+) or minus (−) reduces the possibility of miscalculating months' credit. (Table 9–3 indicates the months' credit assigned at different year levels.)

5. Place a (Q) mark after those responses of the examinee that needed probing.

6. When there is uncertainty about the scoring of a response, place a question mark in the margin and review the scoring after the examination has been completed.

7. Double-check all scoring and calculations (months' credit, MA, CA, and IQ) after completing the examination. This always should be done to avoid serious errors in scoring.

8. Double-check the entries in the summary section of the cover page of the record booklet with the entries at all year levels inside the booklet in order to guard against errors in transcribing credits from the year levels to the cover page. Careful scoring, administration, and checking should be routine procedures to protect the examinee from any adverse decisions that might be made on the basis of erroneous examination results.

THE IQ AS A STANDARD SCORE

One of the noteworthy contributions to the measurement of intelligence in the Form L-M revision was the change in the method of calculating the IQ. Formerly, the IQ represented a ratio of MA to CA multiplied by 100, with provision made for changing the denominator after age 13. The IQ in the current revision is a standard score with a mean of 100 and a standard deviation (SD) of 16; it is termed a "deviation IQ." The normal curve, shown in Figure 9–2, can now be used to interpret IQ's throughout the scale. An IQ of 116 is one standard deviation above the mean (the mean represents the 50th percentile) and therefore falls at the 84th percentile rank (50 + 34 = 84). An IQ of 84, which is one standard deviation below the mean, falls at the 16th percentile rank (50 − 34 = 16). Similarly, an IQ of 132 represents the 97th percentile rank (50 + 47 = 97), and an IQ of 68 represents the 3rd percentile rank (50 − 47 = 3). Table C-29 in the Appendix presents the percentile ranks for IQ's of 63 to 136. This range represents percentile ranks 1 through 99. Figure 9–2 also shows the relationship between the normal curve and z scores, T scores, stanines, and Wechsler subtest scaled scores and deviation IQ's.

The intervals used in the Stanford-Binet to classify intelligence do not follow those proposed by Heber (1961) for classifying levels of mental retardation (see Chapter 22). For example, Terman and Merrill (1960, p. 18) suggested that IQ's between 80 and 89 be considered as "Low Average" while Heber suggested that IQ's between 69 and 83 be considered as "Borderline Retarded." Which system the examiner uses, or whether he uses both, is dependent on a number of factors, including the examiner's personal preferences

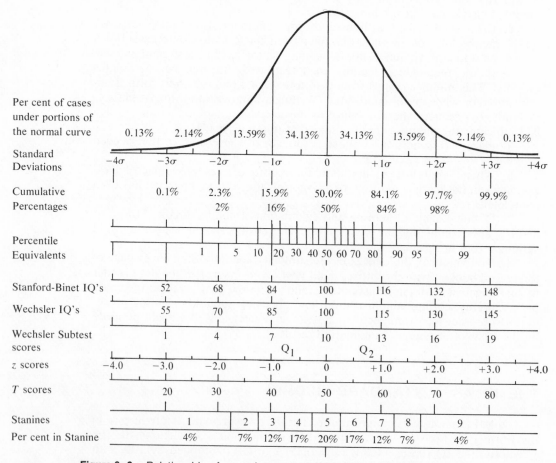

Figure 9–2. Relationship of normal curve to various types of standard scores.

or the particular agency's preference. Usually, the classification system used is the one shown in the test manual. When another system is used, the examiner should clearly indicate in the report the basis for the classification.

SEX DIFFERENCES

McNemar (1942) reported that sex differences in IQ on the 1937 forms tend to be small. This finding therefore supports the intent of the standardization procedure, which was to eliminate sex differences from the scales. Girls are somewhat higher at preschool ages (three points), while boys are somewhat higher at later ages (about two points). In the final two forms of the scales, six tests showed girls significantly surpassing boys, and 18 tests showed boys significantly surpassing girls. The fact that a greater number of tests favored boys rather than girls is accounted for by repetition of the same or similar tests at various year levels and in both forms. Many of the significant findings (and lack of consistent significant findings) could not be explained easily. Sex differences on tests, McNemar concluded, "are apt to be a function of the content of an item rather than of any basic abilities called for by the item [p. 54]."

STANFORD-BINET TESTS PREDICTING WAIS IQ's

Bradway and Thompson (1962) studied a group of 111 subjects who as children had been administered the Stanford-Binet and 25 years later the WAIS. Some tests were found to predict significantly the Verbal Scale IQ; other tests, the Performance Scale IQ; and still other tests, both the Verbal and Performance Scale IQ's. Only one test, Counting Four Objects, was found to be a negative predictor of the Performance Scale IQ, while none of the tests was a negative predictor of the Verbal Scale IQ. The best predictors of adult abilities were verbal tests and memory tests, while number concept tests were unreliable in predicting adult abilities.

STUDIES COMPARING THE STANFORD-BINET AND THE WAIS

The relationship between the Stanford-Binet and WAIS still holds some interest, especially for longitudinal studies of intelligence and for work in the field of mental retardation. The studies listed in Table B-1 in the Appendix can be viewed as comparative validity studies of the Stanford-Binet (or of the WAIS). (The relationship between the Stanford-Binet and other individual tests of intelligence is discussed in Chapters 11, 15, and 18.)

The correlations between the Stanford-Binet and WAIS in samples of mentally retarded individuals are uniformly high, ranging from .74 to .90 (median correlation of .75). However, differences between mean IQ's may be large — by as much as 23 points in favor of the WAIS. Binet IQ's are lower than WAIS IQ's in mentally retarded groups. In contrast, with normal college freshmen and normal adults, the Stanford-Binet has been found to yield higher IQ's than the WAIS, with correlations ranging from .40 to .83 (median correlation of .77). The Stanford-Binet correlates more highly with the Verbal Scale than with the Performance Scale.

SUMMARY

One of the first things to consider in administering the Stanford-Binet is whether the child has the necessary sensory and motor abilities required by the various tests. Tests below year-level VIII usually require vision, while many tests in year-levels II through V require arm-hand use. Older examinees who cannot speak may write their answers if they are capable of doing so. In beginning the test administration, the examiner should find a year level that is of moderate difficulty; the child's chronological age serves as a good guidepost. In addition, the Vocabulary test for older examinees is a good test with which to begin the examination, because it provides information for selecting a tentative basal year level.

It is difficult to evaluate the effects of not having a basal or ceiling year level. In such cases, the IQ can still be reported, with a statement indicating that the results may not be completely valid. The larger the number of tests that are passed at year-level II, or failed at year-level Superior Adult III, the greater the probability is that the results are valid. Extending the range of testing to two basal levels or two ceiling levels may be useful for certain populations (e.g., mentally retarded), but generally these procedures do not appear to provide more reliable and valid results than those obtained by establishing one basal and one ceiling year level.

Administering and scoring the Stanford-Binet requires considerable skill and judgment. Careful study of the test manual is required. Administration and scoring are not routine procedures. Modifying some test procedures may not lead to scores that differ significantly from those obtained with standard test procedures, but modifications should be used only after standard procedures have been attempted. Testing-the-limits procedures, which are to be used after the entire examination has been administered, may be useful on some occasions. Short forms of the Stanford-Binet generally appear to provide reliable and valid IQ's. However, the resulting loss of information may not be compensated by the gain in time. A record booklet that is properly completed provides a useful test record, aids in the writing of a report, and facilitates a review of the scoring. A usable record booklet is a contribution to the assessment process.

The deviation IQ on Form L-M permits expressing IQ's in terms of normalized standard scores throughout the entire range of the scale. Sex differences are minimal on the Stanford-Binet. Verbal and memory tests on the Stanford-Binet are good predictors of WAIS IQ's, while number concept tests are less reliable predictors. While correlations between the Stanford-Binet and the WAIS are generally satisfactory, large differences between mean IQ's have been reported in some studies.

CHAPTER 10

INTERPRETING THE STANFORD-BINET

One of the dilemmas faced by the examiner is how he should present to the reader of the report the kinds of tests found in the Stanford-Binet, without in the process conveying that there are special, separate, reliable cognitive functions being measured by the individual tests or by a cluster of tests. Each examinee has a pattern of successes and failures, and one of the goals of the evaluation is to describe this pattern. Tests passed or failed at year levels at or close to the examinee's chronological age are likely to have less diagnostic significance than tests passed at higher year levels or failed at lower year levels. Another aim, then, is to determine when the examinee's performance represents a deviation from his chronological age level (and from his mental age level when his performance is being evaluated in relation to his own achievements on the scale).

Responses to the Stanford-Binet tests represent the interplay of many functions. The child's apprehension of the test questions, coupled with his answer, involves a complex chain of psychological processes. Specific terms used to describe the functions or processes involved in performance on a test do not convey the complexity of the processes that may be involved when a child responds to a question. In fact, it may not be possible ever to state precisely which factor or factors have contributed to successful performance. In addition, a process used by one child to answer a question may not be the same process used by another child to answer the question.

More detailed descriptions of processes involved in two tests may help to demonstrate the multifaceted elements involved in a response. Dunsdon's (1952) analysis of the Stringing Beads test (year-levels III and XIII) is informative:

The child's response will indicate first whether he has understood an instruction to observe a demonstration of what he himself will be asked to attempt afterwards; secondly, whether he has grasped the principle of "threading," which will involve comprehension of the fact that a sufficient length of the tag must be pushed through the hole before it is possible to change from "pushing" to "pulling"; thirdly, if he can begin on the task, his response will demonstrate his ability to remember instructions and maintain his initial purpose for a period appropriate to the age level at which the test is placed. Even at this early stage therefore, the problem is one of comprehension and direction of attention as much as of purely mechanical skill. . . . The test has now become [at the higher level] a test of form perception and discrimination and of spatial relations and visual memory, rather than merely manipulation [p. 36].

Dearborn's (1926) analysis of responses to the Fables test is relevant to other tests, especially Proverbs (year-levels AA, SA I, and SA III). First, failure may be associated with lowered attention and concentration. Second, bizarre interpretations or irrelevant interpretations may indicate disturbances of conceptual associations. Third, responses may be suggestive of suspicion, evasion, lack of cooperation, negativism, or incoherence. Fourth, responses may reveal the examinee's rational process of inference. Thus, the test involves many processes, including attention, awareness of a whole situation, appreciation of fine shades of meaning, memory, judgment (both practical and ethical forms), interest, vocabulary, and imagination.

The year level at which the test appears also may play a role in evaluating the functions and processes required for successful performance. For example, McNemar (1942) pointed out that repeating digits "may at the early ages depend upon whatever ability is involved in attention and in following directions, whereas at later ages it may depend more upon immediate memory [p. 121]." McNemar is thereby indicating that in later years "attention" and "following directions" are asymptotic as far as repeating digits is concerned, so that the variance in scores at that point is attributable to the remaining, nonasymptotic (in the population) function, immediate memory. NcNemar's analysis shows us the difference between a logical analysis and a factor analysis of test scores. Factor analysis overlooks any "factors" that do not contribute to test variance, despite the fact that a particular function may be absolutely necessary to pass the test. The logical analysis, on the other hand, says nothing about which of the functions isolated account for the observed variance at any given age level. Thus, both approaches have their places, but they tell us different things.

In attempting to describe the examinee's pattern of performance, one can use no fool-proof method to determine which cognitive (or even noncognitive) function or functions are involved in the successes and failures. Each of the principal methods that have been used to determine functions measured by the tests, factor analysis and content analysis (logical analysis of skills measured), has difficulties associated with it, and these will become apparent in this chapter.

Factor analysis is a method of reducing a larger number of variables to a smaller number that "explain" the variance of the respective variables in a more parsimonious way. The remaining variables are called dimensions or factors, depending on whether one is dealing with the geometrical or the algebraic conception. Cluster analysis is a method of grouping objects—whether they be people, rocks, or Binet test items—into clusters of objects that appear to resemble one another, according to certain criteria. Cluster analysis can be done, as in the various instances in this chapter, by logical groupings or by mathematical methods such as distance functions.

This chapter is divided into four parts. The first discusses factor analytic studies of the Stanford-Binet, beginning with the earliest version of the scale. The second presents a review of classification systems that have been developed for the various revisions. The third describes a method for determining the spread of successes, and the fourth considers scatter analysis. The first two parts can be viewed as an attempt to evaluate the functions measured by the Stanford-Binet.

FACTOR ANALYSIS

A number of factor analytic studies of the Stanford-Binet have appeared over the years. Factor analytic approaches are adequate for a number of purposes (such as a study of the composition of test items), but they usually are not adequate for the practical purposes envisaged by examiners who are using the Stanford-Binet. It is important to recognize that naming factors is a subjective process and may lead to interpretations that are just as "subjective" as those resulting from content analyses of the mental skills brought into play by various test items. We now review the findings for the 1916, 1937, and 1960 forms.

1916 Stanford-Binet

Wright (1939) studied the performance of a sample of 10-year-old children on tests appearing at year-levels VII through XII of the 1916 Stanford-Binet. She found one common factor termed "maturation," and six group factors (number, spatial, verbal relations, reasoning, induction, and one not named, but conceivably related to an ability more common to children at a lower level of development).

In Burt and John's (1942) factor analysis, year-levels X and XII of the 1916 Stanford-Binet were studied. A general factor was found to account for about 40% of the variance. Three factors (verbal, spatial, and numerical) had high loadings while three other factors (immediate memory, understanding words, and understanding situations) had low loadings. Burt and John concluded that "an experienced tester may legitimately use the scale, not only to estimate a child's general intelligence, but also to gain sidelights on his special abilities and disabilities [p. 161]."

1937 Stanford-Binet

McNemar (1942) factor analyzed the two forms of the 1937 Stanford-Binet using part of the standardization sample. The results indicated that many of the tests load heavily on a common factor. Minor group factors were evident, but their contributions were difficult to interpret. The common factors at successive year levels appear to be nearly identical. McNemar concluded that IQ's "for individuals of differing mental-maturity levels or for the same individual at different stages of development are comparable quantitatively and qualitatively [p. 123]." The tests with high or low common factor loadings, grouped by year levels, are shown in Table 10–1.

Jones (1949, 1954), in his first study, factor analyzed the performance of four age groups (7, 9, 11, and 13 years of age) on the Stanford-Binet (Form L and Form M). The number of meaningful factors that were found ranged from three to six (e.g., verbal, memory, visualization, spatial, and reasoning), depending on the age group studied. The results suggested that differentiation of mental abilities occurs with increasing age. In his second study of year-levels XII, XIII, and XIV of Form L and Form M, he found nine primary factors (e.g., verbal comprehension, memory span, space visualization, general reasoning, closure, and carefulness). Jones also derived three second-order factors that he thought might represent fundamental components of general intellectual ability. One factor represented the ability to profit from scholastic experience. A second factor represented the ability to synthesize perceptions so as to impose a good gestalt. The third factor indicated a facility for dealing with relations, either of verbal or spatial content. Dean (1950) factor analyzed year-levels VI, VII, and VIII of Form L and found five group factors (verbal, perceptual speed, spatial, reasoning, and memory). These results generally are similar to those obtained by Jones.

Hofstaetter (1954) factor analyzed Bayley's (1949) 18-year growth study data. (In Bayley's study, the Stanford-Binet was administered from ages 2 to 14 years.) Three factors were obtained, which were labeled "sensori-motor alertness" (until 20 months of age), "persistence" (from 20 to 40 months of age), and "manipulation of symbols" (after 48 months of age). Hofstaetter pointed out that during the second decade of life the manipulation-of-symbols

Table 10-1. STANFORD-BINET TESTS (L AND M) WITH HIGH OR LOW
COMMON FACTOR LOADINGS

YEAR LEVELS	HIGH LOADING	LOW LOADING
II–IV–6	Picture Vocabulary, Identifying Objects by Name, Response to Pictures I, Comparison of Sticks, Comparison of Balls, Comprehension I, Opposite Analogies I, Pictorial Identification, Materials	Block Building: Tower, Block Building: Bridge, Three-Hole Form Board: Rotated, Motor Coordination, Copying a Circle, Drawing a Cross, Three Commissions, Stringing Beads
V–XI	Pictorial Likenesses and Differences, Similarities: Two Things, Vocabulary, Verbal Absurdities, Similarities and Differences, Naming the Days of the Week, Dissected Sentences, Abstract Words I	Paper Folding: Triangle, Patience: Rectangles, Copying a Bead Chain, Copying a Bead Chain from Memory I, Picture Absurdities I, Word Naming, Word Naming: Animals, Block Counting
XII–SA III	Vocabulary, Verbal Absurdities II, Abstract Words, Differences Between Abstract Words, Arithmetical Reasoning, Proverbs, Essential Differences, Sentence Building	Problems of Fact, Copying a Bead Chain from Memory II, Memory for Stories: The Acrobat, Enclosed Box Problem, Papercutting, Plan of Search, Repeating Digits, Repeating Digits: Reversed

Adapted from McNemar (1942).

factor accounts for almost all the variance of intelligence test scores. However, Cronbach (1967) observed that the findings obtained by Hofstaetter were an artifact of certain decisions made by Bayley in the testing schedule. Different factorial separations would have appeared at other ages if tests had been selected that were spaced differently along the age continuum. Consequently, in such analyses the ages at which new factors become prominent are based on arbitrary decisions concerning where to begin and end a series of tests. Hofstaetter's findings, therefore, must be questioned.

Stott and Ball (1965) factor analyzed the Stanford-Binet (Form L) performance of children in three age levels (36 months, 48 months, and 60 months). The results indicated that cognitive and memory factors are measured at each of the three ages studied, while an evaluation factor, in addition, appears at 36 months and 48 months, but not at 60 months. A divergent production factor was not measured at any of the three ages studied, while a convergent production factor was measured only at 36 months of age.

1960 Stanford-Binet

Two factor analytic studies have appeared for Form L-M. In one study, Stormer (1966) administered the Stanford-Binet (L-M), together with 27 other tests that measure either specific intellectual abilities or creative abilities, to 15-year-old boys and girls. The results indicated that Stanford-Binet tests in the upper year levels load primarily on a verbal production and verbal reasoning factor. This factor, however, was not sufficiently conclusive to be labeled as a *g* factor. There was little loading on a memory factor and only a small loading on a spatial ability factor. A large number of factors, with few significant loadings, were found. Stormer concluded that the Stanford-Binet in the upper levels appears to identify those who are verbally fluent and those strong in verbal reasoning.

In the other study, Ramsey and Vane (1970) factor analyzed year-levels IV through VI of Form L-M, using a sample of white and Negro children who were between the ages of 3 and 7 years. Seven factors (verbal, visual-motor, cognitive figural systems, visual ability and judgment, aspect of general knowledge, control of impulsivity, and visualization and cognition) were found. Of the 18 tests studied, two-thirds loaded on the first factor. A single common factor, it was concluded, cannot explain all of the performance on the Stanford-Binet in this age range. The results also indicated that Stanford-Binet tests in the lower year levels are factorially complex, with tests depending on one or more aspects of intelligence.

Comment on Factor Analysis

Vernon (1961) observed that factor analyses of the Stanford-Binet agree that a general factor carries most of the variance, but that there are also many small group factors whose make-up depends on the age level studied. Factors that are found usually include a verbal factor, an immediate memory factor, and a spatial-pictorial factor. Vernon did not think that these group factors are sufficiently clear-cut or consistent to justify using the scale diagnostically. Group factor content differs at different year levels of the scale, so that the scale does not always measure the same thing throughout the year levels. Vernon concluded that the Stanford-Binet is as useful as or more useful than group tests in evaluating children partly because its *general* and *verbal-numerical-educational* content is high and partly because it is less affected than group tests by artificial "formal" factors, such as practice effects, speed, and test difficulty.

Vernon was also critical of Jones's (1954) factor analytic approach to the Stanford-Binet. He questioned the value of extracting and rotating factors at a particular year level. Furthermore, he did not feel that it was very meaningful to call a factor "closure," to take one example, unless it can be demonstrated that the factor is representative of some more generally known ability.

An important observation made by Wesman (1968), concerning the factors that may enter into the performance of a seemingly "simple" cognitive act, is related to the problem of applying factor names and classifications to tests that appear on various scales. Wesman's analysis, which is shown below, illustrates why it is so difficult to apply a simple or "pure" factor name or classification to cognitive acts or behaviors. His analysis should be considered in evaluating much of the material that appears in the present chapter and in Chapters 13 and 16, which discuss the interpretation of the WISC and WPPSI.

A 6-year-old who assembles three alphabet blocks to spell out "cat" has employed, at a minimum, verbal and spatial skills; if he is aware that there are three blocks or letters, he has engaged in numerical perception as well. The ability to perform the task has required cognition, memory, convergent thinking, and evaluation. The product is figural, symbolic, and semantic. All this, and we have not yet taken into account such considerations as the motor-manipulative activity, the perception of color, the earlier learning experiences which enabled him to perform the task successfully, or the imagery which the concept "cat" induces in him. We, as analysts, may choose to attend to only a single aspect of the behavior — but the behavior itself remains multifaceted and complex. To assume that we can abstract from a host of such activities a pure and simple entity is to ignore the psychological meaning of intelligent behavior [p. 273].

CLASSIFICATION SYSTEMS

Classification systems have appeared over the years because examiners have been interested in a detailed examination of an examinee's performance.

A classification scheme is a convenient way of describing what the child has done in categories that have some face validity. The fact that the child has done something different does not depend upon factor analytic justification, technically. Without classification schemes, the examiner is left with few options. He can report just the IQ (and behavioral observations and other qualitative material) or discuss performance on specific tests. Classification schemes provide for an evaluation of the examinee's pattern of successes and failures (cf. Cronbach, 1960; Freeman, 1962). The diagnostic role, which is to provide an understanding of the examinee's abilities and to make useful recommendations, can be facilitated by use of classification schemes.

Classification schemes should not be used to determine in any absolute sense special abilities from the Stanford-Binet (cf. Goodenough, 1937). Yet the examiner, in observing the child's performance, attempts to evaluate such things as the examinee's vocabulary level, verbal fluency, conceptualization level, verbal and general reasoning ability, memory, and visual perception (cf. Newland & Meeker, 1964). Pronouncements should not be made about special abilities, but careful attention should be given to the child's pattern of performance in order to have a basis for making more detailed recommendations. The pattern of performance is important, because the IQ cannot satisfy the demands of differential diagnosis of learning failures. Persons with identical IQ's can differ in many ways, including test ranges, skewness of distribution of successful responses, and relative placements of respective abilities (Jastak, 1950). We now discuss the classification schemes that have been developed over the years for the 1916, 1937, and 1960 forms.

1916 Stanford-Binet

Interest in classifying the Stanford-Binet tests began almost from the inception of the scale. One of the first systems, developed by Brigham (1917) for the 1911 Goddard revision, consisted of a nine-category scheme: ideation, judgment, school training, association, memory, imagination, kinaesthetic discrimination, suggestibility, and perception. At least 13 different classification systems (or evaluations of functions or abilities that may be measured by the tests) have been proposed for the 1916 Stanford-Binet (see Pignatelli, 1943). Most of the systems incorporated such categories as comprehension or reasoning, memory, vocabulary, number concept, and imagery.

In addition to the systems described by Pignatelli (1943), other schemes have appeared. Kendig and Richmond (1940) proposed a two-category system. In one category there are *educative tests,* which primarily measure a *g* factor (e.g., vocabulary tests, comprehension tests, problem tests, and abstraction tests). In the other category, *non-educative tests,* the *g* factor is not measured primarily (e.g., memory tests, sensory discrimination tests, visual-imagery tests, and orientation tests). A scheme proposed by Roe and Shakow (1942) also consisted of classifying tests into two categories, which in turn are subdivided. One category, *learned material,* consists of tests that require recall of material learned at some time preceding the test administration. The other category, *thought material,* is represented by tests that involve carrying through a train of ideas to a conclusion.

1937 Stanford-Binet

Various classification systems have appeared for the 1937 Stanford-Binet (Bradway, 1945; Bradway & Thompson, 1962; Davis, 1941; McNemar, 1942; Slutzky, Justman, & Wrightstone, 1953). These systems generally are similar to those proposed for the 1916 Stanford-Binet. An ego-psychology approach to test classification, which evaluates personality variables that may enter into successful or unsuccessful performance on various tests, also has appeared (Fromm, 1960; Fromm, Hartman, & Marschak, 1954, 1957). The system is complex, but it may be useful to those who are particularly interested in exploring the child's psychodynamics as they may be related to performance on particular Stanford-Binet tests.

We will describe briefly McNemar's (1942) work. He evaluated three special scales: a vocabulary scale, composed of all the words from the Vocabulary test of Form L; a nonverbal scale, composed of 20 tests selected by Merrill that do not require verbal responses; and a memory scale, composed of 22 tests that appear to tap memory functions. The latter two scales had two forms. McNemar concluded that the vocabulary scale alone was adequate as a limited special scale. The limited number of nonverbal tests prevents the development of an adequate nonverbal scale, while the development of a memory scale is hampered because it is not known to what extent tests involving memory or immediate memory are actually measuring memory. Tests involving memory apparently measure the same aspects of general intelligence that are measured by the scale as a whole. Scales measuring special abilities, McNemar concluded, must be found in sources other than the Stanford-Binet.

1960 Stanford-Binet

Structure of Intellect Classification

An innovative approach to test classification has recently been presented by Meeker (1969), who used Guilford's (1967) Structure of Intellect model to classify tests in the Stanford-Binet (Form L-M), WISC, and WPPSI. The model's three dimensions, as we have seen in Chapter 2, are operations, contents, and products. Each dimension can be designated by a capital letter (see Table C-28 in the Appendix). A three-letter classification, representing the three dimensions of the Structure of Intellect, is used to classify each test. The first letter refers to operations; the second, contents; and the third, products. For example, the first test in the Stanford-Binet, "Three-Hole Form Board" at year-level II, is designated NFR. This means that the test is classified as measuring convergent production operations (N), figural contents (F), and units products (R). Table C-2 in the Appendix presents the Structure of Intellect designations developed by Meeker for each Stanford-Binet test. Some tests are classified by more than one designation, so that there are 249 classifications (representing the three dimensions) for the 122 tests (without alternates) in Form L-M. The major problems with Meeker's work, as well as with most classification systems, are that the reliability and validity of the classifications are not known.

According to Meeker's classification, tests (excluding alternates) in the Stanford-Binet in the operations dimension are most frequently represented by cognition activities (37%), followed by convergent production (23%), memory (16%), evaluation (15%), and last by divergent production (9%). Tests classified as requiring divergent production do not begin until year-level IV. In the contents dimension, the majority of the test classifications are semantic (60%), followed by figural (26%), and symbolic (14%). In year-levels II through V, only two tests are classified in the symbolic category. The products dimension has a somewhat more even distribution of test classifications among its six categories, namely, units (25%), relations (21%), systems (20%), implications (16%), transformations (11%), and classes (6%). Implications and transformations are not represented by tests until year-level III-6.

Templates for the entire scale are available for providing a quick and convenient way of classifying an examinee's test performance. Meeker discussed how the Structure of Intellect classifications can be useful in analyzing an examinee's strengths and weaknesses and in planning educational programs. While some reports have appeared that have questioned the categories proposed by Meeker (Stormer, 1966; Wikoff, 1971), there is generally little available data to evaluate the system's usefulness. In addition, the criticisms associated with Guilford's model, which are discussed in Chapter 2, may also affect the usefulness of the proposed classifications for the Stanford-Binet tests (and WISC and WPPSI subtests, too). Yet those who are involved in educational planning would do well to study Meeker's work, because it has the potential of making a contribution to the field of individual intelligence testing for the purpose of curriculum planning.

Sattler's Classification Scheme

More traditional classification schemes have also appeared for the 1960 Stanford-Binet. Sattler (1965) presented a classification scheme using seven categories: language, memory, conceptual thinking, reasoning, numerical reasoning, visual-motor, and social intelligence. Valett (1964), working independently of Sattler, classified tests in the Stanford-Binet into one of six categories: general comprehension, visual-motor ability, arithmetic reasoning, memory and concentration, vocabulary and verbal fluency, and judgment and reasoning. Silverstein (1965) noted that the two systems agree in classifying 75% of the total number of Stanford-Binet tests. Lutey (1967) also developed a classification scheme.

Sattler's classification scheme is presented in detail. It is offered as a means of ordering data from the Stanford-Binet and as a convenient way of describing what the child has done in categories that have some face validity. Research studies concerning its usefulness and general validity would be welcome. The scheme is based on somewhat arbitrary groupings of tests, according to test content. Therefore, some tests could be placed in categories other than those shown and other categories also could be developed, if desired. A factor analysis was not performed, nor were judges used for a reliability check on the categorizations. Cronbach (1970) observed that some of the distinctions are subtle, and other interpreters of the scale would no doubt modify Sattler's categories. However, the classifications are in the tradition of those presented for previous revisions, and as Silverstein (1965) noted, the scheme is similar to that presented by Valett, so that there appears to be a satisfactory degree of reliability for the categorizations.

It is important to recognize that the categories should not be used to determine special abilities, since research has generally shown that special groupings of tests are not reliable. In addition, if the category names are used, the examiner should not lose sight of what the individual tests actually require of the examinee (Silverstein, 1965). Wikoff (1971) has concluded that the classification schemes developed by Meeker (1969), Sattler (1965), and Valett (1964) are not valid, because the results of a factor analysis, which used each classification scheme, failed to provide more than one general factor. However, Wikoff also reported that performance on the test categories is differentially related to socioeconomic status. For example, in Sattler's scheme, the correlation between the visual-motor category and socioeconomic status was .17, while the correlation between the language category and socioeconomic status was .34. These results suggest that the categories may be providing somewhat different information.

The schemes developed by Meeker, Sattler, Valett, and Lutey are intended to assist in making interpretations. For example, a child who consistently fails visual-motor tests while passing other types of tests may need further testing to evaluate his perceptual abilities. It is in just such cases that the categorization systems can be useful. The schemes should be used to generate hypotheses about the examinee's performance in order to make more meaningful recommendations; they are not to be used to make diagnoses about special abilities.

Sattler's classification scheme is presented in Table C-2 of the Appendix. The first description in the second column of Table C-2 refers to the category from Sattler's classification scheme. Other relevant descriptions that pertain to test functions and processes also are described. The third column of Table C-2, as we have seen previously, shows the Structure of Intellect designations. The Binetgram, described in the latter part of this chapter, also presents the tests that are classified in each category. Each category in the Sattler scheme represents a general area conveying the nature of the function measured. A short description of each category follows.

Language.   This category includes tests related to maturity of vocabulary (in relation to the prekindergarten level), extent of vocabulary (referring to the number of words the child can define), quality of vocabulary (measured by such tests as abstract words, rhymes, word naming, and definitions), and comprehension of verbal relations.

Memory.   This category contains meaningful, nonmeaningful, and visual memory tests. The tests are considered to reflect rote auditory memory, ideational memory, and attention span.

Conceptual Thinking.   This category, while closely associated with language ability, is primarily concerned with abstract thinking. Such functions as generalization, assuming an "as if" attitude, conceptual thinking, and utilizing a categorical attitude are subsumed.

Reasoning.   This category contains verbal and nonverbal reasoning tests. The verbal absurdity tests are the prototype for the verbal reasoning tests. The pictorial and orientation problems represent a model for the nonverbal reasoning tests. Reasoning includes the perception of logical relations, discrimination ability, and analysis and synthesis. Spatial reasoning may also be measured by the orientation tests.

Numerical Reasoning.   This category includes tests involving arithmetic reasoning problems. The content is closely related to school learning. Numerical reasoning involves concentration and the ability to generalize from numerical data.

Visual-Motor.   This category contains tests concerned with manual dexterity, eye-hand coordination, and perception of spatial relations. Constructive visual imagery may be involved in the paper folding test. Nonverbal reasoning ability may be involved in some of the visual-motor tests.

Social Intelligence.   This category strongly overlaps with the reasoning category, so that consideration should be given to the tests classified in the latter as also reflecting social comprehension. Social intelligence includes social maturity and social judgment. The comprehension and finding reasons tests are seen to reflect social judgment, whereas obeying simple commands, response to pictures, and comparison tests likely reflect social maturity.

Table 10–2 shows the rank order of categories by percentage for each category for the total number of tests ($N = 142$), total number of tests without alternates ($N = 122$), alternates ($N = 20$), and starred tests ($N = 80$) that are used in the short form. The 142 tests are not separate and distinct tests, because many of them have the same item content, but receive differential scoring based on the number of correct responses. Table 10–2 shows that language tests are more frequent than other kinds of tests (rank 1 for the total number of tests, with and without alternates, and rank 1 for starred tests). Numerical reasoning tests, on the other hand, are the least frequently represented tests (rank 7 for the total number of tests, with and without alternates, and rank 7 for alternate tests).

Table 10-2. Rank Order of Categories in Stanford-Binet (L–M)

Rank	Total No. of Tests Category	N	%	Total No. of Tests Without Alternates Category	N	%	Alternates Category	N	%	Starred Tests Category	N	%
1	L	35	25	L	32	26	M	4	20	L	31	39
2	R	25	18	R	22	18	VM	4	20	R	11	14
3	M	21	15	M	17	14	L	3	15	M	11	14
4	CT	18	13	CT	16	13	R	3	15	CT	10	12
5	SI	17	12	SI	14	11	SI	3	15	VM	6	8
6	VM	16	11	VM	12	10	CT	2	10	NR	6	8
7	NR	10	7	NR	9	7	NR	1	5	SI	5	6
	Total	142	101		122	99		20	100		80	101

Note.—Abbreviations are as follows: CT = Conceptual Thinking, L = Language, M = Memory, NR = Numerical Reasoning, R = Reasoning, SI = Social Intelligence, VM = Visual-Motor.

(Reprinted, with a change in notation, by permission of the publisher and author from J. M. Sattler, "Analysis of Functions of the 1960 Stanford-Binet Intelligence Scale, Form L-M," *Journal of Clinical Psychology*, **21**, p. 175. Copyright 1965, Clinical Psychology Publishing Co., Inc.)

Table 10–3 presents a rank ordering, by percentage, of the categories by year-level clusters for the distribution of the total number of tests without alternates ($N = 122$). The four clusters of year levels (II-V, VI-X, XI-XIV, and

Table 10-3. Rank Order of Categories in Stanford-Binet (L–M) by Year Levels (Data for total number of tests without alternates)

Rank	II–V Category	N	%	VI–X Category	N	%	XI–XIV Category	N	%	AA–SA III Category	N	%
1	L	11	26	L	6	20	L	7	30	L	8	31
2	VM	9	21	M	5	17	R	6	26	CT	7	27
3	R	9	21	SI	5	17	M	5	17	NR	4	15
4	SI	7	17	CT	5	17	SI	2	9	R	4	15
5	M	4	10	R	3	10	CT	2	9	M	3	12
6	CT	2	5	NR	3	10	NR	2	9	SI	0	0
7	NR	0	0	VM	3	10	VM	0	0	VM	0	0
	Total	42	100		30	101		24	100		26	99

Note.—Abbreviations are as follows: CT = Conceptual Thinking, L = Language, M = Memory, NR = Numerical Reasoning, R = Reasoning, SI = Social Intelligence, VM = Visual-Motor.

(Reprinted, with a change in notation, by permission of the publisher and author from J. M. Sattler, "Analysis of Functions of the 1960 Stanford-Binet Intelligence Scale, Form L-M," *Journal of Clinical Psychology*, **21**, p. 175. Copyright 1965, Clinical Psychology Publishing Co., Inc.)

AA-SA III), while arbitrary, were designed to reflect broad periods of development.

In each year-level cluster, the language category occupies the first rank. The reasoning and memory categories have at least 10% of the tests in each of the year-level clusters. The visual-motor category ties for rank 2 in year-level cluster II-V, ties for rank 5 in year-level cluster VI-X, and is not represented by any tests in year-level clusters XI-XIV and AA-SA III. The conceptual thinking category moves from rank 6, with 5% of the tests in year-level cluster II-V, to rank 2, with 27% of the tests in year-level cluster AA-SA III. The social intelligence category is stable in the first two year-level clusters and then shows successive decreases in the remaining two clusters (17%, 17%, 9%, and 0%, respectively).

Developmental Analysis of Intelligence

The classification scheme indicates that the early year levels of the scale measure such functions as visual-motor capacities, reasoning, social intelligence, and language ability. These four areas comprise 85% of the tests in year-levels II-V. Language development is assessed through the child's knowledge of common objects that are found in his environment. His knowledge of the social world is reflected, in part, by understanding pictures and by knowing the function of houses, books, eyes, and ears.

During the middle years of childhood, more advanced cognitive functions are developed. Memory ability increases in complexity from simple repetition of digits required during the preschool era to repeating digits backward and to recalling stories and reproducing designs in the middle year era. Conceptual thinking also takes on increasing importance in the scale. Visual-motor tests are still represented during the middle years of development but at a lower frequency than at the preschool era. At first, the relatively simple motor ability is reflected by such tasks as building a tower and bridge of blocks, stringing beads, and copying a circle and straight line. In the middle year period more advanced visual-motor functions are measured, such as copying a diamond, paper cutting, and maze tracing.

The ability to do arithmetic calculations, an ability associated with school learning and measured by block counting and making change, is acquired during the middle years of childhood. This ability partly reflects the child's orientation to his environment, since responsibility for money is one aspect of maturity. In the upper age levels, symbol manipulation, which is partly a function of spatial reasoning and integration, is reflected in the numerical reasoning tests.

Language functions during the period between 2 and 5 years center around simple descriptive phrases concerning common objects in the child's environment. The stimuli used in the tests are perceptual, and one-phrase definitions suffice. However, beginning at 6 years of age, and in all succeeding years, language functions are measured by verbal stimuli, and more complex verbal descriptions and definitions are required for success. Beginning at 9 years of age, more varied tasks occur. The child is expected to apply his language ability in rhyming, defining abstract words, making word combinations, sentence building, and word usage. Many of the tasks that are related to language functions may also reflect reasoning ability.

During the adolescent period, verbal reasoning comes into prominence. The adolescent is expected to have some appreciation of the subtleties in his world, and a knowledge of a world of mores where interpersonal relations are at the forefront. The verbal reasoning required by the verbal absurdities tests is similar to the reasoning required by the tests in the social intelligence category. One of the transitions from the middle years of childhood to the adolescent years, as reflected by the scale, is the greater appreciation of a world of mores, of right and wrong, and of one's expectations where social customs are stressed. Memory functions during adolescence continue to develop along the lines established during the middle years. Longer and more complex sentences must be recalled, along with more difficult recall of perceptually presented material and orally presented digits.

The area most stressed during the postadolescent period, besides language ability, is conceptual thinking. Knowledge of similarities occurs at year-level VII, and opposite analogies tests begin at year-level IV and continue through the last year level of the scale. After year-level XIV, the understanding of proverbs, which requires well developed reasoning, verbal comprehension, and analysis and generalization ability, is examined. Language functions play the predominant role in the postadolescent period, while other areas of intelligence receive relatively less emphasis.

Binetgram

The analysis of functions provided by Sattler (1965) is, in graphic form, termed the "Binetgram." The Binetgram provides a visual picture of the distribution of the examinee's passes and failures. At the present stage of knowledge, there is probably insufficient evidence to reject the Binetgram. Children on the Stanford-Binet are doing different things, and the Binetgram in conjunction with the classification scheme can be used to evaluate the child's performance. The Binetgram, like the classification scheme, is not to be used to make statements about special abilities, but it is useful, in a qualitative way, to describe the child's performance.

The first two lines in the upper left-hand corner of the Binetgram are available for recording "identifying data." The standard deviation (SD) points appropriate for the examinee's performance can be entered in the spaces provided in the upper right-hand corner. (See the next part of this chapter, entitled "Determination of Spread of Successes," for a discussion of the standard deviation method.)

The rows of the Binetgram present the seven categories of the classification scheme, while the columns present the year levels of the scale. The last column is available for recording the total number of tests passed in each category. In each column the Arabic numbers not in parentheses identify the number of the test that is located at the year level; the "A" in the column identifies the alternate test. At year-level II, tests 3, 5, 6, and A appear in the language category; test 2, in the reasoning category; and tests 1 and 4, in the visual-motor category. No tests have been classified in the remaining four categories at this year level.

Cumulative Total.   After each test number another number appears in parentheses. This number represents the cumulative total of tests located in the category. For example, at year-level II, test 3 is the first language test. This is indicated by the "(1)" following the "3." Test 5 at year-level II is the second language test, noted by the "(2)" following the "5," and test 6 is the third language test, noted by the "(3)" in parentheses. Thus, there are three language tests at year-level II. The first test in the reasoning category is test 2 (1) at year-level II, while test 1 (1) and test 4 (2) at year-level II are the first two tests in the visual-motor category. Skipping to year-level V, we find that test 3 (11) is the eleventh language test appearing in the scale. Finally, at year-level SA III, we note that test 1 (32) is the 32nd language test. The cumulative total does not include the alternate tests.

Completing the Binetgram.   The Binetgram is completed after the examination is finished and all scoring and calculations have been checked. The mechanics of completing the Binetgram are relatively simple. Identifying data should be recorded and SD units obtained, if desired. Circle the Roman

BINETGRAM

Instructions: 1. Circle basal year level and ceiling year level.   2. Circle all tests passed by examinee.

Name _____ Date of testing _____ Grade _____ IQ _____ CA _____ MA _____   CA: SD _____ +1 _____ +2 _____ +3 _____ −1 _____ −2 _____ −3

Date of birth _____   MA: SD _____ +1 _____ +2 _____ +3 _____ −1 _____ −2 _____ −3

CATEGORIES	II	II-6	III	III-6	IV	IV-6	V	VI	VII	VIII	IX	X	XI	XII	XIII	XIV	AA	SA I	SA II	SA III	TOTAL TESTS PASSED
Language	3(1) 5(2) 6(3) A	1(4) 2(5) 3(6) 4(7)	2(8)		1(9) 4(10)	A	3(11)	1(12)		1(13)	4(14) A	1(15) 3(16) 5(17)	3(18)	1(19) 5(20) 6(21)	2(22) 5(23)	1(24)	1(25) 3(26) 8(27)	1(28) 3(29) 5(30)	1(31)	1(32)	
Memory		5(1)	4(2) A		2(3) A	5(4)			6(5) A	2(6)	3(7) 6(8)	6(9)	1(10) 4(11)	4(12) A	3(13) 6(14)			4(15)	6(16)	6(17)	
Conceptual Thinking					3(1)	2(2)		2(3) 5(4)	2(5) 5(6)	4(7)			6(8)			6(9)	5(10) 7(11)	6(12) A	3(13) 5(14)	2(15) 3(16) A	
Reasoning	2(1)			1(2) 2(3) 3(4) 5(5) A	5(6)	3(7)	5(8) 6(9)	3(10)		3(11)	2(12)	A	2(13)	2(14)	1(15) 4(16)	3(17) 5(18)	6(19)		2(20) A	4(21) 5(22)	
Numerical Reasoning								4(1)			5(2)	2(3)				2(4) 4(5) A	2(6) 4(7)	2(8)	4(9)		
Visual-Motor	1(1) 4(2)	A					1(7) 2(8) 4(9) A	6(10)	3(11)		1(12)				A	A	A				
Social Intelligence		6(1)		4(2) 6(3)	6(4)	1(5) 4(6) 6(7)		A	1(8) 4(9)	5(10) 6(11) A		4(12)	5(13) A	3(14)							

YEAR LEVEL

numbers for the basal year level and for the ceiling year level (e.g., (VII) when this is the basal year level and (XI) when this is the ceiling year level). Then circle all of the tests passed by the examinee. Finally, if desired, note the cumulative total number of tests passed by the examinee in each category in the last column.

The cumulative total may be obtained by one of two methods. First, the number of tests failed in the category can be subtracted from the number of the highest test passed. For example, suppose that the basal year level is at year-level VII and the ceiling year level at year-level XI. In the language category, test 1 and test 3 have been failed at year-level X, while all other language tests have been passed through year-level X. Since the last language test passed at year-level X is test 5 (17), two (representing the number of tests that were failed) is subtracted from 17. The number entered in the last column in this case is 15, representing 15 language tests credited with success. The other method for obtaining the cumulative total is simply to count the number of tests passed in the category after the basal year level and to enter this number in the last column.

Discussion of Binetgram. All of the difficulties associated with classification systems, of course, pertain to the Binetgram. The Binetgram may be misleading, because it suggests that performance on each test depends on only one aspect of intelligence (cf. Ramsey & Vane, 1970). We have seen previously that performance on any given test may involve a variety of cognitive functions. The Binetgram, therefore, must be used in a tentative manner, primarily to generate gross hypotheses about the examinee's abilities. The Binetgram shows that there are many year levels at which categories are not tapped. For example, tests in the conceptual thinking category do not begin until year-level IV. Numerical reasoning tests, which begin at year-level VI, do not appear again until year-level IX. Language is the most systematically represented category; it appears at every year level, with the exception of year-levels III-6, IV-6, and VII.

The cumulative total provides another source for qualitative analysis. It should be used only as a rough guide. The principle behind the cumulative total is similar to that of any point scale. An example of how the cumulative total may be used is as follows: At year-level X, the language category shows a cumulative total of 17 tests. This total has associated with it a mental age credit of X. A 10-year-old child who obtains a language category score of 12, which is approximately equivalent to a mental age credit of VI, therefore, would be demonstrating below-normal language ability. The SD method can also be used with the cumulative totals. The Binetgram, as presently constructed, does not permit the use of cumulative totals with the short form or with the alternate tests.

DETERMINATION OF SPREAD OF SUCCESSES

One of the aims of the psychological evaluation is to determine the examinee's spread of successes. This task is difficult because the age-level format of the scale does not permit a simple way of calculating significant differences between those tests that are passed and those that are failed. However, some guideposts can be obtained by use of standard deviation units in connection with the examinee's CA and MA. The SD procedure is described in the next part of the chapter.

If the examiner chooses not to use the SD method to determine approximate year levels of strength and weakness, he still should recognize that the distance between the examinee's CA or MA year levels and year levels on the scale do not mean the same thing throughout the scale. For example, the difference between year-level II and year-level III represents a 50 per cent increase in mental development, whereas the difference between year-level X and year-level XI represents a 10 per cent increase in mental development. Thus, a 2-year-old child who obtains an MA of 3–0 receives an IQ of 147, while a 10-year-old child who obtains an MA of 11–0 receives an IQ of 107. The statement "Tests were passed one year level above the examinee's chronological age" fails by not describing the level of mental functioning represented by the successes. For a 2-year-old, passing tests "one year above" may indicate superior functioning, while for a 10-year-old, passing tests "one year above" may indicate normal functioning. Therefore, the aforementioned statement concerning the level at which tests were passed must be elaborated.

Names of year levels after year-level XIV change from Roman numbers to names with "Adult" in them. However, these year levels also represent mental age credits needed to calculate the IQ. Table 10–4 has been prepared to show the respective mental ages for the last four year levels of the scale. The mental age credits received by the examinee represent the total of his entire performance on the scale. An MA of 15–4 can mean theoretically that *all* tests have been passed at the AA-year level, but in actual practice it reflects the total credit received — 15 years and 4 months. At the earlier year levels the same principle applies. An MA of 3–0 means that the child's performance gives him 36 months of credit. However, unlike the meaning of MA for year levels above 15, an MA of 3–0 also theoretically can mean that the child is functioning at a level similar to that of the average 3-year-old child.

When all tests are passed at year-level II, 24 months of credit are given. Mental age credits of 18 months are assumed, and six months are added for the six tests successfully completed at year-level II. The Stanford-Binet is so constructed that whenever a basal year level is established, mental age credits are assumed for all year levels of the scale below the basal year level. This procedure automatically includes the initial 18 months of mental age credit. At year-levels IV-6 and V, a total of 12 months' credit is given for the 12 tests. If all tests of the scale are passed through year-level V and none at higher year levels, five years and zero months (5–0) of mental age credits are given. Year-level VI provides 12 months of mental age credit and thereby bridges the apparent gap between year-level V and year-level VI (i.e., not having a ½ year level between year-level V and year-level VI). A basal year level established at V and one success at year-level VI results in mental-age credits of 5–2 (five years and two months).

The relationship between the child's chronological age and year levels on the scale can, at first, be confusing. However, the confusion can be cleared up readily by noting that a child whose chronological age is 7–0 must pass all tests at the VII-year level in order to achieve an IQ that is approximately equal to 100. Consequently, when all tests are passed at the VIII-year level, the suc-

Table 10-4. Mental Age Credits for Last Four Stanford-Binet (L–M) Year Levels

Year level	Credit earned	MA equivalent
AA	16 months	15–4
SA I	24 months	17–4
SA II	30 months	20
SA III	36 months	23

cesses represent those that are *one* year above the child's chronological age level. The scale is so devised that, for a child to achieve at a level that is consistent with his chronological age, he must pass all of the tests at the year level that is equal to his chronological age. Thus, for example, if an 8-year-old is said to pass tests at his chronological age level, he must pass all of the tests at the VIII-year level. Tests appearing at year-level VII are ones that are one year below his chronological age level. If he passes all tests at year-level VII, but fails all tests at year-level VIII, his IQ would be less than 100, and he would be functioning at a level that is one year below his chronological age level.

Proposals have been made to obtain an Altitude Quotient for the Stanford-Binet by using the altitude age (the highest year level at which tests are passed) as a substitute for the usual mental age in computing the IQ (Berko, 1955b; Diller & Beechley, 1951). Perhaps the Altitude Quotient could be used as a clinical tool for prediction of mental development for brain-injured and other groups of children; however, there is no evidence to support the value of the Altitude Quotient (cf. Mecham et al., 1966).

Standard Deviation (SD) Method

The SD method can be used to facilitate analysis of the examinee's performance on the scale. The year level points obtained from the SD method may be used to obtain probable areas of more or less well-developed abilities in relation to the examinee's CA or MA by mapping the year level points that are one or more SD's above or below the examinee's CA and MA year levels. Tests passed or failed at year levels within the ±1 SD range are not to be considered as significant departures from the baseline year level. Performance on these tests (within the ±1 SD range) may indicate neither more well-developed abilities nor less well-developed abilities but instead may reflect normal variability.

The SD procedure is not exact and its application requires flexibility. In most cases, the SD unit above or below the examinee's CA or MA (e.g., +1 SD or −1 SD) will fall part way in a year level. When this occurs, rounding off may be necessary. After a CA of 15–0, the Revised IQ tables in the Stanford-Binet manual do not provide SD units comparable to those that appear at lower year levels. To take one example, a CA of 16–0 and an MA of 21–0 result in the same IQ as a CA of 18–0 and an MA of 21–0 (IQ = 135). The SD method must be used cautiously with examinees who are older than 15 years of age. (See Chapter 3 for further information concerning mental age.)

Two baselines can be used to evaluate variability. (*a*) The CA baseline (the year level at which the CA falls) is used to interpret variability in relation to the examinee's CA level. For example, the CA baseline for a 9–6-year-old examinee is midway into year-level X of the scale. (*b*) The MA baseline (the year level at which the MA falls) is used to interpret variability in relation to the examinee's MA level. Thus, the MA baseline for an examinee whose MA is 3–7 is one-sixth into year-level IV of the scale. It is necessary to calculate SD year levels only for the examinee's actual performance. Therefore, if all tests are passed at year levels between +1 SD and −1 SD points, one need not calculate year levels for +2 SD and −2 SD points. If tests are not failed below the CA year level, but are passed at year levels above the CA baseline year level, then one should calculate as many SD year level points above the baseline year level as needed (+1 SD, +2 SD, +3 SD, etc.). A similar procedure is followed for tests that are failed at year levels below the baseline year level. Since the IQ tables in the Stanford-Binet manual (Form L-M) represent standard scores, the tables can be used to obtain approximate year level points using the SD method.

Finding +1 SD and −1 SD for CA Baseline

1. Find the page in the Stanford-Binet manual for examinee's CA and for IQ = 116.

2. Note MA for IQ of 116. This MA becomes the year level for +1 SD point.

3. Find the page in the Stanford-Binet manual for examinee's CA and for IQ = 84.

4. Note MA for IQ of 84. This MA becomes the year level for −1 SD point.

Example for +1 SD.   Examinee has a CA of 5–0. An IQ of 116 is found on page 272 of the Stanford-Binet manual for a CA of 5–0. The MA for this IQ is 5–9, and V-9 now becomes the year level point that is the upper limit for +1 SD. A V-9 year level point means that approximately four tests must be passed at year-level VI. Therefore, the end of +1 SD is approximately two-thirds of the way into year-level VI. Tests passed above this point are above the +1 SD point. Using a conservative approach, tests passed at year-level VII and above may be described, for example, as reflecting well-developed abilities or above normal performances (or superior or very superior, as the case may be).

Example for −1 SD.   Examinee has a CA of 5–0. An IQ of 85 (85 is selected because 84 is not shown in the tables) is found on page 267 of the Stanford-Binet manual for CA of 5–0. The MA for this IQ is 4–4, and IV-4 now becomes the year level point that is the lower limit for the −1 SD point. Therefore, the end of −1 SD is two-thirds of the way into year-level IV-6. Tests failed below this point are below the −1 SD point. Using a conservative approach, tests failed at year-levels IV and below can be described, for example, as reflecting poorly developed abilities or below normal performances (or borderline retarded or retarded, as the case may be).

Finding +1 SD and −1 SD for MA Baseline

Exactly the same procedure as that described for the CA baseline is used to obtain ±1 SD for the MA baseline. However, because of the arrangement of the tables in the Stanford-Binet manual, it is more convenient to enter the tables with the CA column even when obtaining year levels for the MA baseline. The steps for obtaining the ±1 SD year level points for the MA baseline are summarized, but examples are not provided because the ones shown for ±1 SD points for the CA baseline are exactly the same, with the exception of substituting the MA for the CA as the beginning point of entry.

1. Find page in the Stanford-Binet manual for examinee's MA in CA column and for IQ = 116.

2. Note MA for IQ of 116. This MA becomes the year level for +1 SD point.

3. Find page in the Stanford-Binet manual for examinee's MA in CA column and for IQ = 84.

4. Note MA for IQ of 84. This MA becomes the year level for −1 SD point.

Use the SD of 16 IQ points to determine further SD points of reference. Thus, in order to determine year levels for the +2 SD point and for the −2 SD point use IQ's of 132 and 68, respectively. For the +3 SD point and for the −3 SD point use IQ's of 148 and 52, respectively. Follow the same procedures as indicated for +1 SD and −1 SD. When the IQ tables do not have the exact IQ (as has been shown in the −1 SD CA baseline example) use the nearest IQ shown in the table to obtain the year level point of reference. Three examples are presented to illustrate how the SD approach can be applied.

Example 1.

CA = 10	CA SD +1 = 12–0	MA SD +1 = 12–0
MA = 10	−1 = 8–7	−1 = 8–7
IQ = 97 ±4		

Year level	Pass	Fail
VIII	Basal	
IX	4 tests	2 tests
X	4 tests	2 tests
XI	4 tests	2 tests
XII		Ceiling

The IQ of 97 ±4 is in the Normal range. (The "±4" refers to precision range; see Chapter 25 for further information.) Whenever the CA and MA are equal, normal functioning is indicated. Since the CA and MA are equal, statements applied to the CA baseline year level also apply to the MA baseline year level. Using the SD method to guide in interpreting significant variability in performance, we find that the point that is +1 SD above the examinee's CA (and MA) baseline level is 12–0, which means through year-level XII, while the point that is −1 SD below the CA (and MA) baseline level is 8–7, which means seven-twelfths into year-level IX. Since tests are not failed below year-level IX or passed above year-level XI, the points for −2 SD and +2 SD are not calculated.

In Example 1, a discussion of strengths and weaknesses is not meaningful, because all tests are passed and failed within one standard deviation (±1 SD) of both the CA and MA baselines. The examinee is generally normal in all areas measured by the tests administered. The two tests failed at year-level IX may point to some minor less well-developed abilities, while the tests passed at year-level XI may suggest areas of minimally better developed ability. However, based upon the SD method, better developed abilities or lesser developed abilities should not be discussed, because the variability in performance is too minimal.

Limited variability (and variability in general) is difficult to interpret. It may indicate simply a narrow range of abilities, or a somewhat narrow or constricted personality style, or nothing more than normal functioning. Variability is merely one index to be used in conjunction with all available sources of data. The meaning of limited variability may become clearer in the course of evaluating the examinee's total performance, and by using other sources of data (e.g., case history material).

Example 2.

CA = 10	CA SD +1 = 12–0	MA SD +1 = 16–4 (SA I)
MA = 14	+2 = 13–8	+2 = 18–8 (SA II)
IQ = 135 ±5	+3 = 15–4 (AA)	−1 = 11–5
	+4 = 17–1 (SA I)	

Year level	Pass	Fail
X	Basal	
XI	4 tests	2 tests
XII	4 tests	2 tests
XIII	3 tests	3 tests
XIV	3 tests	3 tests
AA	4 tests	4 tests
SA I	2 tests	4 tests
SA II	2 tests	4 tests
SA III		Ceiling

The examinee's superior ability means that he has developed intellectual strengths that are significantly above his CA level. The pattern of his successes should be examined in order to determine whether there are any specific areas of strength. Since one SD above his CA baseline is 12–0, tests passed at year-level XIII and above indicate significant areas of better developed abilities. Areas in which he is superior (+2 SD) occur at year levels above the 13–8 point, indicating that the AA-year level and above should be examined for superior performance. Minus SD points are not calculated for the CA baseline, because failures do not occur below the CA year level.

The MA baseline is at 14 (year-level XIV). One SD above this baseline falls at the 16–4 point, which is ten-twenty-fourths into year-level SA I. If we wish to describe tests that are well developed for his mental age level, we would discuss those above the 16–4 point, namely, those at year-level SA II (and year-level SA III if tests had been passed at this year level). One SD below the MA baseline is at 11–5, meaning five-twelfths into year-level XII. Tests failed below this point are relatively less well developed for his mental age baseline, but the failures do not reflect weaknesses, because they occur at a level above his CA baseline level.

The SD method furnishes a guide for locating the year levels at which the examinee's superior abilities lie. In discussing his performance, the examiner should bring out clearly the fact that he is not below average in any test areas. All tests were passed at the year level of the scale corresponding to his CA level. The specific tests (or pattern of tests) passed one, two, three, and four SD's above his CA level may be suggestive of areas of exceptional ability.

Example 3.

CA = 10	CA SD −1 = 8–7	MA SD +1 = 5–9
MA = 5	−2 = 6–11	+2 = 6–6
MA = 5	−3 = 5–2	+3 = 7–2
IQ = 50 ±3	−4 = 3–6	−1 = 4–4
		−2 = 3–7

Year level	Pass	Fail
III	Basal	
III-6	4 tests	2 tests
IV	4 tests	2 tests
IV-6	4 tests	2 tests
V	4 tests	2 tests
VI	2 tests	4 tests
VII	2 tests	4 tests
VIII		Ceiling

The IQ indicates that the examinee is functioning in the mentally retarded range of intelligence. He did not succeed in passing any tests at year levels above the −1 SD point (seven-twelfths of the way into year-level IX). Therefore, it is likely that he is below normal in all areas measured by the tests. The major focus of the report should deal with his deficient ability.

Extremely less well-developed ability, or retarded functioning, is reflected in tests failed at year levels below the −2 SD point, which in this example is 6–11 (eleven-twelfths of the way into year-level VII). Therefore, tests failed at year-level VII and below (this being a less conservative criterion because 6–11 is being rounded off to 7) reflect retarded functioning. Severely retarded functioning is represented by those tests failed at year levels below VI.

The MA baseline is 5 (year-level V). For his level of mental development, tests passed above the one SD point reflect better developed abilities, but abilities that are still below average. In the present example, the +1 SD point is nine-twelfths into year-level VI. Therefore, tests passed at year-level VII and above reflect better developed abilities for his MA level. Whenever the MA baseline is used, be sure that the reader of the report clearly understands that the abilities being discussed reflect *relative* strengths and weaknesses based on the examinee's achievements on the scale. In Example 3, all of the examinee's performances are at the borderline-retarded level, or retarded level, with respect to the normative group.

SCATTER ANALYSIS

Scatter analysis, a method that has been subject to much criticism but one that is still used occasionally, is discussed in this part of the chapter. There are two different kinds of approaches to what might be called "scatter analysis." The first method is the use of specific items or groups of items to determine specific functions in which the child is strong or weak. This method has been described in an earlier part of the chapter. The second is the assessment of variability in relation to the child's own level, disregarding the content of the items or groups of items. The second meaning of scatter is the focus of this part of the chapter.

The Concept of Scatter

Scatter, a qualitative feature of test performance, has been of interest to psychologists almost from the inception of the Binet-Simon scales. On the Stanford-Binet, scatter refers to the range of successes and failures from the basal to the ceiling level. Failing a test at a given year level and passing a test at higher year levels is the basis for deriving scatter scores. Test scatter has been used because it may provide valuable information to supplement quantitative indices of brightness. Scatter analysis incorporates the child's spread of successes, but it is not concerned with determining strengths and weaknesses in relation to the child's chronological and mental ages. In a sense, the evaluation of spread of successes can also be considered as a form of scatter analysis.

History of Scatter Analysis and the Stanford-Binet Scales

The history of scatter may be divided into two periods: the period up until the Harris and Shakow (1937) review, and the period after their review. Scatter has been approached by trying to account for the amount of scatter, that is, for the general unevenness in the distribution of successes and failures.

Period Before Harris and Shakow Review

Harris and Shakow in their review of literature up to 1937 evaluated nine different measures of scatter. The measures included range of scatter (number of age levels from the basal level to the level where all tests are failed), area of scatter (number of tests passed above and failed below the mental age level), and a combination of range and area of scatter. They concluded that research had failed to demonstrate clearly any valid clinical use for numerical measures of scatter. Furthermore, they were unable to recommend even one best measure among the nine.

Period After Harris and Shakow Review

Negative criticisms of the scatter approach to the Stanford-Binet continued to appear after the Harris-Shakow review (e.g., Garner, 1966; Hendriks, 1954; Hunt & Cofer, 1944; Lorr & Meister, 1941; McNemar, 1942). The technical criticisms of the use of scatter are numerous. Scatter may result from a number of factors inherent in the construction of the Stanford-Binet, including lack of perfect correlation among tests, test unreliability, incorrect order of test difficulty, lack of discriminatory power of certain tests, an increase in variability with an increase in absolute mean test performance, the presence of a series of tests that call for some special ability, and systematic errors in testing due to language handicaps, sensory defects, special training, lack of cooperation, and ambiguous scoring instructions. In succeeding revisions of the scale, the problems of test placement at year levels and special ability tests generally have been eliminated (McNemar). Scatter can occur even in the absence of any clinically significant variability in the examinee's responses (Garner). McNemar concluded that it is difficult to see how any clinical meaning can be attached to the concept of scatter. Lorr and Meister were opposed to the use of scatter as even a crude estimate of the measurement of error of the test for an individual examinee. However, in spite of all the negative criticism, Anderson (1951) was of the opinion that the interpretation of scatter still has clinical usefulness.

Research Studies Investigating Scatter

Studies and evaluations of scatter have continued to appear, primarily with exceptional children. Scatter has been found to be greater in emotionally disturbed children than in non-emotionally disturbed children in two studies (Schafer & Leitch, 1948; Vane, Weitzman, & Applebaum, 1966), while in another study scatter was not found to be useful in distinguishing an emotionally disturbed group of children from a normal group of children (Schneider & Smillie, 1959). In mentally retarded children, scatter has been reported to be significantly greater for retardates with organic etiology than either for retardates with familial etiology (Riggs & Burchard, 1952) or for normal children (Satter, 1955). Exogenous brain-injured children were found to have more scatter than endogenous brain-injured children (Berko, 1955a); scatter also has been found to be a measure of learning efficiency in brain-injured children (Berko, 1955b). Finally, with schizophrenic children, scatter has not been found to be useful as an indicator of higher potential ability (Gittleman & Birch, 1967).

Comment on Scatter Analysis

Clinicians and researchers continue to use scatter, although in tentative ways. The weight of evidence indicates that scatter cannot be used with any degree of certainty in assessing an individual examinee, although it may prove useful in generating hypotheses concerning the examinee. Scatter may be more useful in studying groups of examinees than in studying an individual examinee. Scatter, as Liverant (1960) observed, is the rule rather than the exception within any population (cf. Wallin, 1917; Wells, 1927), and may result from the acquisition of certain skills and not from abnormal conditions. Tests developed in the future may enable the examiner to use scatter in more reliable and valid ways.

SUMMARY

Factor analytic studies have appeared for each of the three forms of the Stanford-Binet. The major findings are that many Stanford-Binet tests load on a common factor, and that special group factors—such as verbal, memory, reasoning, and spatial—also appear at various year levels of the scale. The Stanford-Binet (Form L-M) appears to measure mainly verbal fluency and verbal reasoning abilities in the upper year levels, whereas the abilities measured at the lower year levels appear to be more diverse.

The results of factor analytic studies suggest that the factorial composition of a test cannot be prejudged accurately; a problem may be solved through the use of different abilities by different individuals and at different age levels; tests may show fairly high loadings on more than one factor, so that failure cannot be attributed to the lack of any one ability; and some clusters of tests have too low a reliability to have any real diagnostic value. It is important also to recognize that providing a name for a factor does not in the process insure that the factor is representative of some general ability.

Classifying Stanford-Binet tests into categories is a hazardous procedure, for it may lull the examiner into believing that stable and reliable abilities are being measured. Classification systems can serve as provisional, tentative guides for grouping tests in the scale in order to formulate hypotheses about the child's pattern of abilities. If classification systems are used, they should be thought of as rough, crude guideposts. Cognitive acts require complex and multifaceted behaviors. Reducing the act to a simple category name or factor name does not do justice to the psychological processes involved in the task.

One interesting classification system, based on Guilford's Structure of Intellect model, has been developed by Meeker. Another system, by Sattler, classifies Stanford-Binet tests into seven categories. A Binetgram provides a visual picture of the child's pattern of scores. Factor analytic studies and classification systems provide information that may prove to be useful for diagnostic work with the Stanford-Binet. However, the validity, reliability, and even utility of the classification systems are still unknown.

The standard deviation method is a useful procedure for evaluating a child's strengths and weaknesses on the Stanford-Binet. The child's chronological age and mental age can serve as guideposts for evaluating his pattern of performance. The standard deviation method requires flexibility, because the year level format of the Stanford-Binet places standard deviation points at various places within a year level. Even if the standard deviation method is not used, it is still necessary, if areas of strength and weakness are to be evaluated, to recognize that distances between year levels reflect different growth increments, depending on the year levels selected. For example, the distance between year-level II and year-level III, using year-level II as a baseline, represents a change of one-half. However, there is only a one-tenth change in going from year-level X to year-level XI, using year-level X as the baseline. The altitude quotient method has not been shown to be a valid procedure.

Scatter analysis, as applied to the Stanford-Binet, was once thought of as being a useful tool that could aid in the diagnostic process. While many different measures of scatter have been proposed, numerical measures of scatter generally have not been proved to be valid clinical tools. There are many technical reasons inherent in the construction of the Stanford-Binet (e.g., lack of perfect correlations among tests, test unreliability, and limited discriminatory power of some tests) that limit the application of scatter. Investigators occasionally report that scatter is a useful indication of adjustment level or of learning efficiency, but these findings have been based on limited samples of children and, for the most part, have not been replicated.

SECTION 4

WISC, WPPSI, AND OTHER TESTS

The point-scale format reached its peak of popularity with the introduction of the Wechsler scales. Section 4, which covers Chapters 11 through 18, presents a survey of the WISC, WPPSI, and other individual intelligence tests. Chapter 11 documents the early contribution of Yerkes to the development of point scales and shows how Wechsler developed his scales. The remainder of Chapter 11 is devoted to a consideration of the reliability, validity, and assets and limitations of the WISC.

The main theme of Chapter 12 concerns general issues that are involved in administering the WISC. The problems involved in using short forms and suggested ways of increasing their reliability are discussed. The chapter details the physical abilities that are necessary for taking the WISC and WPPSI, and highlights procedures that have been suggested for evaluating deaf or partially-hearing children.

Chapter 13 presents the clinical lore surrounding each of the 12 WISC subtests. Much of the material covered in the chapter is transferred from its cousins, the WAIS and Wechsler-Bellevue. However, the material is potentially useful to both clinical and school psychologists who are called upon to make educated decisions about their examinees. Administrative considerations for each of the 12 subtests also are presented.

Chapter 14 considers several topics related to the WISC. Factor analysis, scatter analysis, experimental attempts to evaluate subtest assumptions, and clinical interpretations are discussed. The approach to scatter analysis emphasizes the need to base subtest comparisons on a statistical foundation.

Chapters 15 through 17 approach the WPPSI with the same concerns that were expressed for the WISC. Because the scale is relatively new and the published literature is limited, it is difficult to evaluate the place that the WPPSI will have in the psychologist's battery. It is a good scale, but it has many of the limitations that are associated with the WISC.

Chapter 18 considers a variety of intelligence tests that are for the most part brief, easy to score, and relatively easy to administer. While the tests discussed in Chapter 18 provide less qualitative information and likely give less reliable and valid IQ's than the Stanford-Binet, WISC, and WPPSI, they are useful on certain occasions. Some of the tests also may be paired to provide a means of assessing language and nonlanguage skills. Examiners are encouraged to administer the tests covered in the chapter (as well as other intelligence tests) on at least one occasion in order to become acquainted with the test materials.

CHAPTER 11

WECHSLER INTELLIGENCE SCALE
FOR CHILDREN (WISC)

In Chapter 2, a brief introduction to the history of intelligence testing was presented, while a detailed history of the Stanford-Binet was presented in Chapter 8. The forces that shaped the Stanford-Binet are part of the heritage of all tests. Consequently, a knowledge of the material presented in Chapters 2 and 8 is required for an understanding of the development of the Wechsler scales, which are point scales. Our survey of the WISC begins by turning to the second decade of the twentieth century, when the major impetus for the construction of point scales developed.

YERKES'S CONTRIBUTION

Soon after the Binet scales were introduced to the United States, discontent with the age-scale format appeared. The leading spokesman against the age-scale format was Robert M. Yerkes (1876–1956), who, with Bridges and Hardwick, published the Point Scale in 1915. Yerkes (1917) believed that the age-scale format was radically different from the point-scale format in three ways: (a) the method of selecting the parts of the test; (b) the method of standardizing the tests or combinations of tests; and (c) the method of measuring the examinee's responses and of expressing his scores. Let us now consider how Yerkes developed these three points.

Tests are selected for the age scale on the basis of proportions of successes and failures in selected age groups. This procedure assumes that important forms of behavior appear at various points in development. In contrast, tests are selected for the point scale on the basis of their ability to measure various functions; the tests in the scale are not considered in relationship to stages of development. The heterogeneity of tests within the Stanford-Binet suggests that measurements made on individuals who differ in age are not strictly comparable, whereas the ideal of a point scale is to measure the same aspects of behavior at every age.

The Stanford-Binet is internally standardized, i.e., tests are selected according to percentage of passes and are grouped according to year level. The Point Scale is externally standardized. Tests are selected that are independent of the development of specific norms. Therefore, the Point Scale was characterized as being more flexible than the Stanford-Binet.

The Stanford-Binet uses an all-or-none scoring procedure for each test, while the Point Scale uses a more-or-less scoring procedure. The point-scale format provides some credit for each correct answer, and thereby was thought to produce a more effective basis for statistical handling of data.

General comparisons between the Binet and point-scale formats are shown in Table 11-1. We have seen that many of the difficulties in the Stanford-Binet to which Yerkes alluded in Table 11-1 have been cleared up in subsequent revisions of the scale. Yerkes's overall criticism was that the constructors of the Binet not only avoided repeating tests, but also avoided including more difficult versions of the same tests. Tests appear to be distributed throughout the year levels in a haphazard manner, and their placement at particular year levels, Yerkes believed, was not based on any scientific principle.

WECHSLER'S SEARCH FOR SUBTESTS

In designing the Wechsler-Bellevue Intelligence Scale, Form I (the forerunner to Form II and the WISC and WPPSI), Wechsler studied the standardized tests that were available during the later 1930's and selected 11 different subtests to form the scale. Sources for the subtests included the Army Alpha (for Information and Comprehension), Stanford-Binet (for Comprehension, Arithmetic, Digit Span, Similarities, and Vocabulary), Healy Picture Completion Tests and other tests having picture completion items (for Picture Completion), Army Group Examinations (for Picture Arrangement), Kohs Block Design test (for Block Design), and Army Beta (for Digit Symbol and Coding). Wechsler designed original material for all subtests, although in some cases items were only slightly modified from those appearing on other scales.

Wechsler's search for subtests was guided by his conception of intelligence, which focused on the global nature of intelligence. Wechsler considered intelligence to be a part of a larger whole, namely personality itself. The WISC was designed to take into account factors that contribute to the total effective intelligence of the individual. However, no attempt was made to design a series of subtests that measure "primary abilities" or to order the subtests

Table 11-1. COMPARISONS BETWEEN BINET AND POINT SCALES

BINET CHARACTERISTICS	POINT SCALE CHARACTERISTICS
Multiple-group, age or year scale	Single graded-test scale
Selection by relation of successes to age	Selection by function measured
Varied, unrelated, ungraded tests	Each test so graded as to be available for wide range of ages
Internally standardized and inflexible	Externally standardized and flexible
All-or-none judgments	More-or-less judgments
Qualitative	Quantitative
Measurements only slightly amenable to statistical treatment	Measurements wholly amenable to statistical treatment
Tests weighted equally	Tests weighted unequally
Implicit assumption, that of appearing functions	Implicit assumption, that of developing functions
Measurements for different ages relatively incomparable	Measurements for different ages relatively comparable

(Reprinted by permission of the publisher from R. M. Yerkes, "The Binet versus the Point Scale Method of Measuring Intelligence," *Journal of Applied Psychology,* **1,** p. 117. Copyright 1917, American Psychological Association.)

into a hierarchy of relative importance (Wechsler & Weider, 1953). The overall IQ obtained from the scale represents an index of general mental ability.

DESCRIPTION OF THE WISC

The WISC (Wechsler, 1949) was developed as a downward extension of the Wechsler-Bellevue Intelligence Scale, and, in particular, of Form II of the adult scales. To make Form II more suitable for children, easier items were added to the low end of the subtests. The WISC is applicable to children between the ages of 5–0 and 15–11 years.

The WISC contains 12 subtests, six of which form the Verbal Scale (Information, Comprehension, Arithmetic, Similarities, Vocabulary, and Digit Span) and the other six, the Performance Scale (Picture Completion, Picture Arrangement, Block Design, Object Assembly, Coding, and Mazes). The IQ tables in the manual are based on 10 of the 12 subtests. The two subtests excluded, Digit Span and Mazes, are supplementary subtests. When more than 10 subtests are administered (or on those occasions when fewer than 10 subtests are administered), prorating is necessary. The last page of the manual provides a table for prorating the scores obtained when four or six subtests are administered.

The WISC was standardized on 2200 white American boys and girls selected to be representative of the 1940 U.S. census. However, in the standardization group there was an overrepresentation of children from the middle and upper socioeconomic levels. Therefore, children from ethnic minority groups, or from lower socioeconomic groups, may be penalized because they were not represented adequately in developing the norms (see Chapter 4 for further discussion of this point).

Wechsler developed the WISC and the other Wechsler scales without using the mental-age concept, which, together with the ratio IQ, he found to be limited in a number of ways. The criticisms associated with the mental-age concept are discussed in Chapter 3. Wechsler, in particular, was willing to accept the mental-age concept if it was limited to a level of test performance (Wechsler & Weider, 1953). However, he believed that more than this operational definition is implied or subsumed. For example, Wechsler rejected the notion that mental age be considered to represent an absolute level of mental capacity, with the assumption, difficult to verify, that the same mental age in different children represents identical intelligence levels.

However, soon after the initial publication of the WISC, Wechsler recognized that mental-age equivalents also would be useful; in subsequent editions of the WISC manual a table of mental-age equivalents was presented. Wechsler considered the mental-age equivalents as guides to facilitate interpreting the examinee's performance, and not as a means for calculating intelligence quotients.

In the Wechsler scales, the IQ is a deviation IQ that is obtained by comparing each examinee's scores with the scores earned by a representative sample of his own age group. IQ's obtained by this method are standard scores, so that the mean IQ's and standard deviations at each age level are equal (100 and 15, respectively). IQ's obtained on successive retests give the examinee's relative position in the age group to which he belongs at each time of testing. This procedure avoided the problems that were associated with the unequal standard deviations found on the Stanford-Binet prior to the 1960 revision. After the raw scores on each subtest are obtained, they are converted to normalized standard scores within the examinee's own age group. Tables in the manual are provided for the conversion by four-month age intervals between ages 5 and 16 years. Each subtest has a mean scaled score of 10 and a standard deviation of 3.

RELIABILITY AND STABILITY

The WISC manual reported split-half reliability coefficients for the three separate scales and for 10 of the 12 subtests, with the exceptions of Coding and Digit Span. For the Coding subtest an alternate-form procedure was used to establish reliability, while reliability was established for the Digit Span subtest by correlating Digits Forward with Digits Backward. Coefficients are presented for ages $7\frac{1}{2}$, $10\frac{1}{2}$, and $13\frac{1}{2}$ years. The reliability coefficients are .92 to .95 for the Full Scale, .88 to .96 for the Verbal Scale, and .86 to .90 for the Performance Scale. The reliabilities for the subtests range from a low of .59 for the Comprehension and Picture Completion subtests at the $7\frac{1}{2}$ age level to a high of .91 for the Vocabulary subtest at the $10\frac{1}{2}$ age level. The standard errors of measurement in IQ points for the three scales range from 3.00 to 5.19.

Reliability and stability studies provide continued support for the WISC as a reliable and stable instrument (e.g., Caldwell, 1954; Gehman & Matyas, 1956; Hagen, 1952; Hite, 1953; Jones, 1962; also see Chapter 22 for studies with mentally retarded children and Chapter 23 for studies with emotionally disturbed children). These data indicate that the WISC is a reliable instrument for normal, emotionally disturbed, and mentally retarded children and that it provides stable IQ's.

VALIDITY

Littell (1960) presented an excellent discussion of the many factors involved in evaluating the content, predictive, concurrent, and construct validities of the WISC. Some of his points are briefly noted and are brought up to date with the citing of current literature.

Content Validity

With respect to content validity, Littell indicated that

the WISC appears to lack any explicitly stated, organized network of intuitive reasons for expecting it to show predictive validity other than the very broad assumption of a general factor which enters into the purposeful solution of all problems — *whether they occur in a test or in the child's life* [p. 135].

Because there is little evidence to judge the extent to which nonintellective factors enter into a child's actual behavior in responding to the test questions, users of the WISC are forced to depend on whatever demonstrated criterion-oriented and construct validity the WISC might have.

Predictive Validity

When Littell wrote his review he indicated that there was little evidence of the value of the WISC as a predictor of subsequent behavior. However, many studies that are covered in this text, especially those reported in Section 5, attest to the predictive validity of the WISC.

Concurrent Validity

The majority of the reports concerning the concurrent validity (or comparative validity) of the WISC usually have correlated the WISC with other well known, standardized, individually administered or group administered tests. In this part of the chapter we present five separate groups of comparisons: (a) the WISC with the Stanford-Binet, (b) the WISC with the Wechsler-Bellevue, (c) the WISC with the WAIS, (d) the WISC with other intelligence tests, and (e) the WISC with other measures of achievement. Studies comparing the WISC and WPPSI appear in Chapter 15, whereas those comparing the WISC and primarily nonverbal tests appear in Chapter 18.

WISC and Stanford-Binet. The bulk of studies have used the Stanford-Binet as the criterion for evaluating the comparative validity of the WISC. Table B-2 in the Appendix lists 47 different studies comparing the WISC and Stanford-Binet. The studies indicate that the two scales are highly comparable (correlation coefficients range from .44 to .92 for the Verbal Scale and Stanford-Binet; .30 to .86 for the Performance Scale and Stanford-Binet; and .43 to .94 for the Full Scale and Stanford-Binet, with a median correlation of .80). The WISC Full and Verbal Scales correlate highest with the Stanford-Binet, followed by the Performance Scale. The studies, however, also indicate that the two scales do not yield comparable mean IQ's. Every study that investigated children scoring in the Superior range on the Stanford-Binet reported mean WISC IQ's that were below those obtained on the Stanford-Binet. In two of those studies, means differed by as much as 16 and 18 points in favor of the Stanford-Binet (Estes, 1965; Estes, Curtin, DeBurger, & Denny, 1961). Children obtaining IQ's in the Bright Normal and Normal ranges on the Stanford-Binet also obtained higher IQ's on the Stanford-Binet than on the WISC. It is only in the ranges below the Normal that the two scales provided mean IQ's that are comparable. The results of the studies shown in Table B-2 indicate that the two scales cannot be considered to provide comparable IQ's.

WISC and Wechsler-Bellevue. The WISC and Wechsler-Bellevue overlap for the chronological ages of 10 through 15 years. Table B-3 in the Appendix lists studies that have compared the two scales for the overlapping year levels and one study for the 17-year-old level. The studies indicate that the two scales appear to be related to a significant degree (.54 to .90 for the Verbal Scales; .41 to .82 for the Performance Scales; and .70 to .89 for the Full Scales, with a median correlation of .78). Wechsler-Bellevue Verbal Scale IQ's (and to a lesser extent, Full Scale IQ's) tend to be lower than WISC IQ's, while Performance Scale IQ's appear to be more similar for the two scales.

WISC and WAIS. The WAIS, which replaced the Wechsler-Bellevue, overlaps with the WISC at the 16-year age level. Studies that have compared the two scales at this age level (or close to this age level), as well as longitudinal studies using the two scales, are listed in Table B-4 of the Appendix. The studies indicate that there is a high degree of comparability between the two scales (.66 to .96 for the two Verbal Scales; .51 to .92 for the two Performance Scales; and .70 to .95 for the two Full Scales, with a median correlation of .84). The WAIS yields IQ's that are, on the average, eight points higher than WISC IQ's in mentally retarded samples. In contrast, WISC IQ's tend to be higher than WAIS IQ's in samples of bright children.

WISC and Other Intelligence Tests. The studies listed in Table B-5 of the Appendix usually have used the WISC as the criterion against which other tests have been validated. The three tests most frequently appearing in the studies listed in Table B-5 are the Columbia Test of Mental Maturity, Draw-a-Man, and Progressive Matrices. The correlations with the WISC Full Scale for these three tests run from .49 to .74 (median correlation of .62), .04 to .59 (median correlation of .36), and .27 to .91 (median correlation of .51), respectively. While some correlations between the WISC and other tests are rather low, they suggest generally that the WISC provides an adequate general measure of intelligence. The Draw-a-Man test has not been found to correlate highly with the WISC in samples of emotionally disturbed children (cf. Hanvick, 1953), possibly because these children may be led by their disturbance to draw the human figure in an idiosyncratic way.

WISC and Measures of Achievement.   Table B-6 of the Appendix lists studies that have correlated the WISC with measures of achievement. Correlations between the WISC Full Scale and measures of achievement range from a low of .14 to a high of .81, with a median correlation of .61. The studies suggest that the WISC is usefully related to scores on academic achievement tests for a variety of groups of children (cf. Littell, 1960).

Construct Validity

There is still limited evidence for the construct validity of the individual subtests that combine to form the scale. However, factor analytic studies from a variety of sources, and some studies evaluating assumptions of WISC subtests, provide support for the factorial distinction between the Verbal and Performance Scales and for some of the construct validity of the WISC (see Chapter 14).

ASSETS AND LIMITATIONS OF THE WISC

The concluding part of this chapter discusses some of the assets and limitations of the WISC, primarily as assessed by reviewers of the scale. The assets of the WISC (as well as its limitations) will become more apparent as one studies the material in Chapters 12, 13, and 14, and in Section 5. The reader may note that in this part of the chapter more space is devoted to the limitations of the WISC than to its assets. This simply is due to the inclusion of details of studies that evaluated various features of the scale. The wealth of studies with the WISC, as is seen throughout the remainder of Section 4 and in Section 5, attests to its popularity and to its value as a scale of intelligence.

Assets of the WISC

The WISC was greeted warmly by most reviewers. Shaffer's (1949) prediction that the scale would be used widely by clinicians and would be evaluated by a wealth of studies has proved to be accurate. The scale was characterized as being modern in construction and in standardization (Delp, 1953b). The subtests generally are easy to administer; the manual is easy to handle, with clear directions and tables; the material is interesting to children; the norms are good; and the record booklet is convenient. Verbal, Performance, and Full Scale IQ's are provided for all age groups. Clinical observations of the child's behavior may also be made. A valuable feature of the WISC is that all children take a comparable battery, which contains all the available subtests (McCandless, 1953b). McCandless believed that the WISC was generally a good test and a useful addition to the testing field.

The method of calculating the IQ, a procedure that is particularly useful in the upper age levels where the mental-age concept breaks down, was found to be valuable (Fraser, 1959). The standardization samples were adequate and the reliability of the scale was good. Fraser concluded:

To sum up: For testing children who are not outstandingly bright or markedly dull, the WISC is a convenient, reliable instrument which uses up-to-date material intrinsically interesting to the child; for very young children, and for children at the extreme ranges of intelligence, this reviewer still recommends the Stanford-Binet [p. 559].

Two other reviewers also were impressed with the scale. Burstein (1965) noted that reliability and concurrent validity studies indicated that the WISC is a well-standardized, stable instrument, correlating well with other tests of intelligence. Patterson (1959) wrote that the scale represents one of the major contributions to the field of intelligence testing with children.

Limitations of the WISC

The WISC, as we have seen, is generally considered to be a very satisfactory instrument, yet there are a number of difficulties with the scale and with the manual that should be recognized. These are considered now.

Applicability of Norms for 5-Year-Old Children

One of the major questions about the WISC concerns the applicability of the norms for children 5 to 6 years old (cf. Anderson, 1953; Delp, 1953b; Fraser, 1959; Garner, 1966; Rabin, 1959; Ross, 1959). In standardizing the WISC, children were tested within 1.5 months of the midyear of their birthdate. Consequently, in the 5-year-old age level the children were past 5 years, 4 months but were not yet 5 years, 7 months—no children were included who were between 5 years, zero months and 5 years, 3 months. Nevertheless, the WISC manual presents norms for this three-month period. Because the standardized scores were arrived at by extrapolation, the norms may not be adequate for this age group.

A study of gifted children between the ages of 5–0 and 5–3 years also suggested that the norms may not be adequate for this age group of children (Beldoch, 1963). The children obtained WISC IQ's that were approximately 10 points lower than gifted children who were older than 5–3. On retest 11 months later, the younger group was at a level that was equal to the older group. Beldoch concluded that gifted children between 5–0 and 5–3 years of age are penalized by the WISC norms.

Limited Floor and Ceiling

A second major problem with the WISC is that the range of IQ's (46 to 154) is insufficient, so that children who have a mental age below five or who are gifted may not be assessed properly. A 5-year-old child can obtain an IQ of 52 without giving any correct answers. Age 12 is the first age at which a raw score of zero does not receive credit on any of the subtests. Even for a Verbal Scale IQ of 80, only a very small sample of the child's ability is tested. Thus, sampling of test performance is inadequate in the lower age groups, particularly among the mentally retarded (Fraser, 1959; Garner, 1966).

The difficulty in assessing gifted children with the WISC was illustrated in a study by Lucito and Gallagher (1960). The children, who were between the ages of 7 and 11 years, had obtained Stanford-Binet IQ's of 150 or higher. Then on the WISC, they obtained a mean Verbal Scale IQ of 139, a mean Performance Scale IQ of 136, and a mean Full Scale IQ of 141. Between 10 and 20 per cent of the children were performing at the ceiling on the Information, Vocabulary, and Block Design subtests, and 30 per cent, on the Similarities subtest. These results indicate that the ceiling on the WISC is too low for gifted children.

To partially remedy the problem of a limited floor and ceiling, reports have provided extrapolated IQ's which extend the IQ tables down to the minimum possible sum of scaled scores (Ogdon, 1960; Silverstein, 1963c) and up to the maximum possible sum of scaled scores (Silverstein, 1968c). Extrapolated IQ's must be used with caution, because they are projected IQ's; i.e., they are not based on the actual performance of children in the standardization group. In addition, as the IQ extrapolated values become lower and lower, the accuracy of the extrapolated values becomes less and less.

Scoring Responses

The WISC manual contains fewer samples of acceptable responses than the Stanford-Binet manual (McCandless, 1953b). Considerable subjectivity is involved in scoring responses for some of the Verbal subtests (Comprehension, Similarities, and Vocabulary, in particular); this topic is considered further in the evaluation of the individual subtests in Chapter 13. A recent study by Sattler and Ryan (1973b) indicated that part of the difficulty in scoring may be connected with the particular examples used to illustrate the scoring criteria.

These investigators selected 20 sample responses from the WISC manual for 10 WISC Vocabulary words and presented the responses, along with the scoring criteria for the Vocabulary subtest, to linguists, English professors, graduate students, and undergraduate students. The raters were not familiar with the WISC. They were asked to score the 20 responses using the WISC scoring criteria. Considerable scoring disagreement was found between the scores given by the raters and those appearing in the manual. Disagreement was most pronounced for three responses that are scored zero in the manual ("a piece on furniture" for "cushion," "clean" for "aseptic," and "get smaller" for "recede"). One or both professional groups, as well as student raters, awarded these responses at least one point of credit. Overall, the four groups gave mean total scores that were from 70% to 117% higher than the mean total scores indicated in the manual. The raters also were highly confident of their ratings. The results suggested that a review of the WISC scoring manual for the Vocabulary subtest needs to be undertaken.

Other Difficulties

Anderson (1953) was, perhaps, the severest critic of the WISC. He suggested that an alternate form of the WISC should have been available before the scale was published. He found directions for administering some of the subtests confusing, because there are double directions for some subtests ("for subjects under 8 and older suspected mental defectives" and "for 8 year olds and over"). Since the norms are based on 10 subtests, there is no way of knowing precisely what the scores mean when 12 subtests are administered. Anderson suggested that only the 10 standard subtests be administered, and suggested prorating when fewer subtests are given. He also questioned the procedure of disregarding days in computing the chronological age, particularly at the lower levels. Anderson concluded: "the inherent weaknesses of the test make it an unsatisfactory instrument which, in the field of testing children, cannot compare with the more adequate Stanford-Binet [p. 363]."

Other difficulties in using the WISC have been noted. WISC norms may not be applicable to children who are from ethnic and cultural groups and from socioeconomic levels that are different from those represented in the standardization group (Garner, 1966; McCandless, 1953b). (Chapter 4 discusses the problems involved in testing ethnic minority group and "culturally disadvantaged children.") When easier items are given to some children and not to others (i.e., in starting with items for children younger than 8 years of age), a procedure is introduced that was not taken into account in the standardization of the scale (Ross, 1959). The manual fails to give means, standard deviations, and frequency distributions for the raw scores (Maxwell, 1961b). While the manual also fails to give adequate validity data (Delp, 1953b; McCandless, 1953b; Shaffer, 1949), subsequent research, as we have seen, attests to the validity of the WISC (cf. Littell, 1960; Zimmerman & Woo-Sam, 1972). There are difficulties in the interpretation of subtest scores (Delp, 1953b) and profiles (McCandless, 1953b). These latter two points are discussed more fully in Chapters 13 and 14, and in the chapters presented in Section 5.

SUMMARY

The WISC was developed as a reaction against the age-scale format of the Stanford-Binet. While Yerkes and his co-workers had recognized early the advantages of the point-scale format, it was Wechsler who systematized and organized a series of subtests into a standardized scale. Wechsler's search for subtests was guided by a conception of intelligence that emphasized its global nature. The forerunner of the WISC was Form II of the Wechsler-Bellevue Intelligence Scale.

The material in the WISC is well suited to the testing of children. Research has shown that it is a reliable, stable, and valid instrument, correlating well with other individually and group administered intelligence and achievement tests. However, the WISC and Stanford-Binet do not provide IQ's that are comparable, especially in the upper IQ ranges. IQ's on the Stanford-Binet are higher than those on the WISC for bright children.

The Verbal, Performance, and Full Scale IQ's on the WISC are standard scores with means of 100 and standard deviations of 15. This procedure for calculating IQ's is particularly valuable, for IQ's at each age level are comparable throughout the range of the test. Mental age equivalents are also available, but are not used in the calculation of the IQ.

The following are some of the major limitations of the WISC:

1. Limited applicability of norms for ages between 5 and 6 years.

2. Limited range of IQ's (46 to 154).

3. Difficulty in scoring responses, especially for the Comprehension, Similarities, and Vocabulary subtests.

4. Limited applicability of norms to ethnic minority group children.

5. Difficulties in interpreting subtest scores.

Overall, the WISC represents a major contribution to the field of intelligence testing of children.

CHAPTER 12

ADMINISTERING THE WISC

The general procedures discussed in Chapters 5, 6, and 7 for administering psychological tests and the procedures discussed in Chapter 9 for the Stanford-Binet should prove to be helpful in administering the WISC. However, there are problems associated with the administration and scoring of the WISC that are not encountered with the Stanford-Binet; for each different test, the special procedures must be mastered. Some confusion may arise in administering the WISC because there are some subtests on the WAIS and WPPSI that are similar to those on the WISC, but that have different instructions and time limits. Extreme care is needed in using the procedures that are appropriate for the particular scale.

PHYSICAL ABILITIES NECESSARY FOR TAKING THE WISC (AND WPPSI)

The physical abilities that are necessary in order for the child to respond to each WISC (and WPPSI) subtest are shown in Table C-9 of the Appendix (Allen & Jefferson, 1962). Vision or hearing (or both) are necessary for most of the Verbal Scale subtests, while vision and arm-hand use are necessary for the Performance Scale subtests. The last two parts of this chapter discuss techniques for administering the WISC to handicapped children.

SUGGESTIONS FOR AND ISSUES INVOLVED IN ADMINISTERING THE WISC

Specific and detailed suggestions supplementing those presented in the WISC manual are covered in Chapter 13 for each WISC subtest. This section discusses some general issues. As a general rule, considerable practice is necessary in order to gain familiarity with the test materials before the scale is actually administered to a child. The Verbal Scale subtests are generally easier to administer than the Performance Scale subtests, but they also are more difficult to score. A stopwatch is very useful in administering the timed WISC subtests.

The problems associated with test administration, test scoring, and completing the record booklet, which have been pointed out in Chapter 9 in discussing the Stanford-Binet, also pertain to the WISC and other similar individually administered tests. The record booklet should be clearly and accurately completed and responses recorded verbatim. Checking all calculations is an absolute necessity, as is the checking of the transformation of raw scores to scaled scores and of scaled scores to IQ's. The correct calculation of the child's chronological age also is, of course, important. Examiners should try to develop proper administrative procedures early in their testing career.

General Problems in Administering the WISC

In administering the WISC, beginning examiners have been observed to display the following problems:
1. Failing to adhere to directions.
2. Making errors in timing.
3. Reading questions too quickly or too slowly.
4. Failing to question ambiguous or vague responses.
5. Failing to clear the table of unessential materials. (At times it looks as though the examiner is hiding behind the materials.)
6. Failing to record responses.
7. Failing to administer the subtests in proper order.
8. Providing too much help for the child.
9. Giving items beyond "discontinuance point."
10. Failing to credit all responses.
11. Making errors in converting raw scores to scaled scores.
12. Prorating errors.
13. Using incorrect time-bonus credits.
14. Using wrong norms.

General Suggestions for Specific Subtests

Comprehension.   Do not probe an obvious one-point response in an attempt to make it a two-point response.

Vocabulary.   Do not spell the Vocabulary words for the child. The word may be repeated as often as necessary. Correct pronunciation of the Vocabulary words is especially important.

Picture Completion.   It is especially important to observe the time limits on the Picture Completion subtest, because the child is allotted only 15 seconds.

Picture Arrangement.   The Picture Arrangement cards should be laid out one at a time from the child's left to right, in the order indicated.

Block Design.   The Block Design subtest requires considerable practice in order to develop administrative skill. It is necessary to scramble the blocks before each new block design is administered. Only the proper number of blocks needed for the item should be placed before the child. The child must be given nine blocks for items requiring this number of blocks.

Object Assembly.   It is important that the child does not see the WISC manual, which contains pictures of the correct objects. The screen used to set up the individual puzzle parts can be the cover of the manual, if desired. Be sure to place the Object Assembly pieces close to the child so that he does not lose time in attempting to reach the pieces.

Discontinuance Procedures

While the manual sets specific cutoff points for discontinuing various subtests, an adequate rationale behind such procedures never has been furnished. A study designed to determine the effects of discontinuance procedures on the WISC (and WAIS) in a sample of children between 5 and 18 years of age, equally divided by sex, found that the cutoffs presently employed for five of the seven WISC subtests that use cutoffs (Comprehension, Arithmetic, Similarities, Digit Span, and Picture Completion) are satisfactory, while the cutoffs for two subtests (Information and Vocabulary) are not (Quereshi, 1968d). More optimal cutoffs could be obtained for the Information and Vocabulary subtests by lowering the cutoffs by one. These results suggest that the discontinuance procedures presently employed in the manual generally are satisfactory.

Scoring WISC Responses

In Chapter 13, scoring suggestions are presented for some of the WISC subtests. Detailed scoring suggestions appear in Appendix A for the Comprehension, Similarities, and Vocabulary subtests. This part of the present chapter evaluates some general findings related to the scoring of WISC responses. Dramatic differences in the scoring standards of examiners have been illustrated in a number of reports. In one study, 99 school psychologists with credentials gave IQ's ranging from 63 to 117 to the same WISC protocol (Massey, 1964). Both graduate-student examiners (Miller, Chansky, & Gredler, 1970) and members of the American Psychological Association (Miller & Chansky, 1972) have been found to vary in the scores given to the same WISC responses. The graduate students gave IQ's ranging from 76 to 93 to the same protocol, whereas the professional raters gave IQ's ranging from 78 to 95. The types of mechanical errors made by the raters are shown in Table 12–1. The most frequent error made in both groups was crediting items after the cutoff criteria. Clerical errors—such as incorrect scoring, additions, and score transformations—have been reported in another study (Hannon & Kicklighter, 1970).

The Scottish Council for Research in Education (1967) reported the results of an investigation in which five trained examiners scored the Vocabulary subtest for 218 protocols. The raters differed by as little as one point on some protocols, and by as much as 17 points on another protocol; the mean difference was 5.13, which was significantly greater than zero. Some raters were

Table 12-1. MECHANICAL ERRORS IN SCORING WISC PROTOCOLS

TYPE OF ERROR	SCHOOL PSYCHOLOGISTS IN TRAINING (N = 99) Frequency of error (%)	PROFESSIONAL PSYCHOLOGISTS (N = 64) Frequency of error (%)
Credited item after cut-off	21	44
Credited an incorrect response	16	3
Calculation error in adding raw scores of subtest	10	5
Failed to check all Coding responses	10	14
Error in converting raw score to scaled score	7	5
Error in adding scaled scores together	3	1
Incorrect prorating procedure	10	3
Failed to credit non-administered passed items	3	5
Omitted scoring a subtest	6	2
Improper credit for a timed item	4	3
Incorrectly converted scaled scores to IQ	3	3
Failed to credit a correct item	6	11

(Reprinted, by permission of the publisher and authors, from C. K. Miller, N. M. Chansky, and G. R. Gredler, "Rater Agreement on WISC Protocols," *Psychology in the Schools,* **7,** p. 192, copyright 1970; and from C. K. Miller and N. M. Chansky, "Psychologists' Scoring of WISC Protocols," *Psychology in the Schools,* **9,** p. 149, copyright 1972, Clinical Psychology Publishing Co., Inc.)

more lenient than others and, at times, the raters did not adhere consistently to their own relative standards. On some occasions, for example, the rater who was generally strict was more lenient than the raters who were generally lenient. An examination of the four protocols that showed the most variability in scoring revealed that the variability appeared to arise from the coincidence of a number of factors. There was a larger-than-usual number of borderline answers, supplementary questioning was not always adequate, instructions were not always followed, and there was an abundance of clerical errors. The Council pointed out that examiners must attempt to be as objective as possible by guarding against interpreting what the child actually said as something that they thought the child wanted to say but could not express (see Chapter 5 for related information).

Other reports have shown that WISC Comprehension, Similarities, and Vocabulary responses, in particular, are difficult to score (Kaspar, Throne, & Schulman, 1968; Mahan, 1963; Sattler, Winget, & Roth, 1969). These studies demonstrate that examiners must be extremely vigilant in administering and scoring the WISC. The findings also indicate that the scoring guides in the manual are not sufficiently detailed to handle the many varied responses that are given by children. The results of many of the studies are striking, for they point out the need for examiners to study the scoring criteria in the manuals very carefully. Improved scoring manuals may help to reduce this source of examiner variability. Appendix A presents some additional scoring suggestions that should be helpful in scoring WISC responses.

MODIFYING STANDARD PROCEDURES

The WISC is begun with the Information subtest, followed by the remaining Verbal Scale subtests in the order indicated in the manual. However, Palmer (1970) suggested that the Vocabulary subtest be administered first, followed by Information, Comprehension, Similarities, and Arithmetic, because such a sequence is more natural than the order specified in the manual. However, Palmer did not present any evidence for his statement. It is recommended that the standard order of administering the subtests be followed, unless there is some compelling reason to use another order. A rearranged order constitutes a departure from standard procedures. (Suggestions for modifying test procedures in administering the WISC to handicapped children are presented in the last two parts of the chapter.)

Revised WISC Vocabulary Subtest

Jastak and Jastak (1964) presented a revised and shortened form of the WISC (and WAIS) Vocabulary subtest. The revised WISC Vocabulary subtest contains 25 words that are scored 0, 1, or 2. The scoring criteria were modified to eliminate the contradictions and inconsistencies that are present in the scoring instructions for the regular WISC Vocabulary subtest. A thorough scoring guide is presented and administrative procedures are changed. Each child begins with the first word on the subtest, and the subtest is discontinued after 10 consecutive failures. A table is presented for converting raw scores on the revised subtest to standard raw scores.

The population used to investigate the validity and reliability of the revised Vocabulary subtest consisted of 1248 children between the ages of 5 and 15 years, 65 per cent of whom had been referred for counseling. Correlation coefficients between the revised and standard subtests for a sample of 100 boys and 100 girls at three age levels ranged from .88 to .93, while split-half reliabilities ranged from .81 to .92. These coefficients are similar to those reported for the standard Vocabulary subtest. Jastak and Jastak's contribution lies, in part, in its careful attention to scoring and discontinuance criteria, and in its demonstration of the importance of qualitative scoring. While many examiners may not wish to substitute the revised Vocabulary subtest for the standard Vocabulary subtest, they will benefit from a careful study of the material presented in the Jastak and Jastak monograph.

Rewording Questions

Suggestions have been made for rewording certain WISC questions. One suggestion is to use the optional wording given in the WISC manual for the Comprehension subtest question, "What is the thing to do if you lose one of your friend's balls?" to "What is the thing to do if you lose a ball that belongs to one of your friends?" because rural children may be penalized by the standard wording (Eisenman & McBride, 1964). ("Balls" is slang for "testicles.") Another suggestion is to change the Information subtest question, "What does C.O.D. mean?" to "What do the letters C.O.D. stand for?" because lower class children may misinterpret the question in its standard form (Coyle, 1965). ("Cod" is a vulgarism for "scrotum."). Neither of these suggested changes was supported with research findings. Therefore, while they are interesting, it is recommended that the standard wording be used and the alternate wording be given in those cases in which misinterpretation was evident. The alternate wording then can be used as a testing-of-limits procedure.

Spreen and Tryk (1970) demonstrated that it cannot be assumed on an *a priori* basis that rewording questions in order to make them more appropriate for a specific population will automatically lead to acceptable items. WISC Information items 17 and 19 were reworded and presented to Canadian children between the ages of 7 and 14 years. One substitution ("How tall is the average Canadian man?" for item 19) was found to be reasonable, but the other was not ("What is celebrated on the first of July?" for item 17).

Procedural Changes

Four of the five studies covered in this part of the chapter found that procedural changes affected scores significantly. One study focused on the effects of having third-grade children talk about the procedure they were using while they were taking three WISC Performance Scale subtests (Post, 1970). The examiner asked such questions as "Tell me about the story," "Tell me what happened next," and "Tell me how you will begin." The group that was encouraged to vocalize achieved scores higher than did those in the control group on the Picture Arrangement and Object Assembly subtests, but not on the Block Design subtest. Because standard time limits were doubled, it is difficult to know whether vocalization would affect performance on subtests that are administered under standard conditions.

When 11-year-old children were asked to think about their answers before responding, they achieved significantly higher scores than did a control group on three of the four subtests studied—namely, Comprehension, Similarities, and Mazes, but not Block Design (Schwebel & Bernstein, 1970). Having children (from 6 through 15 years) explain Picture Arrangement stories has been found to facilitate performance by an average of 2 scaled-score points (Herrell & Golland, 1969). Three different modes of administering the Vocabulary subtest (neutral presentation, examiner's reading aloud the child's responses, and a permissive, encouraging examiner manner) were not found to affect significantly the scores of upper middle class children between the ages of 6 and 8 years (Brodt & Walker, 1969).

The effects of cues on the WISC and Wechsler-Bellevue Picture Arrangement and Block Design subtests were the focus of another investigation
(Sattler, 1969). In the first experiment, only the Block Design subtest was administered. When an item was failed, the children were given one cue (e.g.,
showing how the first row was arranged). This procedure did not significantly
affect the scores on either the initial or repeated administration of the subtest.
In a second experiment, the Picture Arrangement and Block Design subtests
were studied. Instead of one cue, a series of cues was given for each item that
was failed. For example, on the Picture Arrangement subtest the first cue consisted of 50% additional time. If the child again failed a Picture Arrangement
item, a specified number of cards were arranged in the correct order and the
child was asked to complete the sequence. If the child was still unsuccessful,
the examiner arranged a greater number of cards than in the second cue. A similar procedure was used for the Block Design subtest. These procedures
resulted in significantly higher scores on both the initial and repeated administration of both subtests. The results illustrate, in part, the dangers involved
when the examiner deviates from the standard procedures.

TESTING THE LIMITS ON THE WISC: ALTITUDE QUOTIENT

The general testing-of-limits suggestions presented in Chapter 5 can be
applied to the WISC. Additional suggestions and procedures for specific WISC
subtests are presented in Chapter 13. In this part we focus on the Altitude Quotient.

Various methods have been proposed for obtaining an Altitude Quotient
for the WISC. The intent of an Altitude Quotient is to provide an index that
may be a more valid predictor of learning ability than is the standard IQ. One
method consists of averaging the three highest subtest scaled scores and then
multiplying the average by 10 (Salvati, 1960). This method, when applied to a
sample of institutionalized mentally retarded children, failed to predict rate of
learning better than the standard IQ. Consequently, no support was provided
for the hypothesis that the Altitude Quotient was an index of latent capacity or
that it was a better predictor than the standard IQ of rate of learning. Using a
second method, Fisher (1961) averaged the two highest subtest scores to obtain a Full Scale IQ and found that the Altitude Quotient and IQ were highly
correlated ($r = .78$) in a sample of mentally retarded children between 8 and 15
years of age. However, the validity of the Altitude Quotient was not studied.

Two other methods have been proposed for computing Altitude Quotients.
A third one consists of multiplying the highest raw score by 5, the next highest
by 3, and the next highest by 2 (Whiteman, 1950). A fourth method is to multi-
ply the sum of the top two Verbal Scale scores and the top two Performance
Scale scores by 2.5 (Purcell, Drevdahl, & Purcell, 1952). These latter two
methods were reported to produce similar Altitude Quotients (Jurjevich, 1963).
Since the external validity of Altitude Quotient procedures is not known, they
should not be used in any decision-making process. Further studies might
prove to be useful in evaluating the effectiveness of the Altitude Quotient in
selected groups of children.

SHORT FORMS OF THE WISC

Since the publication of the WISC, there has been a plethora of studies
that have attempted to develop or to evaluate abbreviated versions of the scale.

The usual procedure for evaluating a short form has been to rescore complete tests; seldom have the proposed combinations been administered separately. Several methodological problems are evident in the literature concerned with short forms; these problems occur in such areas as adequacy of sampling, validity of short forms, estimates of validity, reliability of short forms, and methods for conversion of scores into IQ's (Levy, 1968; Tellegen & Briggs, 1967). Even with high validities, short forms may misclassify individuals. However, short forms may have higher (or lower) predictive validity than the Full Scale (Levy, 1968).

Because of the many methodological problems associated with the studies investigating short forms, we will not attempt to summarize the available literature. Rather, work by Silverstein (1970b) and by Tellegen and Briggs (1967) is highlighted—in addition to the Yudin abbreviated form and the Vocabulary-Block Design short form—because these investigators have taken into account subtest unreliability, have used the standardization data, or have applied techniques that conform to those employed in the WISC. While the approaches of Silverstein and Tellegen and Briggs do not eliminate the many problems associated with the use of short forms, they do appear to be reliable.

Selecting the Short Form

Silverstein (1970a), using the standardization data and a formula that takes into account subtest unreliability, has published the 10 best combinations of two, three, four, and five WISC subtests. These combinations are shown in Table C-13 of the Appendix. Clinical considerations may guide the examiner in the selection of the short form.

Converting the Composite Scores into Deviation Quotients

After the specific combination of subtests has been selected, there remains the problem of obtaining the Full Scale IQ. According to Tellegen and Briggs (1967), simple prorating and regression procedures should not be used, because these techniques do not deal adequately with the problem of subtest reliability. The more acceptable procedure, they believed, is to transform the short form scores into the familiar Wechsler-type quotient (Deviation Quotient—a mean of 100 and a standard deviation of 15).

The following formula is used to compute the Deviation Quotient for a short form:

(1) Deviation Quotient = $(15/S_c)(X_c - M_c) + 100$, where

(2) $S_c = S_s \sqrt{n + 2 \Sigma r_{jk}}$.

(3) X_c = composite score, and

(4) M_c = normative mean, which is equal to $10n$. Further,

(5) S_c = standard deviation of composite score;

(6) S_s = subtest standard deviation, which is equal to 3;

(7) n = number of component subtests; and

(8) Σr_{jk} = sum of the correlations between component subtests.

This equation considers the number of subtests that were given, the correlations among the subtests, and the total scaled score points that were earned by the examinee. Table C-16 in the Appendix (from Tellegen & Briggs) can assist in calculating the Deviation Quotient. Two constants are used, with constant $a = 15/S_c$ and constant $b = 100 - n(150)/S_c$. Substituting these constants in the formula leads to the following: Deviation Quotient = (composite score $\times a$) + b.

In using Table C-16, first select the appropriate heading corresponding to the number of subtests that are used in the short form. The first column under each heading is Σr_{jk}. This term represents the sum of the correlations between (or among) the subtests making up the composite score. To obtain Σr_{jk}, the WISC correlation table of the group closest in age to the examinee is used (Tables IV, V, and VI on pages 10, 11, and 12 of the WISC manual). With two subtests in the short form, only one correlation is needed. With three subtests in the short form, three correlations are summed (1 with 2, 1 with 3, and 2 with 3). With four subtests in the short form, six correlations are summed (1 with 2, 1 with 3, 1 with 4, 2 with 3, 2 with 4, and 3 with 4). With five subtests in the short form, 10 correlations are summed (1 with 2, 1 with 3, 1 with 4, 1 with 5, 2 with 3, 2 with 4, 2 with 5, 3 with 4, 3 with 5, and 4 with 5). After Σr_{jk} is calculated, the values for the two constants are obtained under the appropriate heading.

The following steps then are needed to obtain the Deviation Quotient.

1. The scaled scores of the subtests in the short form are summed. This constitutes the composite score.

2. The correlations between (or among) the subtests are summed to obtain Σr_{jk}.

3. After Σr_{jk} is obtained, Table C-16 in the Appendix is consulted to find the appropriate a and b constants.

4. The Deviation Quotient is computed using the composite score and the a and b constants.

An example: The examiner selected a three-subtest short form composed of the Arithmetic, Vocabulary, and Block Design subtests. The examinee was 7 years old, and had obtained scaled scores of 7, 12, and 13, respectively, on the three subtests. The steps described in the previous paragraph are illustrated.

1. Summing the three scaled scores yields a composite score of 32.

2. From Table IV (page 10) of the WISC manual, the correlations among the three subtests are obtained (Arithmetic and Vocabulary, .46; Arithmetic and Block Design, .27; and Vocabulary and Block Design, .33). These are summed to yield 1.06 (Σr_{jk}).

3. The appropriate row in Table C-16 in the Appendix is the fifth one under the heading "3 Subtests." There we find the values for the constants a and b (2.2 and 34, respectively).

4. Using the formula, Deviation Quotient = (composite score $\times a$) + b, we obtain a Deviation Quotient of $(32 \times 2.2) + 34 = 104$.

Yudin Abbreviated Procedure

Yudin (1966) proposed a short form of the WISC, which consists of administering every other item on most subtests. The specific procedures are shown in Table C-14 of the Appendix. Every third item is administered on Information, Vocabulary, and Picture Completion; every even item on Arithmetic; every odd item on Comprehension, Similarities, Picture Arrangement, Block Design, and Object Assembly; and all of the items on Digit Span and Coding. Raw scores are multiplied by a constant, and a correction factor is applied to some tests. The scaled scores and IQ's are obtained from the manual in the usual way. The Yudin procedure differs from other short-form procedures in that all of the subtests are used. The advantages are that a representative sample of items is administered, scatter analysis can be applied to the examinee's scores, and the procedure uses approximately 56% of the items that are used in the Full Scale.

Silverstein (1968a), while agreeing that the Yudin procedure has merit, also suggested that some changes should be made in the procedure. These changes also are shown in Table C-14. Changes include elimination of correction factors, administering odd items on the Arithmetic subtest, and eliminating Digit Span and Mazes from the abbreviated form, because these subtests were omitted in establishing the IQ tables. Silverstein reported reliabilities for the abbreviated form of .89 for the Verbal Scale, .83 for the Performance Scale, and .91 for the Full Scale.

Yudin (1966) reported that his procedure yielded satisfactory correlations for a sample of emotionally disturbed children. Correlations between the Yudin short form and the standard form for the individual subtests ranged from .76 to .94, while correlations between the Yudin short form and the standard form for the Verbal, Performance, and Full Scales ranged from .93 to .97. The Yudin procedure also has been found to be satisfactory with samples of brain-damaged and mentally retarded children (Reid, Moore, & Alexander, 1968).

Shortcomings with the Yudin procedure also have been noted. The Yudin procedure may result in lower reliability coefficients, with somewhat less reliable profile data (Tellegen & Briggs, 1967). Although correlations have been found to be highly significant using the Yudin procedure, means obtained on the abbreviated version have been found to differ significantly from those found on the Full Scale (Erikson, 1967). In a study of children in an outpatient psychiatric facility, correlations between the abbreviated and Full Scales were high for the subtests, but they dropped considerably for the Verbal-Performance discrepancies (Gayton, Wilson, & Bernstein, 1970). These results suggest that the usual types of scatter analysis may not be applicable with the Yudin procedure. The Yudin procedure also has been found to be less useful with children having IQ's above the Normal range than with those having IQ's in the Normal range (Satz, Van de Riet, & Mogel, 1967). Examiners need to consider carefully the assets and liabilities of the Yudin abbreviated procedure in deciding whether it should be used.

Vocabulary Plus Block Design Short Form

A popular two-subtest combination for use as a short form for screening purposes is the Vocabulary plus Block Design subtests (cf. Mercer & Smith, 1972; Sells, 1966; Silverstein, 1970b; Simpson & Bridges, 1959; Wight & Sandry, 1962). These two subtests have high correlations with the Full Scale over a wide range and have consistently high reliabilities. If this combination is chosen, Table C-15 in the Appendix can be used for converting the sum of scaled scores on the two subtests directly to an estimate of the Full Scale IQ. Silverstein (1970b) reported a correlation of .85 between the Vocabulary plus Block Design short form and the Full Scale.

Comment on Short Forms of the WISC

Now that we have considered some of the factors involved in the use of short forms, a concluding comment is in order. Short forms are practical, save time, and can serve as screening devices. However, coupled with these advantages are many disadvantages. For example, the IQ's obtained with short forms may be less stable than those obtained with the standard form (Baumeister, 1964). When short forms are used, information about cognitive patterning is lost. For example, the use of the Verbal Scale alone, as a quick estimate of intelligence, does not allow for the assessment of both verbal and performance abilities (Witkin, Faterson, Goodenough, & Birnbaum, 1966). When there is intersubtest scatter, the savings of time may be hazardous and expensive in terms of lost information (Burstein, 1965). With Negro children, it may not be safe to eliminate any one subtest, because the correlations among the subtests have been found to be lower among Negroes than in the standardization group (Caldwell & Smith, 1968).

The following comment by Hutt and Gibby (1965) summarizes some of the shortcomings of short forms, especially from a clinical standpoint.

Any short form of the test reduces the amount of the total information available to the clinician for evaluation. Since the evaluative process should be one which is as complete as possible, and is an exceedingly difficult task at best, the use of a short form of an intelligence test is difficult to condone in the evaluation of a retarded child. It defeats the purpose of an adequate evaluation and has little place in the total assessment process if the results are to have value for the individual [pp. 261–262].

Those interested in using short forms must address themselves to the problem of determining an equation that defines the relationship between validity lost and time saved (Levy, 1968). In addition, it is important to identify the nature of the decision that is to be made on the basis of the test scores. Levy suggested that the efficient testing strategy and the problem of evaluating costs are, in part, dependent upon the goal of the evaluation, i.e., whether it is for (a) a general evaluation of intelligence, (b) classification, (c) selection, (d) saving examinee's time, or (e) saving examiner's time. Educational and clinical situations call for more, rather than less, extensive cognitive evaluation. Therefore, examiners are encouraged to administer the Full Scale, unless there is some compelling reason to administer a short form.

ADMINISTERING THE WISC AND WPPSI TO HANDICAPPED CHILDREN

The adaptive administration of the WISC (and WPPSI) is similar to that of the Stanford-Binet. The examiner attempts to find ways to administer the test without, in the process, providing cues to the child. However, when modifications are needed that go beyond simple alteration in the response modality, it is likely that the norms must be reinterpreted in light of the modifications used. The point-scale format of the WISC (and WPPSI) reduces the need to shift constantly from one test to another, thus making the WISC (and WPPSI) more convenient than the Stanford-Binet for adaptive administration.

All of the Verbal Scale subtests can be administered orally if the child can hear. However, if he cannot hear but can read, the Information, Comprehension, Similarities, and Vocabulary questions can be typed on cards and presented one at a time. It is recommended that the Arithmetic and Digit Span items not be shown to the child because of the time limits involved in these subtests and because visual presentation of the items seems drastically different from oral presentation, especially with Digit Span items. If the child cannot respond orally, I recommend that written replies to any of the Verbal Scale subtests be accepted, although Allen and Jefferson (1962) recommended written replies only for the Arithmetic and Digit Span subtests.

The subtests in the Performance Scale of the WISC and WPPSI require the child to have adequate vision. Adaptations, where possible, center on the child's methods of responding. Block Design, Object Assembly, Coding, Mazes, Animal House, and Geometric Design are not easily adaptable when the child has severe impairment of arm-hand use. The Picture Completion subtest can be given only to a child who is able to see and who can describe the missing part orally or in writing, or point to it. Adaptation of the Picture Arrangement subtest is possible when there is only impairment of arm-hand use. The examiner can arrange the cards in the order indicated by the child. Modifications of the subtests for deaf children are discussed in the next part of the chapter.

The distribution of the subtests into the Verbal and Performance Scales is helpful in testing handicapped children. For example, the Verbal Scale can be administered to blind children and to children with severe motor handicaps. The Performance Scale can be administered to hard-of-hearing children and to children who have little or no speech. In the case of hard-of-hearing children, the Verbal Scale also may be administered, if possible, and a comparison between the two scales might reveal the extent of the child's verbal deficit.

ADMINISTERING THE WISC (AND WPPSI) TO DEAF CHILDREN

Various suggestions have been offered for presenting the WISC Performance Scale subtests to deaf children. (Some of the suggested methods also may be useful in testing hearing children who have difficulty in comprehending the subtest instructions, especially for the Picture Arrangement subtest.) In general, written instructions can be used for children who can read (Murphy, 1957). The specific suggestions that have been made for the five standard Performance Scale subtests are presented below. It is important to recognize that without empirical findings there is no way of knowing how the suggested modifications in standard test procedures affect the reliability and validity of the subtest scores. However, when standard procedures cannot be used because sensory handicaps prevent the child from comprehending the instructions, modifications in instructions should be considered. When modifications are used, the resulting score should be considered as a rough estimate of intelligence. A similar conclusion was reached by Graham and Shapiro (1953) from their investigation of the effects of pantomime instructions on the WISC Performance Scale. Pantomime instructions led to significantly lower scores than standard instructions in a group of normal children. With this brief introduction, we turn to the suggested modifications. (The suggested modifications, where appropriate, may also be useful for the WPPSI.)

Picture Completion

On the Picture Completion subtest, the instructions should help the child to understand that he is required to indicate a missing part. Various procedures have been proposed to obtain this goal. One method is to show the child, before the subtest is administered, a series of pencil drawings of a face, each with a different part missing (Reed, 1970). The missing part can be drawn in for the child, after which he should be allowed to draw in the missing part himself. On the subtest pictures proper, the child can use a dry paint brush to show the missing part. A second method is to present the child with a series of drawings of a man, showing an arm missing or a leg missing, and then to ask the child to point to what is missing or not there (Murphy, 1957). A third method is to show three trial items, with each item showing a picture with a missing detail accompanied by a picture with the detail filled in (e.g., an elephant without a trunk on one side and an elephant with the trunk drawn in on the other side) (Neuhaus, 1967).

Picture Arrangement

In order to help the child to understand the requirements of the Picture Arrangement subtest, a series of numbers can be given to him that should be put in order, then a series of letters, and finally, a series of pictures, each time accompanied by a demonstration of what he has to do (Reed, 1970). After he understands the procedure, the subtest pictures should be administered.

Another suggestion is to pantomime the first item, because this procedure usually gives the child insight into the task (Murphy, 1957). The first major difficulty occurs with the item "SCALE." It is important that the child understand the notion that a story is told by the arrangement of the cards. The "FIGHT" item can be used to teach him the concept of "a story." He also should be taught to indicate to the examiner that he has finished the arrangement, preferably during the demonstration series.

Some children may have difficulty in changing from the A, B, and C series to the D and 1 through 6 series (Neuhaus, 1967). In the latter series they may continue to push the cards together to form a whole, rather than to place them in sequence to tell a story. To help the child to understand that the cards are not to be pushed together, a cardboard strip can be shown to him (see Figure 12–1). The strip should contain the numbers 1, 2, 3, and 4, which are placed in four separate boxes and which are separated by at least ⅝ of an inch. After the A, B, and C series are completed the child should be permitted to have two practice trials using items that are not contained on the test proper.

Object Assembly

Generally, there should be no particular difficulty in helping the child to understand the directions on the Object Assembly subtest (Murphy, 1957). However, when difficulties occur, the picture of a man, for item one, and of a horse, for item two, can be shown to the child (Neuhaus, 1967).

Block Design

On the Block Design subtest it is important for the child to understand that all of the blocks are the same with respect to color (Murphy, 1957). The blocks should be set out in a single line with one color on top. The child should be asked to name the color and should be helped to recognize that all blocks have the same color on top. The same procedure should be followed for the remaining colors. In demonstrating the first design, the examiner should use both hands. The child should be allowed to finish the first design even if the time limit has expired.

Coding

On the Coding subtest the record booklet should be held steady for young children (Murphy, 1957). The child's performance should be observed carefully, and his attention redirected, if necessary, to the task. A soft black pencil

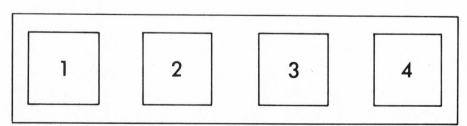

Figure 12–1. Cardboard strip for Picture Arrangement subtest.

should be provided. Young children and mentally retarded children may have difficulty in understanding the importance of speed; throughout the examination the notion of working quickly should be developed. On the sample Coding items, the examiner should demonstrate by his own actions both the method of making the symbol and the speed at which it is to be made. If necessary, the examiner can point quickly to the next symbol after the child has finished the previous one.

SUMMARY

The general suggestions for administering intelligence tests that have been presented in previous chapters of the text also pertain to the WISC. Hearing is necessary for most of the Verbal Scale subtests, although for some subtests vision may be used as a substitute modality. Arm-hand use is a prerequisite for almost all of the Performance Scale subtests, although some adaptations are possible.

The WISC manual generally presents clear directions for administering the various subtests. Beginning examiners tend to make a variety of errors, including improper completion of the record booklet, failure to adhere to directions, failure to probe ambiguous responses, and giving items beyond the discontinuance points. These and other problems are discussed in the chapter. It is important that every examiner develop proper administrative procedures early in his career. General suggestions for administering specific subtests also are noted in the chapter.

One of the more difficult problems encountered in administering the WISC involves the scoring of responses, especially for the Comprehension, Similarities, and Vocabulary subtests. Many studies have pointed out that examiners vary considerably among themselves in their scoring of responses. A careful study of the scoring criteria, along with improved scoring manuals, should help in reducing this source of test unreliability.

A variety of reports dealing with modifying standard procedures has appeared. The most thorough and systematic one has been the development of a revised and shortened Vocabulary subtest by Jastak and Jastak. However, there is little evidence to indicate that the revised form contributes substantially to the validity of the scale. The rewording of some WISC questions has been proposed by some writers but, for the most part, the effects of the proposed modifications have not been tested.

The following procedural changes have been found to increase significantly the child's scores on various WISC subtests: (*a*) asking the child to describe his problem-solving methods on the Picture Arrangement and Object Assembly subtests; (*b*) asking the child to think about his answers before responding on the Comprehension, Similarities, and Mazes subtests; (*c*) having the child explain his Picture Arrangement stories; and (*d*) providing the child with a series of cues on items that were failed on the Picture Arrangement and Block Design subtests. Different modes of administering the Vocabulary subtest were not found to affect performance significantly.

The Altitude Quotient, derived from summing the scores on combinations of the highest subtests, has not proved to be a better predictor of learning efficiency than the IQ.

Short forms of the WISC, while practical, have disadvantages associated with them. IQ's may be less stable, patterning of subtest scores and scaled scores is not available, and scatter analysis is difficult. The majority of the published studies concerned with short forms of the WISC have methodological problems. However, the procedures advocated by Tellegen and Briggs, which are described in the chapter, appear to overcome many of the statistical problems associated with short forms. Table C-13 in the Appendix shows the 10 best combinations of two, three, four, and five WISC subtests, and Table C-15 in the Appendix shows the IQ's for the sum of the scaled scores for the Vocabulary plus Block Design short form.

The Verbal and Performance Scale arrangement of the subtests facilitates the selection of scales in testing handicapped children. Special procedures, which are described in the chapter, are usually needed in administering the Performance Scale to deaf children.

CHAPTER 13

DESCRIPTION AND EVALUATION OF WISC SUBTESTS

Chapter 13 discusses the interpretative rationale, Cohen's (1959) factor analytic findings, Meeker's (1969) Structure of Intellect logically derived classifications, and administrative considerations for each of the 12 WISC subtests. Table C-8 in the Appendix summarizes the functions proposed for each subtest that are described in detail in the chapter.

The analysis of subtest functions is, in part, based on an ego-psychology approach (cf. Blatt & Allison, 1968; Fromm, Hartman, & Marschak, 1957; Rapaport, Gill, & Schafer, 1968). The Wechsler scales, while primarily designed to provide a valid and reliable index of global intelligence, also are considered a means of assessing ego functions. The test questions are relatively neutral and highly structured, and the subtests assess the relative integration and balance of a variety of ego functions such as planning, judgment, attention, concentration, memory, concept formation, and visual-motor integration. The pattern of subtest scores, which may be related to the organization of ego functions, also provides indices of general adaptive processes and of the pathological impairments of these adaptive processes (Rapaport et al., 1968).

Most of the subtests are not reliable measures of specific functions; rather, they are likely to be more reliable estimates of specific abilities when they are combined with other subtests. (Further information concerning this point is discussed in Chapter 14, which considers factor scores.) However, comparisons among subtests permit the development of hypotheses about the examinee's abilities, and such hypotheses may facilitate the assessment process. On the basis of a factor analysis, Cohen (1959) generally advised against making interpretations for individual subtest scores. In clinical and educational settings, however, interpretations that are cautiously made may prove to be of benefit.

As part of the administrative considerations, a number of questions are posed for some subtests so as to aid the examiner in observing the child's performance. The answers to these questions, as well as to similar ones that appear in the text, will serve as a data base for the testing of clinical hypotheses when the test is completed. The examiner may not have many specific questions in mind at the beginning of the testing, but he will at the end. Therefore, he will have to make as complete a record as possible (as has been noted in Chapter 5) in order to be able to answer any questions that arise.

INTERPRETATIVE RATIONALE AND ADMINISTRATIVE CONSIDERATIONS FOR WISC SUBTESTS

Information

The Information subtest of the WISC consists of 30 items. The first three items are administered only to children who are under 8 years or to older suspected mental retardates. The items on the subtest usually can be answered by a simply stated fact; they require circumscribed, precise responses.

Rationale

The questions on the Information subtest appear to provide an adequate sampling of information acquired by a person who has had the usual opportunities in our society (Freeman, 1962). The subtest may reflect the examinee's natural endowment, richness of early environment, extent of schooling, and cultural predilections (Rapaport et al., 1968). Therefore the subtest may measure the wealth of available information, which is acquired largely as a result of native ability and early cultural experience (Blatt & Allison, 1968). High scores may not necessarily be an indication of mental efficiency and competence. Individuals may acquire isolated facts without being able to use them appropriately or effectively (Taylor, 1961).

The Information questions require memory (Rapaport et al., 1968). Some questions tap primarily habitual, overlearned responses (e.g., "How many days are there in the week?"), especially in the case of older children. Inhibition may be noted on the subtest. Thus, for example, answers that may be in the child's repertoire cannot be recalled, because the questions concern conflict-laden material.

Factor Analytic Findings

The Information subtest is the second best measure of g (Cohen, 1959). In young children, when the Information score is deviant by at least three points from the general subtest average, it may be interpreted as reflecting specific verbal knowledge. Cohen advised against making subtest-specific interpretations, such as "he is usually well informed about general facts." Information is seen as a measure of g and as contributing to the Verbal Comprehension I factor.

Structure of Intellect Classification (SOI)

The SOI classifications of the Information subtest are MMU (Memory for Semantic Units—the ability to remember isolated ideas or word meanings), MMR (Memory for Semantic Relations—the ability to remember meaningful connections between items of verbal information), MSS (Memory for Symbolic Systems—the ability to remember the order of symbolic information), MMS (Memory for Semantic Systems—the ability to remember meaningfully ordered verbal information), EMR (Evaluation of Semantic Relations—the ability to make choices among semantic relationships based on the similarity and consistency of the meanings), NMR (Convergent Production of Semantic Relations—the ability to produce a word or idea that conforms to specific relationship requirements), CMU (Cognition of Semantic Units—the ability to comprehend the meaning of words or ideas), and NMU (Convergent Production of Semantic Units—the ability to converge on an appropriate name—or summarizing word—for any given information). The eight classifications are distributed among the 30 items.

Administrative Considerations

The Information subtest is easy to administer. The questions are simple and direct, and timing is not required. Credit should be given to the examinee if he answers correctly an Information subtest question any time during the course of administering the scale (Rapaport et al., 1968). Scoring usually proves to be straightforward. A correct response receives 1 point, an incorrect response, 0. The examinee should always be asked to decide on the best answer whenever two or more answers, one of which is ambiguous or incorrect, are given to the question.

Comprehension

The Comprehension subtest of the WISC consists of 14 questions that deal with a variety of situations, including the body ("What is the thing to do when you cut your finger?"), interpersonal relations ("What is the thing to do if a fellow (girl) much smaller than yourself starts to fight with you?"), and societal activities ("Why are criminals locked up?").

Rationale

The Comprehension subtest is considered to measure judgment or common sense. The tasks consist of comprehending what is involved in the situations and providing answers to the problems. Success depends, in part, on possession of practical information, plus ability to evaluate and use past experience. Success indicates that the child has social judgment and a grasp of social conventionality. These skills imply an ability to use facts in a pertinent, meaningful, and emotionally relevant manner. Extensiveness of cultural opportunities and development of conscience or moral sense may be involved in performance on the subtest.

Factor Analytic Findings

The Comprehension subtest is a moderately good measure of g (Cohen, 1959). The subtest combines with other subtests to measure g and the Verbal Comprehension II factor. Cohen recommended that it should not be interpreted as measuring verbal judgment because of its low subtest-specific variance.

Structure of Intellect Classification (SOI)

The SOI classification of the Comprehension subtest is EMI (Evaluation of Semantic Implications—the ability to judge the adequacy of a meaningful deduction). Every item is so classified.

Administrative Considerations

The Comprehension subtest is one of the three Verbal Scale subtests (Similarities and Vocabulary are the other two) that tax the examiner's scoring ability. Children may give a variety of responses to the Comprehension questions, and scoring is difficult. Sattler, Winget, and Roth (1969), for example, using a sample of 28 WISC Comprehension responses that were potentially ambiguous, reported that two-thirds (6 out of 9) of a sample of Ph.D. clinical psychologists gave the same score to only 57% of the responses. Scoring difficulties arise, in part, from the limited number of examples in the manual, and partly from the difficulty in establishing precise criteria that can be applied to the variety of responses. A careful study of the scoring criteria and scoring examples in the manual, in Massey's (1964) guide, and in Appendix A of this book, which also presents scoring suggestions, is needed before modest scoring proficiency is reached. Comprehension subtest responses receive a 2, 1, or 0 score. The most complete or best response receives a 2, a less adequate response, a 1, and an incorrect response, a 0. If inquiry into a passing response alters the meaning of the response, the response should be scored as it was initially given (Rapaport et al., 1968).

The child's responses should be examined carefully (Taylor, 1961). Does he fail a question because he misunderstood the meaning of a word or the implication of a particular phrase? Does he give an answer or just repeat part of a phrase? Does he respond to part of the question or to the entire question? Do his responses suggest that he wants to appear independent and self-sufficient? Does he seem to be objective, see various possibilities, and then choose the best way?

Unusual responses may be probed by asking the examinee to explain further his responses. Inquiry provides material that may give insight into the examinee's thought processes, but it should not be a routine procedure or be conducted on every response. Extensive inquiry can be conducted as part of the testing of limits after the examination has been completed. It is especially important that the examinee's responses be recorded verbatim both during the initial presentation of the items and during the inquiry phase in order to facilitate restudy and qualitative evaluation.

Arithmetic

The Arithmetic subtest of the WISC consists of 16 problems. The first three problems are given only to children below the age of 8 years or to older suspected mental retardates. All of the problems are timed, with a range of 30 to 120 seconds. The solutions require the use of standard arithmetical operations—addition, subtraction, multiplication, and division.

The problems in the Arithmetic subtest reflect various kinds of skills. Problems 1, 2, and 3 require direct counting of concrete quantities. Problems 5, 6, 7, and 9 require simple addition and subtraction. Problem 8 involves multiplication. Problems 4, 10, and 11 involve small division. Problems 12 through 16 require subtle operations, in addition to automatized number facts, such as seeing relevant relationships immediately at a glance. In problems 10 and 11, the answers may come intuitively to children experienced with facts, while for children who have not yet automatized simple arithmetic facts, the problems require reflection and mental operation (Taylor, 1961).

Rationale

The Arithmetic subtest is a test of reasoning ability plus numerical accuracy in mental arithmetic. These processes involve concentration and, to some extent, attention. Concentration is necessary when the material is complex. Concentration assumes an active relationship with one's environment. The problems require the utilization of skills that have been obtained during the educational process. Like Vocabulary and Information, Arithmetic depends upon memory and prior learning; unlike these two subtests, it requires concentration (to a greater extent than Vocabulary and Information) and active application of select skills to cope with new and unique situations (Blatt & Allison, 1968).

Factor Analytic Findings

The Arithmetic subtest is a moderately good measure of g (Cohen, 1959). At ages $10\frac{1}{2}$ and $13\frac{1}{2}$, when there is substantial departure (e.g., 3 or more scaled score points) of the subtest score from the mean of the other subtests (particularly Verbal Scale subtests), there is some basis for drawing inferences about level of specific arithmetic ability.

Structure of Intellect Classification (SOI)

The SOI classifications of the Arithmetic subtest are MSI (Memory for Symbolic Implications—the ability to remember arbitrary connections between symbols) and CMS (Cognition of Semantic Systems—the ability to comprehend relatively complex ideas). Every item receives both classifications.

Administrative Considerations

If the examinee needs additional time to complete the problems, allow him to do so. The time elapsed after the time limit has expired and the reaching of a correct solution should be recorded. While a correct response after the time limit has expired does not receive credit, such information is important in attempting to differentiate between failures due to "temporary inefficiency" and those due to limited knowledge. Successful performance after the time has expired may indicate temporary inefficiency or a slow, painstaking approach to problems. Inquiry after failures may help to determine the reasons for failure (e.g., lack of knowledge, temporary inefficiency, or carelessness).

Similarities

The Similarities subtest of the WISC consists of 16 questions. The first four questions, which are given only to children below the age of 8 years or to older suspected mental retardates, differ from the remaining 12 in that they require simple analogies, which are based on previously learned associations, and not similarities.

Rationale

The Similarities subtest requires verbal concept formation (i.e., abstract thinking) and logical thinking. The first four questions appear to measure logical thinking, while the remaining 12 questions measure verbal concept formation. Concept formation is a function that permits the individual to place objects and events together in a meaningful group or groups. While concept formation can be a voluntary, effortful process, it can also reflect well-automatized verbal conventions (Rapaport et al., 1968). Performance on the Similarities subtest may be related to cultural opportunities and to interest patterns.

Factor Analytic Findings

The Similarities subtest is a moderately good measure of g (Cohen, 1959). Its major utility lies in its combination with other subtests in forming factor scores. The subtest precludes specific interpretations.

Structure of Intellect Classification (SOI)

The SOI classifications of the Similarities subtest are EMR (Evaluation of Semantic Relations—the ability to make choices among semantic relationships based on the similarity and consistency of the meanings), CMT (Cognition of Semantic Transformations—the ability to see potential changes of interpretations of objects and situations), and CSR (Cognition of Symbolic Relations—the ability to see relations between items of symbolic information). The majority of the items (5 through 15) are CMT items.

Administrative Considerations

The first four questions are scored 1 or 0. Little difficulty is encountered in scoring answers to these questions. Questions 5 through 16 are scored 2, 1, or 0. High conceptual level responses are scored 2, lower conceptual level responses, 1, and failures, 0. The Similarities subtest, like Comprehension and Vocabulary, is difficult to score. Useful scoring suggestions are presented in Appendix A and in Massey's (1964) guide. Sattler et al. (1969) reported that two-thirds (6 out of 9) of the raters gave the same score to only 68% of the 25 responses that were presented.

The examiner should note whether the child understands the task. Children who state that they do not know the answer to a question should be encouraged to think about the question. As in any subtest, the child should not be pressed unreasonably hard. When many responses are given to one question, the examinee should be asked to select the response that he thinks best represents the essential similarity (e.g., "Tell me the one best way in which they are alike"). The score should be based on this answer.

Vocabulary

The Vocabulary subtest of the WISC consists of 40 words. The first nine words are routinely administered only to children below the age of 8 years or to older suspected mental retardates.

Rationale

The Vocabulary subtest, a test of word knowledge, may involve a variety of cognitive functions or features—including learning ability, fund of information, richness of ideas, memory, concept formation, and language development—that may be closely related to the child's experiences and educational environment. The subtest is considered to be an excellent estimate of intellectual capacity. Performance on the subtest is stable over time and relatively resistant to neurological deficit and psychological disturbance (Blatt & Allison, 1968). The subtest is valuable in deriving an index of the examinee's general mental ability.

Factor Analytic Findings

The Vocabulary subtest is an excellent measure of g (Cohen, 1959). It is essentially a g measure and combines with other subtests to form the Verbal Comprehension I and II factors. Cohen suggested that the subtest, by itself, can be used to estimate intelligence in research and in clinical screening batteries.

Structure of Intellect Classification (SOI)

The SOI classification of the Vocabulary subtest is CMU (Cognition of Semantic Units—the ability to comprehend the meanings of words or ideas). Every item is so classified.

Administrative Considerations

It is important to record carefully the examinee's responses to the words. Inquiry is especially important whenever peculiar responses are given. The basis for the examinee's incorrect responses should be determined, because a careful qualitative analysis of the Vocabulary subtest may reveal clues about the examinee's thought processes. It is important to distinguish among the many possible reasons for the responses, including, for example, guesses, clang associations, idiosyncratic associations, or bizarre associations.

The following guides, presented by Taylor (1961), are useful for observing and evaluating responses to the Vocabulary subtest.

Note all responses, whether correct or not. Note whether the child is familiar with the word or whether he knows only about in which area it might belong. If he explains a word, does he try to find one description or definition only, does he try to be precise and brief or does he embark on lengthy explanations? Does he keep it objective or does he get involved in relating personal experiences? Note whether he thinks he knows the word, but confuses it with another that sounds like it to him. If he does not know the word does he try to guess its meaning? Is he ready to say, "I do not know" and try to shake off further demands, or is he puzzled? Note whether or not showing him the word printed helps him to recognize it.

Watch for possible hearing difficulties; listen carefully how he repeats the word, if he does. Has he heard it correctly or with some distortion? Note how he expresses himself. Does he find it easy or difficult to say what he means? Does he have mechanical difficulties getting words said properly or does he seem uncertain about how best to express what he thinks? Does he use gestures to help him illustrate his statements or does he even depend on them exclusively?

Note the content of his definitions. Does he choose a synonym for the stimulus word (for cushion, a pillow), or does he describe an action ("Cushion" — "you put it under your head")? Does he describe some special feature ("Donkey" — "it has four legs"), or does he try to fit it into some category ("Donkey" — "a living creature that is kept in some kind of enclosure or in a special building called a barn")?

Note any emotional overtones, personal experiences or feelings ("Authority" — "they have the power to do anything to you") [p. 485].

The first five Vocabulary words are scored 2 or 0, while the remaining 35 words are scored 2, 1, or 0. Vocabulary is one of the more difficult subtests to score. The manual does not provide a sufficient number of 0, 1, and 2 examples. In addition, it is difficult to implement Wechsler's criteria for scoring the responses. In the study by Sattler et al. (1969), two-thirds (6 out of 9) of the raters gave the same score to only 69% of the 26 Vocabulary responses that were used in the task. The examiner is encouraged to probe borderline responses and to study carefully the scoring guide in the manual, in Massey's (1964) guide, and in Appendix A. These sources will help in resolving some of the scoring problems that arise in the course of administering the subtest, but they will not resolve all problems. The examiner must try to do the best job possible with the available guides.

Digit Span

The Digit Span subtest of the WISC is a supplementary test that consists of a Digits Forward part, with series ranging from three to nine digits in length, and a Digits Backward part, with series ranging from two to eight digits in length. There are two series of digits for each sequence length. The second series is administered only if the examinee fails the first series. The raw score is the sum of the number of digits in the last series passed in the two separate parts. There are no separately scaled scores for Digits Forward and for Digits Backward.

Rationale

The Digit Span subtest is a measure of attention (Rapaport et al., 1968) and short-term memory. An effortless and relaxed performance may enable a child to achieve a high score on the subtest. The task requires of the child the capacity to retain in mind several elements that have no logical relationship to each other (Kubota, 1965). Digits Backward requires not only memory but also remanipulation and reorganization. Taylor (1961) indicated that Digits Backward involves supplementing passive registration and auditory recall "by a more active mental process which, through a predetermined mental set, transforms the initially perceived order of the numbers [p. 434]."

Factor Analytic Findings

The Digit Span subtest has a high loading on the Freedom from Distractibility factor at each of the three age levels ($7\frac{1}{2}$, $10\frac{1}{2}$, and $13\frac{1}{2}$ years) studied by Cohen (1959). However, only at the $13\frac{1}{2}$ year level does it combine with Arithmetic to form the Freedom from Distractibility factor score; at the younger two age levels there is no subtest that can be found to supplement Digit Span to form the factor score. The subtest precludes specific interpretation.

Structure of Intellect Classification (SOI)

The SOI classification of the Digit Span subtest is MSS (Memory for Symbolic Systems—the ability to remember the order of symbolic information). Every item is so classified.

Administrative Considerations

The digits should be read clearly at the rate of one per second. A stopwatch can be used to practice reading speed. It is never permissible to repeat any of the digits on either trial of a series. After the subtest has been completed, it is worthwhile to ask the examinee about his method of recalling the digits. "How did you go about recalling the digits?" is one way of phrasing the question. The examiner should record whether, for example, the examinee visualized the digits, said the digits to himself and reproduced them by use of verbal or motor or auditory techniques, or grouped the digits. Grouping introduces meaning into the task. Thus, instead of separate entities, the digits become numbers, or grouped into hundreds, tens, or other units. If grouping occurs, the function underlying the task may be changed from one of attention to one of concentration (Rapaport et al., 1968).

In the record booklet, the actual number of digits in each series correctly recalled should be recorded by either placing a correct mark above or on each digit correctly recalled or by placing an incorrect mark on each digit missed. This procedure provides another source of qualitative material. For example, an examinee who consistently misses the last digit in a series and then successfully completes the second series in the sequence may differ from one who fails to recall any of the digits in the first series, but successfully completes the second series. The quantitative scores do not distinguish between these two patterns. This is true particularly for the number of digits failed. For example, for scoring purposes, an examinee who misses one digit in the eight-digit sequence receives the same score as one who misses eight digits in the sequence. A qualitative analysis of the two patterns suggests that the second examinee has more inefficiency in his performance than the first examinee, and thereby reveals lapses in attention that may be due to anxiety or to other factors.

In observing the child's performance, the following points should be considered carefully (Taylor, 1961). How does the child respond to the task? Is it interesting to him, boring, or difficult? Is he discouraged easily or stimulated by the increasing length of the series? Does he continue to try? When he makes errors, does he notice them, or does he think that his answers are correct? When he is presented with the Digits Backward series, does he understand the difference between this task and the previous one? Does he make the same type of errors, or do they change? As the series proceeds, does he become stimulated and encouraged, or more tense and anxious?

Picture Completion

The Picture Completion subtest of the WISC consists of 20 drawings; each contains an important missing element. The examinee's task is to discover what is missing in each picture within the 15-second time limit.

Rationale

The Picture Completion subtest involves recognizing the picture, appreciating its incompleteness, and determining the missing part. It is a test of the ability to differentiate essential from non-essential details, and requires concentration, reasoning (or visual alertness), and visual organization and visual memory. Thus, many psychological processes enter into the child's performance, including perception, cognition, judgment, and delay of impulse (Taylor, 1961). The concentration required is directed toward an externalized form, whereas the concentration required on the Arithmetic subtest is a more internalized process. The time limit on the subtest is important, since it places additional demands on the examinee. The child's experiences, such as extensiveness of contact with the environment, may affect performance on the subtest.

Factor Analytic Findings

The Picture Completion subtest is a poor measure of g (Cohen, 1959). The subtest consistently loads on the Verbal Comprehension II factor in all three age levels and on the Perceptional Organization factor at the $10\frac{1}{2}$ year and $13\frac{1}{2}$ year age levels. The subtest precludes specific interpretation.

Structure of Intellect Classification (SOI)

The SOI classifications of the Picture Completion subtest are CFU (Cognition of Figural Units—the ability to perceive or recognize figural entities) and EFS (Evaluation of Figural Systems—the ability to evaluate a system of figural units that have been grouped in some manner). Every item receives both classifications.

Administrative Considerations

Some of the points to consider are as follows (Taylor, 1961): Does the child understand the tasks? Does he say anything that comes to mind or does he search for the right answer? When he fails, who does he find fault with, himself or the picture?

The examinee should be aware that he is being timed, because it is important for him to realize that speed is expected. Allowing him to see the stopwatch is all that is needed. After the subtest is completed, inquire into the examinee's perception of the task. "How did you go about solving the task and deciding when to give the answer?" is one way of asking the question. The examinee's response may provide clues to his perception of being timed. Inquiry should also be made into peculiar answers that are given to any of the subtest pictures.

If an examinee has speech difficulties, such as those that occur in aphasia, the subtest can be administered by having him point to the place where the part is missing. In all cases incorrect respones as well as the time taken to make the response should be recorded. Examinees who characteristically respond in less than five seconds may be brighter than examinees who take more than five seconds. Similarly, examinees who uniformly respond correctly between 16 and 25 seconds do not receive credit, yet they may be brighter than those who respond incorrectly. Because the all-or-none scoring (scoring is either 1 or 0) makes no provision for such individual variations, qualitative factors (e.g., receiving no credit but answering the item correctly) should be carefully evaluated in each case and discussed in the report.

Picture Arrangement

The Picture Arrangement subtest contains 11 items. The first four items (A through D) are given to children below the age of 8 years or to older suspected mental retardates. Three of these four items (A, B, and C), which require the juxtaposition of the parts as in jigsaw puzzles, appear to differ from the remaining eight items (D, 1 through 7), which require arranging parts (complete in themselves) into a meaningful sequence. All 11 items are timed, with items 1 through 7 receiving credit for speed. Items 3, 4, and 6 receive credit for either of two arrangements, and item 7, for any of three different arrangements. Only one of the three arrangements for item 7 (MASTER) receives a time-bonus credit.

On the Picture Arrangement subtest the material is visually presented. The motor action required to solve the problems is simply to change the position of the parts so that they make a meaningful figure, as in the first three items, or story, as in the last eight items.

Rationale

The Picture Arrangement subtest, a test that requires interpretation of social situations, is a nonverbal reasoning test. It measures comprehension of a story as told in pictures. It may be viewed as a measure of planning ability, that is, an ability to comprehend and size up a total situation. Anticipation and visual organization are important factors in the subtest. The former is an ability to anticipate the consequences of initial acts or situations and to interpret social situations. Thus, the subtest may reflect planning ability in social situations. The capacity to anticipate, judge, and understand the possible antecedents and consequences of events is important in providing meaningful continuity in everyday experiences (Blatt & Allison, 1968). Some minimum of cultural opportunities may be necessary for successful performance on the subtest.

Factor Analytic Findings

The Picture Arrangement subtest is the best single measure of g among the Performance Scale subtests (Cohen, 1959). In combination with the Block Design subtest, it can be used to obtain a nonverbal estimate of g. The subtest precludes specific interpretation.

Structure of Intellect Classification (SOI)

The SOI classifications of the Picture Arrangement subtest are EMR (Evaluation of Semantic Relations — the ability to make choices among semantic relationships based on the similarity and consistency of the meanings) and NMS (Convergent Production of Semantic Systems — the ability to order information into a verbally meaningful sequence). Every item receives both classifications.

Administrative Considerations

The subtest is useful in observing how the examinee approaches a performance task involving planning ability. How does the child proceed with the task? Does he look the cards over, come to some decision, and reassess it while he places the cards (Taylor, 1961)? Or does he proceed quickly without stopping to reconsider his decision? Is his failure to understand the task revealed by his leaving the pictures in the order that they were placed by the examiner?

The child's persistence, trial-and-error patterns, degree of discouragement, impulsiveness, or rigidity should be noted. With the train item, for example, does the child observe that the train consists of separate units with the two pieces belonging to the engine? Comparing the child's approach to the Picture Arrangement items with those used on the Block Design and Object Assembly items may prove to be valuable. Does he consistently employ the same patterns in his search for the solutions? If he is not consistent, what may account for the changes? Consider the extent to which the content of the task, fatigability, or mood changes are involved in his approach to the various items.

Inquiry into the examinee's arrangements may elicit useful material, particularly on those items that have been failed. In order to keep the test administration as standardized as possible, inquiry should be conducted after the entire scale has been administered. Select items from those that have been failed or passed, if there is reason to believe that they may reveal insight into the examinee's thought pattern. For older examinees (above 8 years of age), the last two items attempted can routinely be subjected to inquiry. Even in the case of items that have been correctly arranged, incorrect anticipations or lack of understanding may be present (Rapaport et al., 1968). Set up the Picture Arrangement cards for each item separately in the order given by the child. Ask the child "to tell what is happening in the pictures," or "to make up a story," or "to tell the story," or "to tell what the pictures show."

The following questions should be considered in evaluating the stories (Taylor, 1961): Are they logical, fanciful, or bizarre? Is there originality in them or are they conventional? Are emotional attitudes revealed? Are incorrect arrangements due to incorrect perceptions of details in the pictures or to failure to consider some details? Were all relationships in the pictures considered?

Block Design

The Block Design subtest of the WISC consists of 10 items. The first two are given only to children below the age of 8 years or to older suspected mental retardates. For the first two items, the child is required to reproduce the designs from a model constructed by the examiner. For the remaining eight items, the patterns are shown on cards. Only the red and white surfaces of the blocks are used in the construction of the designs.

All of the items are timed. The first three items are given a maximum of 45 seconds, the next four items, 75 seconds, and the last three items, 150 seconds. The last seven items are given time-bonus credit for quick execution. The first three items have a maximum score of 2, while the remaining seven items have a maximum score of 7.

Rationale

Taylor (1961) described the task on the Block Design subtest as follows: "The printed designs' intricate relationships must be perceived, analyzed, broken up in a number of squares, transposed to material (blocks) which differs in size, texture, and manipulative qualities [p. 408]." Simply put, the pattern on the card is broken down and then it is reconstructed. The subtest appears to measure the reproductive aspect of visual-motor coordination. Perceptual organization ability and spatial visualization ability (or abstract conceptualizing ability and generalizing ability) are needed for achievement on the subtest. Thus, the Block Design subtest can be conceived of as a concept formation task involving both analysis and synthesis. Rate of motor activity and color vision may be related to performance on the subtest. Inadequate performance on the Block Design subtest should not be interpreted as direct evidence of inadequate visual form and pattern perception, because the ability to discriminate block designs (i.e., to perceive the designs accurately at a recognition level) may be intact even though the ability to reproduce the designs is impaired (Bortner & Birch, 1962).

Factor Analytic Findings

The Block Design subtest is a useful measure of both g and the Perceptual Organization factor (Cohen, 1959). It can be interpreted as measuring speeded perceptual organization or spatial visualization ability.

Structure of Intellect Classification (SOI)

The SOI classifications of the Block Design subtest are CFR (Cognition of Figural Relations – the ability to recognize figural relations between forms) and EFR (Evaluation of Figural Relations – the ability to choose a form based on the evaluation of what the relations are between the figures or forms in the sequence). Every item receives both classifications.

Administrative Considerations

It is important to have the examinee indicate when he has completed each item. It may be necessary, therefore, to ask him to indicate when he has finished ("Tell me when you have finished"). If testing of the limits is indicated or desired, the specific item or items should be presented *after* the entire examination has been completed. The amount of help the examinee needs in order to complete the design accurately should be determined. Block Design, like Object Assembly, is an excellent subtest for observing the examinee's methods of working. Anxiety, for example, may be revealed by excessive fumbling or by failure to check the pattern. Impulsiveness may be indicated by careless and hurried approaches to the task. Is the child persistent or does he give up easily when faced with possible failure?

The child's approach to the task should be noted by considering the following suggestions (Taylor, 1961): Does he try to copy the design or does he first copy the color scheme and then correct it? Does he retain only a superficial impression of the design? With the two-color designs, does he invert them, later correct them, or ignore them? "Is he quick or slow, patient, orderly, and over-meticulous, or erratic and superficial? Does he continue in one kind of approach, or does he alter it as need arises [p. 408]?" Does he study the designs first? Does he start with a plan? Does he construct units of blocks and arrange them in proper relationship, or does he work in piecemeal fashion?

Object Assembly

The Object Assembly subtest of the WISC consists of four items, each of which is a jigsaw problem. The items are a manikin (five pieces), a horse (six pieces), a face (eight pieces), and an auto (seven pieces).

There is a two-minute time limit for the manikin item and a three-minute time limit for the remaining three items. Time bonuses, up to 3 points, are given for each item. Without time bonuses, 4 points are given for the manikin item and 6 points for the remaining three items.

Rationale

The Object Assembly subtest requires visual-motor coordination. The motor activity is guided by visual perception and sensory-motor feedback. It is a test of perceptual organization ability. The visual organization seems to play a "productive" role, in that something must be produced out of parts not immediately recognizable. In solving the jigsaw puzzles, examinees are required to grasp a whole pattern by anticipating the relationships among the individual parts. The tasks, therefore, require some constructive ability as well as perceptual skill. Rate and precision of motor activity may be related to performance on the subtest.

Factor Analytic Findings

The Object Assembly subtest is a poor measure of g (Cohen, 1959). In combination with the Block Design subtest at the 13½ age level and with the Block Design and Mazes subtests at the younger age levels (7½ and 10½), it is a useful measure of Perceptual Organization. The subtest precludes specific interpretation.

Structure of Intellect Classification (SOI)

The SOI classifications of the Object Assembly subtest are CFS (Cognition of Figural Systems – the ability to comprehend arrangements and positions of visual objects in space), CFT (Cognition of Figural Transformations – the ability to visualize how a given figure or object will appear after given changes, such as unfolding or rotation), and EFR (Evaluation of Figural Relations – the ability to choose a form based on the evaluation of what the relations are between the figures or forms in the sequence). Every item receives all classifications.

Administrative Considerations

As in other subtests, it is sometimes necessary to ask the examinee to indicate when he is finished. In requesting this information, the examiner must be careful not to give any cues to the examinee that indicate approval or disapproval. Are low scores a result of temporary inefficiency, such as reversal of two parts, with the resulting loss of time-bonus credits, or are they due to other reasons? Inquiry should be made of constructions that appear to be peculiar or unusual.

The Object Assembly subtest is an especially good test in which to observe the examinee's modes of perception, trial-and-error methods, and responses to errors (Freeman, 1962). Some examinees anticipate the final pattern immediately and the task becomes one of simple visual-motor coordination. Other examinees engage in trial-and-error maneuvers, if the final pattern is not immediately evident to them (Blatt & Allison, 1968).

The following questions present useful guides for evaluating the child's performance (Taylor, 1961): Does the child recognize immediately what the figures represent, have an idea about the possible figure, or does he manipulate the pieces first? Is his idea correct, or does he have ideas that impede his ability to arrive at a correct solution? Does he study the situation and discover what the figure will be while still experimenting?

Coding

The Coding subtest of the WISC consists of two separate and distinct parts. Coding A is administered to children under the age of 8 years, and Coding B to those who are 8 years of age and over. Each part uses a sample (or key). In Coding A, the sample consists of five shapes (star, circle, triangle, cross, and square). Within each shape, a special mark appears (vertical line, two horizontal lines, horizontal line, circle, and two vertical lines, respectively). The child is required to place within each shape the mark that appears in the sample. Five practice shapes are presented, followed by 43 shapes in the subtest.

In Coding B, the sample consists of boxes containing the numbers 1 through 9, and a symbol below each number. The child is required to write the symbols shown in the sample in boxes that contain a number in the upper part and an empty space in the lower part. There are seven practice boxes, followed by 93 boxes in the subtest proper. The time limit for both Coding tasks is 120 seconds.

Rationale

The Coding subtest of the WISC appears to measure visual-motor coordination, speed of mental operation, and short-term memory. Success depends on visual activity, motor activity, and coordination; the motor factor is given great weight. It is a test of psychomotor speed. Success, too, depends not only on the child's comprehending the task, but also on his skill with pencil and paper.

Factor Analytic Findings

The Coding subtest is relatively low in g (Cohen, 1959). The subtest, by itself, has limited utility. It loads exclusively on the Quasi-Specific factor, a factor which is not interpreted by Cohen.

Structure of Intellect Classification (SOI)

The SOI classifications of the Coding A subtest are NFU (Convergent Production of Figural Units—factorial meaning has not been described) and EFU (Evaluation of Figural Units—the ability to judge units of figural information as being similar or different). The entire subtest receives both classifications.

The SOI classifications of the Coding B subtest are NSU (Convergent Production of Symbolic Units—factorial meaning has not been described) and ESU (Evaluation of Symbolic Units—the ability to make rapid decisions regarding the identification of letter or number sets). The entire subtest receives both classifications.

Administrative Considerations

The examinee's method of proceeding with the task should be observed. If he skips around, filling like shapes or like numbers first, he should be told to proceed in order.

Left-handed children may be penalized on the Coding subtest. They may bend their wrists when writing, cover the sample immediately above the line of writing, and lift their hands repeatedly during the task. Either of two procedures can be used to counteract these difficulties. One method consists of showing the child the sample from another record booklet. A more satisfactory procedure is to cut the sample from another record booklet, mount it on a strip of cardboard, and then position it in a convenient place for viewing (McCarthy, 1961).

The subtest affords an opportunity to study the child's working habits. Observe whether he is impulsive or meticulous, or whether tremor is evident. The pace of his performance should be noted. Does he increase or decrease his speed? An increase in speed, coupled with correct copying of symbols, suggests good ability to adjust to the task. A decrease in speed, coupled with correct copying of symbols, suggests that fatigability is present (Rapaport et al., 1968). Opportunity, too, is provided to study the child's attention, especially when attention difficulties are suspected in a child who had a recent head injury and who previously had no attention difficulties (Taylor, 1961).

The following questions are useful for evaluating the child's performance (Taylor, 1961). Are his marks well done, just recognizable, or wrong? Is he penalized for lack of speed, for inaccuracy, or for both? Does he understand the task? Does he fail because of inadequate form perception or poor attention? Does he check each figure with the samples, or does he try to remember the samples? Does he pick out one figure only and skip others? Does he work smoothly, or does he become confused as he goes along? Does he understand and proceed correctly after explanations have been made?

The actual symbols written by the child should be examined for types and frequency of distortions. Do they appear with one figure only, occasionally, or each time the figure appears? Do distortions appear randomly among the correct markings? Distortions of forms may suggest difficulties in perceptual functioning (Taylor, 1961). Inquiry should be made into any symbol that is peculiarly written, and a determination made of whether the peculiarity is associated with inadequate visual-motor coordination, or whether it has some symbolic meaning to the child.

Mazes

The Mazes subtest of the WISC is a supplementary test consisting of eight mazes, the first two of which are administered to children under the age of 8 years or to older suspected mental retardates. All items are timed, ranging from 30 to 120 seconds.

Rationale

The Mazes subtest of the WISC appears to measure planning ability and perceptual organization (following a visual pattern). Visual-motor control and speed combined with accuracy are in part needed for success.

Factor Analytic Findings

The Mazes subtest is relatively low in g. At younger age levels ($7\frac{1}{2}$ and $10\frac{1}{2}$), it is a useful measure of Perceptual Organization in combination with the Block Design and Object Assembly subtests. Mazes can be interpreted as measuring planning ability, particularly if the score departs by several points from other subtests (from the Block Design and Object Assembly subtests, in particular).

Structure of Intellect Classification (SOI)

The SOI classification of the Mazes subtest is CFI (Cognition of Figural Implications—the ability to foresee the consequences involved in figural problems). Every item is so classified.

Administrative Considerations

The child's performance should be observed carefully. Is there tremor, difficulty with control of the pencil, or nonuniformly drawn lines? Does the child correctly solve the mazes, but not receive credit because the time limit has expired?

SUMMARY

The interpretative rationale, factor analytic findings, Structure of Intellect classifications, and administrative considerations for each of the 12 WISC subtests are discussed in Chapter 13. A summary of the proposed interpretative rationales appears in Table C-8 in the Appendix. An ego-psychology approach is in part the basis for the analysis of subtest functions.

The following is a short summary of some of the important features of each subtest:

1. *Information.* The subtest is considered to measure the wealth of available information acquired as a result of native ability and early cultural experience. Memory is an important aspect of performance on the subtest. The subtest is the second best measure of g. The Structure of Intellect classifications cover eight different categories. The subtest is relatively easy to administer.

2. *Comprehension.* The subtest is considered to measure social judgment: the ability to use facts in a pertinent, meaningful, and emotionally relevant manner. The subtest is a moderately good measure of g. The Structure of Intellect classification is Evaluation of Semantic Implications (EMI) for every item. Scoring requires considerable judgment. The child's responses should be analyzed carefully.

3. *Arithmetic.* The subtest is considered to measure reasoning ability plus numerical accuracy in mental arithmetic. The subtest is a moderately good measure of g. The Structure of Intellect classifications are Memory for Symbolic Implications (MSI) and Cognition of Semantic Systems (CMS) for every item. The subtest is relatively easy to administer.

4. *Similarities.* The subtest is considered to measure verbal concept formation and logical thinking. The subtest is a moderately good measure of g. The primary Structure of Intellect classification is Cognition of Semantic Transformations (CMT). Scoring requires considerable judgment on some items. The child's responses should be evaluated carefully.

5. *Vocabulary.* The subtest is considered to measure a variety of func-

tions, including language ability and fund of information. The subtest is an excellent measure of g. The Structure of Intellect classification is Cognition of Semantic Units (CMU) for every item. The subtest requires skill to administer and score. The child's responses should be evaluated carefully.

6. *Digit Span.* The subtest is considered to measure attention and short-term memory. With older children it is part of the Freedom from Distractibility factor. The Structure of Intellect classification is Memory for Symbolic Systems (MSS) for every item. The subtest is relatively easy to administer.

7. *Picture Completion.* The subtest is considered to measure the ability to differentiate essential from non-essential details and to require concentration, visual organization, and visual memory. The subtest is a poor measure of g. The Structure of Intellect classifications are Cognition of Figural Units (CFU) and Evaluation of Figural Systems (EFS) for every item. The subtest is relatively easy to administer.

8. *Picture Arrangement.* The subtest is considered to measure nonverbal reasoning ability, and it also may be viewed as a measure of planning ability, i.e., the ability to comprehend and size up a total situation. The subtest is the best single measure of g among the Performance Scale subtests. The Structure of Intellect classifications for every item are Evaluation of Semantic Relations (EMR) and Convergent Production of Semantic Systems (NMS). The subtest is easy to administer, and it is amenable to testing-of-limits procedures.

9. *Block Design.* The subtest is considered to measure visual-motor coordination and perceptual organization. The subtest is a useful measure of g. The Structure of Intellect classifications for every item are Cognition of Figural Relations (CFR) and Evaluation of Figural Relations (EFR). The subtest requires skill to administer.

10. *Object Assembly.* The subtest is considered to measure perceptual organization ability. The subtest is a poor measure of g. The Structure of Intellect classifications for all items are Cognition of Figural Systems (CFS), Cognition of Figural Transformations (CFT), and Evaluation of Figural Relations (EFR). The subtest requires skill to administer.

11. *Coding.* The subtest is considered to measure visual-motor coordination, speed of mental operation, and short-term memory. The subtest is relatively low in g. The Structure of Intellect classifications for the entire subtest are Convergent Production of Figural Units (NFU) and Evaluation of Figural Units (EFU). The subtest is easy to administer.

12. *Mazes.* The subtest is considered to measure planning ability and perceptual organization. The subtest is relatively low in g. The Structure of Intellect classification for every item is Cognition of Figural Implications (CFI). The subtest is easy to administer.

CHAPTER 14

INTERPRETING THE WISC

The functions of the WISC subtests, presented in Chapter 13, were based on interpretative rationales developed primarily from an ego-psychology approach to subtest interpretation. Factor analytic results generally provided limited confirmation for the rationales offered for the various subtests. In the present chapter, the general results of factor analytic studies are described, as well as other types of research investigations that have evaluated the interpretative rationales for the WISC subtests. Scatter analytic techniques are reviewed systematically. Because the WISC provides individual subtest scores that are also standardized scores (mean of 10 and standard deviation of 3), statistical techniques can be applied to comparisons between subtest scores. Finally, the latter part of the chapter presents interpretative rationales for comparisons between and among subtests and between the Verbal and Performance Scales.

FACTOR ANALYSIS

In Chapter 13, Cohen's (1959) factor analytic findings, arrived at by a centroid analysis of common factor variance for the 7½, 10½, and 13½ year levels of the WISC and using the total standardization sample reported in the WISC manual, were presented for each individual subtest. In this part of Chapter 14, the general findings of his analyses are described. The five primary factors that were found at each age level are shown in Table 14–1. According to Cohen, the Verbal Comprehension I factor reflects that aspect of verbally retained knowledge that is impressed by formal education. The Perceptual Organization factor is a nonverbal factor and reflects the ability to interpret and/or organize visually perceived material against a time limit. The Freedom from Distractibility factor measures the ability to remain undistracted (to attend or concentrate). The Verbal Comprehension II factor measures the application of judgment following some implicit verbal manipulation. Verbal Comprehension I represents formally learned verbal comprehension, whereas Verbal Comprehension II represents the application of verbal skills to situations that are new to the child. The Quasi-Specific factor has no psychological interpretation.

Other findings indicated that the WISC Full Scale IQ and Verbal Scale IQ are good measures of g, while the Performance Scale IQ is a relatively poor measure of g. The best measures of g among the subtests are Vocabulary and Information, while the poorest are Picture Completion, Mazes, and Object

Table 14-1. Oblique Primary Factors in WISC for the Three Age Groups

Subtest	Factor A Verbal Comprehension I			Factor B Perceptual Organization			Factor C Freedom from Distractibility			Factor D Verbal Comprehension II			Factor E Quasi-Specific		
	7½[a]	10½	13½	7½	10½	13½	7½	10½	13½	7½	10½	13½	7½	10½	13½
Information	41	32	39	-02	02	07	-09	-02	10	02	15	00	17	00	-10
Comprehension	-10	-06	37	-02	-01	-10	-09	06	-07	47	38	20	09	-05	07
Arithmetic	21	41	07	-04	04	-04	17	10	36	-06	-09	02	18	08	-05
Similarities	34	38	26	09	-05	02	09	02	00	-01	08	24	-10	-06	09
Vocabulary	21	05	47	-07	07	00	-04	07	-10	26	30	-01	05	00	08
Digit Span	-04	04	02	-04	00	01	38	44	33	02	-09	00	04	-04	-10
Picture Completion	-06	04	-05	06	43	50	09	-10	04	28	21	27	-10	-04	-10
Picture Arrangement	01	-02	-02	29	07	09	33	-09	-06	-01	09	14	-10	38	33
Block Design	06	02	07	50	55	46	-08	15	01	07	03	10	09	04	-03
Object Assembly	-01	-05	-03	59	49	57	07	32	-09	-05	-05	-08	09	-04	10
Coding	-07	03	01	06	-05	-01	06	09	10	-01	-03	-10	39	23	25
Mazes	05	-02	-05	56	42	03	-04	20	23	-02	02	-03	04	01	10

[a]This row indicates age level.

(Reprinted by permission of the publisher and author from J. Cohen, "The Factorial Structure of the WISC at ages 7-6, 10-6, and 13-6," *Journal of Consulting Psychology*, **23**, p. 287. Copyright 1959, American Psychological Association.)

Assembly. The Perceptual Organization factor consistently is the poorest measure of *g*. Other findings and recommendations pertinent to each individual subtest have been discussed in Chapter 13.

Factor Scores

Cohen (1959) advocated the use of factor scores in place of single subtest scores, which he considered to be unreliable and ambiguous, and in place of the more or less *a priori* Verbal and Performance Scale IQ's. His proposal for factor scores is shown in Table 14-2. The Verbal Comprehension factor score results from the pooling of the Verbal Comprehension I and II factors. The Perceptual Organization factor score includes the Mazes subtest at the two younger age levels. The Freedom from Distractibility factor score is recommended only for the 13½ age level. The Full Scale or the Verbal Scale are recommended as good measures of *g*. At age level 13½ the factor scores are identical to those of the WAIS (see Cohen (1957) for factor analytic results of the WAIS). The standard deviation of the factor scores is 2½, with the exception of the *g* factor score (based on the Full Scale), which has a standard deviation of 2.

After the factor scores are obtained, they can be transformed into Deviation Quotients by a relatively simple procedure (Tellegen & Briggs, 1967). The Deviation Quotients are obtained for each individual factor proposed by Cohen; it is not the same as the Deviation Quotient derived from all of the WISC subtests. (The method is similar to the one proposed to obtain Deviation Quotients for short forms, which is described in Chapter 13. However, since the subtests are the same for each factor score, it is not necessary to obtain the Σr_{jk}, as it is when various short-form combinations are selected.) The procedure avoids the problems associated with prorating formulas and with regression estimates. It is based on the reliabilities of the subtests that form the factor scores. The Deviation Quotient has a mean of 100 and a standard deviation of 15, the same as for the IQ, which also is a Deviation Quotient.

The following formula is used to convert the factor scores into Deviation Quotients:

$$\text{Deviation Quotient} = (\text{Factor score} \times a) + b.$$

Table 14-2. PROPOSED WISC FACTOR SCORES

FACTOR SCORE	AGES	SUBTESTS
Verbal Comprehension	all	Information Comprehension Similarities Vocabulary
Perceptual Organization	7½ and 10½	Block Design Object Assembly Mazes
	13½	Block Design Object Assembly
Freedom from Distractibility	13½	Arithmetic Digit Span
g	all	Full Scale or Verbal Scale

Adapted from Cohen (1959).

The following steps are needed:

1. The factor score is obtained by summing the subtest scaled scores that form the factor.

2. The a and b constants for the appropriate factor score are obtained from Table C-17 in the Appendix.

3. The Deviation Quotient is computed with these three pieces of information.

An example: A 14-year-old examinee obtained scaled scores of 9 and 13 (total = 22) on the Arithmetic and Digit Span subtests, the two subtests in the Freedom from Distractibility factor score. Table C-17 in the Appendix indicates that the a and b constants for this factor score are 3.0 and 40, respectively. When these three figures are substituted in the formula, we have a Deviation Quotient of $106 = (22 \times 3.0) + 40$. The same procedure is followed for computing other factor scores.

Comparison between Centroid and Principal-Factor Methods

Silverstein (1969a) also performed a factor analysis using the entire standardization data, but without dividing the standardization data into age levels. Instead of the centroid method, the principal-factor method was used. We have seen that, in the centroid method of factor analysis, factors are extracted from a correlation matrix in which the first axis passes through the center of gravity of the system. The principal-factor method is a factor analytic method that locates one axis so that it defines a factor which accounts for the maximum possible variance of the correlation matrix, and locates another axis that accounts for the maximum possible amount of the remaining variance. Two principal factors were found. Verbal Scale subtests had the highest loadings on Factor I, while Performance Scale subtests had the highest loadings on Factor II. The average loadings of the subtests and scales on each factor are shown in Table 14-3. Silverstein concluded that the Verbal and Performance Scales constitute actual functional unities in the scale.

Since the two different factor analytic methods yielded different results, it is difficult to know which findings best reflect the organization of the WISC. Silverstein (1969a) noted that neither his approach nor the one by Cohen (1959) is

Table 14-3. AVERAGE LOADINGS OF WISC SUBTESTS

SUBTEST	FACTOR I	FACTOR II
Information	67	−03
Comprehension	57	−01
Arithmetic	57	−01
Similarities	60	−01
Digit Span	41	03
Vocabulary	65	02
Picture Completion	19	33
Block Design	13	53
Picture Arrangement	31	27
Object Assembly	−02	62
Coding	27	16
Mazes	11	40
Verbal Scale	59	00
Performance Scale	17	40

(Reprinted by permission of the publisher and author from A. B. Silverstein, "An Alternative Factor Analytic Solution for Wechsler's Intelligence Scales," *Educational and Psychological Measurement*, **29**, p. 766. Copyright 1969, Fredrick Kuder.)

"right" or "wrong" on mathematical grounds alone. He also pointed out that his Factor I represents a merger of Cohen's Verbal Comprehension I, Memory, and Verbal Comprehension II factors, while Factor II represents a merger of Cohen's Perceptual Organization and Quasi-Specific factors. Those examiners who desire to interpret the Verbal and Performance Scale IQ's as functional unities can find support for such a procedure in Silverstein's results. However, other examiners may wish to use Cohen's approach, which focuses on the use of factor scores. It is also possible to use the approaches of both Cohen and Silverstein in connection with the same protocol to evaluate different types of relationships among the subtests. Finally, examiners also may find it helpful to use a scatter analysis approach, discussed in a later part of this chapter, to evaluate the child's scores; this approach highlights the individual subtests, but it is more unreliable than using the individual scales or the factor scores.

Other Factor Analytic Studies

Factor analytic investigations of the WISC also have appeared that have used the WISC standardization data (Maxwell, 1959), normal samples (Crockett, Klonoff, & Bjerring, 1969; Cropley, 1964; Jackson, 1960; Jones, 1962; Klonoff, 1971; Osborne, 1963, 1965), racial groups (Osborne, 1964, 1966; Semler & Iscoe, 1966), learning disabled children (Leton, 1972), and brain-injured children (Grimaldi, 1970). These studies, for the most part, agree with the findings of Cohen (1959), although there are differences depending on the method used to perform the factor analysis and depending on the sample used. Many of these studies indicate, as Burt (1960) has observed, that it is unjustifiable to assume that a given factor pattern will appear at all age levels and with all types of children.

STUDIES EVALUATING ASSUMPTIONS AND CORRELATES OF WISC SUBTESTS

In Chapter 13, the 12 WISC subtests were described and evaluated. The rationales of the subtests were based primarily on clinical interpretations. For the most part, research investigations were not used to establish the functions associated with each subtest. In this section, a number of studies are reviewed that have investigated some of the assumptions and correlates of the WISC subtests.

Comprehension and Picture Arrangement

A relatively small but significant relationship has been found between Comprehension subtest scores, but not Picture Arrangement subtest scores, and Vineland Social Maturity Scale scores ($r = .27$) in a sample of boys between 8 and 12 years of age who were having reading difficulty (Krippner, 1964). These results suggest that there may be some basis for interpreting Comprehension scores, but not Picture Arrangement scores, as reflecting social skills. However, the use of the Vineland Social Maturity Scale as the criterion for the Comprehension and Picture Arrangement subtests is interesting but by no means crucial for evaluating social comprehension and social anticipation skills.

Digit Span

Digit Span scores have not been found to be related to degree of classroom distractibility in elementary school children (Nalven, 1969; Nalven & Puleo,

1968). However, these studies do not provide adequate tests of the hypotheses concerning the Digit Span subtest. Classroom distractibility may have many causes besides limited attention span. Further, to what extent should a cognitive measure of attention or immediate memory be related to classroom distractibility?

Block Design

Block Design scores are susceptible to training (Schubert, 1967). These findings imply that Block Design scores are dependent on environmental influences.

Object Assembly

The relationship between Object Assembly scores and extensiveness of bodily concerns has been investigated (Blatt, Allison, & Baker, 1965). The seven children in the bodily-concern group were found to have significantly lower Object Assembly scores than the six control-group children, whereas no other significant differences between the two groups were observed on the other subtests. It was concluded that the Object Assembly subtest is susceptible to interference by concerns and preoccupations about body intactness. However, subsequent investigations failed to confirm these findings (Marsden & Kalter, 1969; Rockwell, 1967). Consequently, little can be said about the relationship between bodily concerns and WISC Object Assembly scores.

Coding

A significant correlation has been reported between Coding scores and achievement-orientation ratings ($r = .51$) in a group of 10-year-old physically handicapped children (Oakland, 1969). These results provide some support for the hypothesis that the WISC Coding subtest may involve motivational components.

Subtests and Test Behavior Relationships

Burnes (1971) set out to evaluate the assumptions about WISC subtests as they pertain to the examinees' behavior during the examination. The children were rated on attention, energy level, social skill, task persistence, and concern about performance. The sample consisted of 78 normal 8-year-old Negro and white boys from the upper middle and lower classes. The following relationships were hypothesized: (a) attention with Arithmetic, Digit Span, Picture Completion, Picture Arrangement, Block Design, Object Assembly, Coding, and Mazes; (b) energy level with Coding; (c) social skill with Comprehension and Vocabulary; and (d) task persistence with Picture Completion, Block Design, Object Assembly, and Mazes. No hypothesis was made for the concern-about-performance behavioral rating.

While many significant correlations were obtained, they usually did not follow the predicted relationships. Most of the significant correlations occurred within the lower class group, therefore suggesting that the scores of lower class children are sensitive to their test behaviors. Some of the more substantive findings were that Picture Arrangement scores were positively related to attention, task persistence, and concern about performance, while Coding scores were not related to any of the behavioral scales. The major difficulty in evaluating correlates of WISC subtests by using behavior ratings derived from the examination is that the range of behavior during the examination is restricted.

Block Design, Picture Completion, and Object Assembly as Measures of Field Dependence

Goodenough and Karp (1961) sought to determine whether performance on three WISC subtests (Block Design, Picture Completion, and Object Assembly) was related to the dimension of field dependence. Field-independent persons tend to be active, initiating, and organizing in their relationship toward the environment, whereas field-dependent persons tend to be dependent in their interpersonal relations, suggestible, and conforming. On perceptual tasks, field-independent persons can easily "break up" an organized perceptual field—they can overcome embedding contexts by readily separating an item from its context. Conversely, field-dependent persons accept the prevailing field or context—they do not readily separate an item from its context. When the WISC and measures of field dependence were administered to normal children, the results of a factor analysis indicated that the three subtests loaded on a factor in common with measures of field dependence. Consequently, it was concluded that performance on the Block Design, Picture Completion, and Object Assembly subtests requires a capacity for overcoming embedding contexts.

A closer examination of the three subtests shows how they are related to the capacity for overcoming embeddedness. Goodenough and Karp pointed out that on the Block Design subtest, the stimulus cards are an organized whole that usually must be "broken up" for effective performance. On the Object Assembly subtest, a rigid adherence to a conceptualized image of the solution may impair performance, particularly where the parts that are given to the examinee do not readily correspond to units making up his image of the whole. On the Picture Completion subtest, the solution can be arrived at by analyzing the whole into its components in order to locate the missing part. The Block Design and Object Assembly subtests and, to some extent, the Picture Completion subtest load on the Perceptual Organization factor (Cohen, 1959).

Goodenough and Karp's research suggests that the Block Design, Picture Completion, and Object Assembly subtests reflect the ability to find or to manipulate an item that is embedded within a surrounding context. The ability to overcome embeddedness is an ability that can be considered to reflect a general cognitive style by which performance in many perceptual and intellectual situations might be characterized. A similar view has been expressed by Witkin et al. (1966). They suggested that the ability to overcome an embedding context (that is, to experience items as discrete from an organized field of which they are a part), which the three subtests have as a common requirement, is equivalent to the ability to deal analytically with cognitive tasks.

WISC Subtests and Piagetian Conservation Stages

The relationship between performance on psychometric tests and performance on Piagetian measures of conservation has also been of interest (Orpet & Meyers, 1970). Five WISC subtests (Arithmetic, Digit Span, Vocabulary, Picture Arrangement, and Block Design), along with other tests, were administered to a sample of first- and second-grade middle class children. Only the Picture Arrangement subtest, of the five WISC subtests studied, was found to differentiate significantly between children showing conservation and those not showing conservation. Other variables that were also found to be related to conservation were the Nebraska Picture Association test, Knox Cube Tapping test, and a descriptive global style in explaining pictures. The results suggested that the ability to make inferences from meaningful nonverbal material, but not from material tapping acculturated verbal skills, best distinguished the child who shows conservation from one who does not.

In another investigation studying first- and second-grade children, the WISC Vocabulary subtest and other verbal measures were found to correlate highly ($r = .70$) with Piagetian conservation measures (Sollee, 1969). These results, which appear to conflict with those of Orpet and Meyers (1970), suggest that verbal competence is related to the achievement of stable and generalized levels of conservation, measured either nonverbally or verbally. Another point concerning Piagetian tests and intelligence level is worth mentioning: despite the different goals and the theoretical differences in the construction of the Piaget and WISC measures of intelligence, both appear to be sampling cognitive processes that are highly correlated and that are equally effective in predicting achievement as early as first grade (Dudek, Lester, Goldberg, & Dyer, 1969).

WISC Subtests and Analytic Concepts

Another area of interest has been the relationship between the development of analytic concepts, defined as the ability to determine the shared similarity in a particular objective component among a set of stimuli, and performance on the Information, Vocabulary, Picture Completion, and Picture Arrangement subtests (Kagan, Rosman, Day, Albert, & Phillips, 1964). Only scores on the Picture Arrangement subtest were found to be related significantly to analytic conceptual ability in a sample of first- and second-grade children. According to the investigators, the Picture Arrangement subtest requires a perceptual analysis of component aspects of the pictures. The correct arrangement of the scenes into a coherent theme occurs if the child attends to subtle cues, such as the posture of people and direction of travel of objects. Consequently, success on the Picture Arrangement subtest may reflect analytic conceptual ability.

Comment on Studies Evaluating Assumptions and Correlates of WISC Subtests

The findings of the research investigations concerning the assumptions of WISC subtests are varied; some of the assumptions appear to hold while others do not. For the most part, the studies reviewed cannot be said to be adequate tests of the hypotheses. We have seen that many of the studies have methodological difficulties. However, despite the difficulties in assessing the validity of the subtest assumptions, the studies reviewed are a beginning, and more systematic research would be welcome.

The investigations of the correlates of WISC subtests point out the value of applying theoretical views from fields of personality and cognition to intelligence test performance. The Block Design, Picture Completion, and Object Assembly subtests were found to be related to the capacity for overcoming embeddedness, while performance on the Picture Arrangement subtest was found to be related to both analytic conceptual ability and the ability to show conservation. Both analytic conceptual ability and conservation are highly dependent on a perceptual analysis of stimuli. Research with correlates of subtest scores innervates the field of intelligence testing by placing the wisdom of general psychology at its doorstep.

SCATTER ANALYSIS

The evaluation of irregular performance on intelligence tests has been of interest to psychologists almost from the beginning of the testing movement. We have seen in Chapter 10 that scatter analysis applied to the Stanford-Binet has proven to be, for the most part, of limited value. However, scatter and profile analyses are tools that still are used frequently with the Wechsler scales, although these procedures, as the material in this section of the chapter and in the chapters in Section 5 indicate, must also be used with caution. The cardinal position advocated for use of scatter analysis is that *scatter analysis is dependent upon the presence of statistically significant differences between subtest scaled scores or between Verbal and Performance Scale IQ's.* Thus, before any statements are made about whether the examinee obtained higher (or lower) scaled scores (or IQ's) on one subtest (or scale) than another subtest (or scale), significant differences between the scaled scores (or IQ's) should be present. The emphasis on a statistical approach to scatter analysis comes about because the limited reliability of any one particular subtest means that predictions based on individual subtest scores are likely to be poor. As Littell (1960) pointed out, "any prediction made on the basis of an individual subtest score is little more than a rationalized hunch. A plausible rationale certainly does not make a valid measure [p. 152]."

The WISC has an apparent advantage over the Stanford-Binet for the purposes of scatter analysis and analysis of functions. The items on the WISC are already grouped into subtests that in turn, as Chapter 13 has indicated, might be revealing of specific mental operations. The scaled scores on the subtests permit ready comparisons and preparation of profiles. Scatter refers to the pattern or configuration formed by the subtest scaled scores. One of the most satisfactory approaches to the problem of scatter analysis was offered by Liverant (1960). He suggested that it is

justifiable to regard uneven test profiles as the result of conditions (not necessarily abnormal ones) which have differentially affected the acquisition of certain skills and/or the manifestation of these skills in certain classes of situations. Then the task becomes one of determining what these conditions are and how they operate, rather than ascribing subtest patterns to various types of disease entities which affect another entity (intelligence) [p. 102].

The pattern of subtest scores shown by a child is not fortuitous or random. Rather, the task becomes one of determining which of several possible factors may account for the performance. Ideally it would be necessary to consider to what extent age, sex, racial or ethnic group membership, socioeconomic status, occupation, education, special training, social and physical environment, family background, and nationality have affected the examinee's performance on the scale. Only after the above factors have been considered should diagnostic interpretative hypotheses be sought to account for the examinee's performance (Ogdon, 1967).

Scatter, in interaction with selected examinee variables, has been shown to play a role in influencing psychologists' judgments about the degree to which an obtained IQ represented the examinee's "true IQ." Nalven, Hofmann, and Bierbryer (1969) sent WISC subtest scaled scores (ranging from 6 on Arithmetic and Vocabulary to 13 on Digit Span and Coding) and IQ's (Verbal IQ of 91, Performance IQ of 92, and Full Scale IQ of 91) together with four other pieces of information about an examinee (age, sex, race, and socioeconomic status) to psychologists, who were asked to estimate the examinee's "true IQ" (i.e., his "effective intelligence"). Each respondent ($N = 320$) gave an estimate for only one protocol. The results indicated that the respondents' estimates were differentially influenced by both the examinee's socioeconomic status (lower class or middle class) and race (Caucasian or Negro) but not by his age (8 or 11 years) or sex. The mean estimated IQ was 98. Higher estimates were given to examinees from the lower class (M IQ = 101) than from the middle class (M IQ = 96), and to Negro examinees (M IQ = 100) than to Caucasian examinees (M IQ = 97).

In the Nalven et al. (1969) study, scatter was not an independent variable; consequently the part scatter played in the psychologists' judgments cannot be evaluated. A crucial test of the effects of scatter on psychologists' judgments would entail having them estimate IQ's from profiles that show limited scatter as well as from profiles that show much scatter. Since estimated IQ was on the average higher than computed IQ, there is weak circumstantial evidence that scatter may have played a part in the overestimation. Interestingly, in another study, amount of scatter on the WISC has not been found to be related to scores obtained on group intelligence tests; thus, these results suggest that a markedly uneven pattern of subtest scores should not be interpreted as indicating that the results are an underestimate of the child's ability, at least with respect to scores obtained on group intelligence tests (Lessing & Lessing, 1963).

While the major role of scatter analysis, as Liverant (1960) has indicated, should be one of attempting to determine the conditions that may have led to the particular profile exhibited by the examinee, some psychologists still view scatter analysis as a method of studying the organization of ego functions (cf. Blatt & Allison, 1968). Scatter analysis, as Holt (1967) pointed out, is a method of generating hypotheses (primarily inferences) about personality, thought processes, defenses, and related characteristics. Scatter analysis is seen as providing an additional source for qualitative analysis.

If scatter analysis is used to generate hypotheses about personality, it should be employed as one source of data among several sources of test data that must be integrated and organized. Scatter is likely to be misleading when it fails to be congruent with other test indices. It is important to reiterate that, before any inferences about personality or thought processes are made from scatter analysis, the following should be determined: (*a*) that the scaled scores used to formulate the hypotheses are significantly different from one another; (*b*) that cultural factors are ruled out; and (*c*) that other important factors (e.g., sex, age, special training, and socioeconomic status) are considered in evaluating the test scores. It even may be true that the scatter reflects no particular personality pattern, but simply is a manifestation of factors inherent in the unreliability of the individual subtest scores, examiner variability, situational variability, and the specific make-up of the individual's unique pattern of cognitive development displayed on the scale.

In the early history of the Wechsler and Wechsler-type scales it was hoped that scatter analysis would contribute to the diagnostic process by allowing the clinician to classify examinees into diagnostic categories or to pinpoint their cognitive deficiencies. Soon after the Point Scale (Yerkes et al., 1915) was published, Pressey and Cole (1918a) pointed out that irregularity on the scale might have a number of implications, including poor cooperation, deterioration, negativism, retardation, temporary psychotic disturbance, physical disease or disability, malingering, and illiteracy. However, research studies together with clinical work have failed to provide any firm basis for making predictions derived from scatter or profile analysis (Tyler, 1971). Thus, for example, Frost (1960) reported that scatter analysis applied to the WISC was generally ineffective in differentiating among 10 different categories of emotionally disturbed children. The use of scatter analysis for the WISC and WPPSI (and other Wechsler scales) presents problems because the subtests have relatively low average specific variance (Silverstein, 1968b) and because of the variable internal consistency indices among the subtests (Querishi, 1968c).

Schofield's (1952) critique of scatter analysis of the Wechsler-Bellevue appears to be pertinent for all Wechsler tests. He pointed out that there probably is a limited range within which personality variables may show themselves in intelligence test performance and, consequently, it is difficult to determine their operation. The failure to demonstrate consistent differences among widely different groups, such as normals and psychotics, in their degree of scatter makes it extremely improbable that scatter will be helpful in diagnosing borderline cases. Schofield, however, stated that "it is reasonable to entertain the notion that some of the subtest patterning observed in the Wechsler is reflective of the basic organization of intellective functions [p. 17]." Such an assumption is probably held by many psychologists who administer the Wechsler scales and is one that is favored in the present text.

While we have seen that scatter and profile analysis is fraught with difficulties, it still appears useful to evaluate routinely the pattern of scores obtained by the examinee. The goal of scatter analysis is not to classify or categorize the child; rather, it is to seek clues to guide the evaluation of his abilities. Ideas generated from subtest scatter must be viewed simply as hypotheses to be checked against other information about the examinee. Scatter analysis may assist in arriving at recommendations for clinical treatment, educational programs, or vocational placement. Thus, for example, Mecham et al. (1966) advocated a careful study of scatter on the WISC for the assessment of brain-injured children. They believed that the dynamic and functional nature of the child's learning problems can be better understood by use of scatter analysis. In addition to the subtests, the Verbal and Performance IQ's should be compared and evaluated. Discrepancies between the two scales may be particularly useful, for example, in the study of ethnic minority group children (see Chapter 4) and brain-injured children (see Chapter 21).

Many different patterns are, of course, possible. Some configurations have all subtest scaled scores within three or four points of each other, while other configurations have greater variability, with subtest scaled scores differing from each other by many points. Marked intersubtest variability may be due to temporary inefficiencies, permanent incapacity, or disturbed school experiences (Blatt & Allison, 1968). The examiner in each case will have to seek out the best explanation of the results by using all of the test data and the case history material.

Approaches to Scatter Analysis

The primary methods of scatter analysis include (1) comparing sets of individual subtest scores, (2) comparing the Verbal Scale and Performance Scale IQ's, (3) comparing the average of several subtest scaled scores with one of the subtest scaled scores that is included in the average, and (4) comparing the average of several subtest scaled scores with one of the subtest scaled scores that *is not* included in the average. (The approach described in (3) is similar to the one offered by Rhodes (1969), who devised a scatter profile to assist in determing whether scores obtained on the subtests are significantly different from the level of performance on the Full Scale, Verbal Scale, or Performance Scale.) Additional methods include (5) comparing the average of the Verbal Scale subtest scaled scores with one of the Verbal subtest scaled scores that is included in the average, (6) comparing the average of the Verbal Scale subtest scaled scores with one of the Verbal subtest scaled scores that *is not* included in the average, (7) comparing the average of the Performance Scale subtest scaled scores with one of the Performance subtest scaled scores that is included in the average, (8) comparing the average of the Performance Scale subtest scaled scores with one of the Performance subtest scaled scores that *is not* included in the average, and (9) comparing each subtest scaled score with the Vocabulary subtest scaled score. Since methods 5, 6, 7, and 8 are special cases of method 3 or method 4 and since method 9 is a special case of method 1, only methods 1 through 4 are described.

1. Comparing Sets of Individual Subtest Scores. Comparisons between sets of individual subtest scores permit an assessment of the child's strengths and weaknesses. However, before any statements are made concerning whether one subtest score is different from another, it is necessary to determine whether the magnitude of difference between any two subtest scores is statistically significant. This determination can be made easily by reference to Table C-10 in the Appendix. Table C-10, which was prepared by Newland and Smith (1967), indicates the differences between sets of scaled scores on the WISC subtests that are needed to satisfy the .05 and .01 confidence levels.

Table C-10 should be consulted whenever the examiner desires to compare scaled scores between sets of subtests. It is divided into three sections, each of which represents one of three age levels: 5 through $8^{11}/_{12}$ years, 9 through $11^{11}/_{12}$ years, and 12 through $15^{11}/_{12}$ years. For a child who is between 5 and 9 years of age, the statement, "The child obtained a higher score on the Information than on the Comprehension subtest" should not be made unless there is a 5-point scaled score difference between the Information and Comprehension subtests. As Table C-10 also shows, this difference need be only four scaled score points when the child is between 9 and 12 years of age or between 12 and 16 years of age. Generally, differences between sets of subtest scaled scores do not have to be as large for older children as for younger children in order to reach the .05 or .01 significance levels.

The need for a smaller difference among the subtests with increasing age follows from the increase in reliability of the scaled scores with age. The magnitude of the difference needed at a particular confidence level is dependent on the standard error of measurement of each subtest and scale. The standard error of measurement, in turn, is related to the reliability of the subtest or scale. The subtests are more reliable after the age of 9 years than before the age of 9 years. (See note in Table C-10 for an example of how the magnitude of differences was arrived at.)

2. Comparing the Verbal Scale and Performance Scale IQ's.   Table C-10 in the Appendix should also be consulted to obtain the differences between sets of IQ's on the WISC Verbal, Peformance, and Full Scales that are needed to satisfy the .05 and .01 confidence levels. Differences between any two IQ's, as in the case of differences between sets of subtest scaled scores, should reach, as a minimum, the .05 level of confidence before any statements are made about whether performance on one scale differs from that on another scale. Comparisons between the Full Scale and Verbal Scale or between the Full Scale and Performance Scale are likely to be less important than the Verbal-Performance Scale comparison, because the Full Scale is composed of both of the individual scales.

As in the case of the subtest scaled scores, differences between sets of IQ's need not be as large for older children as for younger children in order to reach the .05 or .01 significance levels. Thus, a 15-point difference is needed between the Verbal and Performance Scales at the .05 level of confidence for a child under 9 years of age, whereas only an 11-point difference between these two scales is needed for a child who is between 9 and 12 years of age or between 12 and 16 years of age.

The procedure advocated by Newland and Smith is similar to the one described by Field (1960) for the Verbal and Performance Scales. Field extended the probability levels to include the range between .001 and .50. The discrepancy scores (or difference scores) between the Verbal and Performance Scales of the WISC and WPPSI associated with these levels are shown in Table C-18 in the Appendix. The difference scores needed for the .05 and .01 levels are the same (except for rounding) as those that appear in Table C-10. Field also noted that it is sometimes of interest to determine the percentage of individuals obtaining a given discrepancy (difference) between the Verbal and Performance Scales. Table C-19 in the Appendix shows these data for the WISC and WPPSI. Tables C-18 and C-19 provide somewhat different information; the nature of the problem will dictate which table is more useful.

3. Comparing the Average of Several Subtest Scaled Scores with One of the Subtest Scaled Scores Included in the Average.   Table C-11 in the Appendix has been prepared to facilitate comparison of the average of several subtest scaled scores with each of the subtest scaled scores that are included in the average. It shows the deviations from the average that are needed at the 5 per cent and 1 per cent confidence levels for a variety of comparisons, including averages that are based on 10, 11, or 12 subtests or on the number of the subtests in the Verbal or Performance Scales.

In order to use Table C-11, the following steps are necessary:

1. When the 10 standard subtests have been given, compute the average of the 10 scaled scores by summing the scaled scores and dividing by 10, the number of subtests.

2. Compute the deviation from the average for each subtest.

3. Check column one of Table C-11, the column for the 10 standard subtests, to determine whether the deviations from the average are significant.

4. Use column two or three when 11 subtests have been given, and column four when 12 subtests have been given. The divisor in these cases for Step 4 will be either 11 or 12, depending on the number of subtests that have been administered. (Use the appropriate column and the correct divisor for comparisons involving averages that are based only on the Verbal or Performance Scale subtests.)

A concrete example, modeled after Davis (1959), illustrates how the significant deviations can be obtained. Suppose the examiner wishes to compare each of the 10 standard WISC subtest scaled scores (excluding Digit Span and Mazes) with the average of the 10 subtest scaled scores. The examinee's subtest scaled scores are shown in the first column of Table 14–4, which is a worksheet that can be used for making the comparisons. We have seen that the significance of the difference between the examinee's average subtest scaled score and any one of the subtest scaled scores that is included in the average can be determined from Table C-11 in the Appendix. This table shows the minimum deviation of each subtest scaled score from the average that can be regarded as significant at the .05 and .01 levels. Since the 10 standard subtests were given, column one of Table C-11 should be used. This column shows that the examinee's scaled scores on the Similarities, Block Design, and Coding

Table 14-4. WORKSHEET FOR COMPARING THE AVERAGE OF SEVERAL SUBTEST SCALED SCORES WITH ONE OF THE SUBTEST SCORES INCLUDED IN THE AVERAGE

SUBTEST	EXAMINEE'S SUBTEST SCALED SCORE	DEVIATION FROM AVERAGE	SIGNIFICANCE LEVEL
Information	10	+ 1.1	Not significant
Comprehension	6	− 2.9	Not significant
Arithmetic	8	− .9	Not significant
Similarities	5	− 3.9	.01
Vocabulary	8	− .9	Not significant
Picture Completion	10	+ 1.1	Not significant
Picture Arrangement	11	+ 2.1	Not significant
Block Design	15	+ 6.1	.01
Object Assembly	12	+ 3.1	Not significant
Coding	4	− 4.9	.01
Sum of scaled scores	89		
Average scaled score	8.9		

Note.—Significance levels obtained from Table C-11 in Appendix.
Adapted from Davis (1959).

subtests deviate sufficiently from his average scaled score to warrant the inference that the difference is attributable to something other than chance. On the Block Design subtest, the score is significantly higher than the average, while on the Similarities and Coding subtests, the scores are significantly lower than the average.

4. Comparing the Average of Several Scaled Scores with One of the Subtest Scaled Scores Not Included in the Average.   It also may be of interest to determine whether the difference between the examinee's average scaled score and a scaled score on a subtest that is *not* included in the average is statistically significant. This type of comparison can be helpful when one or two subtests markedly shift the average scaled score. Table C-12 in the Appendix shows the deviations from average that are needed at the 5 per cent and 1 per cent confidence levels for essentially the same kinds of comparisons that are shown in Table C-11. In order to use Table C-12, the following steps are necessary:

1. When the 10 standard subtests have been given and the first comparison is between the Information subtest scaled score and the average of the remaining nine subtest scaled scores, compute the average of the nine subtest scaled scores by dividing by 9, the number of subtests to be averaged.

2. Compute the deviation from the average for the Information subtest.

3. Check column one of Table C-12, the column for any of the nine standard subtests that have been given in addition to the standard subtest for the comparison, to determine whether the deviation from average is significant.

4. Repeat the same procedure for the remaining subtests, recomputing the average each time.

5. Use columns two or three when 11 subtests have been given, and column four when 12 subtests have been given. The divisor in these cases for Step 5 will be either 10 or 11, depending on the number of subtests that have been administered. (Use the appropriate column and the correct divisor for comparisons involving averages that are based only on the Verbal or Performance Scale subtests.)

COMPARISONS BETWEEN AND AMONG WISC SUBTESTS

In the section on scatter analysis, detailed procedures were described for making comparisons between sets of subtest scaled scores. Interpreting the meaning of differences among subtest scores is not an easy matter. Once significance has been established, the task still remains to translate the statistical findings into meaningful descriptions. Careful study of the material that has been presented for each subtest in Chapter 13 and of the material previously presented in Chapter 14 will facilitate the making of such interpretations. In addition, the material discussed below should prove to be of benefit. However, it is important to recognize that this material, like some of the material presented in Chapter 13, must be viewed with caution. The suggested interpretations should be viewed as hypotheses that may prove to be useful in evaluating the child's performance, but the interpretations that are offered still are in need of further investigation.

Information and Comprehension

Comprehension scores that are significantly above Information scores may suggest the use of repressive defenses. In contrast, Comprehension scores that are significantly below Information scores may suggest a doubt-laden or suspicious individual (Rapaport et al., 1968).

Comprehension and Arithmetic

Both the Comprehension and Arithmetic subtests require reasoning ability, or more specifically, the ability to analyze a set of given material and then to recognize the elements that are needed toward the solution of the specified problem (Freeman, 1962).

Arithmetic and Digit Span

Both the Arithmetic and Digit Span subtests require facility with numbers and ability in immediate recall (Freeman, 1962). Comparing the two subtests may provide an index of the relative balance between attention (Digit Span) and concentration (Arithmetic) (Blatt & Allison, 1968).

Comprehension and Picture Arrangement

Both the Comprehension and Picture Arrangement subtests contain stimuli that are concerned with social interaction. Scores on the two subtests permit comparison of well-learned social conventionalities (Comprehension) with the capacity to anticipate and plan in a social context (Picture Arrangement). High Picture Arrangement scores coupled with low Comprehension scores may indicate an individual who is sensitive to interpersonal nuances, but one who also disregards social conventionality (Blatt & Allison, 1968).

An adequate Comprehension score coupled with a poor Picture Arrangement score suggests that the child can understand social situations in the abstract, but that once he is involved in them he may be unable to decide what they may mean or to decide how to act (Palmer, 1970).

Vocabulary, Information, and Comprehension

A high Vocabulary score and a high Information score coupled with a low Comprehension score may suggest an individual who, in life situations, is not able to utilize fully his verbal facility and general knowledge; he therefore may have impaired judgment (Rapaport et al., 1968).

Block Design, Object Assembly, and Coding

The Block Design, Object Assembly, and Coding subtests of the WISC require visual-motor coordination; that is, they involve motor activity guided by visual organization. A visual direction is involved in the execution of the tasks. The role of visual organization differs in the three subtests (Rapaport et al., 1968). In the Block Design subtest, visual organization is involved in a process consisting of analysis (breaking down the pattern) and synthesis (building the pattern up again out of the blocks). In the Object Assembly subtest, the motor action consists of arranging parts into a meaningful pattern. In the Coding subtest, visual organization is of the same kind that is found in such activities as writing or drawing. Thus, the name "visual organization" does not mean the same function in every case.

EVALUATION OF WISC VERBAL AND PERFORMANCE SCALES

The evaluation of the WISC Verbal and Performance Scales is dependent primarily on the assumptions made for the individual subtests that comprise the respective scales. However, some general observations can be made concerning the scales as a whole. For example, the Verbal Scale is relatively highly structured, is dependent on the child's cumulated experience, and usually requires the child to respond automatically with what he already knows, whereas the Performance Scale is relatively less highly structured, is more dependent on the child's immediate problem solving ability, and requires the child to meet new situations and to apply past experience and previously acquired skills to a new set of demands (Pedersen & Wender, 1968; Silverstein, Mohan, Franken, & Rhone, 1964). The findings obtained from research investigations of Verbal-Performance Scale discrepancies are reported in Chapters 20 through 23, which survey various forms of childhood disturbances and mental retardation.

A promising approach to determining the behavioral correlates of WISC scores has been presented by Pauker (1971). While still at a preliminary stage, Pauker is attempting to determine characteristics—in such areas as health, developmental history, family relationships, and personality—that are associated with WISC profiles. His method, in part, consists of locating a group of subjects with a specific WISC pattern (e.g., Performance Scale higher than Verbal Scale by 15 or more points), matching the target group with a control group on age and Full Scale IQ, and finding descriptive statements in medical records that distinguish the two groups. The results of such studies may prove to be valuable as aids in the diagnostic process.

Weiner (1969) set out to investigate some of the correlates associated with children who have a large Verbal-Performance discrepancy in favor of the Performance Scale (termed "language-deficient group"). A short form of the WISC was administered to white, native-born American children who were between 6 and 8 years of age. The Verbal Scale subtests were Information, Similarities, and Vocabulary; the Performance Scale subtests were Object Assembly, Block Design, and Mazes. The selection criteria for the language-deficient group were as follows: a Performance Scale IQ that was above 80, a Verbal Scale IQ that was below 90, and a Verbal Scale IQ that was 15 points or more below the Performance Scale IQ. In the control group, the children had a Verbal-Performance discrepancy that was less than 10 points. Excluded from both groups were children with motor problems, auditory problems, or uncorrected visual problems, and those with gross incapacitating emotional problems. The IQ's for the language-deficient and control groups were as follows: Verbal Scale M IQ = 74 and 102, respectively; Performance Scale M IQ = 101 and 97, respectively.

A battery of tests was administered to both groups. The results indicated that the language-deficient group was inferior to the control group on auditory conceptual tasks and on auditory perceptual tasks, while the two groups did not differ significantly on tasks involving the visual modality; sensory modality thus was shown to play an important role in the cognitive functioning of language-deficient children.

SUMMARY

Factor analytic investigations of the WISC serve to demonstrate the underlying commonalities that exist in the subtests. Cohen's classic centroid-method factor analysis has provided the basis for evaluating the factor structure of the WISC. The following five primary factors were found: Verbal Comprehension I, Perceptual Organization, Freedom from Distractibility, Verbal Comprehension II, and Quasi-Specific. The contribution of the subtests to each factor is partly a function of age level. Factor scores, which potentially provide additional information about the child's performance, can be obtained and converted to Deviation Quotients. Silverstein, using the principal-factor method, reported that the Verbal and Performance Scales can be considered to constitute actual functional unities.

The few studies that have evaluated assumptions and correlates of WISC subtests are generally disappointing, in that they do not provide any firm foundation for predicting behavorial patterns from WISC scores. Methodological shortcomings, however, are evident in many of these studies. Substantial evidence exists, however, that (*a*) the Block Design, Picture Completion, and Object Assembly subtests are related to field independence—a capacity for overcoming embedding contexts—and (*b*) the Picture Arrangement subtest is related to analytic conceptual ability. Piagetian and WISC measures of intelligence appear to be highly correlated.

Scatter analysis should be based on a statistical approach, which is designed to determine significant differences between sets of subtest scaled scores and between Verbal and Performance Scale IQ's. However, even after such differences are established, it is necessary to consider a variety of factors that may account for a specific profile. Scatter analysis is a method of generating hypotheses about the organization of intellective functions, and, to a much lesser extent, about personality. Scatter analytic findings are only one source for test interpretation, and they must be interpreted in relation to the entire test performance and background data. Various approaches to scatter analysis are described and illustrated in the chapter. Interpreting the findings of scatter analysis requires considerable judgment and skill. Some examples are presented to illustrate how differences between or among subtest scaled scores and between the Verbal and Performance Scale IQ's can be interpreted.

CHAPTER 15

WECHSLER PRESCHOOL AND PRIMARY SCALE OF INTELLIGENCE (WPPSI)

In 1967 the Wechsler Preschool and Primary Scale of Intelligence (WPPSI) was published for use with children aged 4 to 6½ years (Wechsler, 1967). It is a separate and distinct scale, although similar to the WISC in form and content. Three subtests are unique to the WPPSI—Sentences, Animal House, and Geometric Design. Excluded from the WPPSI are the Digit Span, Picture Arrangement, Object Assembly, and Coding subtests that are found in the WISC. The method of computing the IQ and the evaluation of scores are similar to that employed on the WISC.

The WPPSI was standardized on 1200 children, 100 boys and 100 girls in each of six age groups, ranging by half-years from 4 to 6½ years. The 1960 U.S. census data were used to select representative children in the normative sample. Whites and nonwhites were included in the sample based on the ratios found in the census for four geographic regions.

RELIABILITY AND STABILITY

The average reliability coefficients (odd-even correlations with exception of Animal House subtest) for the entire standardization group are between .77 and .87 (median correlation of .82) for the individual subtests. The reliability coefficients (odd-even correlations) for the Verbal, Performance, and Full Scales are .94, .93, and .96, respectively. While the reliability coefficients for the Verbal, Performance, and Full Scales are satisfactory, the reliability of the subtests may not be sufficiently stable to be of much value for individual use (Oldridge & Allison, 1968).

Satisfactory split-half reliability coefficients have been reported with gifted children (Ruschival & Way, 1971) and with preschool mentally retarded children (Richards, 1968). The range of coefficients for the gifted children on the individual subtests was from .41 to .88, while the coefficients for the Verbal, Performance, and Full Scales were .84, .96, and .93, respectively. In the mentally retarded group, the coefficients ranged from .82 to .97 for the subtests, while the coefficients were .93, .92, and .88 for the Verbal, Performance, and Full Scales, respectively. In a sample of 5½-year-old English children, a reliability coefficient of .97 was reported for the Full Scale (Brittain, 1969).

208

Practice effects reported in the WPPSI manual over a mean interval of 11 weeks indicate mean gains of 3.0, 6.0, and 3.6 IQ points for the Verbal, Performance, and Full Scales, respectively, and correlations of .86, .89, and .91 for the three scales. Changes in subtest scaled scores ranged from −.2 (Sentences) to 1.3 (Mazes). The mean scaled score increases on the Information (.7), Similarities (.7), Animal House (.4), Picture Completion (.7), Mazes (1.3), and Block Design (1.0) subtests, but not on the other subtests, have been found to be significant (Wasik & Wasik, 1970). Generally, the Performance Scale subtests show more of a practice effect than the Verbal Scale subtests.

VALIDITY

The WPPSI manual presents minimal information about the validity of the scale. The discussion of the validity of the WISC in Chapter 11 is also pertinent to that of the WPPSI, and should serve as a background for evaluating the WPPSI. Since the publication of the WPPSI, a number of studies have compared the WPPSI with other tests, and these studies are reviewed below. The studies reflect the concurrent or comparative validity of the WPPSI.

WPPSI and Stanford-Binet

The Stanford-Binet has been the most popular scale to serve as the criterion for the WPPSI. The findings of the 13 studies listed in Table B-7 of the Appendix indicate that the correlations between the WPPSI and the Stanford-Binet ranged from .33 to .92 for the Verbal Scale, from .33 to .88 for the Performance Scale, and from .44 to .92 for the Full Scale. Median correlations are .81, .67, and .82 for the Verbal, Performance, and Full Scales, respectively. Thus, the Verbal Scale usually correlates more highly with the Stanford-Binet than does the Performance Scale. The lowest correlations have been reported with samples of gifted children. Overall, these results indicate that the concurrent validity of the WPPSI, using the Stanford-Binet as the criterion, is satisfactory.

When WPPSI and Stanford-Binet IQ's are compared, a somewhat different pattern emerges concerning the interchangeability of IQ's on the two scales. The Stanford-Binet yields higher mean IQ's than the WPPSI (range of +1 to +17). The largest discrepancies were reported in the Superior range (+11 to +17). In the Average and Dull Normal ranges, discrepancies ranged from +1 to +9. Two studies with mentally retarded children reported a +1 discrepancy (Richards, 1968) and a +3 discrepancy (Bach, 1968). The studies comparing the WPPSI and the Stanford-Binet indicate that *WPPSI and Stanford-Binet IQ's are not interchangeable.*

The WPPSI is generally a more difficult test than the Stanford-Binet. The extent of the discrepancy between WPPSI and Stanford-Binet IQ's, as we have seen, appears to be directly related to level of intelligence: the brighter the child, the larger the discrepancy in the IQ in favor of the Stanford-Binet. In one of the studies designed to investigate the effectiveness of the two tests in selecting children for gifted programs in schools, more than half of the gifted children would have met the criterion of an IQ of 130 or more for "gifted programs" on the Stanford-Binet, but only one out of the 21 in the sample would have done so on the WPPSI (Zimmerman & Woo-Sam, 1970). Consequently, school systems may have to revise their cutoff points in selecting students for gifted programs when the WPPSI is used as the measuring device.

WPPSI and WISC

The WPPSI and WISC overlap between the ages of 5 and 6½ years; it is of interest, therefore, to review the studies that have compared the two scales. The findings of the studies listed in Table B-8 in the Appendix indicate that the correlations run from .57 to .91 for the Verbal Scale, from .43 to .82 for the Performance Scale, and from .65 to .90 for the Full Scale (median correlation of .81). These results suggest that the two scales appear to be related to a significant degree. However, this conclusion is somewhat tentative because of the limited number of studies and the restricted populations (primarily Head Start children) that have been used. IQ's appear to be very similar, differing in no case by more than five mean IQ points. Again, because of the restricted ranges of intelligence that were used in the available studies, more information is needed in order to compare the IQ's provided by the two scales.

WPPSI and Other Tests

The relationship between the WPPSI and tests other than the Stanford-Binet and WISC also has been studied. The results of the studies listed in Table B-9 in the Appendix indicate that the correlations between the WPPSI and a variety of other tests ranged from a low of .30 (Progressive Matrices) to a high of .82 (Primary Mental Abilities Test), with a median correlation of .64. In eight of the nine investigations, lower class or ethnic minority group or Head Start children were studied; therefore, it is difficult to know whether the findings are generalizable to other groups of children. WPPSI scores also have been found to be related significantly both to perceptual development and to creativity (Lichtman, 1969; Yule, Berger, Butler, Newham, & Tizard, 1969).

SEX DIFFERENCES

Sex differences have been found on some WPPSI subtests. In the standardization sample, boys obtained significantly higher scores than girls on the Mazes subtest, while girls obtained higher scores than boys on the Animal House, Geometric Design, Block Design, and Sentences subtests (Herman, 1968). Thus, Performance IQ's may be achieved in different ways by boys and girls. In a sample of 5½-year-old English children, boys obtained higher WPPSI IQ's than girls (M IQ = 104 vs. M IQ = 98), thus indicating that the test may be biased in favor of boys when used in England (Brittain, 1969). However, significant sex differences in IQ were not found by Ruschival and Way (1971) in an American sample. Generally, for purposes of individual assessment, sex differences do not appear to play an important role.

ASSETS OF THE WPPSI

The WPPSI has many assets, as well as some limitations. This statement, of course, applies equally well to the WISC and Stanford-Binet. Reviewers and investigators have commented favorably on the WPPSI. We have seen that the WPPSI is a reliable and valid instrument, carefully standardized, and following closely the statistical approaches used in the WISC (cf. Oldridge & Allison, 1968; Yule et al., 1969). The features that made the WISC popular — such as separate Verbal and Performance Scales, deviation IQ's, and a convenient manual — also are part of the WPPSI. Children have been reported to enjoy taking the test, and the mixture of verbal and performance items maintains their interest (Yule et al., 1969). The WPPSI promises to yield useful diagnostic information and to be a clinical instrument of considerable merit (Dokecki, Frede, & Gautney, 1969; Yule et al., 1969). The WPPSI may be useful in planning special school programs, perhaps tapping more developmental or maturational factors that are important for school success in the lower grades than the Stanford-Binet (Corey, 1970).

The WPPSI also appears to be a valid and reliable instrument for the identification of preschool mentally retarded children (Richards, 1968). Oldridge and Allison (1968) concluded: "The WPPSI is a carefully developed and well standardized instrument of general intelligence that warrants widespread acceptance, although the value of the subtest scores for individual use remains yet to be established [p. 348]." Eichorn's (1972) conclusion was that "for the age and ability range covered the WPPSI is the best standardized and most up-to-date individual test available [p. 807]."

LIMITATIONS OF THE WPPSI

We now turn to the limitations of the WPPSI, some of which have been discussed previously for the WISC. As with the WISC, the reader may note that more space is devoted to the limitations of the WPPSI than to its assets. The disproportion is due to detailed explanations that are presented for some of the limitations. Such detailed explanations do not appear to be needed in describing the assets of the WPPSI. As we consider the limitations of the WPPSI, we also should bear in mind the many assets which the scale possesses.

Administration Time

Administration time may be too long for some children, although fatigue often may not be encountered (cf. Eichorn, 1972; Oldridge & Allison, 1968; Fagan, Broughton, Allen, Clark, & Emerson, 1969). With younger children or with handicapped children, two test sessions may be needed. When this procedure is followed, there is no way of determining, for any particular child, whether the break between testing sessions affects the test scores. It is a procedure that differs from the one used in standardizing the scale. However, empirical data would be helpful in clarifying the effect of two test sessions on test scores. In the standardization sample, approximately 10 per cent of the children needed one and one-half hours or more in which to complete the test. Other reports have indicated a mean administration time of 62 minutes (McNamara, Porterfield, & Miller, 1969) or of more than one hour (Fagan et al., 1969).

Limited Floor and Ceiling

Limited Floor. The WPPSI, like the WISC, is limited by having an inadequate floor, i.e., in not clearly differentiating abilities at the lower end of the scale. The IQ equivalents of the scaled scores shown in the manual range from 45 to 155. However, this range is not applicable until the 5½ year level. For example, at the 4-year-age level the lowest Full Scale IQ shown in the manual is 51, the lowest Verbal Scale IQ is 55, and the lowest Performance Scale IQ is 55. A child receives up to four scaled score points for having given *no* correct answers. Wechsler (1967) recognized this problem and therefore recommended that IQ's for each scale be computed only when the child obtains a raw score greater than zero on at least two of the subtests on each of the scales. Similarly, a Full Scale IQ should not be computed unless raw scores greater than zero are obtained on two Verbal and two Performance subtests.

What is the lowest possible IQ that a 4-year-old child can receive on the WPPSI? Following Wechsler's recommended procedure, IQ's were calculated for each of the three scales for a hypothetical 4-year-old child who obtained raw scores of one on the Information, Vocabulary, Animal House, and Picture Completion subtests and a raw score of zero on each of the remaining six subtests. The resulting IQ's were as follows: Verbal Scale IQ = 59 (17 scaled score points), Performance Scale IQ = 60 (21 scaled score points), and Full Scale IQ = 55 (38 scaled score points). Four one-point successes thus yielded an IQ of 55. This example demonstrates that the WPPSI may not provide precise IQ's for children who are functioning two or more standard deviations below the mean. Further research is needed to determine the validity of the WPPSI for moderately mentally retarded children.

Limited Ceiling.   The WPPSI not only has a limited floor but also has a limited ceiling. Between 11 and 19 per cent of a sample of gifted children have been found to obtain the maximum possible scores on the Arithmetic, Mazes, and Block Design subtests (Rellas, 1969). Consequently, the WPPSI may be limited in the assessment of gifted children.

Extrapolated IQ's.   Extrapolated IQ's also have been provided for sums of scaled scores that are below those shown in the WPPSI manual (Silverstein, 1968e) and for scores that are above those shown in the WPPSI manual (Silverstein, 1968c). However, as noted in the discussion of extrapolated IQ's for the WISC, extrapolated IQ's must be used cautiously.

Scoring Responses

As in the WISC, the scoring of responses on some subtests is difficult (cf. Corey, 1970; Fagan et al., 1969; Yule et al., 1969). This is especially true for the Geometric Design subtest, which appears to rely on the examiners' subjective decisions, and for the Vocabulary, Similarities, and Comprehension subtests. Consultation with colleagues is recommended when responses are difficult to score. Difficulties in scoring responses are discussed further in Chapter 16, which evaluates the individual subtests.

Other Difficulties

There are other difficulties with the WPPSI that have been mentioned. The disadvantages of the WPPSI, at least with lower class children, are the changes in instructions and materials in midtest, which make it somewhat difficult to administer; the ambiguity and/or emotional loadings of several Comprehension subtest questions; and the need to ask for additional reasons on several questions, making some of the children uncomfortable (Fagan et al., 1969). Finally, the WPPSI manual fails to provide information concerning how the cutoff criteria were determined (i.e., empirically or intuitively) (Oldridge & Allison, 1968).

SUMMARY

The WPPSI, published in 1967, is the latest test in the Wechsler series. It is designed to be used with children between 4 and 6½ years of age. It follows the basic format of the WISC, providing Verbal, Performance, and Full Scale IQ's. Three new subtests were developed for the WPPSI: Sentences, Animal

House, and Geometric Design. The standardization sample was good. Average reliabilities ranged from .77 to .87 for the individual subtests, and from .93 to .96 for the three scales. Comparative validity studies between the WPPSI and Stanford-Binet indicate that the two scales correlate highly (median $r = .81$). However, Stanford-Binet IQ's are uniformly higher than WPPSI IQ's, thereby indicating that IQ's on the two scales are not interchangeable.

The limited and restricted published studies that have compared the WPPSI with other ability and achievement tests generally indicate satisfactory concurrent validity. Sex differences are minimal on the subtests; when they occur, they are more pronounced on Performance than on Verbal subtests. The limitations of the WPPSI include long administration time, limited floor and ceiling (IQ range of 45 to 155), difficulty in scoring some subtests, and minor administration problems. Research studies with more varied populations, in part focusing on predictive and construct validity, would be useful. Overall, the WPPSI is a well-standardized, carefully developed instrument that should prove to be a valuable tool for the assessment of children's intelligence.

CHAPTER 16

DESCRIPTION AND EVALUATION OF WPPSI SUBTESTS

The interpretative rationale for the WPPSI subtests is similar to the one presented for the WISC subtests. Interpretations of subtest functions must be approached with full recognition of the tentativeness of the underlying functions tapped by the subtests. The reliability coefficient of each subtest should be considered when making statements about the subtest and when making comparisons between the subtests (see section on scatter analysis in Chapter 14). According to Wechsler (1967), the eight WPPSI subtests in common with the WISC (see below) measure the same functions as the corresponding WISC subtests. However, supporting data were not presented by Wechsler. Until factor analytic studies and other evidence are available, the tentativeness of Wechsler's assertion must be recognized.

The eight WPPSI subtests in common with the WISC are Information, Vocabulary, Arithmetic, Similarities, Comprehension, Picture Completion, Mazes, and Block Design. Following Wechsler's position, it is recommended, with certain reservations, that the interpretations, evaluations, and administrative considerations presented for these WISC subtests be applied cautiously to the WPPSI subtests having the same name. However, WPPSI subtests may measure different functions from those found in the WISC. A study of the items contained in the WPPSI subtests suggests that certain interpretations applicable to the WISC subtests may not be applicable to the WPPSI subtests. Such divergencies are noted in the discussion of the particular WPPSI subtest. The discussion of the three new WPPSI subtests—Sentences, Animal House, and Geometric Design—is based on content analysis, material presented in the WPPSI manual, and other published sources. Much less is known about the three new subtests than is known about the eight old subtests.

COMPARISON OF WPPSI AND WISC
STRUCTURE OF INTELLECT DIMENSIONS

A look at the Structure of Intellect (SOI) logically derived dimensions, presented by Meeker (1969) for the WPPSI and WISC, provides information about the comparability of the two scales (see Table 16–1). A comparison of the SOI dimensions indicates that, of the eight subtests with similar names in the two scales, four (Comprehension, Vocabulary, Picture Completion, and Mazes) have the same classifications, while four do not (Information, Arith-

Table 16-1. Comparison of Structure of Intellect Dimensions for WISC and WPPSI Subtests in Common

Subtest	In WISC and WPPSI	In WISC only	In WPPSI only
Information	MMU MMR MSS EMR CMU	MMS NMR NMU	CFS EFU CFU CFC CFR MFU
Comprehension	EMI	—	—
Arithmetic	MSI CMS	—	EFR MSU
Similarities	EMR CMT	CSR	NMS
Vocabulary	CMU	—	—
Picture Completion	CFU EFS	—	—
Block Design	CFR EFR	—	NFR
Mazes	CFI	—	—
Coding/Animal House	NFU EFU	—	—

Note.—See Table C-28 in the Appendix for a description of the Structure of Intellect dimensions.

metic, Similarities, and Block Design). Coding and Animal House also have the same SOI classifications. It will be of interest to learn the results of factor analytic studies that compare the WPPSI and WISC. The SOI classifications suggest that the two scales have both common and unique factors.

INTERPRETATIVE RATIONALE AND ADMINISTRATIVE CONSIDERATIONS FOR THE WPPSI SUBTESTS

In this section of the chapter, we consider, as we have with the WISC, the interpretative rationale, administrative considerations, and Structure of Intellect classifications for the WPPSI subtests. Factor analytic findings are discussed in Chapter 17. A summary of the functions proposed for the WPPSI subtests appears in Table C-22 of the Appendix. It is important to reiterate that the value of subtest scores for individual use remains to be established (cf. Oldridge & Allison, 1968). The analysis of subtest functions, then, should be used as a means of generating hypotheses about the examinee's abilities and not as a means of determining with precision specific cognitive skills.

Information

The Information subtest of the WPPSI contains 23 questions, 12 of which, with minor changes in wording, come from the WISC. As in the WISC, most of the new questions require the child to give a simply stated fact or facts.

Rationale

The rationale presented for the WISC Information subtest appears to apply to the WPPSI Information subtest. However, the WPPSI questions appear to assess that part of the child's knowledge of his environment that he gains from his experiences rather than from education, especially formal education.

Structure of Intellect Classification (SOI)

The SOI classifications of the Information subtest are MMU (Memory for Semantic Units—the ability to remember isolated ideas or word meanings), MMR (Memory for Semantic Relations—the ability to remember meaningful connections between items of verbal information), EMR (Evaluation of Semantic Relations—the ability to make choices among semantic relationships based on the similarity and consistency of the meanings), CMU (Cognition of Semantic Units—the ability to comprehend the meanings of words or ideas), CFS (Cognition of Figural Systems—the ability to comprehend arrangements and positions of visual objects in space), EFU (Evaluation of Figural Units—the ability to judge units of figural information as being similar or different), CFU (Cognition of Figural Units—the ability to perceive or recognize figural entities), CFC (Cognition of Figural Classes—the ability to recognize classes of figural items of information), CFR (Cognition of Figural Relations—the ability to recognize figural relations between forms), MSS (Memory for Symbolic Systems—the ability to remember the order of symbolic information), and MFU (Memory for Figural Units—the ability to remember given figural objects). The 23 items are distributed among the 11 classifications.

Administrative Considerations

Although scoring is 1 or 0, judgment is required in scoring a number of the items. In the manual, acceptable answers to question 4 ("What comes in a bottle?") do not mention things that come in plastic bottles. However, because the term "etc." appears in the manual after the acceptable answers, it seems logical to assume that "shampoo," "liquid soap," and other things that come in plastic bottles should receive credit. Acceptable answers to question 9 ("What shines in the sky at night?") do not include "planet"; yet a planet shines in the sky at night. It is recommended that "planet," "comet," and other astronomical terms be given credit. (The Psychological Corporation, A. S. Kaufman, personal communication, August 1971, has indicated that these are acceptable answers for questions 4 and 9.)

Vocabulary

The Vocabulary subtest of the WPPSI contains 22 words, 14 of which are from the WISC.

Rationale

The rationale presented for the WISC Vocabulary subtest generally applies to the WPPSI Vocabulary subtest. However, formal education appears to play a minor role on the WPPSI, especially below the age of 5 years, in enabling the child to acquire knowledge of words. The young child's experiences are likely to be the major factor in facilitating the acquisition of vocabulary.

Structure of Intellect Classification (SOI)

The SOI classification of the Vocabulary subtest is CMU (Cognition of Semantic Units—the ability to comprehend the meanings of words or ideas). Every item is so classified.

Administrative Considerations

The subtest is started with the first word for all examinees. This procedure differs from the one used in the WISC, where the subtest is started with word 10 for examinees who are 8 years or older and who are not suspected of being mentally retarded.

The general administrative considerations presented for the WISC Vocabulary subtest should be followed for the WPPSI Vocabulary subtest. Scoring differs slightly in the two scales. In the WPPSI, each response is scored 2, 1, or 0, while in the WISC, the first five words are scored 2 or 0. Scoring requires considerable judgment. The WPPSI manual, like the WISC manual, fails to provide a substantial number of sample responses. Because many of the Vocabulary words have near homonyms (words 1, 13, 14, 15, 16, 17, and 22), diction should be watched carefully when pronouncing these words (Yule et al., 1969).

Arithmetic

The Arithmetic subtest of the WPPSI consists of 20 problems, six of which are from the WISC.

Rationale

Problems 1 through 4 measure quantitative concepts without involving the explicit use of numbers (Wechsler, 1967). Problems 5 through 8 require counting. Problems 9 through 20 involve addition and subtraction, although simple division and multiplication also can be used to solve the problems.

The rationale described for the WISC Arithmetic subtest appears to apply generally to the WPPSI Arithmetic subtest. However, the skills required for the WPPSI Arithmetic subtest are likely to be less dependent on formal education than those required for the WISC Arithmetic subtest. The first four WPPSI questions, which require the child to make comparisons and perceptual discriminations, appear to measure nonverbal reasoning ability.

Structure of Intellect Classification (SOI)

The SOI classifications of the Arithmetic subtest are EFR (Evaluation of Figural Relations—the ability to choose a form based on the evaluation of what the relations are between the figures or forms in the sequence), MSU (Memory for Symbolic Units—the ability to remember isolated items of symbolic information, such as syllables and words), MSI (Memory for Symbolic Implications—the ability to remember arbitrary connections between symbols), and CMS (Cognition of Semantic Systems—the ability to comprehend relatively complex ideas). The majority of items (9 through 20) receive the MSI and CMS designations.

Administrative Considerations

The first six problems are administered to children under the age of 6 years or to older suspected mental retardates. The first eight problems are not timed, while problems 9 through 20 have a 30-second time limit.

Scoring, as in the WISC, is for the most part direct, 1 or 0 points. The time taken by the child to solve problems 9 through 20 should be recorded. Correct answers to the problems after the time limit has expired also should be noted. The administrative considerations discussed for the WISC Arithmetic subtest also apply to the WPPSI Arithmetic subtest.

Similarities

The Similarities subtest of the WPPSI consists of 16 questions, seven of which are found in the WISC. The first 10 questions, which require simple analogies and not similarities, are similar to the first four WISC questions.

Rationale

The rationale described for the WISC Similarities subtest generally applies to the WPPSI Similarities subtest. However, because over one-half of the WPPSI questions (1 to 10) require analogies, the subtest may be measuring logical thinking rather than verbal concept formation, especially at the younger age levels of the test (i.e., below 5 years of age).

Structure of Intellect Classification (SOI)

The SOI classifications of the Similarities subtest are EMR (Evaluation of Semantic Relations—the ability to make choices among semantic relationships based on the similarity and consistency of the meanings), NMS (Convergent Production of Semantic Systems—the ability to order information into a verbally meaningful sequence), and CMT (Cognition of Semantic Transformation—the ability to see potential changes of interpretations of objects and situations). Items 1 through 10 all receive the EMR classification, while items 6, 8, and 10 through 16 receive the CMT classification.

Administrative Considerations

The administrative considerations discussed for the WISC Similarities subtest apply generally to the WPPSI Similarities subtest. Scoring procedures, however, differ. Responses to the first 10 questions are scored 1 or 0, and few scoring problems should be encountered for these questions. However, as in the WISC, questions 11 through 16, which deal with similarities, are difficult to score. Responses to these questions are scored 2, 1, or 0. The higher conceptual response (e.g., general classification) receives a 2, a more concrete response (e.g., specific property of the items), receives a 1, and an incorrect response receives a 0.

Comprehension

The Comprehension subtest of the WPPSI contains 15 questions, six of which, with minor changes in wording, are from the WISC. The last WPPSI Comprehension question is the seventh WISC question. The WPPSI Comprehension questions cover a wide variety of situations, including health and hygiene ("Why do you need to wash your face and hands?"), knowledge of environment ("Why do we need clocks?"), and knowledge of activities in society ("Why do people have to work?").

Rationale

The rationale presented for the WISC Comprehension subtest appears to apply generally to the WPPSI subtest. Perhaps linguistic skill and logical reasoning play a more important role in successful performance on the WPPSI Comprehension subtest than they do on the WISC Comprehension subtest.

Structure of Intellect Classification (SOI)

The SOI classification of the Comprehension subtest is EMI (Evaluation of Semantic Implications—the ability to judge the adequacy of a meaningful deduction). Every item is so classified.

Administrative Considerations

The administrative considerations discussed for the WISC Comprehension subtest generally apply to the WPPSI Comprehension subtest. Scoring for all responses is 2, 1, or 0. As in the WISC, responses are difficult to score. Wechsler (1967) recognized that the examiner will have to use judgment in arriving at appropriate scores. He also emphasized that poor verbalization does not detract from the child's score; this is true, of course, for all scoring decisions made for WPPSI and WISC responses.

Sentences

The Sentences subtest of the WPPSI is a supplementary subtest. It is not counted in the final score when it is administered as a sixth Verbal Scale subtest. This procedure is different from the one used for the two WISC supplementary subtests (Digit Span and Mazes). In the WISC, the supplementary subtests can be included in the tabulation of the IQ when they are administered as the sixth subtest in their respective scales, even though they were not included in the development of the norms. The Sentences subtest was not included in establishing the IQ tables, because of Wechsler's desire to keep the composition of the WPPSI as similar to the WISC as possible.

Rationale

The Sentences subtest, which appears to measure immediate recall and attention, is a memory test (Herman, 1968; Lutey, 1967). The child is required to repeat verbatim sentences of increasing length that are read to him. Because success may depend upon verbal facility (Wechsler, 1967), failure may not necessarily reflect poor recall ability. Scores appear to be related primarily to memory ability for children 5 years of age and older, and to verbal knowledge and comprehension, rather than to immediate recall ability *per se*, for children below the age of 5 years (Lutey, 1967).

Structure of Intellect Classification (SOI)

The classification of the Sentences subtest is MMS (Memory for Semantic Systems—the ability to remember meaningfully ordered verbal information). Every item is so classified.

Administrative Considerations

Scoring the child's responses on the Sentences subtest is an exacting procedure. Wechsler (1967) described four types of possible errors that can occur: omission, transposition, addition, or substitution. Responses must be carefully analyzed in order to determine which type of error has occurred.

The subtest is discontinued after three consecutive sentences have been failed. This procedure does not differentiate a child who misses each sentence completely from one who fails by missing only one word in each sentence. Qualitatively, these two performances may be different. Consequently, children with minor temporary inefficiencies (missing one or two words) may be penalized by the discontinuance procedures. Nevertheless, it is still necessary to follow the discontinuance procedures that are stated in the manual.

Animal House and Animal House Retest

The Animal House subtest of the WPPSI is a new Performance Scale subtest that replaces the Coding subtest. It is a timed subtest (maximum time of 5 minutes) in which a premium is placed on speed. A perfect performance in 9 seconds or less is credited with 70 raw score points, while one obtained in 5 minutes is credited with 12 raw score points.

Rationale

The task on the Animal House subtest requires the child to place a cylinder of the appropriate color (the "house") in the hole in front of each animal. As in the Coding subtest of the WISC, the task requires the child to associate sign with symbol. Memory, attention span, goal awareness, concentration, and finger and manual dexterity may all be involved in the task (Herman, 1968; Wechsler, 1967). The subtest is also considered to be a measure of learning ability (Wechsler, 1967).

Structure of Intellect Classification (SOI)

The SOI classifications of the Animal House subtest are NFU (Convergent Production of Figural Units—factorial meaning has not been described) and EFU (Evaluation of Figural Units—the ability to judge units of figural information as being similar or different). Every item is so classified.

Administrative Considerations

Before administering the subtest, it is important, as the WPPSI manual notes, to determine whether the child is right- or left-handed. The child should be encouraged to use his preferred hand. As on all timed subtests, it is not permissible to stop timing once the subtest has begun. However, if for any reason the subtest is spoiled, do not include it in the final calculations. (This is true, of course, for all subtests in the scale.)

The Animal House Retest does not enter into the calculation of the IQ. It is exactly the same subtest as Animal House. When the Animal House subtest is administered a second time, the examiner can compare the child's two performances, and thereby obtain some indication of the child's learning ability or ability to benefit from practice. Table 20 in the manual is used to obtain raw scores for the Animal House and Animal House Retest, but a separate part (last column) of Table 21 in the manual, "Scaled Score Equivalents of Raw Scores," is used to obtain the Animal House Retest scaled score.

An inspection of the scaled scores for Animal House and Animal House Retest indicates that the child needs a higher raw score on the Animal House Retest in order to receive a scaled score that is equivalent to the one earned on Animal House. For example, a raw score of 16 on Animal House is equivalent to a scaled score of 10. The same raw score on Animal House Retest is equivalent to a scaled score of 9. In this example, one scaled score point is lost because there was no improvement on the Retest.

Yule et al. (1969) cautioned against accepting Wechsler's statement that performance on the Animal House Retest may differentiate between slow and fast learners. They believed that this statement is potentially misleading, because it is difficult to assess and predict rate of learning. The validation studies that are needed to support Wechsler's position have not been presented. Yule and his co-workers pointed out that an assessment of learning ability on the Animal House Retest needs to take account of the child's age and initial score. For example, Table 21 of the WPPSI manual indicates that a child aged 4¼ years, with a raw score of −2 sigmas below the mean (raw score of 3) on the initial subtest, maintains his initial status on retest by improving his performance by two raw score points, whereas a child of the same age at zero sigma (raw score of 18) on the initial subtest needs an increase of about 10 raw score points to maintain his position. At age 6¼ years, still other relationships are found. In addition to the child's age and initial score, motivational factors, magnitude of retest change, and, possibly, overall level of ability must be considered as relevant factors that can affect learning ability. Yule and his co-workers concluded that empirical work is needed before meaningful interpretations can be made of scores on the Animal House Retest.

Picture Completion

The Picture Completion subtest of the WPPSI contains 23 pictures, 12 of which come directly from the WISC.

Rationale

The rationale described for the WISC Picture Completion subtest appears to hold for the WPPSI Picture Completion subtest.

Structure of Intellect Classification (SOI)

The SOI classifications of the Picture Completion subtest are CFU (Cognition of Figural Units — the ability to perceive or recognize figural entities) and EFS (Evaluation of Figural Systems — the ability to evaluate a system of figural units which have been grouped in some manner). Every item is so classified.

Administrative Considerations

The administrative considerations discussed for the WISC Picture Completion subtest generally apply to the WPPSI Picture Completion subtest, with the exception of the material related to the time limits. Unlike the WISC Picture Completion subtest, which has a maximum of 15 seconds per card, there is no absolute time limit on the WPPSI Picture Completion subtest. However, Wechsler (1967) suggested that if there is no response within 15 seconds, the next card should be shown. Even though the WPPSI Picture Completion subtest is not timed, it may prove to be valuable for qualitative analysis to record the amount of time taken by the child to make his response.

In administering the second card, it is advisable to repeat the directions given for the first card: "Look at this picture. Some important part is missing. Tell me what is missing." The child is given credit if he correctly points to the missing part. However, if a pointing response is accompanied by a verbal response, the verbal response is given precedence over the pointing response. Therefore, an incorrect verbal response ("hair" to #1) together with a correct pointing response (pointing to the missing tooth) receives a score of 0.

Mazes

The Mazes subtest of the WPPSI consists of 10 mazes, seven of which are from the WISC. The three new mazes are horizontal mazes that have been introduced at the beginning of the subtest, and are intended for younger children. The Mazes subtest in the WPPSI is a standard subtest, while in the WISC it is a supplementary subtest.

Rationale

The rationale described for the WISC Mazes subtest appears to apply to the WPPSI Mazes subtest.

Structure of Intellect Classification (SOI)

The SOI classification of the Mazes subtest is CFI (Cognition of Figural Implications—the ability to foresee the consequences involved in figural problems). Every item is so classified.

Administrative Considerations

While the administrative considerations described for the WISC Mazes subtest apply to the WPPSI Mazes subtest, the administrative *procedures* used in the WPPSI Mazes subtest are not the same as those used in the WISC Mazes subtest. Changes have been made in timing, in scoring, and in other details. For example, mazes 1A, 1B, 2, 4, 5, and 6 each have 45 seconds, mazes 3 and 8 each have 60 seconds, and maze 10 has 135 seconds. Therefore, the examiner must be alert to using the procedures applicable to the specific Wechsler scale (WPPSI or WISC, as the case may be).

It has been recommended, and properly so, that the child be allowed to finish each maze, regardless of the errors made (Yule et al., 1969). Interrupting the child as soon as he makes a mistake on item 2 or after the second mistake on item 3, for example, appears to be bad for continuity and for the child's morale.

Scoring the WPPSI Mazes subtest requires considerable judgment. The examiner must become familiar with special terms, such as "blind alley," "false exit," "alley wall," and "false start," which designate specific features of the mazes or of the child's performance. The types of errors made by the child may be a valuable source of qualitative material. The child's failures should be studied carefully. The examiner should note whether there is a pattern to the child's failure, or whether there are signs of tremor or other visual-motor difficulties. After the entire examination has been administered, the examiner may desire to return to the Mazes subtest to inquire into the child's performance. "Why did you go that way?" is a question that may be asked. Inquiry may be made about the child's performance on any of the mazes that have been failed or about any of the mazes that may be of interest to the examiner.

Geometric Design

The Geometric Design subtest of the WPPSI is a new subtest that consists of 10 items, some of which also appear on the Stanford-Binet (e.g., Copying a Circle, Copying a Square, and Copying a Diamond). The child is asked to copy a circle, square, and other figures from line drawings. There is no time limit for the subtest.

Rationale

The Geometric Design subtest is considered to measure perceptual and visual-motor organization abilities (Wechsler, 1967). Low scores may indicate lags in the developmental process. High scores may be difficult to obtain even by bright young children, because the motor ability needed for successful performance is associated in part with maturational processes that may be independent of the development of cognitive processes.

Structure of Intellect Classification (SOI)

The SOI classification of the Geometric Design subtest is NFU (Convergent Production of Figural Units—factorial meaning has not been described). Every item is so classified.

Administrative Considerations

Scores for items 1 to 5 range from 0 to 2, scores for items 6 and 7 range from 0 to 3, and scores for items 8 to 10 range from 0 to 4. Deciding on the score will tax the ability of even the most competent examiner (cf. Yule et al., 1969). Much practice will be needed in order for the examiner to arrive at reliable scores.

Ordinary quarto folded paper can serve as well as the "special," copyrighted blank paper for the administration of the Geometric Design subtest (Yule et al., 1969). The appropriate number should be written on each drawing, and "top" and "bottom" relative to the child should be indicated on the paper.

Block Design

The Block Design subtest of the WPPSI consists of 10 items. The first two items are given only to children below the age of 6 years or to older suspected mental retardates. Of the 10 items, three are from the WISC, three are from the Wechsler Adult Intelligence Scale, and four are new. For the first seven items, the child is required to reproduce the designs from a model constructed by the examiner. For the last three items, the patterns are shown on cards. The WPPSI blocks are almost two dimensional, while the WISC blocks are three dimensional.

Rationale

The rationale described for the WISC Block Design subtest appears to apply to the WPPSI Block Design subtest.

Structure of Intellect Classification (SOI)

The SOI classifications of the Block Design subtest are CFR (Cognition of Figural Relations—the ability to recognize figural relations between forms), EFR (Evaluation of Figural Relations—the ability to choose a form based on the evaluation of what the relations are between the figures or forms in the sequence), and NFR (Convergent Production of Figural Relations—factorial meaning has not been described). Every item receives all classifications.

Administrative Considerations

The administrative considerations described for the WISC Block Design subtest generally apply to the WPPSI Block Design subtest. All of the items are timed. The first four items are given a maximum of 30 seconds; the next two, 45 seconds; the next two, 60 seconds; and the last two, 75 seconds. Unlike the WISC, there are no time-bonus credits. A score of 2 is given for a successful performance on the first trial, a score of 1, on the second trial, and a score of 0, when both trials are failed.

SUMMARY

The interpretative rationales for the WPPSI subtests are described in this chapter. It is recommended, with certain reservations, that the interpretations, evaluations, and administrative considerations presented for the WISC subtests be applied to the WPPSI subtests with the same name. However, even this recommendation is only tentative, because sufficient research is not available to evaluate the extent to which subtests with common names in both scales measure the same functions. The Structure of Intellect classifications for the WPPSI and WISC subtests with the same name indicate that four of the subtests (Comprehension, Vocabulary, Picture Completion, and Mazes) share the same classifications, while four differ (Information, Arithmetic, Similarities, and Block Design). Coding and Animal House also share the same classifications. A summary of the functions proposed for the WPPSI subtests appears in Table C-22 of the Appendix.

The following summarizes some aspects of each WPPSI subtest:

1. *Information.* Scores on the WPPSI Information subtest may be related more to the child's experiences than to formal education. The Structure of Intellect classifications cover 11 different categories. Judgment is required in the scoring of responses.

2. *Vocabulary.* The child's experiences are likely to play an important role in the acquisition of vocabulary ability. The Structure of Intellect classification for every item is Cognition of Semantic Units (CMU). Scoring requires considerable judgment. Administrative procedures differ from those used on the WISC.

3. *Arithmetic.* The problems involve quantitative concepts. The Structure of Intellect classifications for the majority of items are Memory for Symbolic Implications (MSI) and Cognition of Semantic Systems (CMS). Scoring is direct. Administrative considerations that apply to the WISC also apply to the WPPSI.

4. *Similarities.* The subtest is considered to measure logical thinking as well as verbal concept formation. The Structure of Intellect classifications cover three different categories, with Evaluation of Semantic Relations (EMR) applying to the first 10 items. Scoring procedures differ from those found in the WISC.

5. *Comprehension.*   The rationale for the WISC Comprehension subtest appears to apply to the WPPSI Comprehension subtest, although linguistic skill and logical reasoning may play a more important role on the WPPSI than on the WISC. The Structure of Intellect classification for every item is Evaluation of Semantic Implications (EMI). Scoring requires considerable judgment.

6. *Sentences.*   This is the only supplementary subtest in the scale. It appears to measure immediate recall and attention. The Structure of Intellect classification for every item is Memory for Semantic Systems (MMS). Scoring requires considerable skill.

7. *Animal House and Animal House Retest.*   The subtest is considered to measure memory, attention span, goal awareness, concentration, and finger and manual dexterity. The Structure of Intellect classifications for every item are Convergent Production of Figural Units (NFU) and Evaluation of Figural Units (EFU). Administration is relatively easy. The abilities measured by the Animal House Retest are not known at this time.

8. *Picture Completion.*   The rationale for the WISC Picture Completion subtest appears to apply to the WPPSI Picture Completion subtest. The Structure of Intellect classifications for every item are Cognition of Figural Units (CFU) and Evaluation of Figural Systems (EFS). Administration is relatively easy. There is no time limit.

9. *Mazes.*   The rationale for the WISC Mazes subtest appears to apply to the WPPSI Mazes subtest. The Structure of Intellect classification for every item is Cognition of Figural Implications (CFI). Scoring requires considerable judgment. Administrative procedures differ from those used on the WISC.

10. *Geometric Design.*   The subtest is considered to measure perceptual and visual-motor organization abilities. Maturational lags may be indicated by low scores. The Structure of Intellect classification for every item is Convergent Production of Figural Units (NFU). This subtest may be the most difficult of all WPPSI subtests to score.

11. *Block Design.*   The rationale for the WISC Block Design subtest appears to apply to the WPPSI Block Design subtest. The Structure of Intellect classifications for every item are Cognition of Figural Relations (CFR), Evaluation of Figural Relations (EFR), and Convergent Production of Figural Relations (NFR). The subtest requires skill to administer.

CHAPTER 17

ADMINISTERING AND INTERPRETING THE WPPSI

The administrative procedures and suggestions that have been described in Chapter 12 for the WISC are also appropriate for the WPPSI. Both scales share common problems in administration and scoring. However, as we have seen, the directions that are appropriate for the respective scales must be used. The difficulties involved with administering the new WPPSI subtests have been discussed in Chapter 16. The new WPPSI subtest, Geometric Design, in particular, requires considerable skill to score. The present chapter considers some general administrative questions, short forms, factor analysis, scatter analysis, and the clinical and educational use of the WPPSI.

PHYSICAL ABILITIES NECESSARY FOR THE WPPSI

The physical abilities that are necessary for the WPPSI are, for the most part, the same as those required for the WISC. Table C-9 in the Appendix also presents the functions necessary for the 11 WPPSI subtests. As in the WISC, visual-motor skills are needed for the Performance Scale subtests. The age range of the children for which the WPPSI is applicable limits the ways by which the child can respond to the test questions or by which the examiner can administer the tests. For example, children who cannot speak usually will not be able to write their answers, while those who cannot hear usually will not be able to read the test questions. Much of the material in Chapter 12 that pertains to the common subtests found on the WISC and WPPSI should be reviewed. Especially important are the suggestions for administering the Performance Scale subtests to deaf or partially-hearing children.

TESTING THE LIMITS ON THE WPPSI

The general testing-of-limits suggestions that have been presented in Chapter 5 also can serve for the WPPSI. The Altitude Quotient, discussed in Chapter 12 for the WISC, may have the same limitations for the WPPSI as it has for the WISC. There is currently no way of knowing whether the Altitude Quotient represents an index of latent capacity on the WPPSI, because the question has not been researched.

WPPSI SHORT FORMS

As we have seen with the WISC in Chapter 12, short forms of the scale are open to many criticisms. These same criticisms apply to the WPPSI short forms discussed below. However, there may be occasions when a short form is useful. Silverstein's (1970a) approach to the development of WPPSI short forms appears to be one of the more satisfactory ones, because the standardization data were used to compute correlations with the Full Scale. Table C-26 in the Appendix shows the best WPPSI short forms for two, three, four, and five subtests. The short forms of a given length, for all practical purposes, are mutually interchangeable. Consequently, Silverstein suggested that clinical considerations, on some occasions, can be used to select the short form.

After the short form is selected, the procedures outlined in Chapter 12, which deal with converting WISC composite scores to Deviation Quotients, should be followed. Table C-16 in the Appendix also can be used to obtain the appropriate a and b constants. The same procedure presented for the WISC should be followed for the WPPSI, with the exception that the WPPSI correlation table of the group that is closest in age to the examinee be used to obtain Σr_{jk} (i.e., one of the tables on pages 26 through 31 of the WPPSI manual).

In a study investigating the WPPSI scores of middle class children, the four subtests that make the best short form were found to be Information, Comprehension, Arithmetic, and Geometric Design ($r = .94$ with the Full Scale; Dokecki et al., 1969). In another study that investigated WPPSI scores of lower class children, Information and Geometric Design subtests were found to be the two subtests that make the best short form for predicting reading achievement scores (Plant & Southern, 1968).

Yudin's Procedure for the WPPSI

Yudin's (1966) short form method for the WISC, which reduces the number of items within the subtests, has been applied to the WPPSI by Silverstein (1968a). Table C-27 in the Appendix shows the specific procedures. Raw scores are multiplied by a constant and, as Silverstein suggested for the WISC, a correction factor is not needed. Silverstein suggested that Sentences be excluded from the short form, because the subtest was omitted in establishing the IQ tables. The following reliabilities were reported for the short form: .91 for the Verbal Scale, .91 for the Performance Scale, and .94 for the Full Scale.

Vocabulary Plus Block Design Short Form

The Vocabulary plus Block Design subtests, as a two-subtest short form, may prove to be as popular on the WPPSI as they are on the WISC. When this combination is used, Table C-15 in the Appendix can be used to convert the sum of scaled scores on the two subtests directly to an estimate of the Full Scale IQ. Silverstein (1970b) reported a .82 correlation between the Vocabulary plus Block Design short form and the Full Scale.

FACTOR ANALYSIS

We have seen in Chapter 14 that there are differences in factor analyses, depending on what method and procedures are used. Such differences also are evident in the factor analytic studies of the WPPSI. Factor analyses have been performed on the WPPSI for four different samples of children: children in the standardization group, Negro children, middle class children, and upper and lower class children. These studies are reviewed below.

Standardization Group

Silverstein (1969a), using the standardization data, performed a factor analysis for the entire age range by the principal-factor method. As in the WISC (see Chapter 12), two principal factors were found. The subtests on the Verbal Scale had the highest loadings on Factor I, while the subtests on the Performance Scale had the highest loadings on Factor II. Table 17–1 shows the average loadings of the subtests and scales on each factor. Silverstein came to the same conclusion for these data as he did for the WISC, namely, that the Verbal and Performance Scales constitute actual functional unities in the scale.

Boyd (1970) used the principal-factor method to factor analyze the 5½-year-age group of the standardization population. He found two major factors. Factor A, termed a "Visual-Perceptual Factor," accounted for 57% of the variance, while Factor B, termed a "Perceptual-Motor Factor," accounted for 9% of the variance. The most salient subtests for Factor A were Vocabulary, Similarities, Comprehension, and Animal House, while those for Factor B were Picture Completion, Mazes, Geometric Design, and Block Design. The factor loadings are shown in Table 17–2.

Negro Sample

Boyd (1970) also factor analyzed the WPPSI using a sample of 111 Negro children (59 males and 52 females) who were between the ages of 5 and 7 years ($M = 5$ years, 4 months for the males, and 5 years, 5 months for the females). The sample was primarily "culturally deprived," with 74 of the children enrolled in Head Start programs and the remainder from the kindergarten and first grades. Two major factors were found. Factor A ("Perceptual-Motor Memory Factor") accounted for 54% of the common variance, and was best defined by the Information, Arithmetic, Mazes, and Block Design subtests. Factor B ("Verbal Factor") accounted for 46% of the common variance, and was best defined by the Vocabulary and Similarities subtests. A separate analysis by sex indicated that in addition to the two major factors, a third factor, Fac-

Table 17-1. AVERAGE LOADINGS OF WPPSI SUBTESTS

SUBTEST	FACTOR I Silverstein	FACTOR I Krebs	FACTOR II Silverstein	FACTOR II Krebs
Information	53	77	09	35
Vocabulary	51	78	06	23
Arithmetic	33	56	27	40
Similarities	54	79	−02	21
Comprehension	57	79	01	26
Sentences	47	68	07	24
Animal House	12	33	37	64
Picture Completion	19	36	34	46
Mazes	01	25	49	76
Geometric Design	00	17	53	75
Block Design	09	17	46	66
Verbal Scale	50	—	08	—
Performance Scale	08	—	44	—

(Reprinted by permission of the publisher and author from A. B. Silverstein, "An Alternative Factor Analytic Solution for Wechsler's Intelligence Scales," *Educational and Psychological Measurement,* **29,** p. 766, copyright 1969, Fredrick Kuder; and by permission of author from E. G. Krebs, *The Wechsler Preschool and Primary Scale of Intelligence and Prediction of Reading Achievement in First Grade.* (Doctoral dissertation, Rutgers State University) Ann Arbor, Mich.: University Microfilms, 1969, p. 81. No. 70-3361, copyright 1970, E. G. Krebs.)

Table 17-2. Loadings of WPPSI Subtests for Two Groups

	STANDARDIZATION GROUP 5½-YEAR AGE LEVEL		NEGRO SAMPLE 5 TO 7 YEARS OF AGE	
SUBTEST	Factor A	Factor B	Factor A	Factor B
Information	75	40	64	36
Vocabulary	72	30	00	80
Arithmetic	62	53	69	13
Similarities	77	09	11	70
Comprehension	75	30	36	60
Animal House	69	26	35	47
Picture Completion	27	64	32	55
Mazes	32	61	62	06
Geometric Design	23	71	71	33
Block Design	12	83	73	17

Adapted from Boyd (1970).

tor C ("Verbal Factor") was found only for the female Negro children. This factor accounted for 26% of the common variance. It was best accounted for by the Similarities and Comprehension subtests. The factor loadings for the total group are shown in Table 17–2.

Boyd noted that the Negro children had an inverse factorial relationship with reference to the standardization group. A greater part of the common variance extracted for the Negro children was explained by perceptual-motor-memory aspects, while a greater part of the common variance extracted for whites (primarily represented in the standardization group) was explained by verbal-perceptual aspects. These results suggest that there may be qualitative intellectual differences between black and white children at the age levels studied. However, even this generalization must be restricted to the specific samples employed. The findings do not indicate whether the differences that were found were due to experiential factors or to genetic factors.

Middle Class Children

Dokecki et al. (1969), using the centroid method, performed a factor analysis on the 10 standard WPPSI subtests for a sample of 80 children from the upper middle and lower middle classes. The sample was between 57 and 77 months of age ($M = 66$ months). Three factors were found: Visual Organization (Picture Completion, Mazes, Geometric Design, and Block Design), Verbal Comprehension (Vocabulary, Similarities, and Comprehension), and Undifferentiated Memory (Information, Arithmetic, and Animal House).

Upper and Lower Class Children

Krebs (1969) used a principal-factor method to factor analyze the WPPSI scores (plus other test scores) of 70 upper and lower class children who were between the ages of 53 and 79 months. Two factors were found. The Verbal Scale subtests loaded on Factor I, termed "Verbal Memory and Problem Solving," and the Performance Scale subtests loaded on Factor II, termed "Perceptual-Motor Problem Solving." The factor loadings are shown in Table 17–1.

Comment on Factor Analyses of the WPPSI

The findings of Silverstein (1969a) for the total WPPSI standardization group and of Boyd (1970) for the 5½-year-age group of the standardization group are congruent in some, but not in all, respects. For example, Silverstein reported that none of the average loadings on the Performance Scale subtests were above .19 on Factor I, while Boyd reported loadings ranging from .12 to .69 on his Factor A. Silverstein's Factor II had loadings all below .28 on the Verbal Scale subtests, while Boyd's Factor B had loadings ranging from .09 to .53, with four of the five subtests above .29. However, the pattern of loadings in Boyd's study was similar to that of Silverstein's. The Verbal Scale subtests (with the addition of Animal House from the Performance Scale) formed Factor A, while the Performance Scale subtests (with the exception of Animal House) formed Factor B. Silverstein's and Krebs's results were similar in that the subtests on the Verbal and Performance Scales each loaded on separate factors. However, the loadings were uniformly higher in the Krebs study. Sampling differences may account, in part, for the different findings.

Factor analytic studies are still needed that employ the standardization data for each age level separately. The available results suggest that it is useful to consider the Verbal and Performance Scale designations as representing meaningful labels. It also appears that the pattern of loadings differs with different types of populations.

SCATTER ANALYSIS

Scatter analysis may turn out to be a useful procedure in attempting to assess the child's strengths and weaknesses. However, it is still too early to know the extent to which scatter analysis will be useful. The same considerations that are discussed in Chapter 14 for the WISC pertain to the WPPSI; this material should be studied carefully before scatter analysis is applied to the WPPSI.

Approaches to Scatter Analysis

The techniques used to measure scatter that are discussed in Chapter 14 for the WISC can be applied in the same way to the WPPSI. In order to avoid undue repetition, Chapter 14 should be consulted for an explanation of each of the approaches listed below.

1. Comparing sets of individual subtest scores (see Table C-23 in the Appendix).

2. Comparing the Verbal Scale and Performance Scale IQ's (see Table C-23 in the Appendix). (In the Appendix, Table C-18 presents the probabilities from .001 to .50 that are associated with a given Verbal-Performance Scale discrepancy, and Table C-19 presents the percentage of individuals obtaining a given discrepancy between the Verbal and Performance Scales.)

3. Comparing the average of several subtest scaled scores with one of the subtest scaled scores that is included in the average (see Table C-24 in the Appendix).

4. Comparing the average of several subtest scaled scores with one of the subtest scaled scores that *is not* included in the average (see Table C-25 in the Appendix).

CLINICAL AND EDUCATIONAL USE OF THE WPPSI

Since the WPPSI is a comparatively new instrument, little is known about its usefulness as a clinical tool. The qualitative behaviors indicative of various forms of difficulty, disturbance, or psychopathologic behavior that are manifested during the examination should be carefully noted and reported (see Chapter 19). However, there is no evidence, at present, that indicates that significant differences between Verbal and Performance Scale IQ's or among subtest scaled scores are clinically meaningful (Yule et al., 1969). Research in these areas is needed. Wechsler's (1967) statement that very poor performance on the Animal House subtest will, at times, be associated with organic deficit should not be accepted until research studies are available; it should be regarded as an unconfirmed hypothesis (Yule et al., 1969).

Learning Disabilities and the WPPSI

An interesting contribution by Hagin, Silver, and Corwin (1970) illustrated how the WPPSI can be used in the assessment of cognitive functioning of children with learning disabilities. Three subgroups within the learning disability syndrome were described (specific language disability, brain-injured, and developmental immaturity), and for each subgroup a representative WPPSI profile was, where possible, presented. We now turn to their illustrations.

Specific Language Disability. Children in the specific language disability subgroup have problems in developing body image concepts, in establishing cerebral dominance for language, and in orienting figures in space and sounds in time. Richard (see Table 17–3) is representative of this subgroup. While the neurological examination was negative, evidence was found that indicated gross errors in right-left orientation, mild difficulties in praxis, and abnormal elevation on the extension test. Visual-motor skills were good, but some difficulties were evident in auditory discrimination and sequencing. On the WPPSI, he earned an average IQ (98), but showed a 23-point spread between his Verbal and Performance IQ's (87 and 110, respectively). Within the Verbal Scale, his major difficulties were in areas requiring quantitative reasoning, logical thinking, and social judgment. Range of knowledge and linguistic skill were adequate, although ideas were sometimes awkwardly expressed. His effortful and productive approach to the Performance Scale items suggested that he has

Table 17-3. ILLUSTRATIONS OF WPPSI DEVIATIONS FROM MEAN SCALED SCORE FOR CHILDREN WITH LEARNING DISABILITIES IN FIRST GRADE

SUBTEST	RICHARD: SPECIFIC LANGUAGE DISABILITY	KARL: BRAIN-INJURED	ROSEMARY: DEVELOPMENTAL IMMATURITY
Information	+ .5	− .2	0
Vocabulary	+1.5	+2.8*	−1.0
Arithmetic	−3.5*	− .2	0
Similarities	−3.5*	−3.2*	0
Comprehension	−2.5*	− .2	0
Sentences	−1.5	−2.2*	−1.0
Animal House	+1.5	−2.2*	+4.0*
Picture Completion	+3.5*	− .2	0
Mazes	+2.5*	+3.8*	−1.0
Geometric Design	+1.5	+1.8	0
Block Design	+ .5	− .2	−1.0
M scaled score	9.5	11.2	7.0
Verbal Scale IQ	87	106	80
Performance Scale IQ	110	112	82
Full Scale IQ	98	110	79

*These are significant deviations (see Table C-24 in the Appendix). Adapted from Hagin, Silver, and Corwin (1970).

good potential for learning. It was recommended that educational intervention stress the auditory modality.

Brain-Injured. A second subgroup is the brain-injured. These children demonstrate many of the behaviors of the specific language disability group, but in addition show abnormality on the standard neurological examination. Some children are hyperkinetic, while others are hypokinetic. Generally, the findings do not point to focal brain damage, and specific etiological factors are rarely found in the child's history. The children in this subgroup present special educational problems, because of poor impulse control, limited attention span, inadequate motor coordination, and anxiety.

Karl (see Table 17–3) is an example of a child in the brain-injured subgroup. Because there is no typical "brain-injured child," he was selected simply to illustrate how one brain-injured child performed on the WPPSI. The neurological examination disclosed poor fine and gross motor coordination and severe praxic difficulties. There was confusion in right-left discrimination, restless motion, tremors, and hyperactivity. His verbal communications were, at times, incoherent and circumstantial. On the WPPSI, he obtained a Full Scale IQ of 110. Conceptual thinking, memory, and attention and concentration were areas that were below his average level of performance. His motor problems were especially evident in his difficulty in grasping the pegs in the Animal House subtest and in his four-finger, non-oppositional grip on the pencil in the Geometric Design subtest. His best performances were on the Mazes and Vocabulary subtests, subtests that reflect planning ability and word knowledge, respectively. His performance improved when he became familiar with the task requirements. It was recommended that educational effort emphasize visual-motor and organizational skills.

Developmental Immaturity. The third subgroup focuses on children with developmental immaturity. In this subgroup, there is no clinical or historical evidence of central nervous system damage; rather, there is slowness in reaching developmental landmarks. In physical appearance, in gross and fine motor development, in language, and in social awareness these children seem to be younger than is warranted by their chronological ages. Low birth weight appears frequently in their histories.

Rosemary (see Table 17–3) can be considered to be representative of this subgroup. Neurological difficulties were absent. The extension test was abnormal, and errors in right-left orientation were found. On the WPPSI, she performed in the Borderline range. Her profile of deviations of subtest scaled scores from the mean of her scaled scores is essentially flat; the only significant variation occurred on the Animal House subtest. Recommendations centered on general enrichment, with particular emphasis upon language stimulation.

Reading Disability and the WPPSI

Krebs (1969) investigated the effectiveness of the WPPSI in predicting reading scores. At kindergarten age, 70 children (34 boys and 36 girls), equally divided into lower and upper socioeconomic status groups, were administered the WPPSI. One year later in first grade, the Stanford Achievement Test, which contains sections on reading, and the Gilmore Oral Reading Paragraphs Test were administered. As Table 17–4 shows, all of the subtests and scales were found to be related significantly to reading scores on both tests. When breakdowns were made for socioeconomic class, the WPPSI scores were found to have higher correlations with reading scores in the lower socioeconomic status group than in the upper socioeconomic status group. For example, in the lower socioeconomic status group, the correlations with the total reading score on the Stanford Achievement Test for the Verbal, Performance, and Full Scales were .59, .61, and .66, respectively, whereas in the upper socioeconomic

Table 17-4. Correlations Between WPPSI
and Two Reading Tests

WPPSI SUBTEST	GILMORE ORAL READING PARAGRAPHS TEST	STANFORD ACHIEVEMENT TEST: READING
Information	.49	.52
Vocabulary	.52	.53
Arithmetic	.54	.58
Similarities	.48	.53
Comprehension	.36	.38
Sentences	.54	.55
Animal House	.41	.46
Picture Completion	.43	.47
Mazes	.42	.47
Geometric Design	.52	.54
Block Design	.44	.49
Verbal Scale IQ	.57	.61
Performance Scale IQ	.58	.63
Full Scale IQ	.62	.68

(Reprinted by permission of the author from E. B. Krebs, *The Wechsler Preschool and Primary Scale of Intelligence and Prediction of Reading Achievement in First Grade.* (Doctoral dissertation, Rutgers State University) Ann Arbor, Mich.: University Microfilms, 1969, pp. 73a–73b. No. 70–3361. Copyright 1970, E. G. Krebs.)

status group, they were .32, .35, and .40, respectively. In the total sample, the two best subtests, obtained via multiple regression procedures, that predicted the total reading achievement score on the Stanford Achievement Test were Arithmetic and Geometric Design ($R = .63$).

A study of the WPPSI scores of 57 inadequate readers and 57 adequate readers of Anglo-American and Mexican American ethnic backgrounds revealed few significant findings (Kavajecz, 1969). The children were in preschool, kindergarten, and first grades (M age $= 69$ months), where of both sexes, and were matched on Full Scale IQ. Both reading groups had average intellectual ability. The criterion for reading skill was the teachers' judgment. In the Anglo-American group, the inadequate readers had significantly lower Arithmetic subtest scores than the adequate readers, while in the Mexican American group, the inadequate readers had significantly lower scores on the Animal House subtest than the adequate readers. The WPPSI profiles for the adequate and inadequate reading groups were essentially identical.

Qualitative Analysis of Performance on the WPPSI Mazes Subtest

A careful evaluation of the failures that occur on the Mazes subtest may prove to be useful. Two examples are shown in Figure 17–1. In Example 1, the child failed to complete the maze, but has made no errors as far as his performance goes. In Example 2, the child has entered a blind alley and therefore has made an error. The first performance makes one wonder why the child stopped short before reaching the goal. Perhaps his perseverance is limited, or perhaps he takes things for granted and hopes that others will understand him, or perhaps he was distracted. In contrast, the second performance may be that of an impulsive child who works well until he is about to complete the task, and then is unable to do so correctly. These analyses are, of course, only tentative, subject to modification by a study of the child's performance on the entire subtest, other subtests on the scale, and other sources of data.

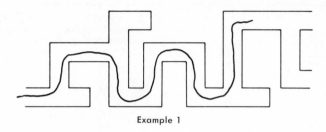

Example 1

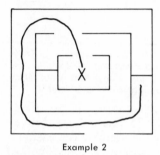

Example 2

Figure 17-1. Two examples of failures on the Mazes subtest. (WPPSI Mazes reprinted by permission of the publisher. Copyright 1949, © 1963, 1967, The Psychological Corporation, New York, N.Y. All rights reserved.)

SUMMARY

The administrative and interpretative considerations that apply to the WISC generally apply to the WPPSI. The younger age group for which the WPPSI is appropriate presents some problems in adapting the subtests to alternate sensory modalities.

Table C-26 in the Appendix shows the best combination of two, three, four, and five WPPSI subtests, and Table C-15 in the Appendix shows IQ's for the sum of the scaled scores for the Vocabulary plus Block Design short form.

The principal-factor method of factor analysis applied to the WPPSI in one study indicated that the Verbal and Performance Scales constitute actual functional unities. However, another study, which used only one age group of the standardization sample, did not entirely replicate these findings. Other factor analytic findings suggest that patterns of factor loadings differ with different types of populations.

The same considerations that apply to scatter analysis on the WISC apply to scatter analysis on the WPPSI. However, even more care should be taken with the WPPSI than with the WISC in using scatter analysis because limited research findings are available.

Illustrations of the clinical use of the WPPSI were presented.

CHAPTER 18

A POTPOURRI OF INDIVIDUALLY ADMINISTERED INTELLIGENCE TESTS

The major emphasis of the text has been placed on providing a thorough and systematic description and evaluation of the three major individually administered intelligence tests—the Stanford-Binet, WISC, and WPPSI. In the present chapter, our survey will be brief, aiming to describe a variety of other individually administered tests that can be valuable additions to the examiner's basket of techniques when it is not feasible or practical to administer one of the major individual intelligence tests.

The chapter considers the following tests: Peabody Picture Vocabulary Test, Quick Test, Pictorial Test of Intelligence, Columbia Mental Maturity Scale, Leiter International Performance Scale, and Slosson Intelligence Test. Some of these tests also provide IQ's for adults; however, the major emphasis in the chapter is on surveying the usefulness of the tests with children below 16 years of age. There are many other individually administered intelligence tests that are not covered in the chapter. *The Mental Measurement Yearbooks,* edited by Buros, are excellent sources of relevant information concerning tests in general.

The tests covered in the chapter can be used for screening devices, for follow-up evaluations, and for assessing handicapped as well as normal children. It is possible, too, that persons not specifically trained in the administration of individual intelligence tests may learn to administer most of the tests quickly and easily. Many of the tests require a simple pointing response, and if this response is not available, there are other means of obtaining a response from the child. Eye movements may be used in some cases. In others, the examiner may point to each alternate choice and ask the child to indicate "yes" or "no" by a prearranged signal. In testing deaf or hard of hearing children, the words for the picture vocabulary tests can be typed on cards and shown to the examinee. Instructions for some tests can be pantomimed.

Although the tests covered in the present chapter provide limited material for qualitative analysis, it is still important for the examiner to try to understand the reason for the child's failures (as well as successes). For example, failure on the part of the child to respond to the Peabody Picture Vocabulary Test items (or to items on other tests) should serve only as a challenge to find out why.

The failure may represent a general lack of mental competence, inability to understand the directions because of an auditory perceptual disability, or inability to respond to the kind of abstraction of which the test material is composed [Bice & Cruickshank, 1966, p. 123].

These possibilities should be evaluated carefully by the examiner.

It is important to recognize that critical decisions should not be based on any of the tests described in the present chapter. The test results should be supplemented by supporting data from other intelligence tests. Some of the tests have limited validities and reliabilities, others have limited normative groups, while still others likely measure only a limited aspect of intelligence. In addition, large discrepancies for individual children have been reported between IQ's obtained on some tests and those obtained on the Stanford-Binet or WISC, even though mean IQ's for the total group may not be significantly different for the tests that are being compared. It is recommended that when the child has the necessary physical capacities and when time is not at a premium, the examiner select the Stanford-Binet, WISC, or WPPSI as the instrument of choice for the assessment of intelligence. This is especially so when the IQ is to be used in making decisions about the child. However, when verbal responses cannot be elicited from the child, when motor handicaps limit the child's performance, when trained examiners are not available, or when time is at a premium and only a screening procedure is needed, picture vocabulary tests, short intelligence tests, and other intelligence tests requiring pointing responses can be useful instruments.

PEABODY PICTURE VOCABULARY TEST

The Peabody Picture Vocabulary Test (PPVT), developed by Dunn (1959, 1965), is a nonverbal, multiple-choice test that was designed to evaluate children between the ages of $2\frac{1}{2}$ and 18 years who have no hearing disabilities and who can indicate "yes" or "no" in some manner. The test was designed to provide an estimate of an individual's verbal intelligence through measuring his hearing vocabulary or receptive knowledge of vocabulary. It measures, in Guilford's terminology, Cognition of Figural Units.

The PPVT consists of 150 plates with four pictures on each plate. The plates are arranged in increasing level of difficulty from one year, nine months to 18 years. There are two forms of the PPVT, Form A and Form B, which differ only in that they use different words. The PPVT was standardized on a population of 4,012 white subjects, aged 2 years, 6 months to 18 years, residing in and around Nashville, Tennessee.

The pictures are clearly drawn, free of fine detail, and pose no figure-ground problems. The test is untimed; it requires no reading ability, and neither pointing nor oral response is essential. Testing time is between 10 and 15 minutes. If the child cannot point, the examiner can administer the test by pointing to each picture and asking the child to designate whether it is correct or incorrect by means of some prearranged signal. These qualities make the test suitable for testing a variety of exceptional children (cf. Bice & Cruickshank, 1966).

The IQ's available in the manual range from 55 to 145. Extrapolated IQ's published in the 1965 manual extend the range from 17 to 171. The standard errors of measurement range from 6.00 to 8.61 IQ points. Because chronological age is classified in 6-month intervals up to 5 years and 12-month intervals after this age, big "jumps" occur in the IQ table. For example, a 5 year, 5 month old child with a raw score of 50 obtains an IQ of 101, whereas a 5 year, 6 month old child with the same raw score obtains an IQ of only 89 (Lyman, 1965).

Reliability and Stability

The PPVT manual reported alternate form reliabilities for age groups 2–6 years through 18–0 years. The coefficients, using raw scores, ranged from .67 at age 6–0 years to .84 at ages 17–0 and 18–0 years. The standard errors of measurement in IQ points range from 6.00 at ages 17–0 and 18–0 years to 8.61 at age 6–0 years. Therefore, age 6–0 years is the least reliable age level, while ages 17–0 and 18–0 years are the most reliable.

Fourteen studies, which are listed in Table B-10 of the Appendix, also have reported alternate form reliabilities for the PPVT with children. The coefficients in these studies range from .37 to .97, with a median of .77. The median coefficient is similar to those reported in the manual. The highest coefficients are with cerebral palsied and mentally retarded groups, whereas the lowest coefficients are with preschool children and with Head Start children.

Test-retest studies, which are listed in Table B-11 of the Appendix, also have appeared, with retest intervals ranging from four weeks to two years. The coefficients in these studies range from .28 to .97, with a median coefficient of .73. Stability of PPVT scores is generally high for mentally retarded children. The findings suggest that the PPVT generally provides stable IQ's.

Validity

The PPVT manual indicates that content validity is high because *Webster's New Collegiate Dictionary* was used as the source for all words whose meaning could be depicted by a picture. The major emphasis in the literature has been on the concurrent validity of the PPVT. Separate tables have been prepared, which appear in the Appendix, that list studies comparing the PPVT and Stanford-Binet, PPVT and WISC, PPVT and other intelligence and ability tests, and PPVT and achievement tests.

PPVT and Stanford-Binet. The Stanford-Binet has been a popular instrument for evaluating the concurrent validity of the PPVT. The 37 studies listed in Table B-12 in the Appendix provide correlations between the PPVT and Stanford-Binet, which range from .22 to .92 with a median correlation of .66. A variety of children are represented in these studies, including white children, ethnic minority group children, and mentally retarded children. The PPVT and Stanford-Binet do not correlate as highly as the WISC and Stanford-Binet.

A comparison of the IQ scores on the PPVT and Stanford-Binet for the studies listed in Table B-12 as well as in other studies shows some interesting trends. In samples of ethnic minority group and "culturally disadvantaged children," the PPVT has consistently been found to yield lower IQ's than the Stanford-Binet. The largest mean discrepancy between mean scores on the two tests was 24 IQ points (mean of 67 on the PPVT and mean of 91 on the Stanford-Binet—Rosenberg & Stroud, 1966). In mentally retarded groups, the PPVT yields IQ's that tend to be somewhat higher than those on the Stanford-Binet. IQ's on the PPVT and Stanford-Binet are not comparable for ethnic minority group children. Furthermore, IQ's on the two tests do not appear to be interchangeable for any groups of children.

PPVT and WISC. The WISC follows the Stanford-Binet in popularity as a test that has been used to evaluate the validity of the PPVT. The findings of studies listed in Table B-13 in the Appendix indicate that the highest correlations are found with the Verbal Scale (range of .36 to .94, median correlation of .66), next highest with the Full Scale (range of .30 to .84, median correlation of .63), and lowest with the Performance Scale (.21 to .74, median correlation of .54). The range of correlations and the median correlations between the PPVT and Full Scale and between the PPVT and Verbal Scale are similar to those found between the PPVT and Stanford-Binet. The relatively low correlations between the PPVT and Performance Scale suggest that the PPVT may not be sensitive to the processes tapped by the Performance Scale (cf. Allen, Haupt, & Jones, 1964).

A comparison of the IQ scores on the PPVT and WISC indicates that in samples of mentally retarded children the PPVT generally yields higher IQ's than the Full Scale WISC. In some studies mean PPVT IQ's were 15 points higher than mean WISC IQ's. It is difficult to compare IQ's on the PPVT and WISC in samples of ethnic minority group children because few investigations studied such groups. As with the PPVT and Stanford-Binet, PPVT and WISC IQ's should not be considered to be interchangeable.

PPVT and Other Intelligence and Ability Tests.   Table B-14 in the Appendix lists studies that have correlated the PPVT and a variety of intelligence and ability tests (other than the Stanford-Binet and WISC). The predominant groups in these studies are exceptional children (i.e., mentally retarded, cerebral palsied, aphasic, and deaf). The variety of tests covered in these studies makes generalizations difficult. Correlations between the PPVT and other tests range from .06 to .90, with a median correlation of .53. The lowest and highest correlations were in mentally retarded samples. Some of the highest correlations were found with other picture vocabulary tests (e.g., Full-Range Picture Vocabulary Test and Van Alstyne Picture Vocabulary Test), with the exception of the Quick Test.

An analysis of the PPVT and Quick Test stimuli may help to explain the low correlations between the two tests that are reported in some studies. The PPVT stimuli appear to have low associative linguistic value and represent the automatic-sequential level (a level requiring the child to deal with non-meaningful use of symbols, principally their long term retention and the short term memory of symbol sequences) in Osgood's model, whereas the Quick Test stimuli have varying associative linguistic values and represent the representational level (a level requiring the child to deal with meaningful symbols) in Osgood's model. Thus, the Quick Test may be sensitive to higher order language skills (Strandberg, Griffith, & Miner, 1969).

The PPVT correlates more highly with the total score of the Illinois Test of Psycholinguistic Abilities than with its individual subtests (Teasdale, 1969). These results suggest that the PPVT may have more value as a measure of language ability than as a measure of a particular language skill. In evaluating language-impaired children, differences between scores on the PPVT and Leiter International Performance Scale (or Columbia Mental Maturity Scale) might be valuable in obtaining an estimate of language deficit (Spellacy & Black, 1972).

PPVT and Achievement Tests and Teachers' Ratings.   Table B-15 in the Appendix lists 21 different studies that have compared the PPVT with various achievement tests and with teachers' ratings. The correlations in these studies range from .00 to .90, with a median correlation of .40. The median correlation of .40 suggests that the PPVT has a reasonable degree of concurrent validity using measures of academic achievement. However, the Stanford-Binet and WISC relate to test-measured academic achievement better than does the PPVT.

General Research Studies

Several investigations have focused on various aspects of the PPVT, including the content of the words, the effects of modifying administrative procedures, and the constancy of the IQ in ethnic minority group children. These topics are reviewed briefly.

Content of Words.   The PPVT contains two categories of words at the preschool level: action words (verbs) and object words (nouns). One investigation compared the proportion of errors in the two categories made by lower class and by middle class Negro preschoolers (Jeruchimowicz, Costello, &

Bagur, 1971). The lower class children made significantly more errors on action words than on object words, whereas the errors of the middle class children were similar for the two types of words. In addition, the lower class children made more errors than the middle class children on both types of words. A story-telling task also was used to evaluate the extent to which the children used action and object words. On this task, socioeconomic status was not found to be a significant variable. The investigators suggested that lower class Negro preschool children may not be significantly different from middle class Negro preschool children "in their tendency to use dynamic concepts or in having experienced them, but they may be deficient in labels for many of the action concepts which they already have [p. 456]."

Another investigation has also shown that lower class Negro preschoolers have more difficulty with action words than with object words (John & Goldstein, 1964). To account for these findings, the investigators hypothesized that verbs are more difficult to learn because their referents are more variable than the referents of nouns. Another study reported that cerebral-palsied children, in comparison to nonhandicapped children, had more difficulty in identifying action words than object words (Melcer & Peck, 1967).

Items on the PPVT also can be classified as having human content or nonhuman content. In a study of institutionalized mentally retarded children who were classified as either emotionally disturbed or nondisturbed, the entire group was found to have more difficulty on items with human content than on those with nonhuman content (Shipe, Cromwell, & Dunn, 1966). However, the emotionally disturbed children had significantly more relative difficulty than the nondisturbed children on items with human content. Either situational anxiety toward test stimuli or a history of selective learning may account for these findings.

Modifying Administrative Procedures.   The PPVT can be adapted for group administration by using conventional group testing procedures (Norris, Hottel, & Brooks, 1960) or by using television (Fargo, Crowell, Noyes, Fuchigami, Gordon, & Dunn-Rankin, 1967) in testing grade-school children who are in the third to fifth grades (and perhaps in other grades as well). The group procedures resulted in IQ's similar to those obtained under individual administration.

Illustration size had no effect on the performance of preschool children (Dunn & Vergason, 1964). However, children with severe visual handicaps were found to obtain higher scores with enlarged pictures ($8\frac{1}{2} \times 11$ inches) than with the standard pictures (Mueller, 1962). Presenting the PPVT by typing the words on cards rather than presenting them orally led to significantly higher scores in a sample of orally deaf children (Hedger, 1965).

Item order, item format, method of establishing basal and ceiling levels, and rapport also have been studied. Reordering of items 70 to 120 resulted in a significant increase in the validity of the item ordering for children in grades four through six (Renzulli & Paulus, 1969). Combining both forms of the PPVT into one test was found to yield greater reliability than the separate forms, although testing time was increased (Tillinghast & Renzulli, 1968). Procedural changes have been found to increase the scores of Negro preschool children (Ali & Costello, 1971; see Chapter 4). Reliability was increased when items 30 through 75 were presented to all children (first graders), without concern for basal and ceiling levels (Klaus & Starke, 1964). Finally, procedures designed to facilitate rapport, induce physical relaxation, and increase motivation generally had little effect on the PPVT scores obtained by mentally retarded and nonmentally retarded children (Woody & Billy, 1970).

IQ Constancy in Ethnic Minority Group Children.   Studies have reported that, as a result of a Head Start program, children from ethnic minority groups make appreciable gains in their scores on the PPVT (mean increase up to 16 points) but not on the Stanford-Binet (Howard & Plant, 1967; Klaus & Gray, 1968; Milgram, 1971). To account for these findings, Milgram suggested that the PPVT "is dependent on consistent attention and control over competing responses. Its multiple-choice format may obscure the loss of attentional set to a greater degree than the relatively more open-ended questions of Binet [p. 325]." Milgram offered several hypotheses to explain the larger rise for the PPVT than for the Stanford-Binet. It may be that (a) after 4 years of age the children are increasingly able to maintain a consistent set; (b) they become more familiar with the verbal items of the PPVT; (c) the practice effect is larger for the PPVT than for the Stanford-Binet; (d) the PPVT stimuli, presented as two-dimensional line drawings, might be less familiar to the young disadvantaged child, but with school experience the stimuli become more familiar. Research is needed to evaluate which of the above hypotheses best accounts for the rise in PPVT IQ's as a result of a Head Start experience.

Comment on PPVT

The PPVT may be useful in measuring extensiveness of vocabulary and degree of cultural assimilation of children (Cole, 1966). The test may serve as a screening device for children with a limited expressive vocabulary or for children who are verbally inhibited in a testing situation. However, PPVT scores should not be considered in isolation from other measures of intelligence or of language ability (cf. Costello & Ali, 1971). Special care must be given in examining ethnic minority group children because they have been found to obtain lower scores on the PPVT than on other intelligence tests (also see Cundick (1970), cited in Chapter 4). Their lower PPVT scores may in part be a reflection of their verbal and experiential deficiencies (Milgram & Ozer, 1967).

Overall, reviewers (e.g., Lyman, 1965; Piers, 1965a) have found the test to be attractive, simple to administer, and easy to score. Piers observed that it is probably the best of its kind, with attractive plates and format and a good manual. The test has been reported to be one of the more widely used instruments for screening purposes in centers for the mentally retarded (Kaufman & Ivanoff, 1968; Silverstein, 1963b). The PPVT, as we have seen, has inspired a great amount of research since its publication in 1959. While it is a useful additional tool, it must be used cautiously in evaluating children's intelligence.

QUICK TEST

The Quick Test (Ammons & Ammons, 1962) is a brief intelligence test based on vocabulary definitions. There are three forms of the test described in the manual, each containing 50 words. In addition, three other forms are available (C. H. Ammons, personal communication, February 1973). Three plates of four drawings each are used, with two forms of the test used for each plate. The words on each of the three forms described in the manual are non-overlapping with one another, or with the Stanford-Binet, WISC, or Full-Range Picture Vocabulary Test. Norms are provided from age 2 years to adult level. The Quick Test is similar to the Full-Range Picture Vocabulary Test (Ammons & Ammons, 1948), but it was independently standardized. There are also several group formats of the test.

A single form of the test can be given in three minutes or less. However, the manual recommends that either two or three forms be used if the test is the only measure of intelligence being used, whereas one form is sufficient if only general information about intellectual ability is desired. The Quick Test is a recognition test for word meaning using pictures of objects and activities.

The test can be administered by persons not specifically trained to administer individual intelligence tests. Suggestions for handling guessing are included in the manual. Since only a pointing response is required, children (and adults) with a variety of handicaps (e.g., speech or motor difficulties) can be evaluated. Mental age norms were based on 458 white children and adults. IQ's are not reported for children. The manual suggests, however, that IQ's can be calculated by the ratio method. Providing deviation IQ's would have been a more satisfactory procedure (cf. Piers, 1965b). The manual suggests that MA's below 2.5 years be interpreted with extreme caution.

Alternate form reliability coefficients reported in the manual range from .60 to .96, with a median coefficient of .70. Alternate form reliabilities published in later studies have ranged from .56 to .99 (median coefficient of .77) in a variety of samples including mentally retarded children, normal children, and inadequate readers (Otto & McMenemy, 1965; Sawyer & Whitten, 1972; Strandberg, Griffith, & Miner, 1969). Test-retest reliabilities have been reported to be from .80 to .89 (with Ns of 74 to 76) in three groups of high socioeconomic status children and from .82 to .83 (with Ns of 39 to 42) in three groups of low socioeconomic status children (C. H. Ammons, personal communication, February 1973). The manual presents standard errors of measurement for raw scores but not for IQ's.

Validity studies are reported in the manual using school grades as one criterion, and such tests as the Full-Range Picture Vocabulary Test, Ohio Psychological Examination, and Iowa Test of Basic Skills. The validity coefficients ranged from .13 to .93, with a median correlation of .48. Validity coefficients based only on the Full-Range Picture Vocabulary Test ranged from .62 to .95, with a median correlation of .85. Additional concurrent validity studies have appeared, which are listed in Table B-16 of the Appendix. The three studies with the Stanford-Binet reported correlations of .17, .61, and .62. Correlations between the WISC and Quick Test have ranged from .31 to .88 with the Verbal Scale, from .22 to .70 with the Performance Scale, and from .35 to .84 (median correlation of .41) with the Full Scale. Generally, the correlations run higher with the Verbal Scale than with the Performance Scale. Studies that have compared the Quick Test with the PPVT (cited in Table B-14 of the Appendix) report correlations ranging from .36 to .84, with a median coefficient of .76. Finally, Mednick (1967, 1969) has found the Quick Test to have acceptable validity coefficients (range of .15 to .68, median coefficient of .36) using a variety of ability tests.

Mean differences between the Quick Test and some of the tests reported in the above studies have varied from as little as .5 point to as much as 14 points. However, in individual cases differences in IQ between the Quick Test and another test may be extreme. A consequence of such discrepancies is that examiners should give more than one type of test whenever there is a doubt about the validity of the score obtained on the Quick Test (or obtained on other similar intelligence tests). In addition, as the manual for the Quick Test advises, local norms should be obtained whenever possible.

In addition to questions concerning the standardization of the test, test-retest reliability, standard errors of measurement, and use of the ratio IQ, other difficulties should be noted. A drawback of the test is its complex and poor quality drawings (Piers, 1965b; Semeonoff, 1964). Semeonoff also pointed out that some of the attributions of meaning, and the cues on which they rest, are highly dubious; the method encourages loose use of language. On the positive side, the test is a good rapport builder (Otto & McMenemy, 1965), has a useful manual (McCandless, 1965), appears to be a promising instrument (Merenda, 1965), and can be administered in a short period of time by individuals not specifically trained to administer individual intelligence tests. The Quick Test appears to be useful as a screening device, that is, when precise estimates of intelligence are not of crucial importance; it should not be used as a substitute for the Stanford-Binet, WISC, or WPPSI. It also appears to be useful in large scale research studies where a simple and quick assessment of intelligence is needed.

PICTORIAL TEST OF INTELLIGENCE

The Pictorial Test of Intelligence (French, 1964) was devised to assess the general intelligence level of normal and handicapped children between the ages of 3 and 8 years. There are six subtests in the scale: Picture Vocabulary, Form Discrimination, Information and Comprehension, Similarities, Size and Number, and Immediate Recall. The standardization sample consisted of 1,830 children stratified by regional area, community size, and father's occupational level to conform with the 1960 census. The subtests are not timed and the test takes approximately 45 minutes to administer.

The items are presented in multiple-choice fashion, thereby making scoring a simple procedure. The arrangement of the alternatives on the response cards facilitates the use of eye movements for recording responses for those children who are not capable of pointing to their choices. The raw score is converted to MA units and then to deviation IQ's ($M = 100$, $SD = 16$).

The manual reports test-retest reliabilities of .90 to .96 for intervals between two and six weeks, while Kuder-Richardson 20 reliabilities were reported to range from .87 to .93. In a study by Sawyer (1968), split-half reliabilities were found to be similar to those in the manual, but test-retest reliabilities were lower, ranging from .77 to .88. Howard and Plant (1967) reported a test-retest coefficient (interval of 90 days) of .74 for children in a Head Start program. Sawyer, in addition, found that the subtest intercorrelations were both lower and higher than those reported in the manual (.35 to .96 versus .57 to .69). Test-retest reliability may not be as adequate as split-half reliability. The test may be least reliable at age 8 years (Himelstein, 1972a).

The concurrent validity of the test was established by correlating it with the Stanford-Binet ($r = .72$), WISC ($r = .65$), and Columbia Mental Maturity Scale ($r = .53$) in a sample of first-grade children. Pasework, Sawyer, Smith, Wasserberger, Dell, Brito, and Lee (1967) reported correlations with the WISC of .75 and .71 in kindergarten and second grade children, respectively, and with the Lorge-Thorndike of .51 and .42 for the same two grades. In grade 2, a coefficient of .23 was found with a reading skill test (Stroud Hieronymous Test). Correlations of .35 and .46 were found with teachers' estimation of IQ in the two grades. Elliott (1969) reported a .77 correlation between the PPVT and the Pictorial Test of Intelligence, using MA scores in a sample of institutionalized mentally retarded children between 7 and 14 years. The predictive validity of the test was also studied by Elliott, using the Wide Range Achievement Test with the same sample. He found the following correlations: .68 with spelling, .56 with reading, and .79 with arithmetic.

The Pictorial Test of Intelligence sustains children's interest (Pasework et al., 1967), although some of the instructions are confusing. Generally, the items appear to be arranged in ascending order, although some easy items appear in the later portions of the subtests (Sawyer, 1968). The need to start each subtest with the first item may add to testing time, and the norms may not be sufficiently specific. The test appears to be useful in evaluating children with motor and speech handicaps (Himelstein, 1972a) and for evaluating the learning aptitude of children from 3 to 6 years of age (Newland, 1972).

COLUMBIA MENTAL MATURITY SCALE

The Columbia Mental Maturity Scale (CMMS), Third Edition (Burgemeister, Blum, & Lorge, 1972), is useful in evaluating children who have sensory or motor defects or who have difficulty in speaking and, to some extent, in reading. The test does not depend on reading skills. It provides age deviation scores (standard scores) for chronological ages between 3 years, 6 months and 9 years, 11 months. The age deviation scores range from 50 to 150, with the mean equal to 100 and the standard deviation equal to 16. The standard error of measurement is 5 points for ages 3½ through 5½ years, and 6 points for ages 6 through 9½ years. A second score, the Maturity Index, which indicates the standardization age group most similar to that of the child in terms of test performance, also is provided. The standardization sample for the Third Edition consisted of 2600 children residing in 25 states. The norming procedures were designed to ensure a representative national sample.

The test contains 92 cards (6 by 19 inches), 50 of which are completely new to the Third Edition. The task is simple, namely, to have the child select the one drawing on each card that is different from the others. The test is untimed, usually takes between 15 and 20 minutes to administer, and is simple to score. The child is required to make perceptual discriminations involving color, shape, size, use, number, missing parts, and symbolic material. There are simple perceptual classification tasks and tasks requiring abstract manipulation of symbolic concepts. Thus, the test appears to measure general reasoning ability. Young children and deaf children may have difficulty in understanding the concept of pointing to the "one that does not belong."

The first version of the CMMS appeared in 1954, and the second in 1959. The test was revised after a five-year period because many questions were raised about the 1954 Edition's validity and reliability, the adequacy of its norms, and the difficult level of its items. The Third Edition was introduced in order to make further improvements on the scale. The manual for the Third Edition is much improved over the former manuals. The manual for the Second Edition, for example, was inadequate in presenting the procedures that were used in developing the norms and in presenting reliability data. However, the manual for the Third Edition is not deficient in any of these ways. Norming procedures are described carefully. Split-half reliability coefficients range from .85 to .91, with a median coefficient of .88. Test-retest reliabilities for three separate groups range from .84 to .86. The manual reports the following validity coefficients for the Third Edition of the CMMS: .31 to .61 (median of .50) with the Stanford Achievement Test; .62 and .69 with the Otis-Lennon Mental Ability Test; .84 with the 1959 CMMS; and .67 with the Stanford-Binet, Form L-M.

Since the Second and Third Editions are highly correlated, it may be useful to examine validity studies for the 1959 Edition. The studies in this paragraph are based on correlations between the CMMS (1959 Edition) and the Stanford-Binet. The manual reports correlations of .65 (using mental age) and .56 (using IQ) with a mentally retarded sample. Bligh (1959) reported correlations of .70 and .59 in samples of 4- and 5-year-old mentally retarded children, respectively. A .88 correlation was reported in a handicapped population (Hirschenfang, 1961), a .39 correlation in a normal sample (Levinson & Block, 1960), and .84 and .87 correlations in neurologically impaired samples (Hirschenfang, Jaramillo, & Benton, 1966). In the above studies (with the exception of the one reported in the manual) IQ's were always higher on the CMMS than on the Stanford-Binet. However, in a sample of Negro kindergarten children, lower IQ's were obtained on the CMMS than on the Stanford-Binet (84 versus 91; Rosenberg & Stroud, 1966). The above results, as well as other findings,

led some of the investigators to suggest that further revision in item arrangement, administration, and scoring were indicated.

The studies listed in Table B-5 of the Appendix that have compared the
1959 CMMS and the WISC report correlations of .50 to .76, with a median coefficient of .64. The samples included Negro children and mentally retarded
children. The median coefficient is similar to the median coefficient ($r = .67$)
reported in the studies above that have compared the CMMS and the Stanford-
Binet.

Newland (1965) had observed that there was some doubt about how well
the 1959 Edition was performing. Because the Third Edition is new, research
studies will be needed to evaluate its effectiveness. The test could be adapted
so that the child could be helped to employ a convenient response modality
(speaking, pointing, looking, or some combination of these). While the psychometric properties of the CMMS are not well established, the scale provides a
means for evaluating intelligence through the use of nonverbal stimuli. It can be
useful as an aid in evaluating handicapped children.

LEITER INTERNATIONAL PERFORMANCE SCALE

The Leiter International Performance Scale (Leiter, 1959) is a nonverbal
test of intelligence that can be used to evaluate children who have sensory or
motor defects or who have difficulty in speaking or reading. The scale also has
been purported to be a culture-free measure of intelligence, although Tate
(1952) reported that the test appeared to be no more culture-free than the Stanford-Binet. The scale contains 54 tests and is arranged in an age-scale format
from year II to year XVIII. The task consists of having the child select the
blocks bearing the appropriate symbols or pictures and insert them into the appropriate recess of a frame that is used in administering the scale. There is no
time limit, and instructions are given in pantomime. The scale appears to
require perceptual organization and discrimination ability. The tests at the
lowest levels of the scale are considered to be tests of the ability to learn, rather
than tests of learned material (Arthur, 1949).

The 1948 revision is the latest in a series of revisions. The initial version of
the scale was reported in 1929 in Leiter's master's thesis. The 1948 revision
was adapted by Arthur (1949), who supplemented the revision with tests from
the Revised Form II of the Point Scale of Performance Tests. The Arthur Adaptation covers the age range between 3 and 8 years, and the tests cover year-
levels II through XII. The adaptation was needed because Arthur found the
norms too high for children between the ages of 3 and 8 years. However, the
test materials for the 1948 revision of the Leiter and the Arthur Adaptation are
exactly the same through year-level XII when the Arthur Adaptation ends. In
principle, the Leiter is a nonverbal Binet scale (Arthur, 1949).

The manual for the Leiter fails to describe adequately the standardization
group, and it also fails to present reliability data or standard deviations for the
various age levels. Sharp (1958) reported a test-retest coefficient (6-month interval) of .91 for a sample of mentally retarded children, and Spellacy and
Black (1972) reported a test-retest coefficient (25 weeks) of .86 for a group of
language-impaired children.

One of the ways in which the validity of the 1948 revision was assessed
was by administering both the 1940 and 1948 versions to a group of 180
"unselected subjects" who were between 8 and 16 years of age. The resulting
correlation of .92 indicated to Leiter (1959) "that the 1948 Revision could be

used with the same confidence that the 1940 Scale was used [p. 58]." The studies listed in Table B-17 in the Appendix that have evaluated the concurrent validity of the 1948 revision of the Leiter by correlating it with the Stanford-Binet and WISC have reported correlations that range from .56 to .92, with a median correlation of .83. The Leiter has been found to correlate more highly with the WISC Performance Scale than with the Verbal Scale.

The scale has been characterized as having the following problems: item difficulty levels may be uneven; certain pictures are outdated; the culture fairness of the scale has not been determined; the abilities measured by the scale are not clear; and the scale contains a small number of tests at each year level (Werner, 1965). These problems are in addition to the lack of information about the reliability of the scale for various age levels. Because the norms underestimate the child's intelligence, Leiter (1959) recommended that five points be added to the IQ obtained on the scale.

While the Leiter has a number of limitations, it does merit consideration as an aid in clinical diagnosis (rather than as a measure of general intelligence), especially in testing handicapped children who cannot be evaluated by the Stanford-Binet, WISC, or WPPSI (cf. Arnold, 1953). The scale is also useful in testing children who may be penalized by picture vocabulary tests (e.g., the illiterate child and perhaps some children from ethnic minority groups or from "culturally deprived groups") (cf. Allen & Jones, 1967).

SLOSSON INTELLIGENCE TEST

The Slosson Intelligence Test (Slosson, 1963) is an age-scale test that provides mental ages from .5 month to 27 years. The two major sources for the items were the Stanford-Binet and the Gessell Institute of Child Development Behavior Inventory. After 4 years of age, all questions are presented verbally and require spoken responses. There are no time limits. It takes between 10 and 30 minutes to administer. Scoring is fairly objective. The test can be used by relatively untrained examiners.

The test places heavy emphasis on language skills for children between 2 and 3 years of age, and consequently may not be valid for children in this age group if they have delayed language development or are not from a middle class environment (Hunt, 1972). Since the publication of the test, there has been little research concerning the issue that Hunt raised. Hunt also indicated that the major problem with the test is for the age period of .5 to 24 months. There are few items at each month's level, and placement of the items does not agree with the placement of similar items on the Bayley Scales of Infant Development.

The Slosson Intelligence Test still maintains the ratio IQ. This type of IQ, which was used with the Stanford-Binet prior to the 1960 revision, has many disadvantages (see Chapters 3 and 8). Another disadvantage with the test is that the manual is deficient in describing the construction of the test and the characteristics of the standardization sample (Himelstein, 1972b). The manual reports a test-retest reliability coefficient of .97, while Hammill, Crandell, and Colarusso (1970) reported a test-retest reliability coefficient of .96 over a three-month period for a sample of 6 to 9 year olds and a split-half reliability coefficient of .91 for the same group.

While the manual lacks adequate data concerning the validity and reliability of the Slosson, the studies listed in Table B-18 of the Appendix have reported satisfactory concurrent validity using an assortment of different tests. The manual reported correlations with the Stanford-Binet (Form L-M) ranging from .90 to .98, while correlations reported in other studies have ranged from

.60 to .94, with a median correlation of .90. These correlations may be spuriously high because the Slosson contains items that are essentially adaptations from the Stanford-Binet. Correlations reported in the studies listed in Table B-18 are uniformly higher with the WISC Verbal Scale than with the WISC Performance Scale. The correlations range from .49 to .93 with the Verbal Scale, from .10 to .76 with the Performance Scale, and from .50 to .84 with the Full Scale (median correlation of .67). Many of the studies in Table B-18 reported means that were relatively similar for the Slosson and Binet and for the Slosson and WISC. The range of correlation coefficients between the Slosson and tests other than the Stanford-Binet and WISC is from .26 to .83, with a median correlation of .59.

The published research suggests that the Slosson Intelligence Test has merit as a quick screening device or perhaps as a device for retesting purposes. Advantages include the short administration time and relative ease of use by personnel with minimal training in the administration of individual intelligence tests. The test, however, should not be used uncritically as a substitute for the Stanford-Binet, WISC, or WPPSI (cf. Himelstein, 1972b).

SUMMARY

The six tests reviewed in Chapter 18 (PPVT, Quick Test, Pictorial Test of Intelligence, CMMS, Leiter International Performance Scale, and Slosson Intelligence Test) serve a limited but useful function in the assessment of children's intelligence. The first five tests that are reviewed are especially valuable in evaluating handicapped children who cannot be tested with the Stanford-Binet, WISC, or WPPSI. Because the tests require relatively little training, persons not specifically trained in the administration of individual intelligence tests can be trained to administer them. Another advantage is that most of the tests, with the exception of the Pictorial Test of Intelligence, can be administered in less than 30 minutes; the Quick Test may take less than three minutes to administer. The IQ's obtained on the tests covered in this chapter should not be considered to be interchangeable with those obtained on the Stanford-Binet and WISC (and likely the WPPSI).

The PPVT, Quick Test, Pictorial Test of Intelligence, and CMMS share one feature in common: they all require a pointing response. However, the PPVT and Quick Test, while only assessing vocabulary ability, appear to measure different facets of language skills. The PPVT may be less sensitive to higher order language skills than the Quick Test. The Pictorial Test of Intelligence may serve as a method of evaluating learning aptitude of children within the age range of 3 to 6 years. The CMMS appears to require visual perceptual skills, ability to abstract, and ability for number concepts. The Leiter, too, requires nonverbal responses. Instead of pointing, the child simply has to move blocks into a recess on a frame. Abilities measured by the Leiter likely include perceptual organization and discrimination skills. The Slosson is the only test covered in the chapter that requires verbal responses. However, it shares with the other tests relatively simple scoring and administrative procedures. Language skills likely are measured by the test.

The chapter reviewed the reliability and validity of each of the six tests by referring both to the test manuals and to published research. The PPVT has generated a vast amount of research, and studies most pertinent to the assessment process were reviewed. However, the review of the PPVT, as well as of the other tests, primarily covered studies evaluating the performance of children below 16 years. Generally, of the six tests covered in the chapter, the most reliable and valid (the latter determined by concurrent validity studies) appear to be the PPVT, Quick Test, and Slosson Intelligence Test. Less information is available about the reliability and validity of the Pictorial Test of Intelligence, CMMS, and Leiter. However, each of these tests also provides a means of assessing handicapped children (and other groups of children as well) who might not otherwise be validly assessed by other types of tests. The assets and limitations of each test selected by the examiner should be evaluated carefully.

SECTION 5

DIAGNOSTIC APPLICATIONS

The assessment of intellectual ability is the primary goal of those who administer an individual intelligence test. However, psychologists who are especially trained in the problems of children (beyond the ordinary ones) usually will evaluate the child's temperament and general test performance (both quantitative and qualitative) on an intelligence test in addition to reporting test scores and test behavior. In a general assessment situation, a battery of tests usually will be administered to a child and the intelligence test results will be integrated with the results of other tests. Thus, hypotheses derived from intelligence tests will be evaluated by the child's performance on a number of specially designed tests (e.g., personality tests, visual-motor tests, and achievement tests). **The material in Section 5 that is related to diagnostic assessment is presented for readers who are thoroughly trained (or in training) in the problems of clinical and, where relevant, educational assessment. This material should not be used by those whose primary goal (or only goal) is to evaluate the child's level of intelligence.**

Section 5 begins with Chapter 19, which considers the diagnostic aspects of intelligence testing. Information obtained during the assessment process from any of a number of diverse sources, including interview material, responses to the test questions, and pattern of test performance, may be indicative of psychopathology. Often clear-cut patterns or signs will not appear, or there may be indications that further testing is warranted to investigate problem areas, such as perceptual or emotional disturbances. Many children, too, will not display any signs suggestive of psychopathology, and there are children with demonstrable forms of psychopathology (e.g., brain injury) who do not display deficits or symptoms on the examination. The assessment of psychopathology is a difficult task. The examiner must be very careful in placing a diagnostic label on a child. In most cases, as we have seen, the intelligence test will not be the sole device employed in the assessment process. A diagnosis should never be made until all relevant information is considered. If a diagnostic label is used in the report, the examiner should recognize that the label will become part of the child's permanent file and may adversely affect opportunities available to the child for many years to come.

Yet, the examiner must be alert to information that can aid him in making useful recommendations and in conveying as clearly as possible the child's resources. The recognition of the possible existence of, for example, emotional disturbance or organic brain damage or perceptual handicaps may be extremely useful in making a recommendation for a special educational program, for a counseling program, or for a more thorough diagnostic work-up. A solution to the labelling problem may lie in describing the child's performance as clearly and as succinctly as possible, highlighting problem areas. "His performance resembles that of children with neurological handicaps" or "His performance is suggestive of a behavioral disorder" are ways to describe two possible categories of psychopathology when appropriate.

The two most severe conditions of psychopathology are childhood schizophrenia and organic brain damage. A third condition, mental retardation, which may or may not be a reflection of psychopathology also occupies an important place in assessment. A child who is functioning at a low level of intelligence may have nothing psychopathological about him at all. He may only be below normal in intelligence. These three conditions are by no means mutually exclusive and, as one studies the material related to them in Chapters 20, 21, and 22, it will become increasingly clear that labels at times represent arbitrary decisions on the part of the diagnostician. Other frequently encountered conditions, including emotional disturbances in children, learning disabilities in children, and physical diseases or disabilities in children are discussed in Chapter 23.

In Chapter 23, we shall see that cognitive abilities are often not severely affected by minor emotional maladjustments or by some types of physical illness. Part of Chapter 23 also summarizes research findings concerning IQ level and physical disabilities. It can be argued that all of the categories described in Chapters 20 through 23 reflect or represent "medical problems." The intent, however, is to follow standard nomenclature, and consequently such labels as "childhood schizophrenia," "organic brain damage," and "mental retardation" are used. We prefer to reserve the label "medical problems" for children with illnesses that have clear organic etiologies.

Each chapter in Section 5 includes, where possible, a discussion of the application of the Stanford-Binet and WISC to the topic under consideration. An attempt has been made to survey systematically the literature relevant to intelligence, child psychopathology, mental retardation, and the Stanford-Binet and WISC.

CHAPTER 19

DIAGNOSTIC ASPECTS OF
INTELLIGENCE TESTING

Not only do individual intelligence tests yield an IQ and a pattern of relative strengths and weaknesses, but they also provide an opportunity to observe the examinee's personality, interpersonal relations, attitudes, language usage, and visual-motor performance. The assessment process incorporates data obtained from behavioral observations and test performance with other available data, such as school and medical reports and family history. However, individual intelligence testing is not designed to establish diagnostic labels (with the exception of those related to level of intellectual functioning) or to assess personality; rather, its purpose is to answer questions about intellectual functioning and to make recommendations that are useful to the report's readers. On many occasions, an individual intelligence test may be given as one of several tests in a battery; consequently, the IQ provides only one index in the assessment process. All possible sources of data that may shed light on the problem should be considered (Garner, 1966). This chapter covers an introduction into the diagnostic process, general methods for observing and for evaluating test performance, and some general diagnostic examples. Material related to the intellectual functioning of specific psychopathological and physically disabled groups is presented in Chapters 20 through 23.

The referral questions in clinical settings usually pertain to issues regarding the management and understanding of the child and not exclusively to the measurement of intellect. Intelligence tests were devised to measure intellectual abilities and should be used primarily for this purpose (Savage, 1968). While cognitive disorders appear in various forms of psychopathology, they are only part of the total picture. The failure of IQ tests to define definitive patterns that are diagnostic of various forms of psychopathology, as we shall see in Chapters 20 through 23, is not surprising, because mental disorders are superimposed on preexisting patterns of cognitive development. The assessment of intelligence is an important function in its own right. The assessment of mental illness as well is an important function in its own right. It is important to recognize that while intelligence test results permit us to determine the level of mental ability of a child, they do not permit us to determine whether or not he has, for example, organic lesions (Savage, 1968).

Almost from the beginning of the testing movement in the United States, psychologists have been aware that it is important not to make diagnoses on the basis of test scores alone (Fearing, 1919). However, the reactions of the examinee during the examination are a valuable source of information, so that performance on an intelligence test constitutes an important part of the clinical picture. Currently, the evaluation of intelligence is still viewed, as it has been since the acceptance of tests as valid measures of intelligence in the second decade of the twentieth century, as one of the key contributions that the psychologist can make to the case study (e.g., Tallent, 1963). The diagnostic process in intelligence testing includes the careful administration of an intelligence test, the observation and evaluation of the child's entire performance, the development of a useful set of recommendations, and the integration of testing material with previous case material (and perhaps with case material obtained in the future).

In the chapters in Section 5 we shall see that neither the Stanford-Binet nor the WISC (or WPPSI) are effective instruments in providing reliable and valid indices that differentiate among various forms of child psychopathology. In an extensive review of studies dealing with a variety of psychological tests, Herbert (1964) concluded that the majority of tests fail to attain an acceptable standard of efficiency. He proposed that the psychologist's main contribution should lie in helping to facilitate the academic and social training of the child. Although current tests are not sufficiently precise, there are behavioral data, case history data, and medical data, along with test data, to assist in the diagnostic process.

The three broad diagnostic categories that cause the most difficulty for differential diagnosis are schizophrenia, mental retardation, and brain injury. It is possible, of course, that any one child may simultaneously be classified in all three categories. There is nothing that prohibits a child from functioning at a retarded level, revealing schizophrenic symptoms, and being brain-injured. However, in psychological evaluations an attempt usually is made to differentiate among the three conditions.

DIAGNOSTIC PROCESS

We have alluded to the findings, presented in detail in Chapters 20 through 23, that there are few uniform patterns of performance on the Stanford-Binet or on the WISC (and WPPSI) that are unique to specific psychopathological groups or to personality-trait groups. These negative findings should not deter us from reporting the qualitative and quantitative features that characterize the examinee's performance. The assessment of intelligence is not a matter of clinical versus actuarial approaches; it is a matter of careful description and interpretation of behavior and test performance. In these ways useful recommendations and decisions concerning the examinee can be arrived at.

Value of Intelligence Testing

An assessment of intellectual functioning lends itself well to the diagnostic process because there are three distinct factors involved in a child's performance on an intelligence test: "(a) formal cognitive processes, (b) informational achievements which reflect the content rather than the formal properties of cognition, and (c) motivational factors which involve a wide range of personality variables [Zigler & Butterfield, 1968, p. 2]." A neurotic process, or a personality disorder, can be understood better by examining its effects on cognitive processes (Tallent, 1963). Terman (1916) recognized that from the Binet tests "the experienced clinical psychologist is able to gain considerable insight into the subject's emotional and volitional equipment, even though the method was designed primarily for another purpose [p. 49]." This same statement applies equally well to the WISC and WPPSI.

Evaluation as a Process of Prediction

The evaluation of intelligence can be viewed as a process of prediction (Doris, 1963). Intelligence testing in a clinical situation requires that specific questions be posed about the individual child. The clinician's task is "to diagnose the problem, to determine what the prognosis will be without intervention, and to decide what kind of intervention will make what kind of change in the prognosis [Doris, 1963, p. 168]." Intelligence testing simultaneously addresses itself to three roles: The evaluation is used (*a*) to predict the child's present level of functioning in problem solving situations, (*b*) to predict future level of functioning, and (*c*) to predict differences in functioning according to variations in internal and external circumstances.

Description of the Diagnostic Process

The following two approaches to the assessment task reflect the opinions of many psychologists. According to Taylor and Teicher (1946), the diagnostic process includes

an analysis of the quantitative and qualitative aspects of test results, the language organization and quality of verbal responses and finally the observations and interpretations of behavior and adjustment traits which emerge during the examination [p. 326].

Carter and Bowles (1948) offered a slightly different analysis:

...the examiner's task in test interpretation is to present a meaningful behavior picture of the child. This involves an evaluation of the adequacy of formal test results, the significance of those results to the extent that the examiner's information permits, and a description of the child's behavior in the examining situation as it may be indicative of his personality characteristics [p. 142].

Evaluation of Personality

It is important to describe the child's personality in connection with an analysis of test performance, because examinees with the same IQ differ in many respects. They may have different distributions of success and failure, different subtest patterns, and different potentialities associated with their IQ level. Thus,

when intelligence level is considered as one part of a functioning, changing, and developing individual, then specific responses to an intelligence test can give valuable insights not only about the present functioning level of intelligence, but also about the relative development of various aspects or components of intelligence, as well as the form in which these components are expressed and mobilized, how they are affected by internal or external stress and how they contribute to or detract from an individual's sense of achievement, satisfaction, or general well-being [Moriarty, 1961, p. 10].

An adequate assessment of intelligence requires a knowledge of the examinee's strengths and limitations, likes and dislikes, attitudes toward himself, and other factors that may be related to his level of functioning. While a complete picture of the examinee will not be obtained from the examination, there will be *some* information available that will aid in making decisions concerning the educational and treatment process.

Hazards of the Diagnostic Process

The diagnostic process, under which we are subsuming personality description, predictions, and recommendations, is by no means a simple process. It is fraught with many hazards because our ability to predict future behavior, to take one example, is extremely limited. R. B. Cattell (1937) rightly cautioned against premature generalizing from the test situation to everyday life:

> The examiner imagines that he can deduce a good deal about the child's disposition and temperament from reactions in the Binet Test situation and in performance tests. There is, however, no proof that the qualities of persistence or impulsiveness shown in these miniature test situations — which themselves do not necessarily have any relation to the child's total conative life pattern — will throw any light on his persistence or impulsiveness in the major situations arising in school and home [p. 119].

Other writers, too, have commented on the limitations of the test situation in diagnosing personality. Stoddard (1943) noted that the nature of the psychometric situation prevents certain personality factors from having an effect on test scores, while the same factors may be of potent influence on intellectual achievement. Weisskopf (1951) illustrated one such possibility:

> The ability to concentrate one's effort and interest over a long period of time on a problem, for example, is a factor which may have little effect on psychometric performances, since each problem in such performances requires only a very short amount of time. On the other hand, the ability to make a persistent effort may be an important factor affecting intellectual achievement outside the test situation [p. 410].

The Diagnostic Process and the Physically Handicapped

The diagnostic process used with physically handicapped children is similar to that used with other children. However, particular attention should be given to examination material that pertains to the child's potentialities for rehabilitation and that will serve as a guide for understanding behaviors that may occur in the rehabilitative program (Berko, 1953). The assessment should provide information that will help in planning a treatment and educational program (Schonell, 1958). The program should not be developed exclusively on the basis of the overall IQ; it is the pattern of successes and failures in conjunction with the overall level of functioning that must be evaluated (Heilman, 1949). As a general frame of reference, prediction should be subordinate to the desire to meet the present needs of the children; *the primary task is assessment rather than diagnosis, present help rather than prediction* (Reynell, 1970).

Structure of the Interpretative Process

Goldman's Model.   An interesting model for understanding the structure of the interpretative process has been described by Goldman (1961). The model is three dimensional, consisting of four kinds of interpretations (descriptive, genetic, predictive, and evaluative), two methods of combining the data to make interpretations (mechanical and nonmechanical), and two sources of data from which interpretations are made (test data and nontest data). The three dimensions form 16 cells, each representing a type of interpretation.

The descriptive interpretation consists of describing the examinee's personality (what he is like) and the test findings. The genetic interpretation is an attempt to explain how the examinee arrived at his present level of functioning. The predictive interpretation refers to statements about the examinee's future performance. The evaluative interpretation attempts to prescribe a course of action for the examinee (advice-giving).

The mechanical treatment of the data, or what may be termed "statistical" or "actuarial," consists of using expectancy tables, regression equations, and tables of norms. Nonmechanical treatment of the data, or what may be termed "clinical," tends to be more subjective, more vague, and sometimes intuitive. The sources of interpretation in a psychological evaluation are usually tests, although a variety of sources may be used. Examples of nontest data sources are the examinee's statements of interest, his motivation, his socioeconomic status, and his family environment. Nontest data, Goldman pointed out, must be validated in the same manner as test data.

The three dimensions can be brought together to make interpretations and, in practice, many of the cells may be combined to yield a simple interpretative inference or hypothesis. While Goldman provided illustrations for each of the 16 cells, only a few illustrations are presented here, following Goldman's suggestions.

1. DESCRIPTIVE-MECHANICAL-TEST DATA

Jim achieved an IQ of 103 ± 5 on the Wechsler Intelligence Scale for Children. This score places him in the 57th percentile.

2. GENETIC-NONMECHANICAL-TEST DATA

Jose, who is a bilingual Mexican American 5-year-old boy, obtained an IQ of 76 ± 5 on the Stanford-Binet Intelligence Scale, Form L-M. At home, Spanish is primarily spoken. The present IQ may not be valid because of his foreign language background.

3. PREDICTIVE-MECHANICAL-NONTEST DATA

The school psychology division at a local district is trying to determine what family variables correlate with IQ scores and grades in school. A formula will be developed using the family variables to predict IQ scores and school grades.

4. EVALUATIVE-NONMECHANICAL-NONTEST DATA

Mr. Smith, a school psychologist, is often asked to advise students on selecting a college. His decision is based on the student's grades, teachers' ratings, his impression of the student, and his impression of the college.

Goldman pointed out that the optimally effective use of clinical interpretative methods requires the following of the examiner:

1. He must know his tests and a great deal about people.

2. He must develop hypotheses and be willing to modify or reject a hypothesis in the light of new data, recognizing that creative skill and scientific rigor and cautiousness are involved in such procedures.

3. He must know the situations about which he makes inferences.

4. He must study himself as an interpreter of test performance and of human behavior.

Goslin's Assessment Paradigm. A paradigm, developed by Goslin (1963), shows how the assessment of intelligence can be viewed as a three-stage process. As Figure 19–1 shows, an examinee's performance on an ability test or on an intelligence test is affected by many variables. Not all variables are equally important, and on some occasions some variables will play a more important role than others.

The paradigm begins with a consideration of innate factors—general and special inherited abilities—and their contribution to test performance. The contribution of inherited ability to the intelligence test score has been of concern since the inception of the testing movement, and at present a factual conclusion, as Goslin pointed out, is not possible. Genetic differences with respect to intelligence do exist among individuals, but the extent to which genetic limitations can be penetrated by environmental programs is not known. (See Chapter 2 for information concerning genetic factors and intelligence.)

Background and environmental factors, which include cultural background, formal training, experience with similar tests, and the physical condition of the examinee, are also found on the input side of the paradigm. Intervening variables, such as personality, situation, test demands, and random

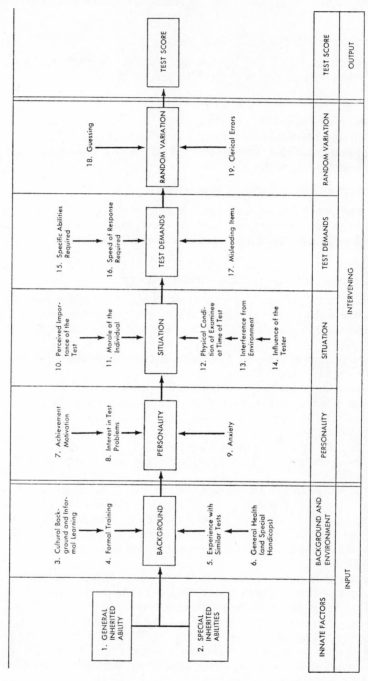

Figure 19–1. A paradigm for the analysis of influencing variables. (Reprinted by permission of the publisher and author from D. A. Goslin, *The Search for Ability: Standardized Testing in Social Perspective*, p. 130. Copyright 1963, Russell Sage Foundation.)

variation, determine what proportion of the examinee's capabilities will be demonstrated on the test. Finally, after considering the input and intervening variables, the output, namely, the test score, is derived. An accurate assessment of intelligence requires consideration of the variables illustrated in the paradigm plus other factors that may be unique to the examinee.

Comment. Goldman and Goslin present overlapping approaches for understanding the interpretative or assessment process. The factors described in the input and intervening parts of Goslin's model are, in Goldman's model, used by the examiner (*a*) in arriving at one or more of the four kinds of interpretations described by Goldman and (*b*) as nontest data sources. The output in Goslin's model, the test score, represents one of the two sources of data in Goldman's model. Thus, the two approaches can be integrated into one conceptual framework.

Comment on the Diagnostic Process

We have seen that the diagnostic process, while extremely important, has its limitations. A thorough understanding of personality dynamics, psychopathology, and child development must be a prerequisite for those using individual intelligence tests and other psychological instruments that focus on children. The reader is encouraged to study intensively the published work in the field of child psychopathology and exceptional children. Before turning to some general guidelines that can assist in the diagnostic process, it is important to recognize that the diagnostic process does not end with a description and an analysis of the child's performance. The entire consultation process, which includes recommendations, also plays an important role in the diagnostic process. In Chapter 26, some factors involved in consultation are considered.

GENERAL TEST PERFORMANCE

The test situation provides diagnostic information from a number of different sources. First, there are qualitative indices, such as the examinee's appearance, general attitude, language usage (which includes content and style of responses), and visual-motor performance. The qualitative scoring systems, illustrated in the text, that have been developed to categorize responses are included in this source. Second, there is the application of test interpretation systems to the Stanford-Binet, WISC, and WPPSI. These systems are described in the present chapter as well as in other chapters that discuss the diagnostic aspects of these tests. Third, there is the examinee's performance on specific tests, or the pattern of his performance on a number of tests or subtests. Thus, for example, comparison may be made of verbal with nonverbal tasks, "tests of attention span and attention to detail with tasks involving more complex judgment and logic, or tasks involving learned skills and information with tasks involving comprehension [Palmer, 1970, p. 104]." (Chapters 10, 13, 14, and 16 consider material related to this third point.) Fourth, material related to factor analysis, classification systems, and scatter analysis is available (see Chapters 10, 14, and 17). Finally, there is the total picture arrived at by integrating all sources of data obtained during the test situation with background information. The remainder of the chapter presents illustrations for each of these sources.

Qualitative Indices

The value of careful observation and analysis of an examinee's performance was well illustrated by Beller (1962):

While two children may answer the same question correctly, one answer will reveal insight into its underlying concept, whereas the other answer will indicate only superficial understanding. Two children may successfully complete a performance task, but only one may grasp the intricate relationship between the parts to be assembled; the other child will solve the problem by trial and error. Similarly, failure may be attributed to lack of knowledge in one child; a simple refusal to answer the question in another; and may be due to bizarre and inappropriate responses, indicating serious intellectual and emotional impairment, in a third child [p. 97].

Carter and Bowles (1948) also discussed the importance of qualitative analysis. "It is much more important for the examiner to know how well a child understands words and under what circumstances he can use them than it is for him to know only that the child either did not respond or that his responses could not be credited [pp. 124-125]." In evaluating the Binet Vocabulary test, they pointed out that "the variety, number, complexity, and preciseness of definitions should be noted. There are, for example, marked qualitative differences between 'lion roars' and 'a loud noise' as definitions for 'roar,' although they receive identical scores [p. 133]." The intelligence test situation provides excellent clues to the examinee's approach to problem-solving tasks. The steps he uses in solving the problem, "his verbalized habits of thinking and reasoning, and his tendency to check upon or ignore the accuracy of his replies furnish a picture of the patient's typical approach to a primarily intellectual situation [Garner, 1966, p. 72]."

Personality features may be revealed through verbal and nonverbal channels. Words, gestures, facial expressions, postures, and bodily movements may provide clues to better understand the examinee. What type of test leads to stammering, blushing, or other s gns of anxiety? Is there a change from the initial meeting between the examinee and examiner to the latter part of the test? If so, what factors might account for the change? Are there any tests that motivate the examinee? How does the examinee relate to the examiner and how does the examiner relate to the examinee? These are some of the questions with which to begin a systematic entry into the diagnostic process. However, it is important to emphasize, as Shapiro (1957) has done, that in making clinical use of observations from test performance, "the psychologist should be under no illusion about what he is doing. He is in fact using an unvalidated and unstandardized test [p. 93]." Careful checking of observations is warranted in all cases.

General Attitude.   The examinee's attitudes toward the testing situation and the examiner should be noted, along with other pertinent attitudes. The material presented in Chapter 25 under *Attitudinal Features* in the section on Test Behavior should prove to be helpful in evaluating the examinee's attitudes during the examination.

Language Usage.   Language usage is a guide to personality style and to thought processes. It is of interest to determine not only how many words the examinee knows, but also the manner in which he presents his answers. Are his responses direct and to the point, vague, roundabout, or free associative in nature? What is the usual tempo of his responses? Does he respond quickly or very slowly? Does he take time to consider his reponses? Does he do his thinking aloud or does he give only his final answer? Is he self-critical? Evaluating such areas together with language patterns will be helpful in the diagnosis of personality patterns and psychopathology.

The following are the major kinds of language distortions that may be observed during the course of an examination:

1. *Speech difficulty* may be shown by stammering, stuttering, or by other types of speech problems, which may indicate aphasic or dysarthric conditions.

2. *Circumlocution* is shown when there are roundabout answers.

3. *Verbal perseveration* is demonstrated by similar definitions to different words.

4. *Rambling* is seen when a topic is introduced after another to which it has little logical relationship; words are not used precisely.

5. In *fragmentation,* incomplete thoughts are presented for complete ones, and the examiner is left to fill in the missing ideas.

6. In *blocking,* an attempt is made to recall the answer but it is not successful. Blocking also may be seen when one word is substituted for another when the child cannot remember the one for which he is searching.

7. *Irrelevant speech* is similar to rambling, except that the degree of disorganization is more intense. Inappropriate topics may be introduced or statements of self-reference may appear.

8. *Bizarreness* is revealed when responses show signs of inconsistency, illogical reasoning, or idiosyncratic associations, or when there is a juxtaposition of disconnected ideas.

9. *Automatic phrases* are repetitive statements that do not serve communication purposes. They may reflect defensiveness or inability to rely on one's own resources.

10. *Perplexity* is signaled by confusion, by an inability to understand the questions, or by an inability to understand what is called for.

11. *Confabulation* is noted in responses that indicate some far-fetched association elaborated on the basis of some superficial similarity to the stimulus.

12. *Circumstantiality* is noted in responses that are indirect. The examinee proceeds indirectly to the answer with many tedious details and parenthetical and irrelevant additions.

13. *Clang associations* are responses that are peripheral to the stimuli, based on similarity of sound.

14. *Over-elaboration* is defined as "the tendency to give alternate meanings and irrelevant details, or to be overly and unnecessarily descriptive [Wechsler, 1958, p. 181]."

15. *Ellipsis* occurs when there is "omission of one or more words (sometimes only syllables) necessary to complete the meaning in a phrase or sentence [Wechsler, 1958, p. 181]."

16. A *self-reference* occurs when personalized elements or details reflecting self-involvement are incorporated into a definition (Wechsler, 1958).

Evaluating the content of the responses can provide information about the extent to which personalized concerns affect cognitive efficiency in relatively routine, impersonal situations, such as the intelligence testing situation (Blatt & Allison, 1968). Impairment of cognitive efficiency, if it appears, will usually occur in severely neurotic or psychotic conditions. The examinee's style of responding, as shown in the following examples provided by Blatt and Allison, is also relevant for personality assessment. An examinee with *obsessive characteristics* may respond in a pedantic, overdetailed manner, and incessantly qualify his responses. A *depressive person* may respond in a hesitant and blocked manner, interspersing self-deprecatory remarks. The *paranoid person* may be querulous, distrustful, and legalistic. The *hypomanic individual* may be expansive, outpouring, and excited. The demarcation between style of responding and content of the responses, however, often is not clear. In addition, judgment must be used in deciding when a response reflects a particular style of responding.

Qualitative Scoring Analysis. Various schemes for analyzing reponses have appeared. One such system, developed by Strauss and Werner (1940), can be applied to responses that are given to a variety of tests (or subtests) that appear on the Stanford-Binet, WISC, and WPPSI, while a system developed by Feifel (1949) is specific for vocabulary-test responses. The two schemes are described in Tables 19–1 and 19–2, respectively; they can be useful in studying children's conceptual level of thinking or general mode of thinking. Research reports using the Strauss and Werner system are described in Chapter 22, while

Table 19-1. STRAUSS AND WERNER'S QUALITATIVE ANALYSIS SCORING SCHEME

CATEGORY	DESCRIPTION	EXAMPLE *(All responses are to the question, "What is the thing for you to do when you have broken something which belongs to someone else?")*
Correct	A correct answer. The principal import of the problem is recognized. The answer is sufficiently specific and comprehensive.	"Give them something instead of it."
Correct-incomplete	A less correct answer than given in the "correct" category, but still satisfactory. The principal import of the problem may not be fully recognized. The answer may lack either specificity or comprehensiveness.	"Paste it."
Superficial	The answer is either irrelevant or based on purely verbal association.	"Tell them."
Wrong	The answer contradicts general facts or specific facts that are involved in the problem.	"Just leave it broken."
Egocentric	The answer indicates a retreat into a personal emotional sphere.	"Be ashamed."
Nonsensical	A logically absurd or meaningless answer.	"Sit down."
Misunderstanding	An answer based on a misunderstanding of the question.	"I tell my mother she should buy me a new one."
Inadequate	An answer reached by adding factors not inherent in the question, or through comprehension of the question from an aberrant point of view.	"Hercules should have helped the driver." Or, "Be kind to your neighbor."
Don't know	The answer is "I don't know."	— —
Ambiguous	Some of the main points of the solution, not explicitly stated, may be inferred. This category is used only in connection with correct and correct-incomplete answers.	"Feel sorry."

(Reprinted by permission of the publisher from A. A. Strauss and H. Werner, "Qualitative Analysis of the Binet Test," *American Journal of Mental Deficiency,* **45**, pp. 50–51. Copyright 1940, American Association on Mental Deficiency.)

Table 19-2. FEIFEL'S QUALITATIVE ANALYSIS SCHEME FOR EVALUATING VOCABULARY RESPONSES

CATEGORY	TYPE OF RESPONSE AND EXAMPLE
Synonym	unmodified: orange = a fruit modified by use: straw = hay that cattle eat modified by description: gown = long dress modified by use and description: eyelash = hair over eye that protects you qualified as to degree: tap = touch lightly
Use and Description	use: orange = you eat it description: straw = it's yellow use and description: orange = you eat it and it's round
Explanation	(no type) priceless = it's worth a lot of money (no type) skill = being able to do something well
Illustration	illustration: priceless = a gem inferior explanation: scorch = hot repetition: puddle = puddle of water demonstration: for words like tap, eyelash, etc.
Error	incorrect demonstration: eyelash = points to eyebrow misinterpretation: regard = protects something wrong definition: orange = a vegetable clang association: roar = raw; skill = skillet repetition without explanation: puddle = puddle omits: the word is left out

(Reprinted by permission of the publisher and author from H. Feifel, "Qualitative Differences in Vocabulary Responses of Normals and Abnormals," *Genetic Psychology Monographs*, **39**, p. 168. Copyright 1949, The Journal Press.)

research using the Feifel system appears in Illustration 8 of this chapter (p. 269).

The Strauss and Werner system consists of a 10-category scheme, with most of the categories describing wrong responses. Feifel's five-category system, in contrast, deals primarily with correct answers. Within most categories, responses can be further classified.

Visual-Motor Performance. Visual-motor ability is assessed by observing all tests involving motor performances. Particular attention should be given to the examinee's reaction time and to his trial-and-error methods. Signs of visual-motor difficulty include much trial-and-error, fumbling, tremor, repetition of copying errors, perseveration, and variable line quality. Visual-motor difficulties may be associated with defects in visual, auditory, or muscular functions, with poor physical condition, or with anxiety.

Berko (1953) observed that perceptual defects can be seen in

figure-ground reversals, confusion in spatial orientation, and specific distortions in form perception. The latter is consistently seen in the children's performances with such items as the Seguin and Binet formboards. The child who is consistently able to adapt the star, the half-circle, and the cross, but who consistently confuses the square, the diamond, and the rhomboid is probably giving evidence of defective perception rather than an inability to make proper associations [p. 15].

General Diagnostic Examples

Murphy (1948) cited the case of a child whose definitions were in highly sensory terms, which suggested that he might have artistic talents; this was later confirmed, but previously had not been suspected. A child who passes difficult items while failing easier ones may be bored by easy material and stimulated by hard material (Murphy, 1948). Hearing difficulty may be disclosed on the memory items if words or numbers are distorted, consonants dropped, or prepositions and other connecting words omitted (Taylor, 1961). Specific learning disabilities may be revealed in

deficient perception and recall of visual patterns, defective visual recognition, poor copying and reproduction of form, and short memory span—all of which are causes of confusion and difficulty in learning to read and in the mastery of other school subjects [Freeman, 1962, p. 324].

Carefully evaluating the child's responses and behavior during the examination is important, especially when emotional difficulties are present. Berko (1953) cited the example of a child with a severe speech defect who answered "knife" instead of "scissors" to one of the Stanford-Binet Picture Vocabulary test cards simply because it was easier for him to say "knife" at that moment. Another child may stare blankly ahead and say nothing when asked comprehension test questions, not because of lack of knowledge, but because he feels unable to respond at the moment. Mecham et al. (1960) pointed out "that the emotionally labile child does not always react to a situation with an appropriate reaction. Thus, laughter, for example, may be an indication of distress rather than joy [p. 42]."

DIAGNOSTIC CONSIDERATIONS ON THE STANFORD-BINET

The Stanford-Binet is useful as a clinical instrument and as a test of intelligence, because much can be learned about the child's personality, resistance to stress, ability to concentrate, and other factors. The scale also lends itself well to "projective" use (McCandless, 1953a). This part of the chapter describes the kinds of materials that are found in the Stanford-Binet, the application of interpretation systems that have been used for a variety of tests to Stanford-Binet tests, the kinds of behavior that may be observed in specific tests, and case illustrations of various facets of the diagnostic and assessment process with the Stanford-Binet.

Observing Behavior on the Stanford-Binet

The examiner has numerous opportunities to observe the child's behavior in the course of administering the Stanford-Binet. In the test situation "the child finds himself in a definitely structured situation with an adult who limits both the area and extent of his operations and who lays down a fairly inflexible set of rules for each game [Brown, 1941, p. 268]." However, because there are varied test materials, the child has the opportunity to react in many different ways, and in the process to reveal some facets of his personality. (Brown presents extensive case material, which describes how children differ in their reactions to the examination. Since only a small portion of his work is described here, it is recommended that his material be read in full.)

Composition of Lower Level Tests

According to Brown (1941), the tests found at the lower year levels of the examination, primarily below year-level IX, can be classified into four general categories that serve to demarcate the kinds of materials with which the child deals. First, there are tests with *materials* (e.g., Sorting Buttons and Stringing Beads), which have a game-like quality and which possess a minimum of authoritative elements. The examiner's attention seems to center on the materials rather than on the child. Some children may resist these materials by simulating active sabotage; buttons or beads may be swept off the table onto the floor. Other children may go beyond the requirements of the tests by making something of their own with the materials. Competition with the examiner, such as seeing who can get the most beads strung, may be triggered off by the Stringing Beads test. Having the child return the materials at the end of a test may reveal such behaviors as tidiness, aggressiveness upon being asked to do a job, or carelessness.

Second, there are *pictorial* tests (e.g., Picture Vocabulary, Discrimination of Animal Pictures, Pictorial Similarities and Differences, Mutilated Pictures, and Picture Absurdities) that direct the child's attention to the pictures. In the process of responding to picture items, the child may free associate or may produce "projective material," which can be helpful in gaining some insight into his personality.

Third, there are *performance* tests (e.g., Picture Completion: Man and Patience: Rectangle) that require the child to respond actively. These tests, more than other types of tests found in the Stanford-Binet, may reveal the child's attitudes toward himself (e.g., degree of self-confidence and self-criticism, aspiration level, or pride in achievement). The drawing tests may bring out confidence in a child who in verbal situations is shy and hesitant.

Fourth, there are tests with questions of *comprehension, memory, definition,* and so forth (e.g., Comprehension I, Repeating 2 Digits, and Definitions). These questions clearly bring out the testing nature of the situation. Reactions to these tests may differ from those found in the performance tests.

Child's Attitudes Reflected in Test Responses

Information about the examinee's personality is acquired not only from his relationship with the examiner, but also from a careful study of the responses given to specific test items, the behaviors accompanying the responses, and the overall test performance. While in theory there is little ambiguity in the test questions, they are open to the child's interpretation (Lejeune, 1955). Because of inherent ambiguity in any test question, responses may reveal personality dynamics. In addition, "Even seemingly neutral stimuli, such as the incomplete man or the mutilated pictures on the Binet, may evoke threatening associations to some children [Palmer, 1970, p. 105]."

Some tests are more likely than others to reveal the child's attitudes. Responses to the Identifying-Objects-by-Use test at year-level II-6 may be especially informative about social factors in the child's environment (Ross, 1959). Attitudes toward the home may be reflected in many responses and, in particular, in those given to the Comprehension test at year-levels III-6 and IV (Ross, 1959). Current interests, family conditions, school relationships, and alertness may be revealed on the Word Naming test at year-level X (Freeman, 1962). Tests requiring the interpretation of pictures may bring out attitudes such as hostility, moralistic preoccupations, and submissiveness (Freeman, 1962).

On the Verbal Absurdities test, which appears at year-level IX, the examinee's responses may reflect his attitudes toward death and toward bodily injury. Some examinees may fail to appreciate the illogicality contained in the statements because of their need to moralize, while other examinees may refuse to accept the statements as even being hypothetical (Kessler, 1966).

Replies to the Comprehension IV test questions, appearing at year-level VII, may reflect the child's inordinate dependency on his mother, a moral or a religious outlook, or an inability to arrive at any solution (Kessler, 1966).

The reply, "Ask my mommy," to a test question may reflect *dependency,* while the reply, "Rest," may reflect *hypochondriacal preoccupations.* The child who responds to the question, "In what way are snake, cow, and sparrow alike?" (Similarities: Three Things, year-level XI) with "They all hurt you," may *view the world as being dangerous.* Responses to the Word Naming test (year-level X) should be examined closely, because they may reveal phantasy forms of preoccupations. *Exhibitionistic* children may produce words referring to dress, parties, and ornaments; *immature* children may produce food related responses; and *aggressive* children may give words referring to weapons and battles (Lejeune, 1955). Lejeune also noted that a *sexually delinquent* girl produced 35 boys' names on the test. High performance on digit span items coupled with low performance on comprehension items may suggest dominance of passive auditory registration over constructive learning ability (Taylor, 1961).

Picture Vocabulary

Taylor (1961) has provided a useful guide, which is shown below, for making a qualitative analysis of a child's performance on the Picture Vocabulary test (year-levels II through IV). Her testing-of-limits suggestions for this test have been presented previously in Chapter 9. It is important to recognize that the guides offered for the Picture Vocabulary test also can be applied to other Stanford-Binet tests as well as to other individual scales of intelligence.

... Note all responses obtained. Does the child find some responses for every picture, or is he apt to say, "I do not know?" Does he try to find a new word for each picture, or does he use the same word several times, successively or at intervals? Does he seem to grope for the correct word, or does he seem to say the first word that comes to his lips? Do his errors show associations easily recognizable as such (spoon for fork) or meaningful to those around him ("Daddy go" for airplane)? Does his naming show that he tends to perceive pictures in a primitive, diffuse, global way, paying attention to "qualities of the whole" rather than fine details (stick for knife)?

Are his errors the result of a carryover from a previous picture or from other familiar verbal patterns? Carefully observe the child's enunciation; note which of the consonants may be missing or defective. Watch for dropped consonants (coa- for coat, fla- for flag). For children with very poor articulation, note and check with the mother on nuances in sound productions which may mean different words to the child even if only barely perceptible to outsiders. Observe gestures and whether they accompany or replace verbal responses. Are they relevant and meaningful or only incidental? If they are the child's only form of response, do they indicate that he is, or is not, familiar with the picture [pp. 308-309]?

Plan-of-Search Test

The Plan-of-Search test at year-level XIII in Form L-M and Form L, called the "Ball and Field" test in the 1916 Stanford-Binet, is valuable for observing how children perform on a relatively minimally structured task (Bühler, 1938; Lejeune, 1955). Bühler described the test as requiring the child "to proceed planfully in a practical situation which is, however, a fictitious and imagined one [p.258]." Children may fail the test because of defective ability to visualize or because of difficulty in working systematically.

Both Bühler and Lejeune described various types of solutions—normal and problematical—that can characterize children's performance. Both investigators, however, failed to present reliability and validity data. The solutions range from primitive to more advanced and mature ones. Lejeune also proposed personality descriptions for the solution-types. Neurotic children, Bühler stated, often have difficulty in organizing their solutions, become stuck in the middle of the field, give up, make random and futile attempts, or are obsessive and unadaptable. Illustrations 1 and 2 in Figure 19–2 are examples of a "helplessly confused" solution and an "ornamentally involved" solution that may be the products of neurotic children. Illustration 3 represents a "giving-up-helplessly" solution that may appear in the performance of mentally retarded children. Illustration 4 is an advanced and thoughtful solution. Examples of solutions that reflect personality dynamics are seen in Illustrations 5 and 6. Lejeune suggested that Illustration 5, "going out of the field," reflects the performance of a timid child whose parents have encouraged his fears and flight reactions, while Illustration 6, "success followed by flight from field," represents the effort of an over-conscientious child or one who has conversion symptoms or school difficulty.

The personality descriptions for the solution types are interesting and potentially useful, but must be viewed as speculations. Utmost caution is urged in interpreting personality dynamics from a child's performance on the Plan-of-Search test. The approaches of Bühler and Lejeune, nevertheless, are valuable, for they enable us to formulate tentative hypotheses that are amenable to further investigation.

Application of Other Test Interpretation Systems

A number of scoring and interpretation systems have been developed for tests that are in some ways similar to those found in the Stanford-Binet. These

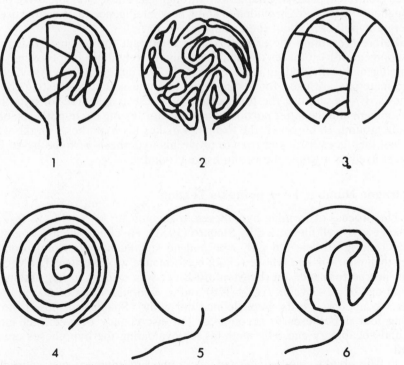

Figure 19–2. Illustrations of types of solutions on the Plan-of-Search test.

systems, if applied with caution, can be helpful in interpreting a child's performance on the Stanford-Binet. The administration and standardization procedures used with other tests differ from those used in the Stanford-Binet. Therefore, information gained by applying such systems to performance on the Stanford-Binet must be viewed in a very tentative light; primarily, the material should be used to generate hypotheses about the examinee's performance.

The examinee's drawings that appear on tests such as Copying a Circle at year-level III, Copying a Square at year-level V, and Copying a Diamond at year-level VIII can be analyzed by applying methods of interpretation associated with the Bender-Gestalt (see Koppitz, 1964). The drawings should be examined for perseveration, closure difficulties, tremor, and other signs of visual-motor impairment.

Guidelines developed for the Children's Apperception Test (see Haworth, 1966) and for other children's tests containing thematic material can be used for interpreting the responses given to picture tests (e.g., Responses to Pictures at year-level III and Picture Absurdities at year-level VII). The child's performance on the Picture Completion: Man test at year-level V can be evaluated for signs of body-image disturbances or confusion of spatial relations (see Machover (1949) for information about interpreting figure drawings).

DIAGNOSTIC ILLUSTRATIONS FOR THE STANFORD-BINET

Further diagnostic approaches to test interpretation are presented in this section. The coverage is not exhaustive; rather, selected examples and approaches that have been used with the Stanford-Binet are discussed. Diagnostic material pertinent to specific psychopathological groups and to mentally retarded children appears in Chapters 20 through 23. These examples, like others throughout the text, are provided to show how intelligence tests can be used to generate hypotheses about the examinee.

Before presenting the examples, it is important to recognize that in the development of hypotheses circular reasoning is sometimes involved, not only in intelligence testing but in research as well. The circularity occurs when the same materials are used for setting up a hypothesis and for testing the hypothesis. If one can use the first portion of a test as a source for hypothesis development and the latter portion as a source for testing the hypothesis, one is on safe ground. If, however, the examiner makes his hypothesis on the whole test and then goes back and tries to prove his hypothesis or hypotheses from the test itself as a whole, he is on unsure ground.

Illustration Number 1—Hypothesis Testing

The process of forming hypotheses to account for variability in test performance was well illustrated by Shapiro (1951). He cited the case of a quiet, rather retiring 10-year-old girl, who had no significant behavioral problems other than enuresis and whose school performance was average. The variability in her performance on the Stanford-Binet was evident in her obtaining a mental age of 12–5 years (IQ = 120) and a vocabulary age of 6 years (only seven vocabulary words were defined correctly). Shapiro proposed the following four hypotheses to account for the discrepancy between her mental age and vocabulary age. His methods for evaluating the hypotheses are also noted.

1. The child's poor social and economic environment has caused her poverty of vocabulary. This first hypothesis can be tested by having a social worker visit the home.

2. An extreme degree of emotional inhibition has produced a breakdown on the Vocabulary items, but not on other items. A group vocabulary test can be administered, and if the obtained score is higher than the Binet Vocabulary score, the second hypothesis would receive some confirmation.

3. The variability is due to a temporary disturbance, and therefore has no diagnostic significance. This hypothesis can be evaluated by administering the Vocabulary test again at the end of the examination.

4. An aphasic disturbance exists. Additional language tests or tests for aphasia may be given to investigate this hypothesis.

Further investigation revealed that the girl's vocabulary ability was commensurate with her IQ, but that a combination of personality factors and peculiarities of the test situation depressed her Vocabulary score. The second and third hypotheses were therefore partly supported. Shapiro's example is an excellent illustration of how clinical hypotheses are formed and how they may be tested.

Illustration Number 2—Development of Hypotheses

Palmer (1970) illustrated how an assessment of the child's cognitive functioning and its relationship with his other ego functions can be made by a study of test successes and failures.

Thus, the seven-year-old child who on the Binet can repeat digits, copy a diamond, answer questions about a story, but has less than a six year old's vocabulary, cannot make the simplest verbal similarities and is not able to fathom "what's foolish about this picture?" may be doing well or even above average work on tasks involving routine learning of one-to-one concrete associations, but the development of his independent judgment and analysis of a situation may be quite retarded [p. 104].

To account for this pattern, Palmer proposed that the child is too dependent emotionally on others to begin to make independent intellectual judgments, or that severe emotional or physiological handicaps deter more complex thought processes. These hypotheses can be tested by examining the quality of his responses and types of failures, and by administering other tests designed to measure social and emotional adjustment.

Illustration Number 3—Interrelationships Among Several Variables

Murphy (1948) emphasized that in any assessment procedure "the total picture is more important than the separate items taken alone [p. 17]." This illustration demonstrates how a number of features of the child's performance can be integrated in arriving at an appraisal of personality.

The child who overcautiously stays within limits on the drawing tests, leans on digits, shows poor insight, defines "obedience" but not aggressive words, may be giving important clues to a personality structure; he may be anxious about authority to the extent of inhibition of normal childish spontaneity, and this would affect work as well as social relations in a modern school [Murphy, 1948, p. 17].

Illustration Number 4—Analysis of Personality Variables

Personality variables, primarily integrative ones, were proposed by Fromm (1960) to account for successful performance on tests appearing at year-level IX. In this illustration, Fromm showed how such personality variables may be deduced from a child's performance.

On the Paper Cutting test an eight year old struggled for a while with the solution. She drew one cut incorrectly, looked at it critically and said, "No, I don't think I have it right." She erased it. She thus showed that, among other variables, she employed *judgment* and *self criticism* in striving for the correct solution. Had she stopped after the first trial with the remarks "Oh, well, I never can do things right," her self criticism would have been an unhealthy one and would have been involved in her failing the item. Instead, she asked the examiner: "Do you know how to do it?" The examiner said she did. The little girl replied in an eager voice, "If you can do it, I want to be able to learn to do it by myself too." Thus she also used the mechanism of *identification* in spurring herself on towards success. She sat there thinking for a few more moments, and suddenly, with a flash of *insight* . . ., exclaimed, "Oh, I know how it goes!" Then she drew the correct pattern. In addition to the variables already discussed, others were involved in her success: *language understanding*—she understood the instructions; *reality-centered concept formation*—she asked herself what is the thing, what does the paper look like when it is opened; and *flexibility of thinking*, which is necessary in order to proceed from the actual stimulus, the folded paper, to the imagined visualization of the opened paper [p. 233].

Illustration Number 5—Comparisons Among Several Tests

An example provided by Escalona (1945) shows how a qualitative analysis of test responses and a comparison of the child's performance on several tests are useful for an assessment of personality. The examinee, a 6½-year-old female whose mother had recently died before she was seen for testing, was in good health, with the exception of severe myopia. Escalona attempted to determine whether failures were a function of physical disability or of emotional disturbance.

While she obtained an IQ of 97±4 on the Stanford-Binet, Form L (CA = 6–6, MA = 6–4), emotional disturbance was reflected by irrelevant and absurd fantasy material appearing in a variety of responses. To the "Man with umbrella" item on the Picture Absurdities I test (year-level VII) she replied, "Nothing is funny about it . . . his hand . . . he has got it cut off . . . sure, when the finger is cut off it hurts." When she was asked to repeat the sentence "Fred asked his father to take him to see the clowns in the circus" (Memory for Sentences II, year-level VIII) she said, "Fred lost his father." She performed poorly on the Copying-a-Square test (year-level V) and failed the Copying-a-Diamond test (year-level VII). The failures on the visual-motor tests might be attributed to her visual handicap, if it were not for the fact that other tests requiring visual acuity were passed (e.g., Maze Tracing, year-level VI; Mutilated Pictures, year-level VI). She adorned the incomplete drawing of a man (Picture Completion: Man, year-level V) with a gun and showed the "smoke from shooting" by violent scribbles across the entire page.

Escalona noted that the Stanford-Binet alone did not reveal the degree to which the child differed from normal children in her capacity to deal with everyday situations. It was the Stanford-Binet in conjunction with other tests that provided a comprehensive picture of the child's psychological functioning. Escalona concluded that the child was emotionally disturbed.

Illustration Number 6—Analysis of Vocabulary Definitions

This illustration, provided by Moriarty (1961), reveals how a qualitative interpretation of test responses is useful for forming hypotheses about the examinee. Compare the two following definitions for the word "orange": (*a*) "Well, it's something that has juice in it and you squeeze it in the squeezing room and then you get the whole juice." (*b*) "That you eat." Both responses are equally correct. However, the first response suggests that the child is aware of uses and values of things, and that he has some original phrases. The second response is short. It "might reflect efficiency, inhibition in verbalizing or a functional orientation in the pattern of thinking [p. 8]."

Illustration Number 7 — Analysis of Verbal Absurdities Responses

Fromm (1960) provided interesting illustrations of how responses to the Verbal Absurdities II test (year-level IX) may reveal personality dynamics. It must be emphasized (and Fromm presents similar cautions) that any interpretations about personality that are made from one or two responses must be tentative, subject to revision or abandonment after making a thorough and systematic analysis of all available material. A 10-year-old boy reveals his impulsiveness in his response to the fireman item ("The fireman hurried to the burning house, got his fire hose ready, and after smoking a cigar, put out the fire." "Why is that foolish?"): "Boy-oh-boy, he'll start a second fire with his cigar! And pretty soon the houses next door will burn down, and then the whole city will burn up like Chicago did when Mrs. O'Leary's cow kicked over the kerosene lamp." To the melting icebergs item ("One day we saw several icebergs that had been entirely melted by the warmth of the Gulf Stream." "Why is that foolish?") he said: "They couldn't have told you that, because when the icebergs melted the water rushed all over the boat and everybody drowned." This latter answer suggested the presence of hostile-aggressive impulses, as well as wild, destructive fantasy; the question does not include any reference to a boat or to drowning people. The following response to the iceberg item by an adolescent girl revealed her anxiety (perhaps concerning sexual feelings), and a religious defense against the anxiety: "God would not allow icebergs to melt when I am so near that I could see them, because God does not want me to get drowned."

Illustration Number 8 — Feifel's Qualitative Analysis Scheme

Feifel and Lorge (1950) applied Feifel's (1949) qualitative analysis scheme (Table 19–2 shows the scheme) to responses given to the Vocabulary test of Form L of the 1937 Stanford-Binet by children in age groups 6 through 14 years. With increasing age, synonym responses increased and, as expected, error responses decreased. After age 9 years, the synonym response occurred more frequently than other types of responses. The use-and-description response was greatest at ages 6 and 7 years. The explanation response was lowest between ages 6 and 9 years, but second in frequency to synonym responses with older children. Demonstration, repetition, illustration, and inferior explanation types of responses were not given frequently at any age. Papania (1954), using Feifel's scheme, studied normal children and institutionalized mentally retarded children. His findings essentially confirm those of Feifel and Lorge. In addition, at all mental age levels normal children responded with proportionately more synonym and explanation type of responses than did retarded children. In Feifel's (1949) study of normal and abnormal adults, normals tended to give synonyms, while abnormals tended to give use-and-description, explanation, and illustration responses.

Illustration Number 9 — Perseveration

Wells and Kelley (1920) presented examples of perseveration. The first illustration of perseveration concerns an examinee who gave the answer "Burning" to the question, "In what way are wood and coal alike?" (Similarities: Two Things, year-level VII). Then to the next question, "In what way are apple and peach alike?" he said "They'll burn all the time." In the second illustration, the child replied to the question, "What's the thing for you to do when you have broken something that belongs to someone else?" (Comprehension IV, year-level VII), with, "Return it and have it fixed." Then to the next question, "What's the thing for you to do when you are on your way to school and see that you are in danger of being late?" he answered, "Hurry up and fix it as quick as I could."

DIAGNOSTIC CONSIDERATIONS ON THE WISC (AND WPPSI)

The diagnostic considerations presented for the Stanford-Binet are also valuable in working with the WISC (and WPPSI). The numerous attempts that have been made to use the WISC as a diagnostic instrument are illustrated in the chapters on psychopathology and mental retardation (Chapters 20 through 23). Chapters 13 and 14 have also considered diagnostic implications of WISC subtest scores (while Chapters 16 and 17 described diagnostic considerations for the WPPSI). In this part of Chapter 19 some general considerations and illustrations concerning diagnostic procedures on the WISC (and WPPSI) are presented.

Cognitive variables involved in the WISC (and WPPSI) subtests (e.g., planning, anticipation, attention, and concentration) are a good source for understanding personality organization. The pattern of scores may reflect general modes of adaptation. The general procedure is to look for consistency among the various aspects of test performance (profile of scores, content of responses, and style of responses).

Some children may show a pattern of missing easy items and succeeding on more difficult items. This pattern may occur in the case of a bright child who may be bored by the easy items, giving careless or even nonsense replies, only to become challenged by more difficult items where he can demonstrate his skills (Palmer, 1970). A number of questions or words on the WISC may arouse associations of violence or hostility (Palmer, 1970). An example of one question is "Why should women and children be saved first in a shipwreck?" which appears on the Comprehension subtest. Examples of words include knife, nitroglycerine, affliction, and hara-kiri, which appear on the Vocabulary subtest.

The response to the Comprehension question, "What is the thing to do if a fellow (girl) much smaller than yourself starts to fight with you?" may reveal the child's ability for social impulse control (Palmer, 1970). On the Object Assembly subtest, children handicapped by motor deficiencies may react emotionally to the manikin item since it may represent a mutilated human figure (Taylor, 1961). The painstaking Coding task may be more difficult for the alert, creative, and intuitive normal child than for the more pedantic, passive, and slower moving one (Taylor, 1961).

DIAGNOSTIC ILLUSTRATIONS FOR THE WISC

The principles of test interpretation that are illustrated in the diagnostic examples presented in this part of the chapter can be generalized to many different types of responses and patterns that may occur on the WISC. The illustrations, as with the Stanford-Binet, cover only a few selected points. As noted above, Chapters 20 through 23 also describe diagnostic uses of the WISC.

Illustration Number 1—Example of a Paranoid Structure

Blatt and Allison (1968) demonstrated how content of responses, style of responses, and pattern of scores are interrelated in a paranoid individual. The content of the responses may reflect suspiciousness regarding the recording of the responses or feelings of being tricked. The style may be cautious, rigid, and legalistic. The pattern of scores may show high scores in areas related to hyperalertness to details (Picture Completion or Picture Arrangement) and to bringing together and relating disparate things (Similarities).

Illustration Number 2 — Interpreting Comprehension Subtest Responses

The following are possible interpretations of Comprehension subtest responses (Taylor, 1961). The interpretations should be viewed as being tentative, subject to modification by an analysis of the child's performance on the entire test.

1. A moralistic response: "What is the thing to do if a fellow (girl) much smaller than yourself starts to fight with you?" Answer, "He should not hit you."

2. A moralistic response: "What is the thing to do when you cut your finger?" Answer, "You should be more careful and not cut your finger."

3. A defensive response: "What is the thing to do if a fellow (girl) much smaller than yourself starts to fight with you?" Answer, "I should not fight."

4. An unrealistic response: "What should you do if you see a train approaching a broken track?" Answer, "I would tell the trainman, perhaps I would telephone."

5. A need-for-help response: "What is the thing to do if a fellow (girl) much smaller than yourself starts to fight with you?" Answer, "I would tell my mother."

Illustration Number 3 — Diagnostic Aspects of the Picture Arrangement Subtest

Correct as well as faulty solutions on the Picture Arrangement subtest allow for an evaluation of the child's developmental level of reasoning (Taylor, 1961). Most failures are due to difficulties in logical reasoning. However, faulty solutions also may be due to inattention (e.g., on the SLEEPER item, failure to see the time on the clock), minimal experience with common events (e.g., on the BURGLAR item, prison picture is placed before court session), or emotional attitudes and preoccupations (e.g., on the BURGLAR item, "He is in prison, got up again, holds up a guy, then tells judge that he did not do it.") The last arrangement, however, may not be an indication of emotional preoccupations because it actually depicts what occurs in many real situations. Children who "miss" the item by using this arrangement may be very close to the experience, especially those coming from lower classes.

Reasoning difficulties are suggested when distorted infantile arrangements occur with regularity in a child who is older than 8 years. This can occur with mentally retarded children, with brain-injured children, and perhaps with psychotic children. Emotionally disturbed children usually produce stories that are logical. However, their arrangements may be conspicuous and unusual, with details being neglected for the sake of a particular theme, which may reveal their anxieties and preoccupations.

Illustration Number 4 — Picture Arrangement Subtest as a Thematic Technique

Craig (1969) described a method for obtaining thematic material from the WISC Picture Arrangement subtest. The method may serve as a useful screening device; it is not intended to replace other thematic techniques (e.g., Thematic Apperception Test or Children's Apperception Test). The method is used *after* the entire WISC has been administered. The procedure involves randomly placing the FIGHT sequence of cards before the child and then asking him to make up a story to *one of the cards* in standard TAT fashion. After completing the story, the cards are removed and the FIRE sequence of cards is placed randomly before him. He is asked to tell a story to one of the cards. This procedure is followed for each of the Picture Arrangement sequences. The procedure differs from the one suggested by Rapaport et al. (1968) and Wechsler (1958), which involves the examinee making up a story that is based on the arrangement of cards in each sequence. The stories are interpreted by following usual methods applied to thematic material (e.g., Arnold, 1962; Haworth, 1966; Murstein, 1963). The method is illustrated in the following case which, with some minor modifications, was presented by Craig.

Case Illustration of the Picture Arrangement Subtest as a Thematic Technique

T. P. is a 12-year-old, male, seventh grade child who was referred for testing because of low motivation for academic work and because his current school progress was judged to be less than that expected in view of his intelligence.

T. P. obtained a Verbal Scale IQ of 110, a Performance Scale IQ of 96, and a Full Scale IQ of 104 ± 4 on the Wechsler Intelligence Scale for Children. This places him in the Average classification and indicates that he exceeds 60% of the children of his age in the standardization group, which was roughly representative of the population of the United States. The chances that the range of scores from 100 to 108 includes his true IQ are about 68 out of 100.

His Verbal Scale IQ is in the Bright Normal range, suggesting that he has the ability to achieve. However, his less adequate Performance Scale IQ suggests that motivation may be somewhat limited. He tended to score lowest in areas where active effort and involvement in tasks are needed for good results (Coding, Object Assembly, and Digit Span). These same tasks also are, for the most part, ones in which there is a concrete pattern to follow and where he is to do what he is told and to conform to a model. This point will take on more significance as the Picture Arrangement stories are discussed. His highest score was on the Comprehension subtest, indicating that his social judgment in uninvolved areas cannot be questioned. His next three highest scores were in areas where little effort is required but where he could succeed by relying on past knowledge and by assuming a somewhat passive orientation (Information, Arithmetic, and Picture Completion). Thus, scoring well in areas requiring factual detail shows that he can excel where passive performance suffices. When concentrated effort is needed and when he has to conform to a model, his performance is reduced.

The Picture Arrangement Stories

The following stories were given by T. P. to the Picture Arrangement cards that he himself had selected. The arrangements of FARMER, PICNIC, and RAIN were omitted because of time limitations. Each story title is identified by its WISC coded title followed by a brief picture description.

FIGHT: Man Being Carried From Arena

Sammy had been practicing for months trying to be a better boxer than he was last time. His two friends were trying to make him a better boxer, because they had a bet on him. Joey, the boxer he fought, had won the world championship. So the night came and fans were going to the fight. The crowds were all cheering for Sammy. The bell rang. In the first round there was no action. In the second round Sammy gave him a good hit in the right jaw but he didn't fall. Then simultaneously Joe gave him a sock in the jaw and Sam fell to the ground. Sam was out cold. His two friends carried him out and Sammy never boxed again.

FIRE: Child Crying

Little Ann woke up in the morning and didn't have anything to do. She walked around the house trying to find something to do. As she was walking she found a book of matches and went up to her room to play. She started to light the matches and by mistake dropped one on the curtain. Her mother was already asleep and didn't hear the fire. Before Ann knew it her house was on fire. Her mother woke up and found her house ablaze. She called the fire department and they put it out. Ann was very sad because now her mother had no arm because it was burnt in the fire.

BURGLAR: Man Climbing Out of Window

Joe, a full-time robber, was going to break in the house tonight. He had it all planned out so at twelve he would break into the Smiths' home who had the money. So at twelve Joe broke in, looked around but couldn't find the safe. Then he heard someone coming down the stairs so he hid. Then he looked around for the safe and he found it. He broke it open and found the money. He had a bag and as he was climbing out of the window a policeman was standing right next to it. Joe was caught. That was very good.

SLEEPER: Man Hurriedly Eating

One morning Jim's alarm clock didn't work so he was late. He got up and ate his breakfast as fast as he could. His wife told him that it was going to rain but he didn't think so and he didn't take an umbrella but he was wrong. For as soon as he walked a block away it started to rain. So he ran as fast as he could all the way home and apologized to his wife for not believing her, and he took the umbrella. As soon as he got out it stopped raining, and he was very late for work.

GARDENER: Man Fishing

One day Mike woke up and said he was going fishing. He got his bait and tackle and walked to go fishing. He got to the lake and he was the only one there. He found a nice spot and took a nap. Then he got a real big bite and it almost pulled him in. He reeled in the fish and it was a 25-pound bass. When he was taking the hook off it slipped out of his hands and back into the lake. He was very disappointed but he tried again. Then he took another nap and another time he got a bite. It was the same fish. He reeled it in and took the hook out very carefully and that night he had bass for dinner.

Analysis of the Picture Arrangement Stories

There are two basic issues in the first story (FIGHT); together they suggest a workable, dynamic hypothesis to account for his underachievement: (1) initiative and direct aggression meet with failure, and (2) people are asking him to do the impossible by leading him into situations wherein he cannot succeed. Note that there is positive effort on his part. He fails, not because he is not trying, but because he is up against impossible odds.

In story two (FIRE) the theme of aggression is dealt with once again, but this time the person must resort to its covert expression if he is to succeed. The sequence of these two stories suggests that he feels people are stacking the odds against him, that direct aggression is futile, and that covert aggression, handled surreptitiously, can bring a modicum of success.

In story three (BURGLAR) the theme of direct aggression is dealt with once again. Although there is the healthy superego-social issue of being caught for one's crimes, the recurrent issue seems to be that initiative and aggression, if directly expressed, is unsuccessful.

Story four (SLEEPER) is basically a repetition of the correct sequential arrangement so that little projective content is revealed in this thema. It does, however, add a new dimension to the idea expressed in story one. Not only does he feel that people are leading him astray, but also that when they are correct in their guidance, their judgment cannot be absolutely trusted.

Story five (GARDENER) seems to suggest what he can do if he "puts his mind to it." The thema seems to say, "If I try, in my own way, maybe I can't do it perfectly, but if I try again and be more careful, I can succeed."

In summary, an analysis of his Picture Arrangement stories reveals that he feels direct aggression does not succeed, people are leading him into situations wherein he cannot succeed, and if he could select his own method of doing things, he could succeed. This is consistent with his low scores on the WISC in tasks requiring him to conform to a model provided him by others. The hypothesis is that he is dealing with his aggression against these people surreptitiously in the form of underachievement.

Recommendations.   It was recommended that more of a choice be given to him, especially a range of subjects that are designed to help him attain success and thereby increase self-esteem and aspiration level. Conferences were held with his parents and teachers in order to discuss ways in which this recommendation could be implemented at home and in school.

Follow-up.   Six months after the date of original testing, T. P. was again given the WISC. Both the Verbal and Performance IQ's were in the Bright Normal range, with little scatter present between subtests. His grades had substantially improved and his teachers were quite pleased with his progress to date.

SUMMARY

Chapter 19 introduces some general principles concerning the diagnostic process, and provides illustrative examples of the application of the diagnostic process to the Stanford-Binet and WISC. However, the principles described are generalizable to the WPPSI and to other assessment techniques. The diagnostic process is broadly conceived as one that incorporates a valid test administration, the observation and evaluation of the child's entire performance, the development of recommendations, and the integration of test findings with case material.

The diagnostic process is by no means simple; it is fraught with hazards because our ability to predict future behavior, for example, is limited. The intelligence testing situation, while limited in many ways, provides structure for observing and describing the child's behavior. The intelligence test, as a diagnostic instrument, provides not only an IQ, but information regarding cognitive processes and motivational factors. In addition, an analysis of the child's personality in connection with his test performance will be useful in bringing out the unique qualities that distinguish one child from another.

Goldman's model for the interpretative process—consisting of different kinds of interpretations, combinations of test data, and sources of test data—is helpful in focusing on a variety of sources that affect test interpretations. Goslin's assessment paradigm, similarly, is useful, for it summarizes the factors that may affect the test score.

Qualitative indices may be useful diagnostic guides. The child's general attitude, language usage, and visual-motor performance should be observed carefully. Specific types of language distortions are illustrated in the chapter, ranging from speech difficulty to self-references.

On the Stanford-Binet there are many different kinds of materials contained in the tests with which the child deals. A careful study of his methods of dealing with the materials may be helpful. The chapter also illustrates how responses to specific Stanford-Binet tests provide another source for evaluating the child's personality. The application of interpretation systems designed for other tests may be helpful when applied to some Stanford-Binet tests. Diagnostic illustrations, which show how the Stanford-Binet can be useful in generating hypotheses about children and in making personality evaluations, also are presented in the chapter.

The WISC lends itself to diagnostic work, not only through a qualitative analysis of the child's performance, but also through an evaluation of the pattern of subtest scores. Cognitive variables involved in the subtests are a good source for understanding personality organization. Selected diagnostic illustrations for the WISC are presented in the chapter.

CHAPTER 20

CHILDHOOD SCHIZOPHRENIA AND EARLY INFANTILE AUTISM

Schizophrenia in childhood is a condition that has been difficult to define, and its recognition as a distinct clinical entity has been problematical (Ekstein, Bryant, & Friedman, 1958). Further, it is not known to what extent childhood schizophrenia constitutes a single disease entity or a number of pathological conditions which, while superficially similar, have different etiologies (Mosher & Feinsilver, 1971). This chapter first summarizes symptoms of childhood schizophrenia and early infantile autism, and then presents a number of studies concerning intelligence and childhood schizophrenia, and intelligence and early infantile autism. These studies are followed by a section which describes some performances on the Stanford-Binet and WISC that have been related to childhood schizophrenia and early infantile autism. The final part of the chapter considers the matter of differential diagnosis.

CLASSIFICATION OF CHILDHOOD SCHIZOPHRENIA

Diagnostic decisions usually are made on a probability basis: The more symptoms present, the more likely it is that a child falls into a certain classification. To assist in diagnosing childhood schizophrenia, Creak (1964) and her group described a set of nine symptoms which, if shown by a child, indicate a high probability of childhood schizophrenia. Goldfarb later (1969) suggested that the diagnosis can be given if more than half of the symptoms are shown. Meanwhile, the nine points were revised by O'Gorman (1967) after he carefully reviewed the available evidence and criticisms of the initial set of symptoms. The features of the schizophrenic syndrome in childhood, according to O'Gorman, are as follows:

(1) Withdrawal from, or failure to become involved with reality; in particular, failure to form normal relationships with people.

(2) Serious intellectual retardation with islets of normal, near normal or exceptional intellectual function or skills.

(3) Failure to acquire speech, or to maintain or improve on speech already learned, or to use what speech has been acquired for communication.

(4) Abnormal response to one or more types of sensory stimulus (usually sound).

(5) Gross and sustained exhibition of mannerisms or peculiarities of movement, including immobility and hyperkinesis, and excluding tics.

(6) Pathological resistance to change. This may be shown by:

(a) Insisting on observance of rituals in the patient's own behaviour or in those around him.

(b) Pathological attachment to the same surroundings, equipment, toys and people (even though the relationship with the person involved may be purely mechanical and emotionally empty).

(c) Excessive preoccupation with particular objects or certain characteristics of them without regard to their accepted functions.

(d) Severe anger or terror or excitement, or increased withdrawal, when the sameness of the environment is threatened (e.g. by strangers) [pp. 13-14].

Bosch (1970), while finding O'Gorman's description of the symptoms succinct and practical, would add a seventh point, which was left out by O'Gorman but included by Creak, namely,

(7) Disturbance in the development of personal identity. This may be shown by abnormal behavior toward self or by repeated self-directed aggression.

The difficulty with the above formulation is that there always is the problem of determining what behaviors are meant by terms such as "serious intellectual retardation," "abnormal response," and "pathological resistance." Consequently, clinical judgment must be used on all occasions.

EARLY INFANTILE AUTISM

The syndrome of early infantile autism, introduced by Kanner in 1943, has received much attention during the ensuing years. Efforts to distinguish the syndrome from childhood schizophrenia have been made (Rimland, 1964), but many problems still remain in considering it as a separate, clearly defined syndrome (Masters & Miller, 1970; Rutter, 1968; Treffert, 1970; Ward, 1970). The following features characterize early infantile autism (Eisenberg & Kanner, 1956):

(1) extreme detachment from human relationships from the beginning of life;

(2) failure to use language for the purpose of communication;

(3) an anxiously obsessive desire for the maintenance of sameness;

(4) fascination for objects which are handled with skill and fine motor movements; and

(5) good cognitive potentials.

The family background is marked by high intelligence, marked obsessiveness, and coldness. Chambers (1969) observed that early infantile autism should be distinguished from childhood forms of schizophrenia which develop beyond the first two years of life. The degree of aloneness constitutes an important prognostic variable in early infantile autism.

INTELLIGENCE AND CHILDHOOD SCHIZOPHRENIA

We have seen that one of the features of childhood schizophrenia is serious intellectual retardation with areas of functioning that are normal or even exceptional. A cognitive criterion also was included in the features of early infantile autism, namely, good cognitive potentials. With these considerations in mind, we would expect that the evaluation of intelligence constitutes an important part of the diagnostic work-up, especially in cases of differential diagnosis. The role of intelligence testing in childhood schizophrenia has been stressed by Goldfarb (1970): "*The best single measure of integrative functioning is the intelligence test* [p. 789]" (italics added).

Studies indicate that between one-third and one-half of schizophrenic children usually obtain IQ's lower than 70, and less than one-quarter obtain IQ's above 90 (Pollack, 1967). The critical variable determining level of intelligence seems to be the age of the child when tested. Preschool children diagnosed as schizophrenic more frequently have been found to have lower scores than those so diagnosed in preadolescent years. There is some suggestive evidence that in a family predisposed to schizophrenia, the child with the lowest IQ is most vulnerable (Offord & Cross, 1971). Intelligence level may also be related to etiology. Schizophrenic children with nonorganic etiologies tend to obtain higher IQ's than those with organic etiologies (Gittleman & Birch, 1967; Goldfarb, 1961).

Deficiencies in Cognitive Processes

Schizophrenic children are seriously deficient in many intellectual processes, including attention and concentration, language usage, associations, and coherent thinking (Beck, 1965). These deficiencies hamper their ability to think purposefully, to test reality, and to synthesize percepts. Impaired thinking is evidenced by dreamlike condensations, circumstantial processes, regressions, confusion, personalized logic, and vague analogies. Beck concluded that schizophrenic children show intellectual aridity, limited spontaneity, and much intellectual pathology.

Beck observed that adult schizophrenics and childhood schizophrenics differ in their thinking patterns. It is rare to find schizophrenic children who are overly concrete in their thinking or who have malignant speech regressions; however, vague analogizing may occasionally appear. Schizophrenic children function more like those adults who have inadequate ego structures, and less like those adults who display excessive intellectual control. Beck characterized schizophrenic children's emotional state as being either labile (feelings easily released) or extremely restricted (absence of emotional display). The labile children appear to have a slightly better prognosis than those with restricted affect.

The schizophrenic child probably will be intellectually retarded because he has closed himself off from the stimulation necessary for intellectual growth. If and when the schizophrenic child enters the real world at a later time in his life, it may be too late for him to develop his intellectual skills "because he has passed the optimum period of 'learning plasticity' of his cortex [O'Gorman, 1967, p. 86]." When withdrawal is only partial or selective, a particular skill may be acquired in one area (e.g., memory, manual dexterity, or musical ability), while the remainder of the child's intelligence remains far behind.

Age and Level of Intelligence

Pollack (1960) studied the relationship between age and level of intelligence in a sample of institutionalized, predominantly middle class schizophrenic ($N = 100$) and nonschizophrenic (psychoneurotic and manic depressive, $N = 60$) children and adults who ranged in age from 6 years through 44 years. The Stanford-Binet (Form L) was administered to the younger groups, while the Wechsler-Bellevue I was given to the older groups. As Table 20–1 shows, a direct relationship was found between intelligence level and age in both groups: the younger the patient, the lower the IQ. Perhaps the more intelligent child is less prone to schizophrenic symptoms in the early years of development than is the less intelligent child.

Table 20-1. RELATIONSHIP BETWEEN IQ AND AGE IN SCHIZOPHRENIC
AND NONSCHIZOPHRENIC PATIENTS

AGE	SCHIZOPHRENIC		NONSCHIZOPHRENIC	
	N	Mean IQ	N	Mean IQ
6–9	15	75	9	94
13–15	21	88	11	98
16–18	31	104	16	106
19–29	21	109	16	112
30–44	12	115	14	112

Note.—Mean IQ's rounded off.

(Reprinted by permission of the publisher and author from M. Pollack, "Comparison of Childhood, Adolescent, and Adult Schizophrenias. Etiologic Significance of Intellectual Functioning," *Archives of General Psychiatry*, **2**, p. 653. Copyright 1960, American Medical Association.)

Level of intelligence was also related to discharge ratings in the schizophrenic group. Patients with IQ's below 90 had a higher probability than those with IQ's above 90 of being discharged as "unimproved." A poor prognosis in the schizophrenic group was associated with a gradual onset of symptoms, long duration of illness prior to hospitalization, flat and inappropriate affect, and low IQ. While caution is needed in interpreting Pollack's findings because of the limited and selected sample, it appears that preadolescent and adolescent schizophrenic children who are hospitalized are likely to have IQ's that are below normal.

Intelligence level and age at the time of onset of psychosis was recently studied. Kolvin, Humphrey, and McNay (1971) reported that onset of psychosis in the first three years of life was found to be associated with major intellectual deficit, whereas later onset was associated with only moderate deficit. A majority (51%; 24 out of 47) with psychosis below the age of 3 years were found to be either untestable or with an IQ below 50, whereas only 3% (1 out of 30) of those with an onset over the age of 3 years were either untestable or with an IQ below 50. In the former group, 43% obtained IQ's between 50 and 89 and 6% obtained IQ's between 90 and 110 (a mean IQ was not calculated because a high percentage of the children were untestable). In the latter group, 40% obtained IQ's between 50 and 89, 43% obtained IQ's between 90 and 110, and 13% obtained IQ's above 110 (*M* IQ = 86).

Rutter and Lockyer's Study of Psychotic Children

Rutter and Lockyer (1967) studied 63 psychotic children who were seen during an eight-year period at Maudsley Hospital in London. The ratio of boys to girls was 4.25 to 1. In comparison with a matched control group of children who had also been seen at the same department in the hospital, the psychotic children were more prone to disturbed interpersonal relationships, retarded speech development, stereotyped activities (ritualistic and compulsive in nature), stereotyped repetitive motor movements, short attention (or poor persistence), and a tendency toward self-injury. The sample had been administered a series of psychological tests, including a test of intelligence. Of the 63 children, 10 were untestable; the remainder had a mean IQ of 62. While this mean was based on an assortment of tests and partial tests, the authors stated that it reflected the general level of functioning of the sample.

Extreme variability in intellectual functioning was more common in the psychotic group than in the control group. The psychotic children did best on manipulative or visual-spatial tests and on immediate memory tests. They were poorest on tests requiring abstract thought, symbolism, or sequential logic. There was some evidence suggestive of organic brain damage in about one-quarter of the psychotic group. Differences in intellectual levels of functioning were associated with relatively few differences in behavioral characteristics; however, the content of the symptoms was related to level of intelligence. For example, the more intelligent children demonstrated more complex and involved rituals and compulsions than the less intelligent children.

Follow-up Studies

The sample described by Rutter and Lockyer (1967) was followed up approximately 10 years later (Rutter, Greenfeld, & Lockyer, 1967). In both groups, over one-third of the children were in long-stay hospitals. Of the 38 psychotic children who were 16 years of age or over, only two had paid jobs; in contrast, over one-third of the control group of similar age had paid jobs. Overall social adjustment was poor in the psychotic group, and they also had obtained less schooling than the control group.

In the psychotic group, IQ was found to differentiate between children with poor and good adjustments: *The lower the IQ when first tested, the poorer the adjustment.* The results of the study strongly indicate that untestable schizophrenic children and schizophrenic children with an IQ below 60 have a very poor prognosis. The authors concluded that IQ and speech development are two very important prognostic signs; defects in cognition and in language may well characterize the development of infantile psychosis.

Havelkova (1968) followed up children who, at preschool age, were diagnosed as having early infantile autism or childhood schizophrenia. The follow-up period ranged from 4 to 12 years. The children were between 8 and 17 years of age at follow-up. Distinguishing different syndromes proved to be very difficult. From the total of 71 children at follow-up, 43 (61%) were found to be functioning with IQ's under 70, and 10 (14%) were in the 70 to 80 range. Intellectual limitation, therefore, was shown to be an additional handicap to the child's emotional and social malfunctioning. Treatment generally was not effective.

A study by Goldfarb, Goldfarb, and Pollack (1969) of the changes in IQ (WISC Full Scale) of 26 schizophrenic children during residential treatment showed that it is unwarranted to assume that IQ's of schizophrenic children are stable. Some children were found to improve, others stayed the same, and others obtained lower scores. The schizophrenic children with IQ's below 60 showed the least change during the three-year period of testing. Two groups of schizophrenic children were differentiated, an organic group ($N = 18$) and a nonorganic group ($N = 8$). On admission and after a three-year period, the organic group of schizophrenic children had IQ's that were considerably lower (by 16 to 18 points) than the nonorganic group of schizophrenic children.

Levy (1969) followed up 100 of an original sample of 113 children (83 boys and 30 girls) eight to 20 years after they had been discharged from a residential treatment center connected with the Menninger Clinic. A variety of severe childhood disturbances (including chronic brain syndrome, psychosis, severe neurosis, personality disorder, neurotic behavior disorder, and emotional maladjustment) characterized the group when they first entered the hospital at ages ranging from 5 to 15 years. Of the 16 children with IQ's below 90, only four had achieved an "ordinary" or a "marginal adjustment." Furthermore, nine of the 16 were institutionalized at the time of follow-up, while in the remainder of the sample only four of the 84 subjects were in an institution. Subjects who were "chronically ill" at follow-up also tended to have low IQ's as children. The poorest prognosis was found for children having a low IQ *and* either a diagnosis of schizophrenic reaction or psychosis of childhood. The data strongly suggested that level of intelligence is related to prognosis in children having severe childhood disturbances that have necessitated hospitalization.

A follow-up by Bender (1970) of 100 individuals who were diagnosed in childhood as schizophrenic, revealed that at the ages of 22 to 46 years, two-thirds remained incapacitated in institutions. The one-third who had been able to remain in the community had a higher level of intellectual functioning than those who were institutionalized.

INTELLIGENCE AND EARLY INFANTILE AUTISM

While many children with early infantile autism function in the mentally retarded range (Kanner, 1943; Rimland, 1964), Rutter (1968) observed that autism or childhood psychosis cannot be regarded as merely another variety of mental retardation. First, between 25% and 33% of autistic children function in the normal range of intelligence. Second, autistic children perform in an extremely variable manner, ranging from above average levels on some tasks (puzzle-type tests like the Block Design and Object Assembly subtests of the WISC) to mentally retarded levels on others (verbal tasks and those that require abstract thought or logic). This pattern probably results from specific defects in language rather than from global deficiency of intellect. Rutter also pointed out that those autistic children who function in the mentally retarded range are as retarded as are any other children who function in this range. The autistic child's retardation is no less "real" than any other child's retardation.

Rutter (1968) concluded from a variety of research that the IQ of the autistic or psychotic child is as stable as it is in any other child. The IQ and level of language development are the two most important factors related to prognosis in infantile autism. First, the lower the IQ, the less favorable is the prognosis. Second, lack of speech by 5 years of age (or no response to sounds in early childhood) indicates that the autistic child is not likely to achieve a normal level of social adjustment by adolescence. The autistic child's pattern of cognitive abilities is characterized by good immediate memory (as measured by digit span) and by poor verbal concepts. Rutter concluded from the available evidence that

of all the hypotheses concerning the nature of autism, that which places the primary defect in terms of a language or coding problem appears most promising. It is suggested that many of the manifestations of autism are explicable in terms of cognitive and perceptual defects [p. 26]."

CHILDHOOD SCHIZOPHRENIA, EARLY INFANTILE AUTISM, AND THE STANFORD-BINET AND THE WISC

The previous sections have illustrated the complexities associated with the syndromes of childhood schizophrenia and of early infantile autism. The IQ, however, plays an important role in prognosis, and as Goldfarb (1961) has noted, it is a measure of the schizophrenic child's current over-all level of organization and integration. On the Stanford-Binet and WISC all sources of information should be considered carefully, especially when there are suggestions of psychopathology. One source for evaluating the presence of schizophrenic symptoms is behavioral observation. Evaluation of the child's language usage, visual-motor performance, and interpersonal relations is required. The symptoms and signs frequently found in childhood schizophrenia, described in this chapter and in Chapter 19, should be carefully studied so that they can be recognized when they occur. Language and speech patterns, to take one example, may reveal echoing, circumlocution, rambling, fragmentation, irrelevant speech, bizarreness, neologisms, blocking, automatic phrases, confabulation, circumstantiality, clang association, over-elaboration, ellipsis, self-reference, confusion or omission of pronouns and connecting words, and mixtures of concrete with abstract words. In some cases, the test results may not give a representative picture of the child's capacity. This may occur in early infantile autism, as Kanner (1957) noted, because of the problems encountered in testing, and because the cognitive abilities of autistic children are masked by their basic disorder.

Davids (1958) illustrated some of the reasons why schizophrenic children do poorly on standardized intelligence tests.

Even the ones who employ a mechanized, intellectualized approach to the world do not do very well on standard tests because their specialized knowledge, obsessive concern for certain specific details, preoccupations with technical gadgets, astronomy, and so forth, does not earn them IQ points in the various areas of general knowledge that are tapped by conventional tests [p. 161]."

Stanford-Binet

On the Stanford-Binet, Des Lauriers and Halpern (1947) reported that no one pattern is diagnostic of childhood schizophrenia. Some children differ little in performance from normal children, while others show considerable unevenness in functioning. In schizophrenic records, some of the following indices may appear:

1. A run of successes and then an unexpected and unpredictable failure followed by later successes. The failures are not related to the difficulty of the task and may occur in an unpredictable manner. The poor responses may be the result of a sudden preoccupation with some small irrelevant detail with neglect of the main issue. The responses may also be manifestations of inner, uncontrollable pressures, with atypical associations and formulations. The answers, therefore, may be not only incorrect, but often illogical.

Questioning may show how the response was arrived at. This can be seen in the following example. To the statement, "A man called one day at the post office and asked if there was a letter waiting for him. 'What is your name?' asked the postmaster. 'Why,' said the man, 'you will find my name on the envelope' [Verbal Absurdities II, year-level IX]," the child responded with, "He shouldn't have called. There was a strike. The people have to work hard." Further questioning revealed that the child had responded to the word "called," had associated this word with telephoning, and from that had gone on to the threatened telephone strike.

2. Correct responses, too, may be arrived at by unusual lines of reasoning. For example, to the question, "What should you do if you found on the streets of a city a three-year-old baby that was lost from its parents? [Comprehension IV, year-level VIII]," a schizophrenic child replied, "Take it to the cops." When asked why he would do this he said, "Blue, they all wear blue." When further questioned, he said that his father was a sailor and that he felt lost. It appeared that he had associated the blue uniforms of the police with the blue sailor uniforms. Thus, answers which on the surface may appear to be satisfactory may be found to be deviant once the reasoning behind the answer is elicited.

3. Disturbances in thinking may appear in response to any test item and are not confined to certain specific ones. The responses seem to indicate that the child is reacting to what catches his awareness at the moment and to what kind of associations the particular stimulus arouses.

4. On the Picture Completion: Man test (year-level V) the child may reveal

the confusion that he manifests concerning himself as a person and the confused distinction between himself and his environment. Disturbed spatial relations, elongated parts, omission of parts, and over-emphasis on parts may be noted.

WISC

Many of the points made by Des Lauriers and Halpern about the Stanford-Binet also pertain to the WISC (and WPPSI). The following short case description of a schizophrenic child's WISC performance was presented by Palmer (1970). The illustration shows the importance of evaluating carefully the child's behavior in the test situation as well as how he responds to the test questions.

The first hint of Phillip's fulminating schizophrenia came during his responses to the WISC. He was a highly verbal youngster (age ten) who was considered to be potentially very brilliant by his teachers but was labeled as "underachiever" because of his unsatisfactory school performance. He talked incessantly about his interest in science, and it was difficult to get him to respond to anything else. He went into great length to explain why there were four seasons in the year, but he was not clear in his explanation, forgot the question, and actually forgot to name one of the four seasons. "What the stomach does?" and "Why oil floats on water?" similarly set him off on a frantic flight of ideas. On other items of this and other subtests, he tended to give only perfunctory responses. All of his subtest scores were in the low average range. Qualitatively, his failures seemed to result either from a disinterest in the topic or a highly cathe[c]ted but very confused concern with how things work and why [p. 221].

Wechsler and Jaros (1965) proposed five signs based on WISC subtest scores and scale scores that could be used to differentiate the performance of schizophrenic children from that of normal children. The signs were as follows: (1) three subtests, each deviating by three or more scaled-score points from the mean; (2) Picture Arrangement > Picture Completion, and Object Assembly > Coding, each by three scaled-score points; (3) Coding > Arithmetic, and Similarities > Arithmetic, each by three scaled-score points; (4) Verbal-Performance discrepancy of ± 16; (5) Sign 1 plus any one of the three other signs. The investigators reported that the signs generally were effective in differentiating the two groups. For example, Sign 5 was able to select 39% of the schizophrenic sample with a false-positive rate of only 2%.

Kissel (1966) attempted to validate the signs by using a sample of delinquent and neurotic acting-out children, but not a sample of schizophrenic children. Because a schizophrenic sample was not included, his study does not provide an adequate test of the signs proposed by Wechsler and Jaros. Kissel reported that false positives increased from four to 11 times over the rates reported by Wechsler and Jaros. The signs selected the emotionally disturbed children with about the same frequency as the schizophrenic children. Kissel suggested that the signs may reflect more a generalized state of emotional disturbance than a schizophrenic syndrome. However, while Kissel's interpretation is interesting, its validity still remains to be demonstrated. Further research is needed to evaluate the WISC signs proposed by Wechsler and Jaros.

DIFFERENTIAL DIAGNOSIS

Generally, efforts to differentiate childhood psychosis from other conditions such as mental retardation, epilepsy, aphasia, brain damage, psychoneurosis, and responses to early deprivation have not been very productive (Goldfarb, 1970). The difficulty, in part, occurs because the diagnosis of childhood psychosis is a symptomatic diagnosis; other childhood behavior disorders also are diagnosed by symptoms which may overlap with those of childhood psychosis. In addition, childhood behavior disorders, themselves, are not precisely defined classes of deviation. Thus, Goldfarb pointed out that children who are mentally retarded and manifest symptoms of psychosis may be placed in either of the categories, depending on the preference of the diagnostician. Similarly, in children who have a severe behavioral disturbance and an intellectual defect as well, the diagnosis — behavior disorder or mental retardation — may be related to the observer's orientation, rather than to the behavior of the child (Bellak, 1958; Pollack, 1958). Autistic children who lack speech may sometimes be diagnosed as mentally retarded (Payne, 1968). Only the occurrence of characteristic behavior patterns seems to justify the diagnostic separation of autistic children from mentally retarded children (Lobascher, Kingerlee, & Gubbay, 1970). Severely retarded children may also resemble autistic children in being inaccessible. However, the severely retarded child can respond successfully if the appropriate level of testing can be found (Haeussermann, 1958).

Childhood schizophrenia may be differentiated from mental retardation in that the child who develops schizophrenia may at first have a normal period of development and ,then deteriorate, whereas the mentally retarded child may remain at the same level throughout the developmental period (Mehr, 1952). Children with organic brain damage may differ from those with childhood schizophrenia in having a history of difficult birth, postnatal anoxia, whooping cough, encephalitis, or other conditions that may lead to brain damage (Mehr, 1952).

SUMMARY

Childhood schizophrenia constitutes the severest form of child psychopathology. Classification of the disorder is difficult, but a worthwhile proposed set of features, initially formulated by Creak and her group, appears to be a useful guide. The symptoms emphasize withdrawal from reality, intellectual retardation with some areas of exceptional skill, failure to acquire speech, abnormal responses to sensory stimuli, exaggerated movements, pathological resistance to change, and disturbed personal identity. Efforts to distinguish early infantile autism from childhood schizophrenia as a separate and distinct syndrome have been made, but many problems remain in differentiating these two conditions clearly.

Schizophrenic children usually perform at a low level of intellectual functioning. Their deficiencies in attention and concentration, language usage, association, and coherent thinking interfere with their performance on intelligence tests. Considerable evidence exists that the younger the schizophrenic child, the lower the IQ; and, the higher the IQ, the more favorable the prognosis. Generally, prognosis is poor for children with childhood schizophrenia. On follow-up, between one-third and two-thirds of schizophrenic children can be expected to remain in hospitals. Autism cannot be regarded simply as a variety of mental retardation. However, the retardation of autistic and schizophrenic children is no less "real" than is any other child's retardation. Further, the IQ of autistic or psychotic children appears to be as stable as it is in other children.

The diagnostic use of intelligence tests in childhood schizophrenia requires the same considerations as in any other assessment situation. All sources of information are evaluated, including language usage, visual-motor performance, and interpersonal relations. Language and speech patterns may be especially revealing of thinking disturbances (e.g., echoing, circumlocution, and neologisms).

Some of the following indices may appear on the Stanford-Binet: (*a*) a series of successes, and then unpredictable failures, followed by later successes; (*b*) correct responses which have unusual lines of reasoning behind them; (*c*) disturbances in thinking on any test; (*d*) body-image disturbances on the Picture Completion: Man test. The patterns described for the Stanford-Binet also apply to the WISC (and WPPSI). A WISC sign approach proposed by Wechsler and Jaros, based on scatter analytic principles, does not appear to be a valid procedure in differentiating schizophrenic children from other emotionally disturbed children.

Efforts to differentiate childhood psychosis from other conditions have not been very fruitful, because many diagnoses are based on symptoms which may be highly overlapping in a number of conditions.

CHAPTER 21

ORGANIC BRAIN DAMAGE

An evaluation of brain damage in children (as well as in adults) should include, as a minimum, the following items: (*a*) nature and locus of lesion, (*b*) age of child, (*c*) condition of rest of the brain, (*d*) time of injury, and (*e*) pretraumatic personality. Each of these can affect the type and extent of disturbance. Time of injury, an especially neglected variable, is important because there can be marked differences in the initial and residual effects of brain lesions (Smith, 1962). The interaction of these variables produces many different consequences. Damage to some parts of the brain may result in no observable sensory, motor, or behavioral changes; damage to other parts may result in specific sensory and motor deficits; and damage to still other parts may result in behavioral changes (Birch & Bortner, 1968).

SYMPTOMS OF BRAIN INJURY

Brain injury produces no single pattern of behavior. Brain-injured children may be hyperactive or lethargic, distractible or perseverative, destructive or meticulous, verbose or mute, and rigid or restless (Haeussermann, 1958). Workers in the field, recognizing that marked variation exists, seem to agree that there are a number of signs and symptoms characteristic of the behavior and performance of brain-injured children (Benton, 1962; Birch, 1964; Clements & Peters, 1962; Eisenberg, 1957; Pond, 1961; Wender, 1971). The following signs and symptoms serve only as a guideline for the purpose of diagnosis. The total case history, medical examination, and test findings must be evaluated before a diagnosis is made.

1. In the *motor sphere,* there may be hyperkinesis (constant movement; inability to sit still; fingering, touching, and mouthing objects; voluble and uninhibited speech), awkwardness in locomotion and in skilled movement (poor printing, writing, and drawing), postural rigidity, and speech difficulties. While the amount of motor activity may be no greater than in normal children of the same age, the activity lacks clear direction. Once a response has begun, the child may have difficulty in shifting his attention or in changing his mode of responding.

2. In the *sensory sphere*, there may be a very short attention span, poor concentration, and distractibility.

3. In the *affective sphere*, there may be lability of mood, reduced frustration threshold, emotional lability (irritability, aggressiveness, or easily moved to tears), and anxiety (occasionally panic reactions). Therefore, behavior may be unpredictable. A decreased ability to inhibit various functions may also manifest itself in impaired sphincter control.

4. In the *cognitive sphere*, there may be some degree of intellectual deficit along with specific learning defects (in reading, spelling, or arithmetic). The child may show interest in and attraction to minute details and demonstrate perseveration and compulsive tendencies. He may lose interest in abstract material and be preoccupied with one verbal topic.

5. In the *social sphere*, there may be interpersonal difficulties. The child may function at a level lower than is expected for his chronological and mental age levels. He may show resistance to social demands, increased independence, and extraversion, and may engage in a power struggle with his parents. Some children face rejection by their peers and others even may appear to be antisocial (lying, stealing, truancy, cruelty, and sexual offenses).

The organic brain syndrome is characterized by impairments in orientation, memory, intellectual functions, and judgment, and by labile and shallow affect. However, the symptoms noted in items 1 through 5 are not found universally in all children with organic brain damage. Some children may display only a few of the symptoms. Children with organic brain damage differ markedly in the extent to which impairments, if any, exist in the above areas (Smith, 1962). For example, intellectual defects vary from highly circumscribed deficits to generalized depression of intelligence (Eisenberg, 1964). Brain-damaged children may also show retarded intellectual functioning because they cannot explore normally their physical and social environment or because they are either overprotected or rejected at home (Richardson, 1964).

MINIMAL BRAIN DYSFUNCTION

The "minimal brain dysfunction" syndrome, according to Clements (1966), refers to children with near average, average, or above average general intelligence who manifest certain learning or behavioral disabilities which are associated with deviations of functions of the central nervous system. Wender (1971) has recently proposed that the term "minimal brain dysfunction" be used to characterize syndromes that have received a variety of labels, including: minimal brain damage, hyperactive or hyperkinetic child syndrome, minimal brain dysfunction, minimal cerebral palsy, minimal cerebral dysfunction, maturational lag, and postencephalitic behavior disorder. The symptoms of the minimal brain dysfunction syndrome may be *exactly* the same as those described in the preceding section for brain-injured children. Thus, Wender characterized the minimal brain dysfunction syndrome as one in which the child shows dysfunction in motor activity and coordination, attention and cognitive functions, impulse control, interpersonal relations, and emotionality. The primary difference between a brain-injured child and a child with the minimal brain dysfunction syndrome is that in the former there is rather clear-cut evidence for brain injury, either in the child's history or in the neurological examination, while in the latter the evidence for brain damage may be circumstantial. In addition, as Clements (1966) noted, the label "minimal brain dysfunction" is usually applied to children whose intellectual ability is close to or above the normal level.

Manifestations of the minimal brain dysfunction syndrome change with age so that, for example, symptoms present at an early age may not be present at a later age. "Soft" neurological signs are prevalent, while "hard" neurological signs occur with approximately normal frequency. "Soft" neurological signs refer to indices that are slight, inconsistently present, and not clearly associated with neuro-anatomical lesions. Soft neurological signs of cerebral dysfunction include poor fine motor coordination, impaired visual-motor coordination, poor balance, clumsiness, strabismus, choreiform movements, and poor speech.

"Hard" neurological signs refer to the classical indices of neurological damage, such as paresis and paralysis, anesthesia, and reflex changes. As many as 50% of minimal brain dysfunction children have no neurological signs or symptoms, including EEG abnormalities. Thus, clear neurological signs of brain damage do not have to appear in order for a child to be labeled as having "minimal brain dysfunction." Wender (1971) indicated that the minimal brain dysfunction syndrome is probably the most common single diagnostic entity seen in child guidance clinics. Not only are the symptoms varied, but the disorder may be masked by neurotic, sociopathic, and learning difficulties.

DIAGNOSTIC DIFFICULTIES

It is much easier to describe symptoms of brain-damaged children than to appraise brain-damaged children for a number of reasons (Diller & Birch, 1964). First, the term "brain-damaged" may refer to a number of subsyndromes, including cerebral palsy, epilepsy, non-familial mental retardation, and hyperkinesis. Second, the behavioral characteristics associated with brain-damaged children also appear in schizophrenic children and in mentally retarded children. Third, the symptoms of brain damage may represent a direct expression of the injury or may reflect coping mechanisms. Fourth, little is known about the effect on behavior of such factors as age of child, duration of injury, and locus, type, and amount of damage. Fifth, it is difficult to measure continuity of processes from age to age because psychological tests are not developmentally oriented. To this list, a sixth point from Pond (1961) can be added: "There are thus no absolutely unequivocal clinical signs, physiological tests, or psychological tests that can prove a relationship between brain damage and any particular aspect of disturbed behaviour [pp. 1454-1455]."

Hertzig, Bortner, and Birch (1969) studied the prevalence of soft and hard neurological signs in a sample of brain-injured children. The sample consisted of 90 children, between 10 and 12 years of age, who were attending a special education facility for brain-injured children. Hard neurological signs were found in 29% of the children, while soft neurological signs were found in 90% of the children. (In a control group of 15 normal children, 33% were also found to have at least one soft neurological sign, but none had hard neurological signs.) The most frequent soft neurological signs involved disturbances of balance, coordination, and speech. The least frequent neurological sign was an abnormality of position sense. Behaviors classifiable as the hyperkinetic behavior disorder syndrome were found in 19 of the 90 children in the special education facility. Those with hyperkinesis had more soft neurological signs than those without hyperkinesis. The investigators concluded that while there was marked variability in the group, the designation "brain-damaged child" is still a useful one.

Ernhart, Graham, Eichman, Marshall, and Thurston (1963) studied the performance of 70 brain-injured and normal children on a variety of tests and found that the brain-injured children performed in an inferior manner on most of the perceptual-motor and verbal tests. (The Stanford-Binet Vocabulary test and Picture Vocabulary test were included in the battery of verbal tests.) Vocabulary ability, perceptual-motor skills, and conceptual ability were impaired equally. Another important finding was that the parents of the brain-injured children did not describe their children as having symptoms associated with the hyperkinetic behavior syndrome, although they perceived them to have undesirable behavior characteristics.

The investigators concluded that the hyperkinetic behavior syndrome is not a typical picture in a heterogeneous group of brain-injured children who incur injuries of heterogeneous etiology between birth and 5½ years of age. The data suggested to Ernhart et al. that "there may be an inverse relation between age at the time of injury and vocabulary impairment and a direct relation between age of injury and perceptual-motor impairment. Further, effects may vary depending upon the age at which an individual is tested and the particular functions measured [p. 33]." This well controlled study shows that the actual behavioral symptoms in brain-injured children are neither as simple nor as invariant as would be suggested by a theoretical formulation associating hyperkinesis with brain damage.

BRAIN DAMAGE AND INTELLIGENCE

Brain-injured children behave in ways that are not always markedly different from those of children who are not brain-injured (Benton, 1962). Even brain-injured children with demonstrable behavior impairment can vary extensively in their range of intelligence. Some are severely mentally retarded, while others have specific disabilities within a setting of superior general intelligence. A lowered IQ in itself can be considered as a behavioral index of brain damage, although not an unequivocal one. That is, if the child is expected to achieve an IQ of 100 and achieves only an IQ of 75, he is consequently functioning at a level that is more than one standard deviation below normal. The proportion of brain-injured children who show a global reduction of intelligence is still not known (Benton, 1962).

Scherer (1961) determined the extent to which IQ and other variables would be effective in predicting academic achievement in brain-injured children. At 5 years of age the children were administered the Stanford-Binet and were rated on test adjustment, qualitative signs of brain damage, general emotional adjustment, social maturity, and physical status (motor efficiency, speech, vision, and hearing). At a later date, after an average of five years, achievement scores were obtained in reading, spelling, and arithmetic. The Stanford-Binet IQ was the only variable that significantly predicted achievement level.

Extent of Injury and Intelligence

Hebb (1942) reviewed the literature concerning the performance of brain-injured adults on the Stanford-Binet. He concluded that large injuries to the mature brain *do not* adversely affect performance on tests requiring definitions of words, comprehension of and memory for complex verbal material, and solution of unspeeded verbal material, but *do* adversely affect performance on tests involving maze tracing, sentence completion, abstract reasoning, speeded completion, speeded block manipulation, and picture absurdities.

Hebb also was interested in determining whether the vocabulary ability of children who had sustained brain injury is as well maintained as it is for brain-injured adults. The sample consisted of children between the ages of 10 and 19 years who had IQ's between 43 and 99 and who had sustained injury to the brain during infancy. Their performance indicated that they had deficient vocabulary ability and, furthermore, that the deficit could not be accounted for by environmental deficiencies. Hebb concluded that large injury to the infant brain appears to have a more widespread and less selective effect than large injury to the adult brain.

SITE OF LESION AND TEST PERFORMANCE

McFie (1961) was interested in determining how the site of lesion was related to the test performance of brain-injured children. The battery of tests included Memory for Designs I located at year-levels IX and XI on the Stanford-Binet, Form L and Form L-M, and the WISC. The sample consisted of 40 children between the ages of 5 and 15 years. Their IQ's ranged from 64 to 91, and they had left or right unilateral lesions acquired after the first year of life. Age of onset of injury was not found to be associated with level of intelligence. On the Memory for Designs test, children with left hemisphere lesions obtained significantly higher scores than children with right hemisphere lesions. These results are similar to those found in adult patients.

When the regions within each hemisphere were studied, high scores on the Memory for Designs test were found to be associated with lesions in the left temporal and frontal regions, while low scores were associated with lesions in the right parietal and right frontal regions. These findings, however, are tentative, because of the small number of children in each lesion-site classification. Site of lesion was not related to performance on the subtests of the WISC (or Wechsler-Bellevue). However, some trends emerged which McFie considered to be important. In comparison with the normative group, children having lesions in the left hemisphere tended to have lower scores on the Digit Span and Similarities subtests, whereas those having right hemisphere lesions tended to have lower scores on the Picture Arrangement and Block Design subtests. Picture Completion subtest scores were not impaired in either group.

BRAIN INJURY AND OTHER SYMPTOMS

Pond (1961) studied the relationship among level of intelligence, neurotic symptoms, and motor difficulties in a group of 58 brain-injured children. Taking an IQ of 80 as a reference point, neurotic symptoms occurred more frequently in children with IQ's above that point, while hyperkinesis was more prevalent in children with IQ's below it. Abnormal aggressiveness was not related to level of intelligence.

The association between organic brain damage and psychiatric disorder was studied in a total community in Great Britain for children between the ages of 5 and 14 years (Graham & Rutter, 1968). Rate of psychiatric disorder (34%) was high for epileptic children, for cerebral-palsied children, and for children with other pathological disorders of the brain. The children with epilepsy had a rate of psychiatric disorder that was five times that of the general population. Organic brain dysfunction appeared to be the reason why the rate of psychiatric disorder was greater in the epileptic group than in other groups. The psychiatric disorders found in the epileptic group were mixed, and included neurotic disorders, antisocial disorders, mixed disorders, hyperkinetic syndrome, and psychosis. No specific pattern of behavior was found that could be considered typical of or exclusive for the brain-damaged or epileptic child.

The behaviors shown by the epileptic children appeared to be a function of their high rate of psychiatric disorder rather than to their motor and cognitive abnormalities. Those epileptic children who developed psychiatric disorders also had low intelligence and severe reading retardation (independently of their low IQ). Bilateral neurological abnormalities were associated more often with psychiatric disorders than were unilateral neurological abnormalities. Finally, family influences, such as mothers with emotional or psychosomatic symptoms or a "broken home," were significantly associated with psychiatric disorders within the epileptic group.

APHASIA IN CHILDREN

Aphasia, a language disorder characterized by difficulty with the symbolic use of language, is thought to be caused by a localized brain lesion; it usually has a congenital origin in children, although it can occur as a consequence of brain damage sustained prenatally, at birth, or postnatally (Myklebust, 1954). Conditions such as anoxia (at birth), rubella (contracted by the pregnant mother), cerebral hemorrhage (at birth), encephalitis, meningitis, and trauma during the childhood years may lead to cortical lesions which affect language areas (Agranowitz & McKeown, 1964). While aphasia may be present from birth, it may not be evident until the stage of language acquisition is reached (Haeussermann, 1958). Aphasic children *fail* to acquire symbolic activity; aphasic adults *lose* normal symbolic activity.

The major forms of aphasia in children (as as well as in adults) include *expressive aphasia*, defined as impaired ability to use spoken or written language, and *receptive aphasia*, defined as impaired ability to understand spoken or written language. *Auditory aphasia* refers to an incapacity to comprehend the meaning of spoken words. *Alexia* refers to a loss of ability to read written or printed language despite an absence of impairment of vision or intelligence. *Agraphia* refers to impairment in the ability to write. In addition to language disorders, brain injury may manifest itself in *agnosia*, defined as disturbances in the perception of the significance of sensory stimuli or defects of imagination, and in *apraxia*, defined as disturbances of the memory of movements.

DIAGNOSTIC INDICATORS OF BRAIN DAMAGE

Diagnostic indicators of brain damage are based upon behavior in the test situation, performance on specific tests and, of course, past history, neurological examination, and school records. The psychologist, in giving tests, makes one of his contributions to the diagnostic process by carefully evaluating the test performance. For the most part, quantitative test indices (e.g., pattern analysis, scatter, or scores on specific tests or subtests), as is documented in the later parts of this chapter, *have not proven useful* in differentiating brain-damaged children from children who are not brain-damaged. Group data, too, may obscure disturbances which are otherwise characteristic of a single child (Strauss & Lehtinen, 1947). Evaluation of the child's total performance on the examination is required, especially when there is a question of brain damage.

During the examination the examiner should be alert for behaviors indicative of motor restlessness. He should consider carefully the extent to which (*a*) special techniques have to be used to secure the child's attention, (*b*) instructions have to be repeated before the child does what he is asked to do, and (*c*) extraneous activity has to be prevented (Hertzig et al., 1969).

When some of the following signs occur in the test situation, brain damage should be considered. The signs include:

(*a*) difficulty in abstracting,

(*b*) difficulty in organizing,

(*c*) difficulty in analyzing and in synthesizing,

(*d*) concrete, rigid, and inflexible thinking,

(*e*) inability to shift (inflexible behavior),

(*f*) inability to learn quickly,

(*g*) retardation in the flow of thoughts,

(*h*) inability to integrate and to see relationships between two or more things,

(*i*) inability to plan ahead and to anticipate (poor foresight and goal direction), (*j*) memory defect (recent, remote, or both),

(*k*) memory defect (visual, auditory, or both),

(*l*) faulty perception,

(*m*) perseveration,

(*n*) turning material around (lacking goal direction in manipulation of objects),

(*o*) closure difficulty,

(*p*) need of external guides (e.g., using fingers to touch and to manipulate),

(*q*) continuous looking at sample, and

(*r*) poor comprehension of instructions.

Failure may be expected even on tests which only tangentially involve sensory perception, since the brain-damaged child usually suffers from a disturbance of figure-ground perception (Fromm, Hartman, & Marschak, 1957). Their sensory disturbances may also lead to failure on tests involving reality awareness, reality testing, and reality mastery. Success may be shown on tests involving interpersonal relations, because of their ability to relate well to adults. Their vocabulary may be as large as that of normal children, but they may have difficulty in combining and in using words (Strauss & Kephart, 1955).

MINIMAL BRAIN DYSFUNCTION AND PSYCHOLOGICAL TESTS

While there is no standard battery of tests or procedures to insure discrimination of children with minimal brain dysfunction from those with psychological or cultural deficits, Conners (1967) recommended that certain tests can be used to facilitate the diagnostic process. He delineated six areas of functioning:

1. General intelligence: WISC or Stanford-Binet, Draw-a-Man test, Porteus Mazes;

2. Achievement: Wide Range Achievement Test and Gray Oral Reading Test;

3. Visual and auditory perception: Bender Visual-Motor Gestalt Test, Frostig Developmental Test of Visual Perception, tests of auditory discrimination and auditory synthesis;

4. Language functions: Illinois Test of Psycholinguistic Abilities;

5. Motor functions: Neurological examination by pediatric neurologist, Lincoln-Oseretsky Motor Development Scale, motor inhibition tests;

6. Memory: Benton Visual Retention Test, Sentence Memory Test.

Clements (1966) essentially agreed with Conners concerning the general areas needed to evaluate children suspected of having minimal brain dysfunction. He added that a psychological evaluation should also include behavioral observations in a variety of settings, additional indices of learning and behavior, and an academic history. Obviously, the above areas of functioning are excellent ones to investigate whenever there are suggestions of brain damage, minimal or otherwise. However, it is still important to recognize that the list of areas and tests is only suggestive. Research studies have provided and will continue to provide us with information about the validity and reliability of the above tests, and new tests that are being developed may supplant the ones that are currently available. Consequently, it is important for the examiner to keep abreast of current developments in the field of evaluation and measurement. It is important to emphasize that in the evaluation of brain damage or suspected brain damage or minimal brain dysfunction a battery of tests is needed; the intelligence test forms only one part of the battery.

Some of the following signs may appear in the records of children with minimal brain dysfunction (Clements, 1966):

(*a*) spotty or patchy intellectual deficits (i.e., achievement may be low in some areas and high in others);

(*b*) below mental-age-level performance on drawing tests;

(*c*) poor geometric drawings in relation to chronological age and intelligence level;

(*d*) poor performance on block design and marble board tests;

(*e*) poor performance on group tests of intelligence, achievement, and reading;

(*f*) marked scatter within each WISC scale, and Verbal Scale-Performance Scale discrepancies in either direction.

Conners (1967) pointed out that there is no single pattern that appears on psychological tests that is solely characteristic of children with minimal brain dysfunction. This conclusion has received support recently in at least two other reports. In one investigation, Verbal-Performance discrepancies did not appear in the WISC records of white upper middle class children diagnosed as having minimal brain dysfunction (Paine, Werry, & Quay, 1968). In the other, WISC Verbal-Performance discrepancies and scatter patterns failed to distinguish middle class groups of dyslexic, minimal brain-damaged, and emotionally disturbed children from one another (Hartlage, 1970). An important criterion in the recognition of minimal brain dysfunction is the child's failure to learn despite adequate general intelligence. Standard achievement tests can be used to document learning failures.

Conners emphasized that intelligence test results cannot be used in a stereotyped way for diagnostic evaluation. He observed that the reasons for the unevenness in performance may be varied, including (*a*) a direct effect of some specific cognitive anomaly, as in the loss of spatial ability found in children with Turner's syndrome (cf. Money, 1963), or (*b*) inattentiveness, impulsiveness, anxiety, or other factors that are related to the testing situation. The examiner must try to determine the reasons for failure on a given subtest, trying to understand the process whereby the examinee arrives at his answer rather than simply obtaining the final score. There are many ways by which one may fail a subtest, and the *type of failure* may be more enlightening than the failure itself.

Qualitative features of performance are particularly important because, although children with MBD [minimal brain dysfunction] may not differ from controls in the level of success on separate test variables, the way these performances are patterned or organized does differ [Conners, 1967, p. 751].

While Verbal-Performance discrepancies may not appear in the WISC performance of children with minimal brain dysfunction, it is of interest to determine what, if any, behavioral characteristics are associated with such discrepancies when they occur. Mordock and Bogan's (1968) data are helpful concerning this point. Their sample consisted of two groups of 11-year-old children with minimal brain dysfunction. In one group the Verbal-Performance discrepancy was in favor of the Verbal Scale, while in the other group the Verbal-Performance discrepancy was in favor of the Performance Scale. The Verbal > Performance group (95 vs. 81), in comparison with the Performance > Verbal group (100 vs. 81), was found to have the following behaviors more frequently: distractibility, need for adult contact, inability to delay impulse for immediate gratification, social aggression, emotional detachment, anxious fearful ideation, messiness-sloppiness, and eating disturbance. The two groups did not differ in coordination, proneness to emotional upset, unethical behavior, and social isolation. Thus, it appears that more behavioral problems are associated with the Verbal > Performance group than with the Performance > Verbal group in children with minimal brain dysfunction.

ORGANIC BRAIN DAMAGE AND THE STAN-FORD-BINET

The Stanford-Binet can serve as a useful but somewhat limited instrument for the assessment of brain injury. During the child's performance, the examiner should be alert for behavioral and qualitative indices (described in an earlier part of the chapter) that are suggestive of brain injury. On the Stanford-Binet there are some tests that may reveal signs of organic damage more readily than others. These tests are discussed below, along with some specific illustrations of signs of brain injury.

Perseveration

Perseveration may be shown on the Mutilated Pictures test when the child correctly answers the teapot item by stating that the handle is missing, and then saying that the handle is missing from the glove item. The mental set to answer by looking for missing details, a set which is correct for the Mutilated Pictures test, may also carry over to other tests. For example, the first test at year-level VII, Picture Absurdities I, requires that the child state what is funny about the picture. If he is perseverating, he might look for missing details on the Picture Absurdities items instead of looking for funny or foolish details (Mecham et al., 1966).

Signs of Confusion

Brain-injured children may demonstrate more confusion on the Similarities, Pictorial Likenesses and Differences, Repeating Digits, Memory for Sentences, Memory for Stories, and Drawing tests than on other Stanford-Binet tests (Burgemeister, 1962).

Reasoning Difficulties

Reasoning difficulties may be shown by brain-injured children on the Similarities, Opposite Analogies, Verbal Absurdities, Orientation, Problem Situation, and Picture Absurdities tests. Failures arise because the children may not be able to coordinate multiple relationships. They may cling to practical details and only attend to one or several parts of a problem without seeing the correct interrelationships among the parts (Taylor, 1961).

Attention to Small Details

Brain-injured children may solve problems involving a small missing detail more easily than problems involving a large missing detail. For example, on the Mutilated Pictures test, pictures may be solved with greater ease which show the missing cleft in the cow's hoof or the rooster's missing spur than pictures containing more obvious incongruities (Taylor, 1961).

Memory Difficulty

(This discussion also pertains to the WISC.) Brain-injured children may obtain higher scores on Repeating Digits Forward than on Repeating Digits Backward (Taylor, 1961). Auditory memory facilitates recall on Digits Forward, but the difficulty brain-injured children have in organizing and in remanipulating mentally what they have memorized may lead to failures on Digits Backward. Digits Backward is also a more demanding task than Digits Forward, and the trauma or illness associated with the brain injury may impede the children's ability to sustain the effort needed for successful completion of the task. Generally, a significant and consistent discrepancy between Digits Forward and Digits Backward, in favor of Digits Forward, may suggest organic involvement. However, it is important to recognize that failure on Digits Backward also may be a function of attention difficulties which stem from causes other than brain injury.

Visual-Motor Difficulties

Children with visual-motor difficulties may establish a basal year level which is several years below their chronological age, because each year level usually includes a test requiring well integrated visual-perceptual-motor skills and organization (Coleman & Dawson, 1969). Examples of tests requiring visual-motor skills are Picture Completion: Man (year-level V), Paper Folding: Triangle (year-level V), Maze Tracing (year-level VI), Copying a Diamond (year-level VII), and Paper Cutting (year-level IX).

Visual-motor handicaps also may be revealed by failures on the Three-Hole Form Board: Rotated (year-level II-6) and on the Block Building: Bridge (year-level III) tests in the context of successful performance on other tests at the same year levels (Reynell, 1970). Children with visual-motor handicaps who are between 2 and 3 years old may refuse to do the spatial tasks on the Stanford-Binet but not other tasks (Gibbs, 1959). Visual-motor difficulties can often be discovered during a routine administration of the Stanford-Binet, especially when inadequate performance is observed on visual-motor tests and possibly on reading tests and on number tests (Langan, 1970). On the Picture Vocabulary test, young children with visual-perceptual difficulties may not be able to name the objects, although they may know the objects; instead, one part of the picture may be named.

ORGANIC BRAIN DAMAGE AND THE WISC

The WISC has become a popular instrument for evaluating the performance of children with organic brain damage. As with the Stanford-Binet, it is important to observe carefully the child's performance for possible behaviors that may be suggestive of brain damage. Although pattern analysis applied to the WISC has not been very successful in differentiating children with brain damage from those without brain damage, as this section indicates, the WISC is an important research and clinical tool, stimulating many valuable and interesting studies and reports.

Integrative Function of the Cerebral Cortex and the WISC

Ross (1959) proposed that the construct of "integrative function of the cerebral cortex" be used to assist in the diagnosis of cerebral pathology. Further, he showed how it applies to performance on the WISC. The construct is composed of two parts. One is *integration,* defined as a physiologically mediated process which enables the individual to combine and relate discrete cues so that a unified response can occur. The other part is *differentiation,* defined as a holding apart of several discrete, simultaneously received cues. Differentiation often precedes integration. Integration is disrupted when there is an "inability to combine and relate discrete cues or aspects of the environment [p. 219]," while differentiation is disrupted when there is "an uncritical over-combination of cues or an indiscriminate over-responsiveness to stimulation [p. 219]." On intelligence tests, children with cerebral pathology may demonstrate defects in integration, in differentiation, or in both.

The Similarities subtest is a good measure of integrative capacity in the Verbal Scale. Ross described the task as follows:

In order to recognize and define relationships between objects, the child must be able to abstract essential from nonessential attributes for each of the two stimulus words (differentiation) and, following this, he must relate them and verbalize the relationship (integration) in an appropriate fashion [p. 228].

An example of inadequate differentiation is seen in a response based on nonessential attributes, such as "Both eat the same food" to the cat-mouse item. Inadequate integration may result in a statement of differences, for example, "They are not alike."

On the Performance Scale, Block Design is a subtest that is sensitive to disturbances in integration. Ross noted that the

design must first be broken up conceptually into its component parts (differentiation) and then reassembled with the blocks into a structural whole (integration). In addition, the test calls for a coordinated (integrated) functioning of perceptual, conceptual, and motor operations, and a break-down anywhere in this sequence will reflect itself in faulty performance [p. 228].

Decker (1964) pointed out that inadequate integrative functions on the Block Design subtest are revealed when the child fumbles as he proceeds to solve the tasks, demonstrates notable angulation difficulties, particularly when dissimilar angles are spatially contiguous, and occasionally shows grossly inaccurate reproduction.

Ross indicated that defects in integration may also be revealed on the Object Assembly and Coding subtests. Object Assembly calls for a complex integrative process. The child must integrate "between the memory of the percept, the discrete pieces before him, and the motor performance necessary to assemble the pieces correctly [pp. 228-229]." The Coding subtest requires sustained attention and perceptual-performance integration. Integration is required between visual perception and motor performance, although immediate memory may play a role in the achievement of high scores.

Other General Observations

Before turning to research studies concerned with pattern analysis, some other general observations and findings related to the WISC and organic brain damage are cited. Children with epilepsy have the three major WISC factors (Verbal Comprehension, Perceptual Organization, and Freedom from Distractibility) that are found in normal children (Dennerll, Den Broeder, & Sokolov, 1964). Brain-injured children have the ability to discriminate the WISC Block Design patterns, even though their ability to reproduce these same designs may be impaired (Bortner & Birch, 1962). The difficulty in reproducing the designs may involve an inability to translate a perceptual organization into an appropriate action pattern. Brain-injured children may be able to copy a design from a model (such as in Designs A and B of the Block Design subtest), but they may not be able to reproduce designs from a picture (Ross, 1959). On the Object Assembly subtest, they may be able to say what the object is supposed to be, but they may not be able to assemble the pieces or complete the entire picture (Ross, 1959).

Taylor (1961) made some excellent observations about the performance of brain-injured children on the Block Design, Picture Completion, and Digit Span subtests. Her observations about the Block Design subtest supplement those noted in the preceding paragraph. On the Block Design subtest, children with perceptual difficulties caused by brain injury may place isolated blocks spaced far apart, lined up in a row, or joined at their angles. They may show reversals and may not benefit from demonstrations. They may be able to copy from memory what has been demonstrated, but be unable to solve the next design correctly.

On the Picture Completion subtest, brain-injured children, because of their attention to small detail, may have more success with items which involve small missing details (e.g., cleft in the hoof of the cow or spur of the rooster) than with items which involve more obvious incongruities (e.g., slit in the screw). Taylor's observations about the Digit Span subtest appear in the previous section of this chapter, which discusses memory difficulty on the Stanford-Binet.

An example of *perseveration* is seen when the child is asked on the Information subtest, "How many pennies make a nickel?," "How many days in a week?," and "How many things make a dozen?," and he answers "five" to all questions (Decker, 1964). *Conceptual difficulties* were also illustrated by Decker.

To the question [on the Information subtest], "What are the four seasons of the year?" a response sequence typical of a loosely bound and "sticky" conceptualization is: "April, May, June." When reminded that those are months, he replies, "Oh, yeah, Let me see now. Uh—summer." ("That's *one* season.") "I can't think of any more." ("What season are we having now?") "Oh, yeah—spring!" "Let me see now, summer, spring, fall (pause) April!" Another of our youngsters may respond initially with, "Spring, summer, October." When told that October is a month, not a season, he may then proceed accurately [p. 56].

A poor score on the Digit Span subtest may reflect conceptual problems rather than difficulty with attention span (Decker, 1964).

An extreme example is the child who has no difficulty repeating digits forward, but when told to repeat them backwards physically *turns his back* to the examiner and repeats them forward. Visually structuring the concept of repeating digits backward usually helps him succeed [p. 56].

A number of signs of visual-perceptual-motor dysfunction on the WISC have been presented by Coleman and Dawson (1969). While caution is needed in using their signs because neither experimental findings nor statistical data were reported, the signs, which are shown in Table 21–1, provide a basis for evaluating perceptual-motor difficulties on the WISC. Table 21–1 indicates that some of the subtests (e.g., Comprehension and Vocabulary) may not reveal deficient functioning.

Hall and LaDriere (1969) studied the performance on the WISC Similarities subtest of 120 emotionally disturbed and 120 brain-damaged children matched on Full Scale IQ, chronological ages (6 to 15 years), and sex. An error-analysis approach, initially formulated by Spence (1963), was used to analyze the incorrect responses (see Table 21–2). Only items 5 through 16 were categorized because items 1 through 4 are analogies items, and not similarities items. Inadequate attempts at conceptualization were made significantly more frequently by the emotionally disturbed children than by the brain-damaged children. This finding held for both males and females. The investigators suggested that the vague, inappropriate, idiosyncratic, and conceptually inadequate responses of the "inadequate conceptual" type reflect the thinking disturbances found in severe psychogenic conditions. No other error category distinguished the two groups. However, when the two groups were divided by sex, brain-damaged boys had more "don't know" responses than emotionally disturbed boys. This finding, the investigators pointed out, is consistent with the literature and is indicative of the impairment of abstract ability, concreteness, and deficient conceptualization in children with organic brain disor-

Table 21-1. SIGNS OF VISUAL-PERCEPTUAL-MOTOR DYSFUNCTION
ON THE WISC (BASED ON CLINICAL OBSERVATIONS)

SUBTEST	SIGN
Information	The child responds to "How many ears have you?" and "How many legs does a dog have?" by feeling his own ears or by counting a dog's legs when he is past the age where such behavior is expected. Counting on fingers the pennies in a nickel, days in a week, or things in a dozen. Naming the days of the week in an incorrect order.
Comprehension	High scores on this subtest.
Arithmetic	Clumsy or awkward or inadequate use of blocks or use of fingers.
Similarities	Failing items; may be due to inability to recall visually.
Digit Span	Difficulty in recalling numbers.
Vocabulary	Can serve as an indication of Verbal IQ.
Picture Completion	Failing items. Responding with "There is nothing wrong. It's all there."
Picture Arrangement	Child's approach to task can be informative (e.g., impulsiveness, many changes in arrangements, bewilderment, etc.)
Block Design	Failing items.
Object Assembly	Inadequate performance: laying pieces on top of each other, reversing pieces, confusion, and frustration.
Coding	Use of fingers to keep place. Skipping items or lines.
Mazes	Crossing over solid lines.

Adapted from Coleman and Dawson (1969).

Table 21-2. CATEGORIES FOR SCORING INCORRECT WISC AND WPPSI
SIMILARITIES RESPONSES

CATEGORY	DESCRIPTION
Denials	Explicit denial of similarity (e.g., "not alike"), or unqualified statements that the items are opposites.
Don't know	Examinee says that he "doesn't know."
Narratives and descriptions	Descriptions of one or both of the items separately or relating the two narratively but without specification of a common property.
Conceptual attempts	Common properties are specified but are too vague, inaccurate, or idiosyncratic to be considered correct.

Note.—An answer containing several types of responses is scored as follows: A positive response takes precedence over a Denial or Don't Know, and a Conceptual Attempts over a Narratives and Descriptions. An answer containing a Don't Know and Denial is scored Denial. Score additional responses elicited by a question only if examinee is clarifying his original answer.

Adapted from Spence (1963).

ders. This interpretation, however, must be restricted by the finding of close to equal frequency of the "don't know" response in the emotionally disturbed girls and brain-damaged girls.

WISC Pattern Analysis and Signs, and Organic Brain Damage

Investigators have been interested in determining whether certain patterns of Wechsler subtest scores might be indicative of organic brain damage. However, the search for patterns that differentiate brain-damaged children from those who are not brain-damaged is difficult because the availability of fairly large homogeneous groups of brain-damaged children is limited (Reed, Reitan, & Kløve, 1965).

Hewson Ratios. Hewson (1949) presented a system of pattern analysis for the Wechsler-Bellevue, which was adapted for adolescents by Bryan and Brown (1957) and termed the "Adolescent ratios." The two systems were applied by Fisher and Parsons (1962) to the Wechsler-Bellevue protocols of 127 white male and female adolescents with a diagnosis of endogenous (familial or undifferentiated) mental retardation. The Hewson ratios failed to differ from chance in their accuracy of diagnoses, while the Adolescent ratios misdiagnosed almost all of the children. McKeever and Gerstein (1958) also could not confirm the validity of the Hewson ratios. Thus, the available findings indicate that the Hewson ratio method does not appear to be of value in determining the presence of brain injury.

WISC Signs. Studies usually have reported that WISC signs (such as Verbal-Performance discrepancies, subtest patterning, or individual subtest scores) have not been able to differentiate brain-damaged children from emotionally disturbed children, normal children, or both (Bortner & Birch, 1969; Caputo, Edmonston, L'Abate, & Rondberg, 1963; Clawson, 1962; Rowley, 1961; Schwartz & Dennerll, 1970). Several studies by Reed and his co-workers (Reed & Fitzhugh, 1966; Reed & Reed, 1967; Reed & Reitan, 1963, 1969; Reed, Reitan, & Kløve, 1965), which have used either the WISC or the Wechsler-Bellevue Intelligence Scale, indicated that (a) brain-damaged children achieve lower scores on the Wechsler tests than children who are not brain-damaged; (b) a neurological lesion in children often may show general effects (e.g., a reduced level of intelligence) rather than selective or specific ones (e.g., lower Verbal than Performance IQ's) since the lesion is imposed on an immature organism; and (c) children classified by lateralized motor deficits do not appear to show systematic differences in their Verbal and Performance IQ's. (Findings similar to those noted in (c) have been reported by Pennington, Galliani, & Voegele, 1965.) The above studies suggest that the intellectual organization of children who have educational designations of brain damage or emotional disturbance may be markedly similar. *Intellectual patterning in itself, therefore, should not be a basis for assigning children to classes for the brain-damaged or for the emotionally disturbed* (cf. Bortner & Birch, 1969).

Variables Associated with Large Verbal-Performance Discrepancies. What are the major characteristics of children who have large Verbal-Performance discrepancies? Holroyd and Wright (1965), in a carefully controlled study, reported that 12-year-old children (M IQ = 98) whose Verbal Scale was greater than their Performance Scale by at least 25 points had significantly more medical diagnoses of brain damage, more pathological signs on neurological examinations, more abnormal electroencephalograms, and poorer performance on many psychological tests sensitive to brain damage than the control group. Children with a Verbal-Performance discrepancy of at least 25 points in favor of the Performance Scale (P > V) did not differ from the controls on any of the indicators of brain injury. Of the 35 variables studied in the investigation, scores on one test, the Lincoln-Oseretsky Motor Development Scale (Sloan, 1955), correlated the highest ($r = -.76$) with neurological examination ratings.

In another study, Holroyd (1968) compared the medical records of 6- to 15-year-old children with a WISC Verbal-Performance discrepancy of 25 or more points in favor of the Performance Scale (P > V) with those of a group whose Verbal-Performance discrepancy was less than 10 points. Both groups had normal intelligence. The medical records indicated that in the P > V group, speech, hearing, and reading problems were prevalent. However, diagnoses of brain damage or of psychiatric difficulties were not found. The latter two diagnoses were more frequently associated with the control group. The results of the two investigations suggest that a WISC Verbal Scale IQ of 25 points more than the Performance Scale IQ may be associated with organic deficit in children. Holroyd recommended that a neurological examination be conducted whenever the Verbal Scale IQ is greater than the Performance Scale IQ by 25 points or more.

EEG and the WISC.   The relationship between the electroencephalogram (EEG) and the WISC has been of interest to investigators (Annett, Lee, & Ounsted, 1961; Braun & Brane, 1971; Hartlage & Green, 1972; Pihl, 1968). The results of these investigations indicate that WISC patterns probably do not have much relation to EEG severity of abnormality.

DIFFERENTIAL DIAGNOSIS

One of the diagnostic problems in the area of brain injury is that some of the symptoms of brain-injured children also are those associated with non-brain-injured children who have psychiatric problems (cf. Pond, 1961). However, on closer examination, subtle differences usually appear between brain-injured and non-brain-injured children. The compulsive behavior of the child with organic dysfunction is qualitatively different from that of the obsessive-compulsive child (Kernberg, 1969). Strict routines, constancy, and perseveration of sameness are, for the brain-injured child, ways to maintain his equilibrium or his control over the environment; for the neurotic child, they may be defenses against the expression of forbidden impulses. Anxiety in neurotic children "is aroused not by physical disarrangement of objects but by the symbolic meaning of order and disorder to the particular child [Kernberg, 1969, p. 521]." Echolalia in the brain-injured child may be an adaptive effort to register the verbal communications; in the schizophrenic child, it may be a means of binding aggression (Kernberg, 1969).

Identifying aphasic children is difficult, because symptoms associated with other conditions (such as hearing deficit, mental retardation, autism, emotional instability, and delayed speech) are similar to those displayed by aphasic children (McGinnis, 1963). For example, the emotionally disturbed behavior of the aphasic child, which may be a consequence of frustration caused by the inability to communicate and to understand language, is difficult to differentiate from the emotionally disturbed behavior of the child who does not have brain damage. However, other conditions can be distinguished from aphasia more easily. The child with psychosis displays aberrant social behavior that sets him apart from the aphasic child. Children who do not speak by 4 or 5 years of age may acquire speech and language rapidly once training has begun. The aphasic child, in contrast, will need much help. A trial teaching or evaluation period should be used whenever there is doubt about diagnosis or prognosis.

De Hirsch's (1967) work is helpful in understanding the language patterns of aphasic and schizophrenic children. The two groups have in common such features as high auditory thresholds for speech, inferior auditory discrimination, feedback distortions, echolalia, limitations in verbal output, and conceptual deficits. However, auditory memory span is poor in aphasia, but may be excellent in schizophrenia. Aphasic children also differ in not presenting "the deviations in pitch, stress and inflection, the manneristic style, and the idiosyncratic use of words which are characteristic of those communicative disturbances that are clearly related to psychopathology [p. 8]." While some behaviors exhibited by the two groups are the same, the behaviors reflect different needs and may serve different purposes.

SUMMARY

The evaluation of brain injury in children (as well as in adults) requires a consideration of the following factors: (*a*) nature and locus of lesion, (*b*) age of child, (*c*) condition of rest of the brain, (*d*) time of injury, and (*e*) pretraumatic personality. These variables interact to produce varied consequences.

While a variety of symptoms may be present in brain-injured children, the following serve as general guidelines: (*a*) in the motor sphere, there may be hyperkinesis and awkwardness in locomotion and in skilled movements; (*b*) in the sensory sphere, there may be short attention span, poor concentration, and distractibility; (*c*) in the affective sphere, there may be lability of mood, reduced frustration threshold, emotional lability, and anxiety; (*d*) in the cognitive sphere, there may be some degree of intellectual and learning deficit; (*e*) in the social sphere, there are interpersonal difficulties. Children with organic brain damage differ markedly in the extent to which impairments, if any, are present in the above areas.

Minimal brain dysfunction, according to Clements, refers to children with near average, average, or above average intelligence who manifest certain learning or behavioral disabilities which are associated with central nervous system difficulties. Symptoms of minimal brain dysfunction are, in part, dependent upon the child's age. Soft neurological signs are more prevalent than hard neurological signs. However, as many as 50% of children with minimal brain dysfunction have no neurological signs or symptoms.

The diagnosis of brain injury is difficult for a variety of reasons. (*a*) Brain damage includes a number of subsyndromes, so that it is not always clear what condition is being referred to. (*b*) Behavioral signs of brain injury also appear in other conditions. (*c*) Some of the symptoms may not be a direct expression of the injury. (*d*) The interaction of anatomical, physiological, and personality factors yields complex behaviors. (*e*) Continuity of development is difficult to measure. (*f*) There are no unequivocal clinical signs that can prove a relationship between brain damage and behavior.

Hebb has concluded that large brain injury to the infant brain appears to have a more widespread and less selective effect than large brain injury to the adult brain.

Epileptic children appear to have a more frequent rate of psychiatric disorder than is found in the general population.

Aphasia refers to language disorders caused by brain injury. Specific types of aphasic disturbances include alexia (difficulty in reading), agraphia (impairment in writing), agnosia (defects in imagination), and apraxia (disturbances of the memory of movements).

Diagnostic indicators of brain damage include a variety of signs, ranging from difficulty in abstracting and organizing, to perseveration and poor comprehension of instructions. A recommended test battery to evaluate children with minimal brain dysfunction includes tests of intelligence, achievement, visual-motor functions, language, motor abilities, and memory. Signs of minimal brain dysfunction on psychological tests may include (*a*) spotty intellectual deficits, (*b*) below mental-age-level performance on drawing tests, (*c*) poor geometric drawings, (*d*) poor scores on intelligence, achievement, and reading tests, and (*e*) marked scatter. However, there is no single pattern that is characteristic of children with minimal brain dysfunction.

The Stanford-Binet serves as a useful but limited instrument in assessing brain injury. Behavioral and qualitative observations may provide useful clues. Tests on the Stanford-Binet may reveal perseveration, signs of confusion, reasoning difficulties, attention to small details, memory difficulty, visual-motor difficulties, and other suggestive indicators of brain injury.

The WISC has proved to be a popular instrument for the assessment of brain injury, primarily because of the format of the scale, which provides individual subtest scores and Verbal and Performance Scale IQ's. The scale, like the Stanford-Binet, is excellent for observing the child's performance. WISC subtests are sensitive to the integrative capacity of the cerebral cortex (e.g., Similarities, Block Design, Object Assembly, and Coding). Like the Stanford-Binet, subtests on the WISC may reveal various signs that are associated with brain injury. Specific illustrations of such signs are described in the chapter. However, pattern analysis has not been successful in differentiating children with brain injury from those without brain injury.

A Verbal Scale IQ that is higher than a Performance Scale IQ by at least 25 points is more likely to be associated with diagnoses of brain damage than are Verbal-Performance discrepancies that are less than 25 points, or large discrepancies that are in favor of the Performance Scale. The Lincoln-Oseretsky Motor Development Scale has been found to be an excellent measure of neurological impairment.

Studies have uniformly reported that WISC patterns are not able to distinguish children with abnormal EEG's from those with normal EEG's.

Distinguishing brain-injured children from those with no brain injuries is a difficult task. However, a careful study of the child's behavior and test performance may provide valuable cues to facilitate the assessment task.

CHAPTER 22

MENTAL RETARDATION

DEFINITIONS OF MENTAL RETARDATION

Many definitions of mental retardation have been proposed over the years (Robinson & Robinson, 1965), and most have included (*a*) some aspect of intellectual subnormality (with or without qualification), and (*b*) an underlying judgment that retardation involves problems in meeting the demands of society (Geloff, 1963). Of the many definitions, Heber's (1961) appears to be one of the most satisfactory: "Mental retardation refers to subaverage general intellectual functioning which originates during the developmental period and is associated with impairment in adaptive behavior [p. 499]." "Subaverage" refers to performance that is more than one standard deviation below the population mean; "general intellectual functioning" is usually assessed by a standard objective intelligence test; and the "developmental period" is regarded as the period between birth and about 16 years of age. For the Stanford-Binet and Wechsler scales, as Table 22–1 shows, five levels of retardation can be delineated, beginning with a "borderline level" and ending with a "profound level." Heber pointed out that before a diagnosis of mental retardation is made, such factors as adaptive behavior and personal-social ability must be considered. Arriving at a diagnosis of mental retardation requires a careful assessment of all relevant factors.

Heber's definition, according to Robinson and Robinson (1970), has many implications. First, the diagnosis of mental status must be only a *description* of present behavior; *prediction* of later intelligence is a separate process. Second, the contribution of individually administered intelligence tests is specifically recognized. Third, diagnosis is tied to the developmental process, with behav-

Table 22-1. MEASURED INTELLIGENCE

LEVEL OF DEVIATION IN MEASURED INTELLIGENCE	RANGE IN STANDARD DEVIATION VALUE	RANGE IN IQ SCORES FOR STANFORD-BINET, FORM L-M	RANGE IN IQ SCORES FOR WISC, WPPSI, AND WAIS
Borderline −1	−1.01 to −2.00	83–68	84–70
Mild −2	−2.01 to −3.00	67–52	69–55
Moderate −3	−3.01 to −4.00	51–36	54–40
Severe −4	−4.01 to −5.00	35–20	< 40
Profound −5	< −5.00	< 20	

(Reprinted by permission of the publisher and author from R. Heber, "Modifications in the Manual on Terminology and Classification in Mental Retardation," *American Journal of Mental Deficiency*, **65**, p. 500. Copyright 1961, American Association on Mental Deficiency.)

ioral descriptions anchored to the individual's own age level. Fourth, emphasis is given to borderline and mild forms of retardation. Fifth, the definition

avoids both the notion of incurability and the necessity for distinguishing between mental retardation and other problems of childhood, such as emotional disturbance and cultural deprivation, which are often associated with limitations of intellectual functioning. Mental retardation is seen as no more or less than a behavioral symptom, not necessarily stable from one time of life to another, and accompanied or caused by any of a number of genetic, physiological, emotional, and experiential factors [p. 616].

CLASSIFICATION OF ADAPTIVE BEHAVIOR

A tentative classification system of adaptive behavior that parallels the classification of measured intelligence, excluding the borderline level, has been developed by Sloan and Birch (1955) and is shown in Table 22–2. The system is presented in reference to developmental ages and degree of debility. The em-

Table 22-2. LEVELS OF ADAPTIVE BEHAVIOR

LEVEL	PRESCHOOL AGE 0–5 MATURATION AND DEVELOPMENT	SCHOOL AGE 6–21 TRAINING AND EDUCATION	ADULT 21 SOCIAL AND VOCATIONAL ADEQUACY
Mild	Can develop social and communication skills; minimal retardation in sensorimotor areas; rarely distinguished from normal until later age.	Can learn academic skills to approximately 6th grade level by late teens. Cannot learn general high school subjects. Needs special education, particularly at secondary school age levels.	Capable of social and vocational adequacy with proper education and training. Frequently needs supervision and guidance when under serious social or economic stress.
Moderate	Can talk or learn to communicate; poor social awareness; fair motor development; may profit from self-help; can be managed with moderate supervision.	Can learn functional academic skills to approximately 4th grade level by late teens if given special education.	Capable of self-maintenance in unskilled or semi-skilled occupations; needs supervision and guidance when under mild social or economic stress.
Severe	Poor motor development; speech is minimal; generally unable to profit from training in self-help; little or no communication skills.	Can talk or learn to communicate; can be trained in elemental health habits; cannot learn functional academic skills; profits from systematic habit training.	Can contribute partially to self-support under complete supervision; can develop self-protection skills to a minimal useful level in controlled environment.
Profound	Gross retardation; minimal capacity for functioning in sensorimotor areas; needs nursing care.	Some motor development present; cannot profit from training in self-help; needs total care.	Some motor and speech development; totally incapable of self-maintenance; needs complete care and supervision.

(Reprinted, with a change in notation, by permission of the publisher and authors from W. Sloan and J. W. Birch, "A Rationale for Degrees of Retardation," *American Journal of Mental Deficiency*, **60**, p. 262. Copyright 1955, American Association on Mental Deficiency.)

phasis is on sensory-motor skills, language and communication, learning, degree of self-sufficiency, and vocational potential. The assessment of multiple capacities may result in placing an individual over several cells within a column. An individual may be in Level III in terms of an intelligence test, but in Level II in terms of motor capacity. The classification of adaptive behavior still remains a difficult task (Scheerenberger, 1964).

The capacities and limitations of mentally retarded adults can be understood by reference to the guide prepared by Kahn and Giffen (1960). The guide, shown in Table 22–3, supplements the work of Sloan and Birch (1955) and can serve in planning training experiences for older retarded children. However, the capacities and limitations shown in Table 22–3 are broad guideposts; each child must be evaluated individually.

GENERAL CONSIDERATIONS

Mentally retarded children are more vulnerable to the development of maladaptive behavior than normal children in all periods of their life (Garfield,

Table 22-3. CAPACITIES AND LIMITATIONS OF MENTALLY RETARDED ADULTS

CAPACITIES	LIMITATIONS
Mild Retardation: IQ from 51 to 70 *(Adult Mental Ages of 7 to 12 Years)*	
Can perform routine factory or farm work. Can learn to read and write. Can evolve into self-supporting citizens under favorable environment.	Do not usually progress past five to six years of schooling. Often incapable of recognizing their moral and legal obligations and therefore apt to become delinquents, prostitutes, and petty thieves when not properly guided. Their physical maturity, in the absence of corresponding mental maturity, predisposes to unregulated and sometimes antisocial behavior.
Moderate to Severe Retardation: IQ from 26 to 50 *(Adult Mental Ages of 3 to 7 Years)*	
Can learn to talk. Can do simple work under supervision, such as mopping floors, rough painting, digging, and simple farm chores. If tractable and closely supervised, may possibly be self-supporting.	Usually do not understand the value of money. Usually should not be permitted to live outside of institutions or away from very close supervision of the families. May be dangerous to self or others when emotionally upset or sexually aroused.
Severe to Profound Retardation: IQ up to 25 *(Adult Mental Age of 2 Years)*	
May learn to eat food without aid. May make themselves understood by grunts or even a few simple words. May learn to dress themselves partially.	Must be institutionalized to avoid common dangers of life. Often have poor physical stamina and are subject to early demise. Usually unable to contribute constructively in any task and require constant supervision.

(Reprinted, with a change in notation, by permission of the publisher and authors from T. C. Kahn and M. B. Giffen, *Psychological Techniques in Diagnosis and Evaluation*, pp. 56–57. Copyright 1960, Pergamon Press Ltd.)

1963; Philips, 1967). They also exhibit schizophrenic reactions of childhood and have emotional disorders that are similar to those occurring in children of normal intelligence. As with normal children, there is considerable variability in the personality and behavior of individuals considered to be retarded. Most children (85%) who are mentally retarded are mildly retarded, with etiologies associated with social, cultural, psychological, or perhaps genetic factors. The remaining 15% of retarded children have moderate to severe deficits, such as microcephaly, mongolism, phenylketonuria, and cerebral agenesis, that are primarily associated with organic etiologies (Philips, 1967).

Mental retardation is not a disease (Payne, 1968); rather, it is a symptom of a wide variety of conditions which interfere with the normal development of the brain, and intellectual impairment is a functional expression of the interference. It also is important to recognize that a low IQ is not synonymous with being passive, acquiescent, and helpless. In an impressive series of experiments, Braginsky and Braginsky (1971) demonstrated that mentally retarded children have the interpersonal awareness and manipulative skills necessary to control, to some extent, their own fate. In one of the experiments, for example, the children were able to appear either "dumb" or "bright" on the Quick Test according to whichever strategy was appropriate to satisfy their personal goals. Mental retardation represents a complex field of study. Simple generalizations about cognitive processes and personality are as difficult to make in the field of mental retardation as they are in any other field of psychology.

BRAIN INJURY AND MENTAL RETARDATION

The research literature concerned with brain-injured mentally retarded children shows the following trends (Gallagher, 1960): Brain-injured mentally retarded children have difficulty in visual-motor perceptual tasks, in integrating perceptual stimuli or in shifting effectively from one stimulus to another (perseveration is evident), and in concept formation, but only when distracted from the task by outside stimuli or when they are in unstructured situations. Brain damage cannot be diagnosed reliably by use of test scatter. Finally, brain-injured mentally retarded children are not significantly poorer in their quantitative concepts than non-brain-injured mentally retarded children.

Gallagher proposed that the perceptual disturbances observed in brain-injured mentally retarded children may be due to damage in the attention mechanisms rather than to damage in the association areas necessary for perception. The incoming message is distorted, and the proper perception of the sensory impulses is prevented. Brain injury clearly affects perceptual processes, but the existing disabilities do not seem to impede the school performance of brain-injured mentally retarded children.

Strauss (1939) has noted that etiologically, there are two major groups of mentally retarded children—exogenous (or secondary) and endogenous (or familial or hereditary—primary). The *exogenous child* may (a) show evidence of prenatal, natal, or postnatal injury to the brain, either of a traumatic nature or due to an inflammatory process; (b) have neurological signs of brain lesion; and (c) have immediate family members who are not mentally retarded. The *endogenous child* may have (a) a normal developmental history; (b) an absence of neurological signs indicative of brain lesions; and (c) immediate family members who are mentally retarded. Brain-injured mentally retarded children may come from more variable sociocultural backgrounds than familial retardates (Rabin, 1967). The restricted sociocultural background of familial retardates may affect their verbal capacities more than it affects other functions measured by standard intelligence tests.

Gallagher (1957), using many different kinds of tests, intensively studied the performance of brain-injured and non-brain-injured mentally retarded children who were between the chronological ages of 6 and 14 years (IQ's from 35 to 76). The mental age score obtained from the Stanford-Binet, which is considered to be indicative of general level of mental development, was found to be more important than any specific intellectual factor or factors in accounting for performance in both groups. Gallagher concluded "that the mental age score remains the best single piece of information an educator can have about a child although it can be made more meaningful by our knowledge of secondary patterns of factors in individual children [p. 67]." Similarities between the groups were found in their quantitative ability, learning aptitude, Stanford-Binet patterns of success and failure, and perceptual ability.

Two areas produced distinctive group differences. First, the brain-injured children obtained personality ratings which were more negative in tone than those of the non-brain-injured children (e.g., more hyperactive, lacking attention, being fearful, less popular, and uninhibited). The reasons for these findings, however, were not clear. It is possible that brain-injured mentally retarded children either had difficulty in perceiving social situations correctly, or had a general lack of inhibition accompanied by impulsivity and unpredictable behavior. Second, the language development—especially the development of concepts—of the brain-injured children was below that of the non-brain-injured children. Gallagher hypothesized that when brain-injured children perform adequately on learning tasks, it may be due to their ability to learn language by listening and repeating in parrot fashion, rather than to adequate associations and conceptualizing ability.

MENTAL RETARDATION AND INTELLIGENCE TESTING

Test Results and Mental Retardation

As early as the first decade of the twentieth century, the National Education Association was concerned with the proper use of intelligence tests in the study of mentally retarded children. A committee of the association formulated a policy concerning the use of tests that is as appropriate today as it was when it was first issued:

Tests of mental deficiency are chiefly useful in the hands of the skilled experimenter. No sets of tests have been devised which will give a categorical answer as to the mental status of any individual. In nearly every instance in which they are used, they need to be interpreted [Bruner, Barnes, & Dearborn, 1909, p. 905].

The committee noted that the tests proposed by DeSanctis, and by Binet and Simon, were of considerable value as tests of general capacity. Today, the testing of intelligence is still one of the important functions in schools and in institutions for the mentally retarded (cf. Baumeister, 1967).

IQ's obtained from either the Stanford-Binet or Wechsler tests have been found to have considerable predictive power for a number of behaviors—such as those involving independent functioning, self-help and helping others, and learning from training experiences—in a large heterogeneous sample of institutionalized mentally retarded individuals (Johnson, 1970). These results suggest that social adjustment and learning efficiency are, in part, related to level of intellectual functioning in institutionalized mentally retarded individuals. Robinson and Robinson (1965) have pointed out that "mental age is in general a fairly good guide to the overall maturity of the child in social and communicative skills, modified of course by the presence of any secondary motor or perceptual handicaps [p. 403]."

Ross (1971) also concluded that mental age is an important index of the ability level of institutionalized mentally retarded children. This conclusion resulted from a study which indicated that decrements in IQ in hospitalized mentally retarded children are, for the most part, spurious, and are due primarily to increases in chronological age. Ross's results conflict with those of Silverstein (1969b), who reported that institutionalization has a negative effect on the IQ's of mentally retarded children. Consequently, mental age appears to be a more meaningful index than IQ in assessing changes in intelligence level of institutionalized mentally retarded children.

While the IQ is an important factor in arriving at recommendations for mentally retarded children, Wallin (1940) emphasized the importance of attempting educational programs, regardless of the specific IQ that is found.

An IQ should never serve as an excuse for complacency or justification for inaction. Ample opportunities should be afforded young retardates and deficients in the literary subjects, using the best remedial techniques, concrete procedures, and interest-provoking activity programs, before such instruction is abandoned and the emphasis diverted to motor training [p. 220].

If retarded children are to be helped in reaching their potentials, it is important that test scores should not be used as a basis for prohibiting a child from participating in programs which can be potentially stimulating. Studies have shown that many children whose test scores fall into the mentally retarded range develop into self-sufficient and desirable citizens as adults (e.g., Charles, 1953, 1957; Muench, 1944). Further, as Masland, Sarason, and Gladwin (1958) noted, "the criteria customarily used to define mental retardation are not adequate to predict social and occupational success or failure except at the extremes [p. 303]."

The results of a psychological evaluation usually are accepted without extensive questioning. We assume that the examiner was competent, and that pertinent factors were considered in arriving at decisions concerning the examinee. However, the results of a study by Garfield and Affleck (1960) suggest that such assumptions are not always accurate. Many problems were found with the psychological reports of 24 individuals who were in an institution for the mentally retarded and who were later released, because re-examination had shown that they were not mentally retarded. The original examinations were inadequate, personality factors were neglected, and the IQ, by itself, was too exclusively relied on to make decisions about the examinee. Their study, however, was not complete, for they failed to note whether psychological reports of children not released from the hospital had similar inadequacies, although similar problems might have been expected. Their study, too, should not be misconstrued to mean that psychological evaluations are more adequate for examinees who are not in an institution. Their suggestion that emotional and environmental factors must be considered in evaluating intelligence test performance is important; however, their data are difficult to interpret.

Children who are referred for intellectual evaluation are more likely to have lower verbal than nonverbal scores, because those with higher verbal scores are less likely to appear to be mentally retarded to lay people and to school teachers (cf. Levine & Dysinger, 1964; Witkin et al., 1966). Verbally handicapped children also are more likely to achieve a low IQ, with the concomitant prospect of being classified as mentally retarded.

IQ Constancy

The question of IQ constancy in mentally retarded individuals has been of considerable interest. Studies agree generally that mentally retarded persons tend to obtain lower scores and to show less change in IQ when retested than persons who are not mentally retarded (cf. Alper & Horne, 1959; Earhart & Warren, 1964; Poull, 1921; Rushton & Stockwin, 1963; Walker & Gross, 1970; Walton & Begg, 1957). This generalization, however, is in part dependent upon the time interval between tests and the type of tests used on each testing occasion. IQ's are likely to be more similar when the interval is short and when the same test is administered each time (cf. Walker & Gross, 1970).

Goals in Evaluating Mentally Retarded Children

The principles of test interpretation illustrated throughout the text also apply to mentally retarded children. It is important to evaluate the child's relative strengths, even though he is mentally retarded (cf. Garfield, 1959). One of the goals in evaluating a mentally retarded child is to contribute to an understanding of why he does not function socially, if that is his problem, and to determine his assets and limitations, so that remedial action can be taken (Gunzburg, 1970). Perhaps the intelligence test plays a more crucial role in the field of mental retardation than in other areas of psychodiagnostic work. Therefore, the examiner will have to be especially careful in obtaining a reliable and valid estimate of intelligence. While the IQ is only one of the factors that are evaluated in arriving at a diagnosis of mental retardation, it is a crucial one.

MENTAL RETARDATION AND THE STANFORD-BINET

One of the Stanford-Binet's principal missions since its inception has been to serve as an instrument which could be used to determine whether children should be placed in mentally retarded classes in the school. Over the years this purpose has been served remarkably well. The latest revision of the Stanford-Binet (Form L-M), like its predecessors, has been found to have substantial relationships with scholastic achievement, social maturity measures, and developmental schedules for mentally retarded children, thus indicating that Form L-M is a good predictor of learning and other facets of intelligence (Himelstein, 1968). Also, the internal consistency of Form L-M with retardates appears to be satisfactory (Silverstein, 1969c). In this section of the chapter, we survey studies and reports which have dealt with various facets of the Stanford-Binet and mental retardation.

Range of Testing with Mentally Retarded

In Chapter 9, the problem of range of testing with the Stanford-Binet was considered. Some of the investigators cited in that chapter advocated obtaining two consecutive ceiling levels instead of one ceiling level. Cruickshank and Qualtere (1950) also believed that the validity of the test results for mentally retarded children can be increased if two consecutive ceiling levels are obtained for mentally retarded children. They studied 100 mentally retarded children, and found that the two-consecutive-ceiling-level procedure resulted in 38% of the sample showing a mean increase of 3.04 months. While this increase was not significant, the investigators recommended use of the two-ceiling procedure. However, as we have seen in Chapter 9, there is not sufficient evidence available to recommend the routine use of the two-consecutive-ceiling-level procedure.

Form Equivalence

Retesting an examinee who had been administered an earlier form of the scale is another task frequently engaged in by psychologists. Budoff and Purseglove (1963) reported that the relationship between IQ's obtained on Form L and Form L-M in a sample of 70 institutionalized mentally retarded children was high ($r = .90$), suggesting that the two forms are equivalent. This result is not surprising, because a majority of the tests on Form L-M are exactly the same as they are on Form L.

Hard and Easy Stanford-Binet Tests for Mentally Retarded

Investigators have been interested in determining which Stanford-Binet tests are relatively hard or easy for mentally retarded children. In a study of the performance of 19- and 20-year-old institutionalized mentally retarded children on Form L and Form M of the 1937 Stanford-Binet (Sloan & Cutts, 1947), the hard tests were ones which appear to reflect verbal ability, memory of a verbal nature, and verbal abstraction, whereas the easy tests were ones that appear to be more concrete. Rote memory tests were at the same level of difficulty as the remaining types of tests. In another study of the Stanford-Binet (Form L) with mentally retarded children in special education classes (Cruickshank & Qualtere, 1950), the easy tests were ones which seem to depend on extended educational or life experiences accompanying increased chronological age, whereas the hard tests were ones which seem to reflect verbal reasoning, singling out significant aspects of particular situations, and the ability to make generalizations.

Mentally Retarded and Normal Children of Similar Mental Age on the Stanford-Binet

Almost from the beginning of the testing movement in the early twentieth century, psychologists have been interested in comparing the performance of mentally retarded and normal children. Jones (1919), for example, recognized that equal mental ages in mentally retarded and normal children may not reflect equal mental abilities. The mentally retarded child has lived longer, has had more varied experiences, has been in school longer, and may have had a poorer family environment. The normal child, in contrast, has a more active mind and is able to gain information more quickly. Jones then compared mentally retarded boys with superior boys, both matched on a mental age of 10 years, and found that the two groups differed on various verbal and sensory tasks.

Other early investigators, using the Goddard revision of the Binet-Simon scale, the Point-Scale examination, or the 1916 Stanford-Binet (Curtis, 1918; Doll, 1917; Elwood, 1934; Hinckley, 1915; Louden, 1933; Martinson & Strauss, 1941; McFadden, 1931; Perkins, 1932; Pressey & Cole, 1918a; Townsend, 1928; Wallin, 1929), failed to report consistent trends, because different year-levels of the scales were used and different types of populations were studied. The results, however, usually indicated that on some tests the mentally retarded children performed differently from the normal children. Some investigators suggested that the mentally retarded children performed better on tests associated with school training (Elwood, 1934) or on those which seem to depend on experience (Martinson & Strauss, 1941; Perkins, 1932), whereas normal children performed better on tests requiring a critical quality of response (Elwood, 1934), verbal reasoning ability (Martinson & Strauss, 1941), or intellectual endowment (Perkins, 1932).

1937 Forms. Studies continued to compare mentally retarded with normal children of similar mental age for the two forms of the 1937 Stanford-Binet.

Laycock and Clark (1942), using Form L, studied the performance of 40 matched pairs of 12-year-old mentally retarded and 7-year-old superior children on tests appearing at year-levels VII through XIII. The mean mental age of the sample was 9.42 years. The results showed that only four of the 36 comparisons were significant.

Kennedy-Fraser (1945), using the Scottish modification of the 1937 Stanford-Binet (Form L), compared the performance of "dull" (IQ's between 71 and 89, $N = 618$) and "bright" (IQ's between 110 and 129, $N = 422$) Scottish children. Year-levels VI through XII were studied. The tests which best discriminated the "bright" from the "dull" (in favor of the bright) were verbal tests, while the poorest discriminating tests were memory tests and visually presented tests.

Thompson and Magaret (1947) and Magaret and Thompson (1950) analyzed the Form L test performance of 441 mentally retarded children, 1326 normal children, and 197 superior children. All three groups were matched on mental age. The normal and superior children were obtained from the standardization samples of the Stanford-Binet. The mentally retarded children had more difficulty than the normal children (of equal mental age) on tests which are more heavily saturated with a common first factor. The tests that were easier for the mentally retarded children than for the normal ones did not appear to be dependent upon past experience; rather, these tests called for more practical knowledge and less abstract reasoning. The mental retardates' failures were not seen as being a manifestation of rigidity, but as being related to a general factor which might be called "mental energy" or "brightness." The mentally retarded children also failed more rote memory tests than did normal ones. Finally, similar trends were noted in comparing the superior group with the other two groups.

Achenbach (1970) noted that the results of the two studies by Magaret and Thompson were inconclusive for the following reasons:

(*a*) the evident absence of matching on sex and race, (*b*) the comparison of retarded subjects having a 12-month range in MA with those in the standardization sample having only a 2-month range at each level (Terman & Merrill, 1937), (*c*) the probable inclusion of brain-damaged and emotionally disturbed subjects in the retarded sample, and (*d*) testing by different examiners in different localities 10 or more years apart. All of these factors could lead to differences in items passed or failed independently of the group differences in chronological age (CA) and IQ [p. 489].

Form L-M. Achenbach (1970) attempted to avoid some of the methodological problems encountered in the studies of Magaret and Thompson in his study of the Stanford-Binet (Form L-M) performance of 54 matched pairs of 5-year-old nonretarded (*M* IQ = 126) and retarded children (*M* IQ = 52). The mean mental age of both groups was 6 years, 4 months. Controls were instituted for sex of subjects, geographic area, period of administration, and examiner. Children who had organic diagnoses or emotional problems were not included in either of the groups. Of the 33 tests studied in year-levels IV-6 through X, seven were found to differ significantly between the two groups. Tests significantly *easier* for the mentally retarded children than for the superior children were as follows: Picture Completion: Man (year-level V), Paper Folding: Triangle (year-level V), Copying a Square (year-level V), and Naming the Days of the Week (year-level VIII). Tests significantly *harder* for the mentally retarded children than for the superior children were the following: Differences (year-level VI), Verbal Absurdities I (year-level VIII), and Similarities and Differences (year-level VIII). Other comparisons indicated that the amount of scatter was not significantly different between the two groups and that the performance of black retardates was not significantly different from that of white retardates.

Achenbach pointed out that finding seven significant tests is not far above chance. However, three of the significant tests were also found by Thompson and Magaret (1947), namely, Paper Folding: Triangle (in favor of retardates), Copying a Square (in favor of retardates), and Similarities and Differences (in favor of normals). Magaret and Thompson (1950) also found retardates significantly higher than superiors on Paper Folding: Triangle and on Copying a Square, but did not find significant differences between the two groups on Similarities and Differences. Achenbach interpreted his findings as indicating that retardates excelled on concrete and practical tests, while nonretardates excelled on abstract tests and on tests involving general intelligence. Overall, the results suggested that "individuals differing in IQ and CA but matched for MA differ little in their performance on the Stanford-Binet, Form L-M [p. 493]." In addition, "Binet performance by individuals obtaining the same MA scores may be generally similar even if they are of different races [p. 494]."

Johnson and Blake (1960) also compared the abilities of mentally retarded and normal children of like mental age by using a variety of tasks—including measures of serial learning, inhibition, transfer, and reasoning—instead of the Stanford-Binet. They concluded from their findings, like Achenbach (1970), that it is difficult to come to any conclusion about the relative abilities of mentally retarded and normal children of similar mental age.

Brain-Injured Mentally Retarded and the Stanford-Binet

A review of studies with the Stanford-Binet that have compared the performance of brain-injured with non-brain-injured mentally retarded children indicates that the Stanford-Binet does not provide many clues for differentiating between the two groups. In an investigation of the 1916 Stanford-Binet, brain-injured and non-brain-injured institutionalized mentally retarded children were found to obtain similar mental ages (Cassel & Danenhower, 1949). In a study of the 1937 Stanford-Binet, the brain-injured mentally retarded group was significantly poorer than the non-brain-injured group only on the Copying-a-Diamond test (year-level VII). Also, scatter was not a significant factor in distinguishing the two groups (Hoakley & Frazeur, 1945). However, in another study, brain-injured mentally retarded children were found to have significantly more scatter on the 1937 Stanford-Binet than non-brain-injured children (Berko, 1955a).

In Gallagher's (1957) study, the two groups differed significantly on only two Stanford-Binet (Form L) tests. The brain-injured mentally retarded group had more failures on Maze Tracing (year-level VI), but more successes on Repeating Four Digits (year-level IV-6), than the non-brain-injured group. Amount of scatter was similar in the two groups. In another study, brain-injured mentally retarded children have been found to be significantly more successful than non-brain-injured mentally retarded children on only one of the many tests studied, namely, Memory for Stories: The Wet Fall (year-level VIII) (Rohrs & Haworth, 1962). The brain-injured mentally retarded children also had significantly more scatter than the non-brain-injured children.

The results of these five studies strongly suggest that the similarities between brain-injured and non-brain-injured mentally retarded children on the Stanford-Binet are much greater than their differences. There is a slight tendency for brain-injured mentally retarded children to have more difficulty than non-brain-injured mentally retarded children on some perceptual tasks. Brain-injured mentally retarded children also appear to have more scatter than non-brain-injured mentally retarded children, but the evidence is not conclusive. Part of the difficulty in evaluating scatter is that the studies usually used different measures of scatter. Overall, there is no single test pattern which clearly differentiates non-brain-injured mentally retarded children from other groups (cf. Sarason, 1953). Inconclusive findings also have resulted from scoring items on a pass-fail basis without taking into account test patterns, and from failing to consider the present and past learning experiences of the children. The evidence suggests that the Stanford-Binet is not sensitive to factors which differentiate brain-injured from non-brain-injured mentally retarded children (cf. Himelstein, 1968). However, qualitative observations of the child's test performance and behavior may provide useful clues (see Chapter 19).

Qualitative Analysis of Stanford-Binet Responses Given by Mentally Retarded and Other Children

Case Illustration.   The following case presents the responses given by a mentally retarded child to some Stanford-Binet tests (Tansley & Gulliford, 1960). It illustrates the usefulness of a qualitative analysis of test responses. Pat, who is an 11-year-old British mentally retarded girl, gave the following replies to questions on the Similarities: Two Things test (year-level VII). To the question, "In what way are apple and orange alike?" she replied, "Round and juicy." To the next question (coal and wood alike), she said, "Coal has got wood in it." To the third question (ship and motor car alike), she said, "Ship sails and car doesn't." To the last question (iron and silver alike), she said, "Silver shines, iron doesn't." These replies suggest that she had difficulty in conceiving relationships, and that she failed to distinguish related concepts on some continuum.

Pat's responses to the Vocabulary test words also were inadequate. Her replies to the first 12 vocabulary words were as follows: *orange* — "Round one; got pips in it"; *envelope* — "Put the letter in it"; *straw* — "Drink through it"; *puddle* — "Paddle in it," and on further questioning she said, "Lake"; *tap* — "Water comes out of it"; *gown* — "What you wear at night"; *eyelash* — "Close it down to go to sleep"; *roar* — "Lion roar"; *scorch* — "Scratch the bottom of your shoes"; *muzzle* — "Put it on the dog's nose to save him from getting away"; *lecture* — "Sit on it"; *Mars* — "Bar chocolate." Her retarded verbal ability was evident by the limited number of words she knew and by her brief and simple answers. She also was confused by words that sound like other words — eyelid for eyelash, scratch for scorch.

Strauss and Werner's Qualitative Analysis Scheme.   Strauss and Werner (1940) applied their qualitative analysis scheme (see page 260 for a description of the scheme) to the responses given by normal, mentally retarded, and delinquent children to tests appearing at the VIII-, IX-, and X-year levels of the 1916 Stanford-Binet. Normal children gave few wrong answers, few nonsensical and ambiguous answers, and a relatively high number of "don't know" answers. Delinquent children gave more wrong answers than normal children, but the same number as the retarded group. The delinquents also gave a similar number of nonsensical and ambiguous responses as the normals, and the number of their "don't know" responses was closer to the number produced by mentally retarded children than by normal children. Mentally retarded children gave more nonsensical and ambiguous answers than children in the normal and delinquent groups. The higher incidence of "don't know" responses which appeared in the normal group than in the other two groups suggested that normal children are more autocritical.

The Strauss and Werner scheme was used, in somewhat modified form, by Martinson and Strauss (1941) in studying the responses of mentally retarded and normal children having mental ages between 7 and 9 years. The tests appeared at year-levels VIII through XII of the 1916 Stanford-Binet. Normal children, in comparison to the retarded children, gave more "don't know" and more correct-superior answers, and detected similarities at an earlier point in their development.

Cruickshank (1947), also using the Strauss and Werner scheme, was interested in studying how mentally retarded and normal children differed in responding to an extremely difficult test. He selected the Ingenuity test (year-level XIV of the Stanford-Binet, Form L), which was approximately four years above the mean mental age of the children. The responses of the mentally retarded group were distributed among the nonsensical (40%), superficial (26%), inadequate (13%), "don't know" (13%), and correct-incomplete (6%) categories, while in the normal group responses were classified only in the "don't know" category (73%) or correct category (26%). Cruickshank, like Strauss and Werner (1940), concluded that mentally retarded children lack an autocritical attitude and have a need to maintain social integrity. Normal children, conversely, are more willing to admit their inability to cope with situations (cf. Cruickshank & Qualtere, 1950).

Vocabulary Scoring.   Badt (1958) applied a five-point scoring system to the Stanford-Binet (Form L) Vocabulary responses of 60 institutionalized, moderately mentally retarded children who were between the ages of 7 and 15 years. An abstraction score was arrived at by giving five points to an abstract definition, three points to a use definition, and one point to a descriptive definition. The following correlations were obtained between the abstraction score and other variables: chronological age ($r = .34$), mental age ($r = .24$), IQ ($r = .28$), and length of institutionalization ($r = -.61$). Only the correlation with mental age was not significant. Badt concluded that institutionalization appears to have a strong depressing effect on retardates' ability to define words abstractly.

MENTAL RETARDATION AND THE WISC

The WISC has proven to be a popular instrument in the assessment of mentally retarded children, although the scale, as we have seen in Chapter 11, was never designed to test severely retarded children because the lowest possible Full Scale IQ in the manual is 46. We now consider how the WISC has been used in the assessment of mentally retarded children.

Reliability and Stability

The WISC appears to be a reliable and stable instrument in evaluating mentally retarded children, as indicated by test-retest studies (Friedman, 1970; Rosen, Stallings, Floor, & Nowakiwska, 1968; Throne, Schulman, & Kaspar, 1962; Whatley & Plant, 1957) and split-half reliability coefficients (Davis, 1966). Correlations in these studies for the Full Scale IQ ranged from .68 to .97 (median correlation of .90).

Validity

Studies generally support the validity of the WISC as a predictor of learning in retardates (Baumeister & Hawkins, 1966; Kimbrell, 1960; McCulloch, Reswick, & Weissmann, 1955; Salvati, 1960; Sandercock & Butler, 1952). However, the low correlations (e.g., .16, .24, and .41) in some studies suggest that the WISC may be unsuitable for clinical predictions of how well a mentally retarded child will learn a skill.

Sex Differences

There are minimal differences in the WISC scores of mentally retarded girls and boys (Finley & Thompson, 1959; Gainer, 1965).

Item Difficulty and Discrimination

The difficulty levels of the WISC items for mentally retarded children have been found to be similar to those reported in the standardization sample (Carleton & Stacey, 1955). However, the item difficulties were not found to be distributed normally. Most of the items also were found to be significant discriminators.

WISC Subtest Patterning in Mentally Retarded

Silverstein (1968d) reviewed 10 studies which examined WISC subtest patterns of mentally retarded children. Vocabulary, Arithmetic, and Information were consistently among the most difficult subtests, whereas Object Assembly and Picture Completion were consistently among the easiest ones. The strengths of the retarded children appeared in the Performance factor (Object Assembly and Picture Completion), while weaknesses appeared in the Verbal (Vocabulary and Information) and Short-term Memory (Arithmetic) factors. The overall ranks were as follows: Information (8), Comprehension (6), Arithmetic (9), Similarities (5), Vocabulary (10), Picture Completion (2), Picture Arrangement (6), Block Design (3), Object Assembly (1), and Coding (4).

Verbal-Performance Scale Discrepancies

Mentally retarded children usually obtain significantly higher WISC Performance Scale IQ's than Verbal Scale IQ's (Alper, 1967; Baroff, 1959; Newman & Loos, 1955; Pastovic & Guthrie, 1951; Shinagawa, 1960; Sloan & Schneider, 1951; Smith, 1959; Stacey & Levin, 1950; Vanderhost, Sloan, & Bensberg, 1953; Webb, 1963; Whatley & Plant, 1957). Nonsignificant differences between the two scales, or higher Verbal than Performance Scale IQ's, also have been reported (Atchison, 1955; Sandercock & Butler, 1952; Seashore, 1951; Young & Pitts, 1951). In a related study, mentally retarded children, ages 11 to 16 years, were found to perform better on the analytical subtests (Block Design, Picture Completion, and Object Assembly) than on the verbal comprehension subtests (Vocabulary, Information, and Comprehension) (Witkin et al., 1966).

Factor Analytic Studies

Baumeister and Bartlett (1962a, 1962b) factor analyzed the WISC scores of 100 noninstitutionalized mentally retarded children between 13 and 14 years of age, 200 normal children from the WISC standardization group, 130 noninstitutionalized mentally retarded children between 11 and 15 years of age, and 714 institutionalized mentally retarded children with a mean chronological age of 12 years. The scores of the retardates were found to be factorially more complex than those of the normals. A strong general factor, a verbal factor, and a performance factor were found in all of the groups. In the retardates, a weaker but reliable fourth factor appeared, which consisted of the Arithmetic, Digit Span, Picture Arrangement, Block Design, and Comprehension subtests. This factor was interpreted as a Number, Concentration, or Stimulus Trace factor. Additional data confirmed the interpretation of the fourth factor as Stimulus Trace or Number (Baumeister, Bartlett, & Hawkins, 1963).

In the institutionalized mentally retarded group, the general and group factors were usually found to be weaker than in normal children; the subtests, too, were found to have relatively low communalities. The low reliability of the subtests in the institutionalized group, due to the presence of a great number of severely retarded children, may account for these findings (Baumeister, 1964).

Osborne and Tillman (1967) also factor analyzed the WISC scores of normal and noninstitutionalized retarded children. In the retarded group there were 264 children between the ages of 8 and 13 years, while in the normal group there were 152 children between the ages of 6 and 7 years. A factor, termed "Attentiveness," with loadings on the Digit Span, Object Assembly, Comprehension, and Coding subtests, was found in the retardates but not in the normals. "Attentiveness" appeared to be a more proper term for the factor rather than memory or numerical facility. The presence of this factor in retardates, but not in normals, was interpreted as reflecting a *deficiency* of ability in retardates. The factor analyses of both Baumeister and his co-workers and of Osborne and Tillman appear to support the stimulus trace theory of Ellis (1963), which hypothesizes that stimulus traces may not persist as long in retardates as they do in normals. Butterfield (1968), however, disagreed with the deficiency interpretation of the stimulus trace theory. In finding that mentally retarded and normal children, matched on MA, obtained similar Digit Span scores, he concluded that the stimulus trace theory reflects a developmental rather than a defect approach.

A note of caution has been expressed by Dingman and Meyers (1966) concerning Baumeister and Bartlett's findings of a Stimulus Trace factor in mentally retarded children but not in normal ones. First, the finding of a factor in the mentally retarded, but not in the normal children, should not be interpreted as a quality in mentally retarded children that is not present in normal ones. Rather, greater variability in the scores of the retarded children than of the normal children can account for the finding. Second, it is risky to identify factors exclusively from the WISC. Third, a short-term memory factor, similar to a stimulus trace factor, has been demonstrated in normal 6-year-old children (Orpet & Meyers, 1966).

Belmont, Birch, and Belmont (1967) factor analyzed the WISC scores of 71 educable mentally retarded children between 8 and 10 years old who were living in Scotland, and compared their results with those obtained by Cohen (1959), who used the standardization sample. The three factors found by Cohen were found to be present in the retarded group (Verbal, Perceptual Organization, and Freedom from Distractibility). However, the attention factor (Freedom from Distractibility) was stronger in the retarded group than in the standardization group. In addition, the verbal and perceptual factors, which were highly associated in the standardization group, were not associated in the retarded group, whereas the perceptual and attentional factors were highly associated in the retarded group but not in the standardization group. The results, which generally were similar to those of Baumeister and Bartlett (1962a, 1962b), indicated that the factorial organization of intellectual ability in educable mentally retarded children is different from that found in normal children.

The factor analytic studies suggest that mentally retarded children may have a pattern of scores that is factorially more complex (or different) than that of children who are not mentally retarded. However, there is some disagreement concerning the interpretation of the WISC factors that are found in mentally retarded groups. Another problem in evaluating the results of factor analytic studies, such as those covered in this and other parts of the text, is that since so much depends upon the values placed in the diagonal cells and upon the number of factors extracted, conclusions drawn from comparisons of one factor analysis with another have to be tempered by the possibility that differences arise from method rather than from the substance of the variables being investigated.

Brain-Injured Mentally Retarded and the WISC

Studies investigating the performance of brain-injured and non-brain-injured mentally retarded children on the WISC have attempted to determine how patterns of scores and overall scores differ between the two groups. The results indicate that characteristic WISC patterns which can reliably distinguish the two groups have not been found (Alper, 1960; Beck & Lam, 1955; Birch, Belmont, Belmont, & Taft, 1967; Newman & Loos, 1955; Spreen & Anderson, 1966). When other kinds of differences are found, it is likely that the brain-injured children obtain lower Full Scale IQ's than non-brain-injured children. Brain damage may be operative in all cases of severe mental retardation, thus hampering the search for differential patterns. The studies suggest that the WISC does not provide reliable patterns that can distinguish etiological factors in mental retardation. However, these findings do not rule out the need to observe carefully the child's performance for relevant behavioral indices, such as are described in Chapter 19.

One study, however, has found some interesting trends in distinguishing between a brain-injured and a brain-deficit group of 10-year-old children (Burns, 1960). In one group, the children were normal until the age of 3 years and then had sustained central nervous system damage. In the other group, children had brain tissue underdevelopment or maldevelopment from birth. The main findings were that in the tissue-underdeveloped group, Block Design scores were higher than Object Assembly scores, whereas in the tissue-injury group, Object Assembly scores were higher than Block Design scores. The tissue-underdeveloped group had lower scores than the tissue-injury group on all of the WISC subtests. Thus, an injury to the brain sustained by an older child who is mentally retarded may interfere with Block Design performance to a greater extent than with Object Assembly performance.

Testing of Limits

Altering the wording of some questions on the Information, Comprehension, and Arithmetic subtests may facilitate the evaluation of educable mental retardates (Volle, 1957). The alteration of the question is in a direction of making it more concrete. The procedure should be used when the examinee shows by his response that he is confused by the question or that he has misunderstood the question. This testing-of-limits procedure, like other similar procedures, should be used *after* the entire examination has been completed. The IQ obtained by this procedure is not a standardized one. Consequently, it may confuse the reader if it is reported. The results of the testing-of-limits procedure should be used to guide the examiner in making recommendations and in his overall assessment of the examinee's ability. The alterations in wording are shown in Table 22–4.

Qualitative Analysis of WISC Vocabulary Subtest

Stacey and Portnoy (1950) used a three-level system to classify responses to the WISC Vocabulary subtest. The levels were concrete or descriptive, functional or usage, and categorical or conceptual. The 10-year-old borderline mentally retarded children (M IQ = 70) who were studied gave significantly more concrete responses than the 12-year-old mentally retarded children (M IQ = 58), while the mentally retarded children gave significantly more functional responses than the borderline retarded children. However, the two groups did not differ significantly in giving categorical responses. The investigators wondered whether the results were restricted to their sample, or whether the three-level classification method was inadequate, because the borderline retarded children gave more concrete responses than the retarded children, a result which was contrary to their hypothesis.

Table 22-4. Testing-of-Limits Procedures on Three WISC Subtests

Item	Procedure
Information Subtest	
3. "How many legs does a dog have?"	Some younger mental retardates, particularly those with brain injury, answer this by saying "Two in front, two in back." If the examiner asks "So, how many does that make?," the correct answer is often given.
4. "From what animal do we get milk?"	Younger mental retardates occasionally miss the "animal" image, and answer "From the store." If the child answers thus, the examiner then asks "Yes, but where does the store get it?"
5. "What must you do to make water boil?"	One occasionally gets the response "Put it in the teakettle." The examiner must check to determine if it is implied that the teakettle is on the stove; i.e., "And where is the teakettle?"
6. "In what kind of a store do we buy sugar?"	In the event of no response to this question, the examiner might ask "Where do we get sugar?," and following the frequent answer "In the store," ask again "Yes, but what *kind* of store?"
10. "How many things make a dozen?"	The answer "Eggs" is common here. The examiner should then ask "How many eggs make a dozen?"
11. "What are the four seasons of the year?"	If confusion is apparent, the examiner should then repeat the question in the form of "Every year has just four seasons. What are they?"
12. "What is the color of rubies?"	Some mental retardates answer this in terms of their favorite color, "Red." In order to determine whether the child really knows the color of rubies, the examiner should ask "What are rubies?"
Comprehension Subtest	
3. "What would you do if you were sent to buy a loaf of bread and the grocer said he did not have any more?"	The wording and length of this question, in addition to the word "grocer," seems to cause confusion to some mental retardates. A suggested question is "What would you do if you were sent to the store to buy a loaf of bread, and the man said he didn't have any more?"
4. "What is the thing to do if a fellow (girl) much smaller than yourself starts to fight with you?"	This is a particularly difficult question for children who have difficulty with concepts such as "larger-smaller," etc. It is suggested that the examiner gesture with his hand in order to portray the height of a youngster "smaller than" the testee. In addition, the question as stated in the manual does not clearly indicate that the smaller child *instigates* the fight. A suggested wording for the question is "What is the thing to do if a fellow (girl) much smaller than yourself (gesture) starts to pick a fight with you?"

Table 22-4. TESTING-OF-LIMITS PROCEDURES ON THREE WISC SUBTESTS
(Continued)

ITEM	PROCEDURE
Comprehension Subtest	
5. "What should you do if you see a train approaching a broken track?"	The word "approaching" here is too much for many of the younger mental retardates. In order to determine if the child actually would respond appropriately (at least verbally), it is often necessary to ask "What should you do if you see a train coming to a broken track?"
7. "Why are criminals locked up?"	A frequent response here is "What does that mean (criminals)?" The examiner may clarify by saying "You know—people they lock up in jail."
8. "Why should women and children be saved first in a shipwreck?"	Responses to this question such as "Because they can't swim" suggest to the examiner that the testee may have overlooked the essential element of the concept—the word "first." The question may be more meaningfully phrased by asking "In a shipwreck, why should the women and children be saved before the men?"
10. "Why is it generally better to give money to an organized charity than to a street beggar?"	In addition to being an awkwardly worded concept, the phrases "organized charity" and "street beggar" add the finishing touch to make this one of the most difficult of all the Comprehension questions for mental retardates. Still, they may be able to grasp the essential concept sought if the question is rephrased and illustrated. "Why is it generally better to give money to charity, like the Red Cross, than to give it to a beggar on the street?"
11. "Why should most government positions be filled through examinations?"	This question is almost incomprehensible to most mental retardates. They do not understand what is meant by "government positions," and neither do they understand the use of the word "filled." Yet, they may rather easily understand "Why should people who want a government job have to take an examination for it?"
12. "Why is cotton fiber used in making cloth?"	Many retardates know what cotton is, but not "cotton fiber." Thus, "Why is cotton used in making cloth?"
Arithmetic Subtest	
8. "At 7¢ each, what will 3 cigars cost?"	Frequent responses to this question seem to suggest generalized confusion, such as "What do you mean?" Re-phrasing the question "If one cigar costs 7¢, how much would 3 of them cost?," often produces the correct answer.

Table 22-4. TESTING-OF-LIMITS PROCEDURES ON THREE WISC SUBTESTS
(Continued)

ITEM	PROCEDURE
Arithmetic Subtest	
10. "Four boys had 72 pennies. They divided them equally among themselves. How many pennies did each boy receive?"	The question as presented from the manual is very difficult for mental retardates, even though they may be able to handle a short division "story problem." The usual source of confusion here, is that the testee does not realize the boys have the pennies *in common*. This is circumvented by suggesting a common *container* for the money. Thus, "Four boys had 72 pennies in a hat (box, etc.). They divided them equally among themselves. How many pennies did each boy get?"
11. "A workman earned $36; he was paid $4 a day. How many days did he work?"	The order of presentation of the numerical values, plus the phrasing of the question here, causes confusion. Re-phrased as follows, many of the older retardates may be able to respond correctly. "If a man gets paid $4 a day and ends up making $36, how many days did he work?"

(Reprinted, with a change in notation, by permission of the publisher and author from F. O. Volle, "A Proposal for 'Testing the Limits' with Mental Defectives for Purposes of Subtest Analysis of the WISC Verbal Scale," *Journal of Clinical Psychology,* **13**, pp. 65–66. Copyright 1957, Clinical Psychology Publishing Co., Inc.).

DIFFERENTIAL DIAGNOSIS

We have seen in the sections on differential diagnosis in Chapters 20 and 21 that schizophrenic children, brain-injured children, and mentally retarded children may display similar forms of behavior. In addition, it is sometimes difficult to differentiate mentally retarded children from emotionally disturbed children, as is shown in Chapter 23. The criteria developed by Heber (1961), which are described in the beginning part of this chapter, as well as a careful study of the material in Chapters 19 through 23 should assist in the diagnostic process.

SUMMARY

A working definition of mental retardation in current use is as follows: "Mental retardation refers to subaverage general intellectual functioning which originates during the developmental period and is associated with impairment in adaptive behavior." This definition implies that the diagnosis is only a description of present behavior, acknowledges the contribution of intelligence tests, ties diagnosis to the developmental process, emphasizes milder forms of retardation, and avoids problems of differential diagnosis. Adaptive behavior, however, still presents an assessment problem. Most (85%) mentally retarded children are mildly retarded, having nonorganic etiologies. The remaining 15% have moderate to severe deficits, with organic etiologies.

Brain-injured mentally retarded children have many difficulties that are associated with brain injury in general. Gallagher's study suggested that brain-injured mentally retarded children have more disturbed personalities and more difficulty with language development than mentally retarded children who are not brain-injured.

IQ's obtained from individually administered intelligence tests have considerable predictive power for a number of behaviors in institutionalized mentally retarded children. Mental age may prove to be a more meaningful index of intelligence than IQ in the assessment of institutionalized mentally retarded children.

Test scores should not be used to deprive mentally retarded children of meaningful educational programs. Prediction of social and occupational success is difficult. Diagnostic decisions, too, should not be based on invalid test results.

Mentally retarded persons tend to show less change in IQ when retested than persons who are not mentally retarded.

The principles of assessment must be carefully applied in cases in which mental retardation is under consideration, because intelligence test results play a very important role in establishing a diagnosis of mental retardation. The Stanford-Binet continues to be an excellent instrument for the assessment of mental retardation. Studies which have investigated hard and easy tests on the Stanford-Binet for mentally retarded children have reported that the harder tests seem to require verbal ability (e.g., reasoning and generalization) to a greater extent than the easier ones.

Comparing the Stanford-Binet performance of mentally retarded and normal children of similar mental age has been of interest to psychologists almost from the beginning of the testing movement. Reports using the 1916 form failed to find consistent trends. Studies using the 1937 forms reported that verbal tests best discriminated bright from dull children; or that tests easier for normal children than for mentally retarded ones were those more heavily saturated with a common first factor, whereas tests easier for mentally retarded children than for normal ones called for more practical knowledge and less abstract reasoning. Using Form L-M and a more stringent methodological design, Achenbach reported that few differences existed between mentally retarded and normal children of similar mental age.

On the Stanford-Binet, brain-injured mentally retarded children, at times, have been reported to display more scatter than non-brain-injured mentally retarded children. Generally, the similarities between brain-injured and non-brain-injured mentally retarded children on the Stanford-Binet are greater than their differences. The Strauss and Werner qualitative scheme for evaluating responses has been applied to groups of mentally retarded and normal children. Normal children have been found to give more "don't know" responses than mentally retarded children. These results have been interpreted to indicate that mentally retarded children lack an autocritical attitude and have a need to maintain social integrity.

The WISC is often used in the assessment of mentally retarded children; however, it was never designed to test severely retarded children. Studies have supported the reliability, stability, and validity of the WISC in evaluating mentally retarded children. Vocabulary, Arithmetic, and Information have been found to be more difficult than Object Assembly and Picture Completion for mentally retarded children. Mentally retarded children usually obtain higher Performance than Verbal Scale IQ's. Factor analytic studies suggest that the factorial organization of mentally retarded children on the WISC is different from that of normal children. The major difference appears to be the addition of a Stimulus Trace factor in mentally retarded children that is usually not found in normal ones.

WISC patterns that can reliably distinguish brain-injured mentally retarded from non-brain-injured mentally retarded children have not been found.

An interesting testing-of-limits procedure for evaluating mentally retarded children on three WISC subtests, proposed by Volle, is described in the chapter.

CHAPTER 23

INTELLIGENCE AND EMOTIONAL DISTURBANCE, LEARNING DISABILITY, AND PHYSICAL DISABILITY

The present chapter considers a variety of problems associated with children, including emotional disturbance, learning disabilities, and physical disease or disability. These broad categories obviously represent heterogeneous groupings of children. In most cases, children in these categories have behavioral symptoms that are less severe than those described in Chapters 20 and 21. In the section of the chapter on medical problems, there is no specific discussion of the Stanford-Binet or WISC, with the exception of material concerning blind children and deaf children; the presentation proposes simply to survey how level of intelligence is related to or affected by physical disease or disability.

EMOTIONALLY DISTURBED

The term "emotionally disturbed children" (or "emotionally handicapped children") covers a heterogeneous group of conditions (Bower, 1969; Kanner, 1962). Emotionally disturbed children are those who demonstrate any one or more of the following characteristics to a marked extent and over a period of time: an inability to learn, unsatisfactory interpersonal relationships, inappropriate behavior, unhappiness, and repetitive illness (Bower, 1969). The two approaches that are described below—the classification of behavior problems in children by Quay (1972) and the list proposed by Weisskopf (1951) to account for factors that may affect intellectual functioning—are only two among a number of approaches that have been used to classify or to evaluate such problems.

A multivariate statistical approach to the classification of behavior disorders in children indicates that the vast majority of deviant behaviors of children and adults can be subsumed under four headings: conduct disorder, personality disorder, immaturity, and socialized delinquency (Quay, 1972). Table 23–1 presents a description of each type, selected behavior traits, and life history characteristics. The patterns are homogeneous, independent, persistent over time, and reliably judged. Basic psychological processes and social behav-

Table 23-1. Classification of Behavior Disorders in Children

Type	Description	Selected behavior traits	Life history characteristics
Conduct disorder	Pattern involving aggressive behavior, both verbal and physical, associated with poor interpersonal relationships	Disobedience, disruptiveness, fighting, destructiveness, temper tantrums, irresponsibility, impertinent, jealous, shows signs of anger, acts bossy, profanity, attention seeking, boisterous	Assaultive, defies authority, inadequate guilt feelings, irritable, quarrelsome
Personality disorder	Pattern involving withdrawal, with general and specific fears	Feelings of inferiority, self-consciousness, social withdrawal, shyness, anxiety, crying, hypersensitive, seldom smiles, chews fingernails, depression, chronic sadness	Seclusive, shy, sensitive, worries, timid, has anxiety over own behavior
Immaturity	Pattern of behaviors inappropriate to the chronological age of the child and society's expectations of him	Preoccupation, short attention span, clumsiness, passivity, daydreaming, sluggish, drowsiness, prefers younger playmates, masturbation, giggles, easily flustered, chews objects, picked on by others, plays with toys in class	Habitually truant from home, unable to cope with a complex world, incompetent, immature, not accepted by delinquent subgroup, engages in furtive stealing
Socialized delinquency	Pattern of behavior in response to environmental circumstances — reinforcement by peers and modeling of behavior of adults and peers	(This category was left blank in the original table.)	Has bad companions, engages in gang activities, engages in cooperative stealing, habitually truant from school, accepted by delinquent subgroups, stays out late at nights, strong allegiance to selected peers

(Reprinted, with a change in notation, by permission of the publisher and author from H. C. Quay, "Patterns of Aggression, Withdrawal, and Immaturity," in H. C. Quay and J. S. Werry (Eds.), *Psychopathological Disorders of Childhood,* pp. 10, 12, 14–15. Copyright © 1972, John Wiley & Sons, Inc.)

ior differ among the patterns. Boys usually score higher on the conduct problem dimension than girls, whereas girls score higher than boys on the personality disorder dimension. Most deviant children differ from their normal peers in the number, and not the kind, of deviant behaviors.

In a study of the prevalence of behavior symptoms in children between the ages of 5 and 8 years, boys were found to have a higher prevalence of acting out or disruptive symptoms, while girls showed a slight excess of neurotic-type symptoms (Werry & Quay, 1971). Boys also had a higher number of symptoms per child than girls. The results suggested that in our society boys have a higher rate of disorder and are more "at risk" than girls.

There are many different kinds of emotional factors that may interfere with the intellectual functioning of children, some of which are described below (Weisskopf, 1951). The list reflects sources of conflict that should be considered when a child appears to be emotionally disturbed. However, the extent to which the factors affect either the overall level of intellectual functioning or specific areas of functioning is not known. The factors include (*a*) lack of parental reward, (*b*) desire to punish the parents, (*c*) desire for self-punishment, (*d*) desire for masochistic gratification, (*e*) desire to maintain an infantile level of gratification, (*f*) displacement of attitudes toward oral and anal impulses upon intellectual processes, (*g*) displacement of inhibitions from specific, threatening aspects of cognition to intellectual activity in general, (*h*) inhibitions caused by failure, (*i*) inhibitions caused by miscellaneous other threats, (*j*) desire to possess "a magic cap of invisibility," (*k*) desire to avoid self-evaluation, and (*l*) desire to be the recipient of love rather than of envy and aggression.

Emotional Disturbance and Level of Intelligence

Attempts have been made to determine the effects of emotional disturbance on intelligence and the extent to which specific behavioral problems are associated with level of intelligence. An early study by Wile and Davis (1938) is of interest, for it attempted to determine whether different types of behavioral problems are associated with bright and dull boys having the same mental age. In the sample of 250 children with a mental age of 10 years, approximately one-half were bright (chronological ages of 7 to 9 years) and the other half dull (chronological ages of 11 to 15 years). The younger age groups were found to have more problems involving tics, enuresis, and physical illness than the older groups. In contrast, the older groups had more problems involving nail biting, stealing, withdrawn behavior, fantasies, intersibling conflict, and unhappiness in school than the younger groups.

Wolf (1965a, 1965b) compared the performance of emotionally disturbed children (diagnosis of neurosis or personality disorder), who were attending a child guidance clinic and who were from the kindergarten, second, and fourth grades, with the performance of their normal siblings. The two groups did not differ significantly either on level of intelligence or on school grades. However, the emotionally disturbed group received lower "effort" grades than the normal group. Granick (1955) also reported that a group of 10-year-old children with relatively mild emotional instability did not differ significantly from a control group in their Stanford-Binet (Form L) scores. However, significantly lower WISC IQ's were found by Woody (1968) for a group of behavioral problem children who were between 8 and 13 years of age than for a group of well behaved children of equivalent age (IQ's of 98 and 110, respectively). Rutter (1964), from his investigation of neurotic children, also concluded that intellectual disturbance was not a major factor of importance in the etiology of childhood behavioral or neurotic disorders.

Children with school phobia usually have above-average intelligence and few academic achievement problems, according to Sarason, Davidson, Lighthall, Waite, and Ruebush (1960). These investigators also observed that there is some tentative evidence "that brighter children have more fears and that they tend to fear actual dangers in their environments whereas duller children tend to have more fears of stimuli with which they could not possibly have had any personal experience [p. 67]."

Manifest Anxiety and Intelligence

Manifest anxiety can be defined as a generalized and diffuse fear response to many aspects of the environment. Its relationship with intelligence has been studied in a number of investigations using the Children's Manifest Anxiety Scale (Castaneda, McCandless, & Palermo, 1956) as the primary tool for measurement. Studies employing group tests of intelligence usually have reported low but significant negative correlations between manifest anxiety and intelligence in school-age children (Feldhusen & Klausmeier, 1962; Hafner & Kaplan, 1959; McCandless & Castaneda, 1956). Sometimes this relationship has been found to be more pronounced in girls than in boys (McCandless & Castaneda) and in low IQ groups than in normal and high IQ groups (Feldhusen & Klausmeier). Nonsignificant findings also have been reported by Malpass, Mark, and Palermo (1960) with normal and retarded children, and by Wirt and Broen (1956) with normal children. However, the nonsignificant findings reported by Wirt and Broen may have been attributable to the fact that the manifest anxiety scores were correlated with IQ's obtained from four to six years before the anxiety scores were collected (Hafner & Kaplan).

Test Anxiety and Intelligence

The evidence generally indicates that test anxiety has some type of interfering effect upon intellectual performance (Sarason et al., 1960). Possibly, the negative correlations that have been found between test anxiety and intelligence are attributable to the fact that "the IQ score, obtained as it is in a test situation, already reflects the interfering effects of anxiety [Sarason, Davidson, Lighthall, & Waite, 1958, p. 112]." Rabin (1967), however, has suggested that the relationship between test anxiety and intelligence is difficult to evaluate because it is possible that "the less intelligent, to begin with, are more anxious in testing situations that are 'designed' to reveal their inadequacies [p. 441]." Test anxiety has been found to be higher in retarded children than in normal children (Knights, 1963). Correlations between test anxiety and either intelligence or achievement test scores are fairly low in primary grades, but increase with grade level (Hill & Sarason, 1966; Sarason, Hill, & Zimbardo, 1964). Studies usually, but not always, have reported small to moderate negative relationships between measures of anxiety and scores on conventional intelligence tests (Ruebush, 1963).

Performance on Group vs. Individual Tests

The difference between scores obtained by emotionally disturbed children on group intelligence tests and those obtained on individual intelligence tests is also of interest from methodological and validity standpoints. Kessler (1966) suggested that children with *obsessional characteristics* may do better in school work and on group intelligence tests than on the Stanford-Binet (and perhaps other individually administered intelligence tests). Her reasoning was as follows:

The direct person-to-person situation reactivates their tendencies to resist authority. Rather than give answers, they quibble, refuse to accept the obvious and hunt for hidden or farfetched interpretations of the questions, or become immersed in the concrete meanings of words or in other irrelevant aspects of the test material [p. 79].

While Kessler's description of obsessive children is helpful, her observations concerning the Stanford-Binet, group intelligence test scores, and school grades must remain as interesting hypotheses until research findings are forthcoming.

In contrast to Kessler's views, the findings of Bower (1969) and of Willis (1970) appear to point to an opposite conclusion; it should be understood, however, that Kessler was addressing herself only to the obsessive form of emotional disturbance in children. Bower studied the intelligence test scores of emotionally disturbed children and children who were not emotionally disturbed; the sample consisted of 5500 children in 75 school districts. The emotionally disturbed group (162 boys and 45 girls) obtained significantly lower scores (*M* IQ = 93) on a group intelligence test than the normal group (*M* IQ = 103). However, the two groups did not differ significantly on the scores they obtained on individually administered intelligence tests.

In Willis's (1970) study, emotionally disturbed children between 8 and 15 years of age were found to obtain a mean IQ that was 15 points higher on the WISC Verbal Scale (*M* IQ = 108) than on the verbal section of the Lorge-Thorndike Intelligence Test (*M* IQ = 93), which is a group administered test. One child obtained a WISC IQ that was 37 points higher than his IQ on the Lorge-Thorndike. Willis suggested that the structure of the individual-test situation, in comparison with the group-test situation, may facilitate the performance of emotionally disturbed children. The results of the Bower and Willis studies suggest that IQ's obtained from group intelligence tests should be interpreted cautiously when the child is emotionally disturbed. Further research would be helpful in determining whether group or individual intelligence tests provide more valid IQ's for emotionally disturbed children.

Delinquency and Intelligence

Delinquent populations in the United States and in Great Britain obtain IQ's that are about eight points lower than those obtained in the general population (Woodward, 1955). To account for such results, Woodward suggested that associated with delinquency are *cultural* factors which adversely affect test scores. She concluded that low intelligence plays a negligible role in delinquency. Merrill's (1947) conclusions generally agree with Woodward's. Merrill also pointed out that (*a*) the rate of mental retardation is higher among delinquents who get caught than among unselected school children; (*b*) institutionalized delinquents have lower IQ's than normal school children; (*c*) delinquents have superior as well as retarded intelligence; and (*d*) intelligence, as measured by the IQ, has little relationship to choice or persistence of a criminal career. In one of the earliest studies using the 1916 Stanford-Binet to study delinquency, mental age was not found to be a factor that differentiated delinquents from nondelinquents (Mateer, 1924).

Comment on Level of Intelligence in Emotionally Disturbed Children

The studies reviewed lead to the conclusion that nonpsychotic conditions do not seriously affect the overall level of intellectual performance, although in the case of delinquency, IQ's may often be found to be lower than those obtained in the general population. Treatment of emotionally disturbed children does not appear to change their IQ's (Hiler & Nesvig, 1961); rate of improvement, too, has not been found to be related to level of intelligence of emotionally disturbed children (Petrie, 1962). The latter finding was based on a study of 7- to 13-year-old children with average intellectual ability who were in a residential treatment center. The children had been in treatment for at least a 12-month period.

General Diagnostic Indicators of Emotional Disturbance During Testing

Attitudes displayed during the examination that are suggestive of emotional disturbance include irritability and suspiciousness, restlessness, lack of spontaneity, variable mood, apathy, regarding the test as "kid stuff," euphoria, and dysphoria. Language difficulties suggestive of emotional disturbance (or of a character disorder) include speech difficulty, rambling, blocking, circumstantiality, clang associations, circumlocution, confabulation, over-elaboration, and self-reference. It is important to recognize that emotional disturbance cannot be diagnosed from an intelligence test alone.

On intelligence tests, children with a *compulsive neurosis* may pass some tests requiring meticulosity and fail other tests because they are either more meticulous than the test requires or too inflexible in their thinking (Fromm, Hartman, & Marschak, 1957). Performance on memory tasks may be enhanced by a *pedantic urge to accuracy* (Cronbach, 1949). Tasks requiring insight and imagination may be failed by children who are *inhibited and who have a fear of being incorrect* (Cronbach, 1949). Failure to answer a question within an allotted period of time may be due to limited intelligence, shyness and timidity, or deliberate intention to be sure, though slow (Burt, 1914). *Dependent or submissive children* may give ready and assured responses to routine materials, but anxious, hesitant, and tentative responses to questions that require judgment and evaluation (Freeman, 1962).

Indications of obsessive tendencies include the following: (*a*) four or five explanations of courses of action in reply to the Comprehension test questions of the Stanford-Binet and Wechsler scales; (*b*) three, four, or more likenesses given to the Similarities questions of the Stanford-Binet and Wechsler scales; (*c*) elaborate and quibbling definitions of Vocabulary words of the Stanford-Binet and Wechsler scales; and (*d*) overdetailed and doubt-laden responses (Freeman, 1962).

Manifestations of an anxiety state include restlessness, apprehensiveness, impaired attention and concentration, and bodily expressions (e.g., tics, nail-biting, fidgeting, and coughing). Indications of an anxiety state in the test situation include difficulty in finding words; impulsively blurting out unfinished, unchecked, or inappropriate replies; and fumbling about for adequate formulations (Freeman, 1962).

Emotional Disturbance, Delinquency, and the Stanford-Binet

Some individual tests on the Stanford-Binet may reveal particular behavioral reactions or personality patterns more readily than other tests. However, no systematic patterns have been found that are indicative of either emotional disturbance or juvenile delinquency. The clinical interpretations cited in the following paragraphs must be viewed cautiously. They are interesting and valuable observations, but they must remain as tentative, unproven formulations until research evidence can sustain them.

On the Obeying Simple Commands test (year-level II-6), *negativism* may be elicited to a greater extent than on other tests. The presence of repetition compulsion, perseveration, or stimulus boundness in children with a *compulsive neurosis* may cause them to fail the Paper Cutting test (year-level IX) (and perhaps other similar tests). These defenses may lead to blocking, overwhelming anxiety, unrealistic wild flights of fantasy, or compulsive meticulosity, reactions which can impede performance (Fromm, 1960). *Overmeticulous, neurotic children* may be absorbed in and anxious about details on reasoning tests (e.g., Reasoning I at year-level XIV, Ingenuity I at year-level XIV). They may become concerned about the burglary itself or about the danger of spilling water, but still may be able to get to the nucleus of the problem and proceed correctly (Taylor, 1961). Children with *castration anxiety* may fail or exhibit anxiety on the Mutilated Pictures test at year-level VI or on the Picture Completion: Man test at year-level V (Fromm et al., 1957).

Aggressive, practical children with a "know-how" for solving problems may have an advantage over *passive, contemplative children* on the Ingenuity tests found at year-levels XIV and above (Taylor, 1961). Some *able but neurotic children* may have more success with Digits Backward than with Digits Forward, because Digits Backward is more difficult and demands more active effort and attention than Digits Forward; consequently, when he performs in this way, the neurotic child may be able to lessen his fears about his ability to do well (Taylor, 1961). Children who are *dependent on authority and precise tangible accomplishments* may have success on digits and on other precisely defined tasks, but fail tests that require insight, while the opposite pattern suggests that "anxiety may have stimulated a concentrated effort to understand and deal with social relations at the expense of routine learning [Murphy, 1948, p. 17]."

The following pattern of failures and successes on tests at year-levels IV through VI may suggest *sexual inhibition: failing* tests which deal directly or indirectly with sex differences (Opposite Analogies at year-level IV; Pictorial Similarities and Differences at year-level IV-6; Picture Completion: Man at year-level V; Mutilated Pictures at year-level VI), while *passing* other tests of equal difficulty. The sexual inhibition is reflected by the child's denying that there are differences or missing parts (Kessler, 1966).

Research studies that have focused on specific Stanford-Binet tests generally have not reported significant differences between emotionally disturbed and normal children. Dunsdon (1953) developed a scoring system based upon the findings of Myers and Gifford (1943) to evaluate the Stanford-Binet (Form L) performance of a sample of maladjusted ($N = 1297$) and nonmaladjusted ($N = 658$) children who were between 7 and 14 years of age. (Myers and Gifford had found a pattern of success and failures that characterized the performance of a group of schizophrenic adults.) The scoring system, for the most part, as well as scatter analysis, failed to differentiate the two groups. Thus, the attempt to apply findings from an adult population to a population of children was not successful.

Wile and Davis (1941) were interested in determining whether emotionally disturbed children have a characteristic pattern of failure on the 1916 Stanford-Binet. They selected from the files of a mental health clinic a sample of 100 reports for children between the ages of 5 and 11 years who had obtained IQ's ranging from 80 to 130. Most of the sample had mental ages between 7 and 9 years. In this mental age range, the two most frequently failed tests were Copying a Diamond (86%) and Repeating Three Digits Reversed (72%). The overall pattern of failures in the entire sample suggested to Wile and Davis that the children's adjustment was impeded by deficient visual memory and deficient visual auditory association.

Pignatelli (1943) studied the performance of 303 problem children (children having a variety of adjustment and learning difficulties) and 303 nonproblem children, matched for CA, MA, and IQ, on year-levels VII, VIII, and IX of the 1916 Stanford-Binet. Tests were classified into one of the nine categories developed by Pignatelli. No significant differences were found between the two groups in their pattern of successes and failures. Consequently, she concluded that the mental functioning of the two groups appears to be the same.

Emotional Disturbance and the WISC

The WISC appears to be a reliable and stable instrument in evaluating emotionally disturbed children (Tigay & Kempler, 1971; Turner, Mathews, & Rachman, 1967). The attempts that have been made to determine whether sub-test scores and scales reveal any characteristic patterns that can differentiate emotionally disturbed children from other groups of children have not been successful. The findings indicate generally that no systematic pattern appears that can distinguish children with generalized emotional disturbance, or specific forms of emotional disturbance, from normal children or from children with other forms of psychopathology (McHugh, 1963; Petrie, 1962; Schoonover & Hertel, 1970; Woody, 1967). However, greater variability of scores may be found in emotionally disturbed children than in normal children (Maxwell, 1960). On the Digit Span subtest, clinical experience indicates that some emotionally disturbed children may have more success with Digits Backward than with Digits Forward (Taylor, 1961). (See previous section on the Stanford-Binet for related material concerning the Digit Span subtest.) On the Block Design subtest, emotionally disturbed children may show rigidity and demonstrate erratic and impulsive decisions. However, their distortions are less gross and their deviations less persistent than those observed in brain-injured children (Taylor, 1961).

A study by Ravenette and Kahn (1962) is of interest because it reported that the extensiveness of the Verbal-Performance discrepancy in emotionally disturbed children may be related to the age of the children. The sample consisted of 128 British working-class children who had been referred to a child guidance clinic. No significant differences between the Verbal and Performance Scales were found in the 7½- and 10½-year-old groups. However, in the 13½-year-old group, boys (but not girls) had a significantly lower Verbal than Performance Scale IQ (90 vs. 102). These results suggest that in a working-class population, verbal ability lags behind nonverbal ability after the age of 12 years, especially in the case of boys. It would be of interest to learn whether similar findings appear in different socioeconomic groups and in an American sample.

The relationships among WISC scores and social, child-parent, and sibling rivalry variables in a sample of 292 British children, the majority of whom had behavior disorders, generally were found to be limited (Maxwell, 1961a). Children who were having difficulty in adjusting to their foster homes were found to have a significantly higher Performance Scale IQ than Verbal Scale IQ, whereas a control group of children who were placed temporarily in a foster home did not manifest a significant discrepancy between the two scales (Williams, 1961).

Studies also have compared the Children's Manifest Anxiety Scale with the WISC. Significant negative correlations between anxiety scores and WISC IQ's have been reported in samples of normal children (Carrier, Orton, & Malpass, 1962) and institutionalized mentally retarded children (Reger, 1966). However, Rowley and Stone (1963) did not find significant correlations between manifest anxiety scores and the WISC (10 subtests and the three scales) in a sample of children who had been referred for child psychiatric services. Hafner, Pollie, and Wapner (1960) also found that in a sample of normal children, only two WISC subtests—Block Design and Coding—were significantly negatively correlated with manifest anxiety scores. The studies with the WISC and Children's Manifest Anxiety Scale indicate that for some samples of children, but not for all, there is a negative relationship between manifest anxiety and WISC scores.

The following interesting case illustrates how an examiner interpreted the performance of an obese 11-year-old child on the WISC.

Betsy made a sour face when the test was introduced and was resistant throughout. "That's too hard!" she would complain, or "How should I know!" With praise and encouragement, she often succeeded even when she had initially rejected a task. Her total IQ was 113, with a Verbal IQ of 115 and a Performance IQ of 110. She achieved scale scores of 12 on Similarities, Vocabulary, and Block Design, indicating that her reasoning and verbalization were more than adequate. Her top score of 16 on the Picture Arrangement showed her acute perception of the social scene. In contrast, several of her responses to the Comprehension subtest were self-centered. She sputtered over the Arithmetic questions, asking for pencil and paper and to have the questions repeated, then claimed that she never had problems like that in school. She dawdled over the Digit Symbol subtest, biting her pencil and looking up at the examiner as if expecting some kind of help [Palmer, 1970, p. 419].

Halpern (1960) illustrated the application of a psychoanalytically oriented approach to the WISC. The interpretations made by Halpern must be viewed as speculative, needing verification by evaluating the examinee's total performance and case history. Further, it should be understood that there are many possible reasons for poor performance on the WISC. For example, in the illustration below, Halpern suggested that repressive activity and blocking may lead to low Block Design and Object Assembly scores. However, low scores on these two subtests may indicate simply inadequate visual-motor skill. The interpretations offered by Halpern should not be made routinely when Block Design and Object Assembly scores are low. Rather, each case must be evaluated carefully before any such interpretations are made. Some examiners may prefer to refrain entirely from making such kinds of interpretations, preferring to evaluate only the child's cognitive performance.

The case presented by Halpern concerned the performance of an anxious, hostile child with a slow, cautious, and circumscribed manner. His cautiousness, meticulousness, and preoccupations may lower his Coding score, and also may hamper his ability to take in information from his surroundings, with a resulting low Information score. Repressive activity and blocking and the resulting inability to see certain relationships may interfere with his performance on the Block Design and Object Assembly subtests. On the other hand, a need to please the environment and to know what the environment expects may facilitate his performance on the Picture Completion, Picture Arrangement, and Comprehension subtests. However, while the Comprehension score may be high, the content of the responses may reflect difficulties, such as dependency on the environment and fear of impulses. For example, when asked what he should do if he cuts his finger, he might say, "I'd go to my mother," rather than attempt to deal with the situation himself. His response to the question, "What would you do if you were sent to buy a loaf of bread and the grocer said he did not have any more?" might be that he would return home for instructions, thereby showing his difficulty in exercising initiative.

Juvenile Delinquency and the WISC

Research studies with delinquent children and the WISC have focused primarily on the Verbal-Performance discrepancy. Studies have reported that delinquents usually have a higher Performance Scale IQ than Verbal Scale IQ (Camp, 1966; Corotto, 1961; Harris, 1957; Henning & Levy, 1967; Kaiser, 1964; Richardson & Surko, 1956; Shinagawa, 1963; Smith, 1969; Wiens, Matarazzo, & Gaver, 1959), although some studies have not found the scales to be significantly different (Frost & Frost, 1962; Talbot, 1960). Delinquents tend to score in the Normal range on the Performance Scale (IQ of about 95) and in the Dull Normal range on the Verbal Scale (IQ of about 88). A significant Verbal-Performance discrepancy has not been found in a black delinquent sample (Henning & Levy, 1967). In female delinquent samples, a significant Verbal < Performance discrepancy has been found in one study (Smith, 1969) but not in another (Camp, 1966). The extensiveness of the Verbal-Performance discrepancy has not been found to be related significantly to the extensiveness of acting-out behavior in delinquents (Fernald & Wisser, 1967).

The fact that a Verbal-Performance discrepancy, in favor of the Performance Scale, is likely to appear in samples of delinquent children does not mean that this pattern should be used as a diagnostic sign of delinquency (Camp, 1966; Henning & Levy, 1967; Prentice & Kelly, 1963). A Verbal < Performance discrepancy, indicating in part a reduction in verbal functioning, may be related to educational retardation, reading disorder, minority group background, or bilingualism, or it may not be related to any particular difficulty. In general, the Verbal < Performance sign may be more diagnostic of learning difficulties that are a relatively frequent concomitant of delinquency than of delinquency itself.

DIFFERENTIAL DIAGNOSIS

We have seen in the sections on differential diagnosis in Chapters 20 and 21 that differentiating schizophrenic children from emotionally disturbed children is not a simple task. Similar difficulties are encountered in differentiating learning disabled children from emotionally disturbed children, although emotionally disturbed children are usually perceived by their teachers as having more problems than learning disabled children (McCarthy & Paraskevopoulos, 1969). The following psychological report, adapted from Sarason and Sarason (1945), illustrates the problem of differentiating mental retardation from emotional disturbance.

Psychological Evaluation

Name: Mary Jones   Date of examination: July 15, 1945
Date of birth: January 15, 1933   Date of report: July 16, 1945
Chronological age: 12–6   Grade: Special class
Test administered: Stanford-Binet Intelligence Scale, Form L

Mary, a cleanly dressed, immature-looking girl with sparkling, brown eyes and a broad, affectionate smile, seemed too preoccupied to concentrate, staring blankly and silently several moments after directions were given without any apparent effort to respond. This made testing difficult, for it was frequently impossible to contact the girl. Even when contact was apparently good she responded impulsively and incorrectly with what seemed to be the first thought that came to her mind. When asked to reconsider her answers and pay closer attention to directions, surprising insight and judgment were revealed. It was necessary to prod her constantly and caution her frequently, since she feared to assert herself and needed reassurance, which was also inferred from her concern about the correctness of her answers. During the session she grinned and laughed inappropriately. She was in good contact, however, when questioned about her personal matters and was capable of carrying on an excellent conversation. Her verbal usage was good and she was able to carry an idea through without confusion. She spoke in a soft voice and her social manner, though childish, was charming and delightful.

Mary, who is 12–6 years of age, earned on the Stanford-Binet Intelligence

Scale (Form L) an MA of 7 years and 9 months with an IQ of 62 ±3, which if strictly interpreted would place her within the Mentally Defective range. The scatter and the total test picture, however, do not warrant such a classification.

As was described previously, the child seemed too preoccupied to concentrate. This was clearly visible on memory and reasoning items, where poor attention and impulsiveness were apparent. The basal level (the lowest level of the examination where all tests are passed) was lowered from year-level VI to year-level IV-6 because of failure on Memory for Sentences at year-level V. The memory pattern on succeeding items was variable. For example, Memory for Stories was failed at year-level VIII and Memory for Sentences was failed at year-levels VIII and IX, but she had success on Repeating 4 and 5 Digits Reversed at year-levels IX and XII, while failing Repeating 6 Digits at year-level X. Difficulty in recall was striking at year-level X, where Mary read a passage beautifully in good time, but could not give an adequate account of it from memory. That variability in memory was probably due to inadequate concentration was even more apparent at year-level XIII, where Mary was able to remember the general pattern of a bead chain but carelessly substituted cylindrically shaped beads for square ones and vice versa. In her work on memory items which involve immediate recall, it is believed that her slow, phlegmatic attitude might also have interfered.

On reasoning problems the girl responded impulsively and without deliberation. When directions were repeated and prodding ensued, surprising insight was revealed. Surprisingly poor judgment was revealed on relatively simple social problems, as on Comprehension at year-levels VII and VIII, and on Finding Reasons at year-level X. These failures are more or less inconsistent with her work on similar and more difficult, practical reasoning problems at year-level XIII, where credit was received. It is noteworthy that on these reasoning problems Mary grasped the main ideas but elaborated each with difficulty, and showed more than ever before her hesitancy to respond and a tendency to interpret a request to qualify a statement as a sign that her responses were completely incorrect. Inconsistencies were also apparent on items which involved abstract thinking. For example, credit was received on Similarities and Differences at year-level VIII but no credit was received at year-level VII on determining the similarities of two things.

The degree of irregularity can be seen at a glance in the unusual scatter of successes. Mary's basal year level was at IV-6 after passing all tests at year-level VI; she then failed all tests at year-level X, but achieved her highest success at year-level XIII. In addition, she was able to do the last part of the Induction series at year-level XIV, but did not receive credit because she was unable to give the principle involved in the solution. This total performance is very unusual and definitely uncharacteristic of a mentally retarded child. The results obtained are more indicative of an unstable, disturbed child, and are at most a minimal representation of what she can do intellectually. The results of the achievement tests, obtained when the child was in better contact, corroborate this contention. If the mental level as obtained on the Stanford-Binet is the true measure, the child would never have been able to do the work she did on the achievement tests. On the basis of the behavior of the girl and of the test results, additional psychological testing is recommended.

LEARNING DISABILITIES

The term "learning disabilities" is difficult to define, for many writers often use it synonymously with the term "minimal brain dysfunction." However, dysfunction of the central nervous system does not have to be included as an essential criterion for the diagnosis and instruction of children with learning disabilities (Myers & Hammill, 1969). Children with specific learning disabilities, according to Bateman (1965), are those who have an educationally significant discrepancy between their estimated intellectual potential and actual level of performance. The disabilities are related to basic disorders in the learning process, which may or may not be accompanied by demonstrable central nervous system damage. The disabilities are not secondary to mental retardation, educational or cultural deprivation, severe emotional disturbance, or sensory loss. Thus, the designation of learning disability should not be made until a number of other conditions have been excluded.

Since learning disabilities and minimal brain dysfunction are so closely related, the material presented in Chapter 21 on minimal brain dysfunction should also be consulted. Children placed in learning disability classes usually (a) have normal or above normal intellectual capacity, as indicated by an IQ above 90; (b) display academic deficiencies in one or more of reading, arithmetic, spelling, and handwriting; and (c) have difficulties, other than those noted in (b), associated with syndromes of learning disabilities, such as hyperactivity, deficits in expressive language, or attentional difficulties (Clements, 1969). The recommended battery of tests for the assessment of children with learning disabilities is similar to the battery recommended for testing children with minimal brain dysfunction. It includes the WISC (at least 10 of the subtests), Bender-Gestalt, Draw-a-Man, Gray Oral Reading Tests, and Wide Range Achievement Test. Tarnopol (1968) also suggested that after educationally handicapped children are identified by the battery of tests, further tests are called for in order to assess specific disabilities. Such tests include the Detroit Test of Learning Aptitude, Illinois Test of Psycholinguistic Abilities, visual perception tests, motor performance tests, concept formation tests, tests of emotional lability, and other tests as indicated.

Classification System for Children with Learning Difficulties

An interesting system for understanding children with learning difficulties in the school has been proposed by Ross (1967). The system has three categories (learning dysfunction, learning disorders, and learning disabilities), with two subdivisions for each one (without and with secondary reactions, primary and secondary, and chronic and reactive, respectively). The system attempts to differentiate among children with perceptual disorders (e.g., minimal brain dysfunction), neurotic learning inhibitions (e.g., school phobia), and psychological disorders which do not primarily focus on learning (e.g., childhood schizophrenia). It is important to recognize that Ross's third category, "learning disabilities," differs from the usual definition of learning disabled children.

Table 23–2 briefly describes the system together with suggestions for treatment. The system applies only to children who have the basic intellectual capacity for academic school work. It does not cover mentally retarded or severely brain-damaged children. "Culturally disadvantaged" children, too, are excluded because, for these children, the source of difficulty lies outside the child, calling for remedial action on the part of society. Careful study of Table 23–2 should be helpful to those engaged in working with children with learning difficulties.

Intelligence Level and Academic Difficulties

Coleman and Sandhu (1965) investigated how intelligence level (obtained from the WISC) is related to a variety of developmental and behavioral factors in a sample of 364 children, including 311 boys and 53 girls, who had been referred to a university remedial clinic for failing one or more basic subjects or

Table 23-2. A Diagnostic Framework for Learning Difficulties

---

1. Learning Dysfunctions
   This category includes children who have perceptual disorders which interfere with their school performance without significantly disrupting their overall intellectual abilities. Included in the category are children with "perceptual motor problems," "cerebral dysfunctions," or "minimal brain damage."
   a. *Learning dysfunctions without secondary reactions.* Secondary psychological problems are not evident. Help consists of modifications in the educational approach designed to overcome or bypass the handicap. Perceptual training and operant conditioning are two such suggested ways.
   b. *Learning dysfunctions with secondary reactions.* Secondary psychological reactions are evident, including aggression with or without hyperactive and disruptive classroom behavior, social withdrawal with expression of inadequacy and inferiority, somatic complaints, and immature and passive behaviors. Help consists of special education plus alleviation of the psychological disorder. Close coordination between the two therapeutic approaches is called for.

2. Learning Disorders
   This category includes children who are usually referred to as having "neurotic learning inhibitions." Academic performance (behavior) is disrupted or prevented by incompatible responses.
   a. *Primary learning disorders.* Learning is aversive. Avoidance of learning or escape behavior to learning situations occurs both in and out of school. The disorder becomes progressively serious because of the pyramidal nature of education. Help consists of intensive treatment aimed at strengthening the learning-appropriate responses and weakening the incompatible behavior, together with remedial education. Close coordination between the treatment and education approaches is necessary.
   b. *Secondary learning disorders.* Behavior prerequisite for learning is disrupted but not learning itself. Classified in this category are children with school phobia or children whose marked hostility toward school or teacher disrupts their ability to learn. Help may consist of problem-focused intervention, with early intervention recommended.

3. Learning Disabilities
   This category includes children whose performance in school is disrupted or made impossible by psychological disorders which do not have their primary focus on learning or on the school situation.
   a. *Chronic learning disabilities.* Children with long-standing and pervasive disorders, such as infantile autism or childhood schizophrenia, are included in this subdivision. While little is known about how to help children with disorders of this type, therapeutic education appears to be a promising treatment modality.
   b. *Reactive learning disabilities.* Reactions to a crisis or trauma in the children's environment interferes with their cognitive processes. Included in this subdivision are children who have anxiety about separating from their mother with the resulting refusal to go to school, and children who experience a traumatic loss of a close relative accompanied by acute depression. Help consists of therapy—addressing itself to the problem which disrupts learning—and, in some cases, tutoring.

Adapted from Ross (1967).

for having a reading deficit. Three groups were studied: Dull Normal (IQ less than 90), Normal (IQ between 90 and 109), and Bright Normal (IQ of 110 and above). Emotional and developmental problems were similar in the three groups. While general health history was good, frequency of nail biting and speech problems differed, with the Bright Normal group having the highest frequency of nail biting and the lowest frequency of speech problems. The behavioral problems shown by the children, while of the same kind that are found in normal children, differed among the three groups. The Bright Normal group tended to have a higher proportion of children with problems such as disobedience, poor routine habits, timidity, and lying than the other two groups. The data suggest that the kinds of behavioral problems found in children with learning disabilities are related to intelligence level. It would be of interest to learn the extent to which the above findings apply to children who do not have learning difficulties.

Learning Disabilities and the WISC

Studies which have evaluated the scores of learning disabled children on the WISC are difficult to evaluate, because the criteria employed to select children have differed among investigators. The criteria have included children (*a*) who have failed school subjects, (*b*) who have a gap between their achievement test scores and grades, (*c*) who have neurological difficulties, and (*d*) who have been designated as being learning disabled without specifying the selection criteria. These difficulties should be considered in evaluating the available findings.

Underachievers have been found to tend to do better on the Performance Scale subtests than on the Verbal Scale subtests, although Comprehension subtest scores may be higher than some Performance Scale subtest scores (Coleman & Rasof, 1963; Jenkin, Spivack, Levine, & Savage, 1964; Landrum, 1963). The lower scores are usually related to school-type learning tasks (e.g., Information and Arithmetic subtests). When learning disabled children between 7 and 18 years of age were classified as having neurological difficulty, having suspected neurological difficulty, or having no neurological difficulty, the three groups were not found to differ on their WISC scale scores or subtest scores (Boshes & Myklebust, 1964).

In an investigation which used only the Verbal Scale, differences between the adolescent underachievers and normal achievers on their WISC subtest scores generally were small, although the underachievers had significantly lower scores than the normal achievers on the Arithmetic (10 vs. 11) and Digit Span (10 vs. 12) subtests (Dudek & Lester, 1968). Underachievers, therefore, may have more difficulty in concentration and attention tasks than normal achievers. These findings, however, should not be used to predict underachievement in learning disabled children. Validation studies are needed to predict underachievement from WISC patterns.

Investigators have been interested in determining the correlates of Verbal-Performance discrepancies in learning disabled children. First, three groups usually are established, namely, (*a*) those whose Performance Scale is greater than their Verbal Scale by a specific number of points (e.g., 9 or more points) (P > V), (*b*) those whose Verbal and Performance Scales are similar (e.g., within plus or minus 5 points) (V = P), and (*c*) those whose Verbal Scale is greater than their Performance Scale (e.g., 9 or more points) (V > P). The three groups usually are matched on Full Scale IQ.

In one study of children between 9 and 14 years of age, a variety of achievement and perceptual tests were administered to learning disabled children in the three groups (Rourke, Young, & Flewelling, 1971). The results showed that the P > V group performed significantly *better* than the V > P group on tasks involving visual-perceptual skills, whereas the V > P group performed significantly *better* than the P > V group on tasks involving verbal and auditory-perceptual abilities. There were no differences between the groups on tests of problem-solving ability. The investigators concluded that WISC Verbal-Performance discrepancies are useful in predicting differential performances on a variety of ability tests for children with learning disabilities.

In another study of 8-year-old children with academic difficulties (Wells, 1970), the P > V group in comparison with the V > P and V = P groups scored significantly *lower* on the Illinois Test of Psycholinguistic Abilities and on the reading section of the Wide Range Achievement Test, whereas the V > P and V = P groups did not significantly differ on these two measures. Frostig Developmental Test of Visual Perception scores were not significantly different among the three groups. The findings of Wells, in part, corroborate those of Rourke et al. (1971).

Reading Disability

Of the many kinds of learning disorders, reading disability is found more frequently than others. Many different kinds of cognitive and perceptual difficulties may be associated with disabled readers. Retardation in reading can be associated with environmental, emotional, and developmental factors.

Lyle and Goyen (1969) defined reading retardation as a "*syndrome of learning disability in children who are bright enough to learn, and who have had the usual learning opportunities* [p. 106]." This definition, then, suggests that an exploration of reading retardation *per se* is of minimal concern when children are dull, have sensory handicaps, or have missed schooling. Lyle and Goyen also pointed out that

the term "reading retardation" may in fact have four meanings: (*a*) slow reading speed, (*b*) limited vocabulary, (*c*) failure to master basic processes such as letter recognition and sound blending, and (*d*) lack of comprehension despite adequate fluency in the mechanics of reading [p. 106].

In studies of children with reading retardation, it is rare to find any who fall into the fourth type. The first and second types can occur through lack of reading practice at older age levels. Therefore, Lyle and Goyen stated that it is the third meaning which should form the basis for the selection criteria in studies of reading retardation.

One of the primary causes of poor school performance and of reading disability, in particular, may be low intelligence (cf. Ames, 1968). Early reading competence may be dependent on the development and mastery of perceptual skills, whereas later reading skills may rely more heavily on conceptual factors, such as comprehension and reasoning (Belmont & Birch, 1966).

Reading Disability and the Stanford-Binet. On the Stanford-Binet, inadequate readers may demonstrate perceptual difficulty, poor recall of visual patterns, poor copying and reproduction of forms, and short memory span. Studying the child's pattern of successes and failures (see the Binetgram in Chapter 10) may provide clues to various kinds of cognitive difficulties. The few studies available concerned with the performance of inadequate readers on the Stanford-Binet seem to support some of the above observations.

In one study, Bond and Fay (1950) matched 50 pairs of good and poor readers on mental age (M MA = 12–0). The children were in grades 4, 5, and 6, and both 1937 forms were studied. Good readers performed better than poor readers on tests dependent upon the knowledge and use of words, while poor readers performed better than good readers on nonverbal and memory tests, but not consistently so.

Rose (1958) investigated the Stanford-Binet performance of a group of 113 poor readers who were between the ages of 6 and 17 years. All children in the sample had a reading level that was two years or more below expectancy (median reading grade was 2.14). The samples' median mental age was 10–0 years, and the median IQ was 104. While statistical tests of significance were not performed, nor was a control group used, the data are interesting in pointing out trends which exist among a group of retarded readers.

Scatter ranged from 3 to 11 year levels; the median amount of scatter was 7.6 year levels. Rose suggested that this range was greater than that found among children who do not have reading difficulties. The wide range may indicate variability in the development of cognitive skills. Hard tests were primarily those related to auditory memory span and to language ability. Easy tests were usually those that required practical reasoning and ingenuity. The studies by Rose and by Bond and Fay (1950) confirm one's expectation that poor readers should have more difficulty on the Stanford-Binet with verbal tests than with other kinds of tests.

Reading Disability and the WISC.   The WISC has proved to be an extremely popular instrument for investigating patterns of retarded readers. However, many of the studies have suffered from a number of methodological weaknesses (Belmont & Birch, 1966; Lyle & Goyen, 1969), including small sample size, lack of a control group, difficulty in determining whether samples were representative of any definable population of readers, failure to specify whether children had any other associated dysfunction in addition to reading disability, wide age ranges, and uncontrolled sex ratios. The problems of sampling bias are therefore prominent. In addition, the studies usually have failed to define adequately the nature of reading retardation. The definition proposed above by Lyle and Goyen (1969) appears to be an excellent one, in so far as one is interested in studying a precisely defined group of children with reading retardation.

Because of the many methodological weaknesses present in the available studies, it is difficult to evaluate what, if any, WISC patterns are associated with retarded readers. However, an attempt will be made. In Table 23–3, ranks and IQ's are reported for studies which have presented WISC subtest scores of inadequate readers. The Mazes subtest is not included because few of the studies used this subtest. In addition to the studies noted in Table 23–3, other studies have reported WISC subtests (without scores) which were either low or high in inadequate readers (Ackerman, Peters, & Dykman, 1971; Hirst, 1960; Huelsman, 1970; McGraw, 1966; Robeck, 1960, 1964), while still others have focused on Verbal-Performance discrepancies (Reed, 1967; Sandstedt, 1964; Warrington, 1967).

The general trend emerging from these studies indicates that inadequate readers have a somewhat distinct pattern of WISC scores. The average ranks of the subtests for the 22 studies are shown at the bottom of Table 23–3. The four easiest subtests are all Performance Scale subtests (Picture Completion, Picture Arrangement, Block Design, and Object Assembly), while three of the four most difficult subtests are Verbal Scale subtests (Information, Arithmetic, and Digit Span). In every study of Table 23–3 which reported Verbal Scale and Performance Scale IQ's, Verbal Scale IQ's were lower than Performance Scale IQ's. This discrepancy could be expected from the rank order data, which showed that the four easiest subtests were Performance Scale subtests. Finally, a review of the studies which did not report subtest scores, but which reported subtests that were significantly low or high, confirms the overall ranks presented in Table 23–3.

A comparison of the ranks of adequate readers with those of inadequate readers indicates that the adequate readers, in the studies which used an adequate reader group, had a different pattern of subtest ranks. On the basis of the standardization data, it would be expected that adequate readers should not show any distinctive pattern.

The hypothesis proposed by Lyle and Goyen (1969) appears to be a reasonable one in interpreting the overall rankings, namely, that the WISC patterns of retarded readers appear to be symptoms correlated with reading disability, primarily of a verbal nature, and not the effects of reading retardation. The low subtests, with the exception of Coding, require verbalization. Lyle and Goyen suggested that inadequate readers may perform poorly on the Coding subtest from "failure to use an effective labeling strategy as a memory aid, resulting in increased time taken in checking the code key for each symbol [p. 111]." Low Digit Span and Arithmetic scores may be due to "failure to use subvocal rehearsal as a strategy for keeping the items in mind [p. 111]."

The pattern of subtest scores noted above for inadequate readers does not mean that all inadequate readers will show the pattern. The ranks reflect an average, based on studies that had either adequate or inadequate research designs. However, the pattern appears to be one which is consistent with the view that reading retardation reflects problems associated with verbal skills.

Table 23-3. WISC Subtest Ranks for Inadequate Readers

Investigator	N	Age	IQ VS	IQ PS	IQ FS	Composition of Ranks	I	C	A	S	V	DS	PC	PA	BD	OA	CO
Altus (1956)	25	Grades 3–8	98	100	99	with DS	9	7	10	8	2	3	1	5	6	4	11
						without DS	8	6	9	7	2	—	1	4	5	3	10
Belluomini (1962)	139	8–15	101	106	103	without DS	9	6	10	1	7	—	2.5	2.5	4	5	8
Belmont & Birch (1966)	150	9–10	92	94	92	with DS	9	11	2.5	5	10	4	1	2.5	7.5	7.5	6
						without DS	8	10	2.5	4	9	—	1	2.5	6.5	6.5	5
Burks & Bruce (1955)	31	Grades 3–8	—	—	101	with DS	8.5	4	8.5	6.5	6.5	11	3	1	2	5	10
						without DS	8.5	4	8.5	6.5	6.5	—	3	1	2	5	10
Corwin (1967)	30	Grades 4–5	97	101	99	with DS	10	8	9	4	3	11	1	2	6	7	5
						without DS	10	8	9	4	3	—	1	2	6	7	5
Dockrell (1960)	34	8–14	101	108	105	without DS	10	2	9	3	7	—	1	4	5	6	8
Ekwall (1966)	21	9–12	88	94	89	with DS	9	7	10	5	8	11	2	1	6	4	3
						without DS	9	7	10	5	8	—	2	1	6	4	3
Graham (1952)	31	8–16	99	102	100	with DS	8	3	11	1	9	7	2	6	4	5	10
						without DS	7	3	10	1	8	—	2	6	4	5	9
Kallos, Grabow, & Guarino (1961)	37	9–14	96	103	99	without DS	10	5.5	8	7	5.5	—	4	2.5	1	2.5	9
Lyle & Goyen (1969)	54	6–12	100	102	101	with DS	8	2.5	7	6	5	11	1	2.5	4	9	10
						without DS	8	2.5	7	6	5	—	1	2.5	4	9	10
McLean (1963)	42	Grades 4–6	96	104	100	with DS	7	3.5	10	5	8	10	1	2	3.5	6	10
						without DS	7	3.5	9.5	5	8	—	1	2	3.5	6	9.5
McLeod (1965)	116	M = 12	94	97	95	with DS	9	5	8	6	10	7	1	4	2	3	11
						without DS	8	5	7	6	9	—	1	4	2	3	10
Muir (1962)	50	8–16	98	104	108	without DS	7	3.5	9	5	8	—	2	6	3.5	1	10
Neville (1961)	35	Not reported	95	106	100	with DS	10	5.5	8	8	5.5	11	2.5	1	2.5	4	8
						without DS	10	5.5	8	8	5.5	—	2.5	1	2.5	4	8

(Table 23–3 continued on next page.)

Table 23-3. WISC Subtest Ranks for Inadequate Readers—Continued

			IQ			COMPOSITION OF RANKS	SUBTEST RANKS										
INVESTIGATOR	N	AGE	VS	PS	FS		I	C	A	S	V	DS	PC	PA	BD	OA	CO
Paterra (1963)	33	6–14	106	108	108	without DS	8	1	9	2.5	10	—	2.5	7	5.5	5.5	4
Reid & Schoer (1966)	87	9–10	—	—	90–110	with DS	7.5	11	9	2.5	6	10	7.5	5	4	1	2.5
						without DS	7.5	10	9	2.5	6	—	7.5	5	4	1	2.5
Richardson & Surko (1956)	105	8–16	87	92	88	with DS	10	5	9	6	11	7	3	2	4	1	8
						without DS	9	5	8	6	10	—	3	2	4	1	7
Robeck (1962)	20	7–14	—	—	93–136	with DS	8	1	11	4	3	9	2	7	5	6	10
						without DS	8	1	10	4	3	—	2	7	5	6	9
	20	Not reported	—	—	—	with DS	8	1	11	2	3	10	4	6	5	7	9
						without DS	8	1	10	2	3	—	4	6	5	7	9
Rogge (1959)	45	14–16	85	94	88	with DS	11	8	10	7	9	6	1	2	4	3	5
						without DS	10	7	9	6	8	—	1	2	4	3	5
Sheldon & Garton (1959)	11	7–14	96	105	100	without DS	9	5	7.5	6	7.5	—	4	3	2	1	10
Silberberg & Feldt (1968)	7	Grade 1	—	—	—	without DS	10	6	6	9	8	—	2	1	6	3	4
	27	Grade 2	—	—	—	without DS	9	7	10	8	4.5	—	2	1	3	4.5	6
	18	Grade 3	—	—	—	without DS	7	10	8	9	4	—	2.5	2.5	5	1	6
Thompson (1963)	24	Grades 1–2	—	—	—	with DS	8.5	6	7	4.5	11	2	10	8.5	1	3	4.5
						without DS	7.5	5	6	3.5	10	—	9	7.5	1	2	3.5
Average rank						with DS	11	6	10	5	7	9	1	2	3	3	4
						without DS	10	6	9	5	7	—	1	2	3	4	8

Note.— Subtests ranked from easiest (1) to most difficult (11). Abbreviations are as follows: VS = Verbal Scale; PS = Performance Scale; FS = Full Scale; I = Information; C = Comprehension; A = Arithmetic; S = Similarities; V = Vocabulary; DS = Digit Span; PC = Picture Completion; PA = Picture Arrangement; BD = Block Design; OA = Object Assembly; CO = Coding.

Two Developmental Syndromes. Among a small number of retarded readers and writers, there appear to exist the following two types of groups with developmental defects, described by Kinsbourne and Warrington (1963).

1. In one group, there is a Verbal-Performance discrepancy on the WISC in favor of the Performance Scale, no difficulty in finger differentiation and with tests of ordering, no selective impairment of arithmetical abilities, impaired language ability (in addition to reading and writing), and delay in the acquisition of speech. This group may be called a "language retardation" group, analogous to the aphasia syndrome in adults.

2. In the second group, the Verbal-Performance WISC discrepancy is in favor of the Verbal Scale, and there is failure on standard tests of finger differentiation and order, difficulty in arithmetic, significant retardation in right-left orientation, and mechanical and constructional difficulty (e.g., copying drawings and matchstick patterns). This group may be called the "developmental Gerstmann syndrome" group, analogous to the acquired Gerstmann syndrome in adults.

The full syndrome of either type need not be present in every case, nor is a Verbal-Performance discrepancy indicative of the syndrome. Neither group appears to represent the syndrome of specific dyslexia or congenital word-blindness. Kinsbourne and Warrington regard the two types of syndromes as corresponding to retarded cerebral development, however caused, and not as representing single diseased conditions. While the two syndromes probably occur only in a minority of children with reading difficulties, distinguishing these two syndromes may facilitate the educational process by helping to plan programs which take into account the nature of the disorder. Table 23–4 summarizes some of the features associated with each syndrome.

Table 23-4. Frequency of Symptoms Occurring in Individuals with Reading and Writing Difficulties as a Function of WISC Verbal-Performance Discrepancy

Symptom	Performance Scale > Verbal Scale (Language retardation group)	Verbal Scale > Performance Scale (Developmental Gerstmann syndrome group)
Language impairment	always	never
Speech reception difficulties	usually	never
Difficulty on constructional tasks (e.g., copying drawings and matchstick patterns)	never	always
Difficulty in writing neatly and in copying written words	never	usually
Difficulty in performing written additions and subtractions	occasionally	always
Right-left disorientation	infrequently	frequently
Difficulty in finger differentiation and order	never	always
History suggestive of birth injury	infrequently	usually
Abnormal motor development	infrequently	occasionally
Delayed speech development	usually	infrequently
Neurological abnormalities	infrequently	occasionally

Note.—Verbal-Performance discrepancy is greater than 20 points.
Adapted from Kinsbourne and Warrington (1963).

PHYSICAL DISEASE OR DISABILITY AND LEVEL OF INTELLIGENCE

This part of the chapter reviews research reports and surveys that have focused on the level of intellectual functioning of children (and at times adults) who have medical problems. Children handicapped by physical disability not only are restricted in their activities, but are also limited in their opportunities for social, cultural, and intellectual stimulation (Broida, 1955; Linde, 1964; Wrightstone, Justman, & Moskowitz, 1953). It is not known to what extent such adverse social and psychological factors affect the validity of the test results. The information which follows is not an exhaustive list of findings; rather, it serves to familiarize the reader with representative findings concerning the relationship between intelligence and illness or physical disability.

Birth Weight

Intellectual impairment is frequently found in children of very low birth weight (e.g., less than 2000 grams), while heavier low-birth-weight children (e.g., 2001 to 2500 grams) have minimal, if any, intellectual impairment (Caputo & Mandell, 1970). High-birth-weight infants (e.g., more than 4100 grams for girls and more than 4250 grams for boys), when tested at the age of 4 years, are more likely to have IQ's below 80 and are more variable in the distribution of their IQ's than children of standard birth weight (Babson, Henderson, & Clark, 1969).

Blindness

Blind children usually obtain a mean IQ in the normal range, but their distribution of scores tends to be bimodal: there are more superior as well as inferior children in the blind group than in the normal group (Crowell, 1957). Partially sighted children tend to obtain IQ's that are slightly below those of normally seeing children (Myers, 1930; Pintner, 1942).

Blind Children and the WISC.   Studies which have investigated the pattern of WISC Verbal Scale subtest scores obtained by blind children have found generally that they perform best on the Digit Span subtest and poorest on the Similarities and, to a lesser extent, on the Comprehension subtest (Gilbert & Rubin, 1965; Hopkins & McGuire, 1966; Tillman, 1967a; Tillman & Bashaw, 1968; Tillman & Osborne, 1969). These results suggest that blind children have well-developed rote memory capacities but are less adequate in conceptual thinking and in social comprehension. The results also suggest that, in investigating the predictive validity of the WISC Verbal Scale IQ with blind children, both the Verbal Scale IQ and the individual subtest scaled scores should be examined. It is possible that the Verbal Scale IQ may not provide as adequate a measure as some of the individual subtests (cf. Tillman & Bashaw, 1968). A factor analysis of the Verbal Scale with a group of blind children indicated that there were fewer factor loadings and weaker communalities on all subtests, with the exception of Arithmetic, than in a sighted group (Tillman, 1967b). These results demonstrate that blind children may have a greater specificity in the organization of abilities sampled by the subtests than sighted children.

WISC and Hayes-Binet.   The WISC Verbal Scale and the Hayes-Binet (a special form of the Stanford-Binet that is used with blind children) have been compared in various samples of blind children. In one sample of children who were between 9 and 15 years, the two scales were highly correlated ($r = .86$), but WISC IQ's ($M = 110$) were about 8 points lower than Hayes-Binet IQ's (M

= 118) (Hopkins & McGuire, 1966). These results were essentially confirmed in another study (Hopkins & McGuire, 1967). The two scales also have been found to yield similar IQ's (*M*'s of 78 and 75 for the Verbal Scale and Hayes-Binet, respectively) in a study of children between the ages of 6 and 14 years (Gilbert & Rubin, 1965) and in a study of young children (*r* = .94; *M*'s of 98 and 99 for the Verbal Scale and Hayes-Binet, respectively) (Lewis, 1957). The Hayes-Binet has been found to be somewhat more valid than the WISC (or Wechsler-Bellevue Intelligence Scale, Form I) when teachers' ratings were used as the criterion (*r*'s of .51 and .37, respectively) (Denton, 1954). The above studies indicate that the WISC and Hayes-Binet cannot be considered to be interchangeable with above-average-ability blind children. For blind children with average or below-average ability, the scales appear to yield more comparable IQ's. Additional studies are needed that are concerned with the prediction of academic achievement in blind children (H. Goldman, 1970).

Cardiac Conditions

Children with cardiac conditions generally tend to have a lower level of intellectual functioning than normal children (Wrightstone et al., 1953). Children with cyanotic congenital heart disease (decreased oxygen levels in the blood) follow this pattern in infancy because performance on infant tests is heavily dependent on gross motor functioning, but after the age of 3 years they do not have lowered IQ's (Rasof, Linde, & Dunn, 1967).

Cerebral Palsy

In cerebral palsy, which is a neuromuscular impairment resulting from some kind of brain injury, children may have severe physical disability with normal intelligence, or little physical disability with subnormal intelligence (Johnson, 1966). Cerebral palsy is associated with lowered intelligence: generally, 25% of the children function in the Normal or Bright Normal range, 30% in the Borderline to Below Normal range, and 45% in the Mentally Retarded range (Heilman, 1952).

Deafness

Studies of the intellectual functioning of deaf children show a diversity of results. However, the findings indicate that deaf children, in comparison with normally hearing children, obtain lower IQ's on verbal tests, while on performance tests they may obtain lower IQ's (median IQ of 91 for 10 studies), similar IQ's (median IQ of 100 for 12 studies), or higher IQ's (median IQ of 110 for three studies) (Meyerson, 1963).

Deaf Children and the WISC. The entire WISC may be useful for the evaluation of both deaf and partially deaf children (Reed, 1970), although the Performance Scale is probably the most suitable part (Murphy, 1957; Vernon & Brown, 1964). The discrepancy between the two scales permits an assessment of the effects of hearing impairment on verbal ability (Reed, 1970). In the case of very deaf children, the Verbal Scale may not provide useful results. Acceptable reliability and validity coefficients have been reported for the WISC Performance Scale with samples of deaf children (Brill, 1962; Evans, 1966; Larr & Cain, 1959; Lavos, 1962; Pickles, 1966).

Hine (1970) studied the WISC scores of 100 partially deaf English children between the ages of 8 and 16 years. The children obtained higher scores on the Performance Scale than on the Verbal Scale (*M*'s = 82 and 98, respectively). Within the Performance Scale, the Picture Arrangement and Object Assembly subtests had the lowest means, while within the Verbal Scale the

Arithmetic subtest had the highest mean. Hine suggested that the relative difficulty of the Picture Arrangement subtest may be a consequence of the ways in which linguistic facility mediates the solution of items on the subtest, while the relative success on the Arithmetic subtest may be associated with nonverbal skills that are involved in the solution of the arithmetic items. Extensiveness of hearing loss was found to correlate negatively with the Verbal Scale ($r = -.31$) but not with the Performance Scale ($r = .08$).

Hine also conducted a factor analysis. Three factors were found: Verbal Ability (Information, Comprehension, Similarities, and Vocabulary), Numerical Ability (Arithmetic and Coding), and Performance Ability (Picture Completion, Picture Arrangement, Block Design, Object Assembly, and Coding). Hine suggested that the three abilities identified in the factor analysis tend to develop relatively more independently in partially hearing children than in nonhandicapped children.

Other investigations have reported that the Coding and Picture Arrangement subtests were two of the most difficult Performance Scale subtests for their samples of deaf or partially deaf children (Clarke & Leslie, 1971; Evans, 1966; Pickles, 1966). Pickles also reported that there was a significant relationship ($r = .33$) between the Performance Scale IQ and the amount of speech available to the children. Reed (1970) observed that the Picture Completion and Picture Arrangement subtests, because of their high verbal loadings, may be more difficult for deaf and partially deaf children than other Performance Scale subtests. However, as we have seen, research studies do not uniformly report this pattern. Reed also noted that, as language development increases in deaf and partially deaf children, the Performance Scale subtest scores do not appreciably differ from each other.

Diabetes Mellitus

Diabetes mellitus acquired before the age of 5 years may result in lowered IQ's, whereas the disease acquired after the age of 5 years does not significantly reduce intellectual functioning (Ack, Miller, & Weil, 1961). (The findings of Worden and Vignos (1962), who tested children older than 5 years of age, corroborated those of Ack et al.) To account for their findings, Ack and his co-workers proposed two hypotheses. First, metabolic disturbances occurring early in life result in damage which, in turn, affects the IQ, whereas disturbances occurring in later childhood do not produce similar damage. Second, diabetes not only reduces energy available for the young child to pursue intellectual activities, but also disrupts the normal growth of independence.

Epilepsy

Epilepsy occurs irrespective of level of intelligence. Individuals who are institutionalized as a result of epilepsy usually have lower IQ's than the IQ's found in the general population, whereas individuals with epilepsy who are not in an institution have IQ's which approximate those found in the general population (Broida, 1955; Burgemeister, 1962). In symptomatic epilepsy (epilepsy as a symptom of organic brain damage), there is greater intellectual impairment than in idiopathic epilepsy (epilepsy without known or specific cause) (Broida, 1955; Collins, 1951). Lower IQ's are associated more with an early age of onset (below 5 years of age) than with a later age of onset, and more with grand mal or psychomotor seizures than with petit mal seizures (Collins & Lennox, 1947). Anticonvulsant medication (such as phenobarbital or Dilantin) does not appear to impair intellectual functioning significantly.

Muscular Dystrophy

Muscular dystrophy, a condition resulting from a biochemical malfunction, is associated with a greater incidence of mental retardation than is found in the normal population. The percentage of children with muscular dystrophy in the Mentally Retarded range has been reported to range from 24% to 63% (Dubowitz, 1965; Worden & Vignos, 1962).

Neonatal Hyperbilirubinemia

Neonatal hyperbilirubinemia (jaundice), incurred without any demonstrable brain damage between the ages of 3 years and 15 years, may result in significantly lower IQ's (M IQ = 103 vs. 110 in a control group) (Van Camp, 1964).

Nutritional Deficiencies

Malnutrition and disease after the birth stage may not retard intellectual growth directly; however, they are more likely to reduce the amount of energy which the growing child can put into learning about the world and concentrating on school learning (Vernon, 1969).

Perinatal Variables

The relationship between perinatal variables (pertaining to, before, during, or after time of birth) and IQ's obtained at 7 years of age has been found to be extremely limited, with race of child and variables associated with the mother (e.g., education, birthplace, occupational status, and psychiatric status) playing a somewhat more significant role than physical complications surrounding the birth (Henderson, Butler, & Clark, 1971). Perinatal stress, as defined by the total number of potentially stressful symptoms experienced during pregnancy, delivery, and puerperium, was not found to be related to IQ's obtained at 4 years and 7 years of age (Colligan, 1969). Perinatal anoxia at birth may result in lower than normal IQ's at the age of 3 years (Graham, Ernhart, Thurston, & Craft, 1962).

Poliomyelitis

Poliomyelitis appears to have a negligible effect on intelligence (Phillips, Berman, & Hanson, 1948).

Rheumatic Fever

Sex and age factors appear to be associated with rheumatic fever and level of intelligence (Reinhart, 1965). Rheumatic fever contracted after 6 years of age does not appear to affect the IQ. However, rheumatic fever contracted before 6 years of age has been found to be associated with lower IQ's for girls, but not for boys. The girls in this age group also had high anxiety scores.

Speech Difficulties

Generalizations concerning the relationship between speech difficulties and intellectual functioning are difficult because speech problems are at times associated with brain injury or with other organic conditions. Retarded children usually have more speech defects than normal children, but not necessarily defects associated with articulatory errors (Ainsworth, 1958). Psychogenic speech defects tend to be associated with lower WISC Verbal Scale scores than Performance Scale scores in children between 6 and 12 years of age (Butler, 1967).

SUMMARY

The first group considered in Chapter 23 was emotionally disturbed children. Emotionally disturbed children may have learning difficulties, unsatisfactory interpersonal relationships, inappropriate behavior, unhappiness, and repetitive illness. Studies have indicated that the vast majority of deviant behaviors of children can be classified under four headings: conduct disorder, personality disorder, immaturity, and socialized delinquency. The extent to which emotional disorders may affect cognitive functioning is unknown, but there are many possible emotional factors which may interfere with the intellectual functioning of children, ranging from lack of parental reward and desire to punish the parents, to desire to avoid self-evaluation and desire to be the recipient of love rather than of envy and aggression.

Research has shown that intellectual disturbance is not usually a major factor of importance in the etiology of childhood behavioral or neurotic disorders.

Studies using group tests of intelligence usually report low but significant negative correlations between manifest anxiety and intelligence in school-age children. Similarly, small to moderate negative relationships have been reported between measures of test anxiety and scores on conventional intelligence tests.

Emotionally disturbed children have been found to obtain *lower* scores on group-administered intelligence tests than on individually administered intelligence tests.

Delinquent children, on the average, obtain IQ's that are about eight points lower than non-delinquent children.

General diagnostic indicators of emotional disturbance that may occur during the testing situation were reviewed. Indicators of emotional disturbance may be derived from attitudes (e.g., irritability and suspiciousness), language (e.g., speech difficulty and rambling), and performance on specific tests or groups of tests (e.g., passing some tests that are congruent with the neurotic pattern, while failing other tests that are not congruent with the neurotic pattern).

No systematic patterns have been found on the Stanford-Binet that are suggestive of emotional disturbance or juvenile delinquency. However, the child's general performance as well as performance on selected tests may prove to be helpful in evaluating cognitive efficiency.

The WISC, like the Stanford-Binet, does not provide any systematic patterns that can distinguish emotionally disturbed children from normal children or from children with other forms of psychopathology. Delinquent children usually obtain higher Performance than Verbal Scale IQ's on the WISC. However, the extensiveness of the discrepancy may not be related to degree of acting-out behavior. The discrepancy may be more diagnostic of learning difficulties than of delinquency *per se*.

Children with learning disabilities are those who have an educationally significant discrepancy between their estimated intellectual potential and their actual level of performance. The learning disability syndrome is closely associated with the minimal brain dysfunction syndrome, and the designations are at times used interchangeably. Ross proposed an interesting system for classifying children with learning difficulties which attempts to differentiate among children with perceptual disorders, neurotic learning inhibitions, and psychological disorders which do not primarily focus on learning. There is some evidence to suggest that the kinds of behavioral problems found in children with learning disabilities are related to intelligence level.

On the WISC, learning disabled children with a Performance > Verbal pattern were found to perform better than those with a Verbal > Performance pattern on tasks involving visual-perceptual skills, while, in contrast, the Verbal > Performance group performed better than the Performance > Verbal group on tasks involving verbal and auditory-perceptual abilities. WISC Verbal-Performance discrepancies thus were found to be useful in predicting differential performances on a variety of ability tests for learning disabled children.

Reading disability has many causes, but the classification which best serves to demarcate a "learning disability syndrome" is the one proposed by Lyle and Goyen, which focuses on reading retardation in children who are bright enough to learn and who have had the usual learning opportunities. Low IQ may be a cause of inadequate reading ability. The two studies investigating the Stanford-Binet pattern of inadequate readers indicate that inadequate readers have more difficulty with verbal tests than with other kinds of tests. Many studies have used the WISC to investigate patterns of subtest scores obtained by inadequate readers, but most suffer from methodological weaknesses. However, the following pattern of subtest scores appears to characterize inadequate readers (from best to poorest): (1) Picture Completion, (2) Picture Arrangement, (3) Block Design, (4) Object Assembly, (5) Similarities, (6) Comprehension, (7) Vocabulary, (8) Coding, (9) Arithmetic, and (10) Information. This pattern is reflected in lower Verbal than Performance Scale IQ's. The "language retardation syndrome" and the "developmental Gerstmann syndrome" are two special syndromes associated with reading and writing retardation.

The WISC Verbal Scale and Hayes-Binet, while correlating highly in samples of blind children, do not, on the average, provide similar IQ's, especially with above-average-ability blind children; IQ's are higher on the Hayes-Binet than on the WISC. Blind children tend to perform best on the WISC Digit Span subtest and poorest on the Similarities subtest. The WISC Performance Scale is very suitable for the evaluation of deaf children, while the Verbal-Performance discrepancy may provide an index of the effects of hearing impairment on verbal ability. Within the Performance Scale, Picture Arrangement appears to be the most difficult subtest for partially hearing children.

Some generalizations are possible concerning the effects of physical disease or physical disability on the IQ. The age at which the disease is contracted appears to be directly related to intelligence level. Before ages 3, 4, 5, or 6 years (depending on specific condition), many conditions result in lowered intelligence. Cardiac conditions after 3 years of age, diabetes mellitis after 5 years of age, idiopathic epilepsy after 5 years of age, and rheumatic fever after 6 years of age seem to have little effect on the IQ. Conditions which do not appear to affect intelligence include perinatal stress and poliomyelitis. Some effect on intelligence, although not very severe, occurs in blindness, deafness, neonatal hyperbilirubinemia, and perinatal anoxia. Severe adverse effects on intelligence occur in cerebral palsy, symptomatic epilepsy, very low birth weight, and muscular dystrophy.

SECTION 6

PSYCHOLOGICAL REPORTS AND CONSULTATION

Section 6 consists of three chapters. Chapter 24 considers the problems involved in synthesizing test findings and in writing reports. Chapter 25 details the structure and content of the psychological report, and presents examples of Stanford-Binet, WISC, and WPPSI reports for normal children and for children with special problems. Chapter 26, which discusses the consultation process, reviews the activities of school psychologists, the role of recommendations in the consultative process, and consultation with parents. It emphasizes the need to base professional work on ethical guidelines developed by the American Psychological Association and on the guidelines for the maintenance and dissemination of pupil records published by the Russell Sage Foundation. We have emphasized research studies throughout the text and continue to do so in Section 6.

While the material in Section 6 should be carefully studied, there is no substitute for the actual writing of a report. Practice may not lead to perfection, but arm-chair learning of do's and don'ts may not bear any fruits. For many students, writing is an effort. But the report usually must be written, so why not make it an interesting, informative, and valuable piece of communication? It is to this end that the material in Chapters 24 and 25 is addressed.

It is important to recognize that the psychological evaluation usually is not based solely on one test. We strongly endorse the use of a battery of tests in the assessment situation, including objective and projective temperament (personality) instruments, an achievement test (or tests), a visual-motor test (or tests), and one or more intelligence tests. Chapter 21 has illustrated typical tests that may be used in a battery. The reports that are illustrated in Chapter 25 are based on one intelligence test because the focus of the text is on intelligence tests. However, the general format of the reports that are illustrated can be used for assessment situations in which a battery of tests has been administered. When a battery of tests is administered, the report then becomes a statement based on an integrated presentation of the findings of the entire battery. In administering tests, we attempt to get a sampling of behavior and infer that our sampling is representative of the child's behavior. It is unlikely that any one test (intelligence or otherwise) can provide a minimally adequate sampling of behavior.

CHAPTER 24

SYNTHESIS OF TEST FINDINGS

The writing of a psychological report represents a process of analysis, synthesis, and integration of the material gathered by the examiner. In the report, the examiner tries to communicate with the reader by presenting material which will aid the reader in working with and providing help for the child. The report serves as a medium through which findings are described and impressions are conveyed as clearly and as concisely as possible (Klopfer, 1959); it should *not* be a medium used to demonstrate the psychologist's erudition and professional competence (cf. Handler, Gerston, & Handler, 1965). The problems encountered in report writing not only are the usual ones we have with spelling, grammar, and proofreading, but also center on the selection of material that will enable us to present clearly and unambiguously the test findings, interpretations, and recommendations. A well-reasoned and well-organized report requires clear formulation.

Much synthesis occurs in report writing. But even before a report is begun, the examiner has tried to make some kind of coherent whole out of what he has found. The report usually will be sent to some professional source. However, in addition to a written report (or, at times, in lieu of a formal written report) the report is made to a staff, or (usually verbally) to the child himself or to his parents or guardian; sometimes it is not sent to any professional or agency. The examiner, it is recommended, always should write a complete report for his records, regardless of whether or not the report will be sent to another individual. This is necessary because at some future date he may be called on to present the results of his evaluation, and the details of the evaluation are likely to be forgotten unless they have been recorded at the time of the evaluation. The actual writing of the report is an activity that is performed by any number of different professionals (who are usually, but not exclusively, in the field of psychology or education) who administer tests.

Over the years, a number of books have appeared which have presented useful material concerning the writing of reports (Hammond & Allen, 1953; Huber, 1961; Klopfer, 1960; Martin, 1972). The reader is encouraged to study these texts, for this chapter only highlights some of the principles, ideas, and research findings pertinent to the reporting and interpretation of the results of intelligence tests.

DECIDING WHAT MATERIAL TO INCLUDE IN THE REPORT

At times it is difficult to determine whether certain material should be included in the report; that is, whether the material is relevant or important.

Judgment and discretion are necessary, but decisions concerning relevancy depend largely upon the needs of the referral source and the current state of knowledge concerning the particular test itself, intelligence-test theory, personality dynamics, and psychopathology. Sargent's (1951) advice is pertinent: "The nature of the referral problem, the object of testing, the background of the persons for whom a report is written (and even their personal preferences) should largely determine the kind of report submitted [p. 175]." Surveys (Lacey & Ross, 1964; Tallent & Reiss, 1959a) have shown that different professional groups (psychiatrists, psychologists, and social workers) differ in their preferences for the type of content that should be included in psychological reports. Therefore, the three areas discussed by Sargent above should be considered in deciding what kinds of material to include in the report.

When is it worthwhile, for example, to describe the examinee's grooming, his handedness, or his body structure? Each case must be considered individually. In some cases, the examinee's handedness may provide information helpful in determining whether mixed dominance or neurological problems exist. In other cases, a discussion of the examinee's grooming may contribute to an understanding of his self-concept, his attitudes, or his family environment; in still other cases, neither handedness nor grooming will be of importance. Therefore, material should be emphasized which pertains to the referral question, which conveys the examinee's individuality, and which reflects unusual behaviors and attitudes. Giving merely a description of appearance and behavior without interpretation should be avoided; similarly, interpretations without supporting evidence should not be made (Burgemeister, 1962). The formulation of every report is a process of incorporating those details, over and above the standard data, that highlight the examinee's unique level of psychological functioning. "Does it serve to *individualize* the patient? [Lodge, 1953, p. 402]" is the question that should be kept in mind.

NOTING EXAMINATION CONDITIONS WHICH MAY HELP EXPLAIN PERFORMANCE

Once the specific focus of the report has been decided, material should be selected that describes and elucidates the main theme or themes. Data that diverge from the main theme can be included if they have important implications. Discrepancy in performance, or more likely variability in performance, is especially useful in guiding predictions, inferences, and recommendations. Suppose, for example, that there is a general pattern of memory difficulty, but not a consistent one; some successes and failures occur both above and below the chronological age (CA) level. In such a case, the variable efficiency should be noted. Diagnostic formulations should take into account the degree of consistency in the test performance. Consistency alerts us to factors present during the examination, such as fatigue, anxiety, or lack of interest, that may partially explain the examinee's successes and failures. The report aims to give a consistent and integrated account of the examinee's abilities. As Mayman (1959) writes: "The report shows internal consistency in its descriptive and explanatory statements, and reveals the careful dialectic synthesis which is usually required before genuine internal consistency is achieved [p. 458]."

Inferences are based upon many different forms of information, including the quality of the interaction between the examinee and examiner, the examinee's responses, and the examinee's case history, which may include previous test results. *Everything observed from the initial encounter to the termination of the contact with the examinee constitutes data for analysis. The examination is to be viewed, not merely as a question-and-answer session, but as an opportunity for interaction between two individuals. This interaction is as much a part of the examination as are the test questions and the examinee's responses.* The examiner must consider how he affects the examinee and how, in turn, the examinee affects him. The nature of the interaction may play an important role in influencing the interpretations of the examiner. It may very well be that on some occasions the examinee's behavior is primarily a reaction to the examiner's behavior rather than a reaction to the test demands. (See Chapter 6 for a discussion of the variables affecting the test situation.) Administering, scoring, and interpreting individual psychological tests like the Stanford-Binet, WISC, and WPPSI are by no means so standardized that we can neglect any aspect of the individual differences among examiners and examinees.

DECIDING WHEN TO REFER TO RAW DATA IN THE REPORT

The steps used in arriving at inferences, conclusions, recommendations, and diagnostic formulations should not be presented in the report. "In scanning the test items successfully completed by the client, it was apparent that . . . " is superfluous. The statement should start with the information which follows after "that." Similarly, it is generally unnecessary to refer to the raw data upon which the inferences were based. Occasionally, however, carefully selected examples from the examinee's responses can enhance the meaningfulness of the report by serving to illustrate the diagnostic formulations. Holzberg, Alessi, and Wexler (1951), in discussing psychological case reporting at staff conferences, noted that including verbatim material helps to clarify the examinee's problems and also serves to clarify specific points. If, for example, an examinee is described as giving over-elaborated responses, including an example of such over-elaboration would be helpful. Sometimes it may be necessary to cite the test question together with the examinee's response in order to facilitate the reader's understanding. Noting the specific question, test, subtest, or year level at which the question occurs is perfectly permissible and at times warranted. It may not be enough to refer to specific tests or subtests by name; instead, *describe* what they measure or require because test or subtest names may have limited meaning to the reader.

DECIDING ON THE DEGREE OF CERTAINTY OF THE STATEMENTS

We turn now to another aspect of report writing, which concerns the confidence of the writer about the statements made in a report. Phrases and words such as "probably," "it appears," "perhaps," and "it seems" are often used to indicate that we are not completely confident of our predictions, conclusions, or inferences. The limited sample of the examinee's behavior obtained during the testing session ordinarily provides inadequate data about his personality. Therefore, as Mayman (1959) noted, "Speculations about explanatory psychodynamics are kept within reasonable bounds and are identified as speculations in the report [p. 458]." However, when definitive data are available, present them confidently. One could write: "The examinee's IQ is in the classification 'Superior.' The chances that the range of scores from 130 to 140 includes his true IQ are about 68 out of 100." (See Chapter 25 for a discussion of standard error of measurement.) As Foster (1951) indicated: "Be positive when sure, qualify when in doubt [p. 195]."

The degree of certainty we have about our conclusions will depend upon the available data. The examinee's test behavior and responses are the observed data, whereas inferred behavior or predicted behavior has not yet been demonstrated. Recognizing the difference between what the examinee actually *did,* that is, his test performance, and what he *may* be able to do, may help in reducing the amount of ambiguity contained in the report and may also help in reducing errors of interpretation. For example, the examiner is certain that the examinee is brown-eyed or that he obtained an IQ of 110. He feels reasonably sure that his true IQ is within the range from 100 to 120. (The chances are about 95 out of 100 that this is true.)

ANCHORING THE REPORT TO THE INTELLIGENCE LEVEL

The IQ obtained is the anchor point for the development of the report. Primary emphasis should be given to the examinee's general level of intellectual functioning. An examinee with an IQ of 130 should appear superior in the report, while one with an IQ of 70 should appear dull. *The examinee's pattern of performance should always be analyzed with reference to his general range of intellectual ability*. In presenting the examinee's strengths and weaknesses, no absolute guidelines can be established, and therefore, the use of relative terms is imperative. Terms such as "relatively less" or "relatively more developed," "in relation to his level of functioning," "in relation to the average child of his age," and "above average in his ... [a specific area such as language, visual-motor, or memory may be cited] functioning" are preferable to terms such as "weak" and "strong." Using these two latter terms presents a number of problems. First, they imply, incorrectly, an absolute quantity. Patterns of ability are relative, either to the examinee's chronological age group or to his mental age group. The reader should clearly know which reference point is being used. Second, the weaknesses or strengths of an examinee with an IQ of 120 are likely to be qualitatively different from the weaknesses or strengths of an examinee with an IQ of 50. One should therefore describe the examinee's ability in reference to the normative group or the examinee's own level of performance, or both. (The discussion of scatter analysis in Chapters 10 and 14 is also pertinent to evaluating the pattern of the examinee's abilities.) If the terms "weak" and "strong" are used, they should be used in conjunction with a description of the child's performance.

AVOIDING COMMON PITFALLS IN REPORT WRITING

This section presents some general suggestions to aid in the art of clear writing. The points in this section may help to eliminate many of the problems that make reports difficult for the reader.

Eliminating Technical Terms

The report's readability can be enhanced by eliminating technical terms, because such terms are difficult to understand for readers not versed in psychological terminology (cf. Hammond & Allen, 1953; Mayman, 1959; Taylor & Teicher, 1946; Thorne, 1960). Historical and technical information about the particular intelligence test, too, should not be included. It is not necessary to mention, for example, that Terman and Merrill revised the Stanford-Binet in 1937, that Pinneau constructed the revised IQ tables for the Stanford-Binet, or that the standard deviation of the IQ's is 16 for the Stanford-Binet or 15 for the WISC. Technical details should be referred to only in exceptional cases. A report on the testing of a foreign-born examinee might recall that the Stanford-Binet, WISC, and WPPSI were standardized on American children.

Focus on What is There, Not on What is Absent

In order to promote clarity, focus on the *presence* of a trait or behavior rather than on its absence. An almost infinite number of things which did not characterize the examinee can be cited. Unless it is expected that the report will contain information about pathological symptoms (e.g., brain damage), citing the absence of an attribute is not illuminating. Describe how the examinee actually performed. However, occasionally there are presenting complaints or reports from parents, schools, physicians, or others that the child has a particular problem. When a thorough examination does not reveal what has been presented originally, comment should certainly be made that a specific attribute or behavior was not apparent or not discernible during the evaluation.

Clarifying Obscure Details

If terms must be used that are obscure or only understood by a limited number of people, be sure to describe them in detail. Thus, for example, do not use abbreviations to stand for special programs or refer to room numbers in buildings without describing the referents in sufficient detail. The reader is likely to become perplexed unless obscure details are either eliminated or clarified.

Integrating the Presentation

Some report writers have a tendency to dissect or fragment the examinee so that he is presented as if various parts of his intellectual ability or personality are independent of each other. The examinee's abilities are always interrelated, but not necessarily in a well-integrated and well-functioning manner. To illustrate the interplay of abilities, use expressions conveying comparison and contrast, such as "however," "but," "on the other hand," "on the one hand," or "in comparison with" to help build an integrated picture of the examinee's abilities.

Avoiding Incomprehensible Sentences

A number of rules for producing *barely* intelligible prose in scientific writing have been published (Anonymous, 1963). The rules, also applicable to report writing, present frequently occurring lapses in writing. These rules are amusing but make a telling point. To insure the reader's frustration:

go through the manuscript grouping short sentences together into longer ones by substituting commas for periods . . . lapse into abbreviations at every opportunity. A sentence that begins "The DRT group, in contrast to the GTR-2 group, showed no trend with respect to the RQ-Z scores . . . is almost sure to lose the reader. The author can enhance the effectiveness of this technique by making sure that each abbreviation is defined ambiguously or incompletely and by scattering the definitions through the body of the paper so that they are difficult to find . . . . Make different clauses in the same sentence non sequitur. For example, "In attempting to explicate memory processes, usual methods of measuring memory for order are markedly artificial in that . . . . " This sentence means that markedly artificial methods of measuring memory for order are attempting to explicate memory processes. Repeatedly use this technique throughout the length of the paper [pp. 313-314].

REVISING THE FIRST DRAFT

After the first draft has been completed, examine the report for errors and for ways to enhance the clarity of the material. Be sure that all findings, interpretations, and recommendations are clearly presented; revise sections that are vague or ambiguous. Like research papers, the psychological report aims "to make the clearest, most comprehensible presentation in the simplest terms, using the smallest possible number of words, dealing only with relevant issues and avoiding undue generalization and speculation. The aim is to clarify and not to make obscure [Thorne, 1960, p. 343]." Some questions to consider are as follows: Can the report be understood by an intelligent layman? Are there ambiguities, redundancies, or misleading phrases? Is the representativeness of the results clearly presented? After the final typing, it is important to proofread the report. Spelling errors, omitted phrases, and grammatical and typing errors should be corrected. With experience, it is less likely that revisions of the report will be needed, but careful proofreading will always be necessary.

GENERAL CONSIDERATIONS

The interplay of the many sources that contribute to the development of psychological reports has been well illustrated by Appelbaum (1970). Appelbaum pointed out that the examiner assumes many roles in writing the psychological report. He may play the role of politician, diplomat, group dynamicist, salesman, artist, and finally, psychologist. Which one or ones of these roles will be displayed is in part dependent upon the particular setting in which the report is written. The key elements or features involved in report writing, according to Appelbaum, include the ability (a) to balance between data and abstraction, (b) to use modulation, (c) to be assertive or modest when necessary, (d) to keep the interest of the reader, (e) to use illustrations wisely, (f) to discuss systematically the individual parts of the report, and (g) to facilitate the decision-making process. Appelbaum views reports as being political, diplomatic, and strategic persuasions that function in a complex sociopsychological context, rather than as being solely technical and scientific documents.

Paralleling the approach of Appelbaum, but yet slightly different, is the interesting and valuable approach to report writing proposed by Fischer (1973). The approach, while not radically different from those offered by other writers or from that offered in this chapter, emphasizes a contextual approach as an alternative to the psychodynamic approach. The social/descriptive/contextual approach highlights in the report the relationship between the examinee and the examiner, the circumstances under which the testing took place, the limited range of opportunities for observation and interaction, and the behavioral bases for the statements made in the report. Concrete recommendations, which have been discussed with the examinee, are emphasized. The report is descriptive and requires extensive samples; it eliminates constructs, causal interpretations, diagnostics, and other jargon. The necessity to select only certain examples and to make specific recommendations confronts the examiner with the issue of values. He must try to balance the goals of the examinee, of society, and of himself. While Fischer's approach may not appeal to all examiners, it does offer to the examiner an orientation to report writing that is likely to be meaningful and helpful.

We have seen that report writing is a process of refining ideas, establishing clarity of expression, and using expertness in decision making. The ability to write a clear and meaningful report is highly valued. The psychologist, through the psychological report, contributes to the educational and treatment process, a process which he shares with other professionals who are also working toward the goal of enhancing and developing the examinee's potentialities.

RESEARCH INVESTIGATIONS

Evaluation of Psychological Reports

Research investigations that have evaluated psychological reports are very instructive in pointing out communication problems occurring in report writing. One series of surveys concerned professional workers' views of reports (Tallent, 1963; Tallent & Reiss, 1959a, 1959b, 1959c). Respondents, who were psychiatrists ($N = 276$), psychologists ($N = 233$), and social workers ($N = 203$), all of whom were associated with the Veterans Administration, reported many specific problems connected with psychological reports (Tallent & Reiss, 1959c). To some extent, the respondent's professional orientation correlated with the frequency with which certain problem areas were reported. Thus, for example, psychologists were found to be critical of reports containing raw data, while psychiatrists were concerned that reports offer too little raw data.

Tallent and Reiss organized the criticisms of psychological reports around six major areas. These areas, along with selected illustrations, were as follows: (1) *problems of content* — too little or too much raw data, improper emphasis, diagnoses not called for, content of minor relevance, unnecessary duplication; (2) *problems of interpretation* — irresponsible interpretation, over-speculation, unlabeled speculation, inadequate differentiation among patients; (3) *problems of psychologist's attitude and orientation* — report not practical or useful, exhibitionistic (revealed by high-flown terminology), too authoritative, too test-oriented, too theoretical, over-abstract; (4) *problems of communication* — problems in word usage, vague (or unclear or ambiguous), report either too long or too short, too technical (or complex), problems with style, problems with organization, hedging; (5) *problems of role conduct* — the psychologist's recommendations reflect his usurping the responsibilities of other professions; (6) *problems of science and profession* — reports reflect the need for advances in the profession.

Lacey and Ross (1964) conducted a survey similar to that of Tallent and Reiss (1959a, 1959b, 1959c), but they sampled psychiatrists ($N = 41$), psychologists ($N = 42$), and social workers ($N = 67$) associated with community child-guidance clinics instead of professional staff members in the Veterans Administration. Similarities as well as differences were found in the two surveys. Both reported that the respondents preferred that the reports (*a*) include descriptive material concerned with the appearance and behavior of the examinee, (*b*) use a factual rather than a literary style, and (*c*) omit specific medical, social, or other psychological data. However, many more of the respondents in the child-guidance clinics were in favor of the reports containing recommendations than were workers in the Veterans Administration: psychologists, 95% vs. 63%, respectively; social workers, 82% vs. 53%, respectively; and psychiatrists, 50% vs. 33%, respectively. More child guidance respondents also preferred to have prognostic statements and citation of raw data in the reports than Veterans Administration respondents. The two surveys reveal that attitudes held by professional workers toward the content of psychological reports are to some extent associated with their work settings.

Another study concerning report writing evaluated the communication value of reports as judged by psychologists, psychiatrists, and psychiatric social workers (Garfield, Heine, & Leventhal, 1954). While variation was found among the judges in their ratings of the adequacy of the reports, they tended to rate a majority of the reports as being only "fair" or below. The raters found such difficulties as (a) lack of supporting data or behavioral referents, (b) poor expression (e.g., use of clichés and jargon, loose use of terms, and vagueness), (c) poor organization, (d) inconsistencies, (e) incorrect use of theory, (f) poor differentiation of test data from other data, (g) making the unconscious sound conscious, (h) failing to answer referral problem, and (i) being too long and irrelevant.

An analysis of 100 psychological reports that were written by six different psychologists working at a Goodwill Industries rehabilitation facility indicated that 44% of all content statements dealt with measures of intelligence (Hartlage & Merck, 1971). Thus, the assessment of intelligence, in this study, occupied an important place in the psychological report. Reports were found to improve when the psychologists became more familiar with the uses to which their reports were to be applied. It was suggested that psychological reports should serve the decision-making needs of the agency.

Recent surveys also indicate that psychological reports continue to be viewed both positively (Olive, 1972; Smyth & Reznikoff, 1971) and negatively (Moore, Boblitt, & Wildman, 1968) by psychiatrists. In a survey of the contribution of psychological reports to patient management in psychiatric facilities for children and adults, the respondents, usually psychiatric residents, were asked to give their reasons for making referrals and to rate the reports on a number of dimensions (Affleck & Strider, 1971). The dimensions used by Affleck and Strider have been summarized in checklist form and are shown in Table 24–1. (The form may be helpful to readers interested in surveying the usefulness of psychological reports.) It was found that intellectual appraisal occupied the first rank as a reason for referral. Other reasons for referral included personality appraisal, diagnostic impression, indications of organic brain damage, psychotherapeutic potential, and educational and vocational suggestions. The reports were viewed generally either as providing new and significant information or as providing information that confirmed information which was previously suspected, but which was not well established. A majority of the reports (52%) were seen as contributing to patient management.

Technical Psychological Language

Cuadra and Albaugh (1956) reported that there are large gaps between report-writers' intentions and the corresponding interpretations made by professional and student judges. Such discrepancies are probably associated with misinterpretation of technical psychological language, a communication difficulty which Rucker (1967a) showed existed among school personnel. He asked school psychologists ($N = 79$) and elementary school teachers ($N = 61$) to select the one best definition out of four for each of 31 terms commonly found in psychological reports. Using a criterion of 50 per cent or more agreement in both groups, only 14 out of the 31 terms were defined similarly. These 14 terms, together with their modal response, are shown in Table 24–2. The 17 terms that showed major disagreements were as follows: "adjusted academic program," "educational retardation," "ego," "hyperactivity,"

Table 24-1. CHECKLIST FOR EVALUATING PSYCHOLOGICAL REPORTS

	CHECK ONE		
CRITERION	Yes	No	Cannot Evaluate
1. Report erroneous, incomplete, or detrimental	☐	☐	☐
2. Report considered to have had no effect	☐	☐	☐
3. Report had no effect because client went AWOL or quit	☐	☐	☐
4. Report had minimal effect	☐	☐	☐
5. Report considered helpful	☐	☐	☐
6. Report confirmed current thinking about client	☐	☐	☐
7. Altered diagnosis and understanding of behavior and dynamics	☐	☐	☐
8. Altered treatment approach to client	☐	☐	☐
9. Altered clincian's (or teacher's or social worker's) personal feelings toward the client	☐	☐	☐
10. Altered plans regarding education or planning for special disabilities	☐	☐	☐
11. Altered nature of contact or activity with the family of the client	☐	☐	☐
12. Report assisted in placement, disposition, or referral to another agency	☐	☐	☐

Note.—The items have the following kinds of implications: negative (item 1), neutral (items 2 and 3), mildly positive (items 4, 5, and 6), strongly positive (items 7 through 12). (Reprinted, with a change in notation, by permission of the publisher and authors from D. C. Affleck and F. D. Strider, "Contribution of Psychological Reports to Patient Management," *Journal of Consulting and Clinical Psychology,* **37,** p. 178. Copyright 1971, American Psychological Association.)

Table 24-2. TERMS AGREED UPON BY MORE THAN 50 PER CENT OF A SAMPLE OF PSYCHOLOGISTS AND TEACHERS

TERM	MODAL RESPONSE
Compulsive	Ritualistic behavior
Counseling	Supportive guidance
Defensive Behavior	Employed to protect self-esteem
Defense Mechanism	Protective device
Emotional Block	Inhibited thinking due to excessive emotions
Emotionally Disturbed	Behavior disorder
Mentally Healthy	Sense of self-respect and self-reliance
Oral Fixation	Failure to progress past oral gratification stage
Potential Achievement Level	Expected achievement for mental age
Remedial Reading	Instruction to correct reading problems
Retarded Reader	Reading level below mental age expectancy
Specific Reading Disability	Reading disability not associated with difficulty in any other academic area
Underachiever	Achievement below mental-age expectation
Visual-Motor Difficulty	Poor developmental level of eye-hand coordination

(Reprinted by permission of the publisher from C. N. Rucker, "Technical Language in the School Psychologist's Reports," *Psychology in the Schools,* **4,** p. 148. Copyright 1967, Clinical Psychology Publishing Co., Inc.)

"motivation," "school phobia," "slow learner," "basal age," "autism," "brain damaged," "school psychological services," "projective tests," "delinquent behavior," "individual differences," "intellectual level," "anxiety," and "functional retardation." These 17 terms, Rucker concluded, "are likely to be misinterpreted if used in a written psychological report in a school setting [p. 149]." Therefore, such terms should be either explained or omitted in reports that are used in school settings.

A similar conclusion is reached from the findings of a study by Shively and Smith (1969). Thirty technical or potentially ambiguous terms were culled from psychological reports that were available from school files. The terms were presented in a multiple-choice test to teachers, counselors, and undergraduate teacher-education majors. The mean number of correct answers ranged from 14 for the teachers to 22 for the counselors. In the total group, only 54% of the terms were identified correctly. Terms understood more frequently by the counselors than by the other two groups included "psychomotor," "etiology," "enuresis," "pathology," "megalomania," "empirical," "basal," "psychosomatic," and "projective tests."

Grayson and Tolman (1950) also demonstrated that psychological terms convey different meanings to professional readers. They culled 50 terms that are frequently used in psychological reports—such as "abstract," "affective," "aggressive," "spontaneity," "subtest," and "superego"—and analyzed the definitions given to these terms by 17 psychiatrists and 20 psychologists. The people sampled varied widely in their definitions: psychologists' definitions were more abstract, more highly conceptualized, more academic, and more technical, while psychiatrists' definitions more often were in "lay" language. Generally, many of the definitions were loose and ambiguous. The authors suggested that the respondents' lack of verbal precision is associated with the complexity of psychological phenomena represented by the terms.

Quality and Style of the Report

Rucker (1967b) also studied the qualities which differentiate adequate from less adequate reports. Experienced ($N = 9$) and inexperienced ($N = 10$) school psychologists, using the same background data and test protocol, each wrote a report that was rated by five elementary-school teachers. While the sample of school psychologists was small and possibly nonrepresentative (since they comprised only 35 per cent and 37 per cent of the original groups contacted), the results furnish some useful suggestions for report writing. First, the quality of the reports was not related to such writer background variables as length of teaching experience, age, sex, marital status, number of graduate hours, or undergraduate and graduate majors. Second, the *best* reports were described by such words or phrases as "understandable," "enjoyable to read," "motivated to follow suggestions," "excellent interpretation of test results," "explained so that the results are understandable even if reader is not familiar with the test," "showed how problem came about," "answered specific referral questions," "recommendations could be implemented in classroom without singling out child," and "conveyed that teacher had asked relevant questions that deserved careful answers." Phrases characterizing the *poorest* reports were "too brief," "lacked form and organization," "results either absent or not explained," "recommendations vague, short, or not answering referral questions," and "unrealistic suggestions made for classroom procedure." The comments indicate that the best reports contained helpful suggestions, clear answers to the referral questions, specific and meaningful interpretations, and awareness of classroom procedures. The poorest reports were overly brief, poorly organized, and inadequate in their presentation of results and recommendations. *Overall, the most important factor in evaluating the utility of the report was the quality of the recommendations.*

Brandt and Giebink (1968) set out to determine what effect the style of the report has on the preferences of school personnel. Four psychological reports were constructed. Two of the reports contained recommendations based on an "affection-attention-acceptance" interpretation and two employed a "control-discipline-authority" interpretation. In addition, one report of each type provided concrete suggestions for the classroom teacher and the other provided abstract recommendations. The raters consisted of 96 teachers and six administrators. Teachers were also classified as accepting or as authoritarian on the basis of their Minnesota Teacher Attitude Inventory scores. Both groups of raters preferred the concrete and accepting style of report, followed by the concrete and authoritarian style of report. The relationship between teachers' style and report style was not significant. These findings indicate that concrete recommendations are very much desired by school personnel.

Two other surveys corroborate Rucker's (1967b) and Brandt and Giebink's (1968) findings concerning the importance of recommendations. Mussman (1964) reported that his sample of teachers believed that the recommendations and suggestions were very useful portions of the report. Baker (1965) received replies from 333 school personnel—administrators, teachers, and guidance staff—to a questionnaire concerned with school-psychology services. The respondents replied that the recommendations contained in the reports were useful and appropriate only about 50 per cent of the time, and that faster service, with a better follow-up program, was needed. The survey revealed that poor communication existed between the school psychologists and school personnel. On some occasions, instead of poor communication, there is no communication at all. Trione (1958) reported that 22 out of a sample of 103 teachers did not even see the psychological reports that were submitted by the school psychologist.

Comment on Recommendations

A concluding comment concerning the place of recommendations is in order. While there is good agreement in the studies by Rucker (1967b), Mussman (1964), Baker (1965), and Lacey and Ross (1964) that personnel associated with schools and child-guidance clinics feel that recommendations are an important part of the psychological report, the findings of Tallent and Reiss (1959c), as we have seen, indicate that a majority of psychiatrists working in adult settings (Veterans Administration) are against the inclusion of recommendations. These psychiatrists, perhaps, view recommendations as encroaching on a "medical" function; tact, therefore, will be especially needed in the phrasing of recommendations when reports are written in medical settings.

The idea that one can make a separate report for every recipient of the report is somewhat idealistic, and it is not recommended. Recognizing that certain recipients may want recommendations and certain ones may not, one can vary the end of the report and make or not make certain recommendations, depending upon who is to receive the report. In writing the report, the examiner tries to be comprehensive in his thinking as to who should receive the report, and then only under very special circumstances should the report be altered.

THE WATCH-OUT-FOR SENTENCES

This section illustrates types of sentences, selected from graduate student reports, that are for a variety of reasons awkward or less than adequate. The problems encountered in sentence content and structure are classified by categories. Although the sentences have been taken out of context, they and the comments that follow them should be carefully studied in order to recognize and avoid potential problems. Some of the sample sentences have more than one problem and some of the categories overlap, so that placement in a specific category is somewhat arbitrary.

Abstractness

Sentences containing abstract ideas and terms present problems for the reader. The reader must strain for meaning. Information may be lost because vagueness and ambiguity, often a result of abstract phrases, have replaced the directness and simplicity of the communication.

Example 1.   "It is recommended that he be tested again after a three- or four-year period to ascertain whether or not maturation will result in an improved operational level." This is a highly abstract way of saying: "Retesting is recommended in order to evaluate developmental changes."

Example 2.   "His seemingly conscious withdrawal from conversation coupled with an outwardly stoic nature yield an impression of social impoverishment." "Conscious withdrawal," "stoic nature," and "social impoverishment" are complex concepts. The examiner must be wary of describing the examinee as having traits which he may not possess, and of making statements which go beyond an accurate account of the examinee's behavior. To avoid any misinterpretation brought about by the use of the word "stoic," it would be less ambiguous if the examinee's behavior was accurately described (e.g., not showing much emotion during the test). Reticence for conversation and a suggested stoical nature need not indicate social impoverishment. The examinee, boxed in stoicism, wrapped and tied in conscious withdrawal, and labeled as socially impoverished, is defenselessly delivered to the reader. Rephrasing in order to achieve clarity is warranted, because the sentence contains abstract ideas and may be misleading.

Ambiguity

The ambiguous sentence does not clearly inform the reader what the examiner wishes to convey. Be alert to any sentences that may be misinterpreted or that have implications other than those desired.

Example 1.   "It is possible that his performance may reflect the lack of proper emotional orientation which is necessary for meaningful and emotionally relevant action." The concept "meaningful and emotionally relevant action" is ambiguous because it has many possible implications that need to be clarified. Furthermore, concrete illustrations of the examinee's performance are needed to enable the reader to understand the interpretation.

Example 2.   "Joe lacks language ability." "Lacks" may mean either "is deficient in" or "shows a complete absence of." Therefore, ambiguity is created when the phrase is used. The examiner, in all probability, does not literally mean that there is a complete absence of language ability; rather, he desires to convey that the examinee is "below average" or "inadequate" or "retarded" or "slow" or something similar. Preferably, he would use one of these terms or would convey as precisely as possible the level at which the examinee is functioning. For example, he may note that the examinee is below average in language ability or say that language functioning is approximately two years below his chronological age. A gifted examinee can be described as being superior in his language ability, or one may say that language functioning is at a level four years above his chronological age. It is, or course, possible that in exceptional cases the examinee does "lack" a particular skill. In these cases, a sentence such as "Joe cannot write, speak, or understand the speech of others" conveys the information.

Apologies

Do not make excuses either for the test or for the examinee's test performance. Report, without apology, the results of the evaluation in as objective a manner as possible.

Example 1. "Jill gave the impression of enjoying herself, and at the same time was willing to try to meet the challenge of the seemingly never-ending questions of the examiner." To whom did the questions seem never-ending? Do not apologize for the examination techniques, since apologetic statements tend to belittle indirectly the examiner's professional status, and perhaps to diminish the value of the report as well.

Example 2. "The examiner is sorry that Jim achieved an IQ of only 85." Why include "sorry" and "only"? The examiner appears to be belittling the examinee's performance. If other information indicated that the examinee was expected to perform at a higher level of functioning, then this expectation should be noted and the relevant information included; doubts about the representativeness of the results should be clearly brought out. With the use of the term "only," the reader is left in doubt, because he does not know why it was included. Perhaps those examinees falling into ranges below the normal do not feel as helpless or as sorry for themselves as we might think they feel. Our personal values should not be imposed or projected on either the examinees or the readers.

Awkwardness

Awkward sentences contain ambiguous, abstract, vague, or superfluous material. Stylistic problems are therefore evident.

Example 1. "His confidence was congruent with his abilities, and although he realized that he was intelligent, he did not appear to overvalue it or undervalue it, but rather seemed to accept it without evaluating it." The examiner appears to be presenting a picture of a normal examinee, yet the statement is so troubled—poor referents and awkward phraseology—that the message is lost. Better: "He displayed a great deal of confidence in his abilities."

Example 2. "He did not appear to be anxious or concerned but was willing to try to succeed within his normal pattern of effort." The examiner does not usually know what is the examinee's "normal pattern of effort." Better: "His motivation was normal."

Content Unimportant

It is often extremely difficult to determine what material to include in the report. Judgment must be used at all times. "I didn't know what to say" is not sufficient justification for including material that is not important. Include only statements that will contribute to an understanding of the test situation, the examinee's performance, or the examinee's personality.

Example 1. "At one time she wanted to use my pencil and draw a picture, but it was explained to her that she must wait to draw until we were finished. After the test she drew a quick picture and took it with her." Unless this information is serving to illustrate a particular point, why include it? It might be a useful exercise for one to imagine himself as the referral source, reading the report and wondering why the material is included.

Example 2. "John told me that he walks to school and that he likes television." Without other relevant details, the information contained in the sentence is not informative. However, if the child's walking to school reflects a recovery from an illness or reflects a development of independence, then such information is valuable and should appear in the report accompanied by an interpretation.

Generalization Inappropriate

Do not overgeneralize from limited data. All available information should be used in arriving at conclusions. Recommendations and interpretations should be based on reliable and sufficient data.

Example 1. "Nancy was weak in areas requiring numerical reasoning, as evidenced by her missing the item on ingenuity at the Average Adult level." Reference to one item is not sufficient justification for concluding that she was weak in numerical reasoning. It is hazardous to generalize from one failure or from one success. A consistent clear-cut *pattern* of failures or successes should be present before reaching conclusions of this kind. The levels at which the successes and failures occurred will help in guiding the interpretations.

Example 2. "The examinee was small for his age and may feel a need to achieve." Again, if smallness is the only bit of data available to the examiner about the examinee's achievement needs, this interpretation should not be made.

Example 3. "On the basis of his Full Scale IQ of 107, it is predicted that Mark will do at least average work in school and that he will excel in athletics." Two inappropriate generalizations are contained in this sentence. First, the 107 IQ indicates that he is *capable* of performing at least at a normal level in school; it does not mean that he *will* perform at that level. Second, the statement about athletics cannot be made on the basis of a child's performance on an intelligence test.

Example 4. "Charles demonstrated good attention span, which indicates that he is free from anxiety." Satisfactory performance on the Digit Span or Sentences subtests, for example, does not indicate that the child is free from anxiety. The best that can be said is that anxiety did not appear to affect the child's performance.

Hedging

Statements about the examinee's performance should be presented in a direct and confident manner when sufficient data are present. Do not hedge when the data are clear. While there are occasions when caution is needed, factual data may be presented simply and precisely.

Example 1. "The Intelligence Quotient of 120 on the Stanford-Binet would seem to indicate a High Average to Superior range of functioning." An IQ of 120 is in the Superior classification according to the classification scheme presented in the Stanford-Binet manual (see page 18 of the manual). There is no need to hedge about this fact or about similar facts. Referring to an IQ of 120 as being in the High Average range is also incorrect. Better: "The Intelligence Quotient of 120 is in the Superior classification on the Stanford-Binet, Form L-M."

Example 2. "The IQ obtained by Jim was approximately 86." The IQ obtained on any one occasion is an estimate of intelligence and, as stressed in this text, should be accompanied by a statement of precision (standard error). However, the examination does permit the calculation of a score, and this score is a specific, exact number. Therefore, in the sentence above, the word "approximately" should be eliminated and in its place a precision range should be written (e.g., 86 ±5). (See Chapter 25 for further information concerning precision range.)

Inexactitude

Inexact sentences include a host of problems, including misleading content and incorrect interpretations.

Example 1. "Her physical appearance suggested no behavioral problems." Rarely will the examinee's physical appearance denote a behavioral problem. Better: "Her appearance was quite ordinary. She was dressed in a loosely fitting sweater and skirt, and her height and weight are normal for her age group."

Example 2. "The examinee achieved an IQ of 112. He has just begun kindergarten and needs to develop listening skills and an approach to solving problems." Since the examinee achieved an IQ of 112, it is difficult to understand how he achieved this score without having developed *some* listening skills and an adequate pattern of solving problems. The examiner may not have meant to relate the two sentences, but may have seen them as two separate facts and failed to indicate this by lack of a transition. If other information leads you to conclude that the examinee is hyperactive or more impulsive than the average examinee of his age, clearly indicate this in the report. To answer the examination questions successfully, the examinee usually must be able to attend to the test questions, concentrate, and respond to the directions. Always consider what the appropriate normative behavior is for the examinee's developmental stage.

Example 3. "Bill's only weakness was shown by his score on the Arithmetic subtest." This sentence was based on WISC scaled scores of 13 or more on all of the subtests, with the exception of a 10 on Arithmetic. The interpretation is incorrect because a scaled score of 10 represents average functioning. This child had no significant weaknesses in relation to the standardization group. His score on the Arithmetic subtest, rather, indicates that he is not as well developed in arithmetical skills as he is in other areas of the test.

Limited or Too General

A virtue in report writing is to be as complete as possible, while recognizing that the report should be kept within manageable bounds and should include only significant information. However, when the material is too sparse, ambiguity may result. Clarity can be achieved, on some of these occasions, by presenting the data on which the interpretation was based. Comments that are "too general," on the other hand, should be eliminated, except when they pertain to some specific question posed by the referral source.

Example 1. "The examiner would recommend that additional information be gathered in regard to her background and her achievement." In and of itself, this recommendation is acceptable. However, the statement should be more specific so that the reader knows *what* information is needed and *why* it is needed. What does the examiner hope to learn by the additional information? What purpose will it serve? Does the examiner wish to see the examinee for further evaluation after the additional information is obtained? Thus, recommendations should incorporate, at times, the rationale used in their formulation.

Example 2. "Bobby shows indications of strength in numerical reasoning and in nonverbal reasoning, and on tests dealing with nonmeaningful memory. Other areas of strength include . . . ." These are tantalizing sentences because the reader is not given information concerning the examinee's absolute strength. It would be helpful to know how strong the examinee was in these areas and in what ways the strengths were shown.

Non Sequitur

Sentences should blend into one another so that abrupt transitions are minimized. Introduce changes in content by use of transitional phrases. The reader should be prepared for what is to follow, and the lead sentence in a paragraph often provides just such preparation.

Example 1. "Richard is above average on memory items. He failed a memory test at a level below his chronological age." The second sentence should be connected with the first sentence by a phrase like "even though."

Example 2. "Jay has excellent conceptual thinking. Another average ability is memory." The second sentence does not easily follow from the first. An "excellent" ability is first presented, and then without any warning an "average" ability is presented. The word "another" is the major problem in the second sentence. It would be better to use the conjunction "but" after the word "thinking" ("but average memory ability") to indicate that another clause is being introduced. Do not jump from one topic to another before describing or interpreting the findings. Then try to make a transition to the next topic.

Technical Terms

Since the psychological report may be read by many nonprofessional people, it is preferable to keep technical matters to a minimum. The goal is to describe the examinee's intellectual skills by minimizing technical details and by maximizing common-sense terms. Always consider whether the reader clearly knows what the technical referents mean.

Example 1. "His language ability should be strengthened, as indicated by his performance on the Minkus Completion test at year-level XII." The examiner, in attempting to illustrate the examinee's below-average language ability, refers to a test that is likely to have little, if any, meaning to the reader. Also, as we have previously noted, it is of limited usefulness to refer to a specific test without illustrating the activities required by the test.

Example 2. "When she reached the ceiling level, she became more restless and serious." The key technical term "ceiling level" may not be understood by the reader. It is preferable to replace "ceiling level" with "When the more difficult levels of the test were reached, she. . . ." If "ceiling level" is used, it can be followed with "(the level at which all tests are failed)" in parentheses.

Example 3. "The child was particularly strong in memory-span tests." Instead of saying "strong in memory-span tests," describe the examinee's abilities as follows: "The child has a good memory span." Discuss the examinee's abilities rather than noting the test names.

TECHNICAL ASPECTS OF REPORT WRITING

It is a truism that conventional grammatical rules must be followed in writing psychological reports. However, there are some aspects of report writing, concerned with grammatical, stylistic, and structural points, that need special emphasis and discussion. A few areas which have been found by this writer to be particularly difficult for the beginning examiner are presented below. A good reference source for technical writing is the American Psychological Association's (1967) *Publication Manual*. Other reference sources should be consulted as needed.

Abbreviations

Abbreviations generally should not be used in the report. Terms such as "etc." can be misleading and should be used only on rare occasions. However,

IQ, MA, and CA may be used, since they pertain to intelligence testing. These three terms are always capitalized and are usually written without periods. Preferably, "examiner" and "examinee" should not be abbreviated because the reader may not understand the meaning of the abbreviations.

Capitalization

Proper names of tests should be capitalized. For example, the "V" in Vocabulary test is capitalized. Other tests that have more than one word in their title present difficulties with respect to capitalization. It is recommended that the first letters of major words of test names be capitalized. For example, the test "Obeying Simple Commands" is written with the first letter of each word in capitals. The classification in which the examinee's IQ falls should be written so that the first letter is capitalized as an attention-aiding device, as in "Normal classification." General areas of intelligence, such as language skills or visual-motor abilities, are not usually capitalized because they do not refer to specific tests in the examination. "Examiner" and "examinee" should not be written in capital letters.

Hyphens

The rules for hyphenation are very complex. It will be helpful to consult a dictionary or other sources, such as *A Manual of Style* published by the University of Chicago Press (1969) or the *Style Manual* published by the United States Government Printing Office (1967). A term such as "7-year-old" is usually hyphenated, especially if it is employed as a compound adjective.

Identifying Data and Test Results

The heading of the report should contain at least the following identifying data: name and address of agency; examinee's name, date of birth, and chronological age; date of examination; date of report; and examinee's grade. In the body of the report, include the IQ, precision range (standard error of measurement), IQ classification, percentile rank, and MA (for the Stanford-Binet). It is also helpful to repeat the child's CA when presenting the test results. Finally, the examiner's name (typewritten and signature) should be placed at the end of the report.

Punctuation

The period and the comma are always placed *before* the closing quotation marks, even when the quotation marks enclose only a single word. For example, "Mark said that he was 'nervous,' and that he is uncomfortable around people." Place colons and semicolons after the quotation mark. Similarly, place a question mark after the quotation mark, unless the question is part of the quoted material.

Spacing

If the report is to be sent to an agency, single spacing is preferred. However, for training purposes reports should be double spaced to allow for corrections and for the supervisor's comments.

Style

Year levels of the examination may be referred to by Roman numerals or by spelling out the numerals. Use of Roman numerals facilitates differentiating the test proper from other information, such as CA and MA, which use Arabic numerals. Thus, for example, when referring to "year-level VIII" write the last term in Roman numerals or use the words "year-level eight" or "the eight-year level."

Tense

The major difficulty encountered in the use of tense is with reference to past and present tenses. When discussing an examinee's level of intelligence, it is preferable to write: "The examinee is of average intelligence." If the past tense had been used in the above sentence, it would sound as if the examinee were deceased or as if he were not average at the time the report was written. In general, more enduring traits such as height, weight, intelligence, and sex should be referred to in the present tense. Thus, "John is a muscular, overweight adolescent who was cooperative on the examination." John's physical characteristics are described as existing at the time the report was written. Test behavior, in contrast, is described in the past tense, because the behavior was displayed on a specific past occasion.

SUMMARY

The psychologist's job is not complete until the efforts of his work with the child are communicated clearly and succinctly to the referral source or to other interested professionals. The psychological report usually serves as the primary vehicle through which the fruits of the evaluation are conveyed. Preparing the report involves skill and a process of decision-making which requires the examiner to sift the hardier substantive findings from the softer peripheral ones, all the while considering how best to convey to the reader the findings and recommendations that have been developed. The report should *report* findings, but it is more than a mere rephrasing of factual material obtained from the record booklet. The report also should be an evaluation; it is one way in which the psychologist serves as a consultant. He brings his wisdom and knowledge to bear on all the phases of the consultation process that are within his domain by incorporating test data with all other sources of information that are available to him.

A number of problems are considered that arise in the formulation of a report. First, it is important to consider the kinds of material necessary to include in the report. Guideposts will include the preferences of the referral source, and material which emphasizes the examinee's individuality. Second, an attempt should be made to synthesize the test findings with behavioral observations. Variability in performance should be noted and an explanation attempted. The interaction between the examiner and examinee constitutes an important part of the testing situation. Third, carefully selected examples of the examinee's performance can enrich the report's readability. Fourth, the certainty of the statements made in the report should be based in part on the type of data that is being referred to. Fifth, the anchor of the report should be the IQ.

The following are some of the ways by which to avoid common pitfalls in report writing: (*a*) eliminate technical terms; (*b*) focus on what is there, not on what is absent; (*c*) clarify obscure details; (*d*) integrate the presentation; and (*e*) avoid incomprehensible sentences.

The examiner should be prepared to revise his first draft. After proficiency in report writing is reached, revisions may not be necessary.

The examiner, in the writing of the report, may play a number of different roles. Which one (or ones) he plays will be dependent in part on the nature of the situation. A contextual approach to report writing, as an alternative to a psychodynamic one, stresses the social and descriptive elements of the assessment situation.

Research investigations have served to point out the numerous problems that are involved in psychological reports. Problems center on content, interpretation, attitude and orientation, communication, role conduct, and science and profession. Professionals in the mental health field have been found to view psychological reports with mixed feelings. School personnel prefer reports which provide useful recommendations. One of the major communication problems that arises in reports is the difficulty readers have in understanding technical concepts.

Specific examples presented in the chapter illustrate sentences which, for a variety of reasons, fail to communicate adequately. The following kinds of difficulties were enumerated: abstractness, ambiguity, apologies, awkwardness, unimportant content, inappropriate generalization, hedging, inexactitude, limited or too general comments, non sequitur, and technical terms. Finally, technical aspects of report writing were discussed.

CHAPTER 25

REPORT WRITING

The psychological report is an essential part of the examination process. The report, containing such information as the examiner's observations, findings, recommendations, and diagnostic formulations, is the vehicle of communication. The report is termed "psychological" rather than "intellectual," because our concern is not only with quantitative test data but also with behavioral data and qualitative data. The report focuses on the individual as an examinee, and not solely on his intellectual ability. When the intelligence test is the only test administered, we are limited, of course, in arriving at personality descriptions and in making diagnostic statements. Yet the objectives of the report remain the same: to answer the referral question, to convey in as much depth as possible a meaningful description of the examinee, and to provide useful recommendations.

THE READER

The reader of the report represents the consumer. He will incorporate the findings into the educational, diagnostic, or treatment program. Primarily, the report will be read and be utilized by the referral source. However, as our population continues to become more mobile and as agencies continue to share more data with one another, it is likely that the same report may be read by professionals of diverse backgrounds. It would be extremely difficult to satisfy all potential readers, but our efforts should be directed toward writing a clear, meaningful, and objective report with a minimum of technical jargon and with a maximum of simplicity. Suggestions for achieving clarity of expression have been presented in Chapter 24. The present chapter focuses on the structure and content of the report.

FOCUS OF REPORT

Reports may have a *test* orientation or a *subject* orientation. Test-oriented reports rely primarily on the presentation of factual material, such as test questions, year levels, and other technical aspects of the examinee's performance. The subject-oriented report makes use of the same data, but instead of referring to the data directly, it uses them to describe the examinee. For example, "John passed the Vocabulary test at year-level VIII of the examination" is a test-oriented statement, while "John's vocabulary knowledge is at the level of an average 8-year-old" is a subject-oriented statement. Regardless of where the focus is placed, the report should aim to describe the examinee as carefully as possible. *How does the examinee with an IQ of 100 differ from other examinees with the same IQ?* A proper answer to such a question fulfills one of the primary objectives of the report: to present a description of the examinee which portrays his unique pattern and style of performance. While this objective may not always be achieved, it is worth striving for.

The subject-oriented report is probably more satisfactory for a psychological evaluation. However, the test-oriented report is not directly opposed to the subject-oriented report; the difference is a matter of emphasis. Even if an agency requires test-oriented reports or, for that matter, if the examiner himself prefers to write test-oriented reports, examinee characteristics should be included. Subject-oriented reports should, in turn, include test data. Subject-oriented reports may require more effort than test-oriented ones.

The goal of the report is to answer the referral questions and to present an integrated and meaningful picture of the examinee's abilities. Therefore, to answer such referral questions as "How can I best deal with John's behavior?" or "What factors are associated with John's low level of academic performance?" the report should discuss material related to the examinee's aptitudes, personality, and other pertinent factors, in addition to the quantitative data obtained from the examinee's performance on the test. In arriving at appropriate recommendations, all relevant factors, such as background information that includes school and medical records and family history, must be considered—not just the test results.

CONTENT OF REPORT

The report focuses on five general areas: (1) test behavior (qualitative aspects), (2) level of present functioning (test results, precision range, and representativeness of findings), (3) areas of strength and weakness, (4) diagnostic implications (whenever possible or necessary), and (5) recommendations (prognostic implications). The report represents a coherent and organized presentation of these five areas.

Test Behavior

The child's behavior during the examination provides important information for judging the validity of the test results, for evaluating the pattern of test performance, and for assessing temperament and motivation. Descriptive material should not be recorded at random; rather, material pertinent to the goals of the evaluation should be included. There are numerous qualitative features that can provide useful material. These include words, gestures, facial expressions, bodily movements, reaction time, and organizational methods. The older examinee's reactions to the test situation often reflect his attitudes toward school and toward intellectual competition.

Attitudinal, language, and visual-motor factors comprise the three major areas of test behavior. This section of the chapter presents, for each of the three areas, specific questions and suggestions that are important to consider. Information obtained in the course of observing the examinee's test behavior will also be useful in arriving at diagnostic formulations, as described in Chapter 19. In evaluating the examinee's behavior, use information obtained from any of the examination sources, such as attitudes toward the test situation, the examiner, and the test material. The following cues are quite numerous and well may bewilder the novice; however, with increased experience the beginning examiner will notice an increasing number of them.

Attitude Toward Examiner:

1a. How does the examinee relate to the examiner and the examiner to the examinee?
1b. Is the examinee shy, frightened, aggressive, or friendly?
1c. Is the examinee negativistic, normally compliant, or over-eager to please?
2. Is there a change from the initial meeting between the examinee and the examiner to the later part of the test situation?
3. Does the examinee try to induce the examiner to give answers to questions?
4. Does the examinee watch the examiner closely to discover whether his responses are correct?

Attitude Toward Test Situation:

1. Is the examinee relaxed and at ease, tense and inhibited, or restless?
2. Is he interested or is he uninvolved?
3. Does he seem confident of his ability?
4. Is he an eager participant or a perfunctory participant?
5. Are the tasks enjoyable to him as games, challenging as chances to excel, or threatening as possible failures?
6. How well does he attend to the test?
7. Is it necessary to repeat instructions?
8. Is it easy or difficult to regain his attention once it is lost?
9. Does he appear to be exerting his best effort?
10. Does he try only when urged on by the examiner?
11. Does he give up easily or does he insist on continuing to work on difficult items?
12. Does his interest vary during the examination?

Attitude Toward Self:

1. Does he have poise and confidence?
2. Does he make frequent self-derogatory or boastful remarks or is he fairly objective toward his achievement?

Work Habits:

1. Has he a characteristic fast or slow work tempo?
2. Does he appear to think about and organize his answers or does he give them impulsively or carelessly?
3. Does he revise any of his answers?
4. Does he think aloud or will he give only his final answer?

Reaction to Test Items:

1. What type of test item produces such reactions as anxiety, stammering, or blushing?
2. Are there any areas of the test in which the examinee feels more comfortable or less comfortable?
3. Is he more interested in some types of items than in others?

Reaction to Failure:

1a. How does the examinee react to failure?
1b. Does he apologize, rationalize, or accept failure calmly?
2. When faced with difficult items, how does he react? Does he retreat,

become aggressive, work harder, try to cheat, become evasive, or openly admit failure?
3. If he becomes aggressive, toward whom or what does he direct his aggression?
4. If questioned further about an item, does he reconsider his answer, defend his first answer, or become silent?

Reaction to Praise:
1. How does the examinee react to praise?
2. Does he accept it gracefully or awkwardly?
3. Does it motivate him to work harder?

LANGUAGE

1a. How clearly and accurately does the examinee express himself?
1b. Is his speech fluent, halting, articulate, inexact, or precise?
1c. Are his responses direct and to the point, or vague, roundabout, or free associative?
2. Does he make any free, spontaneous conversation or does he limit himself to responding only to questions?
3. Does his conversation appear to derive from friendliness or from a desire to evade the test situation?

VISUAL-MOTOR

1. Note the movements he makes with his hands, feet, and face, and how he handles the testing material.
2. Note his handedness.
3. Is his reaction time fast or slow?
4. Does he proceed in a trial-and-error manner?
5. Is he skillful or awkward?
6. Are bilateral movements skillfully executed?

A convenient way of recording the examinee's reactions in the testing situation is to use the Behavior and Attitude Checklist, which is shown in Table 25–1. The Checklist, which was developed from the material described in this section of the chapter, consists of 11 divisions with 37 seven-point scales. The Checklist, completed by placing an "X" in the appropriate space, can be filed with the record booklet for each examinee. The psychological report should include a discussion of the highlights of the Checklist data.

The Behavior and Attitude Checklist, as well as other material discussed in this text, is not meant to cover and cannot cover all contingencies that can arise during the course of the examination. On some occasions the examinee may be described easily by the categories found on the Checklist; however, the examiner should be prepared to encounter examinees who display behaviors that are not covered by the categories described on the Checklist. *The goal in all cases is to capture the examinee's uniqueness.* Statements which describe the examinee's behavior should be distinguished clearly from statements which interpret this behavior; however, both observations and inferences are valuable (Bingham, 1937).

Level of Present Functioning

Present the test results clearly. CA, MA (for the Stanford-Binet), IQ, precision of IQ (standard error of measurement), classification, percentile rank, and representativeness of the findings should be noted routinely. Percentile ranks for Stanford-Binet, WISC, and WPPSI IQ's can be obtained from Table

Table 25-1. BEHAVIOR AND ATTITUDE CHECKLIST
(Developed by Jerome M. Sattler)

Name:	Examiner:
Age:	Date of report:
Test administered:	Date of examination:
IQ:	

Instructions: Place an "X" on the appropriate line for each scale.

I. Attitude toward examiner:

    1. passive   __ : __ : __ : __ : __ : __   aggressive
    2. hostile   __ : __ : __ : __ : __ : __   friendly

II. Attitude toward test situation:

    3. tense   __ : __ : __ : __ : __ : __   relaxed
    4. interested   __ : __ : __ : __ : __ : __   uninvolved
    5. eager   __ : __ : __ : __ : __ : __   perfunctory
    6. enjoyable   __ : __ : __ : __ : __ : __   not enjoyable
    7. tries his best   __ : __ : __ : __ : __ : __   does not try his best
    8. gives up on hard items   __ : __ : __ : __ : __ : __   does not give up on hard items
    9. interest level continuously high   __ : __ : __ : __ : __ : __   interest level variable

III. Attitude toward self:

    10. confident   __ : __ : __ : __ : __ : __   not confident
    11. boastful   __ : __ : __ : __ : __ : __   self-derogatory

IV. Work habits:

    12. fast   __ : __ : __ : __ : __ : __   slow
    13. answers deliberately   __ : __ : __ : __ : __ : __   answers impulsively
    14. thinks aloud   __ : __ : __ : __ : __ : __   thinks silently
    15. careless   __ : __ : __ : __ : __ : __   neat

V. Reaction to test items:

    16. understands directions easily   __ : __ : __ : __ : __ : __   understands directions with difficulty

Table 25-1. BEHAVIOR AND ATTITUDE CHECKLIST—*Continued*

17. sees global details of pictures	__ : __ : __ : __ : __ : __ : __	sees fine details of pictures
18. examiner's questions help examinee express ideas	__ : __ : __ : __ : __ : __ : __	examiner's questions do not help examinee express ideas

VI. Reaction to failure:

19. aware of failure	__ : __ : __ : __ : __ : __ : __	oblivious of failure
20. calm	__ : __ : __ : __ : __ : __ : __	agitated
21. apologetic	__ : __ : __ : __ : __ : __ : __	not apologetic
22. works harder after failure	__ : __ : __ : __ : __ : __ : __	gives up easily after failure

VII. Reaction to praise:

23. accepts gracefully	__ : __ : __ : __ : __ : __ : __	accepts awkwardly
24. works harder after praise	__ : __ : __ : __ : __ : __ : __	retreats after praise

VIII. Language:

25. fluent	__ : __ : __ : __ : __ : __ : __	halting
26. articulate	__ : __ : __ : __ : __ : __ : __	inarticulate
27. responses direct	__ : __ : __ : __ : __ : __ : __	responses vague
28. converses spontaneously	__ : __ : __ : __ : __ : __ : __	only speaks when spoken to
29. bizarre	__ : __ : __ : __ : __ : __ : __	reality oriented
30. errors indicate associations easily recognizable	__ : __ : __ : __ : __ : __ : __	errors indicate associations not easily recognizable

IX. Visual-motor:

31. reaction time slow	__ : __ : __ : __ : __ : __ : __	reaction time fast
32. trial-and-error	__ : __ : __ : __ : __ : __ : __	careful and planned
33. skillful movements	__ : __ : __ : __ : __ : __ : __	awkward movements
34. relevant gestures	__ : __ : __ : __ : __ : __ : __	irrelevant gestures
35. overcontrolled	__ : __ : __ : __ : __ : __ : __	impulsive

X. Overall test results:

36. valid	__ : __ : __ : __ : __ : __ : __	invalid
37. reliable	__ : __ : __ : __ : __ : __ : __	unreliable

XI. Other:

C-29 in the Appendix. Other test data which may be especially helpful to psychologists reading the report may be included. Examples might include the basal and ceiling years and scatter pattern, in the case of the Stanford-Binet, or Verbal and Performance IQ's and subtest scaled scores, in the case of the WISC and WPPSI.

Precision Range.   It is important to inform the reader of the extent to which the obtained score reflects the examinee's "true" IQ. A range of precision, arrived at in part by use of the standard deviation and reliability coefficient of the test, can be used for this purpose. A definition of reliability serves to introduce us to the precision range. "Reliability refers to the consistency of scores obtained by the same individuals when re-examined with the same test on different occasions, or with different sets of equivalent items, or under other variable examining conditions [Anastasi, 1968b, p.71]." Chance factors affect the reliability of the test score, so that efforts made to standardize the test administration (e.g., uniform instructions, time limits, rapport, and satisfactory room conditions) assist in promoting more reliable scores.

The error of measurement associated with a test allows us to predict for each examinee's score the range of fluctuation or precision range likely to occur as a result of chance factors. For the Stanford-Binet, errors of measurement are available for two examinee factors, age and IQ level. Thus, the precision of the obtained IQ for each examinee can be reported in relation to both the examinee's age and his IQ. Table C-1 in the Appendix, based upon McNemar's (1942) work, presents the appropriate multiples of standard errors of measurements for the 68%, 85%, 90%, 95%, and 99% confidence levels as a function of examinee age and IQ level. Table C-1 shows that for the Stanford-Binet the smallest standard errors of measurement are associated with lower IQ's and with higher age levels. The most precise IQ (smallest standard error of measurement) occurs for children in the 14 to 18 year age range having IQ's between 60 and 69. Conversely, the least precise IQ (largest standard error of measurement) occurs for children in the 2½ to 5½ year age range having IQ's between 140 and 149.

The WISC and WPPSI manuals present the reliability scores needed to calculate one-half confidence intervals. Unfortunately, however, the standard errors of measurement are available only for one examinee factor, namely, age. Table C-7 (for the WISC) and Table C-21 (for the WPPSI) in the Appendix present the appropriate multiples of the standard errors of measurements for the 68%, 90%, 95%, and 99% confidence levels as a function of examinee age for each subtest and scale. The WISC, as can be seen in Table C-7, is more precise for ages above 9 years than for ages below 9 years. However, Table C-21 shows that, for the WPPSI, age level does not appear to be related systematically to precision range.

After the IQ is obtained, the examiner should determine the confidence level that he wishes to use. He may use any one or more of the five levels given in the table, or even select some other level. If another level is chosen, Table C-4 in the Appendix should be consulted in order to obtain the appropriate standard error of measurement for the Stanford-Binet, while for the WISC and WPPSI, the appropriate manual should be consulted. To obtain the one-half confidence interval from Table C-1, use both the examinee's chronological age and IQ. For Tables C-7 and C-21 only the examinee's age is used. The error of measurement and the respective precision range can be expressed in the report in a number of different ways. Suppose that Joe, a 4-year-old examinee, obtained an IQ of 100 on the Stanford-Binet, and the examiner wishes to use the 68% level of precision. Table C-1 shows that the appropriate one-half confidence interval for this age and IQ level is 5 for the 68% confidence level. (The actual standard error is 5.3, but all numbers have been rounded off for ease of expression in the report.) The recommended ways of reporting the precision range are as follows:

(1) Joe obtained an IQ of 100 ± 5. The chances that the range of scores from 95 to 105 includes his true IQ are about 68 out of 100.

(2) Joe obtained an IQ of 100 ± 5. The chances that the range of scores from 95 to 105 does not include his true IQ are about 32 out of 100.

If the 85% level is selected, the one-half confidence interval will be 1.44 times greater (5.3 × 1.44 = 8), and the odds for this level are 85 out of 100. The chances that the ± 8 range does not include the true score are 15 out of 100. For the 90% level, the one-half confidence interval will be 1.65 times greater (5.3 × 1.65 = 9), and the odds for this level are 90 out of 100. The chances that the ± 9 range does not include the true score are 10 out of 100.

If the 95% level is selected, the one-half confidence interval will be 1.96 times greater (5.3 × 1.96 = 10), and the odds for this level are 95 out of 100. The chances that the ± 10 range does not include the true score are five out of 100. Similarly, for the 99% level, the one-half confidence interval will be 2.58 times greater (5.3 × 2.58 = 14), and the odds for this level are 99 out of 100. The chances that the ± 14 range does not include the true score are one out of 100. Statement (1) above for the 99% level is written, "Joe achieved an IQ of 100 ± 14. The chances that the range of scores from 86 to 114 includes his true IQ are about 99 out of 100."

Representativeness of Findings. In addition to the precision range, the representativeness or validity of the obtained IQ should be considered. Validity of the IQ for an individual examinee can refer to the extent to which the test results accurately portray his current level of intellectual functioning. However, a statement concerning the validity of the IQ may also imply a long range prediction. Therefore, it is important to recognize that the predictive validity of the IQ can be impaired in a number of ways (Deutsch et al., 1964). First, there are test-related factors, such as test-taking skills, anxiety, motivation, speed, understanding of test instructions, degree of item or format novelty, examiner-examinee rapport, physical handicaps, bilingualism, deficiencies in educational opportunities, unfamiliarity with the test material, and deviation in other ways from the norm of the standardized group. Obviously, the test results are not valid when the examinee is uncooperative, is highly distractible, or fails to understand most of the instructions. In such cases, testing should be discontinued and attempted at some other time with the same test or with a more appropriate test.

A second group of factors that can impede predictive validity is associated with the complexity of the criteria. School grades, a commonly used criterion, are affected by motivation, classroom behavior, personal appearance, and study habits, as well as by intelligence. If the examinee is hampered in any of these areas (which he is likely to be if, for example, he is from an ethnic minority group), the predictive validity will be lowered.

Third, there are intervening events and contingencies which affect criterion validity. This last general area is of special importance in testing "clinical groups." The examiner must consider the extent to which an emotionally disturbed examinee's condition is acute or chronic. Acute states of disturbance often disrupt intellectual efficiency, thereby leading to nonrepresentative test results. When therapeutic intervention — such as drugs, psychotherapy, foster-home placement, or environmental manipulation — is capable of improving the examinee's performance, the validity or representativeness of the initial test results should be questioned. However, chronic conditions, such as irreversible brain damage or chronic schizophrenia, may not necessarily invalidate the test results because in such conditions there may be little that can be done to improve the examinee's performance. Roe and Shakow (1942) suggested that the representativeness of test results obtained for a psychotic patient should be determined as follows: "If his performance today is, from all the evidence available with regard to his psychotic condition, the best he is likely to be able to achieve during the approximate period of the next few weeks, then in this respect the examination is representative [p. 379]." As the work group of the Society for the Psychological Study of Social Issues pointed out,

> if the time interval between the test administration and the criterial assessment is lengthy, a host of situational, motivational, and maturational changes may occur in the interim. An illness, an inspiring teacher, a shift in aspiration level or in direction of interest, remedial training, an economic misfortune, an emotional crisis, a growth spurt or retrogression in the abilities sampled by the test—any of these changes intervening between the testing and the point or points of criterion assessment may decrease the predictive power of the test [Deutsch et al., 1964, pp. 136-137].

In some cases, it may be difficult to determine the validity of the IQ on the basis of only one test session, especially when information about previous test results (e.g., from school records) is not available. If there is sufficient reason to question the validity of the test results, clearly indicate such doubt in the report. Deviation from a premorbid level of functioning does not necessarily invalidate the results, because a level which is either lower than or higher than the premorbid level may be the accurate current level of functioning.

Strengths and Weaknesses

Stanford-Binet. Chapter 10, which discusses factor analysis and classification systems for the Stanford-Binet, should be referred to when writing this section of the report. The material described in Chapter 10 is useful for analyzing the examinee's performance. Try to identify relative strengths and weaknesses. Note successes and failures above and below the CA and MA. Be careful not to exaggerate the importance of either successes or failures near the examinee's own CA level.

WISC and WPPSI. Chapter 14 should be consulted for the WISC and Chapter 17 for the WPPSI to determine patterns of strengths and weaknesses. Tables C-10 and C-23 in the Appendix permit ready comparisons of subtest scores for determining significant differences among subtests.

Diagnostic Implications

A report based primarily on the administration of the Stanford-Binet, WISC, or WPPSI is usually limited diagnostically to an intellectual assessment. However, any clues obtained about problem areas should be carefully noted and discussed. The examiner should not hesitate to offer diagnostic formulations if sufficient evidence is present. On the other hand, do not capriciously place every examinee in a diagnostic category or feel compelled to emphasize psychopathological material. *Not every examinee has serious emotional problems.* If we look hard enough, problem areas may be found, but this is not our task or our function. The evaluation aims to describe significant aspects of the examinee's personality that may be helpful to the reader. The report should help the reader plan a meaningful program. Referral to other sources (e.g., speech therapist, neurologist, or mental-hygiene clinic) may be part of the recommendations ensuing from a consideration of diagnostic factors. The structured nature of the intellectual evaluation usually limits a thorough assessment of personality and adjustment patterns. However, when information related to the examinee's personality is available, present it as meaningfully as possible. Be careful not to make diagnostic statements on the basis of insufficient data.

Recommendations

The recommendation section of the report, as we have seen in Chapter 24, is a very important part of the psychological evaluation. Recommendations can focus on many different factors, such as (*a*) covering specific suggestions for stimulating and enhancing the examinee's psychological growth and development, (*b*) providing information about possible patterns of developmental disturbances, (*c*) indicating that there is a need for retesting or for further evaluation, (*d*) suggesting specific forms of treatment or remedial education, (*e*) pointing out vocational aptitudes and areas of possible academic achievement, and (*f*) including predictions about future behavior. Recommendations should enable the reader to plan a program suitable to the examinee's needs and to his level of functioning. Especially needed in school settings is a specific plan for the teacher, taking into account her capabilities as well as her limitations (Handler et al., 1965).

While, at times, we may desire to make predictions about future levels of intellectual attainment, we must recognize that such predictions are very difficult and are potentially damaging to the child because the reader of the report may be lulled into thinking that a course of development is fixed or unchangeable. Tyler (1965) rightly cautioned: "Those responsible for the guidance of children need to realize that a single intelligence test can never be used as a basis for a definite judgment about what a child will be able to do several years later. Each new decision, at successive stages of development, calls for a recheck [71]." Therefore, while it is important to indicate the examinee's present level of functioning and to make suggestions about what can be expected of him, statements dealing with performance in the far distant future must be made cautiously, if at all. (See Chapter 26 for related material.)

The recommendation section of the report should be written so that the reader recognizes clearly the examiner's degree of confidence in the predictions. Occasionally, it is helpful to cite test data (cf. Morrow, 1954) or behavioral data to enable the reader to understand the recommendations better. Recommendations serve to highlight the findings and their implications. They should be made judiciously.

Summary

A summary is optional. While a summary reviews and integrates the test findings, it also may be repetitious, may unnecessarily lengthen the report, and may detract from the report by allowing the reader to forego reading the main body of the report. Ideally, the report itself should be a lengthy summary: precise, compact, and to the point.

If a summary is written, the following material should be included: CA, MA (for the Stanford-Binet), IQ, precision range, classification, percentile rank, representativeness of the findings, outstanding features of the test performance, and recommendations. Limit the summary to a short, organized, and integrated paragraph. Do not include any new material.

REPORT OUTLINE

The report outline shown below incorporates the material previously discussed. The outline is only suggestive, since other formats may sometimes better describe the findings. While some modifications in the outline may be necessary to serve various agencies' needs, the suggested outline generally can be used as a model for reporting intelligence-test results.

Suggested Report Outline

Psychological Evaluation

Name: Date of examination:
Date of birth: Date of report:
Chronological age: Grade:
Test(s) administered:

1. *Reason for referral.* Note the problem indicated by the referral source, such as suspected retardation, speech difficulty, behavior problem, or perceptual-motor handicap.
2. *General observations.* Include a brief description of the examinee. Note any physical characteristics that might affect test performance. Atypical behaviors, attitudes, and feelings should be described.
3. *Test results.* Present CA, IQ, precision range, classification, percentile rank, and representativeness of the results. In addition, for the Stanford-Binet, present the MA and, if desired, basal and ceiling levels; for the WISC and WPPSI, present, if desired, Verbal and Performance IQ's and subtest scaled scores. Comment on the variability of tests passed and failed if noteworthy or if desired. Note any factors that may have distorted the results. Consider how educational, emotional, and cultural factors have affected the examinee's test performance. Discuss the examinee's strengths and weaknesses, his personality characteristics, diagnostic implications of findings, and other related material.
4. *Recommendations.* Be as specific as possible. Always try to answer the referral questions. Indicate your level of confidence in the predictions and in the recommendations.
5. *Summary.* If included, make the summary a short, one-paragraph integrated statement of test findings and recommendations.

_____
Examiner's Name

ILLUSTRATIVE REPORTS FOR THE STANFORD-BINET

The four sample reports which follow are written in somewhat different styles, but they all conform to the suggested outline for report writing. Some reports are more person-centered, while others are more test-centered. However, they all attempt to give a clear and meaningful presentation of test findings and their implications. A scatter pattern, Binetgram, and other summary data are furnished for each report.

Sample Stanford-Binet Report Number 1 — A Child with Superior Intelligence

Report number 1 is a short, integrated analysis of a superior child. In spite of its brevity, the report presents the main features of the examinee's performance.

Scatter Pattern (Report Number 1)

Name: Kathy   CA $= 9-9$ CA SD $+1 = 11-8$ MA SD $+1 = 15-9$(AA)
      Brown   MA $= 13-4$ $+2 = 13-4$ $+2 = 18-1$(SA I)
               IQ $= 132 \pm 5$ $+3 = 14-11$ $-1 = 11-0$
                                 $+4 = 16-7$(SA I) $-2 = 8-8$

Pass	*Fail*

Year XIII (Basal)
Plan of Search
Abstract Words II
Memory for Sentences
Problems of Fact
Dissected Sentences
Copying a Bead Chain from Memory

Year XIV	*Year XIV*
Vocabulary	Induction
	Reasoning I
	Ingenuity
	Orientation: Direction I
	Reconciliation of Opposites

Year AA	*Year AA*
Essential Differences	Vocabulary
	Ingenuity
	Differences between Abstract Words
	Arithmetical Reasoning
	Proverbs I
	Orientation: Direction II
	Abstract Words III

SA I (Ceiling)
Vocabulary
Enclosed Box Problem
Minkus Completion II
Repeating 6 Digits Reversed
Sentence Building
Essential Similarities

Psychological Evaluation

Name: Kathy Brown   Date of examination: January 18, 1966

Date of birth: April 22, 1956   Date of report: January 26, 1966

Chronological age: 9–9   Grade: Fourth

Test administered: Stanford-Binet Intelligence Scale, Form L-M

Kathy was tested as part of a testing program carried out at Blank School by a class from San Diego State College. Kathy was well dressed, polite, and quite alert. Her physical appearance was average; complexion, fair. Her health appeared to be good. Kathy reacted to the examiner in a friendly manner; she talked freely and did not seem to be shy or afraid. She started the tasks with a moderate amount of interest. As the items on the vocabulary list grew more difficult, she became more absorbed in the work at hand and did not seem to discourage easily. During the test, Kathy engaged readily in conversation about herself and her family; she expressed herself clearly and concisely in a manner that was rather charming.

On Form L-M of the Stanford-Binet Intelligence Scale, Kathy, with a chronological age of 9–9, achieved a mental age of 13–4. This score gives her an Intelligence Quotient of 132 ± 5, which is in the Superior classification. Her level of intellectual functioning exceeds that of 97% of the children of her age in the standardization group, which was roughly representative of the United States population. The chances that the range of scores from 128 to 137 includes her true IQ are about 68 out of 100. Because of the good rapport that was established and the interest that Kathy showed in taking the test, this measure of Kathy's present level of intellectual functioning appears to be valid.

Kathy passed all of the tests at the XIII-year level, passed one test each at the XIV- and Average-Adult year levels, and failed all the tests at the Superior-Adult-I year level. The fact that no failures occurred below the XIV-year level suggests excellent intellectual efficiency.

BINETGRAM

Instructions: 1. Circle basal year level and ceiling year level.   2. Circle all tests passed by examinee.

Name __Kathy Brown__   Date of testing __Jan. 18, 1966__   CA: SD $+_1$11-8 $+_2$13-4 $+_3$14-11$_1$ ___$-_2$___ ___$-_3$___

$+_4 = 16$-7 (SA I)

Date of birth __Apr. 22, 1956__ Grade __4th__ IQ __132__ CA __9-9__ MA __13-4__   MA: SD $+_1$15-9 $+_2$18-1 $+_3$___ ___$-_1$11-0 $-_2$8-8 $-_3$___

(AA)   (SA I)

CATEGORIES	II	II-6	III	III-6	IV	IV-6	V	VI	VII	VIII	IX	X	XI	XII	XIII	XIV	AA	SA I	SA II	SA III	TOTAL TESTS PASSED
Language	3(1) 5(2) 6(3) A	1(4) 2(5) 3(6) 4(7)	2(8)		1(9) 4(10)	A	3(11)	1(12)		1(13)	4(14) A	1(15) 3(16) 5(17)	3(18)	1(19) 5(20) 6(21)	(2(22)) (5(23))	(1(24))	1(25) 3(26) 8(27)	(SA I) 1(28) 3(29) 5(30)	1(31)	1(32)	24
Memory		5(1)	4(2) A		2(3) A	5(4)			6(5) A	2(6)	3(7) 6(8)	6(9)	1(10) 4(11)	4(12) A	(3(13)) (6(14))			4(15)	6(16)	6(17)	14
Conceptual Thinking					3(1)	2(2)		2(3) 5(4)	2(5) 5(6)	4(7)			6(8)			6(9)	5(10) (7)(11) A	6(12) A	3(13) 5(14)	2(15) 3(16) A	9
Reasoning	2(1)			1(2) 2(3) 3(4) 5(5) A	5(6)	3(7)	5(8) 6(9)	3(10)		3(11)	2(12)	A	2(13)	2(14)	(1(15)) (4(16))	3(17) 5(18) A	6(19)		2(20) A	4(21) 5(22)	16
Numerical Reasoning								4(1)			5(2)	2(3)				2(4) 4(5) A	2(6) 4(7)	2(8)	4(9)		3
Visual-Motor	1(1) 4(2)	A	1(3) 3(4) 5(5) 6(6)				1(7) 2(8) 4(9) A	6(10)	3(11)		1(12)			A	A		A				12
Social Intelligence	6(1)			4(2) 6(3)	6(4)	1(5) 4(6) 6(7)			1(8) 4(9)	5(10) 6(11) A		4(12) A	5(13) A	3(14)							14

YEAR LEVEL

Kathy's vocabulary is well developed for her chronological age, inasmuch as she knew as many words as the average 14-year-old. For example, when asked the meaning of "peculiarity," she replied that it was something odd or strange. Another strength was displayed in her ability to provide essential differences between such concepts as an optimist and a pessimist. In answering this question, she displayed a sense of humor in stating that an optimist would think that he might get to skip a unit in the book. This task required good verbal-reasoning abilities in general and, in particular, the perception of logical relationships.

Kathy's attention span and visual memory are also well developed. She was able to copy a bead chain from memory and repeat complex sentences from memory at the XIII-year level. Her knowledge of abstract words also is well developed. For example, she was able to define "revenge," "obedience," and "compare" at the XIII-year level. Because of her superior intellectual abilities it might prove challenging and stimulating to her if she were provided with special projects on a level in keeping with her intellectual capacities.

In summary, on Form L-M of the Stanford-Binet Intelligence Scale, Kathy, with a CA of 9–9 and an MA of 13–4, achieved an IQ of 132 ± 5. These results place her in the Superior classification and at the 97th percentile rank. The chances are about 32 out of 100 that the range of scores from 128 to 137 does not include her true IQ. The results appear to be valid. Kathy demonstrated a well-developed vocabulary, good verbal-reasoning abilities, and good rote memory and attention span. Because of her superior intellectual capacities it is suggested that she be encouraged to undertake special projects or extra work of interest to her.

John Q. Smith, Examiner

Sample Stanford-Binet Report Number 2 — A Child in the Bright Normal Classification

In report number 2, the writer presents many verbatim responses given by the examinee to specific test questions. While this procedure lengthens the report, it facilitates the reader's understanding of the child's method of responding. The recommendations are developed by considering her level of test performance, her test behavior, and her developmental age. The report illustrates how test-oriented statements can well be incorporated with subject-oriented material.

Scatter Pattern (Report Number 2)

Name: Karla CA = 3–11 CA SD +1 = 4–7 MA SD +1 = 5–4
      Jones MA = 4–7   +2 = 5–3   +2 = 6–0
             IQ = 115±11   −1 = 3–11

Pass	*Fail*
Year IV (Basal)	
Picture Vocabulary	
Naming Objects from Memory	
Opposite Analogies I	
Pictorial Identification	
Discrimination of Forms	
Comprehension II	
Year IV-6	*Year IV-6*
Aesthetic Comparison	Opposite Analogies I
Three Commissions	Pictorial Similarities and Differences I
Comprehension III	Materials

Year V
Paper Folding: Triangle
Definitions
Pictorial Similarities and Differences II
Patience: Rectangles

Year V
Picture Completion: Man
Copying a Square

Year VI (Ceiling)
Vocabulary
Differences
Mutilated Pictures
Number Concepts
Opposite Analogies II
Maze Tracing

Psychological Evaluation

Name: Karla Jones   Date of examination: August 1, 1969
Date of birth: August 18, 1965   Date of report: August 4, 1969
Chronological age: 3–11   Grade: Preschool
Test administered: Stanford-Binet Intelligence Scale, Form L-M

Karla's mother permitted her daughter to be tested in order to help the examiner fulfill the requirements of a course offered at San Diego State College.

Karla is an attractive child of average height and weight for her age. There are no apparent physical or sensory defects. Karla was very friendly and talkative throughout the testing session. As preparation was being made to begin testing, she displayed great curiosity regarding the contents of the examiner's kit, inquiring whether or not she would be allowed to play with some of the "toys." She appeared to be quite excited over the prospect of taking the test.

Karla's enthusiasm diminished somewhat when she discovered that the test involved more than just playing with toys. She became quite restless after a short time and it was necessary to interrupt the testing session in order to allow her to walk around and get a drink of water. She frequently shifted about in her chair and, at times, asked to have a question repeated, saying that she had not heard it the first time.

Karla handled failure well. Only on one occasion was there any indication that failure disturbed her. When she was copying a square, she assumed a pouting expression and said, "That's not the same but it's as good as I can do it." She usually responded quickly to the questions, and only rarely did she say that she didn't know an answer. When asked to complete the statement, "The snail is slow, the rabbit is _____," Karla replied quickly, "Elephant." Even when providing such a purely fanciful answer, however, she did not appear to be disturbed by the thought of failure.

With a chronological age of 3–11 and a mental age of 4–7, Karla achieved an Intelligence Quotient of 115 ± 11 on the Stanford-Binet Intelligence Scale, Form L-M. This places her in the Bright Normal classification and indicates that in this respect she exceeds 82% of the children of her age in the standardization group, which was roughly representative of the population of the United States. The chances that the range of scores from 104 to 126 includes her true IQ are about 95 out of 100. The present measure of her level of intellectual functioning appears to be valid, recognizing that there was some restlessness and possible impulsivity during the examination.

Karla passed all of the tests at the IV-year level, three of the six tests at the IV-6-year level, and four of the six tests at the V-year level. She failed all of the tests at the VI-year level. Although she performed at least at the average level for her age in the various areas of the test, there were minor variations in her levels of performance.

Karla's best abilities were in language usage, general reasoning, and visual-motor coordination, although in the latter area there was not a consistent pattern of strength. In each of these areas, she obtained successes at the level representing the average 5-year-old child. For example, good language ability was shown by her satisfactory definitions of the words ball, hat, and stove:

BINETGRAM

Instructions: 1. Circle basal year level and ceiling year level.   2. Circle all tests passed by examinee.

Name Karla Jones   Date of testing Aug. 1, 1966   CA: ___ SD +1 ___ 4-7 +2 5-3 +3 ___

Date of birth Aug. 18, 1962 Grade pre-school IQ 115 CA 3-11 MA 4-7   MA: ___ SD +1 ___ 5-4 +2 6-0 +3 ___   -1 ___ -3-11 -2 ___ -3 ___

CATEGORIES	II	II-6	III	III-6	IV	IV-6	V	VI	VII	VIII	IX	X	XI	XII	XIII	XIV	AA	SA I	SA II	SA III	TOTAL TESTS PASSED
Language	3(1) 5(2) 6(3) A	1(4) 2(5) 3(6) 4(7)	2(8)		1(9) 4(10)	A	3(11)	1(12)		1(13)	4(14) A	1(15) 3(16) 5(17)	3(18)	1(19) 5(20) 6(21)	2(22) 5(23)	1(24)	1(25) 3(26) 8(27)	1(28) 3(29) 5(30)	1(31)	1(32)	11
Memory		5(1)	4(2) A		2(3) A	5(4)			6(5) A	2(6)	3(7) 6(8)	6(9)	1(10) 4(11)	4(12) A	3(13) 6(14)			4(15)	6(16)	6(17)	4
Conceptual Thinking					3(1)	2(2)	2(3) 5(4)		2(5) 5(6)	4(7)			6(8)			6(9)	5(10) 7(11) A	6(12) A	3(13) 5(14)	2(15) 3(16) A	1
Reasoning	2(1)			1(2) 2(3) 3(4) 5(5) A	5(6)	3(7)	5(8) 6(9) A	3(10)		3(11)	2(12)	A	2(13)	2(14)	1(15) 4(16)	3(17) 5(18) A	6(19)	A	2(20) A	4(21) 5(22) A	8
Numerical Reasoning								4(1)			5(2)	2(3)				2(4) 4(5) A	2(6) 4(7)	2(8)	4(9)		0
Visual-Motor	1(1) 4(2)	A	1(3) 3(4) 5(5) 6(6)		6(4)	1(5) 4(6) 6(7)	1(7) 2(8) 4(9) A	6(10) A	3(11)		1(12)				A		A				7
Social Intelligence	6(1)			4(2) 6(3)		1(5) 4(6) 6(7)		A	1(8) 4(9)	5(10) 6(11) A		4(12)	5(13) A	3(14)							6

YEAR LEVEL

ball — "you throw with it"; hat — "to wear it"; and stove — "to cook supper on." Although failing the Vocabulary test at year-level V, she was able to define four words from the vocabulary list: orange ("you eat it"), envelope ("to put what you write in"), straw ("you drink with"), and eyelash (pointed to her own eyelash).

Her good general reasoning ability was shown by her correctly joining two pieces of paper to form a rectangle. However, some evidence of perseveration or lack of adequate comprehension was noted on a general reasoning test at the IV-6-year level. When asked to identify the dissimilar object on a series of pictures in which three objects were identical and the fourth different, Karla correctly pointed to the left-hand object on the first picture and then continued to point, but incorrectly, to the same location on each of the following pictures. These responses were given very quickly and carelessly; the perseveration was in all likelihood only a reflection of restlessness and immaturity.

Her well-developed visual-motor coordination was shown when she correctly made two folds in a square piece of paper to form a triangle, a feat of which she seemed quite proud. However, other tasks requiring visual-motor ability, in part, were failed at year-level V — copying a square and completing a drawing of a man. She approached these tasks in a quick and careless manner. Noting that the man had only one leg, she quickly drew another and said, "There now, he's all done because he has two legs."

Karla displayed good, but somewhat less well-developed, ability in the areas of memory (being able to carry out three simple commands in order), and social intelligence (being able to state that we have eyes "to look with them"). Conceptual thinking ability is average. Thus, at the IV-year level, a test which required the completion of such statements as "In daytime it is light; at night it is _____," and "The sun shines during the day; the moon at _____," Karla responded correctly by saying "dark" and "night," respectively.

If her present behavior persists when she starts school, Karla's teacher should try to teach her a more careful approach to intellectual problems and to help her overcome her restlessness. This will probably involve encouragement together with a warm, accepting approach. With her above-average ability, Karla can be expected to perform at a good level in classroom work if she is given proper attention.

In summary, with a CA of 3–11 and an MA of 4–7, Karla achieved an IQ of 115 ± 11 on the Stanford-Binet Intelligence Scale, Form L-M. This places her in the Bright Normal classification and indicates that in this respect she exceeds 82% of the children of her age in the standardization group, which was roughly representative of the population of the United States. The chances that the range of scores from 104 to 126 does not include her true IQ are about 5 out of 100. The test results appear to give a valid indication of her present level of functioning. She displayed well-developed language and general reasoning abilities, well-developed but variable visual-motor coordination, slightly less well-developed memory and social intelligence, and average conceptual thinking ability. Because of restlessness and possible impulsivity, it was suggested that Karla be given special attention when she enters school.

Jane Q. Smith, Examiner

Sample Stanford-Binet Report Number 3 — A Child with Limited Interest in School

This report illustrates the derivation of clinical hypotheses from the Stanford-Binet. It is primarily a person-centered report, in that test data receive relatively little emphasis.

Scatter Pattern (Report Number 3)

Name: Jack   CA = 6–7   CA SD +1 = 7–7 MA SD +1 = 7–3
White   MA = 6–4   –1 = 5–8   –1 = 5–5
IQ = 95 ± 9

Pass	*Fail*

Year V (Basal)
Picture Completion: Man
Paper Folding: Triangle
Definitions

Copying a Square
Pictorial Similarities and Differences II
Patience: Rectangles

Year VI   *Year VI*
Vocabulary   Differences
Mutilated Pictures
Number Concepts
Opposite Analogies II
Maze Tracing

Year VII   *Year VII*
Picture Absurdities   Similarities: Two Things
Copying a Diamond   Comprehension IV
Opposite Analogies III   Repeating 5 Digits

Year VIII (Ceiling)
Vocabulary
Memory for Stories: The Wet Fall
Verbal Absurdities I
Similarities and Differences
Comprehension IV
Naming the Days of the Week

Psychological Evaluation

Name: Jack White   Date of examination: October 28, 1969
Date of birth: March 22, 1963   Date of report: November 1, 1969
Chronological age: 6–7   Grade: First
Test administered: Stanford-Binet Intelligence Scale, Form L-M

Jack was referred by his teacher at Blank School for a better understanding of his intellectual ability. He does not appear to be interested in his school subjects.

Jack is a well-developed child of average height and weight, who expresses himself clearly. He appeared to be in good health, and his coordination was adequate.

When introduced, Jack appeared shy and hesitant, but he readily went with the examiner to the testing room. His curiosity concerning what was going to happen carried over into the testing situation, where he expressed a desire to play with the contents of the test kit. On being assured that he would have an opportunity to play with the material, Jack settled down to the task at hand.

Jack conversed readily during the testing period and revealed that drawing was his favorite activity in school. His conversation during the test indicated that while he was interested in what he was doing, he was also curious to know what activity his class was taking part in, and he more than once expressed the hope that they had not gone outside to play.

Jack began the test items with average eagerness and seemed to enjoy some of them thoroughly, especially those which involved objective drawing, like completing a picture of a man. However, his reaction to failure was un-

BINETGRAM

Instructions: 1. Circle basal year level and ceiling year level.   2. Circle all tests passed by examinee.

Name ___ Jack White ___   Date of testing ___ Oct. 28, 1966 ___   CA: ___   SD +1 __7-7__ +2 ___ +3 ___ -1 __5-8__ -2 ___ -3

Date of birth __Mar. 22, 1960__   Grade __1st__   IQ __95__   CA __6-7__   MA __6-4__   MA: ___   SD +1 __7-3__ +2 ___ +3 ___ -1 __5-5__ -2 ___ -3

Categories	II	II-6	III	III-6	IV	IV-6	V	VI	VII	VIII	IX	X	XI	XII	XIII	XIV	AA	SA I	SA II	SA III	TOTAL TESTS PASSED
Language	3(1) 5(2) 6(3) A	1(4) 2(5) 3(6) 4(7)	2(8)		1(9) 4(10)	A	(3(11))	(1(12))		1(13)	4(14) A	1(15) 3(16) 5(17)	3(18)	1(19) 5(20) 6(21)	2(22) 5(23)	1(24)	1(25) 3(26) 8(27)	1(28) 3(29) 5(30)	1(31)	1(32)	12
Memory		5(1)	4(2) A		2(3) A	5(4)			6(5) A	2(6)	3(7) 6(8)	6(9)	1(10) 4(11)	4(12) A	3(13) 6(14)			4(15)	6(16)	6(17)	4
Conceptual Thinking					3(1)	2(2)		2(3) 5(4)	2(5) 5(6)	4(7)			6(8)			6(9)	5(10) 7(11)	6(12) A	3(13) 5(14)	2(15) 3(16) A	4
Reasoning	2(1)			1(2) 2(3) 3(4) 5(5) A	5(6)	3(7)	5(8) 6(9) A	(3(10))		3(11)	2(12)	A	2(13)	2(14)	1(15) 4(16)	3(17) 5(18)	6(19)		2(20) A	4(21) 5(22)	10
Numerical Reasoning							(4(1))				5(2)	2(3)				2(4) 4(5) A	2(6) 4(7)	2(8)	4(9)		1
Visual-Motor	1(1) 4(2)	A	1(3) 3(4) 5(5) 6(6)					(6(10))	(3(11))		1(12)				A		A				11
Social Intelligence		6(1)			6(4)	1(5) 4(6) 6(7)		A	1(8) 4(9)	5(10) 6(11) A		4(12)	5(13) A	3(14)							8

usual. Failing a test item seemed to make him become much less enthusiastic and had the effect of decreasing his attentiveness to the task at hand. Despite the examiner's reassurance, this reaction to failure continued throughout the test. His limited attentiveness, when faced with difficult items, suggests that he may withdraw from threatening situations.

Jack, with a chronological age of 6–7, achieved a mental age of 6–4. The resulting IQ of 95 ± 9 is in the Normal classification and falls at the 38th percentile rank of children of his age in the normative group, which was roughly representative of the United States population. The chances that the range of scores from 86 to 104 includes his true IQ are about 95 out of 100. Because of the good rapport which existed between Jack and the examiner, this measure of his present level of intellectual functioning appears to be valid.

Jack passed all tests at the level of difficulty passed by the average 5-year-old and failed all tests at the VIII-year level. This range of successes and failures indicates that he performed at his age level with minimal variability.

While the scope of Jack's abilities was average, there were both quantitative and qualitative indications that he was having some difficulty with attention-span material. Instead of repeating five digits, Jack would repeat two or four, or give no response at all. It is instructive to note that Jack's school records, dated January 1969, reveal that his attention span was short. His teacher felt that his limited attention span might have been caused by his taking medicine that made him drowsy. If it is now being used, the medication may be contributing to his reported learning problem. Furthermore, Jack appeared to give up easily. If the answers did not come immediately, he would say "I don't know" or give no response at all. These indications of attention-span problems suggest that Jack may not fully apply himself to materials which require extended effort. His limited attention span might manifest itself in the classroom in the form of disinterest or in daydreaming. His attention-span difficulties may also be associated with his apparent fear of threatening situations.

In all other areas tested, Jack performed at an average level for his age, as shown by the following samples of his performance. Average language usage was displayed in his ability to define correctly as many vocabulary words as the average 6-year-old. Average nonverbal reasoning ability was evidenced by his correctly naming, at the VI-year level, the parts missing in mutilated pictures. Average conceptual thinking was shown by his providing opposite analogies at the VII-year level. Also average are his numerical reasoning, visual-motor coordination, and social intelligence. Thus, he dealt adequately with number concepts (year-level VI), copying a diamond (year-level VII), and finding the absurdity in pictures (year-level VII).

The factors associated with Jack's limited attention span should be investigated. If he is still taking medicine, his parents should consult their physician concerning the drowsiness reported by the teacher. Jack needs to learn how to accept failure, and also needs to receive rewards for his efforts. Perhaps he does not adequately realize that failure in learning situations is normal and usual and is a way in which he can discover and overcome inadequacies. He may equate failure with punishment. Changing his attitude toward failure would entail helping him to perceive new and difficult situations as challenges to be met and overcome, rather than as threats to be avoided. This should be repeatedly demonstrated. Situations in which reward for persistence is quick and certain should be constructed at first, with increasing persistence very gradually required. A long period of time may be needed before a change in attitude develops.

Jack likes to draw. While average visual-motor performance was evident, he readily completed an incomplete picture of a man on a fairly mature level, and copied well some objective designs such as squares and diamonds. By encouraging use of his visual-motor skills, it may be possible to gain Jack's interest in other classroom activities as well.

In summary, on the Stanford-Binet Intelligence Scale, Form L-M, Jack, with a CA of 6–7 and an MA of 6–4, obtained an IQ of 95 ± 9, which is in the Normal classification and at the 38th percentile rank. The chances that the range of scores from 86 to 104 does not include his true IQ are about 5 out of 100. The results appear to give a valid estimate of his present level of intellectual functioning. His performance was generally average, but he did have some difficulty with attention-span material. Jack will need reassurance and understanding about the meaning of failure and its relationship to learning in order to overcome his poor and unrealistic reactions to failure. The effects of his medication should be investigated. Stimulating Jack to use his visual-motor skills may serve to increase his interest in other classroom activities.

Helen C. Black, Examiner

Sample Stanford-Binet Report Number 4 — A Child in the Borderline-Defective Classification

Report number 4 is more test-oriented than report number 3. However, personality features are described and recommendations are based upon clinical hypotheses derived from test and behavioral data.

Scatter Pattern (Report Number 4)

Name: Mike   CA = 6–7   CA SD +1 = 7–7   MA SD +1 = 5–10
    Johns   MA = 5–1   −1 = 5–8   +2 = 6–7
        IQ = 75 ± 5   −2 = 4–8   +3 = 7–2
                        −3 = 3–9   −1 = 3–7

Pass	*Fail*
Year III-6 (Basal)	
Comparison of Balls	
Patience: Pictures	
Discrimination of Animal Pictures	
Response to Pictures	
Sorting Buttons	
Comprehension I	
Year IV	*Year IV*
Opposite Analogies I	Picture Vocabulary
Pictorial Identification	Naming Objects from Memory
Discrimination of Forms	
Comprehension II	
Year IV-6	*Year IV-6*
Aesthetic Comparison	Opposite Analogies I
Pictorial Similarities and Differences I	Three Commissions
Materials	
Comprehension III	
Year V	*Year V*
Picture Completion: Man	Patience: Rectangles
Paper Folding: Triangle	
Definitions	
Copying a Square	
Pictorial Similarities and Differences II	
Year VI	*Year VI*
Differences	Vocabulary
	Mutilated Pictures
	Number Concepts
	Opposite Analogies II
	Maze Tracing

Year VII
Similarities: Two Things
Opposite Analogies III

Year VII
Picture Absurdities
Copying a Diamond
Comprehension IV
Repeating 5 Digits

Year VIII (Ceiling)
Vocabulary
Memory for Stories: The Wet Fall
Verbal Absurdities I
Similarities and Differences
Comprehension IV
Naming the Days of the Week

Psychological Evaluation

Name: Mike Johns   Date of examination: October 25, 1969
Date of birth: March 22, 1963   Date of report: November 7, 1969
Chronological age: 6–7   Grade: First
Test administered: Stanford-Binet Intelligence Scale, Form L-M

Mike was referred by Blank School for a routine examination of intelligence. The test was conducted as a partial requirement for a course offered at San Diego State College.

Mike is a well-built boy who seems to be in good health. His appearance was neat, and although he was wearing overalls, in contrast to most of the boys in school who wear jeans, he didn't seem self-conscious about being dressed differently—that is, in a relatively old-fashioned way.

Mike has a pronounced speech defect, which made it difficult for the examiner to understand him. While he spoke little, enunciation of "th," "d," and "l" sounds was poor. He seemed to be very self-conscious about speaking.

Mike was very shy when he was introduced to the examiner, and while he overcame some of his shyness as the testing progressed, he continued to be distant. Toward the end of the testing he seemed to want to be more friendly, as noted by his smiling and desire to talk, but he was still unable to relate easily to the examiner.

Mike attended to the instructions, but had difficulty in carrying them out. His interest was best in manual tasks which required little or no talking. However, generally he did not exert his best effort unless he was prodded. He sometimes acted as though he were expected to do poorly. For example, when he was asked to define "hat," he said, "Can't know." But when the question was repeated he said, "Put on head." He tends to give up more easily on verbal tasks than on nonverbal tasks, because the former ones require speaking, and in speaking he reveals his speech difficulties.

Mike's answers were given quickly when only one word was required. But if any type of explanation was required, he would sit and ponder the matter as if gathering courage to answer. Then he would either give a relevant answer, or say "black" or "green." When asked what black meant, he replied that he did not know. The use of such words suggests that Mike feels compelled to say something, no matter how inadequate his remarks may be. Perhaps such remarks occur in anxiety-provoking situations as a means of informing others to move on to a different problem.

Mike, whose chronological age is 6–7, achieved a mental age of 5–1 on the Stanford-Binet Intelligence Scale, Form L-M. His Intelligence Quotient is 75 ± 5, which is in the Borderline Defective classification and which falls at the 6th percentile rank of the children of his age in the normative group, which was roughly representative of the United States population. The chances that the range of scores from 70 to 80 includes his true IQ are about 68 out of 100. There is some doubt about the validity of the test results because emotional factors, as discussed below, appear to be affecting his intellectual efficiency.

BINETGRAM

Instructions: 1. Circle basal year level and ceiling year level. 2. Circle all tests passed by examinee.

Name: Mike Johns Date of testing: Oct. 25, 1965 CA: SD +1 7-7 +2 +3 -1 5-8 -2 4-8 -3 3-9

Date of birth: Mar. 22, 1959 Grade: 1st IQ 75 CA 6-7 MA 5-1 MA: SD +1 5-10 +2 6-7 +3 7-2 -1 3-7 -2 -3

YEAR LEVEL

CATEGORIES	II	II-6	III	(III-6)	IV	IV-6	V	VI	VII	(VIII)	IX	X	XI	XII	XIII	XIV	AA	SA I	SA II	SA III	TOTAL TESTS PASSED
Language	3(1) 5(2) 6(3) A	1(4) 2(5) 3(6) 4(7)	2(8)		(1(9)) (4(10))	A	(3)(11)	1(12)		1(13)	4(14) A	1(15) 3(16) 5(17)	3(18)	1(19) 5(20) 6(21)	2(22) 5(23)	1(24)	1(25) 3(26) 8(27)	1(28) 3(29) 5(30)	1(31)	1(32)	10
Memory		5(1)	4(2) A		2(3) A	5(4)			6(5) A	2(6)	3(7) 6(8)	6(9)	1(10) 4(11)	4(12) A	3(13) 6(14)			4(15)	6(16)	6(17)	2
Conceptual Thinking					(3)(1)	2(2)		(2(3)) (5(4))	(2)(5) 5(6)	4(7)			6(8)			6(9)	5(10) 7(11)	6(12) A	3(13) 5(14)	2(15) 3(16) A	4
Reasoning	2(1)				(5(6))	(3)(7)	(5)(8) 6(9)	3(10)		3(11)	2(12) A		2(13)	2(14)	1(15) 4(16)	3(17) 5(18)	6(19)		2(20) A	4(21) 5(22)	8
Numerical Reasoning								4(1)			5(2)	2(3)				2(4) 4(5) A	2(6) 4(7)	2(8)	4(9)		0
Visual-Motor	1(1) 4(2)	A					(1(7)) (2(8)) (4(9)) A	6(10)	3(11)		1(12)				A		A				9
Social Intelligence		6(1)		(4(2)) (6(3))	(6(4))	(1(5)) (4(6)) (6(7))		A	1(8) 4(9)	5(10) 6(11) A		4(12)	5(13) A	3(14)							7

Mike passed all of the tests at the III-6-year level, four at the IV-year level, four at the IV-6-year level, five at the V-year level, one at the VI-year level, and two at the VII-year level. He failed all tests at the VIII-year level. The range of successes and failures is somewhat greater than normal, and suggests that there is some inefficiency in his cognitive functioning.

Mike is deficient in many areas, including language ability, memory, reasoning, and social judgment. His deficiency in language ability was apparent throughout the test. For example, at the four-year level he was unable to provide the names for the required number of pictured objects in order to receive credit. He recognized a picture of a telephone, but defined it by saying, "Ring, ring, ring." Mike's short attention span would be a disadvantage for him in school.

It is significant to note that Mike was able to pass two tests at the VII-year level, a level which is at his chronological age and above his mental age of 5–1. These tests required him to recognize and report the similarities of objects and to give opposites in the analogies items. Neither of these two tests requires much verbalization; rather they necessitate conceptualizing and drawing conclusions. His success on these two tests suggests that he may know the meanings of more words than are revealed by his performance on the Vocabulary test or by his performance on other tests requiring verbal ability. Mike is able, at times, to evaluate a situation and to draw conclusions from it.

There are some indications that Mike has personality difficulties and emotional problems. It was noted above that he responded in a nonsensical manner to difficult questions, which probably reflects some immaturity. His general behavior and many of his answers also suggested social immaturity. He appears to react to distress by withdrawing, which could be interpreted by others as ignorance of a subject—particularly in classroom activities.

Mike should be given speech therapy. He seems to be aware that he is different from his peers, and this awareness may lead him to feel inferior and, at times, ashamed of himself. These feelings may partly account for his passive, dependent behavior. Mike should be tested again in six to twelve months, particularly if he has speech therapy, because it does not appear that he is operating at his optimum level of intellectual functioning.

In summary, with a CA of 6–7 and an MA of 5–1, Mike achieved an IQ of 75 ± 5, which is in the Borderline Defective classification on the Stanford-Binet Intelligence Scale, Form L-M. His IQ exceeds those of 6% of the children of his age on this test. The chances that the range of scores from 70 to 80 does not include his true IQ are about 32 out of 100. However, while the results probably give a reliable estimate of his present level of functioning, their validity must be questioned because emotional factors may be affecting his efficiency. Mike displayed inadequate verbal, memory, and reasoning abilities, while his perception of logical relations and discriminatory abilities were closer to the average level. Mike should be given speech therapy. His speech problem may be a source of anxiety. It is advisable for him to be tested again in six to twelve months.

Henry J. Green, Examiner

ILLUSTRATIVE REPORTS FOR THE WISC AND WPPSI

There are three sample WISC reports and one sample WPPSI report in this part of the chapter. The writing styles are generally similar. However, the reports were selected to illustrate various types of referral problems that are encountered by school and clinical psychologists. Each report is preceded by some general comments and the scaled scores for each subtest.

Sample WISC Report Number 1 — A Child with Reading Difficulty

The first WISC example is that of a child who was referred to a child guidance clinic because of reading difficulty. The pattern of WISC scores as well as qualitative observations support the picture of a child who has a "learning disability." She meets the requirements of a "reading retardation" classification as proposed by Lyle and Goyen (1969) (see Chapter 23). The test report integrates background information obtained from the mother, statements obtained from the child, test observations, and test data. The results of the evaluation, although not indicated in the report, should be discussed with the mother and child. It is possible, too, that after such a discussion the psychologist may deem it advisable to consider additional testing or even a trial period of counseling involving either the child, the mother, or both. The background information and test results suggest that the problem appears to be one which requires primarily educational intervention. Those engaged in tutorial work with the child, as well as her regular teachers, however, should be provided with any information which will help them to have a better understanding of her attitudes and feelings toward her difficulties.

After the typical identifying data are presented, the report begins in a traditional fashion by indicating the reason for the referral. Selected background information completes the first paragraph. The second paragraph also presents background information. The third paragraph presents relevant information obtained from the child. The fourth paragraph is a brief summarizing statement. The fifth paragraph is based on the examiner's evaluation of the child's behavior during the test session.

The sixth paragraph presents the test results. A statement about the normative group and validity of the test results also appears. The seventh paragraph emphasizes the Verbal-Performance discrepancy and then describes the child's abilities within the Verbal Scale. The eighth paragraph emphasizes the Performance Scale subtests. However, note that the examiner still brings in a qualitative observation in commenting on the child's approach toward the two different scales.

The ninth paragraph describes some qualitative features of the child's performance. The tenth paragraph emphasizes the examiner's recommendations and partially integrates some of the material that has been previously presented in the report. The final paragraph summarizes the report.

The subtest scores were as follows:

Verbal Scale	Performance Scale
Information = 6	Picture Completion = 14
Comprehension = 10	Picture Arrangement = 8
Arithmetic = 5	Block Design =12
Similarities = 7	Object Assembly = 9
Vocabulary = 9	Coding = 10
Digit Span = 9	Mazes = 10

Psychological Evaluation

Name: Eva Smith   Date of examination: July 29, 1972
Date of birth: April 14, 1961   Date of report: August 2, 1972
Chronological age: 11–3   Grade: Fifth
Test administered: Wechsler Intelligence Scale for Children (WISC)

Eva was referred for evaluation by her mother, who indicated that her daughter "just can't read or do other work involving reading." She feels that

Eva is frustrated because of low grades in school and that she has a poor self-image. Mrs. Smith aspires to have her daughter finish school, work for a few years, and then marry.

Eva is the second child in a family of three children; she has one sister who is one year older and another sister who is two years younger. Relationships among the family members are generally satisfactory, although Eva has some discord with her younger sister, showing occasional angry outbursts. The parents are in the process of obtaining a divorce; the father has been away from home for the past year.

Eva's attitude toward school is generally positive. However, she is concerned about missing part of her regular class when she leaves for special help with a remedial reading teacher. In addition, she said that when she tries to get something right in school, she usually fails. She spoke positively about her family and friends and realized that reading is her major problem in school. Her extracurricular activities include camping, Girl Scouts, and 4H activities.

The background information suggests that the major problem centers on the child's reading difficulties. Neither significant emotional problems nor neurological difficulties have been reported.

Eva is a young, pretty girl, with fine brown hair, blue eyes, and a pleasant smile. Throughout the evaluation she was compliant, displayed little emotion, and responded quickly to most questions. Overall, her behavior was that of a friendly yet somewhat distant girl who appears to be aware of her learning difficulties.

On the WISC, Eva, with a chronological age of 11–3, achieved a Verbal Scale IQ of 85, a Performance Scale IQ of 104, and a Full Scale IQ of 93 ± 3. Her level of functioning is in the Average classification and exceeds that of 31% of the children in the standardization group, which was roughly representative of the United States population. The chances that the range of scores from 90 to 96 includes her true IQ are about 68 out of 100. Eva's cooperativeness and willingness to try suggest that the results give a valid picture of her present level of intellectual functioning.

Eva's Full Scale IQ was achieved with a 19-point difference between her verbal and performance abilities, in favor of the latter. Consequently, it is likely that her achievement is more satisfactory in nonverbal situations, which in part require visual-motor and perceptual capacities, than in situations requiring verbal skills. Within the Verbal Scale, her two lowest scores in relation to her average verbal score suggest that her arithmetical skills, which in part require concentration, and her range of knowledge, which in part requires long-range memory, are less adequately developed than are her other verbal skills. In comparison with the above two areas, she is better developed, although still at an average level, in her social comprehension, that is, in her ability to understand social mores and customs.

Her one outstanding ability on the performance subtests suggests that she is perceptually alert in perceiving details in her environment. In addition, she has better than average spatial visualization ability. Other visual-motor abilities are generally within the average range. Interestingly, her interest level was higher on the performance parts of the test than on the verbal parts of the test.

Eva is a girl with direct answers. Both guesses and "I don't know" responses were evident in her incorrect responses. When she knew an answer, she responded very quickly. She answered the arithmetic items that she knew within three seconds. Similarly, one-half of her responses to the Picture Completion subtest were within three seconds. Time-bonus credits were received on the Block Design subtest.

The WISC results are consistent with those expected of a child who has reading difficulties. While her overall level of intellectual development is within the Average classification, three of her verbal skills are below this level. She is particularly inadequate in concentration and in her range of knowledge. However, she makes up for these deficits by having some perceptual and visual-motor skills that are better than average. Her slight antipathy toward verbal tasks suggests that it will not be an easy matter to engage her in remedial work which might enhance her reading skills. Obviously, her current placement with a remedial reading teacher is excellent, even though she seems to have some anxiety about leaving her regular class for tutorial sessions. The present results suggest that continued effort on the part of the school personnel and her mother should be given to helping Eva improve her reading skills. At present, there does not appear to be a need for Eva to receive counseling, although minor emotional difficulties have been reported.

In summary, on the WISC, Eva, who is 11 years old, achieved an IQ of 93 ± 3. These results place her in the Average classification and at the 32nd percentile rank. The chances are about 32 out of 100 that the range of scores from 90 to 96 does not include her true IQ. The results appear to be valid. She has better developed performance abilities than verbal abilities. The overall results are consistent with her learning disability, which centers on inadequate reading ability. She should be encouraged to continue with her remedial reading class.

Jane K. Finley, Examiner

Sample WISC Report Number 2 — A Child with Emotional Disturbance

In this second WISC example, a child with serious behavioral problems did not manifest a pattern on the Verbal Scale that showed extreme variability among the subtest scores, although some variability was shown on the Performance Scale subtest scores. In addition, qualitative analysis did not generally reveal idiosyncratic responses. The few indices that were possibly suggestive of emotional disturbance or preoccupations are described. The report illustrates the finding, noted in Chapter 23, that emotional disturbances may not affect cognitive functioning.

The subtest scores were as follows:

Verbal Scale	Performance Scale
Information = 14	Picture Completion = 12
Comprehension = 12	Picture Arrangement = 13
Arithmetic = 15	Block Design = 14
Similarities =12	Object Assembly = 8
Vocabulary = 13	Coding = 6

Psychological Evaluation

Name: Jim Young   Date of examination: November 20, 1972
Date of birth: July 17, 1965   Date of report: November 21, 1972
Chronological age: 7–4   Grade: Second
Test administered: Wechsler Intelligence Scale for Children (WISC)

Jim is a seven-year-old boy who was referred to the clinic for evaluation because of involuntary defecation, fecal smearing, enuresis, and stealing.

Jim, an illegitimate child who never knew his natural father, was separated from his mother at six months of age, when she developed leukemia from which she died a year later. Since that time Jim has lived with a paternal aunt and her three children, who range in age from 8 to 18 years. At this time, the aunt has been divorced twice. Jim does call his aunt "mother" and thought of her first husband as his father. This man, who had been in the family as long as Jim had, left when he divorced the aunt; Jim was then two and a half years old. During this period of turmoil, incomplete and ineffectual attempts at toilet training were made. Last year Jim's aunt remarried. During the six months that the marriage lasted, Jim formed no attachment to his second step-uncle.

Jim is routinely reported to have bowel movements in the bathtub; he smears feces on the walls or leaves them in trash cans around the house. He also soils himself frequently. He wanders around the house at night and sometimes vanishes for a number of hours from the park or on his way home from school. He has been known to steal food, money, and a stopwatch from the principal's office. He steals routinely and seems to make an effort to be discovered.

Jim is an excellent student, although he is very difficult to handle because of his opposition and defiance. His behavior in the past three months has been changing. There has been a decrease in encopresis and fecal smearing, and an increase in stealing and aggressive behavior.

Jim is a small, thinly built child who appears to be energetic. He was cooperative and friendly during the testing session. His test behavior was characterized by competitiveness, tenacity, and anxiety. He seemed to want to answer all of the questions correctly and was reluctant to give up on any question. For example, on the Information subtest, he responded to "What are the four seasons of the year?" with "Spring" and "Fall," but he could not remember winter and summer. He had to be encouraged to go on to the next question, and three items later he spontaneously returned to the question, adding "Winter" and "Summer." Jim seemed constantly to need assurance from the examiner that he was answering the items correctly. He often asked, "Have I gotten them all right?"

With a chronological age of 7–4, Jim achieved a Verbal Scale IQ of 120, a Performance Scale IQ of 104, and a Full Scale IQ of 114 ± 8 on the WISC. This places him in the Bright Normal classification and indicates that in this respect he exceeds 81% of the children in the standardization group, which was roughly representative of the population of the United States. The chances that the range of scores from 106 to 122 includes his true IQ are about 95 out of 100. The present measure of his level of intellectual functioning appears to be valid.

While there was a 16-point difference between the Verbal and Performance Scales, this difference was primarily associated with his scores on two Performance Scale subtests which were significantly below the average of his other scores. Therefore, while verbal skills are uniformly well developed, performance skills show more variability, with some abilities that are well developed and others that are less well developed. Overall, with the exception of his scores on two of the Performance subtests, Jim consistently obtained above-average scores on the test.

Within the verbal area, his numerical reasoning ability, range of knowledge, and language usage are excellent, while social comprehension and concept formation ability are very adequate. Within the performance area, his analytic and synthetic ability, planning and anticipation ability, and ability to differentiate essential from nonessential details are all well developed. His less adequate skills are associated with visual-motor coordination and with psychomotor speed. It is difficult to account for his lowered scores in these two areas in light of his overall above-average performance. Perhaps the scores reflect temporary inefficiency, such as inefficiency due to fatigue, or perhaps they simply indicate that his abilities in these areas are less adequate than are his other abilities.

A number of responses were particularly interesting. To the question, "Why are criminals locked up?" he said, "Because they steal things that are expensive." In reference to another question concerning charity and a beggar, he said, "Because the beggars might be a burglar." His mention of "stealing" and the specification of "expensive" and "burglar" are notable responses in view of his behavior pattern, which includes stealing. Preoccupation with stealing seems to be intruding into his outlook toward life. One response differed from his general pattern of rather clear-cut, detailed, well-oriented, and direct responses. He said that plum and peach are alike because they "feel the same." The above responses were the only ones that were noteworthy of idiosyncratic tendencies. Overall, he approaches problems by giving detailed answers that are descriptive and include meaningful phrases.

The test results suggest that Jim's behavioral problems, for the most part, have not interfered with his intellectual functioning. While psychomotor speed and visual-motor coordination are less adequately developed than are his other abilities, his overall functioning is very satisfactory. There were some suggestions of preoccupations with stealing, but it is difficult to determine the extensiveness of such preoccupations or the degree to which they may interfere with other forms of cognitive thinking that were not measured by the present test.

On the basis of the present limited evaluation, it is recommended that a personality evaluation be conducted. Further, the seriousness of his behavioral disturbance suggests that therapy should be initiated. Every attempt should be made to obtain further information about his home environment and to determine what factors in the home may be reinforcing his deviant behavior pattern. His aunt should be actively engaged in the development of a treatment program.

In summary, with a chronological age of 7–4, Jim achieved an IQ of 114 ± 8 on the WISC. This places him in the Bright Normal classification and indicates that in this respect he exceeds 81% of the children in the standardization group, which was roughly representative of the population of the United States. The chances that the range of scores from 106 to 122 does not include his true IQ are about 5 out of 100. The test results appear to give a valid indication of his present level of functioning. Verbal skills were uniformly well developed, while there was some variability in his performance skills. There was no evidence that his behavioral problems are significantly interfering with his cognitive skills. An evaluation of personality was recommended, as well as the development of a treatment program that would involve Jim and his aunt.

Adam C. Wills, Examiner

Sample WISC Report Number 3 — A Child with Serious Behavioral Problems

WISC report number 3 illustrates the problem of differential diagnosis. While the examiner did not make a diagnosis on the basis of the WISC, other than indicating the child's intellectual classification, a diagnosis of either childhood schizophrenia or mental retardation might be appropriate, depending upon the prevalence of psychotic symptoms. The examiner reports the results of a previous testing and attempts to account for the discrepancy in findings. Intrasubtest variability is noted. The examiner also makes some broad recommendations about a treatment program.

The subtest scores were as follows:

Verbal Scale	Performance Scale
Information = 5	Picture Completion = 6
Comprehension = 5	Picture Arrangement = 6
Arithmetic = 6	Block Design = 7
Similarities = 3	Object Assembly = 5
Vocabulary = 2	Coding = 4

Psychological Evaluation

Name: Robert Fell   Date of examination: May 11, 1972
Date of birth: March 29, 1960   Date of report: May 13, 1972
Chronological age: 12-2   Grade: Special Class
Test administered: Wechsler Intelligence Scale for Children (WISC)

Robert is a 12-year-old boy who was admitted to the hospital because of a long history of bizarre behavior, such as chanting or yelling obscene language in the public school classroom for no apparent reason, defecating and urinating in various unconventional places around the house, and putting salt in his parents' coffee. In school he also is constantly fighting with other children. His attention span is limited, and outbursts of laughter are likely to occur for no apparent reason. His teacher described him as frequently making facial grimaces and contortions, constantly patting his hands or face, mouthing anything in his hands, acting impulsively, and constantly being in motion — body vibrating or singing and humming most of the time. Medication has not appeared to improve his school behavior. Previous psychiatric evaluation has resulted in a diagnosis of childhood schizophrenia.

Robert's parents have had difficulty with their son for about the last two years. He has also been classified on the basis of a previous psychological evaluation as being mentally retarded. Although he is in a special education class, he has not been doing well at school. In November 1967, the time at which he was first tested, he achieved the following WISC scores: Verbal Scale IQ of 79, Performance Scale IQ of 71, and Full Scale IQ of 72. The report indicated that he was interested in trying to do well and that he seemed to act younger than his age. There was little variability in the pattern of his scores.

Robert cooperated in the testing. He sat quietly in his chair, hands in lap, and moved only when needing to work on one of the various subtests. He often looked at the examiner with a wide-eyed gaze that was always serious, and he spoke in an abrupt, rapid, staccato fashion.

Robert, whose chronological age is 12-2, achieved a Verbal Scale IQ of 63, a Performance Scale IQ of 69, and a Full Scale IQ of 63 ± 6 on the WISC. This IQ is in the Mentally Retarded classification and falls at the first percentile rank of children in the normative group, which was roughly representative of the United States population. The chances that the range from 57 to 69 includes his true IQ are about 90 out of 100. The present test results appear to be valid.

The general pattern of scores is remarkably consistent. Only one subtest score was significantly lower than the average of his other subtest scores, namely, Vocabulary. Thus, his ability to use and understand words effectively, which in part is a reflection of his learning ability, is severely limited. His definitions were simple, concrete, and impoverished. "Nonsense," for example, was defined as "No good" and "diamond" was defined as "shiny thing." He was unable to define such words as "cushion," "fur," and "spade."

There were some indications of impaired thinking. On the Information subtest, he was able to answer "Where does the sun set?" correctly, but he could not answer the easier question, "How many pennies make a nickel?" On a number of other subtests he showed a similar pattern of missing some of the easier items and succeeding on some of the more difficult items. This pattern is sometimes associated with individuals who have a serious impairment in thinking. However, there were no indications of peculiar verbalizations in the content of his responses.

The picture which emerges from the WISC is that of a child with limited intellectual capacities who approaches situations in a concrete fashion. His IQ is nine points lower than the one he obtained four years ago. Perhaps the behavioral disturbance, which had an onset approximately two years ago, has had some effect in decreasing his cognitive efficiency. Because of his limited ability, Robert is likely to experience failure in the classroom and in other situations outside of the classroom. Because of his concrete thinking, he has difficulty understanding ideas that are presented to him in general terms. The present test should be supplemented with other tests in order to obtain information about his personality.

On the basis of the case history material and the results of the present test, the prognosis appears to be guarded. Robert needs an environment which will help him receive rewards for some of his activities. His parents seem willing to help and should be engaged in the planning of a therapeutic program. His ability to attend to the test questions is a favorable sign, because it indicates that in certain situations he can control his restless and impulsive behavior. A structured milieu may help in reducing some of his anxiety.

In summary, Robert, with a chronological age of 12–2, achieved an IQ of 63 ± 6, which is in the Mentally Retarded classification on the WISC. His IQ exceeds those of less than 1% of the children in the normative group. The results appear to provide a valid estimate of his current level of intellectual functioning. Case history material suggests that Robert has a severe behavioral disturbance. On previous occasions he has received a diagnosis of childhood schizophrenia as well as mental retardation. The general pattern of his subtest scores showed minimal variability. A therapeutic program in part could focus on establishing a structured milieu which will provide him with some rewards. While further psychological testing is warranted, the prognosis appears to be guarded.

Nancy Lester, Examiner

Sample WPPSI Report Number 1 — A Child with Developmental Immaturity

This last example illustrates the application of the WPPSI to a problem involving developmental immaturity. The report essentially is similar to the WISC reports that have been presented previously. The first two paragraphs summarize information that had been obtained from the parents and from a kindergarten teacher. The examiner has used discretion in selecting material which she considers to be pertinent. It is not an easy matter to decide on what kind of background information to summarize, but those factors which potentially are most useful in evaluating the child's difficulties should be selected. Both quantitative and qualitative material are cited. Scatter analysis, an evaluation of the child's responses, and examples of test responses appear in the report. The recommendations take into account the test results as well as background information.

The subtest scores were as follows:

Verbal Scale	Performance Scale
Information = 8	Animal House = 5
Vocabulary = 13	Picture Completion = 6
Arithmetic = 10	Mazes = 8
Similarities = 7	Geometric Design = 7
Comprehension = 9	Block Design = 9

Psychological Evaluation

Name: Debbie Adams   Date of examination: June 12, 1972
Date of birth: November 25, 1966   Date of report: June 15, 1972
Chronological age: 5–6   Grade: Kindergarten
Test administered: Wechsler Preschool and Primary Scale of Intelligence (WPPSI)

The evaluation was requested by Debbie's parents, who are concerned about her rate of development. Her parents described her as being a slow learner, and as having a short attention span. In addition, she has motor difficulty, with an unsteady gait and awkwardness of balance. Developmental landmarks were all slightly behind the average. The results of a neurological examination were essentially negative. She is described as being a fairly well-adjusted child who is happy with other children. There is one other sibling in the family, a boy, who is said to be gifted.

The following information was obtained from her kindergarten teacher, who described Debbie as a willing worker when supervised by an adult. However, on her own, her attention often wanders aimlessly. In class, her retention appears to be limited, and she is distracted by anything that crosses her vision. She tends to perceive situations as parts, not wholes, and because she fixes her attention upon small details she fails to understand many situations. Speech problems also are evident. In class she speaks slowly and uses phrases that are more characteristic of a three-year-old than a five-year-old.

The background information suggests that the major concerns focus on patterns which reflect developmental immaturity. Clear-cut patterns of brain injury have not been reported. Learning difficulties also may be present.

Debbie is an attractive youngster, of average height and weight for her age. While a speech impediment was evident, her speech was understandable. She exhibited some awkwardness in motor coordination. Her walking gait was uneven, and she had some difficulty in turning the pages of a test booklet. At times she was restless during the testing. However, she was cooperative and attempted to answer the questions and do the tasks asked of her.

The WPPSI results were as follows: Verbal Scale IQ of 96, Performance Scale IQ of 80, and Full Scale IQ of 87 ± 6. Her IQ is in the Dull Normal classification and falls at the 20th percentile rank of children of her age in the normative group, which was roughly representative of the United States population. The chances that the range of scores from 81 to 93 includes her true IQ are about 85 out of 100. The good rapport which existed between Debbie and the examiner and the child's ability to follow directions and to attempt to respond to the items suggest that the present results are valid.

Debbie's performance skills are not as well developed as are her verbal skills. The 16-point difference between her scores on the verbal and performance parts of the scale suggest that visual-motor ability, perceptual ability, ability to attend to perceptual details, and persistence are at a level of development that is below normal. In contrast, not only do her verbal skills show more variability than her performance skills, but also the overall level of verbal development is within the normal range. Her outstanding strength was her word knowledge. She was able to define words at a level that was higher than normal and above the average of her verbal scaled scores. Thus, for example, she gave satisfactory definitions to such words as "fur," "join," and "diamond." Arithmetic skills appear to be at an average level and above the level of the average of her verbal scaled scores.

Debbie's answers were usually short, precise, and direct. Her failures were manifested both by incorrect answers and by her saying "No" when she did not know an answer. She seemed to experience more difficulty on the Similarities subtest questions than on most other verbal subtests. Instead of giving analogies, she would repeat part of the question in her answer or give associations. For example, to the question, "You ride in a train and you also ride in a − −," she said, "Choo-choo." This one verbal subtest, more than any of the other verbal subtests, reflected her difficulty in grasping concepts and suggested some immaturity in reasoning. She also at first refused to complete the Animal House subtest, but with encouragement and support finally proceeded with the task.

The results of the intelligence test generally confirm the case history material. What appears to be Debbie's principal handicap is a gap between visual-motor skills and verbal skills, in favor of the latter. In school situations she will not likely be perceived as being extremely slow because of her average verbal skills. However, she will need encouragement and attention, because she may tend to remove herself from difficult situations by inattention or by simply refusing to try. Her parents should be helped to accept her present level of development and not place unrealistic demands on her. Special programs to improve her muscle coordination and speech are recommended.

In summary, on the WPPSI, Debbie, with a chronological age of 5–6, obtained an IQ of 87 ± 6 which is in the Dull Normal classification and at the 20th percentile rank. The chances that the range of scores from 81 to 93 does not include her true IQ are about 15 out of 100. The results appear to give a valid estimate of her present level of intellectual functioning. Case history material suggested a pattern of developmental immaturity. The examination revealed that she has better verbal skills than performance skills. Visual-motor coordination and other perceptual skills are less well developed than her vocabulary ability. Immaturity was suggested by some of her responses and behavior patterns. Overall, the results of the test seem to support the case history material. She will need support and encouragement, and her parents should be helped to accept her at her present level of functioning. Special programs were recommended to improve her muscle coordination and speech.

Jane Jones, Examiner

SUMMARY

The major emphasis of Chapter 25 is on the structure and content of the psychological report. Test-oriented reports and subject-oriented reports are rather arbitrary designations; all reports should include both test-related material and subject-related material.

The following areas are usually included in psychological reports: (*a*) test behavior, (*b*) level of present functioning, (*c*) areas of strength and weakness, (*d*) diagnostic implications, and (*e*) recommendations. Each of these areas is discussed briefly.

(*a*) Specific suggestions for observing attitudinal features, language, and visual-motor performance were presented. The Behavior and Attitude Checklist represents a convenient way of recording the examiner's evaluation of the examinee's behavior.

(*b*) The precision range associated with IQ's on the Stanford-Binet, WISC, and WPPSI can be determined easily by reference to the appropriate tables in the Appendix. The IQ should always be accompanied by a statement of precision range. In addition to the precision range, it is important to consider the representativeness of the test findings.

(*c*) The examinee's strengths and weaknesses can be more easily evaluated on the WISC and WPPSI than on the Stanford-Binet. However, in each scale much care must be used in interpreting subtest scatter and in making inferences about specific areas of ability.

(*d*) Diagnostic decisions require considerable skill and judgment. All factors should be considered before arriving at a diagnosis. The aim of the evaluation is careful description, interpretation, and recommendations, not diagnosis *per se*.

(*e*) Finally, recommendations are arrived at by considering all relevant factors. While specificity is important in making recommendations, long range predictions are especially hazardous and should be recognized as such in the report.

Illustrative reports for the Stanford-Binet, WISC, and WPPSI were presented in the last part of the chapter.

CHAPTER 26

CONSULTATION

The diagnostic role does not end with the testing of the child and the writing of a report. The psychologist may be called upon to present his findings at a case conference, to confer with individual teachers regarding the findings, or to meet with parents. In these ways the findings of the psychological evaluation become "alive," and enable the psychologist to contribute to the decision-making process. Even if conferences are not held, readers of the report will make various uses of the findings and recommendations, depending upon the resources available to them.

SERVICES OF SCHOOL PSYCHOLOGISTS

Before turning to the complex issues involved in consultation, it may be helpful to give a brief glimpse of the activities of school psychologists who, by the nature of their school affiliation, must deal with the many facets of the consultation process. A detailed investigation of the services performed by school psychologists was carried out by a research team in a suburban community near New York City (White & Charry, 1966). The period of time covered was one year (1962-1963). The school systems involved in the survey contained approximately 95,000 pupils, although not all school psychologists in these systems participated in the survey. The total sample of pupils referred for psychological services was 2866. The rate of referral was estimated to be 4.8%, based on 13 of the 19 school systems where complete data were available.

Table 26–1 summarizes six facets of school psychology services. The percentages within each breakdown, with the exception of the last, are not independent, because children were classified under more than one category. The largest source of referral to the school psychologists was the school staff (75%) and the major reason for referral was concern over educational performance ("learning difficulties" and "intelligence evaluation"—27% and 14%, respectively). The most frequent diagnostic services were interviewing (41%) and testing (35%). The diagnostic impressions formed by the school psychologists were varied, reflecting normal and abnormal psychological functioning, and cultural and neurological factors. The sources of help recommended were rather evenly balanced between in-school and out-of-school personnel, between public and private facilities, and between psychology and education. The services recommended by the school psychologists were received by 79% of the pupils.

The referral sample was compared with the total school population, and some interesting trends emerged. The referral sample, while representative of

Table 26-1. Summary of School Psychologists' Services

Facet	Breakdown
Sources of referrals	School staff (75%), parent (18%), school psychologist (2%), self (2%), other (2%), community agency (1%)
Reasons for referrals	Learning difficulties (27%), intelligence evaluation (14%), emotionally upset (13%), acting out in classroom (11%), other reasons (10%), class placement (9%), acting out outside classroom (6%), withdrawn behavior (6%), community agency involved (2%), periodic appraisal (1%)
Psychodiagnostic services	Teacher interview (20%), intelligence examination (20%), interview with mother (15%), personality testing (14%), classroom observation (12%), other (10%), interview with father (5%), not seen for lack of time (2%), not seen for lack of family interest (.3%)
Diagnostic impressions	Emotionally disturbed—mild (27%), essentially normal or transient problem (23%), other (16%), emotionally disturbed—severe (10%), culturally deprived (10%), brain damaged (6%), retarded (5%), history of poor physical health (3%)
Recommendations following diagnosis	Special educational help from teacher or staff specialist (21%), counseling for parents (15%), other (10%), counseling by school psychologist (8%), psychotherapy—clinic (7%), psychotherapy—private (6%), referred for further psychological evaluation (5%), special class placement (4%), counseling by other school staff (4%), referred to a community agency (4%), special educational help—outside school (4%), medical evaluation (3%), change in grade level (2%), change in class—same grade level (2%), neurological examination—clinic (2%), private school (1%), neurological examination—private (1%)
Actions following recommendations	Services recommended were received (79%), family did not act upon recommendations (15%), delay due to unavailability of services (4%), school staff did not act upon recommendations (2%), community agency did not act upon recommendations (1%)

Adapted from White and Charry (1966).

the socioeconomic status of the total school population, was slightly lower in intelligence (median IQ of 102 vs. 109 on a variety of tests) and in achievement scores (3:1 ratio of lower to upper achievement). The ratio of boys to girls was higher in the referral sample (2:1) than in the school population (1:1). Other interesting findings in the study were that in the referral sample the correlation between socioeconomic status and IQ was .41, and that the peak of referrals was in grades kindergarten to three. The pupils who were diagnosed as being emotionally disturbed were characterized by higher IQ, higher socioeconomic status, and better achievement than those who were diagnosed as being educationally disturbed.

In a survey by Gross and Farling (1969) of the case loads of school psychologists in the state of Ohio, 177 of the 255 psychologists contacted responded to the questionnaire. The respondents indicated that in 94% of their cases they obtained an intellectual quotient when they were conducting an evaluation. IQ's below 90 were found in 51% of the cases, and in one-third of the cases the IQ's were below 80. Thus, a majority of the children that were seen by the school psychologists in Ohio for evaluation were found to have below-average IQ's. The breakdown of referrals was as follows: class placement (37%), academic problems (27%), intellectual assessment (15%), acting-out behavior (8%), psychosomatic, bizarre, or withdrawn behavior (7%), physical problems (4%), family problems (2%), and community problems (1%). The results of the Gross and Farling survey agree with those of White and Charry (1966) in finding that the primary reasons for referral to school psychologists center on school-related problems. Both surveys also indicated that between 14% and 15% of the referrals were primarily for intellectual evaluation.

An excellent discussion of the problems involved in translating psychological concepts into action in the school (as well as in other settings) appears in the work of Sarason, Levine, Goldenberg, Cherlin, and Bennett (1966). These investigators pointed out that the mental health consultant, in order to be effective in the school, should know as intimately as possible the situation in which change is to take place. A harmonious working relationship with the school personnel, knowledge of the child's classroom behavior, and continuous interactions and feedback with the teacher and parents are all necessary ingredients if consultation is to be maximally successful. Their work is recommended to all who are engaged in psychological services in educational and clinical settings.

INTELLIGENT USE OF TEST RESULTS

Breger (1968) pointed out that the effectiveness of psychological testing is dependent upon the adequacy of its basic assumptions, its helpfulness to the treatment process, and its contributions to actual decision-making about clients; tests should be used when they make a valid contribution to specific decisions. He stated that there is no evidence that psychological testing is helpful in providing recommendations for different types of treatment or for enabling chronic psychiatric patients to function effectively outside of the hospital. However, Breger concluded that testing for those individuals who seek diagnosis or assessment may be quite appropriate (e.g., identification of organic pathology). The most satisfactory uses of test scores are as aids in decision-making and as sources of information on which to base further investigation; test scores alone should not be used to make decisions (Pauker, 1971).

The intelligence test can be a valuable tool when it is used as an index of what needs to be done for a particular child (Clark, 1967). It should be used to determine where one must start in order to bring him up to maximum effectiveness. When intelligence tests are used to deny children the opportunities to learn up to the limits of their ability or to bias teachers away from helping children learn, they are being used incorrectly. As Clark noted, test results should never be used to shackle children. (Chapter 4 also considers the proper use of test results.)

Since some degree of reliance is placed on test results in the decision-making process, it is important to consider the social impact of testing. Goslin (1967) raised four questions that are related to this issue. First, what is the objective influence of tests on the opportunities available to individuals? Second, what part do test scores play in influencing the kinds of advice given to people in schools, counseling agencies, and similar organizations? Third, how is an individual affected by knowledge of his own test scores? Fourth, what is the ultimate effect of the use of objective criteria for evaluating abilities of individuals on society? While Goslin concluded that little is known about the answers to these questions, the examiner must attempt to evaluate such questions as he performs his testing role.

RECOMMENDATIONS

The recommendations made in the report and at case or parental conferences should be as direct and clear as possible. In all cases, the recommendations should emerge from the results of the entire evaluation (which includes case history material), making clear to the reader those which are tentative and those which are firm. Anastasi (1968a) noted that tests are administered in order to determine what the individual is able to do at the time of testing, and not to show causes of behavior or the origins of individual differences in performance. Recommendations are in part dependent on the services available in the community and the financial status of the family.

We have seen in Chapter 24 that recommendations are highly valued by many readers of the report, especially by those in school settings. Also, in school settings, it would be valuable to discuss how the findings may be related to problems in educational planning and in academic functioning (cf. Handler et al., 1965). It is very important, however, that the recommendations be within the teacher's competence and that the concepts that are used in the report be clearly understood by the teacher. Anything short of this can carry implications of blame (Cason, 1945). Whenever possible, it is important also to determine whether recommendations were followed and whether the hypotheses were supported by the child's subsequent performance (Shapiro, 1951).

The process of formulating recommendations which are given to teachers and parents can be assisted by reference to the 50 "typical" recommendations developed by Blanco (1970) for children who have psychological, educational, or physical problems. Considerable judgment must be used in selecting which of the recommendations, if any, are appropriate for a particular child. The recommendations were derived from different theoretical orientations and cover 10 different types of exceptionality: school phobia, underachievement, mild retardation, deaf, blind, aggression, isolate or reject, shyness, minimal cerebral dysfunction, and dull normal. Over one-half of the recommendations presented by Blanco are for school phobia and underachievement.

The psychologist should study carefully which recommendation (or recommendations) is most appropriate for the child. Blanco also indicated the probable effectiveness of each recommendation, the age range for which it is most appropriate, and the recipient of the recommendation. A careful study of these recommendations may prove to be of value in translating the results of the psychological evaluation into a meaningful program of action.

Palmer (1970) suggested that children selected for psychoanalytic treatment should have a higher WISC Verbal than Performance IQ. The Vocabulary, Similarities, and Comprehension subtests, especially, should be in the Bright Normal range. However, verbal competency should be assessed by other tests if it is suspected that a child's low verbal score is the result of negativism. Generally, low intelligence or poor verbal abstract ability may be indications that some forms of psychotherapy, especially those requiring at least average verbal ability, should not be considered (Huber, 1961).

THE ETHICS OF PSYCHOLOGICAL ASSESSMENT

Ethical Standards of Psychologists

The Ethical Standards of Psychologists of the American Psychological Association (1963) serve as a guidepost for psychologists in their professional work. A careful study of the standards will enable the psychologist (and student-in-training) to understand some of the responsibilities associated with his professional role.

American Psychological Association Guidelines

The American Psychological Association (1970) formulated a set of guidelines to aid psychologists engaged in psychological assessment. The statements that are most pertinent to the assessment of intelligence are summarized.

1. The examinee should be protected against unwarranted inferences by persons not equipped with the requisite background knowledge.

2. The examinee should be protected against unfavorable evaluation based on obsolete information.

3. The examinee should be protected against unnecessary intrusions into his privacy.

4. Policies set up to insure the kinds of protection described in statements 1, 2, and 3 should be of such a nature as to maintain conditions that will facilitate research on which new and improved assessment procedures can be based.

5. The examinee's right to decline to be assessed or to refuse to answer questions has never been and should not be questioned. This right should be pointed out to the examinee when the confidentiality of the results are discussed with him.

6. Whenever possible, the examinee should be told who will have access to the information and for what purposes.

7. The examiner is responsible for determining the relevancy of the techniques to the situation for which the examinee is being assessed.

8. Relevance must be weighed and justified in terms of socially accepted values and principles.

9. The competence of the examiner will determine ultimately the extent to which assessment procedures will work.

Goldman (1970), however, objected to the American Psychological Association's guidelines as being too concerned with the needs and rights of psychologists and the institutions on whose behalf they do their assessment, and too little concerned with the rights of the examinee. Goldman proposed that a better document is the *Guidelines for the Collection, Maintenance, and Dissemination of Pupil Records* (Russell Sage Foundation, 1970), which is discussed in the next section.

Russell Sage Foundation Guidelines

The *Guidelines* (1970) concern the many issues involved in the collection of data, classification and maintenance of data, administration of security, and dissemination of information regarding pupils. Careful study of the *Guidelines* is recommended to all professional individuals working in school systems and in other agencies in which psychological and educational material is obtained from children. In this chapter, only a few of the issues in the *Guidelines* are highlighted, those that are concerned with intelligence testing.

The major principle behind the *Guidelines* is that information collected from students should have the prior informed consent of the child and his parents. However, consent can be either "representational" or "individual," depending upon the type of information that is to be obtained. Representational consent, which refers to the consent of organized bodies (e.g., legislature or school board) that make policies for the school, is usually sufficient for aptitude and achievement testing, while personality testing and assessment should always require individual consent (in writing) of the child or his parents, or both.

With respect to intelligence testing, the *Guidelines* indicate that the child should be informed about the implications of testing and the voluntary character of his participation, and that parental consent should be obtained in those situations in which there is reasonable doubt about the child's ability to understand the implications of the situation. Intelligence test results are not considered to be absolutely necessary to the school over a period of time, and therefore, at periodic intervals, the school should consider eliminating such results from the files. At any time, a pupil or his parents should have the right to challenge the validity of the information in the pupil's records. At all times records should be kept locked and under supervision.

The *Guidelines* indicate that the school may, without consent of parents or pupils, release intelligence test scores (and other similar material as well as objective factual data) to other school officials within the district, to the state superintendent, and to other school systems. It is understood that those having access to the files have legitimate educational interests, and that records are kept of all those using the pupil's file. In cases of transfer, the parents should be so notified and should be permitted to receive a copy of the record if they desire. In all other cases, records should not be divulged unless there is written consent from the parents or unless there is a judicial order or an order from agencies having the power of subpoena. Access to intelligence test data should be available to parents and to pupils who have their parents' permission. However, a student over 18 years of age and no longer attending school, or one who is married, has the right to deny parental access to his records, and becomes the one who is solely responsible for giving consent to release his records.

Goldman's Position on Assessment in the Schools

Psychologists working in schools have somewhat different problems from those who work in agencies or are in private practice. Goldman (1971), who closely follows the *Guidelines* of the Russell Sage Foundation, but also presents additional considerations, is concerned with some important issues related to the problems of secrecy and openness in the public schools.

First, the psychologist's role is to assess the child's learning potential by using, when needed, standard ability and achievement tests. Parental permission and concurrence should be sought for any procedures which go beyond this point.

Second, information received in the course of the diagnostic work-up should be protected from everyone, with the exception of the pupils and their parents and the people they think should have it.

Third, the assumption that the school staff knows better than the parents what is good for the child must be replaced with the recognition that it is the parents who are legally and morally responsible for their child. Even when the child desires a confidential relationship, the psychologist (or counselor) should try to help the child to understand the importance of involving the parents in the relationship. Further, the parents must be given the opportunity to refuse the services of the psychologist.

Fourth, the psychologist should recognize that the pupil is not a "client" in the sense that an adult is a "client." A school-age child does not have the same judgment and competence as that of adults.

Fifth, a private practitioner is responsible primarily to the client, and in the case of a child, the client includes the parents. But a school psychologist's position is more complicated. He cannot simply terminate his relationship with the child when the problem is over. For example, he may be called upon to write a letter of recommendation, to discuss the child with a teacher, or to testify about the child at a school meeting. These demands make it impossible for him to promise a confidential relationship, as would be possible if he were in private practice or working in a voluntary agency.

Goldman concluded that the paternalistic stance that has been traditional in the school can no longer be maintained. While some power and control will be forfeited by following the above guidelines, Goldman maintained that power and control should be returned to the proper source, namely, the pupils and their parents who will "retain the power to decide whether they will be helped, what personal information they will divulge, and what the school may release to anyone else [p. 5]."

Other Assessment Considerations

Shah (1970) pointed out that the client has a legal right to obtain test protocols (e.g., the Stanford-Binet record booklet or WISC record booklet). However, the psychologist is entitled to withhold technical information (e.g., test profiles and analyses) from persons not qualified to interpret such data. When psychologists perform an evaluation for an agency, the source material and report belong to the agency. Psychologists working in agencies should be aware that they are not primarily the client's agent. Conflicts that may arise between the psychologist's obligations to the agency and his obligations to the client should be considered. The limits of confidentiality should be discussed with the client.

Assessment in Courts or Correctional Settings

The psychologist who works in courts or in correctional settings is faced with a number of important and somewhat unique issues, which bring into focus situational demands and moral and ethical concerns involved in psychological assessment procedures. These issues are also relevant to the work of psychologists employed in other agencies or in private practice. The following analysis is based on Riscalla's (1971) work.

The duties of the court psychologist include *(a)* making determinations of an individual's competency to stand trial, *(b)* deciding whether a juvenile should remain with his family, and *(c)* recommending whether an offender should be incarcerated or receive probation. The psychologist must decide to what extent concern with the offender's rights may conflict with the rights of the community and with the psychologist's employment by the court. His duties place him in a captive, adversary role, because he may be called upon to support a particular position which is held either by the court or by the offender. He should recognize his own feelings about his role as well as his attitudes toward certain offenses, and should consider how his moral standards will affect his relationship with the offender as well as with the court.

Court psychologists may perceive their role in a number of ways. One is the anti-establishment psychologist who takes sides with the offender by rationalizing the offense on the basis of personality dynamics or adversive environmental conditions. A second is the psychologist who assumes a punitive, self-righteous, superior attitude toward the offender, aiming to protect the rights of society, and wording reports so that the court might take punitive action against the offender. A third role is that of the uninvolved psychologist who is afraid of authority and who preserves his neutrality at any price. The fourth and proper role, according to Riscalla, is that of the psychologist who recognizes his captive, adversary role and yet tries to limit it, insofar as it is possible, by illuminating issues and pointing out ways to constructive alternatives which might lead to solutions.

The psychologist must recognize that as a representative of the court he may be viewed with suspicion and hostility. Sharing the results of the evaluation with the offender before the report is written is one method he can use to reduce evasiveness and to facilitate a more harmonious relationship with the client. As by-products of such a procedure, the accuracy of the assessment may be improved, the recommendations may be more realistic, and the clients may gain insight into their behavior. Clients who do not desire to participate in the evaluation should have their wishes respected.

Riscalla also suggested that the client can be protected further by permitting him, his representative, or other interested authorized individuals to discuss with the psychologist and to examine, if necessary, the psychological report prior to its submission to legal authorities. This procedure may help the psychologist to serve his clients better, to write more understandable reports, and to make the assessment procedure more relevant and meaningful.

The Examinee as a Coevaluator

Fischer (1970), whose views about testing parallel and supplement those of Riscalla, presented suggestions for changing the testing situation from one in which the examinee is placed in a limited restricted role (as traditional testing situations are now constructed) to one in which the examinee is a coevaluator. In order for the examinee to play an active and responsible role in the test situation, a number of important procedures should be followed. First, coadvisement is needed. The examiner describes the reasons for testing, the use of tests, the contents of the report, and the report's readers. The examinee, in turn, is asked to express his view of the purpose of testing. Second, the psychologist, after the tests have been completed, shares with the examinee his impression of the examinee's performance. Third, as has been stressed in the chapter on report writing, everyday language is used in the discussion. The level should be descriptive, with clearly drawn inferences about the examinee. Fourth, the examinee should have the opportunity to give a critique of the written evaluation, and to add his addendum, if he so desires. Fifth, the examinee should be consulted for permission to release the report to specific persons. Fischer recognizes that in the cases of young children, prisoners, and acute psychotics the above recommendations may not be implemented fully. However, she advocates that they be followed within the limits of practical circumstances.

Vane (1971) also favors the approach of giving psychological reports to clients and of including the IQ in the report. However, in conducting a survey of the practices of psychologists, she found that 86% of the respondents ($N = 137$ in the total group) reported that they rarely or never give intelligence test scores to adults, to adolescents, or to parents, and that 88% rarely or never give written reports to their clients. It appears that many psychologists' views will have to be changed before the suggestions of Fischer, Riscalla, and Vane are implemented.

CONSULTATION WITH PARENTS

The psychologist, in many cases, will have to share the results of the psychological evaluation with the child's parents. The psychologist has information which the parents will need in order to make the most appropriate decision for their child. During the conference, the psychologist should help the parents clarify their feelings about their child's problems (Rheingold, 1945). The specific techniques of reporting test results to parents are similar to those used in the test report (Goldman, 1961). The examiner should attempt to understand the purposes of the parents in seeking information about their child. The results of the evaluation should be communicated in language and in concepts which are comprehensible to the parents. The interview can be used both to test the validity of some interpretations and to help the parents to understand and to accept the interpretations (Goldman, 1961).

Consultation with Parents of the Mentally Retarded

Discussing the results of the psychological evaluation with parents of the mentally retarded requires tact and skill. The psychologist's role is to help the parents recognize the problem, formulate a plan, and place the plan into action (Milligan, 1971). It is a traumatic experience for most parents to learn that their child is mentally retarded. The sequence of incorporating this knowledge into the family structure may be one of shock, disbelief, fear and frustration, and then intelligent inquiry (Koegler, 1963); or emotional disorganization, reintegration, and mature adaptation (American Medical Association, 1965). The parents should be informed of the limitations of the findings, and should be encouraged to make tentative plans about the child's future (Doll, 1963; Thurston, 1963). Factual information regarding community resources, referral agencies and institutions, and recommended sources for learning about mental retardation (books and pamphlets) will help parents in planning for their child. In order to be successful, the interview should resemble any other therapeutic interview in which the gaining of insight is the objective (Rheingold, 1945). Especially important in working with mentally retarded children (and with other handicapped children) and their parents is an understanding by the examiner of himself and of his attitude toward handicaps and the handicapped (Thurston, 1963).

Sarason (1959) has provided an extremely thorough and systematic presentation of the many issues involved in communicating test results and in helping the parents of mentally retarded children to recognize and adjust to the realities of their child's condition. His presentation also has much to recommend it to anyone engaged in working with parents of handicapped children. A careful study of his work is recommended because only a partial summary is presented herein. While some of the material discussed by Sarason has been alluded to in the previous paragraph, it is worthy of reemphasis.

The goals of the interview, according to Sarason, include (1) a thorough presentation of the child's condition (etiology, severity, and prognosis); (2) planning of a specific program geared to the child's needs and capabilities; (3) recognizing and dealing with the personal problems of the parents as they affect the child or as they are exacerbated by the child's condition; and (4) planning for periodic discussion. The interview can be conceptualized as covering the following four phases.

I. Initial Phase of the Interview

(1) Every effort should be made to have both parents present at the interview. This will facilitate obtaining a more objective picture of the facts and will help in enabling the parents to share the responsibilities of caring for the child.

(2) The examiner should recognize the frustration and hardships that may have been faced by the parents. They should be made to feel comfortable during the interview and encouraged to talk and to ask questions freely. The examiner should convey to them that they have something important to contribute to the discussion.

(3) The parents' attitudes about the etiology of their child's condition should be obtained, as well as information about how they have handled the problems that the child has presented and what goals they have set for the child.

II. Communicating the Diagnostic Findings

(4) In this phase the examiner should inform the parents that he approves of their participation, prepare them for conflict-arousing information, where indicated, and then help them to express any feelings of anxiety, hostility, disappointment, or despair. The diagnostic findings are used, in part, to help the parents give up erroneous ideas, where present, and to adopt a more realistic approach to their child's problems.

III. Discussion of a Specific Program

(5) The examiner should offer to discuss with the parents a specific program for their child.

IV. Terminating the Interview

(6) The examiner should indicate that he is available for another session or sessions, especially if all of the goals have not been achieved, or if the parents seem to desire further discussion.

(7) In cases in which the parents are unable to accept the results of the evaluation, the examiner should convey to them his understanding of their difficulty in accepting and in adjusting to the material that has been discussed. He should make available to them names of other agencies or professionals should they desire another evaluation.

The particular way in which the above four phases of the interview unfolds will depend upon the needs of the parents and the orientation of the examiner. It is important that the examiner show warmth, understanding, and respect. The crucial test of the effectiveness of the interview, as Sarason pointed out, is whether or not the parents can act on the basis of what they have learned. Erroneous beliefs present before the interview, which have been serving to defend the parents from unpleasant consequences, will probably not be given up after one interview. Consequently, several interviews may be needed, and even a visit to the home may facilitate therapeutic progress.

Future plans should be based on the child's degree of retardation, the etiology of the condition, the size and stability of the family, the emotional and physical health of the mother, and the available facilities and services in the community (Koegler, 1963). Those engaged in communicating the results of psychological evaluations to parents will find their work rewarding, challenging, and, at times, frustrating and heartbreaking. The interview represents an important part of the assessment procedure. It is particularly rewarding, for it allows the psychologist to implement in a purposeful way the results of the evaluation. Following the guidelines presented above will help to alleviate some of the anxieties associated with communication of test results to parents of mentally retarded children, as well as to parents of other handicapped children.

CONCLUDING COMMENTS ON ASSESSMENT

Ackley (1971), chairman of the New York Civil Liberties Union, gave an address at a symposium sponsored by the American Psychological Association. He followed the Russell Sage Foundation *Guidelines* closely and interpreted the American Psychological Association's Code of Ethics as supporting the principle that parents have a right to know the materials that are being used in decisions that affect their child's welfare. Ackley is very aware that ethical considerations are values and principles that pervade one's life and determine one's actions. Belief in the dignity of man and in the worth of each individual is the key to a successful professional life. He reminded us that

the problems of students call for the professional and technical competence of psychologists, but they are much more than technical problems; they are personal problems. They require the understanding of the family—and therefore professional skill of the highest order—for it is the psychologists's function, after he has diagnosed his client's difficulty or promise, to interpret it to each of those situated to lend a hand, including parents. The demands of ethical conduct dovetail with those of professional performance, the rights of parents with the claims of school psychologists [p. 12].

The decade of the 1970's is bringing psychologists to a new awareness of the right of individuals to have access to the results of their psychological evaluation and to voice an opinion about the contents of the evaluation. Also, concern has arisen about problems involved with secrecy, security, and record-keeping, issues which involve many facets of our society. While reservations have been voiced about allowing parents to see psychological reports for fear of watering down reports and diluting the relationship with the child (cf. Thorne, 1961), Valett (1963) has noted that psychological testing of children "is only the beginning of a complex process which must involve the cooperation of the parents, if understanding and desirable follow-up is to be obtained [p. 95]." The weight of opinion from many sources indicates that the parents have the right to see the psychological report.

Allowing the client to see and comment on the psychological report may innervate the assessment process by providing a stimulus for an exciting and productive encounter with the client. With this procedure, the report has a chance of having an impact on another individual and of being subjected to an in-depth and penetrating analysis. Further, the report can serve as an additional vehicle for communication with the client. Although many psychologists may be hesitant to follow such a procedure, it seems to be one that holds meaningful possibilities, and, therefore, should be given a chance.

CONCLUDING REMARKS ON CONSULTATION

The psychologist can be a valuable resource person in many settings. He has the tools to answer specific questions and can be helpful in enabling others to understand the child better by determining, in part, some of the probable factors that may be contributing to the child's problems. One of his most useful tools will be a standardized, individually administered intelligence test, such as those considered in this book. However, he will have to recognize both the assets and limitations of these instruments, and recognize that a great deal of intelligent behavior may not be assessed by the instruments. The recommendations made on the basis of the evaluation play an important role in the consultation process. As Ross (1967) has pointed out, "unless diagnostic efforts lead to constructive intervention they are no more than an academic exercise [p. 92]."

Cason (1945), many years ago, clearly pointed out the responsibilities of psychologists who are working in schools:

The school psychologist's value depends not only on the keenness of his diagnoses, the adequacy of his predictions about future behavior and his own therapeutic work, but also on his ability to stimulate in the school personnel an understanding of the child and a willingness to bring their best efforts to bear upon his needs [p. 137].

We might add that Cason's statement can well apply to any setting in which psychologists perform their duties.

The consultation process begins when the child is first referred to the psychologist. The reason for referral brings about certain expectations in the psychologist, which are augmented by a reading of the material in the child's case file. The psychologist, while using and evaluating all of the information that is available to him, must try to meet the child in as open a manner as possible without undue bias. The child should be permitted every opportunity to express his knowledge, his perceptions, and his anxieties. The assessment situation should be a learning situation for both psychologist and child. A knowledgeable and responsible use of intelligence tests and other psychological and educational tests can be of value to the child, to those responsible for his care and education, and ultimately, to society as a whole.

SUMMARY

Consultation is an inherent part of the work of the psychologist. After the psychological evaluation is completed, the psychologist may still be called upon to follow up on his recommendations, or to develop techniques for implementing his recommendations, or to explain his findings more fully, or to discuss his findings with parents, teachers, and other interested persons.

The consultation process usually begins with a referral. Surveys indicate that children are referred to school psychologists primarily for educational concerns, e.g., learning difficulties and evaluation of intelligence.

The intelligent use of test results is the aim of all psychologists. Test results can aid in decision-making. The IQ is valuable as an index of what needs to be done for a particular child; it fails when it is used to shackle children. It is important to consider the social impact of testing.

Recommendations should be practical, based upon the available services in the community, the resources of the family, and the competencies of the school teacher or agency.

The ethical standards for psychologists and the guidelines for psychological assessment developed by the American Psychological Association, together with the guidelines published by the Russell Sage Foundation, should be studied carefully by all those engaged in professional psychological activities which call for involvement with children (as well as with adults). The rights of the examinee are the key factors to consider in developing an ethical and practical program involving psychological assessment.

The psychologist, before collecting information from children, should have the prior informed consent of the child and his parents. The child and his parents have the right of access to the child's records. Goldman emphasized that it is the parents who are responsible for the child, and this responsibility, in turn, calls for their participation in psychological work with their child. Confidential relationships in school settings are different from those in private practice or agency work, primarily because the school psychologist may continue to be involved with the child's case, even after formal assessment procedures have been completed.

The following are other issues concerned with assessment:

1. The legal rights to the record booklet. Shah indicated that the record booklet belongs to the client.

2. Obligations of psychologist to client vs. agency. It is important to discuss such conflicts with the client.

3. Demands placed on psychologists working in courts or correctional settings. Riscalla suggested that the proper role is for the psychologist to recognize his captive, adversary role, and yet try to limit it, insofar as possible, by developing constructive alternatives.

4. Recognizing the examinee as a coevaluator. Fischer urged that the client become an active participant in the assessment process. This entails, in part, the right of the examinee to see his results and to give a critique of the psychological report.

Consultation with parents is a demanding yet rewarding activity. The results of the psychological evaluation take on a different color when they must be orally communicated to parents. The interaction should be in the nature of a dialogue in which both participants (the examiner and parents) have the opportunity to clarify the results of the evaluation. Working with parents of mentally retarded children requires considerable skill. Sarason's excellent presentation of the issues involved in consulting with parents of the mentally retarded serves as a model of clarity and insight. He emphasized that the psychologist should help the parents to recognize and adjust to the realities of their child's condition.

Psychological assessment is moving out from the closed confines of the office and file cabinet to the open spaces of interpersonal communication. It is not an easy move, and it will be resisted by many professionals. But it is a move which must be attempted if we, as professionals, are going to recognize the rights and responsibilities of our clients. It is the acceptance of similar kinds of responsibilities on the part of the client which we aim for as therapists and counselors; we can ask for no less as assessors of intellectual ability.

CHAPTER 27

OVERVIEW

Our aim in this brief concluding chapter is to consider some general issues that are pertinent to the area of intelligence testing and to assessment in general. While much of the material has been covered or alluded to elsewhere in the book, this chapter serves as a review of some important issues involved in the process of intellectual assessment. We now turn to some of the factors involved in selecting intelligence tests.

FACTORS TO CONSIDER IN SELECTING INTELLIGENCE TESTS

The major problem that the psychologist faces in selecting among the various tests covered in the text (as well as other tests) will be the choice among the Stanford-Binet, WISC, and WPPSI when two or more of these tests are appropriate to evaluate a child. Other tests have more specialized uses. It is these three tests which hold the most promise for obtaining the fullest amount of information about the child, while at the same time providing a measure of intelligence. Surveys, prior to the introduction of the WPPSI, have indicated that both the Stanford-Binet and WISC are highly preferred in hospitals and clinics (Sundberg, 1961; Lubin, Wallis, & Paine, 1971) and in institutions for the mentally retarded (Silverstein, 1963b). In a survey of the preferences of school psychologists in California (Weise, 1960), the Stanford-Binet was preferred to the WISC in testing for giftedness and for mental retardation in kindergarten through second grades. However, starting with the third grade, the WISC was preferred in testing for mental retardation. In testing for giftedness in grades three through six, there was approximately an equal preference for each of the two tests. After grade six, the WISC was preferred in testing for giftedness. The WISC also was preferred to the Stanford-Binet in evaluating problems concerned with differential diagnosis (e.g., learning problem, emotional problem, or neurological problem). The WAIS is preferred to the Stanford-Binet in the testing of adults (British Psychological Society, 1958; McKerracher & Scott, 1966; Mundy & Maxwell, 1958; Nunnally, 1970), although Haworth (1959) noted that the Stanford-Binet is still the best available instrument for assessing mentally retarded adults with mental age levels below six or seven years.

The Stanford-Binet dominated the field of preschool testing until the introduction of the WPPSI (cf. Stott & Ball, 1965). Two recent reports suggest that the Stanford-Binet, in comparison to the WPPSI, is preferred for the evaluation of ethnic minority group children and "culturally disadvantaged children"

(Barclay & Yater, 1969; Fagan et al., 1969). In both investigations, the children obtained higher scores on the Stanford-Binet than on the WPPSI. The explanation of Fagan and her co-workers appears to be a reasonable one for accounting for the advantages of the Stanford-Binet:

The lower-class child is frequently shy, nonverbal, activity-oriented, and sensitive to failure. The frequent switching of materials, the briefer verbal demands, and the less apparent failure experiences made the Binet more appropriate [than the WPPSI] [p. 609].

Ross (1959) preferred the Stanford-Binet to the WISC for children under 8 years of age. The tests in the Stanford-Binet between 2 and 8 years of age are interesting to young children, whereas the WISC directions are somewhat awkward to use for children who are 8 years of age and under. Osborne (1972) is of the opinion that the WISC is the test of choice for use with children in the 6 to 13 age range.

The WISC (and possibly the WPPSI) is easier to administer than the Stanford-Binet, because only 10, 11, or 12 subtests are used rather than the variety of tests that are found on the Stanford-Binet. The breakdown of the IQ into Verbal and Performance components on the Wechsler scales is often helpful, especially when testing exceptional children.

A recent reviewer (Freides, 1972) has predicted the demise of the Stanford-Binet:

The *Stanford-Binet Intelligence Scale* is an old, old vehicle. It has led a distinguished life as a pioneer in the bootstrap operation that is the assessment enterprise. Its time is just about over. *Requiescat in pace* [p. 773].

As has been seen in the text, the Stanford-Binet, in comparison to the WISC, both has better coverage at the lower and upper age levels and provides a more reliable assessment at the extreme ranges of intelligence (cf. Fraser, 1965; Rabin, 1959), is good for children with low mentality (Robinson & Robinson, 1965), and also is used frequently in the evaluation of handicapped children (cf. Braen & Masling, 1959; Schonell, 1958). We also have seen that the Stanford-Binet may have some advantages over the WPPSI. Thus, Freides's prediction appears to be somewhat premature.

The factors that should be considered in selecting a test include the validity, reliability, appropriateness, and familiarity of the tests for the particular examinee (Garner, 1966). Evidence indicates that both the Stanford-Binet and WISC have good predictive efficiency, using as criteria school grades and indices of vocational accomplishment. The basis for choice also will be the validity of the inferences that can be made for each test in the situations in which they are actually used (Thorndike & Hagen, 1969). Thus, the choice of whether to use the Stanford-Binet, WISC, or WPPSI often will boil down to the personal preferences of the clinician (cf. Nunnally, 1970).

OBJECTIVES OF INTELLIGENCE TESTING

The study of intelligence began with rather limited objectives. Binet and Simon sought primarily to classify individuals in relation to one another. Today, much more is demanded from our tests. Not only is classification of intelligence desired, but also information about personality, thinking, language patterns, diagnostic categorizations, and training programs. The list is endless. Certainly, any instrument that can provide reliable information about perceptual processes, language development, thought patterns, social development, and academic skills will become a giant in the field. None of the present tests and, more likely, no one future test will simultaneously reach all of these aims.

But many tests can provide clues and useful leads about some of them. Ideally, the psychological evaluation includes the administration of tests that measure a variety of special abilities and functions. But when only an intelligence test is used, as is occasionally the case, every attempt should be made to observe the child's performance carefully and to evaluate the implications of the performance. In no case should conclusive statements be made about abilities that are not reliably measured by the instrument. The evaluation aims to arrive at a general index of intelligence which, together with other relevant information, can be used as an aid to decision making.

THE IQ

As users of intelligence tests, we must take continuous care not to reify the intelligence quotient. The IQ cannot be used to explain all types of behavior. It is a score on a particular test which has been given at a particular time, and it is subject to change. The IQ, in spite of the numerous criticisms which it has received over the years, continues to serve a useful purpose. Scores on intelligence tests, for example, have good predictive validity for a variety of behaviors and for a variety of groups. Schizophrenic children who have low IQ's have a very poor prognosis, and various social behaviors are significantly related to level of intelligence for mentally retarded individuals in institutions. Until more sophisticated tests appear, the IQ obtained from present tests provides a rather gross but valuable measure to assist us in making meaningful recommendations and decisions about the child.

The IQ is a gross measure of intellectual ability, because it is obtained from tests that tap a restricted sample of intellectual functions. While test scores ably predict educational achievement, they fall down in the prediction of nontest behavior and nonacademic intellectual ability. We should be reminded of Thurstone's statements about the varied nature of intelligence. There are many different kinds of intelligence, including abstract, social, mechanical, verbal, and nonverbal. Current tests of individual intelligence do not provide us with valid scores for the different kinds of intelligence necessary for a person to function in a mature, responsible, and adequate manner. Tyler (1971) similarly noted that the IQ does not permit us to determine how flexible the person is in adapting to new situations, nor does it tell us how he will adjust and learn in many nonschool situations. The IQ obtained on standard intelligence tests, she observed, is not a pure measure of innate capacity; "rather it reflects experience as well as potential, education as well as aptitude [p. 48]."

VALUE OF INTELLIGENCE TESTS IN THE ASSESSMENT PROCESS

The intelligence test, which is considered to be an objective psychological examination, has several advantages in the assessment process (Jastak, 1967). Valuable information is made available in a relatively brief period of time. The kinds of halo effects which arise in the ordinary interview are reduced to a minimum. A record is provided which can be used to check predictions made by the examiner and to compare present with past scores obtained by the examinee. The results of the evaluation can also serve to correct examiner bias concerning the examinee's level of ability. Jastak cautioned that the values of intelligence tests should not prevent us from understanding their limitations in the overall assessment process. They were devised from theoretical frameworks that are relatively limited in scope. Further, the data obtained from intelligence tests cannot be applied systematically to personality evaluation or to psychotherapeutic work.

TESTING PHYSICALLY HANDICAPPED CHILDREN

The method of assessing handicapped children is always dependent upon the child's handicaps. The examiner should initially try to select a test that can be administered without modification and without omitting parts of the test. However, when it becomes necessary to modify the test, either by altering the standard administrative procedures or by omitting certain tests, it also is extremely important to indicate in the report that the test was modified and that the validity of the findings may be in question.

DIAGNOSIS AND ASSESSMENT

The Stanford-Binet, WISC, WPPSI, and other intelligence tests measure only part of the broad spectrum of human abilities. It has been amply demonstrated, for example, that the WISC measures only a few of the many variables that are measured by the Halstead and Reitan neuropsychological test battery (cf. Crockett, Klonoff, & Bjerring, 1969; Klonoff, 1971). The adaptive abilities measured by the Halstead-Reitan battery are distinct from or complement the psychometric-intelligence abilities measured by the WISC. A detailed study of the child, therefore, should incorporate other psychological and educational measures in addition to an intelligence test. In discussing assessment procedures that are used in the evaluation of mentally retarded children, Hutt and Gibby (1965) indicated that assessment

involves much more than the administration of psychological tests and the determination of the level of mental functioning. It involves an exploration of many aspects of a child's life, in order to determine the reasons for the difficulty, the nature of the problem, and prospects for dealing with or improving the condition. It involves a detailed study of the *whole* child [p. 232].

The problem of brain injury and predictable, identifiable, and invariant behavior is complex; there are few generalizations that will hold up across all cases (Sarason & Doris, 1969). The behavior of a child who has a brain lesion should not automatically be attributed to the presence of the lesion. The extent to which the behavior is modifiable is always an empirical question. The category "brain-injured children" includes a variety of children who range from those having brain damage recognizable by neurological examination ("hard signs") to those having no evidence of brain injury, but who have a variety of perceptual and conceptual difficulties that are assumed to be the result of brain injury ("soft signs"). Part of the difficulty in making a differential diagnosis is that, for example, neither the term "brain damage" nor the term "schizophrenia" clearly defines a single syndrome, and overlapping symptoms and signs are frequent occurrences (Baer, 1961). Present tests are not very effective in enabling us to make valid diagnostic decisions (cf. Goldman, 1961).

Severe disturbances during the first years of life are especially difficult to diagnose or to pinpoint in a specific category (Kanner, 1969). While there are a number of syndromes that can be succinctly described, there are still many combinations, overlaps, and fluctuations for which there is no provision for a specific syndrome. Kanner concluded:

The children, not having read those books, do not, for the sake of our convenience, merge into any of the well-known, clear-cut patterns. It is then up to us to go on studying those children as individuals with their own unique peculiarities patiently and pluralistically from every angle, without the air of feigned omniscience, without pressing them into any preconceived diagnostic and etiologic dogma, and with the hope that thus we shall from time to time discover more profiles which speak for themselves [p. 10].

The following is Garner's (1966) excellent summary of the role of intelligence testing in the assessment process.

Intelligence testing in modern clinical psychology, we have seen, is more than the automatic administration of routine test procedures. It begins with a judicious choice of instruments, suited to the patient and constructed to yield valid and reliable results. It requires not only precise knowledge of the characteristics of intelligence scales, but also skill in interpreting test results that are expressed in a variety of ways. It demands an ability to evaluate the results of highly controversial research, and to advance hypotheses to account for a patient's behavior which go beyond unproductive labeling, but stop short of unfounded speculation. The clinician, in diagnosing general intelligence, plays the dual role of a proficient laboratory experimenter and the impartial, understanding observer of human behavior [p. 101].

THE PSYCHOLOGICAL REPORT

The best method for communicating the findings of a psychological evaluation is to report as objectively as possible the child's performances, interpreting and drawing inferences when applicable. Assets and limitations shown by the child should be clearly presented. Labels and jargon should, for most purposes, be eliminated, because they serve only to cloud the picture, detracting from an understanding of the child. The psychological evaluation, by aiming at the identification of the child's particular pattern of cognitive and conative functioning, should lead to the formulation of a program which is directed to developing the child's optimal behaviors (Birch, 1964). Diagnoses give rise to actions—they influence the lives of the examinees (Sarason & Doris, 1969).

FUTURE WORK ON INTELLECTUAL ASSESSMENT

The field of intelligence testing is not a static one. Investigators and theorists continue to explore many diverse pathways, hoping to find more adequate ways of understanding intelligence and more reliable and valid assessment techniques. The field of intellectual assessment appears to have a bright future. However, there is a special need to base future (and current) work on theoretical and experimental foundations which are part of the main body of academic psychology. With this focus, areas of study should include, according to Eysenck (1967), *(a)* an analysis of individual items (e.g., speed of solution, errors, persistence before abandoning items, and similar differential indicators of response style); *(b)* laboratory studies of learning and memory functions; *(c)* evaluation of experimental parameters (e.g., rest and pauses, time from end of learning to recall, rate of presentation, degree of motivation); and *(d)* effects of personality variables (e.g., stability-neuroticism and extroversion-introversion). The systematic study of these areas should help in the diagnosis of individual patterns of cognitive functioning and, it is hoped, contribute to the development of techniques which will enable individuals to enhance their cognitive potentials.

APPENDIX A

SUPPLEMENTARY WISC SCORING CRITERIA

The scoring suggestions presented in the Appendix cover the Comprehension, Similarities, and Vocabulary subtests. The scoring instructions have been obtained from the Scottish Council for Research in Education (1965). Careful study of the supplementary scoring criteria should help the examiner become more proficient in scoring the three subtests. The sample responses shown are supplementary to those appearing in the WISC manual.

COMPREHENSION

The general principle is to give 2 points to responses that are clearly correct by the WISC manual standards, and 0 points to responses that are clearly wrong; 1 point is given to doubtfully correct responses.

1.
  2 points — Put it in a hankie . . . Wash it.
  1 point — Go to hospital.
2.
  2 points — Give him money to buy one . . . Try to find it (Q) if you can't find it, buy him another.
  1 point — Go to the police.
  0 points — Cry . . . Greet . . . Get a row.
4.
  2 points — Don't fight him back, you are older and it would be unfair.
  1 point — Just leave him (Q) don't bother with him.
  0 points — Give her a hit and then go away.

5.
    2 points — Tell it to stop (Q) wave to the driver and say there's a broken line.
    0 points — Stop it (Q) it'll come off the rails.

6.
    2 points — Brick lasts longer (permanence) and stands up to weather better (durability) . . . Brick is warmer (insulation) and wood can get on fire easily (safety).
    1 point — Wood might rot, brick wouldn't (durability) . . . If there was a crash into the house, it would knock down the house while a stone house would still be standing (sturdiness) . . . Because it lasts longer (permanence) and if it's made of wood it might get blown down with winds (no credit).

7.
    2 points — Because they might influence other people (segregation) and be even more wicked than before (deterrent).
    1 point — They might do the same again (deterrent) . . . Because they're bad men (no credit) and could do some damage to people (protection for society). A response mentioning a specific crime, e.g., "because they've murdered someone."

8.
    2 points — Men are stronger and women have to look after the children.
    1 point — They're more important than men (Q) they make the food . . . Because children have still to grow up.

10.
    2 points — Because they know who to give it to best (better position to investigate); the street beggar often pretends, but dosen't really need it (real need).
    1 point — A beggar would spend it on anything, but charity would spend it on people who are lame or diseased (real need) . . . You can help more people by giving it to charity (more orderly).

11.
    2 points — To find out if they're clever enough for the job, and to stop someone getting a good job for a friend.
    1 point — So they know if they've taken on a skilled man . . . To make it quite fair.
    0 points — They might have a disease.

12.
    2 points — It wears hard and takes colors . . . It's nice and cool and it's cheap.
    1 point — It's soft (no credit) and strong (durability).

13.
    2 points — We couldn't all decide on every problem (population too large) but this way everyone has some say (representative government).
    1 point — So we can have one body to take over the country and don't have a lot of little ones (only one principle involved).
    0 points — Because we need government leaders and persons who know about government rights . . . Help make laws . . . To help run our country (Q) to help control the people in the U.S.

SIMILARITIES

The general principle is to give 2 points to responses that are clearly correct by the WISC manual standards, and 0 points to responses that are clearly wrong; 1 point is given to doubtfully correct responses.

5.
> *2 points* – Have vitamin C . . . Grow on fruit trees.
> *1 point* – Make drinks with them . . . Off trees.
> *0 points* – Some apples juicy, like oranges . . . Both sweet.

6.
> *2 points* – Both pets.
> *1 point* – Both tails and I think four legs . . . They have got both tails . . . Both run.
> *0 points* – Long tails.

7.
> *2 points* – Both alcoholics.
> *1 point* – Both drink . . . Both spirits . . . Drunk at New Year.
> *0 points* – Both made in distilleries (or breweries).

8.
> *2 points* – Both play music . . . Both musical things . . . Both musical . . . Both play tunes . . . Music comes from them.
> *1 point* – They play . . . Make some notes . . . Both music . . . Have tunes . . . Give off notes . . . Both strings . . . They have music.
> *0 points* – They play alike.

9.
> *2 points* – You use them to light fire . . . Both burn in fire . . . Both start fire . . . You can set fire with them.
> *1 point* – For fire . . . You light fire easy . . . Make fire.

10.
> *2 points* – Both measures.
> *1 point* – Both in tables . . . In sums . . . Used in arithmetic . . . Both measures of weight *or* length . . . Both scales.

11.
> *1 point* – Same alloys . . . Both made of mineral . . . Same kind of metal.
> *0 points* – Both hard.

12.
> *2 points* – Part of a country.
> *1 point* – Both in country . . . Part of nature . . . Part of the land . . . Beauty spots . . . Natural occurrences . . . In atlas.
> *0 points* – Both places.

13.
> *1 point* – Both chemicals (or chemical substances) . . . Take them with food.
> *0 points* – Both minerals.

14.
> *1 point* – Both things to do with public – things you have . . . Both considered to be good and true . . . Mean rights for people . . . What we fight for.

15.
> *1 point* – Both at the end . . . Both in a race – your place . . . Places.
> *0 points* – Both in a race . . . Used in races – horses.

16.
> *1 point* – Both have square roots . . . Both squares of 7 and 11.
> *0 points* – Both square roots . . . Uneven numbers (though accept "odd" for 1 point) . . . $4 + 9 = 13$ and $12 + 1 = 13$.

VOCABULARY

The general principle is to give 2 points for clearly acceptable responses and 0 points for clearly unacceptable responses; 1 point is given to doubtfully acceptable responses. In items 1 through 5 scoring standards are less rigorous, 0 points being given only where the response is obviously wrong (e.g., *bicycle*—has 2 or 3 wheels; *letter*—it's an envelope; *umbrella*—you put *on* your head) or is very vague (e.g., *bicycle*—a thing that takes you places; *knife*—it's steel, silver; *hat*—has elastic; *letter*—paper with writing).

Supplementary to the WISC manual, the following criteria are useful for scoring items 6 and beyond:

2 points—Clearly definitive responses *or* responses with more than one less definitive response, but cumulatively a fairly clear definition.

1 point —A vague definition *or* one not very definite response.

0 points—Wrong responses *or* response so vague as to describe many other terms, and not indicating that the child knows exactly what he is referring to.

These criteria are illustrated in items 7 and 9.

6.

2 points—Soft to sit on if you have a hard chair ... If you haven't a cushion you could hurt yourself if you fell back on a hard chair, a cushion keeps you comfortable ... For putting on your chair, sit on it ... A thing you put on a chair, it is stuffed with things.

0 points—It is thin.

7.

2 points—To keep two pieces of wood to-gether—iron ... A metal thing you hammer in with a hammer to keep something up ... If you are building something you need a nail to fix them together.	Clearly definitive responses
It's sharp and has a round bit at the top ... It's sharp—joiner uses it ... You hammer it into something, it's pointy ... A sharp thing you push into one thing to make it stick into another thing.	More than one less definitive feature cumulatively giving fairly clear definition
1 point —You hit it with a hammer ... Holds things together ... You hammer it into something ... Thing for hanging pictures on.	A vague definition
It's sharp ... Made of iron ... That you mend wood.	Only one not very definitive feature given
0 points—A thing you hammer *with*.	A wrong definition
A thing that can help to make things.	A description which is so vague that it could describe many other things

8.

    2 points — Some people get rides on it at the seaside . . . A thing that pulls carts sometimes and you can ride on it.

             You ride on it . . . For riding on.

    0 points — A horse . . . has four legs . . . About on the hill . . . Riding on a donkey.

9.

    2 points — The skin of some animals . . . Animal's coat in cold countries . . . Clothing of an animal.
                             Clearly definitive responses

             It can keep you warm, you can put it down as a rug . . . Like mink — its soft and you can wear it . . . It's soft, comes from animals, their outside . . . Something fluffy and you always get it on a bear's back.
                             More than one less definitive feature cumulatively giving fairly clear definition

    1 point — Something on animal's skin . . . It's sort of soft fluff . . . You make a coat with it — from an animal.
                             A vague definition

             It's to keep you warm . . . Sometimes get fur round collar of coat.
                             Only one not very definitive feature given

    0 points — A kind of cloth — warm cloth . . . It's a woolly thing . . . You find it on a coat (Q) sheep . . . Fur off the sheep.
                             A wrong definition

             Something you can wear . . . A fur coat that you can wear . . . Something a lady wears on a coat.
                             A description which is so vague that it could describe many other things

10.

    2 points — A precious stone, it is a jewel . . . Precious thing (Q) it glitters . . . It sparkles, it is in a ring . . . Made of the same kind of stuff as coal, it glitters . . . Can cut glass . . . Something like glass only it is valuable . . . It shines and it is white in color . . . In a ring. You take it out of the ground . . . Shaped like this (indicated).

    0 points — Very beautiful thing, bad people steal it . . . A stone that's red in color and used for necklaces.

11.

    2 points — You put things together . . . Stick together . . . You can join in a game (Q) if someone is playing . . . A game and someone else wants to play they can join in . . . A bit of wool is broken and you join it . . . Join something together . . . For trains, if the carriage is broken you hook it on again.

    1 point — Join hands with someone (Q) to take someone else's hand.

    0 points — Join something . . . A thing to join stuff and join things with it if torn.

12.

    2 points — For digging . . . To dig . . . Digging . . . Dig . . . You dig.

13.

    2 points — You can fence with it and it can stick through you . . . Fight with it (Q) sharp . . . You use it for sword fencing . . . To fence and kill. (Note: "For fencing" gets two points. "For fighting" without further elaboration gets one point.)

    0 points — Soldiers use it . . . To cut wool . . . To chop people's heads off . . . Keep it in a belt . . . Can make one of wood.

14.

2 points — Somebody that keeps bothering you ... Pestering your mother when she's washing ... Someone who keeps tormenting you ... You could torment somebody ... Someone who's not doing things right, in a quiet game he usually talks.

0 points — When you're speaking too much ... Someone people don't like ... You are silly ... It was a nuisance of the football team that they lost ... A boy that can't answer.

15.

2 points — If you do something — save a life — you're brave because there's danger ... Not a coward or not afraid ... If you come back from a war people say you are brave, you will stand up to anything ... Not afraid when fighting ... Not frightened of any big animal.

0 points — Kill somebody and win ... Done something brave ... Hit folk.

16.

2 points — Speaking a lot of rubbish ... You are just blethering ... You say daft things ... Things which don't make sense ... If you say something silly ... Somebody talks foolishly ... Rubbish.

1 point — Can't express it in words.

0 points — When you torment people ... You are just a nuisance ... Not go to school.

17.

2 points — A man that's awful brave ... He kills a giant or something ... A brave person who's usually never forgotten about.

0 points — An Indian (without further elaboration) ... You are funny and make people laugh ... It is a person.

18.

2 points — Have cards you see and play for money ... With cards you lose money or you win money ... To bet money on a race horse or a greyhound or in the pools.

20.

2 points — A thing for magnifying germs — little things.

21.

2 points — Money, British use shillings ... English money.

1 point — It's something like a dollar, but not the very same ... You can spend it, it's a piece of money ... Money — used it in the olden days.

0 points — We don't have it ... Used long ago (Q) we don't have it.

22.

2 points — A short story ... Untrue story.

23.

2 points — A small kind of hut where a bell is on top of a steeple.

27.

2 points — A glitter.

29.

1 point — To get smaller.

30.

1 point — Worry.

33.

2 points — Almost at once.

APPENDIX B

LIST OF VALIDITY AND RELIABILITY STUDIES FOR THE STANFORD-BINET, WISC, WPPSI, PPVT, QUICK TEST, LEITER, AND SLOSSON

Table B-1. Studies Comparing the Stanford-Binet and the WAIS

Brengelmann & Kenny (1961)[a]; Cochran & Pedrini (1969)[b]; Fisher (1962)[b]; Fisher, Kilman, & Shotwell (1961)[b]; Giannell & Freeburne (1963)[a]; Kangas & Bradway (1971)[a,b]; Kroske, Fretwell, & Cupp (1965)[c]; McKerracher & Scott (1966)[b]; Wechsler (1955)[a].

[a]Form L; [b]Form L-M; [c]Form not indicated.

Table B-2. Studies Comparing the WISC and the Stanford-Binet

Arnold & Wagner (1955)[a]; Barclay & Carolan (1966)[b]; Barratt & Baumgarten (1957)[a]; Brittain (1968)[b]; Clarke (1950)[a]; Cohen & Collier (1952)[a]; Davidson (1954)[a]; Estes (1965)[b]; Estes, Curtin, DeBurger, & Denny (1961)[a,b,c]; Frandsen & Higginson (1951)[a]; Gehman & Matyas (1956)[a]; Harlow, Price, Tatham, & Davidson (1957)[a]; Holland (1953)[a,c]; Hunt (1961)[b]; Jones (1962)[b]; Kardos (1954)[a]; Krugman, Justman, Wrightstone, & Krugman (1951)[a]; Kureth, Muhr, & Weisgerber (1952)[a]; Levinson (1959)[a], Mussen, Dean, & Rosenberg (1952)[d]; Nale (1951)[d]; Oakland, King, White, & Eckman (1971)[b]; Pastovic & Guthrie (1951)[a]; Post (1952)[a]; Price (1950)[a]; Pringle & Pickup (1963)[d]; Rapaport (1951)[a]; Reidy (1952)[a]; Rohrs & Haworth (1962)[b]; Rottersman (1950)[a]; Sandercock & Butler (1952)[c]; Schachter & Apgar (1958)[a]; Scott (1950)[a]; Sekyra & Arnoult (1968)[b]; Sharp (1957)[a]; Sloan & Schneider (1951)[a]; Stacey & Carleton (1955)[a]; Stacey & Levin (1951)[a]; Stroud, Blommers, & Lauber (1957)[a]; Tatham (1952)[a]; Triggs & Cartee (1953)[c]; Vanderhost, Sloan, & Bensberg (1953)[d]; Wagner (1951)[a]; Walker & Gross (1970)[d]; Warinner (1952)[a]; Weider, Noller, & Schramm (1951)[a]; Winpenny (1951)[a].

[a]Form L; [b]Form L-M; [c]Form M; [d]Form not indicated.

Table B-3. STUDIES COMPARING THE WISC AND THE WECHSLER-BELLEVUE

Bacon (1954); Delattre & Cole (1952); Knopf, Murfett, & Milstein (1954); Price & Thorne (1955); Quereshi & Miller (1970); Vanderhost, Sloan, & Bensberg (1953).

Table B-4. STUDIES COMPARING THE WISC AND THE WAIS

Fisher (1962); Green (1965); Hannon & Kicklighter (1970); Qureshi (1968a); Qureshi & Miller (1970); Ross & Morledge (1967); Simpson (1970); Stout (1961); Walker & Gross (1970); Webb (1963); Webb (1964).

Table B-5. STUDIES COMPARING THE WISC AND OTHER TESTS
(Not Including the Stanford-Binet and WISC)

Alper (1958)[a]; Altus (1952)[f]; Altus (1955)[f]; Armstrong & Hauck (1960)[d]; Barratt (1956)[g, p]; Brown, Hake, & Malpass (1959)[p]; Cohen & Collier (1952)[b]; Cole, Burkheimer, & Steinberg (1968)[q]; Cooper (1958)[g, n]; Delp (1953a)[m]; Estes (1965)[o]; Estes, Curtin, DeBurger, & Denny (1961)[k, p]; Estes, Kodman, & Akel (1959)[g]; Evans (1966)[p]; Hanvik (1953)[k]; Irwin & Korst (1967)[a, c, r, s, v]; Lehman & Levy (1971)[k]; Malpass, Brown & Hake (1960)[p]; Martin & Wiechers (1954)[p]; McBrearty (1951)[b]; Nalven & Bierbryer (1969)[h]; Pringle & Pickup (1963)[j]; Rottersman (1950)[j]; Schwitzgoebel (1952)[f]; Sekyra & Arnoult (1968)[g]; Sharp (1957)[n]; Sloan & Schneider (1951)[b]; Smith (1961)[g]; Stacey & Carleton (1955)[p]; Stark (1954)[j]; Stempel (1953)[t]; Wallace (1969)[l]; Warren & Collier (1960)[g]; Wilson (1952)[p]; Winpenny (1951)[b, e].

[a]Abstraction Test; [b]Arthur Point Scale of Performance Tests; [c]Articulation Test; [d]Bender Visual-Motor Gestalt Test; [e]Bernreuter-Winpenny; [f]California Test of Mental Maturity; [g]Columbia Mental Maturity Scale; [h]Devereux Elementary School Behavior Rating Scale; [i]Drawing Completion Test; [j]Goodenough Draw-a-Man; [k]Goodenough-Harris Drawing Test; [l]Frostig Developmental Test of Visual Perception; [m]Kent EGY; [n]Leiter International Performance Scale; [o]Otis Quick Scoring Mental Ability Test; [p]Progressive Matrices; [q]Sequin Formboard; [r]Sound Discrimination Test; [s]Speech Tests; [t]SRA Primary Mental Abilities Test; [u]Vocabulary Test.

Table B-6. STUDIES COMPARING THE WISC AND MEASURES OF ACHIEVEMENT

Barratt & Baumgarten (1957)[b]; Clarke (1950)[h]; Conklin & Dockrell (1967)[j]; Cooper (1958)[b]; Egeland, Di Nello, & Carr (1970)[g]; Frandsen & Higginson (1951)[l]; Jenkin, Spivack, Levine, & Savage (1964)[b]; Jones (1962)[m]; Kardos (1954)[b]; Kimbrell (1960)[d]; Mayer (1958)[i, j, k]; Mussen, Dean, & Rosenberg (1952)[g]; Richardson & Surko (1956)[e, l]; Sandercock & Butler (1952)[a]; Smith (1961)[n]; Stroud, Blommers, & Lauber (1957)[l]; Sundean & Salopek (1971)[a]; Thompson (1961)[c].

[a]Achievement Quotient; [b]California Achievement Test; [c]Gates Advanced Primary Reading Tests; [d]Grade Placement; [e]Gray Oral Reading; [f]Iowa Test of Basic Skills; [g]Metropolitan Achievement Test; [h]Progressive Achievement; [i]School and College Ability Tests; [j]School Grades; [k]Sequential Test of Educational Progress; [l]Stanford Achievement Test; [m]Teachers' Rating; [n]Wide Range Achievement Test.

Table B-7. STUDIES COMPARING THE WPPSI AND THE STANFORD-BINET, FORM L-M

Austin & Carpenter (1970); Bach (1968); Barclay & Yater (1969); Dokecki, Frede, & Gautney (1969); Fagan, Broughton, Allen, Clark, & Emerson (1969); Oakland, King, White, & Eckman (1971); Pasewark, Rardin, & Grice (1971); Plant (1967); Prosser & Crawford (1971); Rellas (1969); Richards (1968); Ruschival & Way (1971); Zimmerman & Woo-Sam (1970).

Table B-8. STUDIES COMPARING THE WPPSI AND THE WISC

Anderman, Yater, Boyd, & Barclay (1971); Austin & Carpenter (1970); Oakland, King, White, & Eckman 1971).

Table B-9. STUDIES COMPARING THE WPPSI AND OTHER TESTS
(Not Including the Stanford-Binet and WISC)

Austin & Carpenter (1970)[c]; Bach (1968)[c, d, e, f]; Dokecki, Frede, & Gautney (1969)[c, h]; Krebs (1969)[h]; Lichtman (1969)[k]; McNamara, Porterfield, & Miller (1969)[i]; Plant (1967)[f, g]; Plant & Southern (1968)[j]; Yater, Barclay, & Leskosky (1971)[c]; Yule, Berger, Butler, Newham, & Tizard (1969)[a, b, e].

[a]English Picture Vocabulary Test; [b]Frostig Developmental Test of Visual Perception; [c]Goodenough-Harris Drawing Test; [d]Hiskey-Nebraska Test of Learning Aptitude; [e]Illinois Test of Psycholinguistic Abilities; [f]Peabody Picture Vocabulary Test; [g]Pictorial Test of Intelligence; [h]Primary Mental Abilities Test; [i]Progressive Matrices; [j]Stanford Achievement Test; [k]Torrance Tests of Creative Thinking.

Table B-10. STUDIES EVALUATING PPVT ALTERNATE FORM RELIABILITY

Bashaw & Ayers (1967); Blue (1969); Brown & Rice (1967); Cartwright (1968); Coyle, Dans, & Cork (1968); Dunn & Brooks (1960); Dunn & Harley (1959); Dunn & Hottel (1961); Hartman (1962); Hedger (1965); Ivanoff & Tempero (1965); Kimbrell (1960); Lavitt (1967); Payne, Ball, & Stainback (1972); Tillinghast & Renzulli (1968).

Table B-11. STUDIES EVALUATING PPVT TEST-RETEST RELIABILITY

Bashaw & Ayers (1967); Blue (1969); Bruininks & Feldman (1970); Costello & Ali (1971); Howard & Plant (1967); Milgram & Ozer (1967); Moed, Wight, & James (1963); Moss (1962); Raskin & Fong (1970); Raskin, Offenbach, & Scoonover (1971); Silverstein & Hill (1967); Tillinghast & Renzulli (1968).

Table B-12. STUDIES COMPARING THE PPVT AND THE STANFORD-BINET

Bach (1968)[a]; Blazer (1968)[a]; Borosage (1968)[a]; Brown & Rice (1967)[d]; Bruininks & Feldman (1970)[a]; Burnett (1965)[c]; Cartwright (1968)[d]; Costello & Ali (1971)[a]; Di Lorenzo & Brady (1968)[d]; Dunn & Brooks (1960)[b]; Dunn & Hottel (1961)[b]; English & Kidder (1969)[d]; Hammill & Irwin (1965)[d]; Hartman (1962)[d]; Johnson & Johnson (1971)[d]; Kicklighter (1966a)[a]; Koh & Madow (1967)[a]; Lavitt (1963)[d]; McArthur & Wakefield (1968)[a]; Mein (1962)[b]; Milgram & Ozer (1967)[a]; Moss (1962)[e]; Mueller (1968)[a]; Nelson & Hudson (1969)[d]; Payne, Ball, & Stainback (1972)[a]; Rice & Brown (1967)[d]; Saslow (1961)[a]; Saslow & Larsen (1963)[e]; Sattler & Anderson (1973)[a]; Shotwell, O'Connor, Gabet, & Dingman (1969)[a]; Staffieri (1971)[a]; Taylor (1963)[a]; Throne, Kaspar, & Schulman (1965)[d]; Wells & Pedrini (1967)[a]; Yen (1969)[a]; Zunich & Tolley (1968)[d].

[a]Form L-M; [b]Form L; [c]1937 and 1960 forms used; [d]Form not reported; [e]Form not available.

Table B-13. Studies Comparing the PPVT and the WISC

Anderson & Flax (1968); Ando (1968); Dunn & Brooks (1960); Fitzgerald, Pasewark, & Gloeckler (1970); Gage & Naumann (1965); Garrett (1959); Graubard (1967); Himelstein & Herndon (1962); Hughes & Lessler (1965); Irwin & Korst (1967); Kimbrell (1960); Lavitt (1963); Lavitt (1967); Lindstrom (1961); McArthur & Wakefield (1968); Moed, Wight, & James (1963); Neville (1965); Pasewark, Fitzgerald, & Gloeckler (1971); Reger (1962); Shaw, Mathews, & Kløve (1966); Shipe, Cromwell, & Dunn (1966); Silberberg & Feldt (1966); Throne, Kaspar, & Schulman (1965).

Table B-14. Studies Comparing the PPVT and Other Intelligence and Ability Tests (Not Including the Stanford-Binet and WISC)

Allen (1969)[e]; Bach (1968)[g, i, j]; Burnett (1965)[x]; Carlson (1971)[q]; Carr, Brown, & Rice (1967)[j]; Childers (1966)[l]; Costello & Ali (1971)[j]; Datta (1967)[g]; Deich (1968)[c]; Dunn & Harley (1959)[d, f, w]; Elliott (1969)[o]; English & Kidder (1969)[n]; Garrett (1959)[s]; Giebink & Marden (1968)[j]; Graubard (1967)[j]; Hammill & Irwin (1966)[t]; Hedger (1965)[f, w]; Hubschman, Polizzotto, & Kaliski (1970)[j]; Irwin (1966)[a, b, t]; Irwin & Hammill (1964)[a]; Irwin & Korst (1967)[a, b, t, v]; Ivanoff & Tempero (1965)[c, h]; Johnson & Johnson (1971)[g]; Korst (1966)[k]; Lavitt (1963)[c, x]; Lavitt (1967)[u]; Maloney, Ward, Schenck, & Braucht (1971)[r]; Milgram (1967)[j]; Milgram & Ozer (1967)[j]; Moed, Wight, & James (1963)[f]; Moss (1962)[p]; Moss & Edmonds (1960)[m]; Mueller (1968)[j, m, o, p, q]; Nelson & Hudson (1969)[l]; Nicholson (1970)[d, q]; Scoggins (1960)[f]; Silverstein & Hill (1967)[f, w]; Spellacy & Black (1972)[k]; Staffieri (1971)[r]; Stark, Cohen, & Eisenson (1968)[j]; Strandberg, Griffith, & Miner (1969)[r]; Teasdale (1969)[j]; Throne, Kaspar, & Schulman (1965)[g]; Wells & Pedrini (1967a)[a]; Yen (1969)[g].

[a]Abstraction Test; [b]Articulation Test; [c]California Test of Mental Maturity; [d]Columbia Mental Maturity Scale; [e]Frostig Developmental Test of Visual Perception; [f]Full-Range Picture Vocabulary Test; [g]Goodenough-Harris Drawing Test; [h]Henman-Nelson Test of Mental Abilities; [i]Hiskey-Nebraska Test of Learning Aptitude; [j]Illinois Test of Psycholinguistic Abilities; [k]Leiter International Performance Scale; [l]Otis Beta; [m]Otis Group Intelligence Scale; [n]Paired Association Learning; [o]Pictorial Test of Intelligence; [p]Primary Mental Abilities Test; [q]Progressive Matrices; [r]Quick Test; [s]School and College Abilities Test; [t]Sound Discrimination Test; [u]SRA Tests of Educational Ability; [v]Use Vocabulary Test; [w]Van Alstyne Picture Vocabulary Test; [x]Wechsler-Bellevue Intelligence Scale.

Table B-15. Studies Comparing the PPVT and Achievement Tests and Teachers' Ratings

Bruininks & Feldman (1970)[b]; Childers (1966)[d]; Dunn & Harley (1959)[e]; Dunn & Hottel (1961)[e]; Elliott (1969)[f]; English & Kidder (1969)[e]; Foster (1965)[f]; Garrett (1959)[c]; Graubard (1967)[b]; Hall & Chansky (1971)[d]; Hedger (1965)[d]; Klaus & Starke (1964)[b]; Moss (1962)[b]; Mueller (1968)[f]; Mueller (1969)[f]; Nelson & Hudson (1969)[a]; Panther (1967)[b]; Plant & Southern (1968)[d]; Silverstein & Hill (1967)[e]; Throne, Kaspar, & Schulman (1965)[b]; Wolfensberger (1962)[f].

[a]California Achievement Test; [b]Metropolitan Achievement Test; [c]Sequential Tests of Educational Progress; [d]Stanford Achievement Test; [e]Teachers' Ratings; [f]Wide Range Achievement Test.

Table B-16. Studies Comparing the Quick Test with the Stanford-Binet and WISC

Joesting & Joesting (1971a)[a]; Joesting & Joesting (1971b)[b]; Lamp & Barclay (1967)[b]; Otto & McMenemy (1965)[b]; Pless, Snider, Eaton, & Kearsley (1965)[b]; Sawyer & Whitten (1972)[b].

Note. — See Table B–14 for studies comparing the Quick Test and the PPVT.
[a]Stanford-Binet, Form L-M; [b]WISC.

Table B-17.　Studies Comparing the Leiter with the Stanford-Binet and WISC

Alper (1958)[b]; Arnold (1951)[a]; Bensberg & Sloan (1951)[a]; Bessent (1950)[a]; Beverly & Bensberg (1952)[a]; Gallagher, Benoit, & Boyd (1956)[a]; Sharp (1957)[a, b]; Tate (1952)[a].

[a]Stanford-Binet, Form L; [b]WISC.

Table B-18.　Studies Comparing the Slosson Intelligence Test and Other Intelligence, Ability, and Achievement Tests

Armstrong & Mooney (1971)[k]; Armstrong, Mooney, & Jensen (1971)[k]; Carlisle, Shinedling, & Weaver (1970)[e, k]; DeLapa (1968)[k]; Hammill (1969)[f, h, m]; Hammill, Crandell, & Colarusso (1970)[a, g, j, l]; Houston & Otto (1968)[l, n] Johnson & Johnson (1971)[d, h, k]; Jongeward (1969)[k, n]; Lessler & Galinsky (1971)[n]; Maxwell (1971)[n]; Meissler (1970)[n]; Shepherd (1969)[b, c, m]; Stewart, Wood, & Gallman (1971)[k, m, n]; Swanson & Jacobson (1970)[n].

[a]Abstraction Test; [b]Bender Visual-Motor Gestalt Test; [c]Frostig Developmental Test of Visual Perception; [d]Goodenough-Harris Drawing Test; [e]Kuhlmann Test of Mental Development; [f]Lorge-Thorndike; [g]Miscellaneous IQ scores; [h]Peabody Picture Vocabulary Test; [i]Quick Test; [j]Sound Discrimination Test; [k]Stanford-Binet, Form L-M; [l]Tactile-Kinesthetic Form Discrimination Tests; [m]Wide Range Achievement Test; [n]WISC.

APPENDIX C

MISCELLANEOUS TABLES

Table C-1. ONE-HALF CONFIDENCE INTERVALS FOR STANFORD-BINET IQ'S

| | 2½–5½ | | | | | 6–13 | | | | | 14–18 | | | | |
| | Confidence Level | | | | | Confidence Level | | | | | Confidence Level | | | | |
IQ	68%	85%	90%	95%	99%	68%	85%	90%	95%	99%	68%	85%	90%	95%	99%
140–149	7	10	11	13	18	5	7	8	10	13	4	5	6	7	10
130–139	6	9	11	13	17	5	8	9	10	14	4	6	7	8	11
120–129	6	8	10	12	15	5	8	9	10	14	4	6	7	9	11
110–119	6	8	9	11	14	5	7	8	9	12	4	6	7	9	12
100–109	5	8	9	10	14	4	6	7	9	12	4	6	7	8	11
90–99	5	7	8	10	13	4	6	7	9	11	4	6	6	8	10
80–89	5	7	8	10	13	4	6	7	8	10	3	5	6	7	9
70–79	5	7	8	9	12	3	5	6	7	9	3	4	5	6	7
60–69	5	7	8	10	13	3	4	5	5	7	2	3	4	5	6

AGE LEVEL

Note. – One-half confidence intervals rounded off, with .5 dropped for even numbers. The one-half confidence intervals shown in the table must be preceded with a ± sign in order to represent the confidence level.

The formula for computing the standard error of measurement ($\sigma_{meas.}$), which is used in computing the one-half confidence intervals, is as follows: $\sigma_{meas.} = \sigma_1 \sqrt{1 - r_{11}}$. σ_1 is the standard deviation of the test scores and r_{11} is the reliability coefficient. In order to find the one-half confidence interval which represents the 68% (±1 σ) confidence level on the Stanford-Binet for a 3-year-old child with an IQ of 140, the following procedure is used: $16 \sqrt{1 - .834} = 7$. The standard deviation of the Stanford-Binet is 16, obtained from the manual, while the reliability coefficient for the child's age and IQ is .834, obtained from McNemar (1942). Computed standard errors of measurement for Stanford-Binet IQ's may be found in Table C-4. The one-half confidence interval for the 68% confidence level is also equal to the standard error of measurement. The standard error of measurement is multiplied by the respective z values in order to obtain the one-half confidence intervals for other confidence levels. For example, the one-half confidence interval for the 99% level of confidence (±3σ) is $7 \times 2.58 = 18$. The first term is the standard error of measurement, and the second term is the z value for the 99% level of confidence.

Table C-2. ANALYSIS OF FUNCTIONS OF STANFORD-BINET TESTS
(Form L-M)

TEST	FUNCTIONS AND PROCESSES	STRUCTURE OF INTELLECT DESIGNATION
II, 1. Three-Hole Form Board	Visual-motor ability Recognition and manipulation of forms	NFR
II, 2. Delayed Response	Reasoning Attention Directing ideas in combination with memory span	MFS
II, 3. Identifying Parts of the Body	Language Comprehension of simple speech	CMC
II, 4. Block Building	Visual-motor ability Comprehension of material Spatial relations Ability or desire to imitate and experiment	CFS, EFS, NFR
II, 5. Picture Vocabulary	Language Recall and verbal identification by recognition of familiar objects May reveal child's perceptions and associations, experiences, ability to remember, and special modes of expressing himself	CMU, NMU
II, 6. Word Combinations	Language Meaningful use of two words but not necessarily in a structurally correct manner	NMR
II, A. Identifying Objects by Name	Language Use of verbal symbols in identifying common objects by name	CFU
II-6, 1. Identifying Objects by Use	Language Ability to attach definitions to concrete objects	NMR
II-6, 2. Identifying Parts of the Body	See II, 3	CMC
II-6, 3. Naming Objects	Language Comprehension of simple speech— focus is on specific objects	CFU, NMU
II-6, 4. Picture Vocabulary	See II, 5	CMU, NMU
II-6, 5. Repeating 2 Digits	Memory Passive registration of stimuli Auditory recall Attention Ability to follow directions	MSS, MSU
II-6, 6. Obeying Simple Commands	Social intelligence Purposive response to verbal directions	CMS, MMR
II-6, A. Three-Hole Form Board: Rotated	Similar to II, 1, but requires reorientation	NFR, CFT
III, 1. Stringing Beads	Visual-motor ability Comprehension Direction of attention	CFS, NFU
III, 2. Picture Vocabulary	See II, 5	CMU, NMU
III, 3. Block Building: Bridge	See II, 4	CFS, NFS, NFU
III, 4. Picture Memories	Memory Comprehension Attention	EFU, MFU
III, 5. Copying a Circle	Visual-motor ability Hand-eye coordination	NFU
III, 6. Drawing a Vertical Line	Visual-motor ability Hand-eye coordination Execution by demonstration	NFU
III, A. Repeating 3 Digits	See II-6, 5	MSU
III-6, 1. Comparison of Balls	Reasoning Conceptualization of physical form Identifying relative size	CFR, EFR

Table C-2. ANALYSIS OF FUNCTIONS OF STANFORD-BINET TESTS
(Form L-M)—*Continued*

TEST	FUNCTIONS AND PROCESSES	STRUCTURE OF INTELLECT DESIGNATION
III-6, 2. Patience: Pictures	Reasoning Ability to establish part-whole relationships	CFT, CFU, NMT

III-6, 3. Discrimination of
  Animal Pictures
	Reasoning
	Visual discrimination and perceptual
	  ability
		CFC, EFU

III-6, 4. Response to
  Pictures
	Social intelligence
	Ability to enumerate objects
	Vocabulary
	Fluency of speech
	Sentence combinations
	Perceptions: Ability to interpret single
	  elements of a whole
	Comprehension of situations
		CMC, EMR

III-6, 5. Sorting Buttons	Reasoning Motor manipulation according to verbal direction	NFC
III-6, 6. Comprehension I	Social intelligence Ability to reasonably evaluate a situation and give a pertinent response	CMI, EMT
III-6, A. Comparison of Sticks	Reasoning Visual-perceptual discrimination	EFR
IV, 1. Picture Vocabulary	See II, 5	CMU, NMU
IV, 2. Naming Objects from Memory	Memory	MFU
IV, 3. Opposite Analogies I	Conceptual thinking Associative ability	CMR, NMR, DMS
IV, 4. Pictorial Identification	Language Ability to isolate and eliminate items	CMI, NMR, MFU

IV, 5. Discrimination
  of Forms
	Reasoning
	Ability to compare and contrast visual
	  form perceptions and to apply
	  critical discriminations
		CFC, EFU

IV, 6. Comprehension II	See III-6, 6	CMI, EMR
IV, A. Memory for Sentences I	Memory (immediate auditory recall)	MMS

IV-6, 1. Aesthetic
  Comparison
	Social intelligence
	Comparison and practical judgment
	  involving discriminative ability for
	  aesthetic values
		EMR, EFS

IV-6, 2. Opposite Analogies I	Conceptual thinking Association ability	CMR, NMR, DMS

IV-6, 3. Pictorial
  Similarities and
  Differences I
	Reasoning
	Ability to discriminate differences by
	  use of visual perception
		CFC, CMC, EFU

IV-6, 4. Materials	Social intelligence General information Language comprehension	CMI, CMT

IV-6, 5. Three
  Commissions
	Memory
	Ability to retain and accomplish verbal
	  directions in sequence
		MMS

IV-6, 6. Comprehension III	See III-6, 6	CMI, CMS
IV-6, A. Pictorial Identification	See IV, 4	CMI, NMR, MFU
V, 1. Picture Completion: Man	Visual-motor ability Visual discrimination and perception	CFU, NFI
V, 2. Paper Folding: Triangle	Visual-motor ability Visual-memory and motor coordination	CFT, NFR
V, 3. Definitions	Language Ability to associate verbal symbols with objects General vocabulary	CMU

Table C-2. ANALYSIS OF FUNCTIONS OF STANFORD-BINET TESTS
(Form L-M) — *Continued*

TEST	FUNCTIONS AND PROCESSES	STRUCTURE OF INTELLECT DESIGNATION
V, 4. Copying a Square	Visual-motor ability Hand-eye coordination Appreciation of spatial relationships	EFS, NFU
V, 5. Pictorial Similarities and Differences II	See IV-6, 3	CFC, EFU
V, 6. Patience: Rectangles	Reasoning Manipulation of materials involving spatial relationships and perception	CFS, CFT
V, A. Knot	Visual-motor ability Ability to manipulate and imitate	NFR, CFT
VI, 1. Vocabulary	Language Reasoning Expression of ideas Manner of speech Working habits Personality traits	CMU
VI, 2. Differences	Conceptual thinking Ability to discriminate on an abstract or ideational level	CMT, DMI, CFI, NMC
VI, 3. Mutilated Pictures	Reasoning Perception and part-whole relationships	CFU, MSI
VI, 4. Number Concepts	Numerical reasoning Rote counting ability	MSI, NMR
VI, 5. Opposite Analogies II	See IV-6, 2	CMR, EMR
VI, 6. Maze Tracing	Visual-motor ability Perception General comprehension in making choices	CFI
VI, A. Response to Pictures	See III-6, 4	EMR, CMC
VII, 1. Picture Absurdities I	Social intelligence Ability to isolate incongruities and absurdities of visual material	EMS
VII, 2. Similarities: Two Things	Conceptual thinking	CMT, CSC
VII, 3. Copying a Diamond	Visual-motor ability	EFS, NFU
VII, 4. Comprehension IV	See III-6, 6	EMT, DMI, NMI
VII, 5. Opposite Analogies III	See IV-6, 2	CMR, NMR
VII, 6. Repeating 5 Digits	See II-6, 5	MSU
VII, A. Repeating 3 Digits Reversed	Memory Remanipulation Reorganization	MSU, MSS
VIII, 1. Vocabulary	See VI, 1	CMU
VIII, 2. Memory for Stories: The Wet Fall	Memory Verbal comprehension	MMR, MMU
VIII, 3. Verbal Absurdities I	Reasoning Ability to identify incongruous elements of situations Vocabulary	EMS
VIII, 4. Similarities and Differences	Conceptual thinking Flexibility Comprehension of reversibility Ability to view facts from various angles at the same time and coordinate the multiple relationships involved	CMI, CMT, NMI
VIII, 5. Comprehension IV	See III-6, 6	EMT, NMI, DMI
VIII, 6. Naming the Days of the Week	Social intelligence General information Long-term recall	MMR, MMS

Table C-2. ANALYSIS OF FUNCTIONS OF STANFORD-BINET TESTS
(Form L-M) — *Continued*

TEST	FUNCTIONS AND PROCESSES	STRUCTURE OF INTELLECT DESIGNATION
VIII, A. Problem Situations I	Social intelligence Ability to identify practical elements of a situation	EMR, NMI
IX, 1. Paper Cutting	Visual-motor ability Manipulation in response to verbal directions	CFT, ESR
IX, 2. Verbal Absurdities II	See VIII, 3	EMS
IX, 3. Memory for Designs I	Memory Visuo-memory ability and perception Attention and visual clues combine with recall and motor reproduction	MFU
IX, 4. Rhymes: New Form	Language Controlled association by specific stimulus	DMR
IX, 5. Making Change	Numerical reasoning	NSS, MSI
IX, 6. Repeating 4 Digits Reversed	See VII, A	MFU, MSS
IX, A. Rhymes: Old Form	See IX, 4	DMR
X, 1. Vocabulary	See VI, 1	CMU
X, 2. Block Counting	Numerical reasoning Perception	CFI, NFI, DFC
X, 3. Abstract Words I	Language Ability to select general characteristics by disregarding irrelevant details	CMU
X, 4. Finding Reasons I	Social intelligence Ability to see the relationship between cause and effect in situations with which the child is familiar	MMR, CMI, EMR, DMI, DMU, NMR
X, 5. Word Naming	Language Verbal expression Linguistic facility Free association	DSU
X, 6. Repeating 6 Digits	See II-6, 5	MSU
X, A. Verbal Absurdities III	See VIII, 3	EMS, EMR
XI, 1. Memory for Designs I	See IX, 3	MFU
XI, 2. Verbal Absurdities IV	See IX, 2	EMS, EMR
XI, 3. Abstract Words II	See X, 3	CMU
XI, 4. Memory for Sentences II	Memory Immediate recall of verbal stimuli Familiarity with words Enunciation Auditory accuity Ability to pay attention, to concentrate on a short sequence of stimuli, and to respond to the stimuli	MMS
XI, 5. Problem Situation II	Social intelligence Ability to analyze elements of a situation and to establish relationships	CMI
XI, 6. Similarities: Three Things	Conceptual thinking Ability to test and discard various hypothetical situations Flexibility and factual knowledge	CMT, NMC
XI, A. Finding Reasons II	See X, 4	CMI, MMR, EMR, DMI
XII, 1. Vocabulary	See VI, 1	CMU
XII, 2. Verbal Absurdities II	See VIII, 3	EMR, EMS
XII, 3. Picture Absurdities II: The Shadow	See VII, 1	EFI, EMS
XII, 4. Repeating 5 Digits Reversed	See VII, A	MSS, MSU

Table C-2.   ANALYSIS OF FUNCTIONS OF STANFORD-BINET TESTS
(Form L-M)—*Continued*

TEST	FUNCTIONS AND PROCESSES	STRUCTURE OF INTELLECT DESIGNATION
XII, 5. Abstract Words I	See X, 3	CMU
XII, 6. Minkus Completion I	Language Ability to use abstract words for language completion	CMR, EMR, NMI
XII, A. Memory for Designs II	See IX, 3	MFU
XIII, 1. Plan of Search	Reasoning Ability to analyze the logical requirements of a problem	CFI
XIII, 2. Abstract Words II	See X, 3	CMU
XIII, 3. Memory for Sentences III	See XI, 4	MMS
XIII, 4. Problems of Fact	Reasoning	CMI, EMR
XIII, 5. Dissected Sentences	Language Ability to place the component parts of a sentence in order	NMS, NMR
XIII, 6. Copying a Bead Chain from Memory	Memory Form perception and discrimination Spatial relations	MFS, NFS
XIII, A. Paper Cutting	See IX, 1	CFT
XIV, 1. Vocabulary	See VI, 1	CMU
XIV, 2. Induction	Numerical reasoning Ability to follow a series of events and make a generalization stating the governing principle involved Abstracting a rule from particular instances	CSS, NSR
XIV, 3. Reasoning I	Reasoning	MSS, NMI
XIV, 4. Ingenuity I	Numerical reasoning Application of arithmetic to a realistic, properly visualized situation Manipulation of visual imagery	CSC, DMT, NSI, DST
XIV, 5. Orientation: Direction I	Reasoning	MFS, NFR, CFS
XIV, 6. Reconciliation of Opposites	Conceptual thinking	NMT
XIV, A. Ingenuity II	See XIV, 4	CSC, DMT, NSI, DST
AA, 1. Vocabulary	See VI, 1	CMU
AA, 2. Ingenuity I	See XIV, 4	CSC, DMT, NSI, DST
AA, 3. Differences Between Abstract Words	Language Ability to point out the essential distinction between pairs of stimulus words	CMU, EMU, CMR
AA, 4. Arithmetical Reasoning	Numerical reasoning	CMS, MSI, NSS
AA, 5. Proverbs I	Conceptual thinking Ability to analyze, abstract, and apply result to life situations Rational process of inference	CMI, NMT, DMS
AA, 6. Orientation: Direction II	See XIV, 5	MFS, NFR, CFS
AA, 7. Essential Differences	Conceptual thinking	CMU, EMR, CMT
AA, 8. Abstract Words III	See X, 3	CMU
AA, A. Binet Paper Cutting	Visual-motor ability	CFT
SA I, 1. Vocabulary	See VI, 1	CMU
SA I, 2. Enclosed Box Problem	Numerical reasoning	MSS, MSI, MFT
SA I, 3. Minkus Completion II	See XII, 6	CMR, EMR, NMI

Table C-2. ANALYSIS OF FUNCTIONS OF STANFORD-BINET TESTS
(Form L-M) — *Continued*

TEST	FUNCTIONS AND PROCESSES	STRUCTURE OF INTELLECT DESIGNATION
SA I, 4. Repeating 6 Digits Reversed	See VII, A	MSS, MSU
SA I, 5. Sentence Building	Language	CMU, DMR
SA I, 6. Essential Similarities	Conceptual thinking	CMT, NMT
SA I, A. Reconciliation of Opposites	See XIV, 6	NMT
SA II, 1. Vocabulary	See VI, 1	CMU
SA II, 2. Finding Reasons III	See X, 4	MMR, CMI, EMR, DMI, DMU, NMR
SA II, 3. Proverbs II	See AA, 5	CMI, NMT, DMS
SA II, 4. Ingenuity I	See XIV, 4	CSC, DMT, NSI, DST
SA II, 5. Essential Differences	See AA, 7	CMU, EMR, CMT
SA II, 6. Repeating Thought of Passage I: Value of Life	Memory	MMR, CMS, NMU
SA II, A. Codes	Reasoning	CSR, CMR, NSR
SA III, 1. Vocabulary	See VI, 1	CMU
SA III, 2. Proverbs III	See AA, 5	CMI, NMT, DMS
SA III, 3. Opposite Analogies IV	See IV-6, 2	CMR, CMU, NMR, DMU
SA III, 4. Orientation: Direction III	See XIV, 5	MFS, NFR, CFS
SA III, 5. Reasoning II	See XIV, 3	NSS, MSI, ESR
SA III, 6. Repeating Thought of Passage II: Tests	See SA II, 6	MMR, CMS, NMU
SA III, A. Opposite Analogies V	See IV-6, 2	CMR, CMU, NMU, DMU

Note. — See Appendix C-28 for description of Structure of Intellect designations.

Adapted from Contrucci, Korn, Martinson, and Mathias (1962), Meeker (1969), Sattler (1965), Taylor (1961), and Terman and Merrill (1960).

Table C-3. PHYSICAL ABILITIES NECESSARY AND ADAPTABLE FOR STANFORD-BINET TESTS (L-M)

Test	Vision	Hearing	Oral Speech	Arm-Hand Use	Adaptable
II, 1	X			A	Y
2	X			A	Y
3	X	X			
4	X			X	
5	X		X		
6			X		
A	X	X		A	Y
II-6, 1	X	X		A	Y
2	X	X			
3	X	X	X		
4	X		X		
5		X	X		
6	X	X		A	Y
A	X		X		
III, 1	X		X		
2	X		X		
3	X		X		
4	X	X		A	Y
5				X	
6				X	
A		X	X		
III-6, 1	X	X		A	Y
2	X	X		X	
3	X			A	Y
4	X	X	X		
5	X	A		A	Y
6		X	X		
A	X	X		A	Y
IV, 1	X		X		
2	X	A	X		Y
3		X	X		
4	X	X		A	Y
5	X	A		A	Y
6		X	X		
A		X	X		
IV-6, 1	X	X		A	Y
2		X	X		
3	X	X		A	Y
4		X	X		
5	X	X		X	
6		X	X		
A	X	X		A	Y
V, 1	X	X		X	
2	X			X	
3		X	X		
4	X			X	
5	X	A	A		Y
6	X	X		X	
A	X	A		X	Y
VI, 1	Xr or X		X		
2		X	X		
3	X	X	X or X		
4	X	X		X	
5		X	X		
6	X	X		X	
A	X	X	X		

Table C-3. PHYSICAL ABILITIES NECESSARY AND ADAPTABLE FOR STANFORD-BINET TESTS (L-M)—*Continued*

TEST	VISION		HEARING	ORAL SPEECH	ARM-HAND USE	ADAPTABLE
VII, 1	X		X	X		
2			X	X		
3	X			X		
4	Xr		X	X		
5			X	X		
6			X	X		
A			X	X		
VIII, 1	Xr	or	X	X		
2			X	X		
3			X	X		
4			X	X		
5	Xr	or	X	X		
6	Xr	or	X	X		
A	Xr	or	X	X		
IX, 1	Xr		X		X	
2	Xr	or	X	X		
3	X		X		X	
4	Xr	or	X	X		
5	Xr	or	X	X		
6			X	X		
A	Xr	or	X	X		
X, 1	Xr	or	X	X		
2	Xr	or	X	X		
3	Xr	or	X	X		
4	Xr	or	X	X		
5	Xr	or	X	X		
6			X	X		
A	Xr	or	X	X		
XI, 1	Xr		X		X	
2	Xr	or	X	X		
3	Xr	or	X	X		
4			X	X		
5	Xr	or	X	X		
6	Xr	or	X	X		
A	Xr	or	X	X		
XII, 1	Xr	or	X	X		
2	Xr	or	X	X		
3	X		X	X		
4			X	X		
5	Xr	or	X	X		
6	Xr	or	X		X	
A	X				X	
XIII, 1	Xr	or	X		X	
2	Xr	or	X	X		
3			X	X		
4	Xr	or	X	X		
5	Xr			X		
6	X		A		X	Y
A	Xr	or	X		X	
XIV, 1	Xr	or	X	X		
2	Xr	or	X	X		
3	Xr			X		
4			X	X		
5			X	X		
6	Xr	or	X	X		
A			X	X		

Table C-3. PHYSICAL ABILITIES NECESSARY AND ADAPTABLE FOR STANFORD-BINET TESTS (L-M) — *Continued*

TEST	VISION		HEARING	ORAL SPEECH	ARM-HAND USE	ADAPTABLE
AA, 1	Xr	or	X	X		
2			X	X		
3	Xr	or	X	X		
4	Xr			X		
5	Xr	or	X	X		
6			X	X		
7	Xr	or	X	X		
8	Xr	or	X	X		
A	X		X		X	
SA I, 1	Xr	or	X	X		
2			X	X		
3	Xr	or	X		X	
4			X	X		
5	Xr	or	X	X		
6	Xr	or	X	X		
A	Xr	or	X	X		
SA II, 1	Xr	or	X	X		
2	Xr	or	X	X		
3	Xr	or	X	X		
4			X	X		
5	Xr	or	X	X		
6			X	X		
A	Xr		A		A	Y
SA III, 1	Xr	or	X	X		
2	Xr	or	X	X		
3	Xr	or	X	X		
4	Xr			X		
5	Xr			X		
6			X	X		
A	Xr	or	X	X		

Note.— The following code refers to Table C-3.

X — This ability is absolutely required. Adaptation is not feasible if this function is absent or more than mildly impaired.

A — This ability is not absolutely required. Adaptation is feasible but *only* for the function under which this letter appears. If an item is marked "X A" for two abilities, then the "X" ability must be present for the test to be usable. Adaptation may be made only for the "A" ability.

Y — This test is adaptable, but only for the ability marked "A" and for no other.

Xr — Wherever "Xr" appears it is necessary that vision be accompanied by reading comprehension.

X or X — A test bearing this symbol, always under two abilities, indicates that the task may be administered if one *or* the other ability is present. If "X" or "X" appears under Vision and Hearing, the examinee must be able to see *or* must understand oral speech. "Xr or X" under Vision and Hearing respectively requires reading comprehension only if hearing is impaired.

Reprinted, with a change in notation, by permission of the publisher and authors from R. M. Allen and T. W. Jefferson, *Psychological Evaluation of the Cerebral Palsied Person,* pp. 45–48. Copyright 1962. Courtesy of Charles C Thomas, Publisher, Springfield, Illinois.

Table C-4. STANDARD ERRORS OF MEASUREMENT FOR STANFORD-BINET IQ'S

	AGE		
IQ RANGE	$2\frac{1}{2}$ to $5\frac{1}{2}$	6 to 13	14 to 18
140–149	6.8	5.1	3.8
130–139	6.5	5.3	4.1
120–129	5.9	5.3	4.4
110–119	5.5	4.8	4.5
100–109	5.3	4.5	4.3
90–99	5.0	4.4	3.9
80–89	4.9	4.0	3.4
70–79	4.7	3.4	2.9
60–69	4.9	2.8	2.4

Note.—The formula for computing these standard errors may be found in the note following Table C-1.

Reprinted, with a change in notation, by permission of the publisher and author from Q. McNemar, *The Revision of the Stanford-Binet Scale*, pp. 62–63. Copyright 1942, Houghton-Mifflin Company.

Table C-5. CATTELL-BINET SHORT FORM

AGE LEVEL IN MONTHS	TEST	CREDIT IN MONTHS	YEAR LEVEL	TEST	CREDIT IN MONTHS
2	Voice, attends	1	II	Three-hole Form Board	3
	Follows moving person	1		Picture Vocabulary	3
3	Ring, follows circle	.5	II-6	Picture Vocabulary	3
	Spoon, regards	.5		Naming Objects	3
4	Ball, follows	.5	III	Picture Vocabulary	3
	Toy, activity increases	.5		Copying a Circle	3
5	Bell, turns to	.5	III-6	Comparison of Balls	3
	Ring, attains	.5		Discrimination of Animal Pictures	3
6	Cup, lifts	.5	IV	Picture Vocabulary	3
	Mirror, manipulates	.5		Pictorial Identification	3
7	Ring, inspects	.5	IV-6	Opposite Analogies I	3
	Cube, takes two	.5		Three Commissions	3
8	Ring, string pulls	.5	V	Definitions	3
	Bell, detail interest	.5		Copying a Square	3
9	Spoon, looks	.5	VI	Number Concepts	6
	Bell, rings	.5		Opposite Analogies II	6
10	Cup and cube, combines	.5	VII	Copying a Diamond	6
	Third cube, attempts	.5		Comprehension IV	6
11	Cup and cube, secures	.5	VIII	Vocabulary	6
	Cube in or over cup	.5		Similarities and Differences	6
12	Cubes, in cup, one	.5	IX	Rhymes: New Form	6
	Pencil, marks	.5		Making Change	6
13 & 14	Cube, unwraps	1	X	Vocabulary	6
	Pellet-bottle, imitates	1		Word Naming	6
15 & 16	Formboard, round block	1			
	Pellet-bottle, solves	1			
17 & 18	Cubes, 10 in cup	1			
	Formboard, rotated	1			

Note.—Tests from 2 through 18 months are from the Cattell Infant Intelligence Scale; those from year-level II and above are from the Stanford-Binet Intelligence Scale, Form L-M. Past year-level X any two tests per year level may be used.

Reprinted by permission of the publisher and authors from G. D. Alpern and C. C. Kimberlin, "Short Intelligence Test Ranging from Infancy Levels through Childhood Levels for Use with the Retarded," *American Journal of Mental Deficiency*, **75**, p. 68. Copyright 1970, American Association on Mental Deficiency.

Table C-6. MENTAL AGE EQUIVALENTS OF RAW SCORES ON THE 1937 STANFORD-BINET VOCABULARY TEST

RAW SCORE	MA	RAW SCORE	MA
5	5–4	23	16–4
6	6–3	24	16–10
7	7–2	25	17–4
8	8–0	26	17–10
9	8–10	27	18–4
10	9–7	28	18–11
11	10–2	29	19–5
12	10–9	30	19–11
13	11–3	31	20–5
14	11–9	32	20–11
15	12–3	33	21–5
16	12–9	34	21–11
17	13–3	35	22–5
18	13–9	36	23–0
19	14–3	37	23–6
20	14–9	38	24–0
21	15–3	39	24–6
22	15–10	40	25–0

Note.— Standard error of measurement is approximately 10 IQ points.

Reprinted by permission of the publisher and author from E. E. Cureton, "Mental Age Equivalents for the Revised Stanford-Binet Vocabulary Test," *Journal of Consulting Psychology,* **18**, p. 382. Copyright 1954, American Psychological Association.

Table C-7. ONE-HALF CONFIDENCE INTERVALS FOR WISC SUBTESTS AND SCALES

	AGE LEVEL														
	7½ (5-0-0 through 8-11-29)					10½ (9-0-0 through 11-11-29)					13½ (12-0-0 through 15-11-29)				
	Confidence Level					Confidence Level					Confidence Level				
SUBTEST AND SCALE	68%	85%	90%	95%	99%	68%	85%	90%	95%	99%	68%	85%	90%	95%	99%
Information	2	3	3	3	5	1	2	2	3	3	1	2	2	2	3
Comprehension	2	3	3	4	5	2	2	3	3	4	2	2	3	3	4
Arithmetic	2	3	3	4	5	1	2	2	2	3	1	2	2	3	4
Similarities	2	3	3	3	5	1	2	2	3	3	1	2	2	3	4
Vocabulary	1	2	2	3	4	1	1	1	2	2	1	1	2	2	2
Digit Span	2	3	3	4	5	2	3	3	4	5	2	3	3	4	5
Picture Completion	2	3	3	4	5	2	3	3	3	5	2	2	3	3	4
Picture Arrangement	2	2	3	3	4	2	2	3	3	4	2	2	3	3	4
Block Design	1	2	2	2	3	1	2	2	2	3	1	1	2	2	3
Object Assembly	2	3	3	4	5	2	3	3	4	5	2	2	3	3	4
Coding[a]	2	3	3	4	5	—	—	—	—	—	—	—	—	—	—
Mazes	1	2	2	3	4	1	2	2	3	3	2	2	2	3	4
Verbal Scale IQ	5	7	9	10	13	3	4	5	6	8	3	4	5	6	8
Performance Scale IQ	6	8	9	11	14	5	7	8	10	13	5	7	8	9	12
Full Scale IQ	4	6	7	8	11	3	5	6	7	9	4	5	6	7	9

Note.— The one-half confidence intervals for the subtests are for scaled scores, while those for the scales are for IQ's. The intervals were rounded off, with .5 dropped for even numbers. The one-half confidence intervals must be preceded by a ± sign in order to represent the confidence level. See Table C-1 for an explanation of method used to arrive at confidence intervals.

[a]Coding omitted at 10½ and 13½ age levels because reliability data are not available from WISC manual.

Table C-8.   Summary Analysis of Functions of WISC Subtests (Not based on factor analytic studies)

Subtest	Function	Influencing Factors	Subtest	Function	Influencing Factors
Information	Range of knowledge Long-range memory	Natural endowment Richness of early environment Extent of schooling Cultural predilections Interests	Picture Completion	Ability to differentiate essential from nonessential details Concentration Reasoning Visual Organization	Experiences
Comprehension	Social judgment, social conventionality, or common sense Meaningful and emotionally relevant use of facts	Extensiveness of cultural opportunities Development of conscience or moral sense Ability to evaluate and use past experience	Picture Arrangement	Interpretation of social situations Nonverbal reasoning ability Planning ability	A minimum of cultural opportunities
Arithmetic	Reasoning ability Numerical accuracy in mental arithmetic Concentration Attention Memory	Opportunity to acquire fundamental arithmetic processes	Block Design	Visual-motor coordination Perceptual organization Spatial visualization Abstract conceptualizing ability Analysis and synthesis	Rate of motor activity Color vision
Similarities	Verbal concept formation Logical thinking	A minimum of cultural opportunities Interests and reading patterns	Object Assembly	Visual-motor coordination Perceptual organization ability	Rate of motor activity Precision of motor activity
Vocabulary	Learning ability Fund of information Richness of ideas Memory Concept formation Language development	Early educational environment	Coding	Visual-motor coordination Speed of mental operation Short-term memory	Rate of motor activity
Digit Span	Attention Short-term memory	Ability to passively receive stimuli	Mazes	Planning ability Perceptual organization Visual-motor control	Visual-motor organization

Adapted from Blatt and Allison (1968), Freeman (1962), Glasser and Zimmerman (1967), Ogdon (1967), Rapaport, Gill, and Schafer (1968).

Table C-9. PHYSICAL ABILITIES NECESSARY AND ADAPTABLE FOR WISC AND WPPSI SUBTESTS

SUBTEST	VISION		HEARING	ORAL SPEECH		ARM-HAND USE		ADAPTABLE
Information	Xr	or	X	X	or	Xw		
Comprehension	Xr	or	X	X	or	Xw		
Arithmetic			X	X	or	Xw		
Similarities	Xr	or	X	X	or	Xw		
Vocabulary	Xr	or	X	X	or	Xw		
Digit Span			X	X	or	Xw		
Picture Completion	X			X	or	Xp	or	Xw
Picture Arrangement	X					A		Y
Block Design	X					X		
Object Assembly	X					X		
Coding	X					X		
Mazes	X					X		
Sentences	Xr		X	X	or	Xw		
Animal House	X					X		
Geometric Design	X					X		

Note.—The following code refers to Table C-9:

X—This ability is absolutely required. Adaptation is not feasible if this function is absent or more than mildly impaired.

Xr or X—If the child is too young to read then hearing is necessary. The child who has learned to read comprehendingly may substitute this ability for hearing. If neither is available then this subtest cannot be used.

X or Xw—The examinee should have oral speech *or* be able to write the answers in addition to adequate hearing.

X or Xp—Either oral speech *or* the ability to point is necessary. In the Picture Completion subtest the examiner should not point to the missing part. It must be orally or otherwise indicated by the examinee.

A—This ability is not absolutely required. Adaptation is feasible but *only* for the function under which this letter appears. If an item is marked "X A" for two abilities then the "X" ability must be present for the item to be usable. Adaptation may be made only for the "A" ability.

Y—This test item is adaptable, but only for the ability marked "A" and for no other.

Reprinted by permission of the publisher and authors from R. M. Allen and T. W. Jefferson, *Psychological Evaluation of the Cerebral Palsied Person,* p. 52. Copyright 1962. Courtesy of Charles C Thomas, Publisher, Springfield, Illinois. WPPSI subtests analyzed by the author.

Table C-10. SIGNIFICANT DIFFERENCES AMONG WISC SUBTEST SCORES

AGE LEVEL		I	C	A	S	V	DS	PC	PA	BD	OA	CO
7½	C	5/7										
(5–0–0	A	5/7	5/7									
through	S	5/6	5/7	5/7								
8–11–29)	V	4/6	5/6	5/6	4/6							
	DS	5/7	5/7	5/7	5/7	5/6						
	PC	5/7	5/7	5/7	5/7	5/6	5/7					
	PA	5/6	5/6	5/6	5/6	4/6	5/6	5/6				
	BD	5/5	4/6	4/6	4/5	4/5	4/6	4/6	4/5			
	OA	5/7	5/7	5/7	5/7	5/6	5/7	5/7	5/6	4/6		
	CO	5/7	5/7	5/7	5/7	5/6	5/7	5/7	5/6	4/6	5/7	
	M	4/6	5/6	4/6	4/6	4/5	5/6	5/6	4/5	4/5	4/6	5/6

Box (7½):
	VSIQ	PSIQ
PSIQ	15/20	
FSIQ	13/17	14/18

AGE LEVEL		I	C	A	S	V	DS	PC	PA	BD	OA	CO[a]
10½	C	4/5										
(9–0–0	A	4/5	4/5									
through	S	4/5	4/5	3/5								
11–11–29)	V	3/4	4/5	3/4	3/4							
	DS	5/6	5/6	4/6	5/6	4/5						
	PC	4/6	5/6	4/5	4/6	4/5	5/7					
	PA	4/5	4/6	4/5	4/5	4/5	5/6	5/6				
	BD	3/4	4/5	3/4	3/4	3/4	4/6	4/5	4/5			
	OA	4/6	5/6	4/6	4/6	4/5	5/7	5/7	5/6	4/5		
	M	4/5	4/5	3/5	4/5	3/4	5/6	4/6	4/5	3/4	4/6	—

Box (10½):
	VSIQ	PSIQ
PSIQ	11/15	
FSIQ	9/12	12/16

AGE LEVEL		I	C	A	S	V	DS	PC	PA	BD	OA	CO[2]
13½	C	4/5										
(12–0–0	A	4/5	4/6									
through	S	4/5	4/5	4/5								
15–11–29)	V	3/4	4/5	3/4	3/4							
	DS	5/6	5/7	5/7	5/7	5/6						
	PC	4/5	5/6	4/6	4/6	4/5	5/7					
	PA	4/5	4/6	4/6	4/5	4/5	5/7	5/6				
	BD	3/4	4/5	3/5	3/4	3/4	5/6	4/5	4/5			
	OA	4/5	4/6	4/6	4/5	4/5	5/7	5/6	4/6	4/5		
	M	4/5	4/6	4/5	4/5	3/5	5/7	4/6	4/6	4/5	4/6	—

Box (13½):
	VSIQ	PSIQ
PSIQ	11/14	
FSIQ	9/12	12/15

Note. — Abbreviations: I = Information; C = Comprehension; A = Arithmetic; S = Similarities; V = Vocabulary; DS = Digit Span; PC = Picture Completion; PA = Picture Arrangement; BD = Block Design; OA = Object Assembly; CO = Coding; M = Mazes.

Confidence levels designated as .05/.01. Sample reading: For a child under 9 years of age, a difference of 5 points (or 6 points) between scaled scores on the Information and Comprehension subtests is significant at the 5% level of confidence, while a difference of 7 points is significant at the 1% level of confidence. In like manner, from the small box, a 15-point difference between the Verbal Scale IQ and Performance Scale IQ is needed for the 5% level of confidence, and a 20-point difference is needed for the 1% level of confidence. Digit Span was not included in computation of significant differences for the Verbal Scale and Full Scale, and Mazes was not included in computation of significant differences for the Performance Scale and Full Scale.

The method used to compute the magnitude of differences between any two subtests or scales which can be accepted at a five per cent or a one per cent level of confidence is as follows: Difference Score $= z \sqrt{\sigma_{meas.}^2 + \sigma_{meas.}^2}$. In the case of the five per cent level, $z = 1.96$; in the case of the one per cent level, $z = 2.58$. The standard errors of measurement can be obtained from the WISC manual. For example, to find the difference between the WISC Information and Comprehension subtest scaled scores for the 7½ year age level that is necessary to satisfy the .05 confidence level, the figures used in the formula are $1.96\sqrt{(1.75)^2 + (1.92)^2} = 5$.

[a]Coding omitted because reliability data are not available from WISC manual.

Reprinted, with a change in notation, by permission of the publisher and authors from T. E. Newland and P. A. Smith, "Statistically Significant Differences between Subtest Scaled Scores on the WISC and WAIS," *Journal of School Psychology,* **5,** p. 125. Copyright 1967, Journal of School Psychology, Inc.

Table C-11. DEVIATIONS OF SINGLE SCALED SCORES FROM THE AVERAGE SCORE OF AN INDIVIDUAL EXAMINEE ON WISC

SUBTEST	DEVIATION FROM AVERAGE FOR 10 SUBTESTS[a]		DEVIATION FROM AVERAGE FOR 11 SUBTESTS[b]		DEVIATION FROM AVERAGE FOR 11 SUBTESTS[c]		DEVIATION FROM AVERAGE FOR 12 SUBTESTS	
	5 per cent level	1 per cent level	5 per cent level	1 per cent level	5 per cent level	1 per cent level	5 per cent level	1 per cent level
Information	2.70	3.56	2.72	3.59	2.70	3.56	2.72	3.59
Comprehension	3.16	4.15	3.72	4.90	3.16	4.15	3.18	4.18
Arithmetic	2.74	3.61	2.76	3.64	2.76	3.64	2.76	3.64
Similarities	2.74	3.61	2.76	3.64	2.76	3.64	2.76	3.64
Vocabulary	2.14	2.81	2.14	2.81	2.12	2.79	2.14	2.81
Digit Span	–	–	3.63	4.77	–	–	3.65	4.80
Picture Completion	3.25	4.28	3.27	4.31	3.27	4.31	3.29	4.33
Picture Arrangement	2.94	3.87	2.98	3.92	2.96	3.90	2.98	3.92
Block Design	2.16	2.84	2.18	2.86	2.16	2.84	2.18	2.86
Object Assembly	3.19	4.21	3.23	4.26	3.21	4.23	3.23	4.26
Coding	3.45	4.54	3.49	4.59	3.47	4.57	3.48	4.59
Mazes	–	–	–	–	2.61	3.43	2.63	3.46

SUBTEST	DEVIATION FROM AVERAGE FOR 5 VERBAL SCALE SUBTESTS[c]		DEVIATION FROM AVERAGE FOR 6 VERBAL SCALE SUBTESTS		DEVIATION FROM AVERAGE FOR 5 PERFORMANCE SCALE SUBTESTS[b]		DEVIATION FROM AVERAGE FOR 6 PERFORMANCE SCALE SUBTESTS	
	5 per cent level	1 per cent level	5 per cent level	1 per cent level	5 per cent level	1 per cent level	5 per cent level	1 per cent level
Information	2.53	3.33	2.63	3.46	–	–	–	–
Comprehension	2.88	3.79	3.02	3.97	–	–	–	–
Arithmetic	2.57	3.38	2.67	3.51	–	–	–	–
Similarities	2.57	3.38	2.67	3.51	–	–	–	–
Vocabulary	2.08	3.73	2.14	2.81	–	–	–	–
Digit Span	–	–	3.41	4.49	–	–	–	–
Picture Completion	–	–	–	–	3.06	4.02	3.12	4.10
Picture Arrangement	–	–	–	–	2.82	3.72	2.86	3.77
Block Design	–	–	–	–	2.21	2.92	2.20	2.89
Object Assembly	–	–	–	–	3.02	3.97	3.08	4.05
Coding	–	–	–	–	3.21	4.23	3.29	4.33
Mazes	–	–	–	–	–	–	2.55	3.35

Note.—Table C-11 shows the minimum deviations from an individual's average subtest scaled score that are significant at the .05 and .01 levels.

The following formula, obtained from Davis (1959), was used to compute the deviations from average that are significant at the desired confidence levels: $D = CR \times S_{meas((T/m) - z_I)}$, where D is the deviation from average, CR is the critical ratio desired, and $S_{meas((T/m) - z_I)}$ is the standard error of measurement of the difference between an average subtest scaled score and any one of the subtest scaled scores that entered into the average. The standard error of measurement can be obtained by the following formula:

$$S_{meas((T/m) - z_I)} = \sqrt{\frac{S^2_{meas\,T}}{m^2} + \left(\frac{m-2}{m}\right) S^2_{meas\,z_I}}$$

where $S^2_{meas\,T}$ is the variance error of measurement of the sum of the m subtests, m is the number of subtests, T/m is the average of the subtest scaled scores, and $S^2_{meas\,z_I}$ is the variance error of measurement of any one of the subtest scaled scores. The critical ratio for the 5 per cent level is 1.96, and that for the 1 per cent level is 2.58.

[a] Digit Span and Mazes excluded.
[b] Mazes excluded.
[c] Digit Span excluded.

Table C-12. Deviations of Single Scaled Scores from the Average Score of all other Subtests of an Individual Examinee on WISC

SUBTEST	DEVIATION FROM AVERAGE FOR 9 SUBTESTS[a]		DEVIATION FROM AVERAGE FOR 10 SUBTESTS[b]		DEVIATION FROM AVERAGE FOR 10 SUBTESTS[c]		DEVIATION FROM AVERAGE FOR 11 SUBTESTS	
	5 per cent level	1 per cent level	5 per cent level	1 per cent level	5 per cent level	1 per cent level	5 per cent level	1 per cent level
Information	3.00	3.95	3.00	3.95	2.98	3.92	2.98	3.92
Comprehension	3.49	4.59	3.49	4.59	3.47	4.57	3.47	4.57
Arithmetic	3.06	4.02	3.06	4.02	3.04	4.00	3.04	4.00
Similarities	3.06	4.02	3.06	4.02	3.04	4.00	3.04	4.00
Vocabulary	2.35	3.10	2.35	3.10	2.33	3.07	2.33	3.07
Digit Span	–	–	4.02	5.29	–	–	3.98	5.24
Picture Completion	3.61	4.75	3.61	4.75	3.59	4.72	3.59	4.72
Picture Arrangement	3.27	4.31	3.27	4.31	3.25	4.28	3.25	4.28
Block Design	2.41	3.17	2.39	3.15	2.39	3.15	2.37	3.12
Object Assembly	3.55	4.67	3.55	4.67	3.55	4.67	3.53	4.64
Coding	3.84	5.06	3.82	5.03	3.82	5.03	3.82	5.03
Mazes	–	–	–	–	2.86	3.77	2.86	3.77

SUBTEST	DEVIATION FROM AVERAGE FOR 4 VERBAL SCALE SUBTESTS[c]		DEVIATION FROM AVERAGE FOR 5 VERBAL SCALE SUBTESTS		DEVIATION FROM AVERAGE FOR 4 PERFORMANCE SCALE SUBTESTS[b]		DEVIATION FROM AVERAGE FOR 5 PERFORMANCE SCALE SUBTESTS	
	5 per cent level	1 per cent level	5 per cent level	1 per cent level	5 per cent level	1 per cent level	5 per cent level	1 per cent level
Information	3.16	4.15	3.14	4.13	–	–	–	–
Comprehension	3.61	4.75	3.61	4.75	–	–	–	–
Arithmetic	3.21	4.23	3.19	4.21	–	–	–	–
Similarities	3.21	4.23	3.19	4.21	–	–	–	–
Vocabulary	2.59	3.41	2.55	3.35	–	–	–	–
Digit Span	–	–	4.08	5.37	–	–	–	–
Picture Completion	–	–	–	–	3.80	5.01	3.72	4.90
Picture Arrangement	–	–	–	–	3.51	4.62	3.41	4.49
Block Design	–	–	–	–	2.76	3.64	2.63	3.46
Object Assembly	–	–	–	–	3.76	4.95	3.68	4.85
Coding	–	–	–	–	4.02	5.29	3.94	5.19
Mazes	–	–	–	–	–	–	3.06	4.02

Note.— Table C-12 shows the minimum deviations from an individual's average subtest scaled score (the average excluding the subtest desired for the comparison) that are significant at the .05 and .01 levels.

The following formula, obtained from Davis (1959), was used to compute the deviations from average that are significant at the desired confidence levels: $D = CR \times S_{\text{meas}((T/m) - z_x)}$, where D is the deviation from average, CR is the critical ratio desired, and $S_{\text{meas}((T/m) - z_x)}$ is the standard error of measurement of the difference between an average subtest scaled score and a subtest scaled score that was not included in the average. The standard error of measurement can be obtained by the following formula:

$$S_{\text{meas}((T/m) - z_x)} = \sqrt{\frac{S_{\text{meas T}}^2}{m^2} + S_{\text{meas } z_x}^2},$$

where $S_{\text{meas T}}^2$ is the variance error of measurement of the sum of the m subtests to be averaged, m is the number of subtests to be averaged, T/m is the average of the subtest scaled scores, and $S_{\text{meas } z_x}^2$ is the variance error of measurement of the subtest scaled score that was not included in the average. The critical ratio for the 5 per cent level is 1.96, and that for the 1 per cent level is 2.58.

[a]Digit Span and Mazes excluded.
[b]Mazes excluded.
[c]Digit Span excluded.

Table C-13. RELIABILITY COEFFICIENTS OF PROPOSED WISC SHORT FORMS

DYAD		TRIAD		TETRAD		PENTAD	
Short Form	r	Short Form	r	Short Form	r	Short Form	r
V BD	.856	A V BD	.887	I V PA BD	.904	I A V PA BD	.915
I BD	.836	I V BD	.886	A V PA BD	.903	A S V PA BD	.915
I V	.825	S V BD	.885	A S V BD	.900	I S V PA BD	.913
A V	.822	I V OA	.873	S V PA BD	.900	C A V PA BD	.912
V PA	.822	V PA BD	.873	C A V BD	.897	A S V BD OA	.908
S V	.819	C V BD	.869	I A V BD	.897	I A V BD OA	.908
S BD	.817	I V PA	.867	I S V BD	.896	I S V BD OA	.908
I PA	.816	I C BD	.867	S V BD CO	.892	A S V PC BD	.908
I OA	.811	I S BD	.867	I V PA OA	.892	I C V PA BD	.908
V OA	.811	A V DA	.866	A V PC BD	.891	I A V PA OA	.908

Note.—Abbreviations: I = Information; C = Comprehension; A = Arithmetic; S = Similarities; V = Vocabulary; PC = Picture Completion; PA = Picture Arrangement; BD = Block Design; OA = Object Assembly; CO = Coding.

Reprinted by permission of the publisher and author from A. B. Silverstein, "Reappraisal of the Validity of WAIS, WISC, and WPPSI Short Forms," *Journal of Consulting and Clinical Psychology,* **34,** p. 13. Copyright 1970, American Psychological Association.

Table C-14. YUDIN'S ABBREVIATED PROCEDURE FOR THE WISC

SUBTEST	ITEMS RECOMMENDED BY YUDIN	ITEMS RECOMMENDED BY SILVERSTEIN	MULTIPLY SCORE BY[g]
Information	Every 3rd[a]	Every 3rd	3
Comprehension	Odd only	Odd only	2
Arithmetic	Even only[b]	Odd only	2
Similarities	Odd only	Odd only	2
Vocabulary	Every 3rd[c]	Every 3rd	3
Digit Span	All items	Eliminate	1
Picture Completion	Every 3rd[d]	Every 3rd	3
Picture Arrangement	Odd only[e]	Odd only	2
Block Design	Odd only[f]	Odd only	2
Object Assembly	Odd only	Odd only	2
Coding	All items	All items	1

Note.—Silverstein did not present any correction factors.
[a]Subtract 1 from scaled score.
[b]Add 1 to scaled score.
[c]Subtract 4 from raw score.
[d]Subtract 2 from raw score.
[e]Subtract 3 from raw score.
[f]Subtract 6 from raw score.
[g]This column pertains to both the second and third columns, except for the Digit Span subtest (which is eliminated by Silverstein).

Reprinted, with a change in notation, by permission of the publisher and author from L. W. Yudin, "An Abbreviated Form of the WISC for Use with Emotionally Disturbed Children," *Journal of Consulting Psychology,* **30,** p. 273. Copyright 1966, American Psychological Association. Column three adapted from Silverstein, 1968a.

Table C-15. Estimated WISC and WPPSI Full Scale Deviation IQ's Based on Vocabulary plus Block Design Scaled Scores

Vocabulary plus Block Design scaled score	Estimated WISC Full Scale IQ	Estimated WPPSI Full Scale IQ
1	45	43
2	48	46
3	51	49
4	54	52
5	56	55
6	59	58
7	62	61
8	65	64
9	68	67
10	71	70
11	74	73
12	77	76
13	80	79
14	83	82
15	86	85
16	88	88
17	91	91
18	94	94
19	97	97
20	100	100
21	103	103
22	106	106
23	109	109
24	112	112
25	114	115
26	117	118
27	120	121
28	123	123
29	126	126
30	129	129
31	132	132
32	135	135
33	138	138
34	141	141
35	144	143
36	146	147
37	149	150
38	152	153
39	155	156
40	158	159

Note.—The estimated Deviation IQ's were obtained by the procedure recommended by Tellegen and Briggs (1967). The Deviation IQ's shown in the table differ from those presented by Silverstein (1970b), primarily in that the Deviation IQ's are lower for the low scaled scores and higher for the high scaled scores.

Table C-16. CONSTANTS FOR CONVERTING WECHSLER COMPOSITE SCORES INTO DEVIATION QUOTIENTS

2 SUBTESTS			3 SUBTESTS			4 SUBTESTS			5 SUBTESTS		
Σr_{jk}	a	b	Σr_{jk}	a	b	Σr_{jk}	a	b	Σr_{jk}	a	b
.78–.92	2.6	48	2.16–2.58	1.8	46	3.95–4.85	1.4	44	6.96–8.83	1.1	45
.66–.77	2.7	46	1.79–2.15	1.9	43	3.21–3.94	1.5	40	5.50–6.95	1.2	40
.54–.65	2.8	44	1.48–1.78	2.0	40	2.60–3.20	1.6	36	4.36–5.49	1.3	35
.44–.53	2.9	42	1.21–1.47	2.1	37	2.09–2.59	1.7	32	3.45–4.35	1.4	30
.35–.43	3.0	40	.97–1.20	2.2	34	1.66–2.08	1.8	28	2.71–3.44	1.5	25
.26–.34	3.1	38	.77– .96	2.3	31	1.29–1.65	1.9	24	2.10–2.70	1.6	20
.19–.25	3.2	36	.59– .76	2.4	28	.98–1.28	2.0	20	1.59–2.09	1.7	15

Reprinted by permission of the publisher and authors from A. Tellegen and P. F. Briggs, "Old Wine in New Skins: Grouping Wechsler Subtests into New Scales," *Journal of Consulting Psychology,* **31**, p. 504. Copyright 1967, American Psychological Association.

Table C-17. CONSTANTS FOR CONVERTING WISC FACTOR SCORES INTO DEVIATION QUOTIENTS

VERBAL COMPREHENSION[a] ALL AGES		FREEDOM FROM DISTRACTIBILITY[b] 13½ (12–0–0 through 15–11–29)		PERCEPTUAL ORGANIZATION[c] 7½ & 10½ (5–0–0 through 11–11–29)		PERCEPTUAL ORGANIZATION[d] 13½ (12–0–0 through 15–11–29)	
a	b	a	b	a	b	a	b
1.5	40	3.0	40	2.0	40	2.8	44

Note.—Deviation Quotient = (Sum of subtest scaled scores in factor $\times$ a) + b.
[a]Composed of Information, Comprehension, Similarities, and Vocabulary.
[b]Composed of Arithmetic and Digit Span.
[c]Composed of Block Design, Object Assembly, and Mazes.
[d]Composed of Block Design and Object Assembly.

Reprinted, with a change in notation, by permission of the publisher and authors from A. Tellegen and P. F. Briggs, "Old Wine in New Skins: Grouping Wechsler Subtests into New Scales," *Journal of Consulting Psychology,* **31,** p. 505. Copyright 1967, American Psychological Association.

Table C-18. PROBABILITY OF OBTAINING DESIGNATED DIFFERENCES BETWEEN INDIVIDUAL VERBAL AND PERFORMANCE IQ'S ON WISC AND WPPSI

PROBABILITY OF OBTAINING GIVEN OR GREATER DISCREPANCY BY CHANCE	DIFFERENCES							
	WISC Age Level		*WPPSI Age Level*					
	7½	10½ & 13½	4	4½	5	5½	6	6½
.50	5.1	3.9	3.8	3.7	3.5	3.3	3.3	3.7
.25	8.8	6.7	6.6	6.2	6.0	5.6	5.6	6.2
.20	9.8	7.4	7.3	6.9	6.7	6.2	6.2	7.0
.10	12.5	9.5	9.4	8.9	8.6	8.0	8.0	8.9
.05	15.0	11.4	11.2	10.6	10.3	9.5	9.5	10.7
.02	17.8	13.5	13.3	12.6	12.2	11.3	11.3	12.6
.01	19.7	15.0	14.7	13.9	13.5	12.5	12.5	14.0
.001	25.2	19.1	18.8	17.9	17.3	16.1	16.0	17.9

Note.—Table C-18 is entered in the column appropriate to the examinee's age. The discrepancy that is just less than the discrepancy obtained by the examinee is located. The entry in the same row, first column, gives the probability of obtaining a given or greater discrepancy by chance. For example, the hypothesis that a 13½-year-old examinee obtained a Verbal-Performance discrepancy of 17 by chance can be rejected at the .01 level of significance. Table C-18 is two-tailed. See Table C-10 for an explanation of method used to arrive at magnitude of differences.

WISC material reprinted by permission of the publisher and author from J. G. Field, "Two Types of Tables for Use with Wechsler's Intelligence Scales," *Journal of Clinical Psychology,* **16**, p. 5. Copyright 1960, Clinical Psychology Publishing Co., Inc. WPPSI material provided by the author.

Table C-19. PERCENTAGE OF POPULATION OBTAINING DISCREPANCIES BETWEEN VERBAL AND PERFORMANCE IQ'S ON WISC AND WPPSI

% IN POPULATION OBTAINING GIVEN OR GREATER DISCREPANCY	DISCREPANCY								
	WISC Age Level			WPPSI Age Level					
	$7\frac{1}{2}$	$10\frac{1}{2}$	$13\frac{1}{2}$	4	$4\frac{1}{2}$	5	$5\frac{1}{2}$	6	$6\frac{1}{2}$
50	9.0	8.0	9.4	8.1	8.6	8.7	8.2	7.7	8.8
25	15.4	13.8	16.2	13.8	14.7	14.8	14.0	13.1	15.0
20	17.2	15.4	18.0	15.4	16.3	16.5	15.6	14.7	16.8
10	22.0	19.7	23.1	19.7	21.0	21.2	20.0	18.8	21.5
5	26.3	23.5	27.6	23.5	25.0	25.3	23.9	22.4	25.6
2	31.2	28.0	32.8	27.9	29.6	30.0	28.3	26.6	30.4
1	34.6	31.0	36.3	30.9	32.8	33.2	31.4	29.4	33.7
1	44.1	39.5	46.3	39.6	42.0	42.6	40.2	37.7	43.2

Note.—Table C-19 is entered in the column appropriate to the examinee's age. The discrepancy that is just less than the discrepancy obtained by the examinee is located. The entry in the same row, first column, gives the percentage of the standardization population obtaining discrepancies as large or larger than the located discrepancy. For example, a $13\frac{1}{2}$-year-old examinee with a Verbal-Performance discrepancy of 17 on the WISC will be found in between 20% and 25% of the standardization population.

The method used to compute the discrepancy between the Verbal and Performance Scale IQ's which reflects the percentage of the population obtaining the discrepancy is as follows: Discrepancy $= \sigma_1 z\sqrt{2-2r_{xy}}$ The first term is the standard deviation of the test, the second is the selected z value, and the last is the correlation between the two scales. For example, for a 4-year-old child the discrepancy between the WPPSI Verbal and Performance Scale IQ's which represents 5% of the population is $15(1.96)\sqrt{2-2(.68)} = 23.5$.

WISC material reprinted by permission of the publisher and author from J. G. Field, "Two Types of Tables for use with Wechsler's Intelligence Scales," *Journal of Clinical Psychology,* **16,** p. 4. Copyright 1960, Clinical Psychology Publishing Co., Inc. WPPSI material provided by the author.

Table C-20. ESTIMATED IQ'S AND PERCENTILE RANKS FOR SCALED SCORES ON THE WISC AND WPPSI

SCALED SCORE	IQ	PERCENTILE RANK
20	150	99
19	144	99
18	140	99
17	135	99
16	130	98
15	125	95
14	120	91
13	115	84
12	110	75
11	105	63
10	100	50
9	95	37
8	90	24
7	85	16
6	80	9
5	75	5
4	70	2
3	65	1
2	60	1
1	56	1

Reprinted, with a change in notation, by permission of the publishers and authors from B. Alimena, "A Note on Norms for Scatter Analysis on the Wechsler Intelligence Scales," *Journal of Clinical Psychology,* **17,** p. 61, copyright 1961, Clinical Psychology Publishing Co., Inc.; and from F. Rhodes, *Manual for the Rhodes WISC Scatter Profile,* copyright 1969, Educational and Industrial Testing Services.

Table C-21. One-half Confidence Intervals for WPPSI Subtests and Scales

	AGE LEVEL														
	4 (3-10-16 through 4-2-29)					**4½** (4-3-0 through 4-8-29)					**5** (4-9-0 through 5-2-29)				
	Confidence Level					Confidence Level					Confidence Level				
SUBTEST AND SCALE	68%	85%	90%	95%	99%	68%	85%	90%	95%	99%	68%	85%	90%	95%	99%
Information	1	2	2	2	3	1	2	2	3	3	1	2	2	3	4
Vocabulary	1	2	2	3	3	1	2	2	2	3	1	2	2	3	4
Arithmetic	1	2	2	3	3	1	2	2	3	4	1	2	2	2	3
Similarities	1	2	2	2	3	1	2	2	3	3	1	2	2	2	3
Comprehension	1	2	2	3	4	1	2	2	2	3	1	2	2	3	3
Sentences	1	1	2	2	3	1	2	2	2	3	1	2	2	3	3
Animal House	2	3	3	4	5	2	2	3	3	4	1	2	2	3	4
Picture Completion	1	2	2	2	3	1	2	2	2	3	1	2	2	2	3
Mazes	1	2	2	2	3	1	2	2	2	3	1	1	2	2	3
Geometric Design	1	2	2	3	4	1	2	2	2	3	1	2	2	3	3
Block Design	2	2	3	3	4	1	2	2	3	3	1	2	2	2	3
Verbal Scale IQ	4	5	6	7	9	4	5	6	7	9	4	5	6	7	9
Performance Scale IQ	4	6	7	9	11	4	6	7	8	10	4	5	6	7	10
Full Scale IQ	3	4	5	6	8	3	4	5	6	8	3	4	5	6	7

	AGE LEVEL														
	5½ (5-3-0 through 5-8-29)					**6** (5-9-0 through 6-2-29)					**6½** (6-3-0 through 6-7-15)				
	Confidence Level					Confidence Level					Confidence Level				
SUBTEST AND SCALE	68%	85%	90%	95%	99%	68%	85%	90%	95%	99%	68%	85%	90%	95%	99%
Information	1	2	2	3	3	1	2	2	2	3	2	2	2	3	4
Vocabulary	1	2	2	2	3	1	2	2	2	3	1	2	2	2	3
Arithmetic	1	2	2	2	3	1	2	2	2	3	1	2	2	2	3
Similarities	1	2	2	3	3	1	2	2	2	3	1	2	2	2	3
Comprehension	1	2	2	2	3	1	2	2	3	4	1	2	2	3	4
Sentences	1	2	2	2	3	1	2	2	3	3	1	2	2	2	3
Animal House	1	2	2	3	3	1	2	2	2	3	1	2	2	3	4
Picture Completion	1	2	2	2	3	1	2	2	2	3	1	2	2	3	3
Mazes	1	1	1	2	2	1	2	2	2	3	1	1	2	2	3
Geometric Design	1	2	2	2	3	1	2	2	2	3	1	2	2	3	4
Block Design	1	2	2	2	3	1	1	2	2	3	1	2	2	3	3
Verbal Scale IQ	3	5	6	7	9	3	5	6	7	9	4	5	6	7	10
Performance Scale IQ	3	5	6	7	9	3	5	6	7	9	4	6	7	8	10
Full Scale IQ	3	4	4	5	7	3	4	4	5	7	3	4	5	6	8

Note.—The one-half confidence intervals for the subtests are for scaled scores, while those for the scales are for IQ's. The intervals were rounded off, with .5 dropped for even numbers. The one-half confidence intervals must be preceded by a ± sign in order to represent the confidence level. See Table C-1 for an explanation of the method used to arrive at confidence intervals.

Table C-22. SUMMARY ANALYSIS OF FUNCTIONS OF WPPSI SUBTESTS (Not based on factor analytic studies)

SUBTEST	FUNCTION	SUBTEST	FUNCTION
Information	Range of knowledge Long-range memory	Animal House	Memory Attention Goal awareness Concentration Finger and manual dexterity Learning ability
Vocabulary	Word knowledge Linguistic skill Expressive ability		
Arithmetic	Quantitative concepts Nonverbal reasoning ability Memory	Picture Completion	Alertness to details Visual memory Reasoning Concentration
Similarities	Logical thinking (items 1–10) Verbal concept formation (items 11–16)	Mazes	Planning ability Perceptual organization Visual-motor control
Comprehension	Social judgment Practical knowledge Linguistic skill Logical reasoning	Geometric Design	Perceptual ability Visual-motor organization
Sentences	Memory Attention Verbal facility	Block Design	Visual-motor coordination Perceptual organization Spatial visualization Abstract conceptualizing ability Analysis and synthesis

Adapted in part from Austin (1970), Herman (1968), Massey (1968), and Wechsler (1967).

Table C-23. SIGNIFICANT DIFFERENCES AMONG WPPSI SUBTEST SCORES

AGE LEVEL		I	V	A	S	C	Se	AH	PC	M	GD
4 (3-10-16 through 4-2-29)	V	3/5									
	A	4/5	4/5								
	S	3/4	3/5	4/5							
	C	4/5	4/5	4/5	4/5						
	Se	3/4	3/4	3/4	3/4	4/5					
	AH	4/6	4/6	4/6	4/6	5/6	4/6				
	PC	3/4	3/4	3/5	3/4	4/5	3/4	4/6			
	M	3/4	3/5	4/5	3/4	4/5	3/4	4/6	3/4		
	GD	4/5	4/5	4/5	4/5	4/5	3/5	5/6	3/5	4/5	
	BD	4/5	4/5	4/5	4/5	4/5	4/5	5/6	4/5	4/5	4/5

Boxed (age level 4):

	VSIQ	PSIQ
PSIQ	11/15	
FSIQ	9/12	10/14

AGE LEVEL		I	V	A	S	C	Se	AH	PC	M	GD
4½ (4-3-0 through 4-8-29)	V	4/5									
	A	4/5	4/5								
	S	4/5	4/5	4/5							
	C	4/5	3/5	4/5	4/5						
	Se	3/4	3/4	4/5	3/4	3/4					
	AH	4/5	4/5	4/5	4/5	4/5	4/5				
	PC	3/5	3/4	4/5	3/5	3/4	3/4	4/5			
	M	4/5	3/5	4/5	4/5	3/4	3/4	4/5	3/4		
	GD	4/5	3/5	4/5	4/5	3/4	3/4	4/5	3/4	3/4	
	BD	4/5	4/5	4/5	4/5	4/5	3/5	4/5	4/5	4/5	4/5

Boxed (age level 4½):

	VSIQ	PSIQ
PSIQ	11/14	
FSIQ	9/12	10/13

Table C-23. Significant Differences Among WPPSI Subtest Scores — *Continued*

Age level		I	V	A	S	C	Se	AH	PC	M	GD
5	V	4/5									
(4-9-0	A	4/5	4/5						VSIQ	PSIQ	
through	S	4/5	4/5	3/4				PSIQ	10/13		
5-2-29)	C	4/5	4/5	4/5	4/5			FSIQ	9/12	9/12	
	Se	4/5	4/5	3/4	3/5	4/5					
	AH	4/5	4/5	4/5	4/5	4/5	4/5				
	PC	4/5	4/5	3/4	3/4	4/5	4/5	4/5			
	M	3/5	3/4	3/4	3/4	3/4	3/4	3/4	3/4		
	GD	4/5	4/5	3/5	3/5	4/5	4/5	4/5	4/5	3/4	
	BD	4/5	4/5	3/4	3/4	4/5	3/5	4/5	3/5	3/4	4/5

Age level		I	V	A	S	C	Se	AH	PC	M	GD
5½	V	3/5									
(5-3-0	A	3/4	3/4						VSIQ	PSIQ	
through	S	4/5	3/5	3/4				PSIQ	10/13		
5-8-29)	C	3/5	3/4	3/4	3/5			FSIQ	8/11	9/11	
	Se	3/4	3/4	3/4	3/4	3/4					
	AH	4/5	3/5	3/4	4/5	3/5	3/4				
	PC	3/4	3/4	3/4	3/4	3/4	3/4	3/4			
	M	3/4	3/4	3/4	3/4	3/4	3/4	3/4	3/4		
	GD	4/5	3/4	3/4	4/5	3/4	3/4	4/5	3/4	3/4	
	BD	3/5	3/4	3/4	3/5	3/4	3/4	3/5	3/4	3/4	3/4

Age level		I	V	A	S	C	Se	AH	PC	M	GD
6	V	3/4									
(5-9-0	A	3/5	3/4						VSIQ	PSIQ	
through	S	3/4	3/4	3/4				PSIQ	9/12		
6-2-29)	C	3/5	3/4	3/5	3/5			FSIQ	8/11	9/11	
	Se	4/5	3/4	4/5	4/5	4/5					
	AH	3/4	3/4	3/4	3/4	3/5	4/5				
	PC	3/5	3/4	3/5	3/4	3/5	4/5	3/4			
	M	3/4	3/4	3/4	3/4	3/4	3/5	3/4	3/4		
	GD	3/4	3/4	3/4	3/4	3/4	3/5	3/4	3/4	3/4	
	BD	3/4	3/4	3/4	3/4	3/4	3/4	3/4	3/4	3/4	3/4

Age level		I	V	A	S	C	Se	AH	PC	M	GD
6½	V	4/5									
(6-3-0	A	4/5	3/4						VSIQ	PSIQ	
through	S	4/5	3/4	3/5				PSIQ	11/14		
6-7-15)	C	4/5	4/5	4/5	4/5			FSIQ	9/12	10/13	
	Se	4/5	3/4	3/5	3/5	4/5					
	AH	4/5	4/5	4/5	4/5	4/5	4/5				
	PC	4/5	3/5	4/5	4/5	4/5	4/5	4/5			
	M	4/5	3/4	3/4	3/4	4/5	3/4	4/5	3/4		
	GD	4/5	4/5	4/5	4/5	4/5	4/5	4/5	4/5	4/5	
	BD	4/5	3/5	4/5	4/5	4/5	4/5	4/5	4/5	3/4	4/5

Note. — Abbreviations: I = Information; V = Vocabulary; A = Arithmetic; S = Similarities; C = Comprehension; Se = Sentences; AH = Animal House; PC = Picture Completion; M = Mazes; GD = Geometric Design; BD = Block Design.

Confidence levels designated as .05/.01. Sample reading. For a child 4 years of age, a difference of 3 points (or 4 points) between scaled scores on the Information and Vocabulary subtests is significant at the 5% level of confidence, while a difference of 5 points is significant at the 1% level of confidence. In like manner, from the small box, an 11-point difference between the Verbal Scale IQ and Performance Scale IQ is needed for the 5% level of confidence, and a 15-point difference is needed for the 1% level of confidence. The Sentences subtest was not included in computation of significant differences for the Verbal Scale and Full Scale. See Table C-10 for an explanation of method used to arrive at magnitude of differences.

Reprinted, with a change in notation and with recalculation of significant differences among Verbal, Performance, and Full Scales using corrected standard errors of measurement from WPPSI manual, by permission of the publisher and authors from A. P. Milliren and T. E. Newland, "Statistically Significant Differences between Subtest Scaled Scores for the WPPSI," *Journal of School Psychology, 7*(3), p. 17. Copyright 1969, Journal of School Psychology, Inc.

Table C-24. DEVIATIONS OF SINGLE SCALED SCORES FROM THE AVERAGE SCORE OF AN INDIVIDUAL EXAMINEE ON WPPSI

	DEVIATION FROM AVERAGE FOR 10 SUBTESTS[a]		DEVIATION FROM AVERAGE FOR 11 SUBTESTS		DEVIATION FROM AVERAGE FOR 5 VERBAL SCALE SUBTESTS[a]		DEVIATION FROM AVERAGE FOR 6 VERBAL SCALE SUBTESTS		DEVIATION FROM AVERAGE FOR 5 PERFORMANCE SCALE SUBTESTS	
SUBTEST	5 per cent level	1 per cent level	5 per cent level	1 per cent level	5 per cent level	1 per cent level	5 per cent level	1 per cent level	5 per cent level	1 per cent level
Information	2.43	3.20	2.45	3.22	2.27	2.99	2.35	3.10	—	—
Vocabulary	2.23	2.94	2.25	2.97	2.17	2.81	2.18	2.86	—	—
Arithmetic	2.35	3.10	2.35	3.10	2.21	2.92	2.25	2.97	—	—
Similarities	2.29	3.02	2.29	3.02	2.18	2.86	2.21	2.92	—	—
Comprehension	2.43	3.20	2.45	3.22	2.27	2.99	2.35	3.10	—	—
Sentences	—	—	2.20	2.89	—	—	2.14	2.81	—	—
Animal House	2.65	3.48	2.67	3.51	—	—	—	—	2.45	3.22
Picture Completion	2.29	3.02	2.29	3.02	—	—	—	—	2.16	2.84
Mazes	2.06	2.71	2.06	2.71	—	—	—	—	1.98	2.61
Geometric Design	2.35	3.10	2.35	3.10	—	—	—	—	2.21	2.92
Block Design	2.35	3.10	2.35	3.10	—	—	—	—	2.21	2.92

Note.—Table C-24 shows the minimum deviations from an individual's average subtest scaled score that are significant at the .05 and .01 levels. See note in Table C-11 for an explanation of how the mean deviations were arrived at.

[a]Sentences excluded.

Table C-25. DEVIATIONS OF SINGLE SCALED SCORES FROM THE AVERAGE SCORE OF ALL OTHER SUBTESTS OF AN INDIVIDUAL EXAMINEE ON WPPSI

	DEVIATION FROM AVERAGE FOR 9 SUBTESTS[a]		DEVIATION FROM AVERAGE FOR 10 SUBTESTS		DEVIATION FROM AVERAGE FOR 4 VERBAL SCALE SUBTESTS[a]		DEVIATION FROM AVERAGE FOR 5 VERBAL SCALE SUBTESTS		DEVIATION FROM AVERAGE FOR 4 PERFORMANCE SCALE SUBTESTS	
SUBTEST	5 per cent level	1 per cent level	5 per cent level	1 per cent level	5 per cent level	1 per cent level	5 per cent level	1 per cent level	5 per cent level	1 per cent level
Information	2.72	3.59	2.70	3.56	2.76	3.64	2.74	3.61	—	—
Vocabulary	2.49	3.28	2.47	3.25	2.55	3.35	2.53	3.33	—	—
Arithmetic	2.61	3.43	2.59	3.41	2.67	3.51	2.65	3.48	—	—
Similarities	2.55	3.35	3.51	4.62	2.61	3.43	2.59	3.41	—	—
Comprehension	2.72	3.59	2.70	3.56	2.76	3.64	2.74	3.61	—	—
Sentences	—	—	2.43	3.20	—	—	2.47	3.25	—	—
Animal House	2.94	3.87	2.92	3.84	—	—	—	—	2.98	3.93
Picture Completion	2.55	3.35	3.51	4.62	—	—	—	—	2.61	3.44
Mazes	2.27	2.99	2.25	2.97	—	—	—	—	2.35	3.11
Geometric Design	2.61	3.43	2.59	3.41	—	—	—	—	2.67	3.52
Block Design	2.61	3.41	2.59	3.41	—	—	—	—	2.67	3.52

Note.—Table C-25 shows the minimum deviations from an individual's average subtest scaled score (the average excluding the subtest desired for comparison) that are significant at the .05 and .01 levels. See note in Table C-12 for an explanation of how the mean deviations were arrived at.

[a]Sentences excluded.

Table C-26. RELIABILITY COEFFICIENTS OF PROPOSED WPPSI SHORT FORMS

DYAD			TRIAD			TETRAD			PENTAD		
Short Form		r	Short Form		r	Short Form			r	Short Form				r
I BD		.835	I A PC		.878	I V GD BD			.906	V A S PC GD				.923
I GD		.833	I A MA		.878	I C MA BD			.904	I A C PC MA				.923
I A		.830	A C PC		.877	V A PC GD			.904	V A C PC GD				.923
V A		.828	I V GD		.877	A C PC GD			.904	I V A PC GD				.922
I MA		.828	V A PC		.876	I C GD BD			.904	I A C PC GD				.922
A PC		.828	V A GD		.876	I A PC GD			.904	I A S PC GD				.922
I PC		.823	V A MA		.875	I V A MA			.903	I V A MA BD				.921
A C		.822	A C MA		.875	I A C MA			.903	I V A MA GD				.921
V BD		.822	I V BD		.875	A C PC MA			.903	V A C PC MA				.921
V GD		.820	I C GD		.875	I V MA BD			.903	V A C MA BD				.921

Note. — Abbreviations: I = Information; V = Vocabulary; A = Arithmetic; S = Similarities; C = Comprehension; AH = Animal House; PC = Picture Completion; MA = Mazes; GD = Geometric Design; BD = Block Design.

Reprinted by permission of the publisher and author from A. B. Silverstein, "Reappraisal of the Validity of WAIS, WISC, and WPPSI Short Forms," *Journal of Consulting and Clinical Psychology, 34*, p. 13. Copyright 1970, American Psychological Association.

Table C-27. YUDIN'S PROCEDURE FOR THE WPPSI ABBREVIATED SCALE

SUBTEST	ITEM USED	MULTIPLY SCORE BY
Information	Every 3rd	3
Vocabulary	Every 3rd	3
Arithmetic	Odd only	2
Similarities	Odd only	2
Comprehension	Odd only	2
Animal House	Unchanged	1
Picture Completion	Every 3rd	3
Mazes	Odd only	2
Geometric Design	Odd only	2
Block Design	Odd only	2

Adapted from Silverstein (1968a).

Table C-28. Definitions of Categories in the Structure of Intellect

OPERATIONS

Major kinds of intellectual activities or processes; things that the organism does with the raw materials of information, information being defined as "that which the organism discriminates."

C *Cognition.* Immediate discovery, awareness, rediscovery, or recognition of information in various forms; comprehension or understanding.

M *Memory.* Retention or storage, with some degree of availability, of information in the same form it was committed to storage and in response to the same cues in connection with which it was learned.

D *Divergent Production.* Generation of information from given information, where the emphasis is on variety and quantity of output from the same source. Likely to involve what has been called *transfer.* This operation is most clearly involved in aptitudes of creative potential.

N *coNvergent Production.* Generation of information from given information, where the emphasis is on achieving unique or conventionally accepted best outcomes. It is likely that the given (cue) information fully determines the response.

E *Evaluation.* Reaching decisions or making judgments concerning criterion satisfaction (correctness, suitability, adequacy, desirability, etc.) of information.

CONTENTS

Broad classes or types of information discriminable by the organism.

F *Figural.* Information in concrete form, as perceived or as recalled, possibly in the form of images. The term "figural" minimally implies figure-ground perceptual organization. Visual spatial information is figural. Different sense modalities may be involved; e.g., visual kinesthetic.

S *Symbolic.* Information in the form of denotative signs, having no significance in and of themselves, such as letters, numbers, musical notations, codes, and words, when meanings and form are not considered.

M *seMantic.* Information in the form of meanings to which words commonly become attached, hence most notable in verbal communication but not identical with words. Meaningful pictures also often convey semantic information.

B *Behavioral.* Information, essentially non-verbal, involved in human interactions where the attitudes, needs, desires, moods, intentions, perceptions, thoughts, etc., of other people and of ourselves are involved.

PRODUCTS

The organization that information takes in the organism's processing of it.

U *Units.* Relatively segregated or circumscribed items of information having "thing" character. May be close to Gestalt psychology's "figure on a ground."

C *Classes.* Conceptions underlying sets of items of information grouped by virtue of their common properties.

R *Relations.* Connections between items of information based on variables or points of contact that apply to them. Relational connections are more meaningful and definable than implications.

S *Systems.* Organized or structured aggregates of items of information; complexes of interrelated or interacting parts.

T *Transformations.* Changes of various kinds (redefinition, shifts, or modification) of existing information or in its function.

I *Implications.* Extrapolations of information, in the form of expectancies, predictions, known or suspected antecedents, concomitants, or consequences. The connection between the given information and that extrapolated is more general and less definable than a relational connection.

Table C-29. PERCENTILE RANKS FOR IQ'S

	PERCENTILE RANK			PERCENTILE RANK	
IQ	Stanford-Binet	WISC, WPPSI, or WAIS	IQ	Stanford-Binet	WISC, WPPSI, or WAIS
135	99	98	99	48	48
134	98	98	98	45	45
133	98	98	97	43	43
132	98	98	96	40	40
131	97	98	95	38	37
130	97	97	94	35	35
129	96	97	93	33	32
128	96	96	92	31	30
127	95	96	91	29	28
126	95	95	90	27	26
125	94	95	89	25	24
124	93	94	88	23	22
123	93	93	87	21	20
122	92	92	86	19	18
121	90	91	85	17	16
120	89	90	84	16	15
119	88	89	83	15	13
118	87	88	82	13	12
117	85	87	81	12	11
116	84	85	80	11	10
115	83	84	79	10	9
114	81	82	78	8	8
113	79	80	77	7	7
112	77	78	76	7	6
111	75	76	75	6	5
110	73	74	74	5	5
109	71	72	73	5	4
108	69	70	72	4	4
107	67	68	71	4	3
106	65	65	70	3	3
105	62	63	69	3	2
104	60	60	68	2	2
103	57	57	67	2	2
102	55	55	66	2	2
101	52	52	65	1	1
100	50	50			

PROJECTION OF IQ'S ABOVE THE 99TH PERCENTILE AND BELOW THE 1ST PERCENTILE

	IS EQUALLED OR EXCEEDED BY	
IQ	Stanford-Binet	WISC, WPPSI, or WAIS
160 or 40	11 out of 100,000	4 out of 100,000
155 or 45	34 out of 100,000	26 out of 100,000
150 or 50	9 out of 10,000	5 out of 10,000
145 or 55	25 out of 10,000	13 out of 10,000
140 or 60	6 out of 1,000	4 out of 1,000
136 or 64	1 out of 100	1 out of 100

Note.— The values in this table are based on the assumption of a normal distribution of IQ's in the general population.

REFERENCES

Abramson, T. The influence of examiner race on first-grade and kindergarten subjects' Peabody Picture Vocabulary Test scores. *Journal of Educational Measurement,* 1969, **6**, 241–246.

Achenbach, T. M. Comparison of Stanford-Binet performance of nonretarded and retarded persons matched for MA and sex. *American Journal of Mental Deficiency,* 1970, **74**, 488–494.

Ack, M., Miller, I., & Weil, W. B., Jr. Intelligence of children with diabetes mellitus. *Pediatrics,* 1961, **28**, 764–770.

Ackerman, P. T., Peters, J. E., & Dykman, R. A. Children with specific learning disabilities: WISC profiles. *Journal of Learning Disabilities,* 1971, **4**, 150–166.

Ackley, S. Individual rights and professional ethics. In J. Charry (Chm.), Confidentiality and individual rights: Is the APA Code of Ethics an infringement on the individual's right to know? Symposium presented at the American Psychological Association, Washington, D.C., September 1971.

Affleck, D. C., & Strider, F. D. Contribution of psychological reports to patient management. *Journal of Consulting and Clinical Psychology,* 1971, **37**, 177–179.

Agranowitz, A., & McKeown, M. F. *Aphasia handbook for adults and children.* Springfield, Ill.: Charles C Thomas, 1964.

Ainsworth, S. H. The education of children with speech handicaps. In W. M. Cruickshank & G. O. Johnson (Eds.), *Education of exceptional children and youth.* Englewood Cliffs, N.J.: Prentice-Hall, 1958. Pp. 386–428.

Akhurst, B. A. *Assessing intellectual ability.* New York: Barnes & Noble, 1970.

Ali, F., & Costello, J. Modification of the Peabody Picture Vocabulary Test. *Developmental Psychology,* 1971, **5**, 86–91.

Alimena, B. A note on norms for scatter analysis on the Wechsler Intelligence Scales. *Journal of Clinical Psychology,* 1961, **17**, 61.

Allen, R. M. Psychological assessment procedures for the cerebral palsied. In *Proceedings of the postdoctoral workshop in psychological services for the cerebral palsied.* Coral Gables, Fla.: University of Miami Press, 1959. Pp. 21–24.

Allen, R. M. The mental age–visual perception issue assessed. *Exceptional Children,* 1969, **35**, 748–749.

Allen, R. M., Haupt, T. D., & Jones, R. W. A suggested use and non-use for the Peabody Picture Vocabulary Test with the retarded child. *Psychological Reports,* 1964, **15**, 421–422.

Allen, R. M., & Jefferson, T. W. *Psychological evaluation of the cerebral palsied person.* Springfield, Ill.: Charles C Thomas, 1962.

Allen, R. M., & Jones, R. W. Perceptual, conceptual and psycholinguistic evaluation of the mentally retarded child. In A. A. Baumeister (Ed.), *Mental retardation: Appraisal, education, and rehabilitation.* Chicago: Aldine, 1967. Pp. 39–65.

Alper, A. E. A comparison of the Wechsler Intelligence Scale for Children and the Arthur adaptation of the Leiter International Performance Scale with mental defectives. *American Journal of Mental Deficiency,* 1958, **63**, 312–316.

Alper, A. E. *An analysis of the Wechsler Intelligence Scale for Children with institutionalized mental defectives.* (Doctoral dissertation, University of Florida) Ann Arbor, Mich.: University Microfilms, 1960. No. 60–1895.

Alper, A. E. An analysis of the Wechsler Intelligence Scale for Children with institutionalized mental retardates. *American Journal of Mental Deficiency,* 1967, **71,** 624–630.

Alper, A. E., & Horne, B. M. Changes in IQ of a group of institutionalized mental defectives over a period of two decades. *American Journal of Mental Deficiency,* 1959, **64,** 472–475.

Alpern, G. D. Measurement of "untestable" autistic children. *Journal of Abnormal Psychology,* 1967, **72,** 478–486.

Alpern, G. D., & Kimberlin, C. C. Short intelligence test ranging from infancy levels through childhood levels for use with the retarded. *American Journal of Mental Deficiency,* 1970, **75,** 65–71.

Altus, G. T. A note on the validity of the Wechsler Intelligence Scale for Children. *Journal of Consulting Psychology,* 1952, **16,** 231.

Altus, G. T. WISC patterns of a selective sample of bilingual school children. *Journal of Genetic Psychology,* 1953, **83,** 241–248.

Altus, G. T. Relationships between verbal and nonverbal parts of the CTMM and WISC. *Journal of Consulting Psychology,* 1955, **19,** 143–144.

Altus, G. T. A WISC profile for retarded readers. *Journal of Consulting Psychology,* 1956, **20,** 155–156.

American Medical Association. Conference report on mental retardation: A handbook for the primary physician. *Journal of the American Medical Association,* 1965, **191**(3), 117–166.

American Psychological Association. Ethical standards of psychologists. *American Psychologist,* 1963, **18,** 56–60.

American Psychological Association. *Publication manual.* Washington, D.C.: APA, 1967.

American Psychological Association. Psychological assessment and public policy. *American Psychologist,* 1970, **25,** 264–266.

Ames, L. B. A low intelligence quotient often not recognized as the chief cause of many learning difficulties. *Journal of Learning Disabilities,* 1968, **1,** 735–739.

Ammons, R. B., & Ammons, C. H. The Quick Test (QT): Provisional manual. *Psychological Reports,* 1962, **11,** 111–161.

Ammons, R. B., & Ammons, H. S. *The Full-Range Picture Vocabulary Test.* New Orleans: R. B. Ammons, 1948.

Anastasi, A. *Differential psychology.* (3rd ed.) New York: Macmillan, 1958.

Anastasi, A. Psychological tests: Uses and abuses. *Teachers College Record,* 1961, **62,** 389–393.

Anastasi, A. Psychology, psychologists, and psychological testing. *American Psychologist,* 1967, **22,** 297–306.

Anastasi, A. Culture fair testing. In N. E. Gronlund (Ed.), *Readings in measurement and evaluation.* New York: Macmillan, 1968. Pp. 280–286. (a)

Anastasi, A. *Psychological testing.* (3rd ed.) New York: Macmillan, 1968. (b)

Anastasi, A., & Cordova, F. A. Some effects of bilingualism upon the intelligence test performance of Puerto Rican children in New York City. *Journal of Educational Psychology,* 1953, **44,** 1–19.

Anastasi, A., & Foley, J. P., Jr. *Differential psychology.* (2nd ed.) New York: Macmillan, 1949.

Anderman, S. J., Yater, A. C., Boyd, M. W., & Barclay, A. A comparative study of WPPSI and WISC performances of disadvantaged children. Unpublished manuscript, St. Louis University, 1971.

Anderson, D. E., & Flax, M. L. A comparison of the Peabody Picture Vocabulary Test with the Wechsler Intelligence Scale for Children. *Journal of Educational Research,* 1968, **62,** 114–116.

Anderson, G. L. Qualitative aspects of the Stanford-Binet. In H. H. Anderson & G. L. Anderson (Eds.), *An introduction to projective techniques.* Englewood Cliffs, N.J.: Prentice-Hall, 1951. Pp. 581–603.

Anderson, J. M. Review of the Wechsler Intelligence Scale for Children. In O. K. Buros (Ed.), *The fourth mental measurements yearbook.* Highland Park, N.J.: Gryphon Press, 1953. Pp. 477–479.

Ando, K. A comparative study of Peabody Picture Vocabulary Test and Wechsler Intelligence Scale for Children with a group of cerebral palsied children. *Cerebral Palsy Journal,* 1968, **29**(3), 7–9.

Annett, M., Lee, D., & Ounsted, C. Intellectual disabilities in relation to lateralized features in the E.E.G. In *Proceedings in the Second National Spastics Society Study Group.* London: Heinemann, 1961. Pp. 86–112.

Anonymous, J. D. Psychology of the scientist: VIII. Seven rules for producing barely intelligible prose in scientific writing. *Psychological Reports,* 1963, **13,** 313–314.

Appelbaum, S. A. Science and persuasion in the psychological test report. *Journal of Consulting and Clinical Psychology,* 1970, **35,** 349–355.

Armstrong, R. G., & Hauck, P. A. Correlates of the Bender-Gestalt scores in children. *Journal of Psychological Studies,* 1960, **11,** 153–158.

Armstrong, R. J., & Mooney, R. F. The Slosson Intelligence Test: Implications for reading specialists. *Reading Teacher,* 1971, **24,** 336–340.

Armstrong, R. J., Mooney, R. F., & Jensen, J. A. A short, reliable, easy to administer individual intelligence test for special class placement. *Child Study Journal,* 1971, **1,** 156–163.

Arnold, F. C., & Wagner, W. K. A comparison of Wechsler Children's Scale and Stanford-Binet scores for eight- and nine-year olds. *Journal of Experimental Education*, 1955, **24**, 91–94.

Arnold, G. F. A technique for measuring the mental ability of the cerebral palsied. *Psychological Service Center Journal*, 1951, **3**, 171–178.

Arnold, G. F. Review of the Leiter International Performance Scale. In O. K. Buros (Ed.), *The fourth mental measurements yearbook*. Highland Park, N.J.: Gryphon Press, 1953. Pp. 448–449.

Arnold, M. B. *Story sequence analysis*. New York: Columbia University Press, 1962.

Arthur, G. The Arthur adaptation of the Leiter International Performance Scale. *Journal of Clinical Psychology*, 1949, **5**, 345–349.

Atchison, C. O. Use of the Wechsler Intelligence Scale for Children with eighty mentally defective Negro children. *American Journal of Mental Deficiency*, 1955, **60**, 378–379.

Austin, J. J. *Educational and developmental profile*. Muskegon, Mich.: Research Concepts, 1970.

Austin, J. J., & Carpenter, P. The use of the WPPSI in early identification of mental retardation and preschool special education. In R. S. Morrow (Chm.), Diagnostic and educational application of the Wechsler Preschool and Primary Scale of Intelligence (WPPSI). Symposium presented at the American Psychological Association, Miami, September 1970.

Ayres, L. P. The Binet-Simon Measuring Scale for Intelligence: Some criticisms and suggestions. *Psychological Clinic*, 1911, **5**, 187–196.

Babson, S. G., Henderson, N. B., & Clark, W. M., Jr. Preschool intelligence of oversized newborns. *Proceedings of the 77th Annual Convention of the American Psychological Association*, 1969, **4**, 267–268.

Bach, L. C. *A comparison of selected psychological tests used with trainable mentally retarded children*. (Doctoral dissertation, University of South Dakota) Ann Arbor, Mich.: University Microfilms, 1968. No. 69–3111.

Bacon, C. S. A comparative study of the Wechsler-Bellevue Intelligence Scale for Adolescents and Adults, Form I, and the Wechsler Intelligence Scale for Children at the twelve-year level. Unpublished master's thesis, University of North Dakota, 1954.

Badt, M. I. Levels of abstraction in vocabulary definitions of mentally retarded school children. *American Journal of Mental Deficiency*, 1958, **63**, 241–246.

Baer, P. E. Problems in the differential diagnosis of brain damage and childhood schizophrenia. *American Journal of Orthopsychiatry*, 1961, **31**, 728–737.

Baker, H. L. Psychological services: From the school staff's point of view, *Journal of School Psychology*, 1965, **3**(4), 36–42.

Baldwin, A. L., Kalhorn, J., & Breese, F. H. Patterns of parent behavior. *Psychological Monographs*, 1945, **58**(3, Whole No. 268).

Balinsky, B. Review of L. M. Terman & M. A. Merrill, *Stanford-Binet Intelligence Scale, manual for the third revision, Form L-M. Personnel and Guidance Journal*, 1960, **39**, 155–156.

Baratz, S. S., & Baratz, J. C. Early childhood intervention: The social science base of institutional racism. *Harvard Educational Review*, 1970, **40**, 29–50.

Barclay, A., & Carolan, P. A comparative study of the Wechsler Intelligence Scale for Children and the Stanford-Binet Intelligence Scale, Form L-M. *Journal of Consulting Psychology*, 1966, **30**, 563.

Barclay, A., & Yater, A. C. Comparative study of the Wechsler Preschool and Primary Scale of Intelligence and the Stanford-Binet Intelligence Scale, Form L-M, among culturally deprived children. *Journal of Consulting and Clinical Psychology*, 1969, **33**, 257.

Barnes, E. J. Cultural retardation or shortcomings of assessment techniques. In *Selected convention papers. 47th Annual International Convention. Denver, Colorado, April 1969*. Washington, D.C.: Council for Exceptional Children, 1969. Pp. 35–43.

Barnes, E. J. The utilization of behavioral and social sciences in minority group education: Some critical implications. In W. R. Rhine (Chm.), Ethnic minority issues on the utilization of behavioral and social science in a pluralistic society. Symposium presented at the American Psychological Association, Washington, D.C., September 1971.

Baroff, G. S. WISC patterning in endogenous mental deficiency. *American Journal of Mental Deficiency*, 1959, **64**, 482–485.

Barratt, E. S. The relationship of the Progressive Matrices (1938) and the Columbia Mental Maturity Scale to the WISC. *Journal of Consulting Psychology*, 1956, **20**, 294–296.

Barratt, E. S., & Baumgarten, D. L. The relationship of the WISC and Stanford-Binet to school achievement. *Journal of Consulting Psychology*, 1957, **21**, 144.

Bashaw, W. L., & Ayers, J. B. An evaluation of the norms and reliability of the PPVT for preschool subjects. *Educational and Psychological Measurement*, 1967, **27**, 1069–1075.

Bateman, B. An educator's view of a diagnostic approach to learning disorders. In J. Hellmuth (Ed.), *Learning disorders*. Vol. 1. Seattle: Special Child Publications, 1965. Pp. 219–239.

Bateman, B. "Clinically" obtained IQs versus "production line" IQs in a mentally retarded sample. *Journal of School Psychology*, 1968, **7**(1), 29–33.

Baumeister, A. A. Use of the WISC with mental retardates: A review. *American Journal of Mental Deficiency*, 1964, **69**, 183–194.

Baumeister, A. A. A survey of the role of psychologists in public institutions for the mentally retarded. *Mental Retardation*, 1967, **5**(1), 2–5.

Baumeister, A. A., & Bartlett, C. J. A comparison of the factor structure of normals and retardates on the WISC. *American Journal of Mental Deficiency,* 1962, **66,** 641–646. (a)

Baumeister, A. A., & Bartlett, C. J. Further factorial investigations of WISC performance of mental defectives. *American Journal of Mental Deficiency,* 1962, **67,** 257–261. (b)

Baumeister, A. A., Bartlett, C. J., & Hawkins, W. F. Stimulus trace as a predictor of performance. *American Journal of Mental Deficiency,* 1963, **67,** 726–729.

Baumeister, A. A., & Hawkins, W. F. WISC scores of retardates in relation to learning ability. *Journal of Clinical Psychology,* 1966, **22,** 75–76.

Bayley, N. Consistency and variability in the growth of intelligence from birth to eighteen years. *Journal of Genetic Psychology,* 1949, **75,** 165–196.

Beberfall, L. Some linguistic problems of the Spanish-speaking people of Texas. *Modern Language Journal,* 1958, **42,** 87–90.

Beck, H. S., & Lam, R. L. Use of the WISC in predicting organicity. *Journal of Clinical Psychology,* 1955, **11,** 154–158.

Beck, S. J. *Psychological processes in the schizophrenic adaptation.* New York: Grune & Stratton, 1965.

Beez, W. V. Influence of biased psychological reports on teacher behavior and pupil performance. *Proceedings of the 76th Annual Convention of the American Psychological Association,* 1968, **3,** 605–606.

Beldoch, M. Applicability of the norms of the Wechsler Intelligence Scale for Children to five-year-olds. *Journal of Consulting Psychology,* 1963, **27,** 263–264.

Bellak, L. *Schizophrenia.* New York: Logos Press, 1958.

Beller, E. K. *Clinical process.* New York: Free Press, 1962.

Belluomini, H. M. Wechsler Intelligence Scale for Children: Predicting success in corrective reading. Unpublished master's thesis, Sacramento State College, 1962.

Belmont, I., Birch, H. G., & Belmont, L. The organization of intelligence test performance in educable mentally subnormal children. *American Journal of Mental Deficiency,* 1967, **71,** 969–976.

Belmont, L., & Birch, H. G. The intellectual profile of retarded readers. *Perceptual and Motor Skills,* 1966, **22,** 787–816.

Bender, L. The life course of schizophrenic children. *Biological Psychiatry,* 1970, **2,** 165–172.

Bennett, D. K. *The tester and intelligence testing: An examination of protocol interpretation.* (Doctoral dissertation, Harvard University) Ann Arbor, Mich.: University Microfilms, 1970. No. 70–20,142.

Bennett, G. K. Response to Robert Williams. *Counseling Psychologist,* 1970, **2**(2), 88–89.

Bensberg, G. J., Jr., & Sloan, W. Performance of brain-injured defectives on the Arthur adaptation of the Leiter. *Psychological Service Center Journal,* 1951, **3,** 181–184.

Benson, R. R. The Binet vocabulary score as an estimate of intellectual functioning. *Journal of Clinical Psychology,* 1963, **19,** 134–135.

Benton, A. L. Behavioral indices of brain injury in school children. *Child Development,* 1962, **33,** 199–208.

Berdie, R. F. The Ad Hoc Committee on Social Impact of Psychological Assessment. *American Psychologist,* 1965, **20,** 143–146.

Bereiter, C. The future of individual differences. *Harvard Educational Review,* 1969, **39,** 310–318.

Bergan, A., McManis, D. L., & Melchert, P. A. Effects of social and token reinforcement on WISC Block Design performance. *Perceptual and Motor Skills,* 1971, **32,** 871–880.

Berger, A., & Speevack, M. An analysis of the range of testing and scattering among retarded children on Form L of the Revised Stanford-Binet. *Journal of Educational Psychology,* 1940, **31,** 39–44.

Berger, A., & Speevack, M. An analysis of the range of testing and scattering among retarded children on Form M of the Revised Stanford-Binet Scale. *Journal of Educational Psychology,* 1942, **33,** 72–75.

Berger, M. The third revision of the Stanford-Binet (Form L-M): Some methodological limitations and their practical implications. *Bulletin of the British Psychological Society,* 1970, **23,** 17–26.

Berko, M. J. Some factors in the mental evaluation of cerebral palsied children. *Cerebral Palsy Review,* 1953, **14**(5–6), 6, 11, 15.

Berko, M. J. A note on "psychometric scatter" as a factor in the differentiation of exogenous and endogenous mental deficiency. *Cerebral Palsy Review,* 1955, **16**(1), 20. (a)

Berko, M. J. Psychometric scatter: Its application in the clinical prediction of future mental development in cases of childhood brain injury. *Cerebral Palsy Review,* 1955, **16**(2), 16–18. (b)

Bernreuter, R. G., & Carr, E. J. The interpretation of IQ's on the L-M Stanford-Binet. *Journal of Educational Psychology,* 1938, **29,** 312–314.

Bessent, T. E. A note on the validity of the Leiter International Performance Scale. *Journal of Consulting Psychology,* 1950, **14,** 234.

Beverly, L., & Bensberg, G. J. A comparison of the Leiter, the Cornell-Coxe and Stanford-Binet with mental defectives. *American Journal of Mental Deficiency,* 1952, **57,** 89–91.

Bice, H. V., & Cruickshank, W. M. The evaluation of intelligence. In W. M. Cruickshank (Ed.), *Cerebral palsy: Its individual and community problems.* (2nd ed.) Syracuse, N.Y.: Syracuse University Press, 1966. Pp. 101–134.

Binet, A. Réchèrches sur les mouvements de quelques jeunes enfants. *La Revue Philosophique,* 1890, **29,** 297–309. (a)

Binet, A. Perceptions d'enfants. *La Révue Philosophique,* 1890, **30,** 582–611. (b)

Binet, A. *Introduction a la psychologie expérimentale.* Paris: Alcan, 1894.

Binet, A. *L'étude expérimentale de l'intélligence.* Paris: Schleicher, 1903.

Binet, A. Nouvelles réchèrches sur la mésure du niveau intéllectuel chez les enfants d'école. *L'Année Psychologique,* 1911, **17,** 145–210.

Binet, A., & Henri, V. La mémoire des mots. *L'Année Psychologique,* 1895, **1,** 1–23. (a)

Binet, A., & Henri, V. La mémoire des phrases. *L'Année Psychologique,* 1895, **1,** 24–59. (b)

Binet, A., & Henri, V. La psychologie individuelle. *L'Année Psychologique,* 1895, **2,** 411–465. (c)

Binet, A., & Simon, T. Méthodes nouvelles pour le diagnostic du niveau intéllectuel des anormaux. *L'Année Psychologique,* 1905, **11,** 191–244.

Binet, A., & Simon, T. Le dévèloppement de l'intélligence chez les enfants. *L'Année Psychologique,* 1908, **14,** 1–94.

Binet, A., & Simon, T. L'intélligence des imbéciles. *L'Année Psychologique,* 1909, **15,** 1–147. (a)

Binet, A., & Simon, T. Nouvelle théorie psychologique et clinique de la démence. *L'Annee Psychologique,* 1909, **15,** 168–272. (b)

Bingham, W. V. *Aptitudes and aptitude testing.* New York: Harper, 1937.

Birch, H. G. The problem of "brain damage" in children. In H. G. Birch (Ed.), *Brain damage in children.* Baltimore: Williams & Wilkins, 1964. Pp. 3–12.

Birch, H. G., Belmont, L., Belmont, I., & Taft, L. T. Brain damage and intelligence in educable mentally subnormal children. *Journal of Nervous and Mental Disease,* 1967, **144,** 247–257.

Birch, H. G., & Bortner, M. Brain damage: An educational category? In M. Bortner (Ed.), *Evaluation and education of children with brain damage.* Springfield, Ill.: Charles C Thomas, 1968. Pp. 3–11.

Birch, J. W. The utility of short forms of the Stanford-Binet tests of intelligence with mentally retarded children. *American Journal of Mental Deficiency,* 1955, **59,** 462–484.

Blackwood, B. A study of testing in relation to anthropology. *Mental Measurements Monographs,* 1927, **4,** 1–119.

Blanco, R. F. Fifty recommendations to aid exceptional children. *Psychology in the Schools,* 1970, **7,** 29–37.

Blatt, S. J., & Allison, J. The intelligence test in personality assessment. In A. I. Rabin (Ed.), *Projective techniques in personality assessment.* New York: Springer, 1968. Pp. 421–460.

Blatt, S. J., Allison, J., & Baker, B. L. The Wechsler Object Assembly subtest and bodily concerns. *Journal of Consulting Psychology,* 1965, **29,** 223–230.

Blazer, J. A. Psychological testing in a Head Start program. *Training School Bulletin,* 1968, **65,** 65–70.

Bligh, H. F. Concurrent validity on two intelligence measures for young children. In E. M. Huddleston (Ed.), *The 16th yearbook of the National Council on Measurements Used in Education.* New York: NCMUE, 1959. Pp. 56–66.

Bloom, B. S. *Stability and change in human characteristics.* New York: Wiley, 1964.

Blue, C. M. PPVT temporal stability and alternate form reliability with the trainable mentally retarded. *American Journal of Mental Deficiency,* 1969, **73,** 745–748.

Bond, G. L., & Fay, L. C. A comparison of the performance of good and poor readers on the individual items of the Stanford-Binet Scale, Forms L and M. *Journal of Educational Research,* 1950, **43,** 475–479.

Boney, J. D. Predicting the academic achievement of secondary school Negro students. *Personnel and Guidance Journal,* 1966, **44,** 700–703.

Boring, E. G. *A history of experimental psychology.* (2nd ed.) New York: Appleton-Century-Crofts, 1950.

Borosage, V. *A study of the effect of nursery school experience on intellectual performance at two socioeconomic levels.* (Doctoral dissertation, Michigan State University) Ann Arbor, Mich.: University Microfilms, 1968. No. 68–17,062.

Bortner, M., & Birch, H. G. Perceptual and perceptual-motor dissociation in cerebral palsied children. *Journal of Nervous and Mental Disease,* 1962, **134,** 103–108.

Bortner, M., & Birch, H. G. Patterns of intellectual ability in emotionally disturbed and brain-damaged children. *Journal of Special Education,* 1969, **3,** 351–369.

Bosch, G. *Infantile autism.* New York: Springer-Verlag, 1970.

Boshes, B., & Myklebust, H. R. A neurological and behavioral study of children with learning disorders. *Neurology,* 1964, **14,** 7–12.

Bower, E. M. *Early identification of emotionally handicapped children in school.* (2nd ed.) Springfield, Ill.: Charles C Thomas, 1969.

Boyd, M. W. *A factor analysis of the Wechsler Preschool and Primary Scale of Intelligence.* (Doctoral dissertation, St. Louis University) Ann Arbor, Mich.: University Microfilms, 1970. No. 71–21,372.

Bradway, K. P. Comparison of standard and wide-range testing on the Stanford-Binet. *Journal of Consulting Psychology,* 1943, **7,** 179–182.

Bradway, K. P. IQ constancy on the Revised Stanford-Binet from the preschool to the junior high school level. *Journal of Genetic Psychology,* 1944, **65,** 197–217.

Bradway, K. P. An experimental study of factors associated with Stanford-Binet IQ changes from the preschool to the junior high school. *Journal of Genetic Psychology, 1945*, **66**, 107–128. (a)

Bradway, K. P. Predictive value of Stanford-Binet preschool items. *Journal of Educational Psychology, 1945*, **36**, 1–16. (b)

Bradway, K. P., & Robinson, N. M. Significant IQ changes in twenty-five years: A follow-up. *Journal of Educational Psychology, 1961*, **52**, 74–79.

Bradway, K. P., & Thompson, C. W. Intelligence at adulthood: A twenty-five year follow-up. *Journal of Educational Psychology, 1962*, **53**, 1–14.

Braen, B. B., & Masling, J. M. Intelligence tests used with special groups of children. *Journal of Exceptional Children, 1959*, **26**, 42–45.

Braginsky, D. D., & Braginsky, B. M. *Hansels and Gretels; studies of children in institutions for the mentally retarded.* New York: Holt, Rinehart and Winston, 1971.

Brandt, H. M., & Giebink, J. W. Concreteness and congruence in psychologists' reports to teachers. *Psychology in the Schools, 1968*, **5**, 87–89.

Bransford, L. A. *A comparative investigation of verbal and performance intelligence measures at different age levels with bilingual Spanish-speaking children in special classes for the mentally retarded.* (Doctoral dissertation, Colorado State College) Ann Arbor, Mich.: University Microfilms, 1966. No. 67–1098.

Braun, J. S., & Brane, M. Comparison of the performance of children with dysrhythmia grade 1 and normal EEG on psychological tests. *Proceedings of the 79th Annual Convention of the American Psychological Association, 1971*, **6**, 457–458.

Breger, L. Psychological testing: Treatment and research implications. *Journal of Consulting and Clinical Psychology, 1968*, **32**, 176–181.

Brengelmann, J. C., & Kenny, J. T. Comparison of Leiter, WAIS and Stanford-Binet IQ's in retardates. *Journal of Clinical Psychology, 1961*, **17**, 235–238.

Brigham, C. C. Two studies in mental tests. (I) Variable factors in the Binet test. (II) The diagnostic value of some mental tests. *Psychological Monographs, 1917*, **24**(1, Whole No. 102).

Brigham, J. C. Ethnic stereotypes. *Psychological Bulletin, 1971*, **76**, 15–38.

Brill, R. G. The relationship of Wechsler IQ's to academic achievement among deaf students. *Exceptional Children, 1962*, **28**, 315–321.

Brim, O. G., Jr. American attitudes toward intelligence tests. *American Psychologist, 1965*, **20**, 125–130.

British Psychological Society. Appendix I – the 1937 version of the Stanford-Binet Scale – a critical appraisal. *Bulletin of the British Psychological Society, 1958*, **35**, 13–15.

Brittain, M. A comparative study of the use of the Wechsler Intelligence Scale for Children and the Stanford-Binet Intelligence Scale (Form L-M) with eight-year-old children. *British Journal of Educational Psychology, 1968*, **38**, 103–104.

Brittain, M. The WPPSI: A Midlands study. *British Journal of Educational Psychology, 1969*, **39**, 14–17.

Brodt, A. M., & Walker, R. E. Techniques of WISC vocabulary administration. *Journal of Clinical Psychology, 1969*, **25**, 180–181.

Broida, D. C. Psychological aspects of epilepsy in children and youth. In W. H. Cruickshank (Ed.), *Psychology of exceptional children and youth.* Englewood Cliffs, N.J.: Prentice-Hall, 1955. Pp. 345–390.

Bronner, A. F., Healy, W., Lowe, G. M., & Shimberg, M. E. *A manual of individual mental tests and testing.* Boston: Little, Brown, 1927.

Brooks, F. D. The accuracy of the abbreviated Stanford-Binet Intelligence Scale. *Psychological Clinic, 1929*, **18**, 17–20.

Brown, E. W. Observing behavior during the intelligence test. In E. Lerner & L. B. Murphy (Eds.), Methods for psychology study of personality in young children. *Monographs of the Society for Research in Child Development, 1941*, **6**(Whole No. 4), 268–283.

Brown, F. A comparison of the abbreviated and the complete Stanford-Binet Scales. *Journal of Consulting Psychology, 1942*, **6**, 240–242.

Brown, F. A comparative study of the intelligence of Jewish and Scandinavian kindergarten children. *Journal of Genetic Psychology, 1944*, **64**, 67–92.

Brown, L. F., & Rice, J. A. The Peabody Picture Vocabulary Test: Validity for EMRs. *American Journal of Mental Deficiency, 1967*, **71**, 901–903.

Brown, R., Hake, D., & Malpass, L. F. The utility of the Progressive Matrices Test (1956 Revision). *American Psychologist, 1959*, **14**, 341. (Abstract)

Bruininks, R. H. Auditory and visual perceptual skills related to the reading performance of disadvantaged boys. *Perceptual and Motor Skills, 1969*, **29**, 179–186.

Bruininks, R. H., & Feldman, D. H. Creativity, intelligence, and achievement among disadvantaged children. *Psychology in the Schools, 1970*, **7**, 260–264.

Bruner, F. G., Barnes, E., & Dearborn, W. F. Report of committee on books and tests pertaining to the study of exceptional and mentally deficient children. *Proceedings of the National Education Association, 1909*, **47**, 901–914.

Bruner, J. S. *Toward a theory of instruction.* Cambridge, Mass.: Belknap-Harvard, 1966.

Brunswik, E. *Perception and the representative design of psychological experiments.* (2nd ed.) Berkeley: University of California Press, 1956.

Bryan, G. E., & Brown, M. H. A method for differential diagnosis of brain damage in adolescents. *Journal of Nervous and Mental Disease,* 1957, **125**, 69–72.

Budoff, M., & Purseglove, E. M. Forms L and LM of the Stanford Binet compared for an institutionalized adolescent mentally retarded population. *Journal of Clinical Psychology,* 1963, **19**, 214.

Bühler, C. The Ball and Field test as a help in the diagnosis of emotional difficulties. *Character and Personality,* 1938, **6**, 257–273.

Burgemeister, B. B. *Psychological techniques in neurological diagnosis.* New York: Harper & Row, 1962.

Burgemeister, B. B., Blum, L. H., & Lorge, I. *Columbia Mental Maturity Scale, third edition.* New York: Harcourt Brace Jovanovich, 1972.

Burks, H. F., & Bruce, P. The characteristics of poor and good readers as disclosed by the Wechsler Intelligence Scale for Children. *Journal of Educational Psychology,* 1955, **46**, 488–493.

Burma, J. H. *Spanish-speaking groups in the United States.* Durham, N.C.: Duke University Press, 1954.

Burnes, K. Clinical assumptions about WISC subtest score and test behavior relationships. *Journal of Consulting and Clinical Psychology,* 1971, **36**, 299.

Burnett, A. Comparison of the PPVT, Wechsler-Bellevue, and Stanford-Binet on educable retardates. *American Journal of Mental Deficiency,* 1965, **69**, 712–715.

Burns, R. C. Behavioral differences between brain-injured and brain-deficit children grouped according to neuropathological types. *American Journal of Mental Deficiency,* 1960, **65**, 326–334.

Burstein, A. G. Review of the Wechsler Intelligence Scale for Children. In O. K. Buros (Ed.), *The sixth mental measurements yearbook.* Highland Park, N.J.: Gryphon Press, 1965. Pp. 843–845.

Burt, C. The measurement of intelligence by the Binet tests. *Eugenics Review,* 1914, **6**, 36–50, 140–152.

Burt, C. The latest revision of the Binet intelligence tests. *Eugenics Review,* 1939, **30**, 255–260.

Burt, C. The evidence for the concept of intelligence. *British Journal of Educational Psychology,* 1955, **25**, 158–177.

Burt, C. The inheritance of mental ability. *American Psychologist,* 1958, **13**, 1–15.

Burt, C. The factor analysis of the Wechsler Scale. II. *British Journal of Statistical Psychology,* 1960, **13**, 82–87.

Burt, C., & John, E. A factorial analysis of Terman Binet tests. *British Journal of Educational Psychology,* 1942, **12**, 117–127, 156–161.

Butcher, H. J. *Human intelligence: Its nature and assessment.* London: Methuen, 1968.

Butler, K. G. *Psychogenic articulation disorders related to verbal skills and intelligence as measured by the Wechsler Intelligence Scale for Children.* (Doctoral dissertation, Michigan State University) Ann Arbor, Mich.: University Microfilms, 1967. No. 68–4112.

Butterfield, E. C. Stimulus trace in the mentally retarded: Defect or developmental lag? *Journal of Abnormal Psychology,* 1968, **73**, 358–362.

Caldwell, M. B. An analysis of responses of a southern urban Negro population to items on the Wechsler Intelligence Scale for Children. Unpublished doctoral dissertation, Pennsylvania State University, 1954.

Caldwell, M. B., & Knight, D. The effect of Negro and white examiners on Negro intelligence test performance. *Journal of Negro Education,* 1970, **39**, 177–179.

Caldwell, M. B., & Smith, T. A. Intellectual structure of southern Negro children. *Psychological Reports,* 1968, **23**, 63–71.

Camp, B. W. WISC performance in acting-out and delinquent children with and without EEG abnormality. *Journal of Consulting Psychology,* 1966, **30**, 350–353.

Canady, H. G. The effect of "rapport" on the I.Q.: A new approach to the problem of racial psychology. *Journal of Negro Education,* 1936, **5**, 209–219.

Caputo, D. V., Edmonston, W. E., Jr., L'Abate, L., & Rondberg, S. R. Type of brain damage and intellectual functioning in children. *Journal of Consulting Psychology,* 1963, **27**, 184.

Caputo, D. V., & Mandell, W. Consequences of low birth weight. *Developmental Psychology,* 1970, **3**, 363–383.

Carleton, F. O., & Stacey, C. L. An item analysis of the Wechsler Intelligence Scale for Children. *Journal of Clinical Psychology,* 1955, **11**, 149–154.

Carlisle, A. L., Shinedling, M. M., & Weaver, R. Note on the use of the Slosson Intelligence Test with mentally retarded residents. *Psychological Reports,* 1970, **26**, 865–866.

Carlson, J. S. Some relationships between class inclusion, perceptual capabilities, verbal capabilities and race. *Human Development,* 1971, **14**(1), 30–38.

Carlton, T. Performances of mental defectives on the Revised Stanford-Binet, Form L. *Journal of Consulting Psychology,* 1940, **4**, 61–65.

Carr, D. L., Brown, L. F., & Rice, J. A. The PPVT in the assessment of language deficits. *American Journal of Mental Deficiency,* 1967, **71**, 937–940.

Carrier, N. A., Orton, K. D., & Malpass, L. F. Responses of bright, normal, and EMH children to an orally-administered Children's Manifest Anxiety Scale. *Journal of Educational Psychology,* 1962, **53,** 271–274.

Carroll, H. A., & Hollingworth, L. S. The systematic error of Herring-Binet in rating gifted children. *Journal of Educational Psychology,* 1930, **21,** 1–11.

Carter, J. W., & Bowles, J. W., Jr. A manual on qualitative aspects of psychological examining. *Journal of Clinical Psychology,* 1948, **4,** 109–150.

Cartwright, G. P. A note on the use of the Peabody Picture Vocabulary Test with disadvantaged children. *Journal of Educational Research,* 1968, **61,** 285.

Cason, E. B. Some suggestions on the interaction between the school psychologist and the classroom teacher. *Journal of Consulting Psychology,* 1945, **9,** 132–137.

Cassel, R. H., & Danenhower, H. S. Mental subnormality developmentally arrested: The Primary Mental Abilities Test. *Training School Bulletin,* 1949, **46,** 94–104.

Castaneda, A., McCandless, B. R., & Palermo, D. S. The children's form of the Manifest Anxiety Scale. *Child Development,* 1956, **27,** 317–326.

Cattell, P. Stanford-Binet IQ variations. *School and Society,* 1937, **45,** 615–618.

Cattell, P. *The measurement of intelligence of infants and young children.* New York: Psychological Corporation, 1950.

Cattell, R. B. Measurement versus intuition in applied psychology. *Character and Personality,* 1937, **6,** 114–131.

Cattell, R. B. *Handbook for the Culture Fair Intelligence Test: A measure of "g."* Champaign, Ill.: Institute for Personality and Ability Testing, 1959.

Cattell, R. B. Theory of fluid and crystalized intelligence: A critical experiment. *Journal of Educational Psychology,* 1963, **54,** 1–22.

Chambers, C. H. Leo Kanner's concept of early infantile autism. *British Journal of Medical Psychology,* 1969, **42,** 51–54.

Chandler, J. T., & Plakos, J. Spanish-speaking pupils classified as educable mentally retarded. *Integrated Education,* 1969, 7(6), 28–33.

Charles, D. C. Ability and accomplishment of persons earlier judged mentally deficient. *Genetic Psychology Monographs,* 1953, **47,** 3–71.

Charles, D. C. Adult adjustment of some deficient American children—II. *American Journal of Mental Deficiency,* 1957, **62,** 300–304.

Chavez, S. J. Preserve their language heritage. *Childhood Education,* 1956, **33,** 165, 185.

Childers, P. R. Concurrent validity of a group administered Peabody Picture Vocabulary Test. *Journal of Educational Research,* 1966, **60,** 92–93.

Christiansen, T., & Livermore, G. A comparison of Anglo-American and Spanish-American children on the WISC. *Journal of Social Psychology,* 1970, **81,** 9–14.

Cieutat, V. J. Examiner differences with the Stanford-Binet IQ. *Perceptual and Motor Skills,* 1965, **20,** 317–318.

Cieutat, V. J., & Flick, G. L. Examiner differences among Stanford-Binet items. *Psychological Reports,* 1967, **21,** 613–622.

Claiborn, W. L. Expectancy effects in the classroom: A failure to replicate. *Journal of Educational Psychology,* 1969, **60,** 377–383.

Clark, K. B. Psychodynamic implications of prejudice toward children from a minority group. In M. G. Gottsegen & G. B. Gottsegen (Eds.), *Professional school psychology.* Vol. 1. New York: Grune & Stratton, 1960. Pp. 64–71.

Clark, K. B. *Dark ghetto.* New York: Harper & Row, 1967.

Clark, M. *Health in the Mexican-American culture.* Berkeley: University of California Press, 1959.

Clarke, B. R., & Leslie, P. T. Visual-motor skills and reading ability of deaf children. *Perceptual and Motor Skills,* 1971, **33,** 263–268.

Clarke, F. R. A comparative study of the Wechsler Intelligence Scale for Children and the Revised Stanford-Binet Intelligence Scale, Form L, in relation to scholastic achievement of a 5th grade population. Unpublished master's thesis, Pennsylvania State University, 1950.

Clawson, A. Relationship of psychological tests to cerebral disorders in children: A pilot study. *Psychological Reports,* 1962, **10,** 187–190.

Clements, S. D. Minimal brain dysfunction in children: Terminology and identification. Public Health Service Publication No. 1415, United States Department of Health, Education and Welfare, 1966.

Clements, S. D. The psychologist and case finding. In L. Tarnopol (Ed.), *Learning disabilities: Introduction to educational and medical management.* Springfield, Ill.: Charles C Thomas, 1969. Pp. 171–179.

Clements, S. D., & Peters, J. E. Minimal brain dysfunction in the school-age child. *Archives of General Psychiatry,* 1962, **6,** 185–197.

Cochran, M. L., & Pedrini, D. T. The concurrent validity of the 1965 WRAT with adult retardates. *American Journal of Mental Deficiency,* 1969, **73,** 654–656.

Cohen, B. D., & Collier, M. J. A note on the WISC and other tests of children six to eight years old. *Journal of Consulting Psychology,* 1952, **16,** 226–227.

Cohen, E. Is there examiner bias on the Wechsler-Bellevue? *Proceedings of Oklahoma Academy of Science,* 1950, **31,** 150–153.

Cohen, E. Examiner differences with individual intelligence tests. *Perceptual and Motor Skills*, 1965, **20**, 1324.

Cohen, J. A factor-analytically based rationale for the Wechsler Adult Intelligence Scale. *Journal of Consulting Psychology*, 1957, **21**, 451–457.

Cohen, J. The factorial structure of the WISC at ages 7–6, 10–6, and 13–6. *Journal of Consulting Psychology*, 1959, **23**, 285–299.

Cohen, L. The effects of material and non-material reinforcement upon performance of the WISC Block Design subtest by children of different social classes: A follow-up study. *Psychology*, 1970, 7(4), 41–47.

Cohen, R. A. Conceptual styles, culture conflict, and nonverbal tests of intelligence. *American Anthropologist*, 1969, **71**, 828–856.

Cole, A. A study of preschool disadvantaged Negro children's Peabody Picture Vocabulary Test results. New York State University College, Buffalo. *Child Study Center Bulletin*, 1966, **2**, 61–66.

Cole, D. Communication and rapport in clinical testing. *Journal of Consulting Psychology*, 1953, **17**, 132–134.

Cole, M., & Bruner, J. S. Cultural differences and inferences about psychological processes. *American Psychologist*, 1971, **26**, 867–876.

Cole, S., Burkheimer, G. J., & Steinberg, J. Validity of Seguin Formboard with retarded children. *Psychological Reports*, 1968, **22**, 1143–1144.

Cole, S., & Hunter, M. Pattern analysis of WISC scores achieved by culturally disadvantaged children. *Psychological Reports*, 1971, **29**, 191–194.

Coleman, H. M., & Dawson, S. T. Educational evaluation and visual-perceptual-motor dysfunction. *Journal of Learning Disabilities*, 1969, **2**, 242–251.

Coleman, J. C., & Rasof, B. Intellectual factors in learning disorders. *Perceptual and Motor Skills*, 1963, **16**, 139–152.

Coleman, J. C., & Sandhu, M. Intelligence level and background factors in learning disorders. *Psychological Reports*, 1965, **17**, 69–70.

Colligan, R. C. *Deficits in psychometric performance related to perinatal stress.* (Doctoral dissertation, University of Minnesota) Ann Arbor, Mich.: University Microfilms, 1969. No. 70–15,715.

Collins, A. L. Epileptic intelligence. *Journal of Consulting Psychology*, 1951, **15**, 392–399.

Collins, A. L., & Lennox, W. G. The intelligence of 300 private epileptic patients. *Epilepsy, Proceedings of the Association for Research in Nervous and Mental Disease*, 1947, **26**, 586–603.

Conklin, R. C., & Dockrell, W. B. The predictive validity and stability of WISC scores over a four year period. *Psychology in the Schools*, 1967, **4**, 263–266.

Conners, C. K. The syndrome of minimal brain dysfunction: Psychological aspects. *Pediatric Clinics of North America*, 1967, **14**, 749–766.

Contrucci, V. J., Korn, E. F., Martinson, M. C., & Mathias, D. C. Individual test interpretation for teachers of the mentally retarded. Bulletin No. 18, 1962, Wisconsin State Department of Public Instruction, Madison. ERIC, 1967, No. 11, 41 (EDO11712).

Cook, J. M., & Arthur, G. Intelligence ratings for 97 Mexican children in St. Paul, Minn. *Journal of Exceptional Children*, 1951, **18**, 14–15, 31.

Cooper, G. D., York, M. W., Daston, P. G., & Adams, H. B. The Porteus Test and various measures of intelligence with southern Negro adolescents. *American Journal of Mental Deficiency*, 1967, **71**, 787–792.

Cooper, J. G. Predicting school achievement for bilingual pupils. *Journal of Educational Psychology*, 1958, **49**, 31–36.

Corey, M. T. The WPPSI as a school admissions tool for young children. In R. S. Morrow (Chm.), Diagnostic and educational application of the Wechsler Preschool and Primary Scale of Intelligence (WPPSI). Symposium presented at the American Psychological Association, Miami, September 1970.

Corotto, L. V. The relation of Performance to Verbal IQ in acting out juveniles. *Journal of Psychological Studies*, 1961, **12**, 162–166.

Corwin, B. J. The relationship between reading achievement and performance on individual ability tests. *Journal of School Psychology*, 1967, **5**, 156–157.

Costello, J. Effects of pretesting and examiner characteristics on test performance of young disadvantaged children. *Proceedings of the 78th Annual Convention of the American Psychological Association*, 1970, **5**, 309–310.

Costello, J., & Ali, F. Reliability and validity of Peabody Picture Vocabulary Test scores of disadvantaged preschool children. *Psychological Reports*, 1971, **28**, 755–760.

Costello, J., & Dickie, J. Leiter and Stanford-Binet IQ's of preschool disadvantaged children. *Developmental Psychology*, 1970, **2**, 314.

Coyle, F. A., Jr. Another alternate wording on the WISC. *Psychological Reports*, 1965, **16**, 1276.

Coyle, F. A., Jr., Dans, C., & Cork, E. Form equivalence of the PPVT on children in speech therapy. *Psychological Reports*, 1968, **23**, 1002.

Craig, R. J. An illustration of the Wechsler Picture Arrangement subtest as a thematic technique. *Journal of Projective Techniques and Personality Assessment,* 1969, **33,** 286–289.

Creak, M. Schizophrenic syndrome in childhood. Further progress report of a working party. *Developmental Medicine and Child Neurology,* 1964, **6,** 530–535.

Crockett, D., Klonoff, H., & Bjerring, J. Factor analysis of neuropsychological tests. *Perceptual and Motor Skills,* 1969, **29,** 791–802.

Cronbach, L. J. *Essentials of psychological testing.* New York: Harper, 1949.

Cronbach, L. J. *Essentials of psychological testing.* (2nd ed.) New York: Harper, 1960.

Cronbach, L. J. Year-to-year correlations of mental tests: A review of the Hofstaetter analysis. *Child Development,* 1967, **38,** 283–289.

Cronbach, L. J. Heredity, environment, and educational policy. *Harvard Educational Review,* 1969, **39,** 338–347.

Cronbach, L. J. *Essentials of psychological testing.* (3rd ed.) New York: Harper & Row, 1970.

Cropley, A. J. Differentiation of abilities, socioeconomic status, and the WISC. *Journal of Consulting Psychology,* 1964, **28,** 512–517.

Crow, J. F. Genetic theories and influences: Comments on the value of diversity. *Harvard Educational Review,* 1969, **39,** 301–309.

Crowell, D. H. Sensory defects. In C. M. Louttit (Ed.), *Clinical psychology of exceptional children.* (3rd ed.) New York: Harper, 1957. Pp. 425–491.

Crowell, D. H., & Crowell, D. C. Intelligence test reliability for cerebral palsied children. *Journal of Consulting Psychology,* 1954, **18,** 276.

Crown, P. J. *The effects of race of examiner and standard vs. dialect administration of the Wechsler Preschool and Primary Scale of Intelligence on the performance of Negro and white children.* (Doctoral dissertation, Florida State University) Ann Arbor, Mich.: University Microfilms, 1970. No. 71–18,356.

Cruickshank, W. M. Qualitative analysis of intelligence test responses. *Journal of Clinical Psychology,* 1947, **3,** 381–386.

Cruickshank, W. M., & Qualtere, T. J. The use of intelligence tests with children of retarded mental development. II. Clinical considerations. *American Journal of Mental Deficiency,* 1950, **54,** 370–381.

Cuadra, C. A., & Albaugh, W. P. Sources of ambiguity in psychological reports. *Journal of Clinical Psychology,* 1956, **12,** 109–115.

Cundick, B. P. Measures of intelligence on Southwest Indian students. *Journal of Social Psychology,* 1970, **81,** 151–156.

Cureton, E. E. Mental age equivalents for the Revised Stanford-Binet Vocabulary test. *Journal of Consulting Psychology,* 1954, **18,** 381–383.

Curr, W., & Gourlay, N. Differences between testers in Terman-Merrill testing. *British Journal of Statistical Psychology,* 1956, **9,** 75–81.

Curtis, J. N. Point Scale examinations on the high-grade feeble-minded and the insane. *Journal of Abnormal Psychology,* 1918, **13,** 77–118.

Dangel, H. L. *The biasing effect of pretest information on the WISC scores of mentally retarded children.* (Doctoral dissertation, Pennsylvania State University) Ann Arbor, Mich.: University Microfilms, 1970. No. 71–16,588.

Darcy, N. T. Bilingualism and the measurement of intelligence: Review of a decade of research. *Journal of Genetic Psychology,* 1963, **103,** 259–282.

Datta, L. E. Draw-a-Person Test as a measure of intelligence in preschool children from very low income families. *Journal of Consulting Psychology,* 1967, **31,** 626–630.

Davids, A. Intelligence in childhood schizophrenics, other emotionally disturbed children, and their mothers. *Journal of Consulting Psychology,* 1958, **22,** 159–163.

Davidson, J. F. A preliminary study in statistical comparison of the Revised Stanford-Binet Intelligence Test Form L with the Wechsler Intelligence Scale for Children using the fourteen year level. Unpublished master's thesis, University of Florida, 1954.

Davis, F. B. The interpretation of IQ's derived from the 1937 Revision of the Stanford-Binet Scales. *Journal of Applied Psychology,* 1940, **24,** 595–604.

Davis, F. B. The derivation of three subscores from the 1937 Revision of the Stanford-Binet Scales. *Journal of Consulting Psychology,* 1941, **5,** 287–291.

Davis, F. B. Interpretation of differences among averages and individual test scores. *Journal of Educational Psychology,* 1959, **50,** 162–170.

Davis, L. J., Jr. The internal consistency of the WISC with the mentally retarded. *American Journal of Mental Deficiency,* 1966, **70,** 714–716.

Davis, W. E., Peacock, W., Fitzpatrick, P., & Mulhern, M. Examiner differences, prior failure, and subjects' WAIS Arithmetic scores. *Journal of Clinical Psychology,* 1969, **25,** 178–180.

Davis, W. M., Jr. Are there solutions to the problems of testing black Americans? In M. M. Meier (Chm.), Some answers to ethnic concerns about psychological testing in the schools. Symposium presented at the American Psychological Association, Washington, D.C., September 1971.

Dean, D. A. A factor analysis of the Stanford-Binet and SRA Primary Mental Abilities Battery at the first grade level. In *Pennsylvania State College Abstracts of Doctoral Dissertations, 1950.* State College, Pa., 1950, **14,** 394–397.

Dearborn, G. The determination of intellectual regression and progression. *American Journal of Psychiatry*, 1926, **83**, 725–741.

Decker, R. J. Manifestations of the brain damage syndrome in historical and psychological data. In S. R. Rappaport (Ed.), *Childhood aphasia and brain damage: A definition*. Narberth, Pa.: Livingston Publishing Co., 1964. Pp. 52–57.

de Hirsch, K. Differential diagnosis between aphasic and schizophrenic language in children. *Journal of Speech and Hearing Disorders*, 1967, **32**, 3–10.

Deich, R. F. Correlations between the PPVT and the CTMM. *Psychological Reports*, 1968, **22**, 856.

DeLapa, G. The Slosson Intelligence Test: A screening and retesting technique for slow learners. *Journal of School Psychology*, 1968, **6**, 224–225.

Delattre, L., & Cole, D. A comparison of the WISC and the Wechsler-Bellevue. *Journal of Consulting Psychology*, 1952, **16**, 228–230.

Delp, H. A. Correlations between the Kent EGY and the Wechsler batteries. *Journal of Clinical Psychology*, 1953, **9**, 73–75. (a)

Delp, H. A. Review of the Wechsler Intelligence Scale for Children. In O. K. Buros (Ed.), *The fourth mental measurements yearbook*. Highland Park, N.J.: Gryphon Press, 1953. Pp. 479–480. (b)

Dennerll, R. D., Den Broeder, J., & Sokolov, S. L. WISC and WAIS in children and adults with epilepsy. *Journal of Clinical Psychology*, 1964, **20**, 236–240.

Denton, L. R. Intelligence test performance and personality differences in a group of visually handicapped children. *Bulletin of the Maritime Psychological Association*, 1954, Dec., 47–50.

Des Lauriers, A., & Halpern, F. C. Psychological tests in childhood schizophrenia. *American Journal of Orthopsychiatry*, 1947, **17**, 57–67.

Deutsch, M., Fishman, J. A., Kogan, L., North, R., & Whiteman, M. Guidelines for testing minority group children. *Journal of Social Issues*, 1964, **20**(2), 129–145.

Diller, L., & Beechley, R. M. The constancy of the altitude: A note. *Journal of Clinical Psychology*, 1951, **7**, 191–193.

Diller, L., & Birch, H. G. Psychological evaluation of children with cerebral damage. In H. G. Birch (Ed.), *Brain damage in children*. Baltimore: Williams & Wilkins, 1964. Pp. 27–43.

Di Lorenzo, L. T., & Brady, J. J. Use of the Peabody Picture Vocabulary Test with preschool children. *Psychological Reports*, 1968, **22**, 247–251.

Di Lorenzo, L. T., & Nagler, E. Examiner differences on the Stanford-Binet. *Psychological Reports*, 1968, **22**, 443–447.

Dingman, H. F., & Meyers, C. E. The structure of intellect in the mental retardate. In N. R. Ellis (Ed.), *International review of research in mental retardation*. Vol. 1. New York: Academic Press, 1966. Pp. 55–76.

Dockrell, W. B. The use of Wechsler Intelligence Scale for Children in the diagnosis of retarded readers. *Alberta Journal of Educational Research*, 1960, **6**, 86–91.

Dokecki, P. R., Frede, M. C., & Gautney, D. B. Criterion, construct, and predictive validities of the Wechsler Preschool and Primary Scale of Intelligence. *Proceedings of the 77th Annual Convention of the American Psychological Association*, 1969, **4**, 505–506.

Doll, E. A. A brief Binet-Simon Scale. *Psychological Clinic*, 1917, **11**, 197–211, 254–261.

Doll, E. A. A total program for the mentally retarded. *Training School Bulletin*, 1963, **60**, 13–22.

Donahue, D., & Sattler, J. M. Personality variables affecting WAIS scores. *Journal of Consulting and Clinical Psychology*, 1971, **36**, 441.

Doris, J. The evaluation of the intellect of the brain-damaged child: Historical development and present status. In A. J. Solnit & S. A. Provence (Eds.), *Modern perspectives in child development*. New York: International Universities Press, 1963. Pp. 162–205.

Down, J. L. *On some of the mental affections of childhood and youth*. London: J. & A. Churchill, 1887.

Dreger, R. M., & Miller, K. S. Comparative psychological studies of Negroes and whites in the United States: 1959–1965. *Psychological Bulletin*, 1968, **70**(Monogr. Suppl. 3, Pt. 2).

Dubowitz, V. Intellectual impairment in muscular dystrophy. *Archives of Disease in Childhood*, 1965, **40**, 296–301.

Dudek, S. Z., & Lester, E. P. The good child facade in chronic underachievers. *American Journal of Orthopsychiatry*, 1968, **38**, 153–160.

Dudek, S. Z., Lester, E. P., Goldberg, J. S., & Dyer, G. B. Relationship of Piaget measures to standard intelligence and motor scales. *Perceptual and Motor Skills*, 1969, **28**, 351–362.

Duncan, P. M., & Millard, W. *A manual for the classification, training, and education of the feebleminded, imbecile, & idiotic*. London: Longmans, Green & Co., 1866.

Dunn, L. M. *Peabody Picture Vocabulary Test manual*. Minneapolis: American Guidance Service, 1959.

Dunn, L. M. *Expanded manual for the Peabody Picture Vocabulary Test*. Minneapolis: American Guidance Service, 1965.

Dunn, L. M., & Brooks, S. T. Peabody Picture Vocabulary Test performance of educable mentally retarded children. *Training School Bulletin*, 1960, **57**, 35–40.

Dunn, L. M., & Harley, R. K. Comparability of Peabody, Ammons, Van Alstyne, and Columbia test scores with cerebral palsied children. *Exceptional Children*, 1959, **26**, 70–74.

Dunn, L. M., & Hottel, J. V. Peabody Picture Vocabulary Test performance of trainable mentally retarded children. *American Journal of Mental Deficiency,* 1961, **65,** 448–452.

Dunn, L. M., & Vergason, G. A. Effects of illustration size on test performance. Nashville, Tenn.: George Peabody College for Teachers, *Peabody Papers in Human Development,* 1964, 2(3), 1–7.

Dunsdon, M. I. *The educability of cerebral palsied children.* London: Newnes Educational Company, 1952.

Dunsdon, M. I. A comparison of Terman Merrill scale test responses among large samples of normal, maladjusted and backward children. *Journal of Mental Science,* 1953, **99,** 720–731.

Earhart, R. H., & Warren, S. A. Long term constancy of Binet IQ in retardation. *Training School Bulletin,* 1964, **61,** 109–115.

Earl, C. J. C. *Subnormal personalities.* London: Baillière, Tindall and Cox, 1961.

Ebbinghaus, H. Über eine neue Methode zur Prüfung geistiger Fähigkeiten und ihre Anwendung bei Schulkindern. *Zeitschrift für Angewandte Psychologie,* 1897, **13,** 401–459.

Ebel, R. L. The social consequences of educational testing. *School and Society,* 1964, **92,** 331–334.

Edwards, A. J. Using vocabulary as a measure of general ability. *Personnel and Guidance Journal,* 1963, **42,** 153–154.

Eells, K., Davis, A., Havighurst, R. J., Herrick, V. E., & Tyler, R. W. *Intelligence and cultural differences.* Chicago: University of Chicago Press, 1951.

Egeland, B. Influence of examiner and examinee anxiety on WISC performance. *Psychological Reports,* 1967, **21,** 409–414.

Egeland, B. Examiner expectancy: Effects on the scoring of the WISC. *Psychology in the Schools,* 1969, **6,** 313–315.

Egeland, B., Di Nello, M., & Carr, D. L. The relationship of intelligence, visual-motor, psycholinguistic and reading-readiness skills with achievement. *Educational and Psychological Measurement,* 1970, **30,** 451–458.

Eichorn, D. H. Review of the Wechsler Preschool and Primary Scale of Intelligence. In O. K. Buros (Ed.), *The seventh mental measurements yearbook.* Highland Park, N.J.: Gryphon Press, 1972. Pp. 806–807.

Eisenberg, L. Psychiatric implications of brain damage in children. *Psychiatric Quarterly,* 1957, **31,** 72–92.

Eisenberg, L. Behavioral manifestations of cerebral damage. In H. G. Birch (Ed.), *Brain damage in children.* Baltimore: Williams & Wilkins, 1964. Pp. 61–73.

Eisenberg, L., Berlin, C. I., Dill, A., & Frank, S. Class and race effects on the intelligibility of monosyllables. *Child Development,* 1968, **39,** 1077–1089.

Eisenberg, L., & Kanner, L. Early infantile autism, 1943–55. *American Journal of Orthopsychiatry,* 1956, **26,** 556–566.

Eisenman, R., & McBride, J. W., Jr. "Balls" on the WISC. *Psychological Reports,* 1964, **14,** 266.

Eisenson, J. *Examining for aphasia.* New York: Psychological Corporation, 1954.

Ekren, U. W. The effect of experimenter knowledge of a subject's scholastic standing on the performance of a reasoning task. Unpublished master's thesis, Marquette University, 1962.

Ekstein, R., Bryant, K., & Friedman, S. W. Childhood schizophrenia and allied conditions. In L. Bellak (Ed.), *Schizophrenia.* New York: Logos Press, 1958. Pp. 555–693.

Ekwall, E. E. *The use of WISC subtest profiles in the diagnosis of reading difficulties.* (Doctoral dissertation, University of Arizona) Ann Arbor, Mich.: University Microfilms, 1966. No. 66–10,207.

Elkind, D. Piagetian and psychometric conceptions of intelligence. *Harvard Educational Review,* 1969, **39,** 319–337.

Ellenberger, H. F. Cultural aspects of mental illness. *American Journal of Psychotherapy,* 1960, **14,** 158–173.

Ellenberger, H. F. *The discovery of the unconscious.* New York: Basic Books, 1970.

Elliott, R. N., Jr. Comparative study of the Pictorial Test of Intelligence and the Peabody Picture Vocabulary Test. *Psychological Reports,* 1969, **25,** 528–530.

Ellis, N. R. The stimulus trace and behavioral inadequacy. In N. R. Ellis (Ed.), *Handbook of mental deficiency.* New York: McGraw-Hill, 1963. Pp. 134–158.

Elwood, M. I. A statistical study of results of the Stanford Revision of the Binet-Simon scale with a selected group of Pittsburgh school children. Unpublished doctoral dissertation, University of Pittsburgh, 1934.

Engel, M. Some parameters of the psychological evaluation of children. *Archives of General Psychiatry,* 1960, **2,** 593–605.

English, R. A., & Kidder, J. W. Note on relationships among mental ability scores, teacher's rankings, and rate of acquisition for four-year-old kindergarteners. *Psychological Reports,* 1969, **24,** 554.

Erikson, R. V. Abbreviated form of the WISC: A reevaluation. *Journal of Consulting Psychology,* 1967, **31,** 641.

Ernhart, C. B., Graham, F. K., Eichman, P. L., Marshall, J. M., & Thurston, D. Brain injury in the preschool child: Some developmental considerations: II. Comparison of brain injured and normal children. *Psychological Monographs,* 1963, **77**(11, Whole No. 574).

Escalona, S. K. The use of a battery of psychological tests for diagnosis of maladjustment in young children—a case report. *Transactions of the Kansas Academy of Science,* 1945, **48,** 218–223.

Esquirol, J. E. D. *Des maladies mentales considérées sous les rapports médical, hygiénique et médicolegal.* Paris: Baillière, 1838. 2 vols.

Estes, B. W. Relationships between the Otis, 1960 Stanford-Binet and WISC. *Journal of Clinical Psychology,* 1965, **21,** 296–297.

Estes, B. W., Curtin, M. E., DeBurger, R. A., & Denny, C. Relationships between 1960 Stanford-Binet, 1937 Stanford-Binet, WISC, Raven, and Draw-a-Man. *Journal of Consulting Psychology,* 1961, **25,** 388–391.

Estes, B. W., Kodman, F., & Akel, M. The validity of the Columbia Mental Maturity Scale. *Journal of Consulting Psychology,* 1959, **23,** 561.

Evans, L. A comparative study of the Wechsler Intelligence Scale for Children (Performance) and Raven's Progressive Matrices with deaf children. *Teacher of the Deaf,* 1966, **64,** 76–82.

Exner, J. E., Jr. Variations in WISC performances as influenced by differences in pretest rapport. *Journal of General Psychology,* 1966, **74,** 299–306.

Eysenck, H. J. Intelligence assessment: A theoretical and experimental approach. *British Journal of Educational Psychology,* 1967, **37,** 81–98.

Eysenck, H. J. *The IQ argument: Race, intelligence and education.* New York: Library Press, 1971.

Fagan, J., Broughton, E., Allen, M., Clark, B., & Emerson, P. Comparison of the Binet and WPPSI with lower-class five-year-olds. *Journal of Consulting and Clinical Psychology,* 1969, **33,** 607–609.

Fargo, G. A., Crowell, D. C., Noyes, M. H., Fuchigami, R. Y., Gordon, J. M., & Dunn-Rankin, P. Comparability of group television and individual administration of the Peabody Picture Vocabulary Test: Implications for screening. *Journal of Educational Psychology,* 1967, **58,** 137–140.

Fearing, F. S. The value of psychological tests in psychiatric diagnoses. *Journal of Abnormal Psychology,* 1919, **14,** 190–196.

Feifel, H. Qualitative differences in the vocabulary responses of normals and abnormals. *Genetic Psychology Monographs,* 1949, **39,** 151–204.

Feifel, H., & Lorge, L. Qualitative differences in the vocabulary responses of children. *Journal of Educational Psychology,* 1950, **41,** 1–18.

Feldhusen, J. F., & Klausmeier, H. J. Anxiety, intelligence, and achievement in children of low, average, and high intelligence. *Child Development,* 1962, **33,** 403–409.

Feldman, S. E., & Sullivan, D. S. Factors mediating the effects of enhanced rapport on children's performance. *Journal of Consulting and Clinical Psychology,* 1971, **36,** 302.

Fernald, P. S., & Wisser, R. E. Using WISC Verbal-Performance discrepancy to predict degree of acting out. *Journal of Clinical Psychology,* 1967, **23,** 92–93.

Field, J. G. Two types of tables for use with Wechsler's Intelligence Scales. *Journal of Clinical Psychology,* 1960, **16,** 3–7.

Finley, C., & Thompson, J. Sex differences in intelligence of educable mentally retarded children. *California Journal of Educational Research,* 1959, **10,** 167–170.

Fischer, C. T. The testee as co-evaluator. *Journal of Counseling Psychology,* 1970, **17,** 70–76.

Fischer, C. T. Contextual approach to assessment. *Community Mental Health Journal,* 1973, **9,** 38–45.

Fisher, G. M. The altitude quotient as an index of intellectual potential. II: WISC data for familial and undifferentiated mental retardates. *Journal of Psychological Studies,* 1961, **12,** 126–127.

Fisher, G. M. A note on the validity of the Wechsler Adult Intelligence Scale for mental retardates. *Journal of Consulting Psychology,* 1962, **26,** 391.

Fisher, G. M., Kilman, B. A., & Shotwell, A. M. Comparability of intelligence quotients of mental defectives on the Wechsler Adult Intelligence Scale and the 1960 revision of the Stanford-Binet. *Journal of Consulting Psychology,* 1961, **25,** 192–195.

Fisher, G. M., & Parsons, P. A. The effect of intellectual level on the rate of false positive organic diagnoses from the Hewson and Adolescent ratios. *Journal of Clinical Psychology,* 1962, **18,** 125–126.

Fiske, D. W. The subject reacts to tests. *American Psychologist,* 1967, **22,** 287–296.

Fitch, M. J. *Verbal and performance test scores in bilingual children.* (Doctoral dissertation, Colorado State College) Ann Arbor, Mich.: University Microfilms, 1966. No. 66–12,168.

Fitzgerald, B. J., Pasewark, R. A., & Gloeckler, T. Use of the Peabody Picture Vocabulary Test with the educationally handicapped. *Journal of School Psychology,* 1970, **8,** 296–300.

Flanagan, J. C. Review of *Measuring Intelligence* by Terman and Merrill. *Harvard Educational Review,* 1938, **8,** 130–133.

Flavell, J. H. *The developmental psychology of Jean Piaget.* Princeton, N.J.: Van Nostrand, 1963.

Fleming, E. S., & Anttonen, R. G. Teacher expectancy or My Fair Lady. *American Educational Research Journal,* 1971, **8,** 241–252.

Forrester, B. J., & Klaus, R. A. The effect of race of the examiner on intelligence test scores of Negro kindergarten children. Nashville, Tenn.: George Peabody College for Teachers, *Peabody Papers in Human Development,* 1964, **2**(7), 1–7.

Foster, A. Writing psychological reports. *Journal of Clinical Psychology,* 1951, **7,** 195.

Foster, J. B. Cited by J. F. Jastak & S. R. Jastak, *The Wide Range Achievement Test manual.* (Rev. ed.) Wilmington, Del.: Guidance Associates, 1965.

Frandsen, A. N., & Higginson, J. B. The Stanford-Binet and the Wechsler Intelligence Scale for Children. *Journal of Consulting Psychology,* 1951, **15,** 236–238.

Frandsen, A. N., McCullough, B. R., & Stone, D. R. Serial versus consecutive order administration of the Stanford-Binet Intelligence Scales. *Journal of Consulting Psychology,* 1950, **14,** 316–320.

Fraser, E. D. Review of the Wechsler Intelligence Scale for Children. In O. K. Buros (Ed.), *The fifth mental measurements yearbook.* Highland Park, N.J.: Gryphon Press, 1959. Pp. 558–559.

Fraser, E. D. Review of the Stanford-Binet Intelligence Scale, third revision. In O. K. Buros (Ed.), *The sixth mental measurements yearbook.* Highland Park, N.J.: Gryphon Press, 1965. Pp. 830–831.

Freeman, F. S. *Theory and practice of psychological testing.* (3rd ed.) New York: Holt, Rinehart and Winston, 1962.

Freides, D. Review of the Stanford-Binet Intelligence Scale, third revision. In O. K. Buros (Ed.), *The seventh mental measurements yearbook.* Highland Park, N.J.: Gryphon Press, 1972. Pp. 772–773.

French, J. L. *Manual: Pictorial Test of Intelligence.* Boston: Houghton Mifflin, 1964.

Friedman, R. The reliability of the Wechsler Intelligence Scale for Children in a group of mentally retarded children. *Journal of Clinical Psychology,* 1970, **26,** 181–182.

Fromm, E. Projective aspects of intelligence testing. In A. I. Rabin & M. R. Haworth (Eds.), *Projective techniques with children.* New York: Grune & Stratton, 1960. Pp. 225–236.

Fromm, E., Hartman, L. D., & Marschak, M. A contribution to a dynamic theory of intelligence testing of children. *Journal of Clinical and Experimental Psychopathology,* 1954, **15,** 73–95.

Fromm, E., Hartman, L. D., & Marschak, M. Children's intelligence tests as a measure of dynamic personality functioning. *American Journal of Orthopsychiatry,* 1957, **27,** 134–144.

Frost, B. P. An application of the method of extreme deviations to the Wechsler Intelligence Scale for Children. *Journal of Clinical Psychology,* 1960, **16,** 420.

Frost, B. P., & Frost, R. The pattern of WISC scores in a group of juvenile sociopaths. *Journal of Clinical Psychology,* 1962, **18,** 354–355.

Gage, G. E., & Naumann, T. F. Correlation of the Peabody Picture Vocabulary Test and the Wechsler Intelligence Scale for Children. *Journal of Educational Research,* 1965, **58,** 466–468.

Gainer, W. L. The ability of the WISC subtests to discriminate between boys and girls classified as educable mentally retarded. *California Journal of Educational Research,* 1965, **16,** 85–92.

Gallagher, J. J. A comparison of brain-injured and non-brain-injured mentally retarded children on several psychological variables. *Monographs of the Society for Research in Child Development,* 1957, **22**(2, Whole No. 65).

Gallagher, J. J. *The tutoring of brain-injured mentally retarded children.* Springfield, Ill.: Charles C Thomas, 1960.

Gallagher, J. J., Benoit, E. P., & Boyd, H. F. Measures of intelligence in brain damaged children. *Journal of Clinical Psychology,* 1956, **12,** 69–72.

Gallagher, J. J., & Moss, J. W. New concepts of intelligence and their effect on exceptional children. *Exceptional Children,* 1963, **30,** 1–5.

Galvan, R. R. *Bilingualism as it relates to intelligence test scores and school achievement among culturally deprived Spanish-American children.* (Doctoral dissertation, East Texas State University) Ann Arbor, Mich.: University Microfilms, 1967. No. 68–1131.

Garfield, S. L. Problems in the psychological evaluation of the subnormal individual. *American Journal of Mental Deficiency,* 1959, **64,** 467–471.

Garfield, S. L. Abnormal behavior and mental deficiency. In N. R. Ellis (Ed.), *Handbook of mental deficiency.* New York: McGraw-Hill, 1963. Pp. 574–601.

Garfield, S. L., & Affleck, D. C. A study of individuals commited to a state home for the retarded who were later released as not mentally defective. *American Journal of Mental Deficiency,* 1960, **64,** 907–915.

Garfield, S. L., Heine, R. W., & Leventhal, M. An evaluation of psychological reports in a clinical setting. *Journal of Consulting Psychology,* 1954, **18,** 281–286.

Garner, A. M. Intelligence testing and clinical practice. In I. A. Berg & L. A. Pennington (Eds.), *An introduction to clinical psychology.* (3rd ed.) New York: Ronald Press, 1966. Pp. 67–105.

Garrett, J. Comparison of the Peabody Picture Vocabulary Test and Wechsler Intelligence Scale for Children. Unpublished master's thesis, George Peabody College for Teachers, 1959.

Garrett, J. F. Cerebral palsy. In J. F. Garrett (Ed.), *Psychological aspects of physical disability.* Washington, D.C.: U.S. Government Printing Office, 1952. Pp. 60–67.

Garth, T. R. The problem of racial psychology. *Journal of Abnormal and Social Psychology,* 1922, **17,** 215–219.

Gayton, W. F. An evaluation of two short forms of the Stanford-Binet, Form L-M, for use with a child guidance population. *Psychological Reports,* 1971, **28,** 355–357.

Gayton, W. F., Wilson, W. T., & Bernstein, S. An evaluation of an abbreviated form of the WISC. *Journal of Clinical Psychology,* 1970, **26,** 466–468.

Gehman, I. H., & Matyas, R. P. Stability of the WISC and Binet tests. *Journal of Consulting Psychology,* 1956, **20,** 150–152.

Geloff, M. Comparison of systems of classification relating degree of retardation to measured intelligence. *American Journal of Mental Deficiency,* 1963, **68,** 297–317.

Giannell, A. S., & Freeburne, C. M. The comparative validity of the WAIS and the Stanford-Binet with college freshmen. *Educational and Psychological Measurement,* 1963, **23,** 557–567.

Gibbs, N. Some learning difficulties of cerebral palsied children. *Spastics Quarterly,* 1959, **8,** 21–23.

Giebink, J. W., & Marden, M. L. Verbal expression, verbal fluency, and grammar related to cultural experience. *Psychology in the Schools,* 1968, **5,** 365–368.

Gilbert, J. G., & Rubin, E. J. Evaluating the intellect of blind children. *New Outlook for the Blind,* 1965, **59,** 238–240.

Gillingham, W. H. *An investigation of examiner influence on Wechsler Intelligence Scale for Children scores.* (Doctoral dissertation, Michigan State University) Ann Arbor, Mich.: University Microfilms, 1970. No. 70-20,458.

Ginsburg, R. E. *An examination of the relationship between teacher expectancies and students' performance on a test of intellectual functioning.* (Doctoral dissertation, University of Utah) Ann Arbor, Mich.: University Microfilms, 1970. No. 71–922.

Gittleman, M., & Birch, H. G. Childhood schizophrenia: Intellect, neurologic status, perinatal risk, prognosis, and family pathology. *Archives of General Psychiatry,* 1967, **17,** 16–25.

Glasser, A. J., & Zimmerman, I. L. *Clinical interpretation of the Wechsler Intelligence Scale for Children.* New York: Grune & Stratton, 1967.

Goddard, H. H. The Binet and Simon tests of intellectual capacity. *Training School,* 1908, **5,** 3–9.

Goddard, H. H. A measuring scale of intelligence. *Training School,* 1910, **6,** 146–155.

Goddard, H. H. A revision of the Binet scale. *Training School,* 1911, **8,** 56–62.

Goffeney, B., Henderson, N. B., & Butler, B. V. Negro-white, male-female eight-month developmental scores compared with seven-year WISC and Bender Test scores. *Child Development,* 1971, **42,** 595–604.

Goldfarb, W. *Childhood schizophrenia.* Cambridge, Mass.: Harvard University Press, 1961.

Goldfarb, W. Anxiety and conflict in schizophrenic children. In J. H. Masserman (Ed.), *Childhood and adolescence.* New York: Grune & Stratton, 1969. Pp. 151–162.

Goldfarb, W. Childhood psychosis. In P. H. Mussen (Ed.), *Carmichael's manual of child psychology.* (3rd ed.) New York: Wiley, 1970. Pp. 765–830.

Goldfarb, W., Goldfarb, N., & Pollack, R. C. Changes in IQ of schizophrenic children during residential treatment. *Archives of General Psychiatry,* 1969, **21,** 673–690.

Goldman, H. Psychological testing of blind children. *American Foundation for the Blind, Research Bulletin,* 1970, No. 21, 77–90.

Goldman, L. *Using tests in counseling.* New York: Appleton-Century-Crofts, 1961.

Goldman, L. Position statement on psychological assessment and public policy. *American Psychologist,* 1970, **25,** 874.

Goldman, L. Psychological secrecy and openness in the public schools. In S. L. Brodsky (Chm.), Shared results and open files with the client: Professional irresponsibility or effective involvement? Symposium presented at the American Psychological Association, Washington, D.C., September 1971.

Goodenough, D. R., & Karp, S. A. Field dependence and intellectual functioning. *Journal of Abnormal and Social Psychology,* 1961, **63,** 241–246.

Goodenough, F. L. Review of Terman and Merrill's *Measuring Intelligence. Psychological Bulletin,* 1937, **34,** 605–609.

Goodenough, F. L. The use of free association in the objective measurement of personality. In *Studies in personality contributed in honor of Lewis M. Terman.* New York: McGraw-Hill, 1942. Pp. 87–103.

Goodenough, F. L. *Mental testing.* New York: Rinehart and Company, 1949.

Gordon, L. V., & Durea, M. A. The effect of discouragement on the Revised Stanford-Binet Scale. *Journal of Genetic Psychology,* 1948, **73,** 201–207.

Goslin, D. A. *The search for ability: Standardized testing in social perspective.* New York: Russell Sage Foundation, 1963.

Goslin, D. A. The social impact of testing. *Personnel and Guidance Journal,* 1967, **45,** 676–682.

Gough, H. G., & Domino, G. The D 48 Test as a measure of general ability among grade school children. *Journal of Consulting Psychology,* 1963, **27,** 344–349.

Gozali, J., & Meyen, E. L. The influence of the teacher expectancy phenomenon on the academic performances of educable mentally retarded pupils in special classes. *Journal of Special Education,* 1970, **4,** 417–424.

Graham, E. E. Wechsler-Bellevue and WISC scattergrams of unsuccessful readers. *Journal of Consulting Psychology,* 1952, **16,** 268–271.

Graham, E. E., & Shapiro, E. Use of the Performance Scale of the Wechsler Intelligence Scale for Children with the deaf child. *Journal of Consulting Psychology,* 1953, **17,** 396–398.

Graham, F. K., Ernhart, C. B., Thurston, D., & Craft, M. Development three years after perinatal anoxia and other potentially damaging newborn experiences. *Psychological Monographs,* 1962, **76**(3, Whole No. 522).

Graham, P., & Rutter, M. Organic brain dysfunction and child psychiatric disorder. *British Medical Journal,* 1968, **3,** 695–700.

Granick, S. Intellectual performance as related to emotional instability in children. *Journal of Abnormal and Social Psychology,* 1955, **51,** 653–656.

Graubard, P. S. The use of the Peabody Picture Vocabulary Test in the prediction and assessment of reading disability in disturbed children. *Journal of Educational Research,* 1967, **61,** 3–5.

Grayson, H. M., & Tolman, R. S. A semantic study of concepts of clinical psychologists and psychiatrists. *Journal of Abnormal and Social Psychology,* 1950, **45,** 216–231.

Green, F. The examiner as a possible source of constant error in intelligence testing. In R. L. Cromwell (Ed.), *Abstracts of Peabody studies in mental retardation.* Vol. 2. Nashville: George Peabody College for Teachers, 1960–62. (Abstract No. 36)

Green, H. B., Jr. *A statistical comparison of the Wechsler Intelligence Scale for Children and the Wechsler Adult Intelligence Scale.* (Doctoral dissertation, University of Virginia) Ann Arbor, Mich.: University Microfilms, 1965. No. 66–3187.

Greene, E. B. *Measurements of human behavior.* New York: Odyssey Press, 1941.

Grimaldi, J. *A factor analytic study of WISC patterns in children with CNS dysfunction.* (Doctoral dissertation, St. Johns University) Ann Arbor, Mich.: University Microfilms, 1970. No. 70–25,615.

Gross, F. P., & Farling, W. H. An analysis of case loads of school psychologists. *Psychology in the Schools,* 1969, **6,** 98–99.

Guilford, J. P. The structure of intellect. *Psychological Bulletin,* 1956, **53,** 267–293.

Guilford, J. P. *The nature of human intelligence.* New York: McGraw-Hill, 1967.

Gunzburg, H. C. Clinical mental testing. In C. J. C. Earl (Ed.), *Subnormal personalities.* London: Baillière, Tindall and Cox, 1961. Pp. 243–255.

Gunzburg, H. C. Subnormal adults. In P. Mittler (Ed.), *The psychological assessment of mental and physical handicaps.* London: Methuen, 1970. Pp. 289–317.

Haeussermann, E. *Developmental potential of preschool children.* New York: Grune & Stratton, 1958.

Hafner, A. J., & Kaplan, A. M. Children's manifest anxiety and intelligence. *Child Development,* 1959, **30,** 269–271.

Hafner, A. J., Pollie, D. M., & Wapner, I. The relationship between the CMAS and WISC functioning. *Journal of Clinical Psychology,* 1960, **16,** 322–323.

Hagen, E. P. A factor analysis of the Wechsler Intelligence Scale for Children. *Dissertation Abstracts,* 1952, **12,** 722.

Hagin, R. A., Silver, A. A., & Corwin, C. J. Clinical-diagnostic use of the WPPSI in predicting learning disabilities in grade one. In R. S. Morrow (Chm.), Diagnostic and educational application of the Wechsler Preschool and Primary Scale of Intelligence (WPPSI). Symposium presented at the American Psychological Association, Miami, September 1970.

Hall, B. F. The trial of William Freeman. *American Journal of Insanity,* 1848, **5**(2), 34–60.

Hall, J. C. *A comparative study of selected measures of intelligence as predictors of first-grade reading achievement in a culturally disadvantaged population.* (Doctoral dissertation, Temple University) Ann Arbor, Mich.: University Microfilms, 1969. No. 70–16,669.

Hall, J. C., & Chansky, N. M. Relationships between selected ability and achievement tests in an economically disadvantaged Negro sample. *Psychological Reports,* 1971, **28,** 741–742.

Hall, L. P., & LaDriere, L. Patterns of performance on WISC Similarities in emotionally disturbed and brain-damaged children. *Journal of Consulting and Clinical Psychology,* 1969, **33,** 357–364.

Halpern, F. C. The individual psychological examination. In M. G. Gottsegen & G. B. Gottsegen (Eds.), *Professional school psychology.* Vol. 1. New York: Grune & Stratton, 1960. Pp. 100–112.

Halpern, F. C. Clinicians must listen! *School Psychologist Newsletter,* 1971, **25**(2), 15–17.

Hammill, D. D. The Slosson Intelligence Test as a quick estimate of mental ability. *Journal of School Psychology,* 1969, **7**(4), 33–37.

Hammill, D. D., Crandell, J. M., Jr., & Colarusso, R. The Slosson Intelligence Test adapted for visually limited children. *Exceptional Children,* 1970, **36,** 535–536.

Hammill, D. D., & Irwin, O. C. Peabody Picture Vocabulary Test as a measure of intelligence for mentally subnormal children. *Training School Bulletin,* 1965, **62,** 126–131.

Hammill, D. D., & Irwin, O. C. Relations among measures of language of cerebral palsied and mentally retarded children. *Cerebral Palsy Journal,* 1966, **27**(1), 8–9.

Hammond, K. R., & Allen, J. M. *Writing clinical reports.* New York: Prentice-Hall, 1953.

Handler, L., Gerston, A., & Handler, B. Suggestions for improved psychologist-teacher communication. *Psychology in the Schools,* 1965, **2,** 77–81.

Hannon, J. E., & Kicklighter, R. H. WAIS versus WISC in adolescents. *Journal of Consulting and Clinical Psychology,* 1970, **35,** 179–182.

Hanvik, L. J. The Goodenough Test as a measure of intelligence in child psychiatric patients. *Journal of Clinical Psychology,* 1953, **9,** 71–72.

Harlow, J. E., Jr., Price, A. C., Tatham, L. J., & Davidson, J. F. Preliminary study of comparison between Wechsler Intelligence Scale for Children and Form L of Revised Stanford Binet Scale at three age levels. *Journal of Clinical Psychology,* 1957, **13,** 72–73.

Harriman, P. L. Irregularity of successes on the 1937 Stanford Revision. *Journal of Consulting Psychology,* 1939, **3,** 83–85.

Harris, A. J., & Shakow, D. The clinical significance of numerical measures of scatter on the Stanford-Binet. *Psychological Bulletin,* 1937, **34,** 134–150.

Harris, R. A comparative study of two groups of boys, delinquent and non-delinquent, on the basis of their Wechsler and Rorschach test performances. *Bulletin of the Maritime Psychological Association,* 1957, **6,** 21–28.

Hartlage, L. C. Differential diagnosis of dyslexia, minimal brain damage and emotional disturbances in children. *Psychology in the Schools,* 1970, **7,** 403–406.

Hartlage, L. C., & Green, J. B. EEG abnormalities and WISC subtest differences. *Journal of Clinical Psychology,* 1972, **28,** 170–171.

Hartlage, L. C., & Merck, K. H. Increasing the relevance of psychological reports. *Journal of Clinical Psychology,* 1971, **27,** 459–460.

Hartman, B. *Comparative investigation of the Peabody Picture Vocabulary Test with three etiologic groups of institutionalized mentally retarded students.* (Doctoral dissertation, Indiana University) Ann Arbor, Mich.: University Microfilms, 1962. No. 62–5043.

Hartsough, W. R., & Fontana, A. F. Persistence of ethnic stereotypes and the relative importance of positive and negative stereotyping for association preferences. *Psychological Reports,* 1970, **27,** 723–731.

Hata, Y., Tsudzuki, A., Kuze, T., & Emi, Y. Relationships between the tester and the subject as a factor influencing on the intelligence test score: I. *Japanese Journal of Psychology,* 1958, **29,** 99–104.

Havelkova, M. Follow-up study of 71 children diagnosed as psychotic in preschool age. *American Journal of Orthopsychiatry,* 1968, **38,** 846–857.

Havighurst, R. J., & Janke, L. L. Relations between ability and social status in a midwestern community. I. Ten-year-old children. *Journal of Educational Psychology,* 1944, **35,** 357–368.

Haworth, M. R. Review of the Revised Stanford-Binet Scale. In O. K. Buros (Ed.), *The fifth mental measurements yearbook.* Highland Park, N.J.: Gryphon Press, 1959. Pp. 546–547.

Haworth, M. R. *The CAT: Facts about fantasy.* New York: Grune & Stratton, 1966.

Hebb, D. O. The effect of early and late brain injury upon the test scores, and the nature of normal adult intelligence. *Proceedings of the American Philosophical Society,* 1942, **85,** 275–292.

Hebb, D. O. *A textbook of psychology.* (2nd ed.) Philadelphia: Saunders, 1966.

Heber, R. Modifications in the manual on terminology and classification in mental retardation. *American Journal of Mental Deficiency,* 1961, **65,** 499–500.

Hedger, M. F. An analysis of three picture vocabulary tests for use with the deaf. In J. Rosenstein & W. H. MacGinitie (Eds.), *Research studies on the psycholinguistic behavior of deaf children.* CEC Research Monograph, Series B, No. B-2, 1965, 12–19.

Heidbreder, E. *Seven psychologies.* New York: Century, 1933.

Heilman, A. E. Appraisal of abilities of the cerebral palsied child. *American Journal of Mental Deficiency,* 1949, **53,** 606–609.

Heilman, A. E. Intelligence in cerebral palsy; a new interpretation of research studies. *Crippled Child,* 1952, **30**(2), 11–13, 28.

Henderson, N. B., Butler, B. V., & Clark, W. M., Jr. Relationships between selected perinatal variables and seven-year intelligence. *Proceedings of the 79th Annual Convention of the American Psychological Association,* 1971, **6,** 139–140.

Henderson, N. B., Butler, B. V., & Goffeney, B. Effectiveness of the WISC and Bender-Gestalt Test in predicting arithmetic and reading achievement for white and nonwhite children. *Journal of Clinical Psychology,* 1969, **25,** 268–271.

Hendriks, J. *De kwalitatieve analyse van de intelligentie-test van Terman en Merrill.* (The qualitative analysis of the intelligence test of Terman and Merrill.) Amsterdam: N. V. Standaardboek-handel, 1954.

Henning, J. J., & Levy, R. H. Verbal-Performance IQ differences of white and Negro delinquents on the WISC and WAIS. *Journal of Clinical Psychology,* 1967, **23,** 164–168.

Herbert, M. The concept and testing of brain-damage in children: A review. *Journal of Child Psychology and Psychiatry,* 1964, **5,** 197–216.

Herman, D. O. A study of sex differences on the Wechsler Preschool and Primary Scale of Intelligence. *Proceedings of the 76th Annual Convention of the American Psychological Association,* 1968, **3,** 455–456.

Herrell, J. M., & Golland, J. H. Should WISC subjects explain Picture Arrangement stories? *Journal of Consulting and Clinical Psychology,* 1969, **33,** 761–762.

Herring, J. P. *Herring revision of the Binet-Simon tests.* Yonkers-on-Hudson, N.Y.: World Book, 1922.

Hersh, J. B. Effects of referral information on testers. *Journal of Consulting and Clinical Psychology,* 1971, **37,** 116–122.

Hertzig, M. E., & Birch, H. G. Longitudinal course of measured intelligence in preschool children of different social and ethnic backgrounds. *American Journal of Orthopsychiatry,* 1971, **41,** 416–426.

Hertzig, M. E., Bortner, M., & Birch, H. G. Neurologic findings in children educationally designated as "brain-damaged." *American Journal of Orthopsychiatry,* 1969, **39,** 437–446.

Hewitt, P., & Massey, J. O. *Clinical clues from the WISC*. Palo Alto, Calif.: Consulting Psychologists Press, 1969.

Hewson, L. R. The Wechsler-Bellevue Scale and the Substitution Test as aids in neuropsychiatric diagnosis. *Journal of Nervous and Mental Disease,* 1949, **109,** 158–183, 246–266.

Higgins, C., & Sivers, C. H. A comparison of Stanford-Binet and Colored Raven Progressive Matrices IQs for children with low socioeconomic status. *Journal of Consulting Psychology,* 1958, **22,** 465–468.

Hiler, E. W., & Nesvig, D. Changes in intellectual functions of children in a psychiatric hospital. *Journal of Consulting Psychology,* 1961, **25,** 288–292.

Hilgard, E. R. *Introduction to psychology.* (2nd ed.) New York: Harcourt, Brace, 1957.

Hill, K. T., & Sarason, S. B. The relation of test anxiety and defensiveness to test and school performance over the elementary-school years: A further longitudinal study. *Monographs of the Society for Research in Child Development,* 1966, **31**(2, Whole No. 104).

Himelstein, P. Research with the Stanford-Binet, Form L-M: The first five years. *Psychological Bulletin,* 1966, **65,** 156–164.

Himelstein, P. Use of the Stanford-Binet, Form LM, with retardates: A review of recent research. *American Journal of Mental Deficiency,* 1968, **72,** 691–699.

Himelstein, P. Review of the Pictorial Test of Intelligence. In O. K. Buros (Ed.), *The seventh mental measurements yearbook.* Highland Park, N.J.: Gryphon Press, 1972. Pp. 748–749. (a)

Himelstein, P. Review of the Slosson Intelligence Test. In O. K. Buros (Ed.), *The seventh mental measurements yearbook.* Highland Park, N.J.: Gryphon Press, 1972. Pp. 765–766. (b)

Himelstein, P., & Herndon, J. D. Comparison of the WISC and Peabody Picture Vocabulary Test with emotionally disturbed children. *Journal of Clinical Psychology,* 1962, **18,** 82.

Hinckley, A. C. The Binet tests applied to individuals over twelve years of age. *Journal of Educational Psychology,* 1915, **6,** 43–58.

Hine, W. D. The abilities of partially hearing children. *British Journal of Educational Psychology,* 1970, **40,** 171–178.

Hirsch, E. A. The adaptive significance of commonly described behavior of the mentally retarded. *American Journal of Mental Deficiency,* 1959, **63,** 639–646.

Hirsch, J. Behavior-genetic analysis and its biosocial consequences. *Seminars in Psychiatry,* 1970, **2**(1), 89–105.

Hirschenfang, S. Further studies on the Columbia Mental Maturity Scale (CMMS) and Revised Stanford Binet (L) in children with speech disorders. *Journal of Clinical Psychology,* 1961, **17,** 171.

Hirschenfang, S., Jaramillo, S., & Benton, J. G. Comparison of scores on the Revised Stanford-Binet (L), Columbia Mental Maturity Scale (CMMS) and Goodenough Draw-a-Man Test of children with neurological disorders. *Psychological Reports,* 1966, **19,** 15–16.

Hirst, L. S. The usefulness of a two-way analysis of WISC sub-tests in the diagnosis of remedial reading problems. *Journal of Experimental Education,* 1960, **29,** 153–160.

Hite, L. Analysis of reliability and validity of the Wechsler Intelligence Scale for Children. Unpublished doctoral dissertation, Western Reserve University, 1953.

Hoakley, Z. P., & Frazeur, H. A. Significance of psychological test results of exogenous and endogenous children. *American Journal of Mental Deficiency,* 1945, **50,** 263–271.

Hofstaetter, P. R. The changing composition of "intelligence": A study in T-technique. *Journal of Genetic Psychology,* 1954, **85,** 159–164.

Holland, G. A. A comparison of the WISC and Stanford-Binet IQ's of normal children. *Journal of Consulting Psychology,* 1953, **17,** 147–152.

Holland, W. R. Language barrier as an educational problem of Spanish-speaking children. *Exceptional Children,* 1960, **27,** 42–50.

Holroyd, J. When WISC Verbal IQ is low. *Journal of Clinical Psychology,* 1968, **24,** 457.

Holroyd, J., & Wright, F. Neurological implications of WISC Verbal-Performance discrepancies in a psychiatric setting. *Journal of Consulting Psychology,* 1965, **29,** 206–212.

Holt, R. R. Diagnostic testing: Present status and future prospects. *Journal of Nervous and Mental Disease,* 1967, **144,** 444–465.

Holtzman, W. H. The changing world of mental measurement and its social significance. *American Psychologist,* 1971, **26,** 546–553.

Holzberg, J. D., Alessi, S. L., & Wexler, M. Psychological case reporting at psychiatric staff conferences. *Journal of Consulting Psychology,* 1951, **15,** 425–429.

Honzik, M. P. Environmental correlates of mental growth: Prediction from the family setting at 21 months. *Child Development,* 1967, **38,** 337–364.

Honzik, M. P., Macfarlane, J. W., & Allen, L. The stability of mental test performance between two and eighteen years. *Journal of Experimental Education,* 1948, **17,** 309–324.

Hopkins, K. D., & McGuire, L. Mental measurement of the blind: The validity of the Wechsler Intelligence Scale for Children. *International Journal for the Education of the Blind,* 1966, **15,** 65–73.

Hopkins, K. D., & McGuire, L. IQ constancy and the blind child. *International Journal for the Education of the Blind,* 1967, **16,** 113–114.

Hoskins, R. G., & Jellinek, E. M. The schizophrenic personality with special regard to psychologic and organic concomitants. *Association for Research in Nervous and Mental Disease Proceedings,* 1933, **14,** 211–233.

Houston, C., & Otto, W. Poor readers' functioning on the WISC, Slosson Intelligence Test and Quick Test. *Journal of Educational Research,* 1968, **62,** 157–159.

Howard, J. L., & Plant, W. T. Psychometric evaluation of an Operation Headstart program. *Journal of Genetic Psychology,* 1967, **111,** 281–288.

Huber, J. T. *Report writing in psychology and psychiatry.* New York: Harper, 1961.

Hubschman, E., Polizzotto, E. A., & Kaliski, M. S. Performance of institutionalized retardates on the PPVT and two editions of the ITPA. *American Journal of Mental Deficiency,* 1970, **74,** 579–580.

Hudson, L. Intelligence, race, and the selection of data. *Race,* 1971, **12,** 283–292.

Huelsman, C. B., Jr. The WISC subtest syndrome for disabled readers. *Perceptual and Motor Skills,* 1970, **30,** 535–550.

Huey, E. B. The Binet scale for measuring intelligence and retardation. *Journal of Educational Psychology,* 1910, **1,** 435–444.

Hughes, R. B., & Lessler, K. A comparison of WISC and Peabody scores of Negro and white rural school children. *American Journal of Mental Deficiency,* 1965, **69,** 877–880.

Humphreys, L. G., & Dachler, H. P. Jensen's theory of intelligence. *Journal of Educational Psychology,* 1969, **60,** 419–426.

Hunt, D. The comparative performance of a ten-year-old group of children on the Wechsler Intelligence Scale for Children and the Revised Stanford-Binet Scale of Intelligence, Form L-M. Unpublished master's thesis, University of Saskatchewan, 1961.

Hunt, J. McV. *Intelligence and experience.* New York: Ronald Press, 1961.

Hunt, J. McV. Has compensatory education failed? Has it been attempted? *Harvard Educational Review,* 1969, **39,** 278–300.

Hunt, J. McV., & Cofer, C. N. Psychological deficit. In J. McV. Hunt (Ed.), *Personality and the behavior disorders.* Vol. II. New York: Ronald Press, 1944. Pp. 971–1032.

Hunt, J. V. Review of the Slosson Intelligence Test. In O. K. Buros (Ed.), *The seventh mental measurements yearbook.* Highland Park, N.J.: Gryphon Press, 1972. Pp. 766–767.

Hutt, M. L. A clinical study of "consecutive" and "adaptive" testing with the Revised Stanford-Binet. *Journal of Consulting Psychology,* 1947, **11,** 93–103.

Hutt, M. L., & Gibby, R. G. *The mentally retarded child.* (2nd ed.) Boston: Allyn and Bacon, 1965.

Ireton, H., Thwing, E., & Gravem, H. Infant mental development and neurological status, family socioeconomic status, and intelligence at age four. *Child Development,* 1970, **41,** 937–945.

Irwin, O. C. A language test for use with cerebral palsied children. *Cerebral Palsy Journal,* 1966, **27**(5), 6–8.

Irwin, O. C., & Hammill, D. D. An abstraction test for use with cerebral palsied children. *Cerebral Palsy Review,* 1964, **25**(4), 3–9.

Irwin, O. C., & Korst, J. W. Correlations among five speech tests and the WISC Verbal Scale. *Cerebral Palsy Journal,* 1967, **28**(5), 9–11.

Ivanoff, J. M., & Tempero, H. E. Effectiveness of the Peabody Picture Vocabulary Test with seventh-grade pupils. *Journal of Educational Research,* 1965, **58,** 412–415.

Jackson, M. A. The factor analysis of the Wechsler Scale. I. *British Journal of Statistical Psychology,* 1960, **13,** 79–82.

Janke, L. L., & Havighurst, R. J. Relations between ability and social status in a midwestern community. II. Sixteen-year-old boys and girls. *Journal of Educational Psychology,* 1945, **36,** 499–509.

Jastak, J. F. The endogenous slow learner. *American Journal of Mental Deficiency,* 1950, **55,** 269–274.

Jastak, J. F. Intelligence tests and personality structure. In J. Zubin & G. A. Jervis (Eds.), *Psychopathology of mental development.* New York: Grune & Stratton, 1967. Pp. 282–297.

Jastak, J. F., & Jastak, S. R. Short forms of the WAIS and WISC Vocabulary subtests. *Journal of Clinical Psychology,* 1964, **20,** 167–199.

Jenkin, N., Spivack, G., Levine, M., & Savage, W. Wechsler profiles and academic achievement in emotionally disturbed boys. *Journal of Consulting Psychology,* 1964, **28,** 290.

Jenkins, J. J., & Paterson, D. G. (Eds.) *Studies in individual differences.* New York: Appleton-Century-Crofts, 1961.

Jensen, A. R. How much can we boost IQ and scholastic achievement? *Harvard Educational Review,* 1969, **39,** 1–123.

Jensen, A. R. A theory of primary and secondary familial mental retardation. In N. R. Ellis (Ed.), *International review of research in mental retardation.* Vol. 4. New York: Academic Press, 1970. Pp. 33–105. (a)

Jensen, A. R. Another look at culture-fair testing. In J. Hellmuth (Ed.), *Disadvantaged child.* Vol. 3. New York: Brunner/Mazel, 1970. Pp. 53–101. (b)

Jensen, A. R. Can we and should we study race differences? In J. Hellmuth (Ed.), *Disadvantaged child.* Vol. 3. New York: Brunner/Mazel, 1970. Pp. 124–157. (c)

Jeruchimowicz, R., Costello, J., & Bagur, J. S. Knowledge of action and object words: A comparison of lower- and middle-class Negro preschoolers. *Child Development,* 1971, **42,** 455–464.

Joesting, J., & Joesting, R. Comparison of scores on Quick Test and Stanford-Binet, Form L-M. *Psychological Reports,* 1971, **29,** 1178. (a)

Joesting, J., & Joesting, R. The Quick Test as a screening device in a welfare setting. *Psychological Reports,* 1971, **29,** 1289. (b)

John, V. P., & Goldstein, L. S. The social context of language acquisition. *Merrill-Palmer Quarterly,* 1964, **10,** 265–275.

Johnson, D. L., & Johnson, C. A. Comparison of four intelligence tests used with culturally disadvantaged children. *Psychological Reports,* 1971, **28,** 209–210.

Johnson, E. B. *Pygmalion in the testing setting: Nonverbal communication as a mediator of expectancy-fulfillment.* (Doctoral dissertation, University of Michigan) Ann Arbor, Mich.: University Microfilms, 1970. No. 71–15,190.

Johnson, G. O. Mental retardation and cerebral palsy. In W. M. Cruickshank (Ed.), *Cerebral palsy: Its individual and community problems.* (Rev. ed.) Syracuse, N.Y.: Syracuse University Press, 1966. Pp. 498–537.

Johnson, G. O., & Blake, K. A. Learning and performance of retarded and normal children. Syracuse University special. *Educational Rehabilitation Monographs,* 1960, No. 5.

Johnson, R. C. Prediction of independent functioning and of problem behavior from measures of IQ and SQ. *American Journal of Mental Deficiency,* 1970, **74,** 591–593.

Johnson, R. C., & Medinnus, G. R. *Child psychology: Behavior and development.* New York: Wiley, 1965.

Jones, C. T. Very bright and feeble-minded children: The study of qualitative differences. *Training School Bulletin,* 1919, **16,** 137–141, 155–164, 169–180.

Jones, H. E., Conrad, H. S., & Blanchard, M. B. Environmental handicap in mental test performance. *University of California Publication in Psychology,* 1932, **5,** 63–99.

Jones, L. V. A factor analysis of the Stanford-Binet at four age levels. *Psychometrika,* 1949, **14,** 299–331.

Jones, L. V. Primary abilities in the Stanford-Binet, age 13. *Journal of Genetic Psychology,* 1954, **84,** 125–147.

Jones, S. The Wechsler Intelligence Scale for Children applied to a sample of London primary school children. *British Journal of Educational Psychology,* 1962, **32,** 119–132.

Jongeward, P. A. A validity study of the Slosson Intelligence Test for use with educable mentally retarded students. *Journal of School Psychology,* 1969, **7**(4), 59–63.

Jordan, J. S. Reliability of Stanford-Binet intelligence quotients derived by student examiners. *Journal of Educational Research,* 1932, **26,** 295–301.

Jurjevich, R. An analysis of the altitude IQs of delinquent girls. *Journal of General Psychology,* 1963, **69,** 221–226.

Kagan, J. On cultural deprivation. In D. C. Glass (Ed.), *Environmental influences.* New York: Rockefeller University Press, 1968. Pp. 211–250.

Kagan, J. Inadequate evidence and illogical conclusions. *Harvard Educational Review,* 1969, **39,** 274–277.

Kagan, J. *Understanding children.* New York: Harcourt Brace Jovanovich, 1971.

Kagan, J., Rosman, B. L., Day, D., Albert, J., & Phillips, W. Information processing in the child: Significance of analytic and reflective attitudes. *Psychological Monographs,* 1964, **78**(1, Whole No. 578).

Kagan, J., Sontag, L. W., Baker, C. T., & Nelson, V. L. Personality and IQ change. *Journal of Abnormal and Social Psychology,* 1958, **56,** 261–266.

Kahn, T. C., & Giffen, M. B. *Psychological techniques in diagnosis and evaluation.* Elmsford, N.Y.: Pergamon Press, 1960.

Kaiser, M. D. *The Wechsler Intelligence Scale for Children as an instrument for diagnosing sociopathy.* (Doctoral dissertation, Florida State University) Ann Arbor, Mich.: University Microfilms, 1964. No. 64–10,571.

Kallos, G. L., Grabow, J. M., & Guarino, E. A. The WISC profile of disabled readers. *Personnel and Guidance Journal,* 1961, **39,** 476–478.

Kangas, J., & Bradway, K. P. Intelligence at middle age: A thirty-eight-year follow-up. *Developmental Psychology,* 1971, **5,** 333–337.

Kanner, L. Autistic disturbances of affective contact. *Nervous Child,* 1943, **2,** 217–250.

Kanner, L. *Child psychiatry.* (3rd ed.) Springfield, Ill.: Charles C Thomas, 1957.

Kanner, L. Emotionally disturbed children: A historical review. *Child Development,* 1962, **33,** 97–102.

Kanner, L. The children haven't read those books: Reflections on differential diagnosis. *Acta Paedopsychiatrica,* 1969, **36,** 2–11.

Kardos, M. S. A comparative study of the performance of twelve-year-old children on the WISC and the Revised Stanford-Binet, Form L, and the relationship of both to the California Achievement Tests. Unpublished master's thesis, Marywood College, 1954.

Kaspar, J. C., Throne, F. M., & Schulman, J. L. A study of the inter-judge reliability in scoring the responses of a group of mentally retarded boys to three WISC subscales. *Educational and Psychological Measurement,* 1968, **28,** 469–477.

Katz, E. A "Survey of Degree of Physical Handicap." *Cerebral Palsy Review,* 1954, **15**(11), 10–11.

Katz, E. Success on Stanford-Binet Intelligence Scale test items of children with cerebral palsy as compared with non-handicapped children. *Cerebral Palsy Review*, 1955, **16**(1), 18–19.

Katz, E. The pointing scale method: A modification of the Stanford-Binet procedure for use with cerebral palsied children. *American Journal of Mental Deficiency*, 1956, **60**, 838–842.

Kaufman, H. I., & Ivanoff, J. M. Evaluating the mentally retarded with the Peabody Picture Vocabulary Test. *American Journal of Mental Deficiency*, 1968, **73**, 396–398.

Kavajecz, L. G. *A study of results on the Wechsler Preschool and Primary Scale of Intelligence of inadequate readers*. (Doctoral dissertation, Colorado State College) Ann Arbor, Mich.: University Microfilms, 1969. No. 70–7135.

Keller, J. E. The relationship of auditory memory span to learning ability in high grade mentally retarded boys. *American Journal of Mental Deficiency*, 1957, **61**, 574–580.

Kendig, I., & Richmond, W. V. *Psychological studies in dementia praecox*. Ann Arbor, Mich.: Edwards, 1940.

Kennedy, W. A., Moon, H., Nelson, W., Lindner, R., & Turner, J. The ceiling of the new Stanford-Binet. *Journal of Clinical Psychology*, 1961, **17**, 284–286.

Kennedy, W. A., Van de Riet, V., & White, J. C., Jr. Use of the Terman-Merrill abbreviated scale on the 1960 Stanford-Binet Form L-M on Negro elementary school children of the Southeastern United States. *Journal of Consulting Psychology*, 1963, **27**, 456–457.

Kennedy-Fraser, D. *The Terman-Merrill Intelligence Scale in Scotland*. Malham House, Bickely Kent: University of London Press, 1945.

Kent, G. H. Suggestions for the next revision of the Binet-Simon scale. *Psychological Record*, 1937, **1**, 409–433.

Kent, N., & Davis, D. R. Discipline in the home and intellectual development. *British Journal of Medical Psychology*, 1957, **30**, 27–33.

Kernberg, P. F. The problem of organicity in the child: Notes on some diagnostic techniques in the evaluation of children. *Journal of the American Academy of Child Psychiatry*, 1969, **8**, 517–541.

Kessler, J. W. *Psychopathology of childhood*. Englewood Cliffs, N.J.: Prentice-Hall, 1966.

Keston, M. J., & Jimenez, C. A study of the performance on English and Spanish editions of the Stanford-Binet Intelligence Test by Spanish American children. *Journal of Genetic Psychology*, 1954, **85**, 263–269.

Kicklighter, R. H. Correlation of Peabody Picture Vocabulary Test scores and Stanford-Binet Intelligence Scale, Form L-M scores in an educable mentally retarded population. *Journal of School Psychology*, 1966, **5**, 75–76. (a)

Kicklighter, R. H. Problems in psychological evaluation of children. *Psychology in the Schools*, 1966, **3**, 164–167. (b)

Kidd, A. H. The culture-fair aspects of Cattell's test of g: Culture-free. *Journal of Genetic Psychology*, 1962, **101**, 343–362.

Killian, L. R. WISC, Illinois Test of Psycholinguistic Abilities, and Bender Visual-Motor Gestalt Test performance of Spanish-American kindergarten and first-grade school children. *Journal of Consulting and Clinical Psychology*, 1971, **37**, 38–43.

Kimbrell, D. L. Comparison of Peabody, WISC, and academic achievement scores among educable mental defectives. *Psychological Reports*, 1960, **7**, 502.

Kinnie, E. J. *The influence of nonintellective factors on the IQ scores of middle- and lower-class children*. (Doctoral dissertation, Purdue University) Ann Arbor, Mich.: University Microfilms, 1970. No. 71–9414.

Kinsbourne, M., & Warrington, E. K. Developmental factors in reading and writing backwardness. *British Journal of Psychology*, 1963, **54**, 145–156.

Kirkendall, D. R., & Ismail, A. H. The ability of personality variables in discriminating among three intellectual groups of preadolescent boys and girls. *Child Development*, 1970, **41**, 1173–1181.

Kissel, S. Schizophrenic patterns on the WISC: A missing control. *Journal of Clinical Psychology*, 1966, **22**, 201.

Klapper, Z. S., & Birch, H. G. The relation of childhood characteristics to outcome in young adults with cerebral palsy. *Developmental Medicine and Child Neurology*, 1966, **8**, 645–656.

Klaus, R. A., & Gray, S. W. The early training project for disadvantaged children: A report after five years. *Monographs of the Society for Research in Child Development*, 1968, **33**(4, Whole No. 120).

Klaus, R. A., & Starke, C. Experimental revision of the Peabody Picture Vocabulary Test as a predictor of first grade reading ability. Unpublished manuscript, George Peabody College, Psychology Department, 1964.

Klineberg, O. *Race differences*. New York: Harper, 1935.

Klineberg, O. Tests of Negro intelligence. In O. Klineberg (Ed.), *Characteristics of the American Negro*. New York: Harper, 1944. Pp. 25–96.

Klonoff, H. Factor analysis of a neuropsychological battery for children aged 9 to 15. *Perceptual and Motor Skills*, 1971, **32**, 603–616.

Klopfer, W. G. The psychological report as a problem in interdisciplinary communication. *Journal of Nervous and Mental Disease*, 1959, **129**, 86–88.

Klopfer, W. G. *The psychological report.* New York: Grune & Stratton, 1960.

Klugman, S. F. The effect of money incentive versus praise upon the reliability and obtained scores of the Revised Stanford-Binet test. *Journal of General Psychology,* 1944, **30,** 255–269.

Knights, R. M. Test anxiety and defensiveness in institutionalized and noninstitutionalized normal and retarded children. *Child Development,* 1963, **34,** 1019–1026.

Knopf, I. J., Murfett, B. J., & Milstein, V. Relationships between the Wechsler-Bellevue Form I and the WISC. *Journal of Clinical Psychology,* 1954, **10,** 261–263.

Koegler, S. J. The management of the retarded child in practice. *Canadian Medical Association Journal,* 1963, **89,** 1009–1014.

Kogan, K. L. Repeated psychometric evaluations of preschool children with cerebral palsy. *Pediatrics,* 1957, **19,** 619–621.

Koh, T. H., & Madow, A. A. Relationship between PPVT and Stanford-Binet performance in institutionalized retardates. *American Journal of Mental Deficiency,* 1967, **72,** 108–113.

Kohlberg, L., & Zigler, E. The impact of cognitive maturity on the development of sex-role attitudes in the years 4 to 8. *Genetic Psychology Monographs,* 1967, **75,** 89–165.

Kolvin, I., Humphrey, M., & McNay, A. VI. Cognitive factors in childhood psychosis. *British Journal of Psychiatry,* 1971, **118,** 415–419.

Koppitz, E. M. *The Bender Gestalt Test for young children.* New York: Grune & Stratton, 1964.

Korst, J. W. A comparison of results from the Peabody Vocabulary Test and Leiter International Performance Scale with children having functional articulatory disorders. *Cerebral Palsy Journal,* 1966, **27**(1), 3–5.

Krebs, E. G. *The Wechsler Preschool and Primary Scale of Intelligence and prediction of reading achievement in first grade.* (Doctoral dissertation, Rutgers State University) Ann Arbor, Mich.: University Microfilms, 1969. No. 70–3361.

Krippner, S. WISC Comprehension and Picture Arrangement subtests as measures of social competence. *Journal of Clinical Psychology,* 1964, **20,** 366–367.

Kroske, W. H., Fretwell, L. N., & Cupp, M. E. Comparison of the Kahn Intelligence Tests: Experimental form, the Stanford-Binet, and the WAIS for familial retardates. *Perceptual and Motor Skills,* 1965, **21,** 428.

Krugman, J. I., Justman, J., Wrightstone, J. W., & Krugman, M. Pupil functioning on the Stanford-Binet and the Wechsler Intelligence Scale for Children. *Journal of Consulting Psychology,* 1951, **15,** 475–483.

Krugman, M. Some impressions of the Revised Stanford-Binet Scale. *Journal of Educational Psychology,* 1939, **30,** 594–603.

Kubota, M. Memory span and intelligence. *Japanese Journal of Psychology,* 1965, **36**(2), 47–55.

Kuhlmann, F. A revision of the Binet-Simon system for measuring the intelligence of children. *Journal of Psycho-Asthenics Monograph Supplement,* 1912, **1**(1), 1–41.

Kuhlmann, F. Some results of examining a thousand public school children with a revision of the Binet-Simon tests of intelligence by untrained examiners. *Journal of Psycho-Asthenics,* 1914, **18,** 233–269.

Kuhlmann, F. *A handbook of mental tests.* Baltimore: Warwick & York, 1922.

Kureth, G., Muhr, J. P., & Weisgerber, C. A. Some data on the validity of the Wechsler Intelligence Scale for Children. *Child Development,* 1952, **23,** 281–287.

Kvaraceus, W. C. Pupil performances on the abbreviated and complete new Stanford-Binet Scales, Form L. *Journal of Educational Psychology,* 1940, **31,** 627–630.

Labov, W. The logic of nonstandard English. In F. Williams (Ed.), *Language and poverty.* Chicago: Markham Publishing Co., 1970. Pp. 153–189.

Lacey, H. M., & Ross, A. O. Multidisciplinary views on psychological reports in child guidance clinics. *Journal of Clinical Psychology,* 1964, **20,** 522–526.

LaCrosse, J. E. Examiner reliability on the Stanford-Binet Intelligence Scale (Form L-M) in a design employing white and Negro examiners and subjects. Unpublished master's thesis, University of North Carolina, 1964.

Lamp, R. E., & Barclay, A. The Quick Test as a screening device for intellectually subnormal children. *Psychological Reports,* 1967, **20,** 763–766.

Landrum, J. P. *A study of the WISC performance of under-achievers in comparison to average-achievers and over-achievers.* (Doctoral dissertation, University of Colorado) Ann Arbor, Mich.: University Microfilms, 1963. No. 63–4884.

Langan, W. Visual perceptual difficulties. In P. Mittler (Ed.), *The psychological assessment of mental and physical handicaps.* London: Methuen, 1970. Pp. 375–401.

Lantz, B. Some dynamic aspects of success and failure. *Psychological Monographs,* 1945, **59**(1, Whole No. 271).

Larr, A. L., & Cain, E. R. Measurement of native learning abilities of deaf children. *Volta Review,* 1959, **61,** 160–162.

Larrabee, L. L., & Kleinsasser, L. D. The effect of experimenter bias on WISC performance. Unpublished manuscript, Psychological Associates, St. Louis, 1967.

Lavitt, J. A. Comparison of the Peabody, Wechsler, Binet, and California tests of intellectual ability among 7th to 9th grade pupils. Unpublished manuscript, Westfield Public Schools, 1963.

Lavitt, J. A. *A comparative evaluation of the Peabody Picture Vocabulary Test as a measure of ability for children of differing reading proficiency levels.* (Doctoral dissertation, Oklahoma State University) Ann Arbor, Mich.: University Microfilms, 1967. No. 68-8443.

Lavos, G. W.I.S.C. psychometric patterns among deaf children. *Volta Review,* 1962, **64,** 547–552.

Laycock, S. R., & Clark, S. The comparative performance of a group of old-dull and young-bright children on some items of the Revised Stanford-Binet Scale of Intelligence, Form L. *Journal of Educational Psychology,* 1942, **33,** 1–12.

Lehman, E. B., & Levy, B. I. Discrepancies in estimates of children's intelligence: WISC and human figure drawings. *Journal of Clinical Psychology,* 1971, **27,** 74–76.

Lehmann, I. J. Rural-urban differences in intelligence. *Journal of Educational Research,* 1959, **53,** 62–68.

Leiter, R. G. Part I of the manual for the 1948 Revision of the Leiter International Performance Scale: Evidence of the reliability and validity of the Leiter tests. *Psychological Service Center Journal,* 1959, **11,** 1–72.

Lejeune, Y. A. Projective interpretation of intelligence tests. *Journal of South African Logopedic Society,* 1955, **3,** 9–12.

Leland, H. Testing the disadvantaged. In W. C. Rhodes (Chm.), Use and misuse of standardized intelligence tests in psychological and educational research and practice. Symposium presented at the American Psychological Association, Washington, D.C., September 1971.

Lesser, G. S., Fifer, G., & Clark, D. H. Mental abilities of children from different social-class and cultural groups. *Monographs of the Society for Research in Child Development,* 1965, **30**(4, Whole No. 102).

Lessing, E. E., & Lessing, J. C. WISC subtest variability and validity of WISC IQ. *Journal of Clinical Psychology,* 1963, **19,** 92–95.

Lessler, K., & Galinsky, M. D. Relationship between Slosson Intelligence Test and WISC scores in special education candidates. *Psychology in the Schools,* 1971, **8,** 341–344.

Leton, D. A. A factor analysis of ITPA and WISC scores of learning-disabled pupils. *Psychology in the Schools,* 1972, **9,** 31–36.

Leventhal, T., Slepian, H. J., Gluck, M. R., & Rosenblatt, B. P. The utilization of the psychologist-patient relationship in diagnostic testing. *Journal of Projective Techniques,* 1962, **26,** 66–79.

Levine, D., & Dysinger, D. W. Patterns of intellectual performance and the outcome of institutionalization in the mentally retarded. *American Journal of Mental Deficiency,* 1964, **68,** 784–788.

Levine, M. Psychological testing of children. In M. L. Hoffman & L. W. Hoffman (Eds.), *Review of child development research.* Vol. 2. New York: Russell Sage Foundation, 1966. Pp. 257–310.

Levinson, B. M. A comparison of the performance of bilingual and monolingual native born Jewish preschool children of traditional parentage on four intelligence tests. *Journal of Clinical Psychology,* 1959, **15,** 74–76.

Levinson, B. M., & Block, Z. Research note on Columbia Mental Maturity Scale (CMMS) and Revised Stanford Binet (L) in a preschool population. *Journal of Clinical Psychology,* 1960, **16,** 158–159.

Levy, E. Z. Long-term follow-up of former inpatients at the Children's Hospital of the Menninger Clinic. *American Journal of Psychiatry,* 1969, **125,** 1633–1639.

Levy, P. Short-form tests: A methodological review. *Psychological Bulletin,* 1968, **69,** 410–416.

Lewis, L. L. The relation of measured mental ability to school marks and academic survival in the Texas School for the Blind. *International Journal for the Education of the Blind,* 1957, **6,** 56–60.

Lichtman, M. V. *Intelligence, creativity, and language: An examination of the interrelationships of three variables among preschool, disadvantaged Negro children.* (Doctoral dissertation, George Washington University) Ann Arbor, Mich.: University Microfilms, 1969. No. 70-13,956.

Liddle, G. P. The school psychologist's role with the culturally handicapped. In J. F. Magary (Ed.), *School psychological services in theory and practice.* Englewood Cliffs, N.J.: Prentice-Hall, 1967. Pp. 488–522.

Linde, T. Mental evaluation in cerebral palsy. *Journal of Rehabilitation,* 1964, **30**(2), 17.

Lindstrom, A. E. A comparison of the Peabody Picture Vocabulary Test and the Wechsler Intelligence Scale for Children. *Studies in Minnesota Education,* 1961, 131–132.

Lipsitz, S. Effect of the race of the examiner on results of intelligence test performance of Negro and white children. Unpublished master's thesis, Long Island University, 1969.

Littell, W. M. The Wechsler Intelligence Scale for Children: Review of a decade of research. *Psychological Bulletin,* 1960, **57,** 132–156.

Liverant, S. Intelligence: A concept in need of re-examination. *Journal of Consulting Psychology,* 1960, **24,** 101–110.

Livingston, J. S. *An evaluation of a photographically enlarged form of the Revised Stanford-Binet Intelligence Scale for use with the partially seeing child.* (Doctoral dissertation, New York University) Ann Arbor, Mich.: University Microfilms, 1957. No. 21,712.

Lobascher, M. E., Kingerlee, P. E., & Gubbay, S. S. Childhood autism: An investigation of aetiological factors in twenty-five cases. *British Journal of Psychiatry,* 1970, **117,** 525–529.

Lodge, G. T. How to write a psychological report. *Journal of Clinical Psychology,* 1953, **9,** 400–402.

Lord, E. E. *Children handicapped by cerebral palsy.* New York: Commonwealth Fund, 1937.

Lorge, I. Difference or bias in tests of intelligence. In A. Anastasi (Ed.), *Testing problems in perspective: 25th anniversary volume of topical readings from the Invitational Conference on Testing Problems.* Washington, D.C.: American Council on Education, 1966. Pp. 472–480.

Lorr, M., & Meister, R. K. The concept scatter in the light of mental test theory. *Educational and Psychological Measurement,* 1941, **1**, 303–310.

Lorr, M., & Meister, R. K. The optimum use of test data. *Educational and Psychological Measurement,* 1942, **2**, 339–348.

Louden, M. V. Relative difficulty of Stanford-Binet vocabulary for bright and dull subjects of the same mental level. *Journal of Educational Research,* 1933, **27**, 179–186.

Louttit, C. M. *Clinical psychology of exceptional children.* (3rd ed.) New York: Harper, 1957.

Lubin, B., Wallis, R. R., & Paine, C. Patterns of psychological test usage in the United States: 1935–1969. *Professional Psychology,* 1971, **2**, 70–74.

Lucito, L., & Gallagher, J. J. Intellectual patterns of highly gifted children on the WISC. *Peabody Journal of Education,* 1960, **38**, 131–136.

Lutey, C. L. *Individual intelligence testing: A manual.* Greeley, Colo.: Author, 1967.

Lyle, J. G., & Goyen, J. Performance of retarded readers on the WISC and educational tests. *Journal of Abnormal Psychology,* 1969, **74**, 105–112.

Lyman, H. B. Review of the Peabody Picture Vocabulary Test. In O. K. Buros (Ed.), *The sixth mental measurements yearbook.* Highland Park, N.J.: Gryphon Press, 1965. Pp. 820–821.

Machover, K. A. *Personality projection in the drawing of the human figure.* Springfield, Ill.: Charles C Thomas, 1949.

Madden, R. A note on the eight and nine year levels of Stanford-Binet. *School and Society,* 1932, **36**, 576.

Madsen, W. *Mexican-Americans of South Texas.* New York: Holt, Rinehart and Winston, 1964.

Magaret, G. A., & Thompson, C. W. Differential test responses of normal, superior and mentally defective subjects. *Journal of Abnormal and Social Psychology,* 1950, **45**, 163–167.

Mahan, T. W., Jr. Diagnostic consistency and prediction: A note on graduate student skills. *Personnel and Guidance Journal,* 1963, **42**, 364–367.

Maloney, M. P., Ward, M. P., Schenck, H. U., & Braucht, G. N. Re-evaluation of the use of the Quick Test with a sample of institutionalized mentally retarded subjects. *Psychological Reports,* 1971, **29**, 1155–1159.

Malpass, L. F., Brown, R., & Hake, D. The utility of the Progressive Matrices (1956 Edition) with normal and retarded children. *Journal of Clinical Psychology,* 1960, **16**, 350.

Malpass, L. F., Mark, S., & Palermo, D. S. Responses of retarded children to the Children's Manifest Anxiety Scale. *Journal of Educational Psychology,* 1960, **51**, 305–308.

Manuel, H. T. *Spanish-speaking children of the Southwest: Their education and the public welfare.* Austin: University of Texas Press, 1965.

Margach, C., & Kern, K. C. Visual impairment, partial-sight and the school psychologist. *Journal of Learning Disabilities,* 1969, **2**, 407–414.

Marine, E. L. The effect of familiarity with the examiner upon Stanford-Binet test performance. *Teachers College Contributions to Education,* 1929, No. 381.

Marks, E. S. Sampling in the revision of the Stanford-Binet Scale. *Psychological Bulletin,* 1947, **44**, 413–434.

Marsden, G., & Kalter, N. Bodily concerns and the WISC Object Assembly subtest. *Journal of Consulting and Clinical Psychology,* 1969, **33**, 391–395.

Martin, A. W., & Wiechers, J. E. Raven's Colored Progressive Matrices and the Wechsler Intelligence Scale for Children. *Journal of Consulting Psychology,* 1954, **18**, 143–144.

Martin, M. F. Gaining rapport in the school clinic. *Mental Hygiene,* 1941, **25**, 251–255.

Martin, W. T. *Writing psychological reports.* Springfield, Ill.: Charles C Thomas, 1972.

Martinson, B., & Strauss, A. A. A method of clinical evaluation of the responses to the Stanford-Binet Intelligence Test. *American Journal of Mental Deficiency,* 1941, **46**, 48–59.

Masland, R. L., Sarason, S. B., & Gladwin, T. *Mental subnormality.* New York: Basic Books, 1958.

Masling, J. M. The effects of warm and cold interaction on the administration and scoring of an intelligence test. *Journal of Consulting Psychology,* 1959, **23**, 336–341.

Massey, J. O. *WISC scoring criteria.* Palo Alto, Calif.: Consulting Psychologists Press, 1964.

Massey, J. O. *WPPSI test profile.* Palo Alto, Calif.: Consulting Psychologists Press, 1968.

Masters, J. C., & Miller, D. E. Early infantile autism: A methodological critique. *Journal of Abnormal Psychology,* 1970, **75**, 342–343.

Mateer, F. *The unstable child.* New York: D. Appleton & Co., 1924.

Maurer, K. M. Mental measurement of children handicapped by cerebral palsy. *Physiotherapy Review,* 1940, **20**, 271–273.

Maxwell, A. E. A factor analysis of the Wechsler Intelligence Scale for Children. *British Journal of Educational Psychology,* 1959, **29**, 237–241.

Maxwell, A. E. Discrepancies in the variances of test results for normal and neurotic children. *British Journal of Statistical Psychology,* 1960, **13**, 165–172.

Maxwell, A. E. Discrepancies between the pattern of abilities for normal and neurotic children. *Journal of Mental Science,* 1961, **107**, 300–307. (a)

Maxwell, A. E. Inadequate reporting of normative test data. *Journal of Clinical Psychology,* 1961, **17,** 99–101. (b)

Maxwell, M. T. The relationship between the Wechsler Intelligence Scale for Children and the Slosson Intelligence Test. *Child Study Journal,* 1971, **1,** 164–171.

Mayer, R. W. A study of the STEP Reading, SCAT and WISC tests, and school grades. *Reading Teacher,* 1958, **12,** 117, 142.

Mayman, M. Style, focus, language and content of an ideal psychological test report. *Journal of Projective Techniques,* 1959, **23,** 453–458.

McArthur, C. R., & Wakefield, H. E. Validation of the PPVT with the Stanford-Binet-LM and the WISC on educable mental retardates. *American Journal of Mental Deficiency,* 1968, **73,** 465–467.

McBrearty, J. F. A comparison of the WISC with the Arthur Performance Scale, Form I, and their relationship to the Progressive Achievement Tests. Unpublished master's thesis, Pennsylvania State College, 1951.

McCandless, B. R. Review of the Revised Stanford-Binet Scale. In O. K. Buros (Ed.), *The fourth mental measurements yearbook.* Highland Park, N.J.: Gryphon Press, 1953. Pp. 464–465. (a)

McCandless, B. R. Review of the Wechsler Intelligence Scale for Children. In O. K. Buros (Ed.), *The fourth mental measurements yearbook.* Highland Park, N.J.: Gryphon Press, 1953. Pp. 480–481. (b)

McCandless, B. R. Review of the Quick Test. In O. K. Buros (Ed.), *The sixth mental measurements yearbook.* Highland Park, N.J.: Gryphon Press, 1965. Pp. 825–826.

McCandless, B. R., & Castaneda, A. Anxiety in children, school achievement, and intelligence. *Child Development,* 1956, **27,** 379–382.

McCarthy, D. Administration of Digit Symbol and Coding subtests of the WAIS and WISC to left-handed subjects. *Psychological Reports,* 1961, **8,** 407–408.

McCarthy, J. M., & Paraskevopoulos, J. Behavior patterns of learning disabled, emotionally disturbed, and average children. *Exceptional Children,* 1969, **36,** 69–74.

McConnell, R. E. The origin of mental tests. *Education,* 1930, **50,** 464–473.

McCulloch, T. L., Reswick, J., & Weissmann, S. Studies of word learning in mental defectives: II. Relation to scores on digit repetition, the Stanford-Binet, M, and the WISC Verbal Scale. *American Journal of Mental Deficiency,* 1955, **60,** 140–143.

McDiarmid, G. L. The hazards of testing Indian children. In F. L. Denmark (Chm.), Implications of minority group testing for more effective learning. Symposium presented at the American Psychological Association, Washington, D.C., September 1971.

McFadden, J. H. Differential responses of normal and feebleminded subjects of equal mental age on the Kent-Rosanoff Free Association Test and the Stanford Revision of the Binet-Simon Intelligence Test. *Mental Measurements Monographs,* 1931, No. 7.

McFie, J. Intellectual impairment in children with localized post-infantile cerebral lesions. *Journal of Neurology, Neurosurgery, and Psychiatry,* 1961, **24,** 361–365.

McGinnis, M. A. *Aphasic children.* Washington, D.C.: Alexander Graham Bell Association for the Deaf, 1963.

McGraw, J. J. *A comparison of mean subtest raw scores on the WISC of regular and over-achieving readers with under-achieving readers.* (Doctoral dissertation, University of Oklahoma) Ann Arbor, Mich.: University Microfilms, 1966. No. 66–14,229.

McHugh, A. F. WISC performance in neurotic and conduct disturbances. *Journal of Clinical Psychology,* 1963, **19,** 423–424.

McIntire, J. T. The incidence of feeble-mindedness in the cerebral palsied. *American Association on Mental Deficiency Proceedings,* 1938, **43**(2), 44–50.

McKeever, W. F., & Gerstein, A. I. Validity of the Hewson Ratios: Investigation of a fundamental methodological consideration. *Journal of Consulting Psychology,* 1958, **22,** 150.

McKerracher, D. W., & Scott, J. I.Q. scores and the problem of classification. *British Journal of Psychiatry,* 1966, **112,** 537–541.

McLean, T. K. *A comparison of the subtest performance of two groups of retarded readers with like groups of non-retarded readers on the Wechsler Intelligence Scale for Children.* (Doctoral dissertation, University of Oregon) Ann Arbor, Mich.: University Microfilms, 1963. No. 64–5402.

McLeod, J. A comparison of WISC sub-test scores of pre-adolescent successful and unsuccessful readers. *Australian Journal of Psychology,* 1965, **17,** 220–228.

McNamara, J. R., Porterfield, C. L., & Miller, L. E. The relationship of the Wechsler Preschool and Primary Scale of Intelligence with the Coloured Progressive Matrices (1956) and the Bender Gestalt Test. *Journal of Clinical Psychology,* 1969, **25,** 65–68.

McNemar, Q. *The revision of the Stanford-Binet Scale.* Boston: Houghton-Mifflin, 1942.

McNemar, Q. Lost: Our intelligence? Why? *American Psychologist,* 1964, **19,** 871–882.

Mecham, M. J., Berko, M. J., & Berko, F. G. *Speech therapy in cerebral palsy.* Springfield, Ill.: Charles C Thomas, 1960.

Mecham, M. J., Berko, M. J., Berko, F. G., & Palmer, M. F. *Communication training in childhood brain damage.* Springfield, Ill.: Charles C Thomas, 1966.

Mednick, M. T. Relationship of the Ammons Quick Test of intelligence to other ability measures. *Psychological Reports,* 1967, **20,** 523–526.

Mednick, M. T. The validity of the Ammons' Quick Test of intelligence. *Psychological Reports,* 1969, **24,** 388–390.

Meeker, M. N. *The structure of intellect.* Columbus, Ohio: Charles E. Merrill, 1969.

Mehr, H. M. The application of psychological tests and methods to schizophrenia in children. *The Nervous Child,* 1952, **10,** 63–93.

Mein, R. Use of the Peabody Picture Vocabulary Test with severely subnormal patients. *American Journal of Mental Deficiency,* 1962, **67,** 269–273.

Meissler, G. R. *A correlation of the Slosson Intelligence Test and the Wechsler Intelligence Scale when administered to atypical children.* (Doctoral dissertation, Catholic University of America) Ann Arbor, Mich.: University Microfilms, 1970. No. 70-22,140.

Meister, R. K., & Kennedy, V. An evaluation of a short administration of the Revised Stanford Binet. *American Psychologist,* 1947, **2,** 424.

Meister, R. K., & Kurko, V. K. An evaluation of a short administration of the Revised Stanford-Binet Intelligence Examination. *Educational and Psychological Measurement,* 1951, **11,** 489–493.

Melcer, D., & Peck, R. F. Sensorimotor experience and concept formation in early childhood. Final report, February 1967, University of Texas at Austin, Project No. 6-8493, U.S. Department of Health, Education, and Welfare.

Mercer, J. R. Sociocultural factors in labeling mental retardates. *Peabody Journal of Education,* 1971, **48,** 188–203.

Mercer, J. R., & Smith, J. M. Subtest estimates of the WISC Full Scale IQ's for children. U.S. Department of Health, Education, and Welfare, Public Health Service, 1972, No. (HSM)72-1047 (Series 2, No. 47).

Merenda, P. F. Review of the Quick Test. *Educational and Psychological Measurement,* 1965, **25,** 268–271.

Merrill, M. A. *Problems of child delinquency.* Boston: Houghton Mifflin, 1947.

Messick, S., & Anderson, S. Educational testing, individual development, and social responsibility. *Counseling Psychologist,* 1970, **2**(2), 80–88.

Meyerson, L. A psychology of impaired hearing. In W. M. Cruickshank (Ed.), *Psychology of exceptional children and youth.* (2nd ed.) Englewood Cliffs, N.J.: Prentice-Hall, 1963. Pp. 118–191.

Michal-Smith, H. Problems encountered in the psychometric examination of the child with cerebral palsy, *Cerebral Palsy Review,* 1955, **16**(3), 15–16, 20.

Milgram, N. A. A note on the PPVT in mental retardates. *American Journal of Mental Deficiency,* 1967, **72,** 496–497.

Milgram, N. A. Danger: Chauvinism, scapegoatism, and euphemism. *Clinical Child Psychology Newsletter,* 1970, **9**(3), 2–3.

Milgram, N. A. IQ constancy in disadvantaged Negro children. *Psychological Reports,* 1971, **29,** 319–326.

Milgram, N. A., & Ozer, M. N. Peabody Picture Vocabulary Test scores of preschool children. *Psychological Reports,* 1967, **20,** 779–784.

Miller, C. K., & Chansky, N. M. Psychologists' scoring of WISC protocols. *Psychology in the Schools,* 1972, **9,** 144–152.

Miller, C. K., Chansky, N. M., & Gredler, G. R. Rater agreement on WISC protocols. *Psychology in the Schools,* 1970, **7,** 190–193.

Miller, C. K., McLaughlin, J. A., Haddon, J., & Chansky, N. M. Socioeconomic class and teacher bias. *Psychological Reports,* 1968, **23,** 806.

Miller, H. R. WISC performance under incentive conditions: Case report. *Psychological Reports,* 1969, **24,** 835–838.

Miller, J. M. A comparison of the WAIS, WISC, and WBII. Unpublished master's thesis, Marquette University, 1969.

Miller, J. O., & Phillips, J. A preliminary evaluation of the Head Start and other metropolitan Nashville kindergartens. Unpublished manuscript, George Peabody College for Teachers, 1966.

Milligan, G. E. Counseling parents of the mentally retarded. In J. H. Rothstein (Ed.), *Mental retardation.* (2nd ed.) New York: Holt, Rinehart and Winston, 1971. Pp. 492–502.

Milliren, A. P., & Newland, T. E. Statistically significant differences between subtest scaled scores for the WPPSI. *Journal of School Psychology,* 1969, **7**(3), 16–19.

Mitchell, B. C. The Metropolitan Readiness Tests as predictors of first-grade achievement. *Educational and Psychological Measurement,* 1962, **22,** 765–772.

Mitchell, M. B. Irregularities of university students on the Revised Stanford-Binet. *Journal of Educational Psychology,* 1941, **32,** 513–522.

Moed, G., Wight, B. W., & James, P. Intertest correlations of the Wechsler Intelligence Scale for Children and two picture vocabulary tests. *Educational and Psychological Measurement,* 1963, **23,** 359–363.

Money, J. Cytogenetic and psychosexual incongruities with a note on space-form blindness. *American Journal of Psychiatry,* 1963, **119,** 820–827.

Moore, C. H., Boblitt, W. E., & Wildman, R. W. Psychiatric impressions of psychological reports. *Journal of Clinical Psychology,* 1968, **24,** 373–376.

Moore, J. W. *Mexican Americans.* Englewood Cliffs, N.J.: Prentice-Hall, 1970.

Mordock, J. B., & Bogan, S. Wechsler patterns and symptomatic behaviors of children diagnosed as having minimal cerebral dysfunction. *Proceedings of the 76th Annual Convention of the American Psychological Association,* 1968, **3,** 663–664.

Moriarty, A. E. Coping patterns of preschool children in response to intelligence test demands. *Genetic Psychology Monographs,* 1961, **64,** 3–127.

Morrow, R. S. The diagnostic psychological report. *Psychiatric Quarterly Supplement,* 1954, **28,** 102–110.

Mosher, L. R., & Feinsilver, D. *Special report on schizophrenia.* Washington, D.C.: U.S. Dept. of Health, Education, and Welfare, 1971.

Moss, J. W. An evaluation of the Peabody Picture Vocabulary Test with the PMA and 1937 Stanford-Binet on trainable children. Unpublished paper, University of Illinois, 1962.

Moss, J. W., & Edmonds, P. The Peabody Picture Vocabulary Test with English children. *British Journal of Educational Psychology,* 1960, **30,** 82.

Mueller, M. W. Effects of illustration size on test performance of visually limited children. *Exceptional Children,* 1962, **29,** 124–128.

Mueller, M. W. Validity of six tests of ability with educable mental retardates. *Journal of School Psychology,* 1968, **6,** 136–146.

Mueller, M. W. Prediction of achievement of educable mentally retarded children. *American Journal of Mental Deficiency,* 1969, **73,** 590–596.

Muench, G. A. A followup of mental defectives after eighteen years. *Journal of Abnormal and Social Psychology,* 1944, **39,** 407–418.

Muir, M. The WISC test pattern of children with severe reading disabilities. *Reading Horizons,* 1962, 2(Winter), 67–73.

Mundy, L., & Maxwell, A. E. Assessment of the feebleminded. *British Journal of Medical Psychology,* 1958, **31,** 201–210.

Münsterberg, H. Zur Individualpsychologie. *Centralblatt fur Nervenheilkunde und Psychiatrie,* 1891, **14,** 196–198.

Murdoch, K. Rate of improvement of the feeble-minded as shown by standardized educational tests. *Journal of Applied Psychology,* 1918, **2,** 243–249.

Murphy, G. Psychological views of personality and contributions to its study. In E. Norbeck, D. Price-Williams, & W. M. McCord (Eds.), *The study of personality.* New York: Holt, Rinehart and Winston, 1968. Pp. 15–40.

Murphy, K. P. Tests of abilities and attainments. In A. W. G. Ewing (Ed.), *Educational guidance and the deaf child.* Manchester: Manchester University Press, 1957. Pp. 213–251.

Murphy, L. B. The appraisal of child personality. *Journal of Consulting Psychology,* 1948, **12,** 16–19.

Murstein, B. I. *Theory and research in projective techniques.* New York: Wiley, 1963.

Mussen, P. H., Dean, S., & Rosenberg, M. Some further evidence on the validity of the WISC. *Journal of Consulting Psychology,* 1952, **16,** 410–411.

Mussman, M. C. Teachers' evaluations of psychological reports. *Journal of School Psychology,* 1964, 3(1), 35–37.

Myers, C. R., & Gifford, E. V. Measuring abnormal pattern on the Revised Stanford-Binet Scale (Form L). *Journal of Mental Science,* 1943, **89,** 92–101.

Myers, E. T. *A survey of sight-saving classes in the public schools of the United States.* New York: The National Society for the Prevention of Blindness, 1930.

Myers, P. I., & Hammill, D. D. *Methods for learning disorders.* New York: Wiley, 1969.

Myklebust, H. R. *Auditory disorders in children.* New York: Grune & Stratton, 1954.

Nale, S. The childrens-Wechsler and the Binet on 104 mental defectives at the Polk State School. *American Journal of Mental Deficiency,* 1951, **56,** 419–423.

Nalven, F. B. Classroom-administered Digit Span and distractibility ratings for elementary school pupils. *Psychological Reports,* 1969, **24,** 734.

Nalven, F. B., & Bierbryer, B. Predicting elementary school children's classroom comprehension from their WISC results. *Journal of Clinical Psychology,* 1969, **25,** 75–76.

Nalven, F. B., Hofmann, L. J., & Bierbryer, B. The effects of subjects' age, sex, race, and socioeconomic status on psychologists' estimates of "true IQ" from WISC scores. *Journal of Clinical Psychology,* 1969, **25,** 271–274.

Nalven, F. B., & Puleo, V. T. Relationship between digit span and classroom distractibility in elementary school children. *Journal of Clinical Psychology,* 1968, **24,** 85–87.

Nava, J. Cultural backgrounds and barriers that affect learning by Spanish-speaking children. In J. H. Burma (Ed.), *Mexican-Americans in the United States: A reader.* Cambridge, Mass.: Schenkman Publishing Co., 1970. Pp. 125–133.

Neale, M. D. Review of *Stanford-Binet Intelligence Scale, third revision (1960) – Form L-M. Australian Journal of Education,* 1962, **6,** 233–234.

Nelson, C. M., & Hudson, F. G. Predicting the reading achievement of junior high school EMR children. *American Journal of Mental Deficiency,* 1969, **74,** 415–420.

Neuhaus, M. Modifications in the administration of the WISC Performance subtests for children with profound hearing losses. *Exceptional Children,* 1967, **33,** 573–574.

Neville, D. A comparison of the WISC patterns of male retarded and non-retarded readers. *Journal of Educational Research,* 1961, **54,** 195–197.

Neville, D. The relationship between reading skills and intelligence test scores. *Reading Teacher,* 1965, **18,** 257–262.

Newland, T. E. Psychological assessment of exceptional children and youth. In W. M. Cruickshank (Ed.), *Psychology of exceptional children and youth.* (2nd ed.) Englewood Cliffs, N.J.: Prentice-Hall, 1963. Pp. 53–117.

Newland, T. E. Review of the Columbia Mental Maturity Scale. In O. K. Buros (Ed.), *The sixth mental measurements yearbook.* Highland Park, N.J.: Gryphon Press, 1965. Pp. 801–803.

Newland, T. E. Testing minority group children. *Clinical Child Psychology Newsletter,* 1970, **9**(3), 5.

Newland, T. E. Review of the Pictorial Test of Intelligence. In O. K. Buros (Ed.), *The seventh mental measurements yearbook.* Highland Park, N.J.: Gryphon Press, 1972. Pp. 749–750.

Newland, T. E., & Meeker, M. N. Binet behavior samplings and Guilford's Structure of the Intellect. *Journal of School Psychology,* 1964, **2,** 55–59.

Newland, T. E., & Smith, P. A. Statistically significant differences between subtest scaled scores on the WISC and the WAIS. *Journal of School Psychology,* 1967, **5,** 122–127.

Newman, J. R., & Loos, F. M. Differences between Verbal and Performance IQ's with mentally defective children on the Wechsler Intelligence Scale for Children. *Journal of Consulting Psychology,* 1955, **19,** 16.

Nichols, R. C. The effect of ego involvement and success experience on intelligence test results. *Journal of Consulting Psychology,* 1959, **23,** 92.

Nicholson, C. L. Correlations among CMMS, PPVT, and RCPM for cerebral palsied children. *Perceptual and Motor Skills,* 1970, **30,** 715–718.

Norris, R. C., Hottel, J. V., & Brooks, S. T. Comparability of Peabody Picture Vocabulary Test scores under group and individual administration. *Journal of Educational Psychology,* 1960, **51,** 87–91.

Nunnally, J. C., Jr. *Psychometric theory.* New York: McGraw-Hill, 1967.

Nunnally, J. C., Jr. *Introduction to psychological measurement.* New York: McGraw-Hill, 1970.

Oakland, J. A. WISC Coding as a measure of motivation. *Journal of Clinical Psychology,* 1969, **25,** 411–412.

Oakland, T. D., King, J. D., White, L. A., & Eckman, R. A comparison of performance on the WPPSI, WISC, and SB with preschool children: Companion studies. *Journal of School Psychology,* 1971, **9,** 144–149.

Offord, D. R., & Cross, L. A. Adult schizophrenia with scholastic failure or low IQ in childhood: A preliminary report. *Archives of General Psychiatry,* 1971, **24,** 431–436.

Ogdon, D. P. WISC IQs for the mentally retarded. *Journal of Consulting Psychology,* 1960, **24,** 187–188.

Ogdon, D. P. *Psychodiagnostics and personality assessment: A handbook.* Los Angeles: Western Psychological Services, 1967.

O'Gorman, G. *The nature of childhood autism.* London: Butterworths, 1967.

Oldridge, O. A., & Allison, E. E. Review of the Wechsler Preschool and Primary Scale of Intelligence (WPPSI). *Journal of Educational Measurement,* 1968, **5,** 347–348.

Olive, H. Psychoanalysts' opinions of psychologists' reports: 1952 and 1970. *Journal of Clinical Psychology,* 1972, **28,** 50–54.

Olivier, K., & Barclay, A. Stanford-Binet and Goodenough-Harris Test performances of Head Start children. *Psychological Reports,* 1967, **20,** 1175–1179.

Orpet, R. E., & Meyers, C. E. Six Structure-of-Intellect hypotheses in six-year-old children. *Journal of Educational Psychology,* 1966, **57,** 341–346.

Orpet, R. E., & Meyers, C. E. Discriminant function analysis of conservation stages by structure of intellect and conceptual style variables. *Proceedings of the 78th Annual Convention of the American Psychological Association,* 1970, **5,** 279–280.

Osborne, R. T. Factorial composition of the Wechsler Intelligence Scale for Children at the preschool level. *Psychological Reports,* 1963, **13,** 443–448.

Osborne, R. T. WISC factor structure for normal Negro pre-school children. *Psychological Reports,* 1964, **15,** 543–548.

Osborne, R. T. Factor structure of the Wechsler Intelligence Scale for Children at pre-school level and after first grade: A longitudinal analysis. *Psychological Reports,* 1965, **16,** 637–644.

Osborne, R. T. Stability of factor structure of the WISC for normal Negro children from pre-school level to first grade. *Psychological Reports,* 1966, **18,** 655–664.

Osborne, R. T. Review of the Wechsler Intelligence Scale for Children. In O. K. Buros (Ed.), *The seventh mental measurements yearbook.* Highland Park, N.J.: Gryphon Press, 1972. Pp. 802–803.

Osborne, R. T., & Tillman, M. H. Normal and retardate WISC performance: An analysis of the stimulus trace theory. *American Journal of Mental Deficiency,* 1967, **72,** 257–261.

Otto, W., & McMenemy, R. A. An appraisal of the Ammons Quick Test in a remedial reading program. *Journal of Educational Measurement,* 1965, **2,** 193–198.

Paine, R. S., Werry, J. S., & Quay, H. C. A study of 'minimal cerebral dysfunction.' *Developmental Medicine and Child Neurology,* 1968, **10,** 505–520.

Palmer, J. O. *The psychological assessment of children.* New York: Wiley, 1970.

Palmer, M., & Gaffney, P. D. Effects of administration of the WISC in Spanish and English and relationship of social class to performance. *Psychology in the Schools,* 1972, **9,** 61–64.

Panther, E. E. Prediction of first-grade reading achievement. *Elementary School Journal,* 1967, **68,** 44–48.

Papania, N. A qualitative analysis of the vocabulary responses of institutionalized mentally retarded children. *Journal of Clinical Psychology,* 1954, **10,** 361–365.

Pasewark, R. A., Fitzgerald, B. J., & Gloeckler, T. Relationship of Peabody Picture Vocabulary Test and Wechsler Intelligence Scale for Children in an educable retarded group: A cautionary note. *Psychological Reports,* 1971, **28,** 405–406.

Pasewark, R. A., Rardin, M. W., & Grice, J. E., Jr. Relationship of the Wechsler Pre-School and Primary Scale of Intelligence and the Stanford-Binet (L-M) in lower class children. *Journal of School Psychology,* 1971, **9,** 43–50.

Pasewark, R. A., Sawyer, R. N., Smith, E. A., Wasserberger, M., Dell, D., Brito, H., & Lee, R. Concurrent validity of the French Pictorial Test of Intelligence. *Journal of Educational Research,* 1967, **61,** 179–183.

Pastovic, J. J., & Guthrie, G. M. Some evidence on the validity of the WISC. *Journal of Consulting Psychology,* 1951, **15,** 385–386.

Paterra, M. E. A study of thirty-three WISC scattergrams of retarded readers. *Elementary English,* 1963, **40,** 394–405.

Patterson, G. R. Review of the Wechsler Intelligence Scale for Children. In O. K. Buros (Ed.), *The fifth mental measurements yearbook.* Highland Park, N.J.: Gryphon Press, 1959. Pp. 559–560.

Pauker, J. D. Behavioral correlates of standardized intelligence test scores. In W. C. Rhodes (Chm.), Use and misuse of standardized intelligence tests in psychological and educational research and practice. Symposium presented at the American Psychological Association, Washington, D.C., September 1971.

Payne, J. S., Ball, D. W., & Stainback, W. C. Note on reliability and congruent validity of the Peabody Picture Vocabulary Test with disadvantaged preschool children. *Psychological Reports,* 1972, **30,** 22.

Payne, R. The psychotic subnormal. *Journal of Mental Subnormality,* 1968, **14,** 25–34.

Pedersen, D. M., Shinedling, M. M., & Johnson, D. L. Effects of sex of examiner and subject on children's quantitative test performance. *Journal of Personality and Social Psychology,* 1968, **10,** 251–254.

Pedersen, F. A., & Wender, P. H. Early social correlates of cognitive functioning in six-year-old boys. *Child Development,* 1968, **39,** 185–193.

Pedrini, D. T., & Pedrini, L. N. *The Pedrini supplementary aid to the administration of the Stanford-Binet Intelligence Scale (Form L-M): A handbook.* Los Angeles: Western Psychological Services, 1970.

Peisach, E. C. Children's comprehension of teacher and peer speech. *Child Development,* 1965, **36,** 467–480.

Pelosi, J. W. *A study of the effects of examiner race, sex, and style on test responses of Negro examinees.* (Doctoral dissertation, Syracuse University) Ann Arbor, Mich.: University Microfilms, 1968. No. 69-8642.

Pennington, H., Galliani, C. A., & Voegele, G. E. Unilateral electroencephalographic dysrhythmia and children's intelligence. *Child Development,* 1965, **36,** 539–546.

Perales, A. M. The audio-lingual approach and the Spanish-speaking student. *Hispania,* 1965, **48,** 99–102.

Perkins, R. E. A study of the relation of brightness to Stanford-Binet test performance. *Journal of Applied Psychology,* 1932, **16,** 205–216.

Peterson, J. *Early conceptions and tests of intelligence.* Yonkers-on-Hudson, N.Y.: World Book, 1925.

Petrie, I. R. J. Residential treatment of maladjusted children: A study of some factors related to progress in adjustment. *British Journal of Educational Psychology,* 1962, **32,** 29–37.

Pettigrew, T. F. *A profile of the Negro American.* Princeton: D. Van Nostrand, 1964.

Philips, I. Psychopathology and mental retardation. *American Journal of Psychiatry,* 1967, **124,** 29–35.

Phillips, E. L., Berman, I. R., & Hanson, H. B. Intelligence and personality factors associated with poliomyelitis among school age children. *Monographs of the Society for Research in Child Development,* 1948, **12**(Whole No. 2).

Pickles, D. G. The Wechsler Performance Scale and its relationship to speech and educational response in deaf slow-learning children. *Teacher of the Deaf,* 1966, **64,** 382–392.

Pierce, H. O. Errors which can and should be avoided in scoring the Stanford-Binet Scale. *Journal of Genetic Psychology,* 1948, **72,** 303–305.

Piers, E. V. Review of the Peabody Picture Vocabulary Test. In O. K. Buros (Ed.), *The sixth mental measurements yearbook.* Highland Park, N.J.: Gryphon Press, 1965. Pp. 822–823. (a)

Piers, E. V. Review of the Quick Test. In O. K. Buros (Ed.), *The sixth mental measurements yearbook.* Highland Park, N.J.: Gryphon Press, 1965. Pp. 826–827. (b)

Pierstorff, P. A study of the effects of discouragement upon the Stanford-Binet test performance. Unpublished master's thesis. University of Wisconsin, 1951.

Pignatelli, M. L. A comparative study of mental functioning patterns of problem and non-problem children seven, eight, and nine years of age. *Genetic Psychology Monographs*, 1943, **27**, 69–162.

Pihl, R. O. The degree of the Verbal-Performance discrepancy on the WISC and the WAIS and severity of EEG abnormality in epileptics. *Journal of Clinical Psychology*, 1968, **24**, 418–420.

Pintner, R. *Intelligence testing*. (2nd ed.) New York: Henry Holt, 1931.

Pintner, R. Intelligence testing of partially-sighted children. *Journal of Educational Psychology*, 1942, **33**, 265–272.

Pintner, R., Dragositz, A., & Kushner, R. Supplementary guide for the Revised Stanford-Binet Scale (Form L). *Applied Psychology Monographs*, 1944, No. 3.

Plant, W. T. Cited by D. Wechsler, *Manual for the Wechsler Preschool and Primary Scale of Intelligence*. New York: Psychological Corporation, 1967. P. 34.

Plant, W. T., & Southern, M. L. First grade reading achievement predicted from WPPSI and other scores obtained 18 months earlier. *Proceedings of the 76th Annual Convention of the American Psychological Association*, 1968, **3**, 593–594.

Pless, I. B., Snider, M., Eaton, A. E., & Kearsley, R. B. A rapid screening test for intelligence in children: A preliminary report. *American Journal of Diseases of Children*, 1965, **109**, 533–537.

Plumb, G. R., & Charles, D. C. Scoring difficulty of Wechsler Comprehension responses. *Journal of Educational Psychology*, 1955, **46**, 179–183.

Pollack, M. Brain damage, mental retardation and childhood schizophrenia. *American Journal of Psychiatry*, 1958, **115**, 422–428.

Pollack, M. Comparison of childhood, adolescent, and adult schizophrenias. Etiologic significance of intellectual functioning. *Archives of General Psychiatry*, 1960, **2**, 652–660.

Pollack, M. Mental subnormality and childhood schizophrenia. In J. Zubin & G. A. Jervis (Eds.), *Psychopathology in mental development*. New York: Grune & Stratton, 1967. Pp. 460–494.

Pond, D. A. Psychiatric aspects of epileptic and brain-damaged children. *British Medical Journal*, 1961, **2**, 1454–1459.

Portenier, L. G. Psychological factors in testing and training the cerebral palsied. *Physiotherapy Review*, 1942, **22**, 301–303.

Porteus, S. D. *Studies in mental deviations*. Vineland, N.J.: The Training School, 1922.

Post, D. P. A comparative study of the Revised Stanford Binet and the Wechsler Intelligence Scale for Children administered to a group of thirty stutterers. Unpublished master's thesis, University of Southern California, 1952.

Post, J. M. *The effects of vocalization on the ability of third grade students to complete selected performance subtests from the Wechsler Intelligence Scale for Children*. (Doctoral dissertation, University of South Carolina) Ann Arbor, Mich.: University Microfilms, 1970. No. 70-19,602.

Poull, L. E. Constancy of I.Q. in mental defectives, according to the Stanford-Revision of Binet tests. *Journal of Educational Psychology*, 1921, **12**, 323–324.

Prentice, N. M., & Kelly, F. J. Intelligence and delinquency: A reconsideration. *Journal of Social Psychology*, 1963, **60**, 327–337.

Pressey, S. L., & Cole, L. W. Irregularity in a psychological examination as a measure of mental deterioration. *Journal of Abnormal Psychology*, 1918, **13**, 285–294. (a)

Pressey, S. L., & Cole, L. W. Are the present psychological scales reliable for the examination of adults? *Journal of Abnormal Psychology*, 1918, **13**, 314–323. (b)

Pressey, S. L., & Teter, G. F. A comparison of colored and white children by means of a group scale of intelligence. *Journal of Applied Psychology*, 1919, **3**, 277–282.

Price, A. C. A preliminary study in statistical comparison of the Revised Stanford-Binet Intelligence Test Form L with the Wechsler Intelligence Scale for Children using the ten year age level. Unpublished master's thesis, University of Florida, 1950.

Price, J. R., & Thorne, G. D. A statistical comparison of the WISC and Wechsler-Bellevue, Form I. *Journal of Consulting Psychology*, 1955, **19**, 479–482.

Pringle, M. L. K., & Pickup, K. T. The reliability and validity of the Goodenough Draw-a-Man Test: A pilot longitudinal study. *British Journal of Educational Psychology*, 1963, **33**, 297–306.

Prosser, N. S., & Crawford, V. B. Relationship of scores on the Wechsler Preschool and Primary Scale of Intelligence and the Stanford-Binet Intelligence Scale Form LM. *Journal of School Psychology*, 1971, **9**, 278–283.

Purcell, C. K., Drevdahl, J., & Purcell, K. The relationship between altitude–I.Q. discrepancy and anxiety. *Journal of Clinical Psychology*, 1952, **8**, 82–85.

Quay, H. C. Patterns of aggression, withdrawal, and immaturity. In H. C. Quay & J. S. Werry (Eds.), *Psychopathological disorders of childhood*. New York: Wiley, 1972. Pp. 1–29.

Quay, L. C. Language dialect, reinforcement, and the intelligence-test performance of Negro children. *Child Development*, 1971, **42**, 5–15.

Quereshi, M. Y. The comparability of WAIS and WISC subtest scores and IQ estimates. *Journal of Psychology*, 1968, **68**, 73–82. (a)

Quereshi, M. Y. Intelligence test scores as a function of sex of experimenter and sex of subject. *Journal of Psychology*, 1968, **69**, 277–284. (b)

Quereshi, M. Y. The internal consistency of the WISC scores for ages 5 to 16. *Journal of Clinical Psychology,* 1968, **24,** 192–195. (c)

Quereshi, M. Y. The optimum limits of testing on the Wechsler Intelligence Scales. *Genetic Psychology Monographs,* 1968, **78,** 141–190. (d)

Quereshi, M. Y., & Miller, J. M. The comparability of the WAIS, WISC, and WBII. *Journal of Educational Measurement,* 1970, **7,** 105–111.

Rabin, A. I. Review of the Wechsler Intelligence Scale for Children. In O. K. Buros (Ed.), *The fifth mental measurements yearbook.* Highland Park, N.J.: Gryphon Press, 1959. Pp. 560–561.

Rabin, A. I. Assessment of abnormalities in intellectual development. In J. Zubin & G. A. Jervis (Eds.), *Psychopathology of mental development.* New York: Grune & Stratton, 1967. Pp. 429–446.

Ramirez, M., III, & Gonzalez, A. Mexican-Americans and intelligence testing: Racism in the schools. Unpublished manuscript, University of California at Riverside, 1971.

Ramirez, M., III, Taylor, C., Jr., & Petersen, B. Mexican-American cultural membership and adjustment to school. *Developmental Psychology,* 1971, **4,** 141–148.

Ramsey, P. H., & Vane, J. R. A factor analytic study of the Stanford Binet with young children. *Journal of School Psychology,* 1970, **8,** 278–284.

Rapaport, D., Gill, M. M., & Schafer, R. *Diagnostic psychological testing.* (Rev. ed.) New York: International Universities Press, 1968.

Rapaport, I. A comparison of performance on the Wechsler Intelligence Scale for Children and the Revised Stanford-Binet Scale. Unpublished master's thesis, University of Pittsburgh, 1951.

Raskin, L. M., & Fong, L. J. Temporal stability of the PPVT in normal and educable-retarded children. *Psychological Reports,* 1970, **26,** 547–549.

Raskin, L. M., Offenbach, S. I., & Scoonover, D. L. A developmental study of PPVT temporal stability over two 6-mo. intervals. *Psychological Reports,* 1971, **28,** 501–502.

Rasof, B., Linde, L. M., & Dunn, O. J. Intellectual development in children with congenital heart disease. *Child Development,* 1967, **38,** 1043–1053.

Raven, J. C. *Guide to using the Standard Progressive Matrices.* London: Lewis, 1960.

Ravenette, A. T., & Kahn, J. H. Intellectual ability of disturbed children in a working-class area. *British Journal of Social and Clinical Psychology,* 1962, **1,** 208–212.

Read, K. H. *The nursery school.* (3rd ed.) Philadelphia: Saunders, 1960.

Reed, H. B. C., Jr., & Fitzhugh, K. B. Patterns of deficits in relation to severity of cerebral dysfunction in children and adults. *Journal of Consulting Psychology,* 1966, **30,** 98–102.

Reed, H. B. C., Jr., & Reitan, R. M. Intelligence test performances of brain damaged subjects with lateralized motor deficits. *Journal of Consulting Psychology,* 1963, **27,** 102–106.

Reed, H. B. C., Jr., Reitan, R. M., & Kløve, H. Influence of cerebral lesions on psychological test performances of older children. *Journal of Consulting Psychology,* 1965, **29,** 247–251.

Reed, J. C. Reading achievement as related to differences between WISC Verbal and Performance IQ's. *Child Development,* 1967, **38,** 835–840.

Reed, J. C., & Reed, H. B. C., Jr. Concept formation ability and non-verbal abstract thinking among older children with chronic cerebral dysfunction. *Journal of Special Education,* 1967, **1,** 157–161.

Reed, J. C., & Reitan, R. M. Verbal and Performance differences among brain-injured children with lateralized motor deficits. *Perceptual and Motor Skills,* 1969, **29,** 747–752.

Reed, M. Deaf and partially hearing children. In P. Mittler (Ed.), *The psychological assessment of mental and physical handicaps.* London: Methuen, 1970. Pp. 403–441.

Reeves, J. W. *Thinking about thinking.* London: Secker and Warburg, 1965.

Reger, R. Brief tests of intelligence and academic achievement. *Psychological Reports,* 1962, **11,** 82.

Reger, R. WISC, WRAT, and CMAS scores in retarded children. *American Journal of Mental Deficiency,* 1966, **70,** 717–721.

Reid, W. B., Moore, D., & Alexander, D. Abbreviated form of the WISC for use with brain-damaged and mentally retarded children. *Journal of Consulting and Clinical Psychology,* 1968, **32,** 236.

Reid, W. R., & Schoer, L. A. Reading achievement, social-class and subtest pattern on the WISC. *Journal of Educational Research,* 1966, **59,** 469–472.

Reidy, M. E. A validity study of the Wechsler-Bellevue Intelligence Scale for Children and its relationship to reading and arithmetic. Unpublished master's thesis, Catholic University of America, 1952.

Reinhart, R. A. Some relationships between early rheumatic fever, intelligence and anxiety scores. *Journal of Child Psychology and Psychiatry,* 1965, **6,** 243–250.

Rellas, A. J. The use of the Wechsler Preschool and Primary Scale (WPPSI) in the early identification of gifted students. *California Journal of Educational Research,* 1969, **20,** 117–119.

Renzulli, J. S., & Paulus, D. H. A cross-validation study of the item ordering of the Peabody Picture Vocabulary Test. *Journal of Educational Measurement,* 1969, **6,** 15–20.

Reynell, J. Children with physical handicaps. In P. Mittler (Ed.), *The psychological assessment of mental and physical handicaps.* London: Methuen, 1970. Pp. 443–469.

Rheingold, H. L. Interpreting mental retardation to parents. *Journal of Consulting Psychology,* 1945, **9,** 143–151.

Rhodes, F. *Manual for the Rhodes WISC scatter profile*. San Diego, Calif.: Educational and Industrial Testing Service, 1969.

Rice, J. A., & Brown, L. F. Validity of the Peabody Picture Vocabulary Test in a sample of low IQ children. *American Journal of Mental Deficiency*, 1967, **71**, 602–603.

Richards, J. T. *The effectiveness of the Wechsler Preschool and Primary Scale of Intelligence in the identification of mentally retarded children*. (Doctoral dissertation, University of Virginia) Ann Arbor, Mich.: University Microfilms, 1968. No. 60-4019.

Richardson, H. M., & Surko, E. F. WISC scores and status in reading and arithmetic of delinquent children. *Journal of Genetic Psychology*, 1956, **89**, 251–262.

Richardson, S. A. The social environment and individual functioning. In H. G. Birch (Ed.), *Brain damage in children*. Baltimore: Williams & Wilkins, 1964. Pp. 100–115.

Riessman, F. *The culturally deprived child*. New York: Harper, 1962.

Riggs, M. M., & Burchard, K. A. Intra-scale scatter for two kinds of mentally defective children. *Training School Bulletin*, 1952, **49**, 36–44.

Rimland, B. *Infantile autism*. New York: Appleton-Century-Crofts, 1964.

Riscalla, L. M. The captive psychologist and the captive patient: The dilemma and alternatives. In S. L. Brodsky (Chm.), Shared results and open files with the client: Professional irresponsibility or effective involvement? Symposium presented at the American Psychological Association, Washington, D.C., September 1971.

Robeck, M. C. Subtest patterning of problem readers on WISC. *California Journal of Educational Research*, 1960, **11**, 110–115.

Robeck, M. C. Children who show undue tension when reading: A group diagnosis. *International Reading Association Conference Proceedings*, 1962, **7**, 133–138.

Robeck, M. C. Intellectual strengths and weaknesses shown by reading clinic subjects on the WISC. *Journal of Developmental Reading*, 1964, **7**, 120–129.

Roberts, J. A. F., & Mellone, M. A. On the adjustment of Terman-Merrill I.Q.s to secure comparability at different ages. *British Journal of Psychology Statistical Section*, 1952, **5**, 65–79.

Robinson, H. B., & Robinson, N. M. *The mentally retarded child: A psychological approach*. New York: McGraw-Hill, 1965.

Robinson, H. B., & Robinson, N. M. Mental retardation. In P. H. Mussen (Ed.), *Carmichael's manual of child psychology*. (3rd ed.) New York: Wiley, 1970. Pp. 615–666.

Roca, P. Problems of adapting intelligence scales from one culture to another. *High School Journal*, 1955, **38**, 124–131.

Rockwell, G. J., Jr. WISC Object Assembly and bodily concern. *Journal of Consulting Psychology*, 1967, **31**, 221.

Roe, A., & Shakow, D. Intelligence in mental disorder. *Annals of the New York Academy of Sciences*, 1942, **42**, 361–490.

Rogge, H. J. *A study of the relationships of reading achievement to certain other factors in a population of delinquent boys*. (Doctoral dissertation, University of Minnesota) Ann Arbor, Mich.: University Microfilms, 1959. No. 60-944.

Rohrs, F. W., & Haworth, M. R. The 1960 Stanford-Binet, WISC, and Goodenough Tests with mentally retarded children. *American Journal of Mental Deficiency*, 1962, **66**, 853–859.

Rose, F. C. The occurrence of short auditory memory span among school children referred for diagnosis of reading difficulties. *Journal of Educational Research*, 1958, **51**, 459–464.

Rosen, M., Stallings, L., Floor, L., & Nowakiwska, M. Reliability and stability of Wechsler IQ scores for institutionalized mental subnormals. *American Journal of Mental Deficiency*, 1968, **73**, 218–225.

Rosenberg, L. A., & Stroud, M. Limitations of brief intelligence testing with young children. *Psychological Reports*, 1966, **19**, 721–722.

Rosenthal, R. *Experimenter effects in behavioral research*. New York: Appleton-Century-Crofts, 1966.

Rosenthal, R., & Jacobson, L. *Pygmalion in the classroom*. New York: Holt, Rinehart and Winston, 1968.

Ross, A. O. *The practice of clinical child psychology*. New York: Grune & Stratton, 1959.

Ross, A. O. Learning difficulties of children: Dysfunctions, disorders, disabilities. *Journal of School Psychology*, 1967, **5**, 82–92.

Ross, R. T. IQ changes in hospitalized mental retardates. *Developmental Psychology*, 1971, **5**, 395–397.

Ross, R. T., & Morledge, J. Comparison of the WISC and WAIS at chronological age sixteen. *Journal of Consulting Psychology*, 1967, **31**, 331–332.

Rottersman, L. A comparison of the IQ scores on the new Revised Stanford-Binet, Form L, the Wechsler Intelligence Scale for Children, and the Goodenough "Draw a Man" Test at the six year age level. Unpublished master's thesis, University of Nebraska, 1950.

Rourke, B. P., Young, G. C., & Flewelling, R. W. The relationships between WISC Verbal-Performance discrepancies and selected verbal, auditory-perceptual, visual-perceptual, and problem-solving abilities in children with learning disabilities. *Journal of Clinical Psychology*, 1971, **27**, 475–479.

Rowley, V. N. Analysis of the WISC performance of brain damaged and emotionally disturbed children. *Journal of Consulting Psychology*, 1961, **25**, 553.

Rowley, V. N., & Stone, F. B. A further note on the relationship between WISC functioning and the CMAS. *Journal of Clinical Psychology,* 1963, **19,** 426.

Rucker, C. N. Technical language in the school psychologist's report. *Psychology in the Schools,* 1967, **4,** 146–150. (a)

Rucker, C. N. Report writing in school psychology: A critical investigation. *Journal of School Psychology,* 1967, **5,** 101–108. (b)

Ruebush, B. K. Anxiety. In H. W. Stevenson (Ed.), Child psychology. *The sixty-second yearbook of the National Society for the Study of Education.* Part I. Chicago: University of Chicago Press, 1963. Pp. 460–516.

Ruschival, M. L., & Way, J. G. The WPPSI and the Stanford-Binet: A validity and reliability study using gifted preschool children. *Journal of Consulting and Clinical Psychology,* 1971, **37,** 163.

Rushton, C. S., & Stockwin, A. E. Changes in Terman-Merrill I.Qs. of educationally sub-normal boys. *British Journal of Educational Psychology,* 1963, **33,** 132–142.

Russ, J. D., & Soboloff, H. R. *A primer of cerebral palsy.* Springfield, Ill.: Charles C Thomas, 1958.

Russell Sage Foundation. *Guidelines for the collection, maintenance, and dissemination of pupil records.* New York: RSF, 1970.

Rutter, M. Intelligence and childhood psychiatric disorder. *British Journal of Social and Clinical Psychology,* 1964, **3,** 120–129.

Rutter, M. Behavioural and cognitive characteristics of a series of psychotic children. In J. K. Wing (Ed.), *Early childhood autism: Clinical, educational and social aspects.* London: Pergamon Press, 1966.

Rutter, M. Concepts of autism: A review of research. *Journal of Child Psychology and Psychiatry,* 1968, **9,** 1–25.

Rutter, M., Greenfeld, D., & Lockyer, L. A five to fifteen year follow-up study of infantile psychosis: II. Social and behavioural outcome. *British Journal of Psychiatry,* 1967, **113,** 1183–1199.

Rutter, M., & Lockyer, L. A five to fifteen year follow-up study of infantile psychosis: I. Description of sample. *British Journal of Psychiatry,* 1967, **113,** 1169–1182.

Sacks, E. L. Intelligence scores as a function of experimentally established social relationships between child and examiner. *Journal of Abnormal and Social Psychology,* 1952, **47,** 354–358.

Salvati, S. R. *A comparison of WISC I.Q.'s and altitude scores as predictors of learning ability of mentally retarded subjects.* (Doctoral dissertation, New York University) Ann Arbor, Mich.: University Microfilms, 1960. No. 60–5292.

Sanchez, G. I. Bilingualism and mental measures. *Journal of Applied Psychology,* 1934, **18,** 765–772.

Sandercock, M. G., & Butler, A. J. An analysis of the performance of mental defectives on the Wechsler Intelligence Scale for Children. *American Journal of Mental Deficiency,* 1952, **57,** 100–105.

Sandstedt, B. Relationship between memory span and intelligence of severely retarded readers. *Reading Teacher,* 1964, **17,** 246–250.

Sarason, E. K., & Sarason, S. B. A problem in diagnosing feeblemindedness. *Journal of Abnormal and Social Psychology,* 1945, **40,** 323–329.

Sarason, S. B. *Psychological problems in mental deficiency.* (2nd ed.) New York: Harper, 1953.

Sarason, S. B. *Psychological problems in mental deficiency.* (3rd ed.) New York: Harper, 1959.

Sarason, S. B., Davidson, K. S., Lighthall, F. F., & Waite, R. A test anxiety scale for children. *Child Development,* 1958, **29,** 105–113.

Sarason, S. B., Davidson, K. S., Lighthall, F. F., Waite, R. R., & Ruebush, B. K. *Anxiety in elementary school children.* New York: Wiley, 1960.

Sarason, S. B., & Doris, J. *Psychological problems in mental deficiency.* (4th ed.) New York: Harper & Row, 1969.

Sarason, S. B., Hill, K. T., & Zimbardo, P. G. A longitudinal study of the relation of test anxiety to performance on intelligence and achievement tests. *Monographs of the Society for Research in Child Development,* 1964, **29**(7, Whole No. 98).

Sarason, S. B., Levine, M., Goldenberg, I. I., Cherlin, D. L., & Bennett, E. M. *Psychology in community settings: Clinical, educational, vocational, social aspects.* New York: Wiley, 1966.

Sargent, H. D. Psychological test reporting: An experiment in communication. *Bulletin of the Menninger Clinic,* 1951, **15,** 175–186.

Saslow, H. L. The comparability of the Peabody Picture Vocabulary Test and Revised Stanford-Binet, Form L-M, with cerebral palsied children. Paper presented at the meeting of the American Psychological Association, New York, 1961.

Saslow, H. L., & Larsen, E. T. The comparability of the Peabody and Children's Picture Tests, Stanford-Binet, and Vineland Scales with cerebral palsied children. Paper presented at the meeting of the Rocky Mountain Psychological Association, 1963.

Satter, G. Psychometric scatter among mentally retarded and normal children. *Training School Bulletin,* 1955, **52,** 63–68.

Sattler, J. M. Analysis of functions of the 1960 Stanford-Binet Intelligence Scale, Form L-M. *Journal of Clinical Psychology,* 1965, **21,** 173–179.

Sattler, J. M. Statistical reanalysis of Canady's "The effect of 'rapport' on the I.Q.: A new approach to the problem of racial psychology." *Psychological Reports,* 1966, **19,** 1203–1206. (a)

Sattler, J. M. Comments on Cieutat's "Examiner differences with the Stanford-Binet IQ." *Perceptual and Motor Skills,* 1966, **22,** 612–614. (b)

Sattler, J. M. Effects of cues and examiner influence on two Wechsler subtests. *Journal of Consulting and Clinical Psychology,* 1969, **33,** 716–721.

Sattler, J. M. Racial "experimenter effects" in experimentation, testing, interviewing, and psychotherapy. *Psychological Bulletin,* 1970, **73,** 137–160.

Sattler, J. M. Intelligence testing of ethnic minority-group and culturally disadvantaged children. In L. Mann and D. Sabatino (Eds.), *The first review of special education.* Vol. 2. Philadelphia: The JSE Press, 1973. Pp. 161–201. (a)

Sattler, J. M. Examiners' scoring style, accuracy, ability, and personality scores. *Journal of Clinical Psychology,* 1973, **29,** 38–39. (b)

Sattler, J. M. Racial experimenter effects. In K. S. Miller & R. M. Dreger (Eds.), *Comparative studies of blacks and whites in the United States.* New York: Seminar Press, 1973. Pp. 8–32. (c)

Sattler, J. M., & Anderson, N. E. Peabody Picture Vocabulary Test, Stanford-Binet, and Stanford-Binet Modified with normal and cerebral palsied preschool children. *Journal of Special Education,* 1973, **7,** in press.

Sattler, J. M., Hillix, W. A., & Neher, L. A. Halo effect in examiner scoring of intelligence test responses. *Journal of Consulting and Clinical Psychology,* 1970, **34,** 172–176.

Sattler, J. M., & Martin, S. Anxious and nonanxious examiner roles on two WISC subtests. *Psychology in the Schools,* 1971, **8,** 347–349.

Sattler, J. M., & Ryan, J. J. Scoring agreement on the Stanford-Binet. *Journal of Clinical Psychology,* 1973, **29,** 35–38. (a)

Sattler, J. M., & Ryan, J. J. Who should determine the scoring of WISC Vocabulary responses? *Journal of Clinical Psychology,* 1973, **29,** 50–54. (b)

Sattler, J. M., & Theye, F. Procedural, situational, and interpersonal variables in individual intelligence testing. *Psychological Bulletin,* 1967, **68,** 347–360.

Sattler, J. M., & Tozier, L. L. A review of intelligence test modifications used with cerebral palsied and other handicapped groups. *Journal of Special Education,* 1970, **4,** 391–398.

Sattler, J. M., & Winget, B. M. Intelligence testing procedures as affected by expectancy and IQ. *Journal of Clinical Psychology,* 1970, **26,** 446–448.

Sattler, J. M., Winget, B. M., & Roth, R. J. Scoring difficulty of WAIS and WISC Comprehension, Similarities, and Vocabulary responses. *Journal of Clinical Psychology,* 1969, **25,** 175–177.

Satz, P., Van de Riet, H., & Mogel, S. An abbreviation of the WISC for clinical use. *Journal of Consulting Psychology,* 1967, **31,** 108.

Saunders, B. T., & Vitro, F. T. Examiner expectancy and bias as a function of the referral process in cognitive assessment. *Psychology in the Schools,* 1971, **8,** 168–171.

Saunders, L. *Cultural difference and medical care: The case of the Spanish-speaking people of the Southwest.* New York: Russell Sage Foundation, 1954.

Savage, R. D. *Psychometric assessment of the individual child.* Baltimore: Penguin Books, 1968.

Sawyer, R. N. An investigation of the reliability of the French Pictorial Test of Intelligence. *Journal of Educational Research,* 1968, **61,** 211–214.

Sawyer, R. N., & Whitten, J. R. Concurrent validity of the Quick Test. *Psychological Reports,* 1972, **30,** 64–66.

Schachter, F. F., & Apgar, V. Comparison of preschool Stanford-Binet and school-age WISC IQs. *Journal of Educational Psychology,* 1958, **49,** 320–323.

Schafer, R. *Psychoanalytic interpretation in Rorschach testing.* New York: Grune & Stratton, 1954.

Schafer, S., & Leitch, M. An exploratory study of the usefulness of a battery of psychological tests with nursery school children. *American Journal of Psychiatry,* 1948, **104,** 647–652.

Scheerenberger, R. C. Mental retardation: Definition, classification, and prevalence. *Mental Retardation Abstracts,* 1964, **1,** 432–441.

Scherer, I. W. The prediction of academic achievement in brain injured children. *Exceptional Children,* 1961, **28,** 103–106.

Schmideberg, M. The socio-psychological impact of IQ tests. *International Journal of Offender Therapy,* 1970, **14,** 91–97.

Schneider, J., & Smillie, D. The use of scatter on the Stanford-Binet. *Psychological Service Center Journal,* 1959, **11,** 73–75.

Schofield, W. Critique of scatter and profile analysis of psychometric data. *Journal of Clinical Psychology,* 1952, **8,** 16–22.

Schonell, F. E. *Educating spastic children.* London: Oliver and Boyd, 1956.

Schonell, F. E. Intelligence testing. In R. S. Illingworth (Ed.), *Recent advances in cerebral palsy.* Boston: Little, Brown, 1958. Pp. 132–145.

Schoonover, S. M., & Hertel, R. K. Diagnostic implications of WISC scores. *Psychological Reports,* 1970, **26,** 967–973.

Schroeder, H. E., & Kleinsasser, L. D. Examiner bias: A determinant of children's verbal behavior on the WISC. *Journal of Consulting and Clinical Psychology, 1972,* **39,** 451–454.

Schubert, J. Effect of training on the performance of the W.I.S.C. 'Block Design' subtest. *British Journal of Social and Clinical Psychology,* 1967, **6,** 144–149.

Schwartz, M. L. The scoring of WAIS Comprehension responses by experienced and inexperienced judges. *Journal of Clinical Psychology,* 1966, **22,** 425–427.

Schwartz, M. L., & Dennerll, R. D. Neuropsychological assessment of children with, without, and with questionable epileptogenic dysfunction. *Perceptual and Motor Skills,* 1970, **30,** 111–121.

Schwartz, R. H., & Flanigan, P. J. Evaluation of examiner bias in intelligence testing. *American Journal of Mental Deficiency,* 1971, **76,** 262–265.

Schwebel, A. I., & Bernstein, A. J. The effects of impulsivity on the performance of lower-class children on four WISC subtests. *American Journal of Orthopsychiatry,* 1970, **40,** 629–636.

Schwitzgoebel, R. R. The predictive value of some relationships between the Wechsler Intelligence Scale for Children and academic achievement in fifth grade. Unpublished doctoral dissertation, University of Wisconsin, 1952.

Scoggins, B. J. A comparative study of the Full-Range Picture Vocabulary Test and the Peabody Picture Vocabulary Test. Unpublished master's thesis, Vanderbilt University, 1960.

Scott, G. R. A comparison between the Wechsler Intelligence Scale for Children and the Revised Stanford-Binet Scales. Unpublished master's thesis, Southern Methodist University, 1950.

Scottish Council for Research in Education. *Manual for Scottish standardisation of the Wechsler Intelligence Scale for Children.* Edinburgh: SCRE, 1965.

Scottish Council for Research in Education. *The Scottish standardisation of the Wechsler Intelligence Scale for Children.* London: University of London Press, 1967.

Seashore, H. G., Differences between Verbal and Performance IQs on the Wechsler Intelligence Scale for Children. *Journal of Consulting Psychology,* 1951, **15,** 62–67.

Sekyra, F., & Arnoult, J. F. Negro intellectual assessment with three instruments contrasting Caucasian and Negro norms. *Journal of Learning Disabilities,* 1968, **1,** 564–569.

Sells, S. B. Evaluation of psychological measures used in the Health Examination Survey of children ages 6–11. U.S. Department of Health, Education, and Welfare, Public Health Service, 1966, No. 1000 (Series 2, No. 15).

Semeonoff. B. Review of R. B. Ammons & C. H. Ammons, The Quick Test (QT). *British Journal of Psychology,* 1964, **55,** 117.

Semler, I. J., & Iscoe, I. Structure of intelligence in Negro and white children. *Journal of Educational Psychology,* 1966, **57,** 326–336.

Shaffer, L. F. Review of the WISC. *Journal of Consulting Psychology,* 1949, **13,** 453–454.

Shah, S. T. Privileged communications, confidentiality, and privacy: Confidentiality. *Professional Psychology,* 1970, **1,** 159–164.

Shapiro, M. B. An experimental approach to diagnostic psychological testing. *Journal of Mental Science,* 1951, **97,** 748–764.

Shapiro, M. B. Experimental method in the psychological description of the individual psychiatric patient. *International Journal of Social Psychiatry,* 1957, **3,** 89–102.

Sharp, H. C. A comparison of slow learner's scores on three individual intelligence scales. *Journal of Clinical Psychology,* 1957, **13,** 372–374.

Sharp, H. C. A note on the reliability of the Leiter International Performance Scale 1948 Revision. *Journal of Consulting Psychology,* 1958, **22,** 320.

Sharp, S. E. Individual psychology: A study in psychological method. *American Journal of Psychology,* 1898, **10,** 329–391.

Shaw, D. J., Mathews, C. G., & Kløve, H. The equivalence of WISC and PPVT IQs. *American Journal of Mental Deficiency,* 1966, **70,** 601–604.

Sheldon, M. S., & Garton, J. A note on "A WISC profile for retarded readers." *Alberta Journal of Educational Research,* 1959, **5,** 264–267.

Shepherd, C. W., Jr. Childhood chronic illness and visual motor perceptual development. *Exceptional Children,* 1969, **36,** 39–42.

Shinagawa, F. A statistical study of discrepancy between Verbal IQ and Performance IQ on WISC. *Japanese Journal of Child Psychiatry,* 1960, **1,** 403–411.

Shinagawa, F. Studies on the relationship between intelligence structure and personality traits: An analysis of WISC discrepancy. *Japanese Psychological Research,* 1963, **5,** 55–62.

Shipe, D., Cromwell, R. L., & Dunn, L. M. Responses of emotionally disturbed and nondisturbed retardates to PPVT items of human versus nonhuman content. *Journal of Consulting Psychology,* 1966, **30,** 439–443.

Shively, J. J., & Smith, A. E. Understanding the psychological report. *Psychology in the Schools,* 1969, **6,** 272–273.

Shore, M. F. The utilization of the patient-examiner relationship in intelligence testing of children. *Journal of Projective Techniques,* 1962, **26,** 239–243.

Shotwell, A. M. Arthur performance ratings of Mexican and American high-grade mental defectives. *American Journal of Mental Deficiency,* 1945, **49,** 445–449.

Shotwell, A. M., & McCulloch, T. L. Accuracy of abbreviated forms of the Revised Stanford-Binet Scale with institutionalized epileptics. *American Journal of Mental Deficiency,* 1944, **49,** 162–164.

Shotwell, A. M., O'Connor, G., Gabet, Y., & Dingman, H. F. Relation of the Peabody Picture Vocabulary Test IQ to the Stanford-Binet IQ. *American Journal of Mental Deficiency*, 1969, **74**,
39–42.

Shuey, A. M. *The testing of Negro intelligence*. (2nd ed.) New York: Social Science Press, 1966.

Sievers, D. J. Psychometric problems related to cerebral palsy. Unpublished master's thesis, University of New Mexico, 1950.

Sigel, I. E. How intelligence tests limit understanding of intelligence. *Merrill-Palmer Quarterly*,
1963, **9**, 39–56.

Silberberg, N. E., & Feldt, L. S. The Peabody Picture Vocabulary Test as an IQ screening technique for primary grade referral cases. *Journal of School Psychology*, 1966, **5**, 21–30.

Silberberg, N. E., & Feldt, L. S. Intellectual and perceptual correlates of reading disabilities. *Journal of School Psychology*, 1968, **6**, 237–245.

Silverstein, A. B. An evaluation of two short forms of the Stanford-Binet, Form L-M, for use with
mentally retarded children. *American Journal of Mental Deficiency*, 1963, **67**, 922–923. (a)

Silverstein, A. B. Psychological testing practices in state institutions for the mentally retarded.
American Journal of Mental Deficiency, 1963, **68**, 440–445. (b)

Silverstein, A. B. WISC and WAIS IQs for the mentally retarded. *American Journal of Mental
Deficiency*, 1963, **67**, 617–618. (c)

Silverstein, A. B. Comparison of two item-classification schemes for the Stanford-Binet. *Psychological Reports*, 1965, **17**, 964.

Silverstein, A. B. A further evaluation of two short forms of the Stanford-Binet. *American Journal
of Mental Deficiency*, 1966, **70**, 928–929.

Silverstein, A. B. Validity of a new approach to the design of WAIS, WISC, and WPPSI short
forms. *Journal of Consulting and Clinical Pychology*, 1968, **32**, 478–479. (a)

Silverstein, A. B. Variance components in five psychological tests. *Psychological Reports*, 1968,
23, 141–142. (b)

Silverstein, A. B. WISC and WPPSI IQs for the gifted. *Psychological Reports*, 1968, **22**, 1168. (c)

Silverstein, A. B. WISC subtest patterns of retardates. *Psychological Reports*, 1968, **23**, 1061–
1062. (d)

Silverstein, A. B. WPPSI IQs for the mentally retarded. *American Journal of Mental Deficiency*,
1968, **73**, 446. (e)

Silverstein, A. B. An alternative factor analytic solution for Wechsler's Intelligence Scales. *Educational and Psychological Measurement*, 1969, **29**, 763–767. (a)

Silverstein, A. B. Changes in the measured intelligence of institutionalized retardates as a function
of hospital age. *Developmental Psychology*, 1969, **1**, 125–127. (b)

Silverstein, A. B. The internal consistency of the Stanford-Binet. *American Journal of Mental
Deficiency*, 1969, **73**, 753–754. (c)

Silverstein, A. B. Reappraisal of the validity of the WAIS, WISC, and WPPSI short forms. *Journal
of Consulting and Clinical Psychology*, 1970, **34**, 12–14. (a)

Silverstein, A. B. Reappraisal of the validity of a short short form of Wechsler's Scales. *Psychological Reports*, 1970, **26**, 559–561. (b)

Silverstein, A. B., & Fisher, G. M. An evaluation of two short forms of the Stanford-Binet, Form
L-M, for use with mentally retarded adults. *American Journal of Mental Deficiency*, 1961, **65**,
486–488.

Silverstein, A. B., & Hill, T. V. Comparability of three picture vocabulary tests with retarded
school children. *Training School Bulletin*, 1967, **64**, 58–61.

Silverstein, A. B., Mohan, P. J., Franken, R. E., & Rhone, D. E. Test anxiety and intellectual performance in mentally retarded school children. *Child Development*, 1964, **35**, 1137–1146.

Simmons, O. G. Mutual images and expectations of Anglo-Americans and Mexican-Americans.
Daedalus, 1961, **90**, 286–299.

Simon, W. E. Expectancy effects in the scoring of vocabulary items: A study of scorer bias. *Journal
of Educational Measurement*, 1969, **6**, 159–164.

Simpson, R. L. Study of the comparability of the WISC and the WAIS. *Journal of Consulting and
Clinical Psychology*, 1970, **34**, 156–158.

Simpson, W. H., & Bridges, C. C., Jr. A short form of the Wechsler Intelligence Scale for Children.
Journal of Clinical Psychology, 1959, **15**, 424.

Sloan, W. The Lincoln-Oseretsky Motor Development Scale. *Genetic Psychology Monographs*,
1955, **51**, 183–252.

Sloan, W., & Birch, J. W. A rationale for degrees of retardation. *American Journal of Mental
Deficiency*, 1955, **60**, 258–264.

Sloan, W., & Cutts, R. A. Test patterns of mental defectives on the Revised Stanford-Binet Scale.
American Journal of Mental Deficiency, 1947, **51**, 394–396.

Sloan, W., & Schneider, B. A study of the Wechsler Intelligence Scale for Children with mental
defectives. *American Journal of Mental Deficiency*, 1951, **55**, 573–575.

Slosson, R. L. *Slosson Intelligence Test (SIT) for children and adults*. New York: Slosson Educational Publications, 1963.

Slutzky, J. E., Justman, J., & Wrightstone, J. W. Screening children for placement in special classes
for the mentally retarded: A preliminary report. *American Journal of Mental Deficiency*, 1953,
57, 687–690.

Smith, A. Ambiguities in concepts and studies of "brain damage" and "organicity." *Journal of Nervous and Mental Disease,* 1962, **135,** 311–326.

Smith, B. S. The relative merits of certain verbal and non-verbal tests at the second-grade level. *Journal of Clinical Psychology,* 1961, **17,** 53–54.

Smith, E. H. A normative study of the WISC with high grade retarded boys. Unpublished manuscript, Wayne County Training School, Northville, Mich., 1959.

Smith, H. W., & May, W. T. Individual differences among inexperienced psychological examiners. *Psychological Reports,* 1967, **20,** 759–762.

Smith, H. W., May, W. T., & Lebovitz, L. Testing experience and Stanford-Binet scores. *Journal of Educational Measurement,* 1966, **3,** 229–233.

Smith, N. C., Jr. *Factors underlying WISC performance in juvenile public offenders.* (Doctoral dissertation, Ohio State University) Ann Arbor, Mich.: University Microfilms, 1969. No. 69–15,966.

Smyth, R., & Reznikoff, M. Attitudes of psychiatrists toward the usefulness of psychodiagnostic reports. *Professional Psychology,* 1971, **2,** 283–288.

Snow, R. E. Review of R. Rosenthal and L. Jacobson, *Pygmalion in the classroom. Contemporary Psychology,* 1969, **14,** 197–199.

Solkoff, N. Frustration and WISC Coding performance among brain-injured children. *Perceptual and Motor Skills,* 1964, **18,** 54.

Solkoff, N., & Chrisien, G. Frustration and perceptual-motor performance. *Perceptual and Motor Skills,* 1963, **17,** 282.

Solkoff, N., Todd, G. A., & Screven, C. G. Effects of frustration on perceptual-motor performance. *Child Development,* 1964, **35,** 569–575.

Sollee, N. D. *Verbal competence and the acquisition of conservation.* (Doctoral dissertation, Boston University) Ann Arbor, Mich.: University Microfilms, 1969. No. 69–18,718.

Sontag, L. W., Baker, C. T., & Nelson, V. L. Personality as a determinant of performance. *American Journal of Orthopsychiatry,* 1955, **25,** 555–562.

Sontag, L. W., Baker, C. T., & Nelson, V. L. Mental growth and personality development: A longitudinal study. *Monographs of the Society for Research in Child Development,* 1958, **23**(2, Whole No. 68).

Spache, G. Serial testing with the Revised Stanford-Binet Scale, Form L, in the test range II-XIV. *American Journal of Orthopsychiatry,* 1942, **12,** 81–86.

Spache, G. The Vocabulary tests of the Revised Stanford-Binet as independent measures of intelligence. *Journal of Educational Research,* 1943, **36,** 512–516.

Spache, G. Methods of predicting results of full scale Stanford-Binet. *American Journal of Orthopsychiatry,* 1944, **14,** 480–482.

Spaulding, P. J. Comparison of 500 complete and abbreviated Revised Stanford Scales administered to mental defectives. *American Journal of Mental Deficiency,* 1945, **50,** 81–88.

Spearman, C. E. *The abilities of man.* New York: Macmillan, 1927.

Spellacy, F., & Black, F. W. Intelligence assessment of language-impaired children by means of two nonverbal tests. *Journal of Clinical Psychology,* 1972, **28,** 357–358.

Spence, J. T. Patterns of performance on WAIS Similarities in schizophrenic, brain-damaged and normal subjects. *Psychological Reports,* 1963, **13,** 431–436.

Spreen, O., & Anderson, C. W. Sibling relationship and mental deficiency diagnosis as reflected in Wechsler test patterns. *American Journal of Mental Deficiency,* 1966, **71,** 406–410.

Spreen, O., & Tryk, H. E. WISC Information subtest in a Canadian population. *Canadian Journal of Behavioural Science,* 1970, **2,** 294–298.

Stablein, J. E., Willey, D. S., & Thomson, C. W. An evaluation of the Davis-Eells (Culture-Fair) Test using Spanish and Anglo-American children. *Journal of Educational Sociology,* 1961, **35,** 73–78.

Stacey, C. L., & Carleton, F. O. The relationship between Raven's Colored Progressive Matrices and two tests of general intelligence. *Journal of Clinical Psychology,* 1955, **11,** 84–85.

Stacey, C. L., & Levin, J. Performance of retarded individuals on Stanford-Binet and Wechsler-Bellevue Intelligence Scales. *American Journal of Mental Deficiency,* 1950, **55,** 123–131.

Stacey, C. L., & Levin, J. Correlation analysis of scores of subnormal subjects on the Stanford-Binet and Wechsler Intelligence Scale for Children. *American Journal of Mental Deficiency,* 1951, **55,** 590–597.

Stacey, C. L., & Portnoy, B. A study of the differential responses on the Vocabulary sub-test of the Wechsler Intelligence Scale for Children. *Journal of Clinical Psychology,* 1950, **6,** 401–403.

Staffieri, J. R. Performance of preschool children on the Quick Test (QT). *Psychological Reports,* 1971, **29,** 472.

Stark, J., Cohen, S., & Eisenson, J. Performances of aphasic children on the PPVT and Auditory Decoding tests. *Journal of Special Education,* 1968, **2,** 435–437.

Stark, R. A comparison of intelligence test scores on the Wechsler Intelligence Scale for Children and the Wartegg Drawing Completion Test with school achievement of elementary school children. Unpublished master's thesis, University of Detroit, 1954.

Stempel, E. F. The WISC and the SRA Primary Mental Abilities Test. *Child Development,* 1953, **24,** 257–261.

Stern, W. *The psychological methods of testing intelligence.* Baltimore: Warwick & York, 1914.

Sternlicht, M. A downward application of the 1960 Revised Stanford-Binet with retardates. *Journal of Clinical Psychology,* 1965, **21,** 79.

Stewart, K. D., Wood, D. Z., & Gallman, W. A. Concurrent validity of the Slosson Intelligence Test. *Journal of Clinical Psychology,* 1971, **27,** 218–220.

Stoddard, G. D. *The meaning of intelligence.* New York: Macmillian, 1943.

Stodolsky, S. S., & Lesser, G. S. Learning patterns in the disadvantaged. *Harvard Educational Review,* 1967, **37,** 546–593.

Stoke, S. M. The eight and nine year levels of the Stanford-Binet Scale. *School and Society,* 1933, **37,** 459–461.

Stormer, G. E. *Dimensions of the intellect unmeasured by the Stanford-Binet.* (Doctoral dissertation, University of Illinois) Ann Arbor, Mich.: University Microfilms, 1966. No. 66–12,432.

Stott, L. H., & Ball, R. S. Infant and preschool mental tests: Review and evaluation. *Monographs of the Society for Research in Child Development,* 1965, **30**(3, Whole No. 101).

Stott, M. B. The relation between intelligence and proficiency in Binet-Simon testing. *British Journal of Educational Psychology,* 1940, **10,** 135–142.

Stout, D. H. The Wechsler Intelligence Scale for Children and the Wechsler Adult Intelligence Scale: A comparison study. Unpublished master's thesis, Fresno State College, 1961.

Strandberg, T. E., Griffith, J., & Miner, L. Child language and screening intelligence. *Journal of Communication Disorders,* 1969, **2,** 268–272.

Strauss, A. A. Typology in mental deficiency. *American Association on Mental Deficiency Proceedings,* 1939, **44**(1), 85–90.

Strauss, A. A., & Kephart, N. C. *Psychopathology and education of the brain-injured child.* Vol. 2. *Progress in theory and clinic.* New York: Grune & Stratton, 1955.

Strauss, A. A., & Lehtinen, L. E. *Psychopathology and education of the brain-injured child.* New York: Grune & Stratton, 1947.

Strauss, A. A., & Werner, H. Qualitative analysis of the Binet test. *American Journal of Mental Deficiency,* 1940, **45,** 50–55.

Strong, A. C. Three hundred fifty white and colored children measured by the Binet-Simon Measuring Scale of Intelligence: A comparative study. *Pedagogical Seminary,* 1913, **20,** 485–515.

Strother, C. R. Evaluating intelligence of children handicapped by cerebral palsy. *Crippled Child,* 1945, **23,** 82–83.

Stroud, J. B. The intelligence test in school use: Some persistent issues. *Journal of Educational Psychology,* 1957, **48,** 77–85.

Stroud, J. B., Blommers, P., & Lauber, M. Correlation analysis of WISC and achievement tests. *Journal of Educational Psychology,* 1957, **48,** 18–26.

Sundberg, N. D. The practice of psychological testing in clinical services in the United States. *American Psychologist,* 1961, **16,** 79–83.

Sundean, D. A., & Salopek, T. F. Achievement and intelligence in primary and elementary classes for the educable mentally retarded. *Journal of School Psychology,* 1971, **9,** 150–156.

Swanson, M. S., & Jacobson, A. Evaluation of the S.I.T. for screening children with learning disabilities. *Journal of Learning Disabilities,* 1970, **3,** 318–320.

Sweet, R. C. *Variations in the intelligence test performance of lower-class children as a function of feedback or monetary reinforcement.* (Doctoral dissertation, University of Wisconsin) Ann Arbor, Mich.: University Microfilms, 1969. No. 70–3721.

Talbot, S. C. A cross validation study with the Wechsler Intelligence Scale for Children of the diagnostic signs for the syndrome sociopathy. Unpublished master's thesis, Drake University, 1960.

Talerico, M., & Brown, F. Intelligence test patterns of Puerto Rican children seen in child psychiatry. *Journal of Social Psychology,* 1963, **61,** 57–66.

Tallent, N. *Clinical psychological consultation.* Englewood Cliffs, N.J.: Prentice-Hall, 1963.

Tallent, N., & Reiss, W. J. Multidisciplinary views on the preparation of written clinical psychological reports: I. Spontaneous suggestions for content. *Journal of Clinical Psychology,* 1959, **15,** 218–221. (a)

Tallent, N., & Reiss, W. J. II. Acceptability of certain common content variables and styles of expression. *Journal of Clinical Psychology,* 1959, **15,** 273–274. (b)

Tallent, N., & Reiss, W. J. III. The trouble with psychological reports. *Journal of Clinical Psychology,* 1959, **15,** 444–446. (c)

Tansley, A. E., & Gulliford, R. *The education of slow learning children.* (2nd ed.) London: Routeledge & Kegan Paul, 1960.

Tarnopol, L. Testing the educationally handicapped child. *Academic Therapy Quarterly,* 1968, **3,** 81–89.

Tate, M. E. The influence of cultural factors on the Leiter International Performance Scale. *Journal of Abnormal and Social Psychology,* 1952, **47,** 497–501.

Tatham, L. J. A preliminary study in statistical comparison of the Revised Stanford-Binet Intelligence Test—Form L with the Wechsler Intelligence Scale for Children using the six and one-half year level. Unpublished master's thesis, University of Florida, 1952.

Taylor, E. M. *Psychological appraisal of children with cerebral defects.* Cambridge, Mass.: Harvard University Press, 1961.

Taylor, J. L., & Teicher, A. A clinical approach to reporting psychological test data. *Journal of Clinical Psychology,* 1946, **2,** 323–332.

Taylor, J. R. Screening intelligence. *Journal of Speech and Hearing Disorders,* 1963, **28,** 90–91.

Teahan, J. E., & Drews, E. M. A comparison of northern and southern Negro children on the WISC. *Journal of Consulting Psychology,* 1962, **26,** 292.

Teasdale, G. R. Validity of the PPVT as a test of language ability with lower SES children. *Psychological Reports,* 1969, **25,** 746.

Tellegen, A., & Briggs, P. F. Old wine in new skins: Grouping Wechsler subtests into new scales. *Journal of Consulting Psychology,* 1967, **31,** 499–506.

Terman, L. M. The Binet-Simon scale for measuring intelligence: Impressions gained by its application. *Psychological Clinic,* 1911, **5,** 199–206.

Terman, L. M. *The measurement of intelligence.* Boston: Houghton Mifflin, 1916.

Terman, L. M. A symposium. Intelligence and its measurement. *Journal of Educational Psychology,* 1921, **12,** 127–133.

Terman, L. M., & Childs, H. G. A tentative revision and extension of the Binet-Simon Measuring Scale of Intelligence. *Journal of Educational Psychology,* 1912. II **3,** 61–74, 133–143, 198–208, 277–289.

Terman, L. M., & Merrill, M. A. *Measuring intelligence.* Boston: Houghton Mifflin, 1937.

Terman, L. M., & Merrill, M. A. Tests of intelligence. B. 1937 Stanford-Binet Scales. In A. Weider (Ed.), *Contributions toward medical psychology.* Vol. 2. New York: Ronald Press, 1953. Pp. 510–521.

Terman, L. M., & Merrill, M. A. *Stanford-Binet Intelligence Scale.* Boston: Houghton Mifflin, 1960.

Thomas, A., Hertzig, M. E., Dryman, I., & Fernandez, P. Examiner effect in IQ testing of Puerto Rican working-class children. *American Journal of Orthopsychiatry,* 1971, **41,** 809–821.

Thomas, H. Psychological assessment instruments for use with human infants. *Merrill-Palmer Quarterly,* 1970, **16,** 179–223.

Thompson, B. B. *The relation of auditory discrimination and intelligence test scores to success in primary reading.* (Doctoral dissertation, Indiana University) Ann Arbor, Mich.: University Microfilms, 1961. No. 61–3228.

Thompson, B. B. A longitudinal study of auditory discrimination. *Journal of Educational Research,* 1963, **56,** 376–378.

Thompson, C. W., & Magaret, G. A. Differential test responses of normals and mental defectives. *Journal of Abnormal and Social Psychology,* 1947, **42,** 285–293.

Thorndike, E. L. Intelligence and its measurement. *Journal of Educational Psychology,* 1921, **12,** 124–127.

Thorndike, E. L. *The measurement of intelligence.* New York: Bureau of Publications, Teachers College, Columbia University, 1927.

Thorndike, R. L. Review of R. Rosenthal and L. Jacobson, *Pygmalion in the classroom. American Educational Research Journal,* 1968, **5,** 708–711.

Thorndike, R. L. Educational measurement for the seventies. In R. L. Thorndike (Ed.), *Educational measurement.* (2nd ed.) Washington, D.C.: American Council on Education, 1971. Pp. 3–14.

Thorndike, R. L., & Hagen, E. P. *Measurement and evaluation in psychology and education.* (3rd ed.) New York: Wiley, 1969.

Thorne, F. C. Operational psychological report writing. *Journal of Clinical Psychology,* 1960, **16,** 343–349.

Thorne, F. C. The privileged nature of psychological records. *Journal of Clinical Psychology,* 1961, **17,** 211–212.

Throne, F. M., Kaspar, J. C., & Schulman, J. L. The Peabody Picture Vocabulary Test in comparison with other intelligence tests and an achievement test in a group of mentally retarded boys. *Educational and Psychological Measurement,* 1965, **25,** 589–595.

Throne, F. M., Schulman, J. L., & Kaspar, J. C. Reliability and stability of the Wechsler Intelligence Scale for Children for a group of mentally retarded boys. *American Journal of Mental Deficiency,* 1962, **67,** 455–457.

Thurston, J. R. Counseling the parents of mentally retarded children. *Training School Bulletin,* 1963, **60,** 113–117.

Thurstone, L. L. Primary mental abilities. *Psychometric Monographs,* 1938, No. 1.

Tiber, N., & Kennedy, W. A. The effects of incentives on the intelligence test performance of different social groups. *Journal of Consulting Psychology,* 1964, **28,** 187.

Tigay, B., & Kempler, H. L. Stability of WISC scores of children hospitalized for emotional disturbance. *Perceptual and Motor Skills,* 1971, **32,** 487–490.

Tillinghast, B. S., Jr., & Renzulli, J. S. Reliability of a group form of the Peabody Picture Vocabulary Test. *Journal of Educational Research,* 1968, **61,** 311–314.

Tillman, M. H. The performance of blind and sighted children on the Wechsler Intelligence Scale for Children: Study I. *International Journal for the Education of the Blind,* 1967, **16,** 65–74. (a)

Tillman, M. H. The performances of blind and sighted children on the Wechsler Intelligence Scale for Children: Study II. *International Journal for the Education of the Blind,* 1967, **16,** 106–112. (b)

Tillman, M. H., & Bashaw, W. L. Multivariate analysis of the WISC scales for blind and sighted children. *Psychological Reports,* 1968, **23,** 523–526.

Tillman, M. H., & Osborne, R. T. The performance of blind and sighted children on the Wechsler Intelligence Scale for Children: Interaction effects. *Education of the Visually Handicapped,* 1969, **1,** 1–4.

Towbin, A. P. Psychological testing from end to means. *Journal of Projective Techniques,* 1964, **28,** 86–91.

Townsend, R. R. Tests of the Stanford Revision of the Binet-Simon scale most frequently failed by children in orthogenic backward classes. *Psychological Clinic,* 1928, **17,** 200–203.

Treffert, D. A. Epidemiology of infantile autism. *Archives of General Psychiatry,* 1970, **22,** 431–438.

Triggs, F. O., & Cartee, J. K. Pre-school pupil performance on the Stanford-Binet and the Wechsler Intelligence Scale for Children. *Journal of Clinical Psychology,* 1953, **9,** 27–29.

Trione, V. One hundred eighty cases: A follow-up by a rural school psychologist. *California Journal of Educational Research,* 1958, **9,** 86–90.

Tsudzuki, A., Hata, Y., & Kuze, T. A study of rapport between examiner and subject. *Japanese Journal of Psychology,* 1956, **27,** 22–28.

Tuddenham, R. D. The nature and measurement of intelligence. In L. J. Postman (Ed.), *Psychology in the making.* New York: Knopf, 1962. Pp. 469–525.

Turner, G. H., & Penfold, D. J. The scholastic aptitude of the Indian children of the Caradoc Reserve. *Canadian Journal of Psychology,* 1952, **6,** 31–44.

Turner, R. K., Mathews, A., & Rachman, S. The stability of the WISC in a psychiatric group. *British Journal of Educational Psychology,* 1967, **37,** 194–200.

Tyler, L. E. *The psychology of human differences.* (3rd ed.) New York: Appleton-Century-Crofts, 1965.

Tyler, L. E. *Tests and measurements.* (2nd ed.) Englewood Cliffs, N.J.: Prentice-Hall, 1971.

Tyson, M. H. *The effect of prior contact with the examiner on the Wechsler Intelligence Scale for Children scores of third-grade children.* (Doctoral dissertation, University of Houston) Ann Arbor, Mich.: University Microfilms, 1968. No. 69–784.

United States Government Printing Office. *Style manual.* (Rev. ed.) Washington, D.C.: USGPO, 1967.

University of Chicago Press. *A manual of style.* (12th ed.) Chicago: UCP, 1969.

Valentine, C. A. Deficit, difference, and bicultural models of Afro-American behavior. *Harvard Educational Review,* 1971, **41,** 137–157.

Valett, R. E. *The practice of school psychology: Professional problems.* New York: Wiley, 1963.

Valett, R. E. A clinical profile for the Stanford-Binet. *Journal of School Psychology,* 1964, **2,** 49–54.

Van Camp, D. Psychological evaluation of children who had neonatal hyperbilirubinemia. *American Journal of Mental Deficiency,* 1964, **68,** 803–806.

Vanderhost, L., Sloan, W., & Bensberg, G. J., Jr. Performance of mental defectives on the Wechsler-Bellevue and the WISC. *American Journal of Mental Deficiency,* 1953, **57,** 481–483.

Vane, J. R. What information do school and clinical psychologists give to individuals evaluated? A report of a survey. In J. Charry (Chm.), Confidentiality and individual rights: Is the APA Code of Ethics an infringement on the individual's right to know? Symposium presented at the American Psychological Association, Washington, D.C., September 1971.

Vane, J. R., Weitzman, J., & Applebaum, A. P. Performance of Negro and white children and problem and nonproblem children on the Stanford Binet Scale. *Journal of Clinical Psychology,* 1966, **22,** 431–435.

Varon, E. J. Development of Alfred Binet's psychology. *Psychological Monographs,* 1935, **46**(3, Whole No. 207).

Vernon, M., & Brown, D. W. A guide to psychological tests and testing procedures in the evaluation of deaf and hard-of-hearing children. *Journal of Speech and Hearing Disorders,* 1964, **29,** 414–423.

Vernon, P. E. The Stanford-Binet Test as a psychometric method. *Character and Personality,* 1937, **6,** 99–113.

Vernon, P. E. *The structure of human abilities.* New York: Wiley, 1950.

Vernon, P. E. *The structure of human abilities.* (2nd ed.) London: Methuen, 1961.

Vernon, P. E. Ability factors and environmental influences. *American Psychologist,* 1965, **20,** 723–733.

Vernon, P. E. *Intelligence and cultural environment.* London: Methuen, 1969.

Volle, F. O. A proposal for "testing the limits" with mental defectives for purposes of subtest analysis of the WISC Verbal Scale. *Journal of Clinical Psychology,* 1957, **13,** 64–67.

Voyat, G. IQ: God-given or man-made? In J. Hellmuth (Ed.), *Disadvantaged child.* Vol. 3. New York: Brunner/Mazel, 1970. Pp. 158–162.

Wagner, W. K. A comparison of Stanford-Binet mental ages and scaled scores on the Wechsler Intelligence Scale for Children for fifty Bowling Green pupils. Unpublished master's thesis, Bowling Green State University, 1951.

Walker, K. P., & Gross, F. L. I.Q. stability among educable mentally retarded children. *Training School Bulletin,* 1970, **66,** 181–187.

Walker, R. E., Hunt, W. A., & Schwartz, M. L. The difficulty of WAIS Comprehension scoring. *Journal of Clinical Psychology,* 1965, **21,** 427–429.

Wallace, G. *A study of the relationship of selected visual perceptual capabilities and intelligence to achievement in reading of educable mentally retarded children.* (Doctoral dissertation, University of Oregon) Ann Arbor, Mich.: University Microfilms, 1969. No. 70–2548.

Wallin, J. E. W. A practical guide for the administration of the Binet-Simon Scale for Measuring Intelligence. *Psychological Clinic,* 1911, **5,** 217–238.

Wallin, J. E. W. The phenomenon of scattering in the Binet-Simon scale. *Psychological Clinic,* 1917, **11,** 179–195.

Wallin, J. E. W. A statistical study of the individual tests in ages VIII and IX in the Stanford-Binet Scale. *Mental Measurements Monographs,* 1929, No. 6.

Wallin, J. E. W. The results of multiple Binet re-testing of the same subjects. *Journal of Exceptional Children,* 1940, **6,** 211–222.

Walton, D., & Begg, T. L. Cognitive changes in low-grade defectives. *American Journal of Mental Deficiency,* 1957, **62,** 96–102.

Ward, A. J. Early infantile autism: Diagnosis, etiology, and treatment. *Psychological Bulletin,* 1970, **73,** 350–362.

Warinner, E. M. A comparison of test performance of dull children on the Revised Stanford-Binet and the Wechsler Intelligence Scale for Children. Unpublished master's thesis, University of Chicago, 1952.

Warren, S. A., & Collier, H. L. Suitability of the Columbia Mental Maturity Scale for mentally retarded institutionalized females. *American Journal of Mental Deficiency,* 1960, **64,** 916–920.

Warrington, E. K. The incidence of verbal disability associated with retardation reading. *Neuropsychologia,* 1967, **5,** 175–179.

Wasik, J. L., & Wasik, B. H. A note on use of the WPPSI in evaluating intervention programs. *Measurement and Evaluation in Guidance,* 1970, **3,** 54–56.

Watson, R. I. *The clinical method in psychology.* New York: Harper, 1951.

Webb, A. P. A longitudinal comparison of the WISC and WAIS with educable mentally retarded Negroes. *Journal of Clinical Psychology,* 1963, **19,** 101–102.

Webb, A. P. Some issues relating to the validity of the WAIS in assessing mental retardation. *California Journal of Educational Research,* 1964, **15,** 130–135.

Wechsler, D. *Manual for the Wechsler Intelligence Scale for Children.* New York: Psychological Corporation, 1949.

Wechsler, D. *Manual for the Wechsler Adult Intelligence Scale.* New York: Psychological Corporation, 1955.

Wechsler, D. *The measurement and appraisal of adult intelligence.* (4th ed.) Baltimore: Williams & Wilkins, 1958.

Wechsler, D. *Manual for the Wechsler Preschool and Primary Scale of Intelligence.* New York: Psychological Corporation, 1967.

Wechsler, D., & Jaros, E. Schizophrenic patterns on the WISC. Journal of Clinical Psychology, 1965, **21,** 288–291.

Wechsler, D., & Weider, A. Tests of intelligence. C. Wechsler Intelligence Scale for Children. In A. Weider (Ed.), *Contributions toward medical psychology.* Vol. II. New York: Ronald Press, 1953. Pp. 522–529.

Weener, P. D. Social dialect differences and the recall of verbal messages. *Journal of Educational Psychology,* 1969, **60,** 194–199.

Weider, A., Levi, J., & Risch, F. Performances of problem children on the Wechsler-Bellevue Intelligence Scales and the Revised Stanford-Binet. *Psychiatric Quarterly,* 1943, **17,** 695–701.

Weider, A., Noller, P. A., & Schramm, T. A. The Wechsler Intelligence Scale for Children and the Revised Stanford-Binet. *Journal of Consulting Psychology,* 1951, **15,** 330–333.

Weiner, P. S. The cognitive functioning of language deficient children. *Journal of Speech and Hearing Research,* 1969, **12,** 53–64.

Weise, P. Current uses of Binet and Wechsler tests by school psychologists in California. *California Journal of Educational Research,* 1960, **11,** 73–78.

Weisskopf, E. A. Intellectual malfunctioning and personality. *Journal of Abnormal and Social Psychology,* 1951, **46,** 410–423.

Wells, C. G. *A comparative study of children grouped by three basic score patterns on the Wechsler Intelligence Scale for Children.* (Doctoral dissertation, University of Northern Colorado) Ann Arbor, Mich.: University Microfilms, 1970. No. 71–14,543.

Wells, D. G., & Pedrini, D. T. Relationships between the S-B, L-M, G-H, and PPVT with institutionalized retardates. *American Journal of Mental Deficiency,* 1967, **72,** 412–415. (a)

Wells, D. G., & Pedrini, D. T. Where to begin testing on the 1960 Stanford-Binet L-M. *Journal of Clinical Psychology,* 1967, **23,** 182–184. (b)

Wells, F. L. *Mental tests in clinical practice.* Yonkers-on-Hudson, N.Y.: World Book, 1927.

Wells, F. L., & Kelley, C. M. Intelligence and psychosis. *American Journal of Insanity,* 1920, **77,** 17–45.

Wender, P. H. *Minimal brain dysfunction in children.* New York: Wiley, 1971.

Wender, P. H., Pedersen, F. A., & Waldrop, M. F. A longitudinal study of early social behavior and cognitive development. *American Journal of Orthopsychiatry,* 1967, **37,** 691–696.

Wentworth, M. M. Two hundred cases of dementia precox tested by the Stanford Revision. *Journal of Abnormal and Social Psychology,* 1924, **18,** 378–384.

Werner, E. E. Review of the Arthur adaptation of the Leiter International Performance Scale. In O. K. Buros (Ed.), *The sixth mental measurements yearbook.* Highland Park, N.J.: Gryphon Press, 1965. Pp. 814–816.

Werner, E. E., Honzik, M. P., & Smith, R. S. Prediction of intelligence and achievement at ten years from twenty months pediatric and psychologic examinations. *Child Development,* 1968, **39,** 1063–1075.

Werry, J. S., & Quay, H. C. The prevalence of behavior symptoms in younger elementary school children. *American Journal of Orthopsychiatry,* 1971, **41,** 136–143.

Wesman, A. G. Intelligent testing. *American Psychologist,* 1968, **23,** 267–274.

Whatley, R. G., & Plant, W. T. The stability of the W.I.S.C. IQ's for selected children. *Journal of Psychology,* 1957, **44,** 165–167.

Whipple, G. M. *Manual of mental and physical tests.* Baltimore: Warwick & York, 1910.

Whipple, G. M. The amateur and the Binet-Simon tests. *Journal of Educational Psychology,* 1912, **3,** 118–119.

White, M. A., & Charry, J. (Eds.) *School disorder, intelligence, and social class.* New York: Teachers College Press, 1966.

Whiteman, M. Altitude as a reference point in scatter analysis. *Journal of Clinical Psychology,* 1950, **6,** 160–164.

Wiener, G., Rider, R. V., & Oppel, W. Some correlates of IQ changes in children. *Child Development,* 1963, **34,** 61–67.

Wiens, A. N., Matarazzo, J. D., & Gaver, K. D. Performance and Verbal IQ in a group of sociopaths. *Journal of Clinical Psychology,* 1959, **15,** 191–193.

Wight, B. W., & Sandry, M. A short form of the Wechsler Intelligence Scale for Children. *Journal of Clinical Psychology,* 1962, **18,** 166.

Wikoff, R. L. Subscale classification schemata for the Stanford-Binet, Form L-M. *Journal of School Psychology,* 1971, **9,** 329–337.

Wile, I. S., & Davis, R. M. A study of the behavior of 250 children with mental age ten years. *American Journal of Orthopsychiatry,* 1938, **8,** 689–709.

Wile, I. S., & Davis, R. M. A study of failures on the Stanford Binet in relation to behavior and school problems. *Journal of Educational Psychology,* 1941, **32,** 275–284.

Willard, L. S. A comparison of Culture Fair Test scores with group and individual intelligence test scores of disadvantaged Negro children. *Journal of Learning Disabilities,* 1968, **1,** 584–589.

Willerman, L., Broman, S. H., & Fiedler, M. Infant development, preschool IQ, and social class. *Child Development,* 1970, **41,** 69–77.

Williams, E. B. Testing of the disadvantaged: New opportunities. In F. H. Wright (Chm.), Uses and abuses of psychology: A program for constructive action. Symposium presented at the American Psychological Association, Washington, D.C., September 1971.

Williams, J. M. Children who break down in foster homes: A psychological study of patterns of personality growth in grossly deprived children. *Journal of Child Psychology and Psychiatry,* 1961, **2,** 5–20.

Williams, R. L. Danger: Testing and dehumanizing black children. *Clinical Child Psychology Newsletter,* 1970, **9**(1), 5–6. (a)

Williams, R. L. From dehumanization to black intellectual genocide: A rejoinder. *Clinical Child Psychology Newsletter,* 1970, **9**(3), 6–7. (b)

Williams, R. L. Black pride, academic relevance and individual achievement. *Counseling Psychologist,* 1970, **2**(1), 18–22. (c)

Williams, R. L. Abuses and misuses in testing black children. *Counseling Psychologist,* 1971, **2**(3), 62–73.

Willis, J. Group versus individual intelligence tests in one sample of emotionally disturbed children. *Psychological Reports,* 1970, **27,** 819–822.

Wilson, L. A comparison of the Raven Progressive Matrices (1947) and the Performance Scale of the Wechsler Intelligence Scale for Children for assessing the intelligence of Indian children. Unpublished master's thesis, University of British Columbia, 1952.

Winpenny, N. An investigation of the use and the validity of mental age scores on the Wechsler Intelligence Scale for Children. Unpublished master's thesis, Pennsylvania State College, 1951.

Wirt, R. D., & Broen, W. E., Jr. The relation of the Children's Manifest Anxiety Scale to the concept of anxiety as used in the clinic. *Journal of Consulting Psychology,* 1956, **20,** 482.

Wissler, C. The correlation of mental and physical tests. *Psychological Review,* 1901, 3(Monogr. Suppl. 16).

Witkin, H. A., Faterson, H. F., Goodenough, D. R., & Birnbaum, J. Cognitive patterning in mildly retarded boys. *Child Development,* 1966, **37,** 301–316.

Witmer, J. M., Bornstein, A. V., & Dunham, R. M. The effects of verbal approval and disapproval upon the performance of third and fourth grade children on four subtests of the Wechsler Intelligence Scale for Children. *Journal of School Psychology,* 1971, **9**, 347–356.

Wolf, M. G. Effects of emotional disturbance in childhood on intelligence. *American Journal of Orthopsychiatry,* 1965, **35**, 906–908. (a)

Wolf, M. G. Emotional disturbance and school achievement. *Journal of School Psychology,* 1965, **4**(1), 16–18. (b)

Wolf, T. H. An individual who made a difference. *American Psychologist,* 1961, **16**, 245–248.

Wolf, T. H. Alfred Binet: A time of crisis. *American Psychologist,* 1964, **19**, 762–771.

Wolf, T. H. The emergence of Binet's conception and measurement of intelligence: A case history of the creative process. *Journal of the History of the Behavioral Sciences,* 1969, **5**, 113–134. (a)

Wolf, T. H. The emergence of Binet's conceptions and measurement of intelligence: A case history of the creative process. Part II. *Journal of the History of the Behavorial Sciences,* 1969, **5**, 207–237. (b)

Wolfensberger, W. The correlation between PPVT and achievement scores among retardates: A further study. *American Journal of Mental Deficiency,* 1962, **67**, 450–451.

Woodrow, H. H. *Brightness and dullness in children.* Philadelphia: J. B. Lippincott, 1919.

Woodward, M. The role of low intelligence in delinquency. *British Journal of Delinquency,* 1955, **5**, 281–303.

Woody, R. H. Diagnosis of behavioral problem children: Electroencephalography and mental abilities. *Journal of School Psychology,* 1967, **5**, 116–121.

Woody, R. H. Diagnosis of behavioral problem children: Mental abilities and achievement. *Journal of School Psychology,* 1968, **6**, 111–116.

Woody, R. H., & Billy, H. T. Influencing the intelligence scores of retarded and nonretarded boys with clinical suggestion. *American Journal of Clinical Hypnosis,* 1970, **12**, 268–271.

Worden, D. K., & Vignos, P. J., Jr. Intellectual function in childhood progressive muscular dystrophy. *Pediatrics,* 1962, **29**, 968–977.

Wright, C. A modified procedure for the abbreviated Revised Stanford-Binet Scale in determining the intelligence of mental defectives. *American Journal of Mental Deficiency,* 1942, **47**, 178–184.

Wright, R. E. A factor analysis of the original Stanford-Binet Scale. *Psychometrika,* 1939, **4**, 209–220.

Wrightstone, J. W. *A supplementary guide for scoring the Revised Stanford-Binet Intelligence Scale, Form L.* New York: Board of Education, 1941.

Wrightstone, J. W., Justman, J., & Moskowitz, S. *Studies of children with physical handicaps; the child with cardiac limitation.* New York: Board of Education, 1953.

Yater, A. C., Barclay, A., & Leskosky, R. Goodenough-Harris Drawing Test and WPPSI performance of disadvantaged preschool children. *Perceptual and Motor Skills,* 1971, **33**, 967–970.

Yen, S. M. Y. *A comparative study of test variability with Peabody Picture Vocabulary Test, Goodenough's Draw-a-Man Test, and Stanford-Binet Intelligence Scale as intellectual measurement with a group of urban low socio-economic status pre-school pupils.* (Doctoral dissertation, Catholic University of America) Ann Arbor, Mich.: University Microfilms, 1969. No. 69-19,728.

Yerkes, R. M. The Binet versus the point scale method of measuring intelligence. *Journal of Applied Psychology,* 1917, **1**, 111–122.

Yerkes, R. M., Bridges, J. W., & Hardwick, R. S. *A Point Scale for measuring mental ability.* Baltimore: Warwick & York, 1915.

Young, F. M., & Bright, H. A. Results of testing 81 Negro rural juveniles with the Wechsler Intelligence Scale for Children. *Journal of Social Psychology,* 1954, **39**, 219–226.

Young, F. M., & Pitts, V. A. The performance of congenital syphilitics on the Wechsler Intelligence Scale for Children. *Journal of Consulting Psychology,* 1951, **15**, 239–242.

Yudin, L. W. An abbreviated form of the WISC for use with emotionally disturbed children. *Journal of Consulting Psychology,* 1966, **30**, 272–275.

Yule, W., Berger, M., Butler, S., Newham, V., & Tizard, J. The WPPSI: An empirical evaluation with a British sample. *British Journal of Educational Psychology,* 1969, **39**, 1–13.

Zigler, E., & Butterfield, E. C. Motivational aspects of changes in IQ test performance of culturally deprived nursery school children. *Child Development,* 1968, **39**, 1–14.

Zimmerman, I. L., & Woo-Sam, J. The utility of the Wechsler Preschool and Primary Scale of Intelligence in the public school. *Journal of Clinical Psychology,* 1970, **26**, 472.

Zimmerman, I. L., & Woo-Sam, J. Research with the Wechsler Intelligence Scale for Children: 1960–1970. *Psychology in the Schools,* 1972, **9**, 232–271(Special Monogr. Suppl.).

Zintz, M. V. Problems of classroom adjustment of Indian children in public elementary schools in the Southwest. *Science Education,* 1962, **46**, 261–269.

Zunich, M., & Tolley, J. Performance on the Peabody Picture Vocabulary Test and Stanford-Binet by institutionalized mentally retarded children. *Psychological Reports,* 1968, **22**, 1212.

NAME INDEX

SUBJECT INDEX